UNIVERSITY OF NOTTINGHAM
60 0044733 8
TELEPEN
KU-080-384
WITHDRAWN FROM THE LIBRARY

DATE DUE FOR RETURN

06 FEB 97

UNIVERSITY LIBRARY
- 1 FEB 2000
SEM HALL 22

UNIVERSITY LIBRARY
HALL
THIS ITEM IS DUE FOR RETURN ON
30/9/98

UNIVERSITY LIBRARY
- 1 FEB 2000
SEM HALL 12

UNIVERSITY LIBRARY
- 4 FEB 1999
HALL

UNIVERSITY LIBRARY
- 1 FEB 2000
SEM HALL 12

UNIVERSITY LIBRARY
- 1 FEB 2000
SEM HALL 22

This book may be recalled before the above date

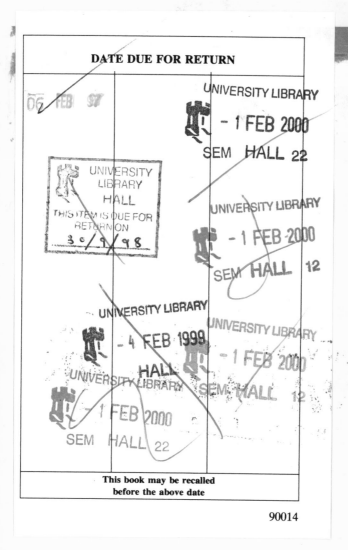

90014

Population and Economic Change in Developing Countries

A Conference Report
Universities–National Bureau
Committee for Economic Research

Number 30

National Bureau of Economic Research

Population and Economic Change in Developing Countries

Edited by Richard A. Easterlin

The University of Chicago Press

Chicago and London

Richard A. Easterlin is the William P. Kenan, Jr., Professor of Economics at the University of Pennsylvania. He is the author of *Population, Labor Force, and Long Swings in Economic Growth* and of many scholarly articles.

The University of Chicago Press, Chicago 60637
The University of Chicago Press, Ltd., London

© 1980 by the National Bureau of Economic Research
All rights reserved. Published 1980
Printed in the United States of America
84 83 82 81 80 5 4 3 2 1

Library of Congress Cataloging in Publication Data

Conference on Population and Economic Change in Less Developed Countries, Philadelphia, 1976.
Population and economic change in developing countries.

(A Conference report of the Universities-National Bureau Committee for Economic Research)
Sponsored by the Universities-National Bureau Committee for Economic Research.
Includes index.
1. Underdeveloped areas—Population—Congresses.
2. Population—Economic aspects—Congresses.
I. Easterlin, Richard Ainley, 1926– II. Universities-National Bureau Committee for Economic Research.
III. Title. IV. Series: Universities-National Bureau Committee for Economic Research. A conference report of the Universities-National Bureau Committee for Economic Research.
HB849.C59 1976 301.32′9′1724 79-12569
ISBN 0-226-18026-3

National Bureau of Economic Research

Arthur F. Burns, *honorary chairman*
James J. O'Leary, *chairman*
Eli Shapiro, *vice-chairman*
Martin Feldstein, *president*
Charles E. McLure, Jr., *vice-president*
Charles A. Walworth, *treasurer*
Sam Parker, *director of finance and administration*

Directors at Large

Moses Abramovitz
Atherton Bean
Andrew F. Brimmer
Otis F. Brubaker
Arthur F. Burns
George T. Conklin, Jr.
Solomon Fabricant
Martin Feldstein
Eugene P. Foley
Edward L. Ginzton
David L. Grove
Walter W. Heller
Walter E. Hoadley
Roy E. Moor
Geoffrey H. Moore
James J. O'Leary
Peter G. Peterson
Robert V. Roosa
Richard N. Rosett
Bert Seidman
Eli Shapiro
Arnold M. Soloway
Stephen Stamas
Lazare Teper

Directors by University Appointment

Gardner Ackley, *Michigan*
G. L. Bach, *Stanford*
Charles H. Berry, *Princeton*
Otto Eckstein, *Harvard*
Walter D. Fisher, *Northwestern*
John H. Kareken, *Minnesota*
J. C. LaForce, *California, Los Angeles*
Robert J. Lampman, *Wisconsin*
Maurice W. Lee, *North Carolina*
James L. Pierce, *California, Berkeley*
Almarin Phillips, *Pennsylvania*
Lloyd G. Reynolds, *Yale*
Robert M. Solow, *Massachusetts Institute of Technology*
Henri Theil, *Chicago*
William S. Vickrey, *Columbia*

Directors by Appointment of Other Organizations

Eugene A. Birnbaum, *American Management Associations*
Carl F. Christ, *American Economic Association*
Robert G. Dederick, *National Association of Business Economists*
Stephan F. Kaliski, *Canadian Economics Association*
Franklin A. Lindsay, *Committee for Economic Development*
Paul W. McCracken, *American Statistical Association*
Douglass C. North, *Economic History Association*
Rudolph A. Oswald, *American Federation of Labor and Congress of Industrial Organizations*
Charles A. Walworth, *American Institute of Certified Public Accountants*
G. Edward Schuh, *American Agricultural Economics Association*
James C. Van Horne, *American Finance Association*

Directors Emeriti

Percival F. Brundage
Emilio G. Collado
Frank W. Fetter
Thomas D. Flynn
Gottfried Haberler
Albert J. Hettinger, Jr.
George B. Roberts
Murray Shields
Boris Shishkin
Willard L. Thorp
Joseph H. Willits
Theodore O. Yntema

Since this volume is a record of conference proceedings, it has been exempted from the rules governing critical review of manuscripts by the Board of Directors of the National Bureau (resolution adopted 6 July 1948, as revised 21 November 1949 and 20 April 1968).

Universities–National Bureau Committee for Economic Research

This committee is a cooperative venture of universities and the National Bureau. Its guiding objective is the encouragement of economic research on problems susceptible of objective treatment and of sufficiently broad scope to merit attention by institutions serving a scientific and public interest.

Participating Universities and Their Representatives

Brown, Jerome L. Stein
California (Berkeley), Daniel McFadden
California (Los Angeles), J. C. La Force
California (San Diego), Robert E. Engle
Carnegie-Mellon, Edward C. Prescott
Chicago, Lester G. Telser
Columbia, Robert Mundell
Cornell, S. C. Tsiang
Duke, T. Dudley Wallace
Harvard, John V. Lintner
Illinois, Robert Resek
Indiana, Franz Gehrels
Iowa State, Dudley G. Luckett
Johns Hopkins, Carl F. Christ
Maryland, Barbara Bergman
Massachusetts Institute of Technology, Richard S. Eckaus
McGill, Alex G. Vicas
Michigan, Harold T. Shapiro
Michigan State, Victor Smith
Minnesota, James M. Henderson
New School for Social Research, Thomas Vietorisz
New York, M. Ishaq Nadiri
New York State (Buffalo), Daniel Hamberg
North Carolina, Henry A. Latané
Northwestern, Robert Eisner
Ohio State, Donald O. Parsons
Pennsylvania, Jere R. Behrman
Pittsburgh, S. H. Chou
Princeton, Edwin S. Mills
Purdue, Patric H. Hendershott
Queen's, Martin F. J. Prachowny
Rochester, Walter Y. Oi
Stanford, Moses Abramovitz
Texas, Samuel L. Myers, Jr.
Toronto, Richard Bird
Vanderbilt, Anthony M. Tang
Virginia, Richard T. Selden
Washington (Saint Louis), Hyman Minsky
Washington (Seattle), Richard W. Parks
Wisconsin, Leonard W. Weiss
Yale, Richard Ruggles

National Bureau of Economic Research Representative

Robert E. Lipsey

Members at Large

Irma Adelman
Bela A. Balassa
Carl E. Beigie
Daniel Creamer
Frank de Leeuw
Walter S. Salant
George J. Stigler

The officers of the Universities–National Bureau Committee are: Edwin S. Mills, chairman; Leonard W. Weiss, vice-chairman; and Christine Mortensen, secretary. The members of the Executive Committee are: Irma Adelman, Richard Bird, Robert Eisner, Robert E. Lipsey, Dudley G. Luckett, Edwin S. Mills, and Leonard W. Weiss.

Contents

Prefatory Note

This volume contains the papers presented at the Conference on Population and Economic Change in Less Developed Countries held in Philadelphia 30 September to 2 October 1976, sponsored by the Universities–National Bureau Committee for Economic Research. Funds for the conference were provided by the National Science Foundation; we are indebted for its support. We also thank Richard A. Easterlin, who served as chairman of the conference and editor of this volume.

Executive Committee, October 1976
Edwin S. Mills, chairman
Irma Adelman
Richard Bird
Robert Eisner
Dudley G. Luckett
Leonard W. Weiss
Robert E. Lipsey, NBER representative

Introduction

Richard A. Easterlin

The concerns behind the papers in this volume are as old as economics itself. Like the present authors, the classical economists wrestled with the causes and consequences of population change in the course of economic development. What is different here is the absence of simple answers. To some this will be a disappointment, but to others it will seem a mark of progress. In the study of population, as in many other areas of economic inquiry, growing awareness of the variety of human experience has had a chastening effect. What is common to the papers assembled here—as befits an NBER volume—is a respect for facts and an effort to match theory with reality.

Peter Lindert's study "Child Costs and Economic Development" provides an appropriate point of departure. It starts with the most challenging subject in the whole field of population, which appears and reappears throughout this volume, the "demographic transition"—the shift from high to low mortality and fertility repeatedly observed in the history of developing areas. It focuses on the possible role in this transition of the variable most natural to an economist's viewpoint, the cost of children. Lindert utilizes the sophisticated theoretical notion of cost that has emerged particularly from recent advances in what has been called "the new home economics." Unlike most of this work, however, Lindert's paper takes seriously the problem of measuring costs, thus fusing theory and measurement.

Lindert's paper, in its stress on cost considerations in fertility determination, conforms to economic orthodoxy. The paper by Easterlin, Pollak, and Wachter, while not rejecting the possible relevance of costs,

Richard A. Easterlin is associated with the Population Studies Center, University of Pennsylvania.

advances, so far as economists are concerned, some less orthodox views—the need in the study of fertility behavior for fuller attention to determinants of preferences, and to factors relating to the fecundity or reproductive capacity of women. A broader framework encompassing such factors is presented. This framework, the authors claim, makes more tractable such problems as the postwar American baby boom and the variability of fertility in less developed countries. Perhaps most disturbing to orthodox economic precepts is the argument and evidence advanced that in many times and places, observed fertility is not a product of deliberate choice.

In the standard formulation of the demographic transition, the decline in mortality leads that in fertility. Causal inferences have frequently been drawn from this pattern—for example, that if, in a regime of high mortality, parents view high fertility as necessary to compensate for child deaths, a reduction in child mortality will reduce the fertility required for replacement purposes. Yoram Ben-Porath's paper makes it clear that the possible analytical links between child mortality and fertility are much more complicated than this simple replacement notion suggests. The Israeli immigration experience, providing a dramatic change in the environment of different population groups, offers an unusual opportunity to explore some of the issues, drawing on both cross-sectional and time-series data. Of special interest is the comparison between immigrants of Afro-Asian origin and those of European origin.

Most empirical research on the economics of fertility in the last decade has focused on developed countries. The paper by T. Paul Schultz seeks to adapt a widely used "value of time" model to the experience of a less developed country undergoing the demographic transition. Schultz sets himself a more ambitious goal than the usual cross-sectional explanation—he seeks to account for the actual declines over time in age-specific fertility rates. Supporters of this model will be pleased at the consistency of his results with prior research on the relation of fertility to husband's and wife's education. As Schultz carefully notes, however, interpreting education's effect solely in terms of the "price of time" is questionable, and we need to get directly at the mechanisms by which education influences fertility.

The central issue in the first four papers is the determinants of human fertility. Although the revival of economic research on this topic is new—dating only from the 1950s—economic research on mortality is even newer. Samuel Preston's paper is one of a few recent attempts to apply economic analysis to the study of mortality. The result is impressive. In the subject of economic growth a standard conceptual approach is to partition the growth in productivity into movements along a "production function" and shifts in the "production function" itself, these shifts often being identified with technological change. Preston utilizes an analogous framework to derive a quantitative answer to an issue that has long beguiled students of mortality—the comparative roles in life expectancy improvement of higher per capita income (movement along a function) and improvements in public health and medicine (shifts in the function due to "technological change" in the biomedical area). Whether or not Preston's specific answer stands up to future scrutiny, his paper represents an important breakthrough from qualitative speculation to quantitative analysis of this problem.

Michael Todaro's study shifts attention to the remaining component of population change, migration. Here the volume enters terrain more customary for economists. Todaro provides a major service in distilling the extensive migration-model literature, summarizing the results of empirical tests, and, on the basis of this, identifying major priorities for research on internal migration.

With the paper by Allen Kelley, the volume turns its primary focus from the causes of population change to its effects. Kelley's paper deals specifically with the effects of alternative family sizes and structures on saving and income in urban Kenya. One might suppose that investigation of such effects of demographic variables would require no more than harvesting the results of earlier work, for there is a long history of economic speculation on such topics. But that is the catch—economic speculation, yes; systematic empirical study, no. Whereas econometric study has become the hallmark of most areas of economic research, questions of the effects of population change have heretofore been left largely to a priori theorizing. Kelley's paper represents an important departure—a rejection of preconceived answers and an attempt to match theory to the facts. This includes an attempt to recognize the possible interdependence between household decisions about saving and fertility. As with Preston's paper, Kelley's contribution lies not only in the specific answers he obtains, but in the approach he suggests for future research on the subject.

In contrast to Kelley's paper, where the approach is new but the problem is old, Simon Kuznets's paper takes up a subject that economists (the classical economists aside) have seriously neglected—the distributive implications of demographic change. That developing nations experience a demographic transition is well established; surprisingly little thought, however, has been given to the effects of this transition on income inequality within a country. Kuznets's concern is whether the size and incidence by class of the dramatic mortality and fertility declines during the demographic transition tend to heighten or reduce income inequality. As befits a pioneering venture on this topic, his paper is particularly concerned with establishing the facts, and in so doing it identifies important gaps in empirical knowledge. It also offers some suggestive speculations on the subject, some of which challenge one's initial predilections.

Ronald Lee's paper is perhaps the most ambitious one in the volume, for it seeks to bring together causes and effects of population change in an econometric model of economic-demographic interrelations. The empirical focus is premodern England, and the question is whether there may have been a self-regulating mechanism that made for a balance between population and economic resources. If, for example, an exogenous decline in mortality set in motion more rapid population growth, did the economic effects of this growth feed back on fertility or mortality in a way that brought population growth to a halt? Although his results are not necessarily definitive, Lee shows how theory and data may be used to move such questions from speculation to serious analysis. He notes that international economic interdependence and rapid technological change in the contemporary world caution against automatically extending his results to today's less developed areas.

In the original conference plan, each paper was to be written by an economist and commented on by both an economist and a demographer (the two categories, of course, are not wholly mutually exclusive). The intent was to retain in some degree the interdisciplinary flavor of a predecessor U-NBER conference on population and economic change (in developed countries) some two decades ago. As it turns out, there is less representation of demographers' views in this volume than was hoped for, but the distinctive flavor of their contribution is well illustrated in several comments. To speed publication, the editorial committee precluded authors' replies. This committee, the same as the conference planning committee, consisted of Allen Kelley, T. Paul Schultz, Robert Willis, and Richard A. Easterlin, chairman. Christine Mortensen provided extensive help in organizing the conference, which was held at the University of Pennsylvania Population Studies Center, 30 September through 2 October 1976.

As a whole the papers and accompanying comments demonstrate what economics brings to the study of population—new theoretical ideas, greater logical consistency, fuller perception of interrelations, more precise specification of problems, and a methodology that fosters confrontation of theory and the quantitative record. If one takes the earlier conference volume as a benchmark, the papers show that economic research on population has moved from fledgling status to become full grown. One may note, too, a growing sensitivity of economic research to the value and importance of demographers' contributions.

1 Child Costs and Economic Development

Peter H. Lindert

1.1 The Delayed Fertility Transition

Many who are concerned about rapid population growth in developing countries have hoped and expected that economic development would be an effective contraceptive. If it is, then population policy can confine itself to the libertarian stance of subsidizing family-planning propaganda and contraceptive means. While experience has shown that family-planning programs achieve only very modest fertility reductions when large families are desired, the task of reducing desired family size might be left to policies aimed at economic development. By fostering education, industrialization, income growth, and female employment outside the home, general development policies may be a prompt and efficient way to cut fertility. But if economic development fails to bring prompt and sustained fertility reductions, developing countries will have more reason to consider tougher antinatal measures, such as Singapore's stiff birth disincentives of 1972–73 or, beyond them, compulsory sterilization. The social costs of these measures would have to be weighed against the perceived social-insurance benefits of faster fertility reduction as a means of lessening congestion and income inequality.

Peter H. Lindert is Professor of Economics at the University of California at Davis.

The author wishes to thank Michael R. Haines, Allen C. Kelley, Barry M. Popkin, Bryan Boulier, Dov Chernichovsky, and Kathryn E. Walker for their help in making available several sets of survey data for this study. Also gratefully acknowledged is the financial support of the Rockefeller Foundation, the Population Council (with funds from the United States Agency for International Development), the Institute for Research on Poverty at the University of Wisconsin (United States Office of Economic Opportunity), and the University of Wisconsin Graduate School for the earlier United States–related portions of this research.

There is a consensus that economic development *ultimately* prevents births, both by improving the supply of contraceptive means and by raising the perceived costliness of extra children. Ignoring George Stigler's lemma that "there are not ten good reasons for anything," we rattle off long lists of well-known reasons why economic development makes children seem more costly and less of an economic asset.[1] Economic development pulls women out of the home, giving them a greater sense of control over their lives, greater access to contraceptive information, and a heightened sense of the earnings they stand to lose by having children. Economic development pulls older children out of jobs and into school, thus cutting their direct economic contribution to their parents' households. It also raises couples' awareness that social mobility depends on per capita family expenditures that would be dragged down by the arrival of extra children. Their "consumer aspirations" are raised, both by income growth itself and by greater exposure to new luxury goods. This exposure is fostered by the migration from farm to city, by industrialization, and by education. Children become less valuable as insurance of old-age support as the development of asset markets and social security gives parents cheaper ways to assure themselves that support. Greater geographic mobility replaces the extended family with the nuclear family, raising the cost and difficulty of arranging for supplementary child care. Meanwhile, reductions in infant and child mortality cut the number of births necessary to achieve any desired number of surviving children.

The individual arguments linking fertility decline to economic development through child costs are not always well spelled out, or documented, or logically aligned with each other—a shortcoming that will be partly remedied here. But they are at least well agreed upon. Indeed, "economic" as these links may sound to some, their importance in explaining the secular fertility decline is not a subject that divides the disciplines.

Much less resolved is the explanation of the earlier part of the fertility transition that most directly worries antinatal scholars and policy-makers in developing countries today. The secular fertility decline often begins rather late in the "development" or "modernization" process. Just how late depends on how one defines development and modernization.

If the onset of development is signaled by a sustained drop in mortality, then the lag of the fertility decline behind the start of development is often long and highly variable. Figure 1.1 and table 1.1 remind us of this by returning to the varied chronologies of crude birthrates and death rates, the most available proxies for fertility and mortality rates across wide stretches of time and space.

Among the early-developing countries, some had no lag between the onset of death rate decline and that of birthrate decline, whereas others

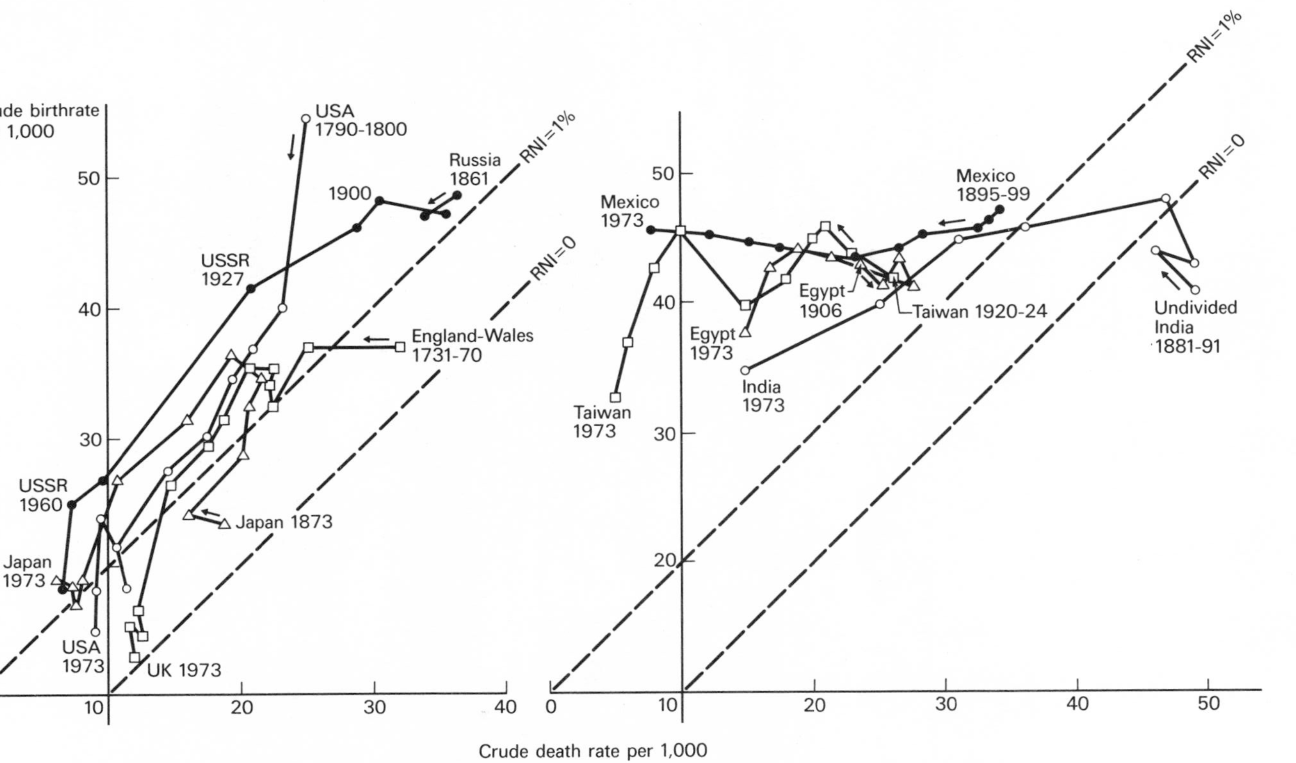

Fig. 1.1 Crude birthrates and death rates in eight countries. Selected peacetime dates.

Table 1.1 **Crude Birthrates and Death Rates in Eight Countries: Selected Peacetime Dates**

Country	Year or period	Crude birth rate/ 1,000	Crude death rate/ 1,000	Source
England/ Wales	1731–70	37	32	Brownlee, via Kuznets 1966, table 2.3
	1781–1820	37	25	Brownlee, via Kuznets 1966, table 2.3
	1841–50	32.6[a]	22.4	Postan and Habakkuk 1965, table 9
	1851–60	34.1[a]	22.2	Postan and Habakkuk 1965, table 9
	1861–70	35.2[a]	22.5	Postan and Habakkuk 1965, table 9
	1876–80	35.3	20.8	Postan and Habakkuk 1965, table 9
	1886–90	31.4	18.9	Postan and Habakkuk 1965, table 9
	1896–1900	29.3	17.7	Postan and Habakkuk 1965, table 9
	1906–10	26.3	14.7	Postan and Habakkuk 1965, table 9
	1926–30	16.7	12.1	Postan and Habakkuk 1965, table 9
	1936–40	14.7	12.5	Postan and Habakkuk 1965, table 9
	1951–55	15.2	11.7	Postan and Habakkuk 1965, table 9
UK	1973	13	12	UN, via Population Reference Bureau 1976
USA	1790–1800	55	25	Grabill et al., via Kuznets 1966, table 2.3
	1870–75	40.8	21.8	Easterlin 1968, p. 189
	1880–85	36.9	21.0	Easterlin 1968, p. 189
	1890–95	34.3	19.5	Easterlin 1968, p. 189
	1900–1905	30.0	17.6	Easterlin 1968, p. 189
	1910–15	27.5	14.7	Easterlin 1968, p. 189
	1925–30	21.5	10.6	Easterlin 1968, p. 189
	1935–40	18.3	11.3	Easterlin 1968, p. 189
	1945–50	24.5	9.9	Easterlin 1968, p. 189
	1955–60	24.6	9.4	Easterlin 1968, p. 189
	1973	15	9	UN, via Population Reference Bureau 1976
Russia[b]	1861	48.8	36.1	Biraben, via Heer 1968, table 1
	1870	47.0	34.0	Biraben, via Heer 1968, table 1
	1880	47.2	34.8	Biraben, via Heer 1968, table 1
	1890	47.2	35.4	Biraben, via Heer 1968, table 1
	1900	48.1	30.2	Biraben, via Heer 1968, table 1
	1910	46.0	28.7	Biraben, via Heer 1968, table 1
USSR	1927	41.6	20.9	Biraben, via Heer 1968, table 1
	1950	26.5	9.6	Biraben, via Heer 1968, table 1
	1960	24.9	7.1	Biraben, via Heer 1968, table 1
	1965	18.5	7.3	Biraben, via Heer 1968, table 1
	1973	18	9	UN, via Population Reference Bureau 1976

[a]Possible underregistration mentioned explicitly by source.
[b]Adjusted to postwar boundaries of USSR.

Table 1.1 (continued)

Country	Year or period	Crude birth rate/ 1,000	Crude death rate/ 1,000	Source
Japan	1873	23.1	18.9	Bank of Japan 1966, pp. 12–13
	1880	24.1	16.5	Bank of Japan 1966, pp. 12–13
	1890	28.7	20.7	Bank of Japan 1966, pp. 12–13
	1900	32.4	20.8	Bank of Japan 1966, pp. 12–13
	1910	34.8	21.6	Bank of Japan 1966, pp. 12–13
	1925	36.3	19.4	Bank of Japan 1966, pp. 12–13
	1940	31.4	16.0	Bank of Japan 1966, pp. 12–13
	1950	26.8	10.5	Bank of Japan 1966, pp. 12–13
	1955	19.0	7.9	Bank of Japan 1966, pp. 12–13
	1960	17.1	7.5	Bank of Japan 1966, pp. 12–13
	1964	18.6	7.3	Bank of Japan 1966, pp. 12–13
	1973	19	6	UN, via Population Reference Bureau 1976
Undivided India	1881–91	49	41	Kingsley Davis, via Postan and Habakkuk 1965, table 16
	1891–1901	46	44	Kingsley Davis, via Postan and Habakkuk 1965, table 16
	1901–11	49	43	Kingsley Davis, via Postan and Habakkuk 1965, table 16
	1911–21	48	47	Kingsley Davis, via Postan and Habakkuk 1965, table 16
	1921–31	46	36	Kingsley Davis, via Postan and Habakkuk 1965, table 16
	1931–41	45	31	Kingsley Davis, via Postan and Habakkuk 1965, table 16
Independent India	1950–55	40	25	UN, via Postan and Habakkuk, table 16
	1973	35	15	UN, via Population Reference Bureau 1976
Mexico	1895–99	47.3	34.4	Collver 1965, table 41
	1900–04	46.5	33.4	Collver 1965, table 41
	1905–09	46.0	32.9	Collver 1965, table 41
	1920–24	45.3	28.4	Collver 1965, table 41
	1925–29	44.3	26.7	Collver 1965, table 41
	1935–39	43.5	23.5	Collver 1965, table 41
	1940–44	43.8	21.8	Collver 1965, table 41
	1945–49	44.5	17.8	Collver 1965, table 41
	1950–54	45.0	15.4	Collver 1965, table 41
	1955–59	45.8	12.5	Collver 1965, table 41
	1973	46	8	UN, via Population Reference Bureau 1976
Egypt	1906	43.2	23.6	Nassef 1970, table D.2
	1913	41.6	25.4	Nassef 1970, table D.2

Table 1.1 (continued)

Country	Year or period	Crude birth rate/ 1,000	Crude death rate/ 1,000	Source
Egypt (*cont.*)	1925	43.5	26.5	Nassef 1970, table D.2
	1935	41.3	26.4	Nassef 1970, table D.2
	1950	44.2	19.0	Nassef 1970, table D.2
	1960	42.9	16.9	Nassef 1970, table D.2
	1973	38	15	UN, via Population Reference Bureau 1976
Taiwan	1920–24	42	26	Gille 1967, table 1; UN (1973), table V.4
	1925–29	44	23	Gille 1967, table 1; UN (1973), table V.4
	1930–34	46	21	Gille 1967, table 1; UN (1973), table V.4
	1935–39	45	20	Gille 1967, table 1; UN (1973), table V.4
	1940–44	42	18	Gille 1967, table 1; UN (1973), table V.4
	1945–49	40	15	Gille 1967, table 1; UN (1973), table V.4
	1950–54	46	10	Gille 1967, table 1; UN (1973), table V.4
	1955–59	43	8	Gille 1967, table 1; UN (1973), table V.4
	1960–64	37.2	6	Gille 1967, table 1; UN (1973), table V.4
	1973	23	5	UN, via Population Reference Bureau 1976

had long lags. In some cases the fact that birthrates were already declining when death rates began their sustained descent can be attributed to frontier conditions that made fertility higher at the outset than it was as settlement proceeded. An early frontier stimulus to fertility may help explain why birthrates were already falling from high levels by the time death rates began their decline in the United States, Canada, Argentina, Chile, Australia, New Zealand, and the Russian empire. Less obvious are the reasons why France was already experiencing declining fertility by the late eighteenth century, before or contemporaneous with the sustained improvement in life expectancy.

In sharp contrast, other early developers appear to have had prolonged periods in which the fall in death rates was not matched by a fall in birthrates. As shown in figure 1.1 and table 1.1, England and Wales were in this transitional position between the late eighteenth century[2] and the 1870s. The lag in fertility decline was at least as long in Japan, where birthrates began to fall slightly only after 1925 and did not drop much until after the defeat of 1945. Japanese experience deserves considerable attention in any overview of the transition. It appears that even with some allowance for early underregistration of births and infant deaths, birthrates and death rates were both below 30 per thousand from the mid-eighteenth century to the early Meiji era.[3] Across the Meiji and Taisho eras (1868–1925), the birthrate rose noticeably while the death rate either rose slightly or fell slightly, depending on the extent of early underregistration. Japan thus experienced either a prolonged period of high fertility with declining birthrates or a prolonged period of rising fertility with stable or slightly rising death rates, depending again on the extent to which births and deaths were underregistered together in earlier eras. There was also a noticeable lag of the secular fertility decline behind the fall in death rates in Denmark, Norway, and Sweden, where death rates dropped from the mid-eighteenth century and birthrates did not fall significantly until the 1860s or later. Germany also experienced stable birthrates and falling death rates across the period from the 1860s to about 1900.[4]

A lag of fertility decline behind mortality decline is much more common among recently developing nations and has generated higher rates of natural increase than ever prevailed in the transition period for England, Japan, or the Scandinavian countries. Figure 1.1 and table 1.1 review this point for four recently developing countries. Across the interwar period, British India experienced rapid reductions in death rate without any downward trend in the birthrate. Only since independence has India had declining birthrates, and the decline has not been large enough to halt the rise in the rate of natural increase. The same experience was shared by Egypt, whose birthrates failed to decline before the Nasser coup and have declined only slightly since. Taiwan also cut its death rate without cutting births between the 1920s and the early 1950s, though Taiwan has achieved impressive birthrate reductions in the postwar era since the flood of immigrants arrived from mainland China. The most dramatic holdout among those countries in figure 1.1 is Mexico, whose birthrates have not dropped over three-quarters of a century of declining peacetime mortality. Developing countries cannot find any prompt or predictable response of birthrates to death rates in this array of national experiences.

If the onset of development is marked by an accelerated rise in literacy rates or a trend toward urbanization and industrialization, the same picture emerges as with the birthrate/death rate comparison. All the settings in which death rates were declining were ones of rising literacy, school attendance, urbanization, and industrialization. Defining development in terms of these changes merely reestablishes that the modern periods of declining mortality without reductions in birthrates were also periods when "development" was occurring without cutting birthrates in the aggregate.[5]

Defining the onset of development as the turning point at which national product per capita began a sustained rise reduces, but does not eliminate, the cases of nonfalling birthrates accompanying development. In England and Wales, product per capita, like the other development indicators, rose from the mid-eighteenth century to the delayed downturn in birthrates in the early 1880s.[6] The length of this transition period would be reduced, however, if we had data on the income progress of the lower-income, higher-fertility groups: real wage rates, with or without allowing for shifts in the occupational structure, probably did not begin a sustained ascent until about 1815.[7] The period when development by all measures touched most segments of English society without bringing a drop in the aggregate birthrate might thus have been as short as 1815–80—but this is still a long transition period. Using the product-per-capita and real-wage yardsticks does not shorten the transition period for Japan, since both indicators were rising over most of the period 1873–1925.[8] There was probably also an extended period in the nineteenth century when by any yardstick economic development was proceeding in Denmark, Norway, and Sweden without a decline in the crude birthrate, but there are not enough pre-1860 data on product per capita and real wage rates for a more positive statement. At any rate, among the early developers there are some clear cases of birthrate decline lagging far behind any measure of economic development, whereas no lag at all occurred in other cases.

Among more recently developing countries, using the product-per-capita or wage yardsticks does narrow the range of experiences involving development without birthrate declines. In particular, these yardsticks separate out the cases of India and Egypt. Product per capita did not begin a sustained rise in India until independence,[9] a quarter-century after the beginning of the decline in crude death rates. Similarly, neither agricultural product per person nor real agricultural wage rates rose in Egypt from the turn of the century to 1940.[10] Only after midcentury did product per capita and real wage rates drift upward in both India and Egypt—and only in this same recent period did birthrates begin a gradual decline. As far as India and Egypt are concerned, properly including real income growth in the definition of development eliminates the transitional phase: birthrates declined when true development began.

Yet other recently developing countries have still had the transitional phase, violating any simple prediction that development means fertility decline. Taiwan apparently had rising average incomes as well as rising literacy for two or three decades before World War II and before the onset of the fertility decline in the 1950s. Several countries in Latin

America and the Caribbean have also had development without declining birthrates. Specifically, since the early 1950s the following twelve countries had birthrates above 30 per 1,000 and not falling faster than half a point a year, while also having growth rates in GNP per capita above 1% a year as well as rising literacy and urbanization: Brazil, Colombia, Dominican Republic, Ecuador, Guatemala, Honduras, Jamaica (to 1969), Mexico, Nicaragua, Panama, Peru, and Venezuela.[11]

1.2 Three Views of the Lag in Fertility Decline

Both the frequent occurrence and the high variance of the lag of fertility decline behind development pose serious empirical problems for any integrated theory relating fertility to modernization. If we are to know what governs the timing of the start of the eventual fertility decline, our knowledge must be based on a model consistent with the lag and its variations across social groups and nations, as well as with the eventual decline. There are at least three theories of the lag in fertility decline that incorporate a submodel designed to explain why fertility does drop later on.

The first interpretation of high fertility during early development posits a *threshold of economic consciousness*; before this point, attitudinal inertia prevents any conscious individual control of family size. According to this view, which is a vague presence in the relevant literature rather than an explicit contender, couples do not regulate their fertility except in conforming to traditional rules regarding marriage, intercourse, and breast-feeding. The early diffusion of modern values has little influence on family formation practices, perhaps even among those becoming literate, urbanized, and more prosperous. Whether children are becoming more or less costly or valuable is irrelevant simply because it is not perceived. Only after the development process has passed some threshold do couples think of the costs and benefits of children as something that should affect their behavior, and by this time children are in fact becoming more costly, more of an impediment to the attainment of the new aspirations. This view contains no obvious way of predicting which groups or societies will take longer to reach the threshold of economic consciousness, except possibly by juggling the definition of development so that the same threshold matches the onset of falling fertility in all cases. It also seems to conflict with other evidence that even in traditional societies families respond to economic opportunities and even view children largely in economic terms. It is, however, one not implausible way of explaining the sometime lag in fertility decline, one that has not been refuted by any conclusive test.

The second interpretation of the sometime lag has been incorporated in a recent model of demographic development by Riad Tabbarah and

Richard Easterlin.[12] This model identifies a threshold at which fertility switches from being determined by the *supply of children* (or the "potential output of children") to being driven downward by the declining demand for children. On this interpretation *Homo economicus* is not born after development has advanced to the threshold. He (and she) already exists in traditional society and in the early phase of modernization as well. In these early settings, however, couples see children as beneficial enough so that they want a larger family than they can achieve. The perceived benefits are not spelled out as economic or noneconomic, but the early constraints on fertility and completed family size are viewed as definitely social and biological. Couples' fertility is, as in the first interpretation, constrained by social codes governing marriage, intercourse, and breast-feeding, and by their fecundity. Within these constraints they leave fertility "unregulated" in order to have as many children as possible, "as many as God wills."

The dawn of economic development raises fertility, in this model,[13] at the same time that it cuts the optimal number of children. Better living standards raise natality by raising fecundity and possibly by relaxing some of the social restrictions on marriage. Development further raises the probability that children will survive to adulthood, causing completed family sizes to rise faster than fertility. Yet, at the same time, economic development is also pulling the desired number of children down toward the attainable maximum, presumably through the same socioeconomic mechanisms that bring the secular fertility decline later on. The threshold arrives when the desired number of children drops below the attainable number, or when couples perceive this and begin to bring unwanted births under individual control.

It is possible to conduct a partial test of the underlying assumption that the supply of children falls below the desired number in the era before the onset of fertility decline. The partial test consists of calculating the actual average net economic benefits or costs of an extra child at the average completed family size. If it turns out that an extra child brings a net economic cost in this setting, supporters of the supply-of-children view would be compelled to assert and show either that extra children would have been of overriding net benefit on noneconomic grounds or that couples' perceptions were biased toward greater appreciation of child benefits than of child costs. If, on the other hand, it turns out that extra children would have brought net economic gains to their parents, critics of the supply-of-children view would have to fall back to the shakier position that children brought an overriding net noneconomic cost or that couples perceived economic costs more fully than they perceived economic benefits. No such test has ever been conducted, though preliminary tests are sketched below. Such tests aside, it can be agreed that this hypothesis is at least partly correct in focusing on basic fecundity and social mores as fertility determinants in the early phases of development.

I will argue that the evidence makes room for a third interpretation of the delayed fertility transition, one arguing that the *relative costs of extra children* at given parity may not rise until well into the development process. It may be that the average desired number of surviving children was never above the potential number. It may be that fertility and child survival were widely "regulated" all along by society and by individual couples through the traditional crude devices—postponement of marriage, abstinence, withdrawal, and, in some societies, induced abortion and infanticide. Perhaps succeeding generations of couples were always vaguely aware of the economic consequences of child-rearing and were not given strong new incentives to prevent births until well into the development process. Neither the available evidence on patterns of birth timing, nor that on stated social norms, nor that on child costs and benefits yet allows us to reject this view.

This interpretation has not been given the empirical tests it deserves, partly because the relative cost concept has not been operationally defined and partly because sufficient data have not been gathered on the economic role of children within households in developing countries. In the next section I shall define a measure of the relative cost of extra children that embodies most of our theoretical intuitions about how changes in the economy affect couples' choices between extra children and other acquisitions. The measure is next quantified in detail and applied to aggregate twentieth-century patterns in United States fertility. Subsequent sections survey some empirical evidence on child-cost patterns in developing countries. It turns out that the relative-child-cost interpretation escapes rejection in some crude initial tests and poses again some puzzles that are already before us. Beyond the slight support given to this interpretation of the delay in fertility transition, the measure of relative child cost offers a theoretically convenient, and often empirically workable, way of bringing order to a host of previously disorderly arguments about how child costs evolve with economic development.

Let me stress in advance that the sections that follow pose only very crude tests of the importance of relative-child-cost movements, and that even these limited tests caution against the belief that movements in relative costs explain all of the most interesting aggregate fertility patterns. To test the influence of the relative-child-cost measure, one should place the measure into direct competition with other socioeconomic and demographic variables in regressions explaining parts of observed fertility patterns. That kind of test has been performed only for the twentieth-century United States, not for the earlier development contexts that are of prime concern here. The usefulness of the relative-cost measure, and its more available proxies, in accounting for the frequent occurrence of a lag in the fertility decline is subjected only to a rough test of raw correlation. It more or less passes this rough test by showing good reasons why the relative cost of an extra child is likely not to have risen in many early-development settings, yet has surely risen much later on.

Even these limited tests—a few regressions for the United States and a looser documentation of the correlation between likely relative-cost movements and fertility trends in developing countries—seem to limit the explanatory power of arguments about movements in child costs. Movements in relative child costs cannot explain away all of the cross-sectional fertility patterns in twentieth-century America. Nor can they account for the postwar baby boom and bust, though they play a partial role. Nor do they pass all the simple tests of raw correlation in the experience of developing countries: they cannot, for example, explain why fertility has begun to decline somewhat in Egypt and India but not in Mexico.

It appears that, when this measure is polished up and given its chance, we will still have to divide our explanations of the most important fertility patterns over time and across socioeconomic groups among these categories of contributing forces: (1) patterns in relative child costs; (2) patterns in the relationship of couples' current income prospects to their prior living standards, a force that can be viewed either as a proxy for their information costs about different life-styles and modes of child-rearing or more simply as a parameter of their tastes regarding inputs per family member; (3) other taste variables; (4) differences in the supply of the means of contraception; and (5) differences in fecundity. The relative-child-cost measure does not promise a monocausal explanation of fertility patterns; it only offers a way to organize the standard vague economic arguments linking secular fertility decline with modernization and to supplement these with a method of accounting for some of the absence of fertility decline in many early-development settings.

1.3 The Concept of Relative Child Cost

1.3.1 Basic Features

Rich as our intuitions are about how changes in the economic environment affect couples' natality incentives, our progress toward converting these intuitive arguments into a manageable and measurable concept has been surprisingly slow. Calculations have been made of the absolute dollar costs and benefits of an extra child. Recently these calculations have been sharpened to include time costs and, in some cases, to be appropriately specific to different birth orders and parental incomes, especially in the United States.[14] The arguments about child costs and economic development are often stated as assertions that changes in the economy drive up a child's absolute net cost to his parents. Yet this is an awkward way of discussing child costs for the purposes of analyzing fertility behavior. If a concept of child cost is to be usable as part of a choice-theoretic framework for analyzing controlled fertility, it must at least separate out price influences in the couples' environment from influences stemming proximately from their tastes and incomes. Treating child costs as an absolute net dollar magnitude fails to meet this standard, even though knowing the absolute magnitude has other uses. Even if there were no change in the price signals couples receive from the economic environment, improvements in their income prospects alone would affect the amounts they spent on each child. Shifts in tastes would do the same. When people's incomes go up at fixed prices of time and commodities, leading them to spend more on each child, we say that they can afford higher-input children. We do not say that the "costs" of children have risen in this case, any more than the higher food expenditures of the rich mean that food "costs" the rich more. Similarly, if couples' tastes shift toward higher inputs of time and commodities per family member with given income, referring to this as a shift that raises the "cost" of a child threatens to confuse taste effects with couples' responses to changes in the prices they face when trading with the outside world.

Thus, if needed repairs are to be made to the vague economic concept of child costs, the first step answers the question, Costs of *what kind* of child? For the cost concept to focus on the effect of changing prices that couples face, it must be an index of the cost of one particular set of time and commodity inputs, one characteristic of a relevant birth order, child life expectancy, parental income level, and so forth. It is more workable when defined as an input price index, not as a measure of net economic value or of psychic cost or value.

A second step is to resolve the question, Cost to whom? Since the concept is being developed to analyze private fertility behavior, an index of the costs facing young couples will be pursued rather than an index of the costs to society. To limit the task of the present paper, I will focus more narrowly on the private child costs facing young married couples over the rest of their lives. No discussion will be given to the possible domination of husband or wife in marital fertility decision-making or to the decisions of unmarried couples regarding intercourse and marriage, though changes in child costs might even have an effect on these premarital decisions.

The final question to be faced in deciding on the basic features of a workable child-cost measure is, Cost relative to what? The arguments about the evolution of child costs presume that this evolution affects fertility decision-making within a context of household choice, analogous to the models of consumer choice that derive demand functions from taste, relative prices, and an income constraint. For this analogy to retain its value it is essential that the price concept be one of relative price, again not one of absolute value of expenditures. The relative cost of an extra child can be said to change only if exogenous changes in the prices of goods and services change the ratio of the input price of a child to the input price of the bundle of activities with which an extra child competes. And it is with some other activities, not with "goods" or "commodities," that children compete. Parents' enjoyment of children is a home activity, an output, produced with both time and commodity inputs, competing with other activities using time and commodities. An extra child competes for couples' time and commodity resources with the further development of parents' enjoyment of already-born children and with activities not related to children.

1.3.2 The Relative-Cost Formula

These basic considerations lead to a formula for the relative cost of an extra child, a ratio of price indexes that fits into any of several household optimization models, even ones in which couples choose fertility regulation strategies rather than childbirth outcomes.[15] The first price index is an index of the prices of the inputs that go into an *N*th family member in a family of given potential income. It is based on the absolute discounted cost of a child's inputs at the expense of his parents' household, net of the child's economic contribution, over the parents' entire expected lifetime in some base period.[16] The absolute cost of the child in the base period is:

(1)
$$\text{Cost}_N = \sum_{t=0}^{T} \frac{\left[\sum_{n=1}^{N} s_t w_{nt} L^N{}_{nt} + \sum_{j=1}^{J} s_t p_{jt} C^N{}_{jt}\right]}{(1+r)^{t+1}},$$

where T = the number of years until the couple's lifetime planning horizon;

s_t = the probability that the child will survive (and remain in the parents' household) to age t;

w_n = the after-tax dollar wage rate of the nth family member, valued at the rate being earned by workers with that member's attributes at the time of decision;[17]

$L^N{}_{nt}$ = the nth family member's time input into the extra child in the tth year, for $n = 0, \ldots, N-1$; for $n = N$, L^N equals *minus* the work time contributed by the Nth family member while still within the household, either at paid work or at household chores that would have to have been performed whether or not this extra child existed;

$C^N{}_{jt}$ = the input of the jth commodity into the extra child in the tth year; for the years after the child has left the home, this set of variables reflects the net flow of transfers from parents to child (parents' gifts and bequests minus support by this child's family);

p_j = its price, at the decision time one year before birth of the Nth family member; and

r = the rate of discount, discussed below.

The related concept of the absolute cost of a *surviving* child equals this same formula with all the survival probabilities, the s_t's, set at unity.

Note that this absolute input cost is measured net of the child's own economic contribution to his parents' household and is not a gross measure of inputs as would be more appropriate for studies of the formation of human capital in children. While the extra child is still a member of his parents' household, his contributions of time for paid work and for chores that would have to be done with or without him are to be subtracted from the time other family members devote to him, in order to arrive at an estimate for the net time input into him. His earnings at paid work must also be included in the income of the expanded family when deducing the effect of the extra child on the family's commodity consumption. His earnings are implicitly viewed as a substitute for the same value of earnings on the part of other family members, as though they are permitted to work less for the same total commodity consumption if he exists. If his contribution to his parents' household turns out to outweigh the gross discounted cost of his inputs, then of course the formula yields the child's asset value (times minus one) if the discount rate is the appropriate rate of return on alternative assets.

Since our present interest is in using this absolute cost formula as part of a price-ratio index, let us define a cost index of these same child inputs as

(2)
$$P_N = \sum_{i=1}^{N+J} c_i p_i \qquad (\Sigma c_i = 1.00),$$

where P_N is the index of child input cost,

p_i is the price index for the ith child input, whether the time of a family member or one of the J commodity classes, and

c_i is the share of the ith input in total cost in the base period.

The base period can be a fixed one, as in the 1960-based index used below. A somewhat better alternative is to use a divisia index as a way of allowing the share weights in the inputs to vary across temporal and spatial comparisons. Adjusting the weights as frequently as possible is especially desirable in view of the systematic shifts in relative weights during the development process, to be documented further below.

The next task is to set up a similar input price index, P_H, for the inputs going into the "alternative bundle," the extra enjoyment of various home activities without the extra child. At the level of any one family, it would be impossible to observe both this alternative bundle and the bundle of inputs going into the extra child. If the family has the extra child, we cannot observe the alternative bundle, the time and commodity inputs they would have devoted to extra travel, living room furniture, landownership, and so forth without the child. If they do not have the extra child, we cannot observe the inputs of time and commodities into that child. Estimating the impact of an extra child on the family's time and commodity allocation, like any other estimation of impacts or effects or causes, involves a counterfactual comparison.

To observe the alternative bundle for comparison with the child input bundle, use is made of a standard assumption of cross-sectional analysis. It is assumed that any couple that in fact had, say, a third child would have followed the same time path of time and commodity inputs over the (cross-sectionally derived) life cycle as do (two-child) couples with all the same attributes except for having a third child. In theoretical terms, this amounts to assuming that the constrained two-child and three-child optima being compared by the two-child couple in its decision-making about fertility regulation correspond to the time paths revealed for couples like them (in schooling, age, race, residence, etc.) having two and three children.

Using this cross-sectional assumption, it is in fact possible to reveal the time and commodity inputs in the alternative bundle by estimating all the effects of the extra child on the household's "foreign trade and payments"—its imports of goods and services, its exports of labor services and home-produced goods, and its net savings.

An extra child will raise some commodity imports into the home and lower others. Imports are raised for those goods used more in child-rearing than in other home activities. As we shall see below, rearing an extra child raises food imports considerably, has a smaller effect on imports of clothing and shelter, and greatly reduces imports of other commodities. Knowing these import effects allows us to reveal the commodity inputs into the alternative bundle. Using the superscript H for the whole set of activities that are the alternative to having the extra child, we can express the following identity for each year t

Value of the *i*th input taken away from other home activities by having the extra child	=	Value of the *i*th input devoted to raising the child	−	Increase in imports of the *i*th input caused by having the extra child

in terms of symbols as follows:

$$(3) \qquad -C^H{}_i \equiv C^N{}_i - (C^H{}_i + C^N{}_i).$$

The term on the left side can be revealed by estimating the items on the right. The $C^N{}_i$ values are estimated by studies trying to quantify the commodity inputs into individual children. The net import effects can be derived from household expenditure surveys showing the variation of family expenditures with the number of children for comparable income and age classes. The resulting figures for the $C^H{}_i$'s can be cross-checked for plausibility against independent estimates of income elasticities of expenditure.

In calculating the effects of a child on the family's commodity imports, considerable care must be taken to specify correctly the income the family would have without the child. One cannot simply compare consumption patterns of families with the same income and different family size, since family size affects income, both through hours worked and through wage rates. The arrival of an extra child is often accompanied by an immediate reduction in family income, since the wife often drops out of the labor force. Further family income losses result because the wife's job is interrupted when the baby arrives. The reduction in her job experience means that she will tend to receive a lower hourly wage than if she had not had the child. This job-interruption effect on her wage rate, like the loss of work hours, lowers the family's income. Partly offsetting these losses of the wife's income is the net increment to the father's income: fathers tend to work slightly longer hours to support their larger families.[18] All these effects on the family's labor export earnings must be taken into account in deriving estimates of the family's commodities with and without the extra child. The two bundles thus involve different time paths of household income.

The time taken away from other home activities each year by an extra child can be estimated by using another identity. For any nth family member other than the extra child, the fact that total living hours per year are fixed means:

$$(4) \qquad L^N{}_{nt} + L^H{}_{nt} + \Delta L_{nt} = = \Delta \bar{L}_{nt} = 0,$$

where the N superscript is for inputs of time into the Nth family member, the H is for activities that are alternatives to having another child, the L's without superscripts are time spent working for pay in the labor force, and the bar is for total available time. The value of home time taken from other home activities during the year t $(-L^H{}_{nt})$ can be derived by subtracting any reduction in labor exports from the estimate of the time put into the extra child $(L^N{}_{nt})$. The reduction in labor time exports can be estimated from studies of labor force participation, and the time spent on an extra child can be estimated from time-use studies.

In this way figures can be derived for all the inputs, both time and commodity, into the alternative activities. The absolute cost of the alternative bundle of inputs can then be measured by the formula:

(5)
$$\text{Cost}_H = \sum_{t=0} \frac{\left[\sum_{n=1}^{N-1} w_{nt}L^H{}_{nt} + \sum_{j=1}^{J} p_j C^H{}_{jt}\right]}{(1+r)^{t+1}}.$$

The discounted values of the two bundles are not necessarily equal. They will differ by the effects of the extra child on the family's total earning potential (for given labor-force participation rates), the effects of the child on the parents' taxes (in particular, the tax exemption per dependent), and a technical discrepancy arising from any difference between the discount rate and the rate of return earned on the parents' savings, which shift resources between time periods.

The index-number counterpart to cost_H, or the index of the prices of inputs into the alternative activities with which the extra child is revealed to be competing, is

(6)
$$P_H = \sum_{i=1.00}^{N+J} d_i p_i \left(\sum_{i=1}^{N+J} d_i = 1.00\right),$$

where P_H is the index of absolute cost of the alternative to having another child, p_i is defined as before, and d_i is the share of the ith input in the total cost of the H bundle in the base period.

Now that we have defined indexes for the input costs of the two alternatives to be compared, the definition of the *relative cost index* for an extra child is simply

(7)
$$P_C = P_N/P_H.$$

Since P_C is a *relative* price index, we need be concerned only with the *differences* in the shares of each input in the two component indexes. It can be shown that the effect of a given percentage movement in the price (or wage) of one home input yields a percentage change in the relative cost of an extra child governed only by the difference in the shares of that input in the numerator and denominator bundles of inputs:

(8)
$$\left(\frac{\Delta P_c}{P_c}\right) \approx \sum_{i=1}^{N+J} \left(\frac{\Delta P_i}{P_i}\right) \times (c_i - d_i).$$

This is a useful simplification of the formula. It means that the magnitudes crucial to the behavior of the relative cost index are the net effects of an extra child on family members' paid work and the household's total consumption of various classes of commodities, represented by the term $(c_i - d_i)$. These effects on the household's foreign trade patterns are easier to estimate than the actual child inputs, which require considerable assumptions about how time and commodities are divided up within the home. The fact that only differences in the shares make the index respond to relative input price movements further means that the weight differences (again, the $c_i - d_i$ terms) do not obsolesce so rapidly as households' incomes grow. Income growth will raise the quantities of commodities going into a child of given parity, but it will also raise the quantities going into the activities with which children compete, leaving smaller net effects on the weight differences. It will turn out below that just a few shifts in weight differences seem to occur with the process of economic development and income growth, making the relative cost index move in accordance with a few key movements in relative prices and weight shifts.

In the event that children turn out to be a net economic asset in the base period, the formula would have to be modified slightly. In this situation, the appropriate measure would be an index ratio relating to the returns from, and the gross inputs into, an extra child. In the numerator would be an index of the prices of the goods and services delivered by the child to the parents' household, and in the denominator would be a price index of the gross inputs into the child. Movements in wages and price would affect this benefit-cost index.

It is worth pausing to reflect on how this concept would be aligned with the more common household-production frameworks recently used to develop models of fertility behavior. Within such frameworks the household budget constraint is often put in nonlinear form. Abstracting from the specific stage of the life cycle, this budget constraint is something like:

$$I = p_z z + p_q q n, \tag{9}$$

where I is the household's total potential income, p_z is an index vector of the prices of inputs into the parents' child-unrelated activities (smoking, adult entertainment, etc.), z is a vector of the amounts of these child-unrelated inputs, p_q is an index vector of the prices of inputs into the children, q is a vector of the average level of inputs per child, and n is the number of children.[19] Abstracting further from the effect of an extra child on income potential itself and from distinctions between current children and surviving children, it is clear that the relative cost of an extra child, the Nth child is

$$P_C = \frac{q p_q}{p_q\,(N-1)\,(\Delta q) + p_z\,(\Delta z)}, \tag{10}$$

where the average inputs level in the numerator (q) is evaluated in the situation with the extra child and the changes in q and z are caused by the need to fit the extra child into the budget constraint. This expression becomes the overall scalar index of relative child cost by letting the p's vary and using the remaining expressions to define the base-period budget weights.

The input price index in the denominator of expressions 7 and 10 is a weighted average of the prices of inputs into extra child-unrelated activities and the prices of inputs into the already-born $N - 1$ children. The procedure outlined above for estimating the alternative bundle does not separate inputs into child-unrelated activities from extra inputs into raising earlier children. In the present state of our knowledge, it is important to avoid trying to make that separation. It is very difficult in practice to identify just which inputs go into child-unrelated activities and which are inputs into children, the more so since so many home activities are shared by all family members. Given this difficulty, it is hard to know to what extent an extra child beyond the first is competing with "adult consumption aspirations" and to what extent he competes with higher average inputs for the earlier children, sometimes unhelpfully labeled "child quality."[20]

1.3.3 Actual versus Perceived Costs

The relative cost measure just sketched calls for immense detail on the average costs of a child to his parents, costs that are "actual" costs if one accepts the assumed accuracy of effects derived from survey cross sections. Computing the costs of the child-input bundle and the alternative bundle is an expensive operation. It took a research assistant and myself hundreds of hours to settle on a satisfactory set of estimates for urban United States families in 1960. I would not embark on such a task just before a fertility-relevant bedtime, and I doubt any peasants would either. The process of making the calculations is itself economically unprofitable, since its costs exceed the expected value of the extra information to the average couple. Of what use can the measurement of actual child-cost patterns be if young couples could not perceive the true magnitudes facing them?

To judge the value of measure of actual child costs for fertility analysis, we must begin by rejecting both extreme views. It is as unreasonable to believe that significant movements in actual relative child costs would be totally irrelevant as it is to assume that couples make calculations like the ones sketched here. The shares of parents' income taken up by the inputs into an extra child are impressive by any measure. It would be much harder to ignore a given percentage movement in the cost of an extra child than it would be to ignore a price increase on matches or cooking pans. The budget constraint is too real, especially at low income levels. Even illiterate villagers can count, and they know they have no choice but to make choices.

Interview responses also seem to show some awareness of the economic costs and benefits of children in all societies, both when respondents are asked about these and when they are just asked to extemporize about the pluses and minuses of children.[21] The recent surveys conducted through the East-West Institute suggested that the tendency to describe the gains and losses from children in explicitly economic terms was even greater in rural and lower-income groups than in the more modern settings.[22] Furthermore, many responses that are not explicitly put in monetary terms nonetheless reflect a direct awareness of the time costs and benefits of children, as when couples mention "too much responsibility," "career conflicts," "fear of doing a bad job as a parent" (to previous children), "general freedom and fun conflicts," and "interference with husband/wife affiliative relationship."

It seems advisable to take an intermediate position, believing that couples are somehow made aware of some rough outlines of the economic costs and benefits of extra children. Since they cannot conceivably get their information from a direct calculation of these costs and benefits, the best guess is that they gather them indirectly, by hearing about and observing the fortunes of other couples. Women will tend to hear more about the agonizing conflict between children and career development in settings in which wage rates away from home are high enough to make the conflict real. Peasants will more readily accept the argument that feeding an extra child is a terrible burden "in times like these" when their ability to buy or grow food with child labor is indeed low than when real wages in terms of food have been higher for some time. Where housing is rationed and extra rooms are especially scarce, urban couples will hear from others, if not see for themselves, what problems come home with an extra child. There are, in other words, plausible mechanisms through which couples who would never speak in terms of cost-benefit analysis would nonetheless respond to child costs and benefits, like the man who spoke prose without knowing it.

There remains the problem of deciding which aspects of the actual costs and benefits couples perceive more clearly and which they tend to overlook. This problem is not easily resolved. The only workable strategy here is to pursue the various actual cost considerations as far as the data allow, on the assumption that the perceived importance of any part of the cost calculation is proportional to its actual quantitative importance.

1.3.4 The Discount Rate and Parents' Savings

The issue of perceptions carries over into another aspect of the relative cost formula, an aspect not easily resolved by standard economic theory. In the formulas for the base-period costs of child inputs and inputs into the alternative inputs, all magnitudes were discounted back to a decision-making date one year before the would-be birth. What is the appropriate discount rate?

To some noneconomists, the issue of a discount rate may seem to be just another symptom of overinvestment in elaborate economic theorizing. Yet the issue is as inescapable as it is knotty. Its difficulty was exemplified when one recent seminar participant tried to wave aside the discount rate as irrelevant on the grounds that "Everybody knows that people don't plan very far ahead, so it's obvious that the discount rate is zero." The confusion goes deeper than a mere semantic misunderstanding over how the economist defines the discount rate, especially when the behavior of peasants and other low-income groups is being discussed. On one hand, it is traditional to view them as myopic, which would make them give much more attention to the early costs of infant-rearing than to later child costs and benefits. On the other, it is also traditional to say that children are valued mainly for their income support for the parents in the distant future. Given the limits on the actual ratios of future support from children to early child-rearing costs, it is hard to argue that the discount rate is both high and low.

Economic theory does not suggest a clear choice of discount rate for the effects of children. The usual guideline is that any investment's stream of expected costs and returns should be compared with the expected rates of return on other assets having the same perceived degree of effect on the riskiness of the decision-maker's entire portfolio. This is a weak guideline here, since the returns from the child are more noneconomic than for most other assets. The procedure followed in my child-cost calculations for the urban United States in 1960 has been to calculate all values under a wide range of discount rates running from the unlikely zero rate up to 18% per annum, with preferred rates being 13% for low-income couples (near the private rate of return on college) and 8% per annum for high-income couples (near the private rate of return on graduate education).[23] In what follows, readers will want to note that their own views about the myopia or hyperopia of young couples will tip the scales toward or away from those effects of a child that come soon after birth.

Also complicated, but having lesser effect on the quantitative patterns in child costs, is the issue of the effect of children on their parents' savings in nonhuman form. Over the years in their parents' household, children tend to reduce the parents' savings, though this tendency is mitigated by the children's contribution to family capital formation in many agricultural settings. A careful calculation of the whole lifetime streams of costs and benefits of an extra child must weigh in the fact that the child may cause the parents to dissave and pull their use of resources toward the present at the expense of consumption and leisure in the more distant future. Less clear is whether parents make up this dissaving by the end of their expected life-span. If they had strict targets for the inheritances to be left to each child, they would more than make up the lost saving in order to allow the extra child his target bequest. If they do not or cannot meet such targets, the effect of the extra child on their savings may be negative even by the time they die. The impact of family size on the final bequests of decedents is empirically unresolved, and an assumption about terminal savings would have to be made for any detailed calculation of child costs. Elsewhere I have assumed that terminal savings are unaffected by the extra child, though the quantitative importance of this assumption looks slight.[24]

1.3.5 The Rise of Average Child Inputs and the Role of Tastes

The relative-cost concept thus defined may seem too narrow to capture all that we think of when discussing the effect of rising child costs on fertility. In particular, one may suspect that there are aspects of the secular rise in average inputs per child that ought to be called a rise in average child "costs" facing succeeding generations of young adults. This suspicion of narrowness has taken two forms in past discussion of the cost issue.

One suspicion, prompted by the use of other household-production-function models, is that the concept as defined here overlooks the simple point that increases in average child inputs drive up the "price" of an extra child. In the language usually used in such models, increases in child quality drive up the shadow price on child quantity. Yet this way of putting it does not specify either the alternatives with which children are being compared or the reasons why higher average inputs per child clearly raise their unit price relative to any commodity, though not relative to an hour of time. Average inputs are on the rise not only for a child, but for other home activities as well. Vacations, entertainment, home improvements, and other activities also absorb rising average inputs. It is not clear that children are rising in price relative to these activities, except to the extent that changes in input prices make such an overall relative price change show in the measure as defined here. In addition, the rise in average inputs, when it occurs for reasons not related to changes in relative input prices, is a force that needs to be explained in terms of tastes and incomes.

The other suspicion is that as incomes grow and development proceeds, people find children increasingly costly in the sense that their upbringing and social position leave them "no choice" but to buy more "costly" children. These forces are real enough. They could in fact be defined as shifts in tastes or as shifts in relative child cost, though this latter approach would have to follow an unconventional route. To make the influence of upbringing and social surroundings an influence on child *costs*, one would have to erect a plausible but empirically elusive argument about information costs. One could plausibly argue that being brought up on, and surrounded by, higher living standards raises the cost to young couples of finding out how they could manage to rear a child with lower inputs. Conversely, their greater familiarity with high-input modes of child-rearing lowers the cost to them of such children relative to lower-input children and the alternatives to lower-input children. Yet any such attempt to work the influence of upbringing and social surroundings into a cost concept overburdens the concept and removes it from its usual choice-theoretic role. It is simpler, and more productive of interdisciplinary cooperation in research on fertility, to put such influences into the categories of income effects and taste effects, leaving the cost measure to pick up only shifts in observable input price ratios.

1.4 An Application to the United States in the Twentieth Century

To clarify how child costs have changed with the process of economic development, I shall first take advantage of the relative abundance of survey data for the postwar urban United States. It is possible to calculate the entire lifetime profiles of parents' use of time and commodities for a first child, a third child, and the activities these replace, for "low-income" and "high-income" couples in the urban United States in 1960. Several data bases have been combined to generate the lifetime profiles. First a low-income and a high-income husband were chosen with reference to 1960 census data on incomes, the former having an hourly rate of pay rising from $1.31 at age 23 to a peak of $2.28 by age 47 and the second earning from $2.25 an hour at age 23 to $5.15 by age 52. Their wives were given corresponding wage rates. The wives' wage rates, their working hours, and husbands' working hours were all allowed to vary with childbearing experience in accordance with estimates derived from cross-sectional studies. Given these family income profiles (and some savings effects caused by child-rearing), the next step was to estimate the time and commodity inputs into a first child, born on the parents' 24th birthday, and a third child, born on the parents' 30th birthday. The time inputs were estimated from the 1967–68 Cornell time-use survey in Syracuse, and the commodity inputs and net effects of the child on family consumption patterns were estimated from the 1960–61 Survey of Consumer Expenditures and some USDA guesses about child inputs based on the same data. The child was assumed to survive his parents in each case. This set of procedures generated the set of 1960 estimates shown in tables 1.2 through 1.5.[25]

The tables reveal several patterns in the differences between child inputs and the inputs into alternative activities. Regarding commodity inputs, all four tables show that an extra child raises the family's consumption of food, regardless of income level, birth order, or the discount rate. That is, a greater value of food enters as an input into the child than would have been purchased by the household in pursuit of other extra enjoyments without the child. This food intensity of extra children is not confined to the United States. Household budget surveys from at least 17 countries have also shown that extra children raise the share budgeted for food.[26] The prevalence of this pattern suggests a not-so-surprising corollary to Engel's law: extra dependents, like poverty, raise the share spent on food.

The effect of an extra child on housing expenditures proves slightly negative in all cases except the first child of a low-income couple. This negative effect prevails in most other household budget surveys as well. It runs counter to the natural belief that extra children require more room and should force their parents into purchasing it. The negative shelter effect does not really contradict this belief. The extra children are simply forcing their parents to make cuts somewhere in order to feed them, and part of the cuts come at the expense of total shelter expenditures. Detailed studies of the demand for specific housing characteristics seem to resolve the puzzle by showing that larger families in fact consume more site space as well as more rooms yet cut their expenditures on centrality of location and other dimensions of housing quality so much as to bring a net reduction in shelter expenditures with larger family size.[27] This means that merely following the overall consumer price index for shelter may hide important information about the drift in the relative cost of the kind of housing that is most relevant to children. If site space and extra rooms are rising faster in price, or becoming more severely rationed, than housing in general, then the relative cost of extra children may be rising in a way that the available figures cannot reveal.

Another clear pattern of commodity intensity is that children are luxury-sparing rather than luxury-intensive. That is, they tend to reduce household consumption of highly income-elastic commodities, as shown by the negative share differentials for "all other" on the right in tables 1.2 through 1.5. It would be highly desirable to break down this large residual category further to identify more fully just which luxury goods are most strongly associated with the alternative input bundle. With such information, it would be possible to be more selective in choosing price indexes for measuring the relative cost of an extra child across time and space. For the present, however, it is necessary to stick to the general observation that luxury goods are heavily associated with the alternative life-styles with which extra children compete.

Tables 1.2 through 1.5 also quantify the time inputs into children and into the alternatives to children. The gross adult time cost accounts for about half the total cost of either a first or a third child at the preferred discount rates (13% in tables 1.2 and 1.3, 8% in tables 1.4 and 1.5). The number of hours represented by this time cost is of course greater

Table 1.2 **Cost Shares, "Low-Income" Couple's First Child and Alternative Activities, Based on 1960 Urban Cross-Sectional Data for the United States**

		Child Inputs (N Bundle)			Alternative-Activity Inputs (H Bundle)			Differences in Shares (%) (N – H)		
Discount Rate		0%	13%	18%	0%	13%	18%	0%	13%	18%
Total amount, all inputs	$	21,102	9,069	7,365	28,138	8,135	6,417			
	%	100	100	100	100	100	100	—	—	—
Adult time inputs	$	8,569	4,591	3,970	2,603	1,644	1,493			
	%	40.6	50.6	53.9	9.3	20.2	23.3	31.3	30.4	30.6
Child's chore and paid work contribution	$	−1,849	−333	−188	—	—	—			
	%	−8.8	−3.7	−2.6	—	—	—	−8.8	−3.7	−2.6
Net time inputs	$	6,720	4,258	3,782	2,603	1,644	1,493			
	%	31.8	47.0	51.4	9.3	20.2	23.3	22.5	26.8	28.1
Food	$	4,267	1,378	1,008	4,630	930	706			
	%	20.2	15.2	13.7	16.5	11.4	11.0	3.7	3.8	2.7
Shelter	$	3,562	1,304	990	4,604	1,144	858			
	%	16.9	14.4	13.4	16.4	14.1	13.4	0.5	0.3	0.0
Medical care	$	1,107	618	544	1,182	281	189			
	%	5.2	6.8	7.4	4.2	3.5	2.9	1.0	3.3	4.5
All other commodities	$	5,446	1,511	1,041	15,119	4,136	3,171			
	%	25.8	16.6	14.1	53.7	50.8	49.4	−27.9	−34.2	−35.3

Table 1.2 (continued)

		Child Inputs (N Bundle)			Alternative-Activity Inputs (H Bundle)			Differences in Shares (%) (N − H)		
Discount Rate		0%	13%	18%	0%	13%	18%	0%	13%	18%
Child clothing	$	3,043	nc	nc	—	—	—			
	%	14.4	nc	nc	—	—	—	14.4	nc	nc
Utilities	$	1,649	nc	nc	2,514	nc	nc			
	%	7.8	nc	nc	8.9	nc	nc	−1.1	nc	nc
Transportation	$	0	0	0	2,475	nc	nc			
	%	0	0	0	8.8	nc	nc	−8.8	nc	nc
Recreation	$	628	nc	nc	383	nc	nc			
	%	3.0	nc	nc	1.4	nc	nc	1.6	nc	nc
Education	$	126	nc	nc	00	00	00			
	%	0.6	nc	nc	00	00	00	0.6	nc	nc
Total commodity inputs	$	14,382	4,811	3,583	25,535	6,491	4,924			
	%	68.2	53.0	48.6	90.7	79.8	76.7	−22.5	−26.8	−28.1
Difference in total bundle values[a]	$	7,036	−934	−948						

Note: nc = not calculated. — = zero by definition. 0 = zero by assumption. 00 = zero by estimation.

[a]The reduction in the mother's rate of pay as a result of the child times the hours she would have worked without the child, *minus* the value of the income-tax exemption per child.

Table 1.3 **Cost Shares, "Low-Income" Couple's Third Child and Alternative Activities, Based on 1960 Urban Cross-Sectional Data (Three-year Child Spacing)**

		Child Inputs (N Bundle)			Alternative-Activity Inputs (H Bundle)			Differences in Shares (%) (N − H)		
Discount Rate		0%	13%	18%	0%	13%	18%	0%	13%	18%
Total amount, all inputs	$	15,050	6,801	5,533	16,059	6,721	5,556			
	%	100	100	100	100	100	100	—	—	—
Time inputs by adults and older siblings	$	6,043	3,331	2,842	4,195	2,534	2,280			
	%	40.1	49.0	51.4	26.1	37.7	41.0	14.0	11.3	10.4
Child's chore and paid work contribution	$	−1,650	−297	−168	—	—	—			
	%	−11.0	−4.4	−3.0	—	—	—	−11.0	−4.4	−3.0
Net time inputs	$	4,393	3,034	2,674	4,195	2,534	2,280			
	%	29.2	44.6	48.3	26.1	37.7	41.0	3.1	6.9	7.3
Food	$	4,047	1,304	954	2,079	670	536			
	%	26.9	19.2	17.2	12.9	10.0	9.6	14.0	9.2	7.6
Shelter	$	2,532	902	686	2,907	1,172	888			
	%	16.8	13.3	12.4	18.1	17.4	16.0	−1.3	−4.1	−3.6
Medical care	$	1,012	586	507	757	272	189			
	%	6.7	8.6	9.2	4.7	4.0	3.4	2.0	4.6	5.8
All other	$	3,066	975	712	6,121	2,073	1,663			
	%	20.4	14.3	12.9	38.1	30.9	29.9	−17.7	−16.5	−17.0

Table 1.3 (continued)

		Child Inputs (N Bundle)			Alternative-Activity Inputs (H Bundle)			Differences in Shares (%) (N − H)		
Discount Rate		0%	13%	18%	0%	13%	18%	0%	13%	18%
Child clothing	$	1,300	nc	nc	567	nc	nc			
	%	8.6	nc	nc	3.5	nc	nc	5.1	nc	nc
Utilities	$	1,413	nc	nc	1,562	nc	nc			
	%	9.4	nc	nc	9.7	nc	nc	−0.3	nc	nc
Transportation	$	0	0	0	583	nc	nc			
	%	0	0	0	3.6	nc	nc	−3.6	nc	nc
Recreation	$	271	nc	nc	299	nc	nc			
	%	1.8	nc	nc	1.9	nc	nc	−0.1	nc	nc
Education	$	82	nc	nc	97	nc	nc			
	%	0.5	nc	nc	0.6	nc	nc	−0.1	nc	nc
Total commodity inputs	$	10,657	3,767	2,859	11,864	4,187	3,276			
	%	70.8	55.4	51.7	73.9	62.3	59.0	−3.1	−6.9	−7.3
Difference in total bundle values[a]	$	+1,009	−80	+23						

Note: nc = not calculated. — = zero by definition.
[a]The reduction in the mother's rate of pay as a result of the child times the hours she would have worked without the child, *minus* the value of the income-tax exemption per child.

Table 1.4 **Cost Shares, "High-Income" Couple's First Child and Alternative Activities, Based on 1960 Urban Cross-Sectional Data for the United States**

		Child Inputs (N Bundle)			Alternative-Activity Inputs (H Bundle)			Differences in Shares (%) (N − H)		
Discount Rate		0%	8%	13%	0%	8%	13%	0%	8%	13%
Total amount, all inputs	$	41,520	21,402	15,890	68,658	18,873	13,121			
	%	100	100	100	100	100	100	—	—	—
Adult time inputs	$	16,131	10,523	8,647	4,898	3,682	3,357			
	%	38.9	49.2	54.4	7.1	19.5	25.5	31.8	29.7	28.9
Child's chore and paid work contribution	$	−3,684	−1,229	−661	—	—	—			
	%	−8.9	−5.7	−4.2	—	—	—	−8.9	−5.7	−4.2
Net time inputs	$	12,446	9,294	7,986	4,898	3,682	3,357			
	%	29.9	43.4	50.3	7.1	19.5	25.5	22.8	23.9	24.8
Food	$	6,423	2,969	2,027	11,614	2,460	1,553			
	%	15.4	13.9	12.8	16.9	13.0	11.8	−1.5	0.9	1.0
Shelter	$	4,630	2,325	1,657	8,765	2,315	1,492			
	%	11.1	10.9	10.4	12.8	12.3	11.4	−1.7	−1.4	−1.0
Medical care	$	1,563	976	794	3,969	776	489			
	%	3.8	4.6	5.0	5.8	4.1	3.7	−2.0	0.5	1.3
All other commodities	$	16,458	5,838	3,426	39,412	9,640	6,230			
	%	39.5	27.3	21.6	57.4	51.1	47.6	−17.9	−23.8	−26.0

Table 1.4 (continued)

Discount Rate		Child Inputs (N Bundle) 0%	8%	13%	Alternative-Activity Inputs (H Bundle) 0%	8%	13%	Differences in Shares (%) (N – H) 0%	8%	13%
Child clothing	$	4,891	nc	nc	—	—	—			
	%	11.7	nc	nc	—	—	—	11.7	nc	nc
Utilities	$	3,223	nc	nc	3,408	nc	nc			
	%	7.8	nc	nc	5.0	nc	nc	2.8	nc	nc
Transportation	$	0	0	0	4,334	nc	nc			
	%	0	0	0	6.3	nc	nc	–6.3	nc	nc
Recreation	$	1,498	nc	nc	432	nc	nc			
	%	3.6	nc	nc	0.6	nc	nc	3.0	nc	nc
Education	$	6,846	nc	nc	3	nc	nc			
	%	16.4	nc	nc	0.0	nc	nc	16.4	nc	nc
Total commodity inputs	$	29,074	21,108	7,904	63,760	15,191	9,764			
	%	70.1	56.6	49.7	92.9	80.5	74.5	–22.8	–23.9	–24.8
Difference in total bundle values[a]	$	27,138	–2,529	–2,769						

Note: nc = not calculated. — = zero by definition. 0 = zero by assumption.
[a]The reduction in the mother's rate of pay as a result of the child times the hours she would have worked without the child, *minus* the value of the income-tax exemption per child.

Table 1.5 **Cost Shares, "High-Income" Couple's Third Child and Alternative Activities, Based on 1960 Urban Cross-Sectional Data (Three-year Child Spacing)**

		Child Inputs (N Bundle)			Alternative-Activity Inputs (H Bundle)			Differences in Shares (%) (N − H)		
Discount Rate		0%	8%	13%	0%	8%	13%	0%	8%	13%
Total amount, all inputs	$	32,108	16,628	12,341	36,650	14,748	11,560			
	%	100	100	100	100	100	100	—	—	—
Time inputs by adults and older siblings	$	11,324	7,583	6,268	8,022	5,717	4,789			
	%	35.3	45.6	50.1	21.9	38.8	41.4	13.4	6.8	8.7
Child's chore and paid work contribution	$	−3,013	−1,011	−546	—	—	—			
	%	−9.4	−6.1	−4.4				−9.4	−6.1	−4.4
Net time inputs	$	8,311	6,572	5,722	8,022	5,717	4,789			
	%	25.9	39.5	45.7	21.9	38.8	41.4	4.0	0.7	4.3
Food	$	6,053	2,806	1,917	5,214	1,607	1,136			
	%	19.0	16.9	15.5	14.2	10.9	9.8	4.8	6.0	5.7
Shelter	$	3,423	1,684	1,195	5,357	2,089	1,499			
	%	10.7	10.1	9.7	14.6	14.2	13.0	−3.9	−4.1	−3.3
Medical care	$	1,084	930	761	1,798	833	616			
	%	3.4	5.6	6.2	4.9	5.6	5.3	−1.5	0.0	0.9
All other	$	13,237	4,636	2,746	16,259	4,502	3,520			
	%	41.3	27.9	22.2	44.4	30.5	30.4	−3.1	−2.6	−8.2

Table 1.5 (continued)

		Child Inputs (N Bundle)			Alternative-Activity Inputs (H Bundle)			Differences in Shares (%) (N − H)		
Discount Rate		0%	8%	13%	0%	8%	13%	0%	8%	13%
Child clothing	$	2,780	nc	nc	1,088	nc	nc			
	%	8.7	nc	nc	3.0	nc	nc	5.7	nc	nc
Utilities	$	2,837	nc	nc	4,190	nc	nc			
	%	8.8	nc	nc	11.4	nc	nc	−2.7	nc	nc
Transportation	$	0	0	0	1,859	nc	nc			
	%	0	0	0	5.1	nc	nc	−5.1	nc	nc
Recreation	$	885	nc	nc	1,221	nc	nc			
	%	2.8	nc	nc	3.3	nc	nc	−0.5	nc	nc
Education	$	6,735	nc	nc	259	nc	nc			
	%	21.0	nc	nc	0.7	nc	nc	−20.3	nc	nc
Total commodity inputs	$	23,797	10,056	6,619	28,628	9,031	6,771			
	%	74.1	60.5	54.3	78.1	61.2	58.6	−4.0	−0.7	−4.3
Difference in total bundle values[a]	$	4,542	−1,880	−781						

Note: nc = not calculated. — = zero by definition. 0 = zero by assumption.

[a]The reduction in the mother's rate of pay as a result of the child times the hours she would have worked without the child, *minus* the value of the income-tax exemption per child.

for a first child than for a third. Virtually all these hours fall as a burden on the mother, since the Syracuse time-use survey, like every other time-use survey, shows that the mother's child-care time far outweighs that of the father and accounts for most of the total care time, regardless of socioeconomic class or nation of residence.[28]

It is also clear that an extra child, especially a firstborn, is time intensive in the postwar urban United States. That is, the time inputs into the child exceed in economic value the time supplied by the child. Figure 1.2 develops this point further by showing an age profile of the time costs and contributions of the child, which will be compared with similar measures for other countries below. Figure 1.2 shows not only that a child is time-intensive in this setting, but also that he causes a net reduction in the household's earnings, even after his own slight teenage earnings are taken into account. Firstborns take a greater share of their total time demands away from the parents' paid work than do third-borns on the average, since firstborns tend to pull the mothers away from a job while third-borns tend to pull already housebound mothers away from other household work and leisure.[29]

The net time-intensity of these modern prototypes looks even higher at positive discount rates, since the time costs are concentrated in infancy while the time contributions from each child come at a much later age. Another adjustment would also raise the time-intensity somewhat. The calculations in tables 1.2 through 1.5 have valued the time inputs into the child at the wife's child-burdened wage rate. This convention makes no allowance for the fact that the arrival of the child cuts the mother's wage rate, through lost work experience, as well as her hours of work. This loss of her earning potential equals a large figure something like the differences in total bundle values at the bottoms of tables 1.2 through 1.5. This loss of on-the-job investment in subsequent pay raises could reasonably be added to the value of the time inputs into the child. Doing so would raise the time-intensity of a child and make the relative cost index more sensitive to movements in real wage rates than it is here.

The 1960 weights for time and commodity inputs in tables 1.2 through 1.5 can be combined with aggregate price and wage series to generate a relative cost index that moves over time. Using the weights from tables 1.2 and 1.3, covering the more representative lower-income families, yields the time series on relative child costs shown in figure 1.2 and table 1.6.

The one time period in which the fixed bundles of child inputs clearly became cheaper relative to the alternative bundle was during World War II. The cheapening of children was caused by the sudden entry of a majority of families into the ranks of income-tax-payers between 1940 and 1945. For the new taxpayers the income-tax exemptions for dependents became relevant for the first time, dropping the cost of a first-born by 9% and the cost of a third-born by 16%—more than enough to outweigh the increases in relative child cost implied by the wartime rise in real wage rates.

Aside from World War II, there has been a slow but unmistakable rise in relative child costs, caused by the leverage of rising real wage rates on the cost of time-intensive children. This suggests that economic development may monotonically raise relative child costs by raising real

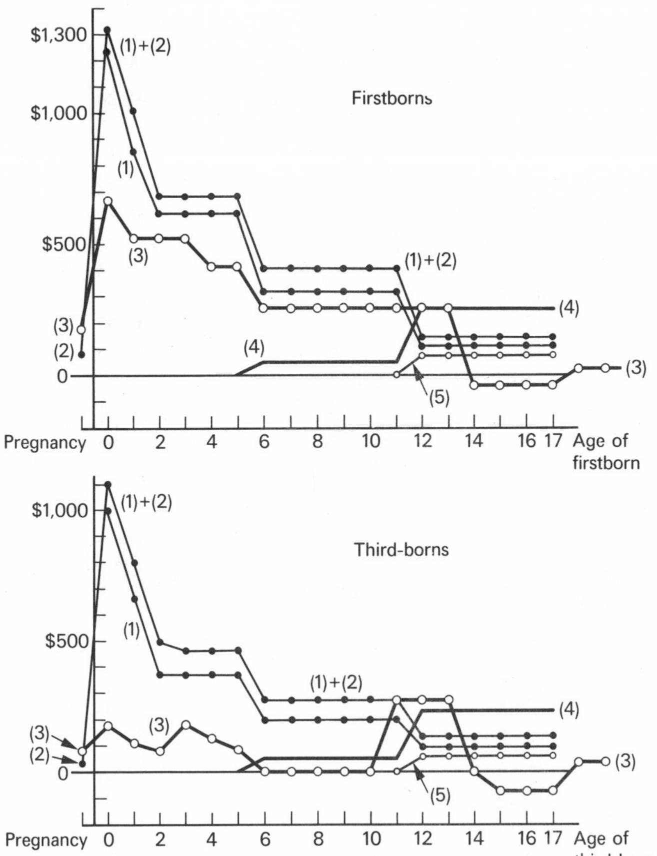

Fig. 1.2 Value of time taken and supplied by firstborn and third-born children, urban United States children, 1967–68 time use and 1960 work effects at 1960 "low-income" wage rates. From Lindert (1978). (1) child-care time by all persons, at wife's wage rates; (2) other chore time increases for wife; (3) net loss of paid work by parents; (4) child's chore plus paid work contribution; (5) child's paid work, a part of (4).

Table 1.6 Relative Cost Indexes for a First and a Third Child, Urban United States, 1900–1970

Year	(1) Price of Inputs into the Child (P_N)	(2) Ditto, Adjusted for Income-Tax Exemption (P'_N)	(3) Price of Inputs into Alternative Activities (P_H)	(4) Relative Child Cost Index (P'_N/P_H)
First Child				
1970	137.32	138.56	134.83	1.0276
1965	111.09	111.85	108.57	1.0302
1960	100.00	100.00	100.00	1.0000
1955	87.10	87.13	88.24	.9996
1950	75.21	75.80	77.48	.9783
1945	52.86	51.74	57.10	.9061
1940	41.72	44.59	45.64	.9771
1935	39.20	41.90	43.88	.9549
1933	35.23	37.66	41.46	.9083
1930	43.78	46.80	49.63	.9929
1925	45.10	48.21	50.76	.9844
1922	42.36	45.28	48.97	.9246
1920	43.82	46.84	49.38	.9485
1919	41.09	43.92	43.85	1.0016
1914	23.74	25.38	27.15	.935
1910	22.39	23.93	26.03	.919
1900	18.92	20.22	22.86	.885
Third Child				
	(1)	(2)	(3)	(4)
1970	137.06	139.21	136.18	1.0223
1965	110.90	112.22	110.16	1.0187
1960	100.00	100.00	100.00	1.0000
1955	87.36	87.40	87.44	.9996
1950	75.68	76.72	75.70	1.0134
1945	53.09	51.04	54.54	.9357
1940	41.59	46.61	43.80	1.0643
1935	39.29	44.04	41.28	1.0668
1933	35.19	39.44	38.22	1.0319
1930	44.10	49.43	46.68	1.0589
1925	45.45	50.94	48.09	1.0593
1922	42.61	47.76	45.71	1.0448
1920	45.00	50.44	45.61	1.1058
1919	42.03	47.11	41.83	1.1262
1914	24.12	27.03	25.47	1.0612
1910	22.69	25.43	24.31	1.0461
1900	19.10	21.41	20.96	1.0215

wage rates. Yet, as we shall see below, this implication cannot be drawn for early stages of development, since children have become time-intensive only in later stages.

Figure 1.3 and table 1.6 might seem to encourage the view that movements in relative child costs explain the United States postwar fertility waves, in view of the wartime dip just before the onset of the baby boom and the rise in costs before the baby bust of the 1960s and 1970s. Yet several alternative regressions reported elsewhere assign only a more limited role to relative cost movements. The most generous regression result credits the wartime decline in the relative cost of a third-born with a significant but small part of the fertility rise of the 1940s and of the fertility decline across the 1960s.[30] Across the 1950s, on the other hand, fertility rose slightly while relative costs also rose. These results suggest that movements in relative costs have played a role in recent fertility fluctuations, yet fall far short of fully accounting for them.

1.5 Are Extra Children Ever Economic Assets?

The cost of a surviving child in the contemporary United States is so high that the initial question to ask about the evolution of child costs with development is simply whether a newborn child offered more expected benefits than costs to his parents in a context of economic underdevelopment. This is commonly presumed but has never been empirically demonstrated. It is not easy to quantify the net gains from a child in a setting in which much of the economic exchange between children and adults never enters the marketplace. Either of two kinds of data would be required. One would be detailed survey data on time use within households in a less developed economy, supplemented by data on the commodity consumption patterns of the same households. The other would be market valuations of child services and child support in settings where children are managed for profit by nonparents. Fortunately, both kinds of data are just now becoming available, some from the early history of the currently industrialized countries and some from contemporary surveys in developing countries. The data are so scattered across nations and time that the present empirical picture must be a very incomplete mosaic.

A starting point for judging the cost or asset value of a newborn child in an underdeveloped economy is the available historical data on the economics of managing a child for profit. Slaveowners in the United

Source: Table 1.6 and figure 1.3 were calculated from the 1960 "low-income" bundle weights in tables 1.2 and 1.3, plus time series on tax exemptions, wage rates, and price indexes for food, shelter, and all other commodities as given in *FSA*, app. F.

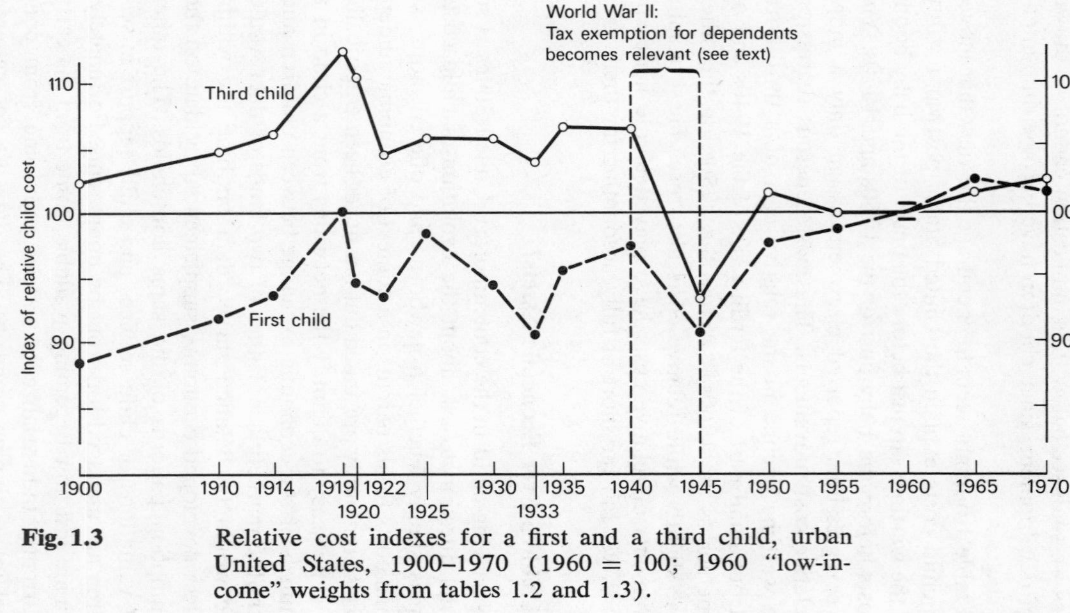

Fig. 1.3 Relative cost indexes for a first and a third child, urban United States, 1900–1970 (1960 = 100; 1960 "low-income" weights from tables 1.2 and 1.3).

States South had a great stake in correct appraisal of the survival chances, work capacity, and costs of support of slave children. They had to appraise not only the child's consumption and productivity in producing salable crops, but also his potential for chores on the plantation and the minimal time spent by all adults in supervising the child at the expense of other tasks. Given these considerations and the child-labor-intensity of cotton to be documented further below, one can assume that if any newborn children were a net asset, slave children were.

The fact that newborn slave children had a positive market value in the antebellum South shows an extreme upper bound on the average value of a newborn to his parents in an agriculture where modernization has not proceeded beyond such implements as the cotton gin. This market value shows what a parent could expect from a live birth if he not only worked his child like a slave but kept receiving all the returns from the productivity of any surviving child beyond slave-level consumption for the child until the parent's death. This is an extreme case of parent exploitation, of course, since most children leave home at about age twenty and give their parents much less support than was extracted by slaveowners. To improve the analogy with the parent's investment, one must look more closely at the effects of a slave child in his first twenty years, temporarily setting aside old-age support for the parent.

The cost and earnings of a slave child were roughly quantified for 1846–50 in the pioneering work of Conrad and Meyer.[31] Their estimates of the costs and returns from slave children by age and sex can be combined with Robert Evans's estimates of age-specific survival rates for slave children in 1850.[32] The Conrad-Meyer estimates imply that over the first twenty years of life, including the initial costs in nursery and the mother's work loss, a surviving slave child brought an undiscounted net return of $194. The rate of return on a guaranteed survivor was just below 8% per annum, while the rate of return on a live birth given the infant and child mortality rates works out to have been between 6% and 7%. These rates of return, while below those reckoned on adult slaves (8–14%), are positive and imply that a child raised in the manner of a slave could be a slight net asset even without including any expected value of old-age support. And the true rate of return over the slave's life may have been slightly higher than this synthetic cross-sectional estimate for 1846–50, given the moderate growth in slave productivity across the antebellum era. Thus far, a slave childhood seems to have been slightly profitable to the slaveowner.

These estimates of slave-child profitability should be cross-checked against other data on the same issue, since the Conrad-Meyer estimates are really their own interpolations based on adult slave productivity and scraps of information on the ages at which slave children began work and began to make back their upkeep. We can judge the profitability of a slave's childhood years from the more reliable data on slave purchase prices in the New Orleans slave market, hire rates and upkeep costs for adult slaves, and, again, Evans's survival rates. Given that prospective slaveowners had the alternative option of buying adult slaves, it is reasonable to assume that they would have discounted the expected returns and costs of a slave childhood at a rate of return similar to that earned on an adult slave. While the original profitability estimates for adults by Conrad and Meyer had been exposed to a number of criticisms, there is general agreement that the cross-sectional rate of return on adult slaves for the 1850s would be between 8% and 14% per annum.[33] Given this range of the adult rate of return, r, we can relate the market prices on newborns (P_0) and 20-year-olds (P_{20}) to the implied present value of the first twenty years of the slave child's life ($PV_{0\text{-}20}$) by the formula

$$P_0 = PV_{0\text{-}20} + \frac{s_{20}P_{20}}{(1 + r)^{20}}, \tag{11}$$

where s_{20} is the perceived share of newborns surviving to age 20, assumed to equal Evans's estimate for 1850. In this case we get something close to a zero net profit on a slave childhood. The present value of the childhood years, $PV_{0\text{-}20}$, is $-\$42$ if the survival-weighted value of a 20-year-old is discounted at 8%, and $+\$47$ if a discount rate of 14% is applied.[34] I infer that if parents in an agricultural setting like that of the antebellum South had discounted uncertain future costs and returns at rates like those revealed by cross sections of slaveownership, and had exploited their children like slaves, the net economic value of raising a child who would leave the home at 20 would be about zero.

The economic flows between a freeborn child and his parents in underdeveloped settings can only be judged, as mentioned, with the help of extensive data on the exchanges of time use within the household. Fortunately, rural time-use studies have recently been conducted in the Philippines, Java, and Nepal.[35] Of these, the most extensively surveyed was also the most affluent. A survey in rural Laguna in the Philippines gathered data on time use in 571 households in May, June, and July 1975. The surveyed barrios were rural, but not remote: just south and east of Los Baños, and within transistor-radio distance of Manila, about 60 miles away. The season was one of intensive crop cultivation, perhaps raising work time by women and children above the annual average. On the other hand, school began in June, probably cutting productive work time by some of the children. The survey measured the allocation of time across several activities for a recent week. While there were some problems in coding time spent on several activities at once, the data are not too different in concept from those from recent United States time-use surveys. Earnings were estimated directly, and the values of other home productive work were imputed with the help of data on likely wage rates for hiring out different home tasks.[36]

Tentative regression results from the Laguna survey reveal the time costs and contributions of a second-born or later-born child.[37] These are plotted in figure 1.4. The time spent by the parents on child care (series 1) refers to care of preschool children only.[38]

Perhaps surprisingly, the extra child does not reduce the parents' earnings over his first twenty years in their household.[39] There is a noticeably positive effect of extra children on the working hours of fathers in Laguna. Whether owing to a feeling of extra responsibility or to a greater desire to get away from the house and children, this "moonlighting father" effect appears to be somewhat stronger in Laguna than in the postwar nonfarm United States.[40] A clearer contrast with contemporary United States patterns of behavior is the effect of the extra child on the mother's income-generating work. This effect is negative, as one would expect, for the first year after birth (a work loss of 5.3 hours a week) but is essentially zero thereafter. The explanation seems to be simply that in rural Laguna, as in all the other rural settings for which relevant data have been gathered, the mother's various productive tasks are all so close to home that she can juggle her schedule and combine tasks so as to avoid any great personal work loss from an extra child. The net result is that an extra child, although he has a positive adult-time cost within the home, actually raises the parents' work hours and earnings.[41]

The extra child contributes to his parents' household a good deal more time than he takes. Here it is only possible to report the average value of productive time use by all children over the age of 7 rather than to give a detailed age profile. It is nonetheless clear from figure 1.4 that children contributed more time, both in all productive tasks and in income-earning work, than they took from their parents. Children in rural Laguna are clearly time-supplying, not time-intensive like their urban United States counterparts. In such a setting, any general increase in rural real wage rates on common labor would apparently make an extra child look *less* costly relative to the alternative life-styles with which he competed in his parents' household.

To judge whether the net time contribution of the extra child is sufficient to make him a net asset, we need data on the commodity inputs concerned. Values of the food, clothing, educational, and other inputs into an extra child in Laguna are now being tabulated. As a preliminary conservative guess, one can combine Lorimer's crude consumption-equivalence scales for children and adults with the Laguna income data to put peso values on the likely consumption of commodities by the extra child.[42] The resulting provisional figures are plotted as series 3 of figure 1.4.

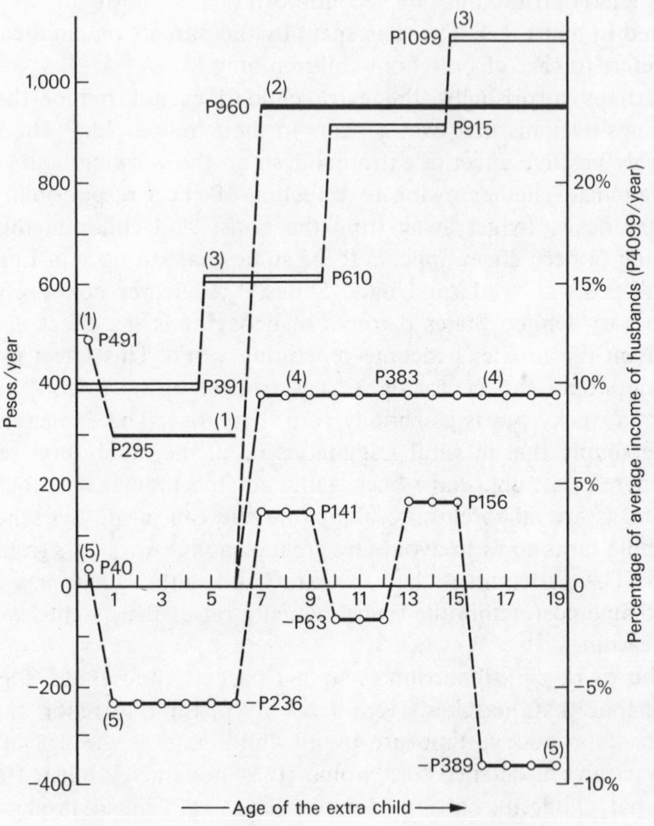

Fig. 1.4 Average time-use effects, commodity consumption, and work effects of an extra child in a household with children, by age of the extra child—rural Laguna, Philippines, 1975. From Boulier 1976, tables IA, IIA, IIIA. (1) preschool child care time by the parents (+ = cost); (2) average time contribution of a child over 7, all productive work; (3) crude estimate of the child's commodity consumption, using Lorimer consumption-equivalent scales; (4) average earnings of a child over 7; (5) effect on earnings of the two parents (+ = loss of earnings). Net cost of the child is approximated by (1) + (3) − (2).

It tentatively appears that a surviving later-born child would bring a slight net cost to his parents while growing up within their household, since the excess of the child's time contribution over time cost is not quite sufficient to match the commodity cost. To be sure, the net cost of the child turns out to be much lower as a share of household income or of an adult male's average earnings than in the postwar United States. Yet thus far it appears that the extra rural Filipino child is not a net economic asset to his parents while still a child. If this conclusion stands up to further evidence, it contrasts the freeborn rural child to the slave child. More important, it provides some tentative support for Eva Mueller's suspicions against the view that a newborn child is a net economic asset in underdeveloped rural economies.[43]

The net preadult costs of an extra child in the rural Laguna area would be reinforced by some conservative biases in the measures shown in figure 1.4. First, the time costs of the child have been underestimated by the exclusion of care for them by nonparents, by excluding measures of their effect on the mother's cleaning-up chores and meal preparation time, and by the already-noted bias related to the care of younger siblings by older siblings. Second, a firstborn child would receive more time inputs than the later-borns. Third, the figures all refer to a surviving child, and any net benefits from a child at the older ages that might appear if the estimates in figure 1.4 were optimistically revised would be reduced by mortality in greater proportion than the clearly positive net costs in the infant years. Finally, if one takes the position that parents psychically discount more distant effects at a positive discount rate, then the immediate net costs of pregnancy (omitted here) and infancy loom proportionately larger.

Some additional useful fragments of information on the net-asset issue are provided by two other recent time-use surveys, one for a Javanese village and another for the low-ranking Thami caste in a Nepalese village, both conducted in 1972–73.[44] These data sets have the advantage of applying to a less-developed rural setting than the Philippine sample. They are also based on extensive interviews spread out over more than a year. They have the disadvantage of relating to fewer households—20 in Java and 45–50 in Nepal—and supplying less detailed information on some key variables. Nonetheless, they do offer another look into the uses of time within rural households, beyond what data on market work alone can reveal.

Table 1.7 sketches the time contributions of children over 6 years old in these two villages. Their overall contribution ("all work") is a much larger share of adult male work time than would be contributed by the same ages and sexes in the postwar United States, and even a somewhat larger share than contributed in the rural Philippine sample.

It is also larger than the total child-care time per household contributed by all adults in the village in Java, suggesting that the children in the Javanese and Nepalese cross sections, like those in the rural Philippines, are net suppliers of time and not time-intensive activities for their parents' household.[45] These time contributions, however, must be weighted by the average wage rate or productivity of the working children, who presumably earned at a lower hourly rate than adult males. Table 1.7 reminds us that the work-time ratios greatly overstate the work-value ratios of children to adults, by showing how the fact that the average child's wage rate was only half the adult male rate cut into the relative value of children's work contribution in rural Egypt in 1964–65.

To reach a conclusion about the net economic value of the hypothetical cross-sectional newborn child in rural Java or Nepal, one would again need data on commodity consumption by children and also on their survival chances. These are currently lacking for the Java and Nepal samples. One can only suggest that if the ratios of consumption patterns to adult male earnings are comparable to those in Laguna, the somewhat higher time contribution of the Javanese and Nepalese children would bring them closer to the margin of being net assets to their parents.

It thus appears possible that in underdeveloped rural settings an extra child could have been a slight net asset. The Philippine data tentatively argue in favor of the opposite view, but for the United States slave economy and Javanese and Nepalese villages, the net benefits may have been positive. At the moment, the net-asset issue remains unresolved for truly underdeveloped economies.[46] Yet two clear patterns are emerging: children were much less of a net burden as a share of family or adult male income in these cases than in developed countries, and children were clearly time supplying.

Rough calculations like these serve to bring out a further point relating to the historical decline in infant and child mortality. It is common to argue that couples set a target number of surviving children and respond, with a lag, to declining infant and child mortality by having fewer births now that fewer are needed to achieve the target. The presumption deserves further empirical tests, in view of the ease of presuming an opposing model of tastes in which couples react to the death of children by becoming less sanguine about having others. The age profiles of child costs and benefits now remind us of another basis for challenging the usual view: children invariably start out as a net cost and become net benefits only after nine or more years. This means that high mortality is a force holding up the net costliness of a live birth or pregnancy by limiting the shares surviving to the net-benefit phase. When infant and child mortality decline with the onset of modernization, the improve-

Table 1.7 **The Work Inputs of Rural Javanese, Nepalese, and Egyptian Children of Various Age-Sex Groups Expressed as Percentages of the Average Work Inputs of Male Adults**

	6–8 Years	9–11 Years	12–14 Years	15–19 Years
		A. Javanese Village		
		All Work		
Boys	43	38	56	91
Girls	39	62	99	120
		Directly Productive Work		
Boys	23	24	42	71
Girls	15	39	59	86
		B. Nepalese Village		
		All Work		
Boys	37	65	73	93
Girls	47	82	96	110
		Directly Productive Work		
Boys	37	61	69	93
Girls	30	71	81	98

	6–11 Years	12–15 Years	16–19 Years
	C. Rural Egypt, 1964–65		
	All Work Outside the Household		
Boys, % of adult male work inputs	14.1	69.3	92.2
% of adult male earnings:[a]	7.1	34.9	46.4
Girls, % of adult male work inputs	8.7	33.2	na
% of adult male earnings:[a]	4.4	16.7	na

Sources: Table 7: a and b, Nag 1976, table 5; c, Mueller 1976, table III-3, and Hansen 1969, p. 308. The reference to adult males in Java and Nepal is to an average work input for all sampled males over 15. This input into "all work" was about 8.5 hours a day in the Javanese village and about 10 hours a day in the Nepalese village.

Note: na = not available.

[a]Assuming that the average ratio of child to adult-male daily wage rates of .503 applied to all age-sex groups.

ment in survival chances may make a newborn seem like more of a net asset or less of a liability. There are, in other words, good theoretical reasons for remaining agnostic on the link between child mortality and fertility. The facts have also held back their support: infant mortality shows a significantly positive effect on fertility in some cross sections but not others and remains subject to suspicions of having taken credit for influences that are due to omitted variables.

1.6 Old-Age Support

It is traditional to argue that in underdeveloped economies parents expect and receive considerable support from their surviving children in their old age. This is assumed to be one of the main reasons why children are net assets in less developed countries. The decline in this reliance on children is traditionally thought to be one of the main ways economic development reduces fertility. The evidence for this view comes in three forms.

The most directly relevant evidence comes from interviews on the perceived importance of old-age support and its relationship to the case for having children. The evidence seems to form a neat pattern: time, development, and urbanization all reduce the stated importance of future old-age support from children. In the East-West Center's surveys in East Asia and Hawaii in the early 1970's, old-age support was more frequently mentioned as an advantage of having children by rural than by urban respondents, and its frequency by nation correlated inversely with national income per capita.[47] A generation of family-planning surveys in Japan found young wives' "willingness to depend" on their children in their old age steadily declining from over half in 1950 to a quarter in 1971, with rural wives more willing to depend than urban.[48]

A second kind of evidence is cross-sectional regression evidence that fertility is significantly lower in countries with social insurance benefits established for the elderly, other variables held equal.[49]

The final form of evidence is data on coresidence of parents and grown children. Elderly parents clearly live with their children more often in less developed economies.[50] The breakup of intergenerational coresidence over the course of development is even more pronounced than the usual data on residence in the same household can reveal, since the tendency of elderly parents to live nearby in the same village has also declined, a fact that has complicated recent research on the evolution from extended toward nuclear families.

If one were simply to accept the decline in old-age support as fact, then it fits neatly into the relative-cost concept and into the delay and ultimate arrival of the fertility transition. The old-age support can be incorporated into the relative-cost measure, data permitting, as a supply of work from the children, one that comes in the parents' old age, after the children have become adults. In the early phase of development, when this support looms large in the perception of benefits from an extra child, its economic value is in fact raised by two trends. Declining mortality raises the probability that any one child will live long enough to deliver the kind of support one expects on the assumption that one will live a long time. Meanwhile the secular rise in real wages raises the purchasing power that any surviving child can command as a parent-supporting adult, raising the economic value of any given work on the parent's behalf. These trends contribute to maintaining higher fertility in the early stages. At the same time, income growth makes the share of parents needing and expecting such support decline with each generation. By the later phases of growth this old-age-support effect has given away to a taste effect: the rising standards the succeeding generations of couples have for support of each child also involve increasing consciousness of the need to leave a nonhuman wealth legacy as well as the need for development of human skills in growing children. This effect helps feed the ultimate fertility decline, buttressed of course by the ultimate rise of social security programs.

Before adding a layer of theory to an argument enjoying moderate empirical support, however, it must be noted that the importance of this argument is hard to quantify. And when one looks closer at problems of quantifying on the importance of old-age support, one finds reason to wonder whether this argument for peasants' having more children is as traditional among peasants as among scholars studying them.

The direct evidence need not convince. It is cheap for interview respondents to say they feel old-age support from children is one of the advantages of having children. (Saying so may even have its own advantages if the children are present at the interview.) The responses about old-age support may also express the anticipation of future companionship as much as future economic support. The international regression evidence is also vulnerable to the suspicion that social security programs are correlated with the fertility-reducing influences owing to such omitted variables as socialism, the position of women, housing scarcity, and so forth.

When one looks more closely at the evidence on coresidence, one discovers a host of reasons for wondering whether the actual old-age support was ever great enough to decline greatly, reasons that inevitably color one's impressions about *perceived* support as well. The fact that grown-up children and their parents live together tells us little about the economic flows between the generations. It can even be argued that in the majority of cases the elderly parents were more than paying their way by retaining ownership of the property. In Tokugawa Japan, for example, the elderly widower or husband living with his children, adopted children, and servants ruled as a patriarch over a complex household in which he implicitly exchanged the rental of his property for labor services.[51] In America in the eighteenth century and early nineteenth century, a bare majority of decedents died with some noticeable amount of personal and real estate, indirectly raising again the question of how great a share of them were not recipients of aid from their children.

These clues about the extent of actual old-age support serve to raise anew the question of how widely the old-age benefits of children are perceived. Young couples in the process of family formation may well heavily discount the putative old-age benefits, through ordinary psychological myopia, through a realization that the extra child may not survive them, and through a reasonable fear that extra births may drag down the ability of any one surviving child to give resources to his parents much later on. The old-age support hypothesis is in need of further testing. Yet it remains an unrefuted consensus view, one that is easily incorporated into the concept of relative child cost.

1.7 Shifting Prices

Any overview of the influence of economic development on relative child costs must supply information on how relative input prices have drifted as well as on how the weights in the child-input and alternative bundles have shifted. The clearest drift in relative prices relevant to relative child costs has been the rise in real wage rates, or the cost of an hour of human time in terms of all commodities. Even common unskilled labor has enjoyed a doubling and redoubling in its purchasing power, and average wage rates have risen even faster with the rise of average skills.

A natural subject of interest in relating wage movements to changes in fertility is whether the wage rates facing adult females have risen faster than those facing children during the course of economic growth. If they have, then the relative cost measure might use this information to quantify the extent to which this drift in wage structure has raised the costliness of children. The average-wage ratio of adult women to children has indeed probably risen, though apparently only through the obvious mechanism of the upward drift in adult skills. There are abundant isolated estimates of the ratio of adult female *unskilled* wage rates to the wage rates for generally unskilled children, both for agriculture and in industry. It is hard to find a trend in these estimates for unskilled wage rates, since they refer to children of different ages in different settings. And as long as the adult females and the children in question are really both unskilled, it is doubtful that there could be any sustained movement in the pay ratio of such close substitutes. It is safer to return to the obvious: the average skill levels of adult females have drifted up relative to those of teenagers, meaning that the wage rates attached to the time costs of an extra child have risen relative to those on the time contributed by the extra child.[52]

While the likely upward drift in the ratio of adult female to child wage rates clearly implies rising relative child cost with economic development, the clearer rise in *all* real wage rates has a different impact on child costs in the early and late phases of development. In the early phases, children are time supplying on balance, as in the survey data for the rural Philippines. In this context, the general rise of real wage rates *reduces* the relative cost of a child by magnifying his net time contribution relative to his net commodity cost. Yet at the later phases, as in the United States postwar data, children have become time-intensive and are made more costly by any further rises in real wage rates. We return to this implication in the next section, when pursuing the evidence on just when the shift from time-supplying to time-intensive children occurs.

Another relative price movement that would affect the relative cost measure would be a change in the price of food relative to luxuries. Since an extra child is invariably food-intensive and luxury-replacing, a rise in the relative price of food would raise child costs. Theory would tend to predict such a drift toward more costly food, as long as it presumes that the more rapid growth in productivity in the supply of luxuries than of food, rather than the demand-side tug-of-war between Engel effects of income growth and the food-favoring demand effects of population growth, dominates the terms of trade between food and luxuries.

The usual available wholesale and retail price indexes show no clear long-run trend in the ratio of food prices to luxury prices, at least in the United States and Japan. The ratio of food price indexes to various "all other" categories has had little net change since the early nineteenth century, despite a historical peak about 1910–14 and some wide fluctuations since. In urban Japan the relative price of food showed no prewar trend, rose moderately across the wartime era, and changed little across the 1950s and 1960s.[53] Taken at face value, the standard price indexes would imply that the food intensity of children has happened to be irrelevant to the course of fertility decline in the past.

The usual indexes are likely to be biased, however, in the direction of underestimating the relative decline in the price of luxuries. Luxuries other than the consumption of traditional personal services are generally "new goods" and goods experiencing considerable quality improvement over time. The usual price series fail to capture the effect of the arrival of newly available goods and of quality improvements. To follow the prices of a fixed bundle of goods over many years, the usual Laspeyres indexes must overlook those goods not existing in early years and those whose quality is changing. Thus indexes of the price of transportation will continue well into the age of the bicycle and automobile before adding these modes to the bundle. Indexes of housing costs will go to some lengths to follow rents on a fixed set of deteriorating dwellings;

new units are added to the bundle in due course, but their initial availability and higher quality are not allowed to pull down the overall rate of inflation. At the same time, urbanization, improved communications, and the rise of mail-order shopping greatly cut the seldom-measured information costs on most income-elastic goods. The noneconomist's hunch that exposure to new "goods aspirations" makes children seem costly would have a direct counterpart in a true measure of relative child cost if the data were available. In all likelihood, a decline in the cost of luxuries relative to staples, correctly measured, set in with the earliest stages of economic development and has proceeded ever since.

Another price ratio of possible relevance to fertility is the price of land relative to commodities and to labor. Little is known about the long-run trends in land scarcity, despite the natural Malthusian intuition that rising population densities should be accompanied by a rise in the price of land. Within urban areas, data from the United States and Japan show an unmistakable and almost monotonic rise in the price of land relative to the price of commodities. In postwar Japan, urban site values (not adjusted for capital investments in real estate) have skyrocketed at real rates of increase of about 17% per annum.[54] And since urban site values are far above rural ones, urbanization has shifted large shares of national populations toward locations charging a higher relative price for lot space and room area. Both of these trends, urbanization and the rise in urban site values, have contributed to an unmeasured upward drift in the relative cost of an extra child, since extra children are living-space-intensive, as one would expect and as noted above, even though they reduce their parents' total expenditures on shelter.

An issue deserving further investigation is the relationship of the relative price of rural land to the course of fertility in rural areas. Studies of United States rural fertility in the nineteenth century by Yasuba, Easterlin, Leet, and others have shown generally good raw and partial correlations between various measures of land availability and human fertility.[55] The measures of land availability have sometimes been land prices and sometimes been demographically derived measures of population density or "population pressure." If these neat empirical patterns have actually identified an underlying mechanism linking greater land scarcity to fertility decline, this is a very important result. It means that rising population pressure on the land tends to check itself by cutting rural fertility. Whether one believes in the hypothesis affects one's view of the future of population growth in currently developing countries.

Easterlin's interpretation of the land-scarcity correlation is that it indeed identifies a basic mechanism underlying rural decision-making about family size. The pattern is viewed as a reflection of the basic desire of prospective parents to be able to set their children up with assets like those they themselves possess, so that greater "population pressure" puts pressure on them either to postpone marriage or to limit fertility within marriage. They have, in other words, an inheritance motive somehow tied to the availability of land, a motive presumed to outweigh the importance of children as potential old-age support.

It is not clear whether the empirical results warrant an interpretation couched in terms of land inheritance, or whether land scarcity would always have the effect of rural fertility ascribed to it in these studies. Land availability may simply have been a convenient proxy for the ratio of current to prior living standards in United States cross sections in the twentieth century. This interpretation is consistent with fertility's seeming to have been highest not in the initial settlement of raw frontier but in the next-least-settled areas. Gains in income prospects over prior incomes would have been highest not in the initial clearing of soil but soon thereafter when the high yields of the new lands were secured. If this is the real meaning of the nineteenth-century United States rural patterns, then they represent a rediscovery of the "relative-income" hypothesis and would not imply declining rural fertility as population fills up the land in developing countries unless income growth were decelerating.

The land-inheritance interpretation is essentially a relative-cost rather than a relative-income hypothesis. It argues that an extra child is viewed as land intensive, in the sense that a couple would tend to demand more acres of land if it had an extra child than if it did not. This has not been demonstrated. Nor could a simple correlation between farm size and family size confirm the land intensity, since the earnings of extra children may make it possible to work or buy more land.

If land defined in acres rather than value did not prove an important share of rural child-input bundles, then one could quantify the contribution of rising land values to relative child costs. One question to be answered first is, Relative to what is land said to be scarce in a way relevant to fertility? The tentative answer seems to be: relative to luxuries, which children replace, and to common labor, of which children are net suppliers in less developed rural settings. It is possible that land scarcity, thus incorporated into a relative-child-cost measure, has been an important preventer of births. This is possible because land has indeed been most scarce relative to luxuries, though not always relative to child labor,[56] in the rural areas with highest fertility. So says the United States rural cross section for the mid-nineteenth century. So also say the upward drifts in the price of land relative to luxuries, but not labor, in the United States between 1800 and World War I and in Japan since the 1880s. *If* the land-intensity of an extra child can be demonstrated sufficiently to reject suspicions to the contrary, then the relative-cost index will prove to be an analytical link between rising land scarcity and declining fertility. The empirical tasks have not been completed, however.

1.8 The Shift toward Time-Intensity

Given the rise in real wage rates with development, and the slight evidence that extra children shift from being time-supplying to being time intensive, it is important to add further documentation of this apparent shift. If it really occurred, it is important to get a better idea of when it occurred, in order to judge roughly when the upward drift of real wage rates might have stopped lowering and started raising the relative cost of an extra child.

One way of bringing additional evidence to bear on the issue of time-intensity is to settle for less direct evidence on the net time costs like those graphed in figures 1.2 and 1.4 above. Time-use studies probing the interior of households will be rare. We can find more abundant data, however, on net *earnings* effects, as proxies for true net *time cost* effects. It is likely that the evolution of the total time children contribute to their parents' households will parallel that of their earnings in the marketplace. And the net effect of an extra child on parents' paid work is, conveniently, more relevant to the issue of time intensity than the missing data on parents' total time inputs into the child.

It should be possible to gather several household surveys from developing countries giving breakdowns of household income among household members, allowing regressions to determine the contributions of children and their effect on the working hours of their parents. Their effect on parents' rates of pay can also be quantified if one can solve the issue of simultaneity between number of children present and parents' rates of pay.

Until surveys with income breakdowns by household member are analyzed, the only additional sources for currently developing countries are those simply reporting total household income and the ages and numbers of children present, plus variables other than income or family composition. Such data sets will show, for almost any less-developed country, that extra children, especially extra older children, are associated with higher total household income. One example of this kind of indirect evidence is a set of regressions run using survey data from Indian village surveys: Naurangdeshar, Rajasthan, 1968–69, and Ankodia, Gujarat, 1967–68.[57] The regressions, which could be repeated using any of several developing-country surveys, ran total income against the male head's age, his age squared, his literacy (Ankodia) or years of schooling (Naurangdeshar), the age and age squared of any adult male relatives present, value of land, tractor ownership, the value of other assets—and the number of children in each of several age-sex groups. The terms relating to children look at a glance like age profiles of net annual income contributions, rising with the child's age and significantly positive for males 16–25. The magnitudes also related to average household income and adult male earnings in proportions near the shares of the net earnings effects shown for the Philippines in figure 1.4. While children thus appear time supplying and income increasing again in these Indian villages, this form of evidence remains vulnerable to the obvious charge of simultaneity. One could argue that the same results show that higher-income parents of given age and other attributes felt they could have more children and had them earlier.[58]

The more satisfactory kind of evidence, which at least breaks down household income by household member, can be gleaned from the earlier history of Europe and the United States. One such data source is the unusual survey taken of agricultural workers' families in England between 1787 and 1796 by the Reverend David Davies and Sir Frederick Morton Eden, just as the French Revolution, bad harvests (1795–96), food price inflation, and Malthus's first essay on population were beginning to work their effects on the English countryside.[59] Parish vicars and rectors were asked to find half a dozen or so families of agricultural laborers who were poor yet generally working enough to avoid extreme dependence on the parish. The purpose was to estimate family consumption, saving or dissaving, and sources of income. The sample was apparently defined by the income range of the male head (except for the observations on widows' families), which varied less than total family income. Considerable effort was devoted to accounting for all income despite the difficulties of estimating home production and to allocating this income to individual family members as far as practicable. The survey also yielded parish- and date-specific data on food and rent prices in most cases, allowing deflation of earnings by the price of a loaf of wheat bread or, in some cases, its price equivalent in wheat flour or oatmeal.[60]

Table 1.8 shows some apparent earnings effects of an extra child in an English agricultural laborer's family in the late eighteenth century. The figures are subject to several cautions. The effects of children on husbands' work and earnings could not be estimated, given the nature of the sample. Some of the children's earnings were reported only for the group of children, and in some cases only the ages of the oldest and youngest children were given, requiring some age interpolation based on the number of middle children.[61] And, despite the efforts of the interviewers, it is likely that some of the children's and wives' earnings were attributed to the husband, owing to the widespread practice of group home production (e.g., "husband earns 1s. 6d. a week weaving with spinning help by eldest daughter").

It appears from table 1.8 that a surviving third-born child would have been earnings supplying, though perhaps less so than the extra Filipino child hypothesized in figure 1.4 above. A third live birth might also have been a net supplier of earnings, though infant and child mortality was severe enough in that setting to make the net earnings effect of the extra birth hinge critically on one's choice of a discount rate. If one accepts

Table 1.8 **Children's Earnings and the Effect of Children on Wives' Earnings, 169 Agricultural Workers' Families, England, 1787–96**

A. Children's Earnings

Age	Average Earnings, Loaves/Year	Average Earnings, % of Adult Male Earnings	Estimated Number of Children
8	11.6	3.2	38
9	12.7	3.5	34
10	26.9	7.3	33
11	32.9	8.9	35
12	41.4	11.2	28
13	71.4	19.4	21
14	54.8	14.9	20
15	67.1	18.2	13
16–18	84.4	22.8	14
19–22	72.9	19.8	6

B. Wives' Earnings, by Number of Children and Age of Youngest

	Number of Children			
Age of Youngest Child	1 or 2	3	4	5 or More
0–1, or "infant" loaves	33.8	39.3	32.6	31.5
% of adult male	9.2	10.7	8.9	8.6
number of observations	12	21	20	35
2–5 loaves	56.7	42.0	41.4	45.9
% of adult male	15.4	11.4	11.2	12.5
number of observations	12	4	13	22
6 or older loaves	44.8	42.9	27.8	29.1
% of adult male	12.2	11.7	7.6	7.9
number of observations	13	3	3	1

C. Implied Effect of a Third-born on Mother's Earnings, Three-year Spacing

	Effect on Mother's Earnings	
Age of Third-born	Loaves/Year	% of Adult Male Earnings
0–1	−17.4	−4.7
2	−14.7	−4.0
3–5	− 2.8	−0.8
6–11	− 1.9	−0.5
12 up	0	0

Note: loaves/year = half-peck loaves of wheat bread (7.3 to 8.3 lbs) per year; adult male earnings = 368.1 loaves/year.

the further assumption that an extra child contributed more value in chore help (not counted as earnings in the survey) than he demanded from the (housebound) mother, then the time-supplying nature of a child in rural eighteenth-century England seems reinforced.

For later dates in England and America we have only scraps of information on the earnings effects of an extra farm or rural child. Reviewing the evidence for twentieth-century America elsewhere, I have found that an extra farm child was still a net supplier of earnings in the 1920s and not an earnings reducer or time intensive until about the 1960s.[62] The available shreds of information thus imply that rural children remained time supplying and earnings supplying throughout most of the course of economic development. If further investigation supports this tentative view, it appears that rural child costs are *reduced* by the upward drift in farm wage rates over most of economic development. This throws the burden of explaining the observed decline in rural fertility back onto other variables: taste-formation mechanisms, the cheapening of new luxury goods, possibly land scarcity, and so forth.

Within the rural sector, it would be worth while to pursue the issue of which economic activities most enhance the net time supply of a child, thereby possibly retarding fertility decline when real wage rates are rising. One obvious suspicion is that abundant opportunities for cottage industry and farm household by-employments, as flourished in Britain in the eighteenth and early nineteenth centuries and in Tokugawa and and Meiji Japan, raised the net time contribution of a child by raising his productive employment by more than his interference with the time use of adults.

The choice of crop may also have been a historically important influence on the economic benefits of children. So far, the one fairly clear pattern linking crop to reliance on child labor is that cotton agriculture is perhaps the major crop with the highest share of its labor performed by children, as well as being very intensive in the use of all labor per acre. The child-labor intensity of cotton has been noted by several observers of Egyptian agriculture since at least the 1940s.[63] The link between children and cotton has also been stressed in a study of the cotton areas of Texas in the 1920s.[64] It may be that forces stimulating a shift to cotton cultivation may buoy up children's earning power and even increase fertility for entire rural regions.

Outside of agriculture the transition from earnings-supplying children to earnings-reducing children came earlier, but still not until the late phases of economic development. Elsewhere I have presented data for United States industrial families' earnings patterns, tentatively concluding that the switch to earnings-reducing children, and presumably time-intensive children if all flows were measured, did not come until World War I or later.[65] Further regression results reported by Michael Haines now appear to confirm that, as of the large United States government survey of industrial workers' families in 1889–90, children were still net earnings suppliers to their parents' households in a subsample from five West European countries as well as in the United States.[66] Only after the upward drift of adult skills and wartime demands for female labor had pulled much larger numbers of wives away from home did an extra child come to take more earnings and, presumably, total time from his parents than he supplied.

Within the industrial sector, there appears to be a pattern relating natural-fiber textiles to heavier net earnings effects for an extra child, whether in factories or in cottages. This is what observers thought about cotton mills and woolen mills in nineteenth-century Massachusetts and Lancashire, and about silk-spinning in rural homes in Meiji Japan. It is a pattern now seemingly confirmed by regressions run on the 1889–90 industrial workers' sample. These regressions find much heavier average earnings by children in cotton and woolen textile families than in the glass, ferrous metal, and mining industries, after allowing for the ages of children and wives, husband's relative income, and regional variables.[67] While the textile industries also made heavier use of adult female labor, their effect on the earnings lost by a mother owing to an extra child was smaller than their effect on child earnings. If this pattern is confirmed by studies on contemporary developing countries, it appears that specialization in textiles, like cotton agriculture, may be a force holding fertility up as wage rates advance in some textile-oriented economies.

Although the shift to earnings-reducing and time-intensive children remains somewhat uncertain, there is little doubt that it has occurred. Figure 1.5 brings this out by summarizing the earnings effects of an extra child in the home in four survey samples widely spread over time and space. In the postwar urban United States a firstborn child is clearly earnings-reducing, as already shown in figure 1.2 above. Yet in the other three settings, corresponding to earlier stages of development, extra children are earnings-supplying. As the dates in figure 1.5 also imply, the shift has come late in the development process. Just how late is an empirical question of considerable importance for forecasting fertility in developing countries.

1.9 Conclusions

1.9.1 Patterns

A careful and straightforward definition of the relative cost of an extra child holds considerable potential for organizing otherwise vague arguments about how changes in the economic environment should affect

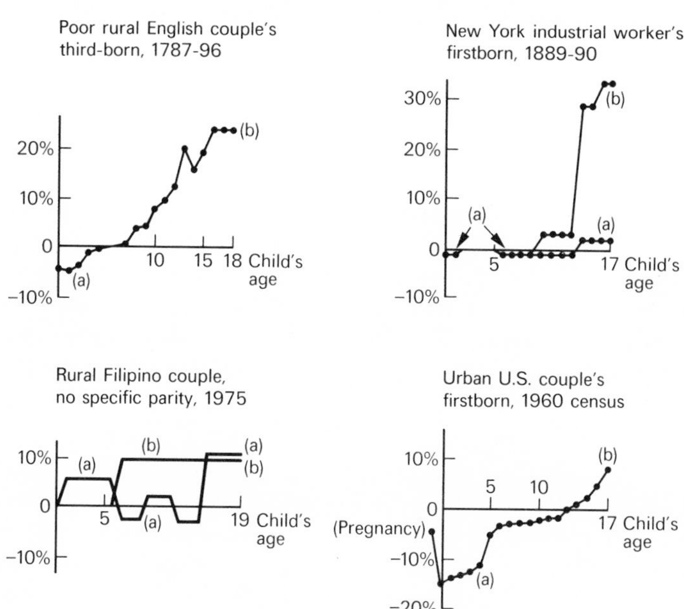

Fig. 1.5 Estimated effects of an extra child in the home on family members' earnings. Selected survey results. (*a*) net effect of the child on earnings of parents (− = loss; on mother's earnings only in England and New York); (*b*) child's own earnings. Vertical axes measure these effects as a percentage of average earnings of the adult males in the sample (in the United States, 1960, as a percentage of an adult male's annual earnings of $4,000).

Poor rural English couple's third-born, 1787–96; see table 1.8 and accompanying text. New York industrial worker's firstborn, 1889–90: see *FSA*, table 4–5 and app. B. The percentages are (*a*) ages 0–1: −2.0%, ages 2–5: 0%, ages 6–13: −1.1%, ages 14–17: 1.6%; and (*b*) ages 10–13: 2.3%, ages 14–15: 28.7%; ages 16–17: 32.5%. Rural Filipino couple, no specific parity, 1975: see fig. 1.4 and accompanying text. Urban United States couple's firstborn, 1960 census: *FSA*, tables 4–5 and E–1. The percentages are: (*a*) pregnancy: −4.7%, under 1: −16.5%, age 1: −13.6%, age 2: −13.2%, age 3: −12.6%, age 4: −10.9%, age 5: −5.1%, age 6: −3.1%, age 7: −2.6%, age 8: −2.3%, age 9: −2.0%, age 10: −1.8%, age 11: −1.5%, age 12: −1.3%, ages 13–17: −0.1%; (*b*) age 14: 1.0%, age 15: 2.5%, age 16: 5.4%, age 17: 8.3%.

fertility incentives. The relative cost concept also seems capable of contributing to our understanding of why fertility failed to decline in the early stages of so many countries' development, and it also partly explains the ultimate secular fertility decline.

Matching the relative cost concept with historical information on price and wage trends and on shifts in the net effects of a child on family allocations of home time and commodities suggests forces that steadily reduce fertility incentives throughout development and also forces whose incentive effect has reversed itself. From the earliest stages of modern economic development, likely declines in the prices of luxury goods relative to staples should have made children seem more costly, other things equal. Yet the implications of improvements in real wages and child survival rates would have had an opposite effect in the early stages of development. With children still time-supplying as defined here, early increases in real wage rates for common labor would have made children seem cheaper relative to the home activities with which they compete. It may have been, for example, that wage gains undercut the case for holding down family size in England's industrial revolution, as the dismal scientists advancing the iron law of wages feared. By contrast, in the later stages of development children have become time-intensive, especially outside of agriculture, translating further improvements in real wage rates into increasing awareness of the costs of a child in terms of the mother's career. As far as we can judge from crude comparisons of time-use studies across classes and nations, this shift to time-intensity has not been due to any marked rise in the gross time inputs into a child of given birth order and spacing. Rather, it has been due to the decline in child time contributions to parents' households and to the drift toward less time-intensive, more commodity-intensive alternatives to an extra child.

The relevant-cost concept is thus able to string together reasons for predicting an early lag in fertility decline as well as the later decline. There is thus at least preliminary support for not rejecting the third of three interpretations of the early persistence of high fertility offered above. This interpretation argues that succeeding generations of young couples may have exercised crude fertility controls all along and simply found no net new incentives to reduce births in the early stages of economic development. This interpretation remains a competitor with the view that couples never thought in terms of child costs and benefits until a development threshold was passed, and with the view that early development finally gave them the social and physical ability to have as many children as they wanted.

The evidence presented here is extremely fragmentary and falls far short of establishing that arguments about relative child costs, as defined here, unlock the many mysteries in fertility patterns over time and across groups. It does indicate, however, the kind of evidence waiting to be pursued in the study of fertility in developing countries.

1.9.2 Child-Cost Proxies and the Identification Problem

The usefulness of the concept of relative child cost will depend on the availability of appropriate empirical proxies that allow one to isolate its influence on fertility without going through the tedious process of actually calculating the various time and commodity costs of children and alternatives to them. This paper has advanced several suggestions for choosing proxies, suggestions that can translate into choices of special interaction terms for fertility regressions.

At the "micro" level of samples consisting of individual households, the relative-cost concept is not likely to bring great changes in our choices or interpretations of independent variables. The relative-cost measure combines information about couples' economic environment that is not likely to be observable at the individual household level, except as a transformation on place of residence and some of the couple's attributes, such as schooling. Using, for example, the wage rate of the wife as a measure of the relative price of time inputs, or schooling as a proxy for lower-cost access to information about luxury goods and services, will accomplish little, since wage rates and schooling have already been surrounded by a host of competing interpretations in work on fertility.

The inability of the relative cost concept to untie Gordian knots at the "micro" level reflects not so much the limitations of the concept as the limitations of microtesting. Many of the questions bearing most directly on population policy are questions of how changes in the aggregate economic environment will affect aggregate fertility. The organizing issue of this paper, for example, was how economic development might affect aggregate fertility by changing the market signals facing whole groups. Similar in its aggregation and its reference to time-series analysis is the issue of the overall effectiveness of deliberate policies toward fertility. Micro cross sections often fail to yield answers to such questions by not letting the independent variables of interest vary and be measured.

For more aggregate testing on changes in fertility over time, where the units of observations are socioeconomic groups, regions, or nations, the relative cost can be proxied, though perhaps only part by part. Since group wage rate data are more often available than group data on prices for commodities, a logical starting place for proxying relative cost patterns is with interaction terms multiplying the earnings intensity of an extra child by the change in a real wage rate for the group or region or nation. For this purpose it would be desirable to proxy the earnings intensity by a gap between the change in the labor force participation of wives caused by the presence of, say, a child under 6 and the participation rate for teenagers. Yet the participation rates for wives are seldom available by presence-of-children categories. One is likely to be forced further down the shopping list of suitable proxies. If it happens that there is evidence that only the real wage rate changes, and not the earnings intensity of an extra child, vary across groups, then the wage rate change alone proxies the change in relative cost. If not, one must look for further suitable participation-rate proxies, such as the rate for single young adult females (again versus that for teenagers). In a setting in which the earnings intensity of an extra child is suspected of varying, yet the only participation rates for women are overall age-group averages, the hunt for a time-cost proxy would have to be abandoned, since the overall female participation rate is simultaneously bound up with the dependent variable, fertility. In many cases, though, proxies can be had and may improve fertility forecasting.

Notes

1. A convenient overview of our eclectic consensus on how development cuts fertility is United Nations (1973, 1:88–106). Theorizing about the evolution of child costs and benefits with the development process goes back at least as far as Harvey Leibenstein's (1957) remarks on this theme. Stigler's lemma was enunciated by George Stigler (1969, p. 266) and helpfully cited (but not observed) by Donald N. McCloskey (1976, p. 434).

2. The Brownlee estimates in table 1.1 and figure 1.1 imply that the death rate in England and Wales fell dramatically from 1731–70 to 1780–1820. The dating of the decline in the death rate and age-standardized mortality rates remains the subject of debate, however, with some scholars putting the turning point as late as the 1810s and arguing that the birthrate may also have been higher in the late eighteenth century and early nineteenth century than is shown here.

3. On Tokugawa fertility rates, see Hanley and Yamamura (1977). Revised estimates of Meiji vital rates under varying assumptions about reporting biases are given in Morita (1963).

4. Habakkuk and Postan (1965, vol. 6, part 1, table 9); and Kuznets (1966, table 2.3).

5. A similar point was made by Kuznets (1975, p. 391). The present statements do not mean, of course, that literacy and urban residence did not reduce fertility among literate and urban households.

6. Deane and Cole (1969, chaps. 1, 2, 9).

7. Gilboy (1934); Bowley (1900); and Flinn (1974).

8. On national product per capita, see Bank of Japan (1966, parts 1 and 10). On real agricultural wages, see Ohkawa, Shinohara, and Umemura (1966–72, 8:135, 9:220). On industrial wage rates, see Minami (1973, pp. 306–8). Product per capita grew at 2% per annum or a bit less, depending on whose estimates one accepts in the controversy over rice production figures. The real wage rate for male day-hired agricultural workers grew at the following rates: 1886–88 to 1900–

1903: 2.84% per year; 1900–1903 to 1910–13: 0.54% per year; 1910–13 to 1924–27: 1.96% per year. Female wage rates in agriculture grew slightly faster. The real daily wage rates in manufacturing generally grew at the following rates calculated for female textile workers: 1900–1903 to 1910–13: 1.22% a year; 1910–13 to 1924–27: 3.60% per year.

9. Maddison (1971, app. A and B), reworking the production estimates of Blyn and Sivasubramonian.

10. Richards (1975, chaps. 3–5); O'Brien (1968).

11. Oechsli and Kirk (1975, p. 410). See also Kirk (1971); and Beaver (1975, chaps. 6–8). It should be noted that the fertility lag under discussion here is evident in the data reviewed by Oechsli and Kirk, even though their article advanced the view that the fertility transition is really more predictable and prompt among today's developing countries than others have suggested. Their deemphasis on the lag is made possible by the simple expedient of constructing "development indexes" standardized so that an index of zero is not achieved until the country has already experienced considerable increases in ten development indicators.

12. Tabbarah (1971, 1976); and Easterlin (1975).

13. Tabbarah's 1976 version of the model actually posits a rise in fertility as well as in completed surviving family size before the threshold is reached. This rise in fertility is hard to observe empirically, leaving it little support over the null hypothesis of no early change in fertility. Yet his model is easily altered to posit no change in maximum attainable births, a rise in child survival chances, and a decline in desired number of children.

14. For extensive citations to the estimates of absolute child costs and benefits, see chapter 4 of Lindert (1978), hereafter cited as *FSA*.

15. The role of the child-cost concept within a model of optimal fertility regulation with uncertain birth outcomes is shown more formally in *FSA*, chap. 3.

16. I assume that the parents expect to live until after their surviving children have left the home as adults.

17. If the family member in question does not in fact work for pay, then the shadow price of his time may of course differ from the market wage for working persons with his attributes. Yet, as shown elsewhere (*FSA*, chap. 4, n. 4), the choice of time price matters to the measurement of relative child costs only where it applies to family members whose paid work is in fact affected by the child's existence. This being the case, the relevant margins of time use here will be ones for which wage rates (plus possible effects of time allocation on future earning power) are the appropriate time prices.

18. Estimates of the positive effect of children on the working hours of postwar United States husbands are reviewed in *FSA*, appendix B. An estimate for the rural Philippines in 1975 is given in section 1.5 below.

It has not yet proved possible to quantify an effect of children on their fathers' pay rates per unit of time from cross-sectional data, because simultaneity in the relationship between husband's income and the number of children threatens to distort any measure of so subtle an effect. Panel data may help isolate this effect. Or an effect of children on a husband's wage rate could be quantified synthetically if one were to take the estimates of the effects on hours and then separately estimate the effects of hours upon the husband's rate of pay, ignoring any other effect from fatherhood to rate of pay.

19. A budget constraint of this type has been developed, for example, in Becker and Lewis (1973).

20. The term "quality" is more suggestive of child attributes, or of child "outputs" in the household-production-function framework, than of inputs into the

child. Even at that level, it invites unhelpful controversy by labeling as human "quality" such narrower observable attributes as schooling achievement and income potential.

21. See, for example, Caldwell (1968, chap. 6); Mainichi Newspapers (1972, chap. 1); and especially Fawcett et al. (1974).

22. Fawcett et al. (1974, appendix, especially tables A1, A2).

23. *FSA*, chap. 4, sec. 4.

24. *FSA*, app. E.

25. The calculations underlying tables 1.2 through 1.5 are laid out in *FSA*, app. A–E.

26. Houthakker (1957); and *FSA*, app. D.

27. Data on house purchases in New Haven, Connecticut, between 1967 and 1970 show that larger family size significantly raises the consumption of lot size and room space while lowering the consumption of location and other housing quality. See Goodman (1976, table 4.8); and King (1975, table 5.1). Several other studies have confirmed that more children lead to the consumption of more rooms despite the reduction in shelter expenditures, among them David (1962).

28. On patterns in child-care time in the United States and other countries, see the sources cited in *FSA*, chap. 4 and app. C, plus Walker and Woods (1976); Szalai (1972); Dodge (1966, pp. 91–99); Kingsbury and Fairchild (1935, chap. 13 and appendix); and the studies of rural Philippines, Java, and Nepal cited below.

29. Note that the estimated effects of a child on the mother's earnings are an average over many households. In some cases the appearance of, say, a firstborn child causes wives to drop out of the labor force and actually raises the amount of time they devote to nonchild home activities. In other cases the arrival of the firstborn merely takes some time of an already unpaid mother away from other home activities. It is the averaging of such cases that yields a time cost exceeding the effect of the child on parents' paid work.

30. *FSA*, chap. 5.

31. Conrad and Meyer (1958).

32. Evans (1962, pp. 208–14). It should be noted that Evans's estimates of slave life expectancy in 1850, which are the ones used by Fogel and Engerman (1974), are higher than any others given in Evans's secondary sources or in the life-table estimates of Eblen and Meeker.

33. Conrad and Meyer (1958); Evans (1962, pp. 214–21); Butlin (1971); and Fogel and Engerman (1974, vol. 1, chap. 3, and vol. 2, pp. 62–87).

34. The predicted values for slaves in the New Orleans slave market are those based on sales in the 1850s reported in Kotlikoff (1976, table 3; regression for the 1850s based on 775 group and individual sales). A 20-year-old was valued at $823.25, and 76.535% of newborns were estimated to survive to their 20th birth day in 1850.

35. The most promising historical data base on time use within rural households, outside the United States farm household surveys of time use from the 1920s on, is several of the zemstvo household surveys taken in prerevolutionary Russia. Those taken in Vologda and Volokolamsk, for example, seem to have separate time-use data on men, women, boys, and girls, to judge from their citation by Chayanov (1966, pp. 179–82). A guide to the contents of dozens of untapped zemstvo surveys is given in Svavitskii (1961, especially appendixes).

36. For a fuller description of the Laguna sample, see Boulier (1976); and Popkin (1976). I am grateful to Drs. Boulier and Popkin for making their tentative results available to me and for running several supplementary regressions.

In the calculations underlying figure 1.4, I have valued the time of family members at their income per hour worked at any productive task: P1.595 for husbands, P0.938 for wives, and P1.31 for working children. For adults, these averages, which partly reflect lower-paid home work, are below the market wage rates for jobs away from home: P1.89 for working fathers and P1.94 for working mothers.

37. The regressions run thus far have not been able to identify the (presumably higher) time costs of a "firstborn"; that is, of the only child present in the home at the time of survey.

38. The regressions run thus far do not reveal any clear net difference between the amount of time spent on the care of an extra preschool child by all persons between the Laguna survey and the time-use survey in Syracuse, New York, in 1967–68. Slight differences in methods of data collection and in model specification make such comparisons hazardous in any case.

39. Figure 1.4 implies that the child leaves home on his or her 20th birthday. It is difficult to know the modal or mean ages of home-leaving in the contemporary rural Philippines. The age of 20 was chosen because the Laguna sample happened to show very little dropoff in the numbers of children present by age until age 20. The choice of a hypothetical home-leaving age does not seem to matter greatly to the discussion of the net benefits derived from a child by his parents as long as children are more or less earning what they themselves consume in their teens and across their early twenties.

40. An extra child in a household already having children makes the father work an extra 3.16 hours a week in its first year, an extra 2.24 for ages 1–6, 0.12 hours less (i.e., no real effect) for ages 7–9, an extra 2.05 hours a week for ages 10–12, 0.17 hours less for ages 13–15, and an extra 5.23 hours a week for ages 16–19 (Boulier [1976, table IIC]). Multiplied by 52 weeks, thus ignoring seasonal effects, one gets a stronger effect than the 8–50 hours of extra work a year estimated for the father of a later-born child in various United States studies (*FSA*, app. B).

41. Preliminary unreported regressions showed no net effect of extra children on the hourly rate of pay for working mothers. This may be the result of (*a*) model misspecification, (*b*) a genuine lack of such an effect, and/or (*c*) the fact that the hourly rates of pay for different tasks were imputed rates at which outsiders would have to be hired to perform those tasks, rather than personal market wage rates facing the mothers.

42. The Lorimer scales, based on 1950 expenditure data from India, and given in Lorimer (1967) and cited in Mueller (1976, table II–1). On these scales, the average household composition in Laguna had 4.242 adult-equivalent consumption units. Assuming that consumption was 90% of reported income in the Laguna households would make each Lorimer "unit" cost P1221. This peso value was then applied to the age-and-sex -specific scales to estimate commodity inputs into the extra child.

43. Mueller (1976).

44. The data for the Javanese village, near Jogjakarta, were gathered and are currently being analyzed by Benjamin White, in his doctoral dissertation at Columbia. Those from Nepal were gathered by Robert Creighton Peet. I am indebted to Moni Nag for reporting the results used here in his paper cited in table 1.7.

45. In the Javanese village, all adults devoted only 2.0 hours a day to child care, or less than a quarter of the adult male work input average. These two hours of household child care time were spread across more than one child, but the number of children under 6 years is not reported.

46. Whether an extra child is a net economic asset to his parents in less developed economies may be as unclear to the parents as it is to scholars. Interviews with 1,497 males and 1,499 females in the partially urbanized Western and Lagos states in Nigeria in 1973 showed both sexes evenly divided in their responses to questions about the net asset issue:

Measure	*Response*	*Males*	*Females*
Whether another child would make the	Richer	32%	32%
parents richer or poorer	The same	44%	44%
	Poorer	25%	25%
Whether children who have reached adulthood have returned more wealth	Yes, more	46%	30%
than that spent on them (parents with	The same	16%	27%
such children only)	No, less	38%	43%

(Okediji et al. [1976, p. 127]). This suggests at least some conformity between what the cross-sectional estimates so far imply and what couples perceive, since it is hard to imagine contemporary United States couples' responding so neutrally about the net economic effects of an extra child.

47. Fawcett et al., *The Value of Children . . . Comparative Perspectives* (1974, table A5).

48. Mainichi Newspapers (1972, chap. 1).

49. Hohm (1975).

50. On the decline of intergenerational coresidence in the United States, see Stern, Smith, and Doolittle (1975); Beresford and Rivlin (1966); Taeuber and Taeuber (1971, table VI–7); and Edward Pryor's estimates from Rhode Island census data in Laslett (1972). On the intermediate patterns in industrial Lancashire in the mid-nineteenth century, see Anderson (1971, pp. 139–40).

On the more extensive coresidence in developing Asian countries, see Nag (1976); Kessinger (1974); and the chapters on Serbia and early Japan in Laslett (1972).

51. Smith (1959).

52. Another structural change raising the relative time cost of an extra child is the trend toward greater geographic separation of young couples from their relatives, a change that raises the transactions costs of purchasing child-care time in a way not revealed by the available wage series.

53. Adams (1944, pp. 33–34); U.S. Bureau of the Census (1976, vol. 1, chap. E); and Ohkawa et al. (1966, vol. 8).

54. Lindert (1974); Ohkawa et al. (1966, vol. 9); Bank of Japan (1966); Mills and Ohta (1976, p. 700).

55. Yasuba (1962); Easterlin (1971, 1976); Leet (1976).

56. Note that the empirical relevance of child wage rates to relative child costs is to be judged, in rural settings where children are net labor suppliers, by patterns in the purchasing power of labor time in terms of the inputs in which rural children are intensive—food (and possibly land). The contribution of wage-rate differences to fertility differences must thus begin by comparing wage rates with the prices of food. In the United States cross sections for the mid-nineteenth century, it is inappropriate to examine nominal wage rates across regions, as Easterlin has done (Easterlin [1976, pp. 61–62]). Wage rates without board must be compared with the cost of food, which was indeed lower in the frontier areas, leaving a positive correlation between the real value of a child's net labor supply and fertility.

57. The data are described and analyzed in Chernichovsky (1975, pp. 69 ff.). I am grateful to Dr. Chernichovsky for running additional unreported regressions on these data at my request.

58. In his paper for the present conference, Allen C. Kelley has reduced the simultaneity problem by applying two-stage least-squares regression techniques to survey data from urban Kenya in 1968–69. His structural equations show positive and sometimes significant effects of extra children of unspecified age on total family income (tables 2, 3, A–1, and A–2). This result at least resembles the result obtained by ordinary least squares from the two rural Indian villages, though differences in models and data bases obviously complicate the comparison.

59. Davies (1795); Eden (1797).

60. In a minority of cases it was necessary to use a bread or flour price for the same year from elsewhere in the same county or an adjoining county. The bread-flour-oatmeal price ratios were based on parishes reporting more than one of these prices.

61. My interpolations of the ages of middle-born children and allocations of children's earnings among the older children may have affected the age profile of children's earnings in unknown ways, but they would not affect the undiscounted average earnings at all.

62. *FSA*, chap. 4.

63. Richards (1975, citing 1943–44 data); Ghomeny (1953, table 26, citing alternative 1943–44 data); and Hansen (1969, p. 503, referring to the early 1960s).

64. "Children are the backbone of the labor supply . . . and in a large measure determine the extent of the cotton crop. . . . [About 45% of all workers are children, and] the median age of all child workers was only 11 years, 5 months" (Gibbons and Armentrout 1925, p. 30).

One source failing to confirm the child-labor intensity of cotton relative to other crops was the University of Nanking's massive farm survey of 1929–33. It failed to record a higher share of labor performed by children in the one locality (out of about 160) that specialized in cotton, or a higher share in several localities having a larger-than-average minority share of their area planted in cotton Buck (1937, chaps. 6, 8). This is not a very satisfactory test, since cotton was not heavily represented in the sample. More generally, however, the Buck *Statistics* volume remains an underutilized resource for studying the division of labor by crop and a host of other issues relating to peasant farm productivity and land tenure.

65. *FSA*, chap. 4 and app. B.

66. Haines (1976).

67. Haines (1976).

Comment Eva Mueller

Professor Lindert's paper is valuable in many ways. One cannot help admiring his ability to draw on data from many countries and many historical periods. The choice-theoretic framework he employs is an immense aid to logical thinking, even if one is critical of its narrow focus on economic variables. Lindert's major conclusion—that at early stages

Eva Mueller is professor of economics and research associate at the Population Studies Center, University of Michigan.

of development the value of children may rise because they may earn more income—is important and, I believe, correct.

Relative cost, the concept central to Lindert's paper, is merely a weighted price index. An advantage of this concept is that changes in weights can be ignored as long as there is reason to believe the weights change to the same extent in the numerator and the denominator. For example, I find myself in agreement with Lindert's assumption that the shares of "other goods" in the bundle of child inputs and the bundle of alternative inputs probably move in more or less parallel fashion. Thus, for rough comparisons, changes in quantities of goods inputs need not be measured. Relative changes in time inputs are much more problematic, as we shall see.

Rather than confining myself to relative cost, I will remark on changes in absolute costs of children in the course of development. Absolute cost is a much more comprehensive concept than relative cost. Rather than focusing exclusively on *prices*, it also focuses on *quantities* of time and other resources that must be sacrificed to raise a child (net of the time and resources derived from the child). Absolute cost is affected by the quality of child the couple chooses or feels it must have. It is a concept that helps us consider "taste" factors, such as the attractiveness of goods that are alternatives to children. Most important, absolute cost has important policy implications. If the net absolute cost of a marginal child up to the time of adulthood exceeds his contribution to household income, economic development is likely to be retarded by large family size, since the household's ability to accumulate physical and human capital is reduced. The noneconomic satisfactions of raising children may of course override absolute child costs, as far as the household is concerned; but parents may not be aware of the macroeffects of a society-wide preference for large family size on the economy and hence on their own family's chances of attaining a higher standard of living. In many less-developed countries governments are in a quandary when they must decide whether to pursue an energetic family planning program or adopt a politically expedient "do-nothing" stance on the family planning issue. As economists we have a serious responsibility to produce research that aids correct policy decisions. For this, absolute cost measurements are more useful than relative cost measurements.

Lindert himself seems intrigued with the question whether children are ever an economic asset, and he goes beyond the relative-cost framework to present some pertinent calculations. My own work (Mueller 1976) has made me skeptical of the proposition that children are an economic asset, and I emphatically share his desire for more data that might throw light on this problem. The question that needs to be answered is not whether children are ever an economic asset but, under what conditions are children an economic asset and under what conditions are they an economic liability?

Let us consider *changes* in child costs during the course of development, without being constrained by the narrow focus of the relative-cost concept. We may think of two kinds of communities: type I is a stagnant, traditional community where there is little technological change, little accumulation of physical and human capital, and little unused land of acceptable quality. In this stagnant community the marginal productivity of capital and labor is very low (as T. W. Schultz argued years ago). Tastes are static. Type II is a community that is modernizing its agriculture or industries or both; the demand for labor and capital is growing; incomes are growing; a taste is developing for new kinds of goods and children of higher quality. Communities in less developed countries range on a continuum from type I to type II. Usually, within the same country, there are type I and type II localities as well as subgroups of the population.

Starting with labor, in a type I community wages and the marginal productivity of labor are low. An additional child reduces per capita income, thereby increasing the marginal utility of income. In consequence, the family is forced to engage in additional work that has very low productivity and that, in the absence of the child, would not be considered worth undertaking. There is increasing evidence of a positive correlation between part-time work by women and higher fertility among poor households (Smith 1976). Husbands may also work longer hours as family size grows, and children may share in the work. In this sense an additional child is time releasing; but it imposes a burden of additional work on the family that is an opportunity cost, since in the absence of the child the family would have preferred to work less.

As we move toward a type II community, the demand for labor and the productivity of labor rise. Thus there is an income effect on labor force participation and a price effect. The strength of the income effect depends on the culture and on the kinds of employment opportunities generated by development. In some LDCs, but not in others, work by women or children, especially manual work, is considered demeaning and a sign of low status. As income rises, therefore, women may work less. Urbanization and industrialization tend to reduce work opportunities for women, especially work that is compatible with child-rearing (Boserup 1970). When women do not want to work for a combination of reasons relating to social status and the characteristics of available jobs, market wages greatly exaggerate the cost of child-care time. If education is highly valued, increasing income may lower children's participation in the labor force. However schooling does not seem to interfere seriously with work by children until it is extended beyond ages

10–12. Thus the result of development may be that the mother has more time for child care, or the children work less, or both. To be sure, there are other type II communities where work by women and children does not have negative status implications. In that case the incentive effect of higher wages on labor force participation may outweigh the income effect. Children and women will then be more willing to engage in market work and children may be time releasing until a later stage of economic development.

In all, the transition from a type I to a type II community may have four combinations of consequences for labor force participation and hence for the cost of children:

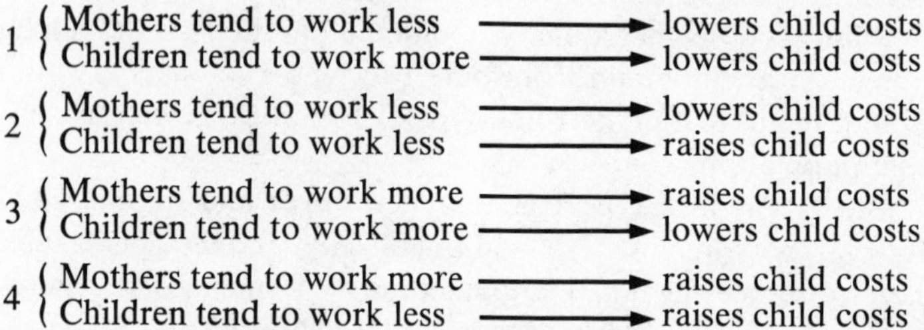

1 Mothers tend to work less → lowers child costs
Children tend to work more → lowers child costs
2 Mothers tend to work less → lowers child costs
Children tend to work less → raises child costs
3 Mothers tend to work more → raises child costs
Children tend to work more → lowers child costs
4 Mothers tend to work more → raises child costs
Children tend to work less → raises child costs

In case 1 children become less costly, and fertility may be stimulated by development. Perhaps Egypt and some Latin American countries resemble case 1. Case 2 may be more common than case 1; here the effects of changes in labor force participation on child costs are mixed. Taiwan during the 1960s is an example. Case 3 also is mixed. In case 4 children become more costly and fertility is discouraged on that account. Contemporary Western communities are typical of case 4. The point is that the transition from type I to type II communities may be accompanied by diverse changes in work patterns. In consequence, the effect of development on child costs via work patterns and wages is not uniform for all countries. In the long run all type II communities may move toward case 4; how long this will take depends on cultural attitudes toward women's work, educational aspirations for children, and the kinds of jobs economic development opens up for women and children.

Turning now to the rate of return on capital, as a less developed community moves from type I to type II, it benefits from new methods of production and other innovations. Hence the demand for capital is increased. In a type I community a farmer may have little need for additional capital, and resources in old age may be as valuable to him as resources now. In a type II community the farmer may profit greatly if he has money to buy hybrid seeds, fertilizer, a water pump, and so forth; a small businessman may profit similarly if he can buy an electric motor. Thus children start to compete with capital accumulation. The discount rate rises and, since child costs are concentrated in the early years and returns from children follow later, the cost of children rises relative to the "alternative H bundle." While the relative-cost framework in principle allows for a discount rate, it has the shortcoming that child costs are compared explicitly only with the bundle of alternative H services. The other possible trade-off—between the marginal child and a higher rate of capital accumulation—is neglected. High discount rates may not fully reflect the difficulty a farmer or artisan has in obtaining capital. Capital markets are imperfect in LDCs, and for the lower income groups access to capital is sometimes as much of a problem as exorbitant interest rates. Thus, while children may work more and at higher wages as development proceeds and therefore become cheaper, the opportunity cost of the funds required for their early upbringing is bound to rise.

Finally, changes in tastes need to be brought into the picture. In a type I community, a very limited assortment of H enjoyments is available. As the amount of traditional H services acquired increases, there may be diminishing marginal utility. Another child may be much more gratifying than an increase in the alternative H bundle. When new consumer goods become available and education for children is desired, the attractiveness of the trade-off is altered. To be sure, this is a taste rather than a price effect. Nevertheless, in the eyes of parents the marginal child becomes more costly because the things that must be sacrificed for it are more highly valued in type II communities.

In sum, in the course of development the growing demand for capital and new consumption aspirations make children more costly, while rising wages and increasing employment opportunities may raise or lower child costs. The total effect of development on child costs depends on such factors as social attitudes toward work by women and children, the kind of jobs the particular economy creates for women and children, the characteristics of the capital market, and the availability of new consumer goods. Further, it depends on the extent to which type II conditions have penetrated the economy. In Mexico, for example, in spite of a relatively high per capita income, the poorer segments of the population still live under close to type I conditions.

Returning briefly to Lindert's method, a major advantage of the relative-cost concept is that it lends itself to comparisons that range widely over time and space. This is interesting; but it seems that studies that compare distant times and widely differing geographic areas and cultures do not deserve high priority in future research. Research to date suggests that the kind of economic variables that enter our models have only limited power to explain fertility change. Noneconomic factors and structural characteristics of the economy play a large role and interact with economic variables. Hence we need very intensive microlevel studies that explore how economic factors help explain differences in fertility decisions between households that share the same culture, and where the remaining differences in the social and economic environment can be explicitly taken into account in the analysis.

In addition, studies of perceived costs deserve some attention. I agree with Lindert that actual movements in absolute and relative child costs are major determinants of changes in perceived costs. However, measures of perceived cost would not give us exactly the same information as measures of actual costs. First, there is bound to be a time lag between changes in actual and perceived costs; and changes in some costs may be perceived more quickly than changes in some other costs. Since time lags are the most puzzling, as well as the most crucial, aspect of the demographic transition, any data that throw light on time lags are of interest. Second, as Lindert suggests, studies of perceived costs may help us learn which parts of the actual costs and benefits of children are salient to couples and which ones they tend to overlook. Third, perceived costs and benefits are affected by a couple's time horizon and time preference—matters we can only guess about when we work with traditional economic data. Last, while perceptions of costs and benefits reflect to some extent economic and demographic factors that can be measured directly, they also reflect a variety of environmental influences that often cannot be brought into the analysis in a more direct way. Thus it appears that much might be learned from studies of perceived costs and benefits, especially if data on actual and perceived costs could be collected for the same population.

References

Adams, T. M. 1944. *Prices paid by Vermont farmers . . . 1790–1940; Wages of Vermont farm labor, 1780–1940*. Burlington, Vt.: Vermont Agricultural Experiment Station.

Anderson, Michael. 1971. *Family structure in nineteenth century Lancashire*. Cambridge: Cambridge University Press.

Bank of Japan, Statistics Department. 1966. *100-year statistics of Japan*. Tokyo: Bank of Japan.

Beaver, Steven E. 1975. *Demographic transition theory reinterpreted: An application to recent natality trends in Latin America*. Boston: Lexington Books.

Becker, Gary S., and Lewis, H. Gregg. 1973. On the interaction between quantity and quality of children. *Journal of Political Economy* 81, no. 2, part 2 (March/April): S279–88.

Beresford, John C., and Rivlin, Alice M. 1966. Privacy, poverty, and old age. *Demography* 3:247–58.

Boserup, Ester. 1970. *Woman's role in economic development.* New York: St. Martin's Press.

Boulier, Bryan L. 1976. Children and household economic activity in Laguna, Philippines. University of the Philippines, Institute of Economic Development and Research, Discussion Paper no. 76–19 (29 July).

Bowley, Arthur W. 1900. *Wages in the United Kingdom in the nineteenth century.* Cambridge: Cambridge University Press.

Buck, John Lossing. 1937. *Land utilization in China: Statistics.* Chicago: University of Chicago Press.

Butlin, Noel G. 1971. *Ante-bellum slavery: A critique of a debate.* Canberra: Australian National University, Research School of Social Sciences.

Caldwell, John C. 1968. *Population growth and family change in Africa.* Canberra: Australian National University Press.

Chayanov, A. V. 1966. *The theory of peasant economy.* Homewood, Ill.: Richard Irwin.

Chernichovsky, Dov. 1975. Fertility behavior in developing economies: An investment approach. Ph.D. diss., City University of New York.

Collver, O. Andrew. 1965. *Birth rates in Latin America.* Berkeley: University of California Press.

Conrad, Alfred H., and Meyer, John R. 1958. The economics of slavery in the ante-bellum South. *Journal of Political Economy* 66, no. 2 (April): 95–122.

David, Martin H. 1962. *Family composition and consumption.* Amsterdam: North-Holland.

Davies, David. 1795. *The case of labourers in husbandry.* London.

Deane, Phyllis, and Cole, W. A. 1969. *British economic growth, 1688–1959.* 2d ed. Cambridge: Cambridge University Press.

Dodge, Norton T. 1966. *Women in the Soviet economy.* Baltimore: Johns Hopkins University Press.

Easterlin, Richard A. 1968. *Population, labor force and long swings in economic growth.* New York: Columbia University Press.

———. 1971. Does human fertility adjust to the environment? *American Economic Review* 61, no. 2 (May): 399–407.

———. 1975. An economic framework for fertility analysis. *Studies in Family Planning* 6, no. 3 (March): 54–63.

———. 1976. Population change and farm settlement in the northern United States. *Journal of Economic History* 36, no. 1 (March): 45–75.

Eden, Sir Frederick Morton. 1797. *The state of the poor.* Original ed. Vols. 2 and 3. London: J. Davis.

Evans, Robert, Jr. 1962. The economics of American Negro slavery. In *Aspects of labor economics*, ed. H. Gregg Lewis. Princeton: Princeton University Press.

Fawcett, James T., et al. 1974. *The value of children in Asia and the United States: Comparative perspectives.* Institute Paper no. 32. Honolulu: East-West Population Institute.

Flinn, Michael W. 1974. Trends in real wages, 1750–1850. *Economic History Review* 27, no. 3 (August): 395 ff.

Fogel, Robert W., and Engerman, Stanley L. 1974. *Time on the cross.* Boston: Little Brown.

Ghomeny, M. R. 1953. Resource use and income in Egyptian agriculture. Ph.D. diss., North Carolina State University.

Gibbons, Charles E., and Armentrout, Clara B. 1925. *Child labor among cotton growers of Texas.* New York: National Child Labor Committee.

Gilboy, Elizabeth W. 1934. *Wages in eighteenth century England.* Cambridge: Harvard University Press.

Gille, Halvor. 1967. Twentieth-century levels and trends of fertility in developing countries. In *World population conference, 1965.* New York: United Nations Department of Economic and Social Affairs.

Goodman, Allen C. 1976. Neighborhood effects, hedonic prices, and the residential housing choice. Ph.D. diss., Yale University.

Habakkuk, H. J., and Postan, M., eds. 1965. *Cambridge economic history of Europe.* Vol. 6, part 1. Cambridge: Cambridge University Press.

Haines, Michael R. 1976. Industrial work and the family cycle, 1889–1890. Paper given at the annual cliometrics conference, Madison, Wisconsin, 24 April.

Hanley, Susan B., and Yamamura, Kozo. 1977. *Economic and demographic change in preindustrial Japan, 1600–1868.* Princeton: Princeton University Press.

Hansen, Bent. 1969. Employment and wages in rural Egypt. *American Economic Review* 59, no. 3 (June): 298–313.

Heer, David M. 1968. The demographic transition in the Russian Empire and the Soviet Union. *Journal of Social History* 1, no. 3 (Spring): 193–240.

Hohm, Charles F. 1975. Social security and fertility: An International perspective. *Demography* 12, no. 4 (November): 629–44.

Houthakker, Hendrik S. 1957. An international comparison of household expenditure patterns, commemorating the centenary of Engel's law. *Econometrica* 25, no. 4 (October): 532–51.

Kessinger, Tom G. 1974. *Valyatpur, 1848–1968: Social and economic change in a north Indian village.* Berkeley: University of California Press.

King, A. Thomas. 1975. The demand for housing: Integrating the roles of journey-to-work, neighborhood quality, and prices. Conference draft of his paper by the same title in *Household production and consumption*, ed. Nestor Terleckyj. NBER Studies in Income and Wealth, vol. 40. New York: Columbia University Press.

Kingsbury, Susan M., and Fairchild, Mildred. 1935. *Factory, family, and woman in the Soviet Union*. New York: Putnam.

Kirk, Dudley. 1971. A new demographic transition? In *Rapid Population Growth*, ed. National Academy of Sciences, pp. 123–47. Baltimore: Johns Hopkins University Press.

Kotlikoff, Laurence J. 1976. Toward a quantitative description of the New Orleans slave market. Paper presented at the annual cliometrics conference, Madison, Wisconsin, 23 April.

Kuznets, Simon. 1966. *Modern economic growth*. New Haven: Yale University Press.

———. 1975. Fertility differentials between less developed and developed regions: Components and implications. *Proceedings of the American Philosophical Society* 119, no. 5 (October): 363–96.

Laslett, Peter, ed. 1972. *Household and family in past time*. Cambridge: Cambridge University Press.

Leet, Don R. 1976. The determinants of the fertility transition in antebellum Ohio. *Journal of Economic History* 36, no. 2 (June): 359–78.

Leibenstein, Harvey. 1957. *Economic backwardness and economic growth*. New York: Wiley.

Lindert, Peter H. 1974. Land scarcity and American growth. *Journal of Economic History* 34, no. 4 (December): 851–81.

———. 1978. *Fertility and scarcity in America*. Princeton: Princeton University Press.

Lorimer, Frank. 1967. The economics of family formation under different conditions. In *World population conference, 1965*, vol. 2 New York: Department of Economic and Social Affairs.

McCloskey, Donald N. 1976. Does the past have useful economics? *Journal of Economic Literature* 14, no. 2 (June): 434–61.

Maddison, Angus. 1971. *Class structure and economic growth: India and Pakistan since the Moghals*. New York: W. W. Norton.

Mainichi Newspapers, Population Problems Research Council. 1972. *Summary of eleventh national survey on family planning*. Tokyo: Mainichi Newspapers.

Mills, Edwin S., and Ohta, Katsutoskh. 1976. Urbanization and urban problems. In *Asia's new giant*, ed. Hugh Patrick and Henry Rosovsky, p. 700. Washington, D.C.: Brookings Institution.

Minami, Ryoshin. 1973. *The turning point in economic development: Japan's experience*. Tokyo: Kinokuniya Bookstore.

Morita, Yuzo. 1963. Estimated birth and death rates in the early Meiji period of Japan. *Population Studies* 17, no. 1 (July): 33–56.

Mueller, Eva. 1976. The economic value of children in peasant agriculture. In *Population and development*, ed. Ronald G. Ridker. Baltimore: Johns Hopkins University Press.

Nag, Moni. 1976. Economic value of children among Javanese and Nepalese peasants: An anthropological inquiry. Revised draft of a paper presented to the annual meeting of the American Association for the Advancement of Science, Boston, 18–24 February.

Nassef, Abdel-Fattah. 1970. *The Egyptian labor force*. Philadelphia: University of Pennsylvania Population Studies Center.

O'Brien, Patrick. 1968. The long term growth of agricultural production in Egypt, 1821–1962. In *Political and social change in modern Egypt*, ed. P. M. Holt, pp. 162–95. New York: Oxford University Press.

Oechsli, Frank W., and Kirk, Dudley. 1975. Modernization and the demographic transition in Latin America and the Caribbean. *Economic Development and Cultural Change* 23, no. 3 (April): 391–419.

Okhawa, K.; Shinohara, M.; and Umemura, M. 1966–72. *Estimates of long term economic statistics of Japan since 1868*. 12 vols. Tokyo: Tokyo Keizai Shinpo Sha.

Okediji, F. O.; Caldwell, John; Caldwell, Pat; and Ware, Helen. 1976. The changing African family project: A report with special reference to the Nigerian project. *Studies in Family Planning* 7, no. 5 (May): 126–36.

Popkin, Barry M. 1976. The production of child welfare in rural Filipino households. University of the Philippines, Institute of Economic Development and Research, Discussion Paper no. 76–17 (July).

Population Reference Bureau. 1976. *1976 world population data sheet*. Washington, D.C.: Population Reference Bureau.

Postan, M. M., and Habakkuk, H. J., eds. *The Cambridge economic history of Europe*. Vol. 6. *The industrial revolutions and after*. Cambridge: Cambridge University Press.

Richards, Alan R. 1975. Accumulation, distribution and technical change in Egyptian agriculture, 1800–1940. Ph.D. diss., University of Wisconsin, Madison.

Smith, Stanley. 1976. The interaction between female labor force participation and fertility in Mexico City. Ph.D. diss., University of Michigan.

Smith, Thomas C. 1959. *The agrarian origins of modern Japan*. Stanford: Stanford University Press.

Stern, David; Smith, Sandy; and Doolittle, Fred. 1975. How children used to work. *Law and Contemporary Problems* 39, no. 3 (summer): 93–117.

Stigler, George. 1969. Does economics have a useful past? *History of Political Economy* 1 (fall): 217–30.

Svavitskii, N. A. 1961. *Zemskii podvornye perepisi.* Moscow: Gosstatizdat.

Szalai, Alexander, ed. 1972. *The use of time.* The Hague: Mouton.

Tabbarah, Riad. 1976. Population education as a component of development policy. *Studies in Family Planning* 7, no. 7 (July): 197–201.

———. 1971. Toward a theory of demographic development. *Economic Development and Cultural Change* 19, no. 2 (January): 257–76.

Taeuber, Irene B., and Taeuber, Conrad. 1971. *People of the United States in the twentieth century.* Washington, D.C.: GPO.

United Nations, Department of Economic and Social Affairs. 1973. *The determinants and consequences of population trends.* New York: United Nations.

United States Bureau of the Census. 1976. *Historical statistics of the United States, colonial times to 1970.* Washington, D.C.: Government Printing Office.

Walker, Kathryn E., and Woods, Margaret E. 1976. *Time use.* Washington, D.C.: American Home Economics Association.

Yasuba, Yasukicki. 1962. *Birth rates of the white population in the United States, 1800–1860: An economic study.* Baltimore: Johns Hopkins University Press.

2 Toward a More General Economic Model of Fertility Determination: Endogenous Preferences and Natural Fertility

Richard A. Easterlin, Robert A. Pollak, and Michael L. Wachter

This paper develops a general model of marital fertility, from which, with appropriate empirical restrictions, implications are drawn for research and welfare analysis. The model builds to a considerable extent on prior economic research, but it differs from much of the economic literature on fertility in its emphasis on endogenous preferences and natural fertility. We feel there is need for a formal statement of such a model to serve as an alternative to the "Chicago-Columbia" approach that dominates the current work on economics of fertility (e.g., Schultz 1974). Throughout the paper we shall frequently contrast our framework with this approach. The first section outlines our argument; the second presents a formal statement of the model; the third classifies fertility determination into four special subcases; the fourth discusses some of the general research implications; and finally, an outline of the welfare implications of our model is contrasted with those of the Chicago-Columbia approach.

2.1 Overview

In section 2.2 we will present a general model of the determinants of marital fertility and completed family size. The determinants are seen as working through a family's preferences for consumption, children, and fertility regulation, and through four constraints:

Richard A. Easterlin, Robert A. Pollak, and Michael L. Wachter are associated with the University of Pennsylvania. Michael L. Wachter is a research associate of the National Bureau of Economic Research.

The research this paper reports was funded by NICHHD grant HD–05427, NSF grants SOC 74–20292 and SOC 75–14750, and Rockefeller Foundation Grant

1. a budget constraint that reflects the limitations implied by the market prices of goods and services, the wage rates of family members, any nonlabor income, and the time at the disposal of household members;
2. the household's technology, which enables it to convert market goods and the time of family members into the basic commodities that are the arguments of its utility function;
3. a "births function" or "fertility production function" that expresses the number of live births as a function of frequency of intercourse, reproductive span of the household, fertility regulation practices, and the commodities, goods, and practices that govern the probability of conception and the nonsusceptible period of the wife;
4. an "infant" mortality function that expresses infant and child mortality through adulthood as a function of such variables as health and nutrition. Subtracting mortality from fertility gives completed family size.

Maximizing the utility function subject to the budget constraint, the household's technology, the births function, and the infant mortality function yields the optimal solution values for the household's decision variables. We denote the optimal solution values for births by b^0 and for completed family size by N^0.

The model is presented (as in the Chicago-Columbia approach) in a single-period decision-making framework. Parents are viewed as making their basic fertility decisions at the beginning of the marriage and then not altering their behavior over their lifetimes. This requires, however, a distinction between results perceived or anticipated when the decisions are made and the actual outcomes. The distinction reflects the fact that families may not correctly perceive the constraints of the maximization problem. The theoretical model of section 2.2 is developed in terms of perceived magnitudes. Conceptually the model can be altered in a straightforward manner to deal with the actual results. This is an important consideration, since the empirical data are usually for the actual rather than the perceived concepts.

In developing a general model of fertility determination, we concentrate on two considerations that we believe are empirically important but that have been largely ignored in much of the economics literature. First, a family's utility function, whose arguments include a vector of commodities and completed family size, is viewed as endogenous to the society in which it lives. In our model this relationship is incorporated

72029. We are grateful for assistance to Debbie Faigen, Stacy Hinck, Neil Weintraub, and Deborah C. K. Wenger, and for helpful comments and suggestions to Ronald Demos Lee, Harvey Leibenstein, Warren Sanderson, Morton Owen Schapiro, and Anne D. Williams. This paper extends previous work by the authors; see Easterlin (1975, 1978) and Wachter (1972*b*).

through an interdependent preference mechanism, which allows for the transmission of aspirations from one family to another and from one generation to another. Past behavior, whether in a "socialization" or a purely intrafamily framework, determines a family's tastes. Second, a family does not always understand or acknowledge the relationship between its fecundity and its consumption decisions because it lacks accurate information concerning the determinants of births and infant mortality. The composition of the consumption bundle has both a direct effect on utility and an indirect effect that operates through the births production function. When household decisions fail to recognize the fecundity effects, in part or in full, there is a problem of "unperceived jointness."

Interdependent preferences and the births and infant mortality functions, with a given level of unperceived jointness, enrich and complicate the optimal solution function. For example, as we shall see, maximizing the family's utility function subject to the appropriate constraints does not yield demand functions for completed family size (or births) as generally construed in the literature.

Needless to say, practical application of such a model is constrained by the limited amount of available data. On fairly reasonable assumptions, however, various subcases of the general model can be distinguished and estimated. Although they are not necessarily realized in pure form, we think these subcases may often constitute useful approximations to reality. In section 2.3 we develop this classification scheme and discuss its empirical relevance.

The concepts of desired fertility and natural fertility play a central role in our classification scheme. The concepts, although prominent in empirical demographic research, have received little attention from economists. We make these concepts an integral part of our analysis. Desired fertility, b^d, is defined as the number of births a family would choose in a situation termed by demographers a "perfect contraceptive society" (Bumpass and Westoff 1970); that is, one in which the family has access to a contraceptive technology with no economic costs and free of preference drawbacks.

Natural fertility, b^n, is defined as the number of births a family believes it would have if it made no deliberate attempt to influence its fertility. Natural fertility is less than the biological maximum and is consistent with the existence of "social controls" on fertility, such as an intercourse taboo. It constitutes uncontrolled fertility only in the sense that the family itself makes no *deliberate* effort to influence its fertility. Contraceptive devices are not utilized, and unperceived jointness or social taboos or both exclude other methods of deliberately influencing family size. If families did perceive the relationship between their consumption pattern and their fecundity, they would alter the former in order to change their fertility. Conscious and deliberate variations by families in the level of their fertility, however, are not compatible with the concept of a *natural* level of fertility. From the standpoint of the family, b^n is constant and is independent of its family-size preferences.

Natural fertility may be greater than, less than, or equal to desired fertility; that is, a family's desires may range from more to fewer children than it thinks it could produce if its fertility were uncontrolled. If the solution for births is below the family's perceived natural fertility ($b^0 < b^n$), then it practices deliberate fertility control. An optimal solution for births above the desired level ($b^0 > b^d$) implies the existence of "excess" or "unwanted" fertility, as the term is used in the demographic literature.

We utilize our generalized fertility model and the associated concepts of natural and desired fertility to classify societies or populations within societies into several categories. The categorization is useful in that it implies restrictions on the coefficients of the variables that appear in the optimal solution functions. Some groups, especially in less developed countries, may be at or close to their natural fertility levels. These groups can be divided into two subcategories. First there are those that lack the motivation to practice fertility regulation because desired fertility is greater than or equal to the optimal solution. Second, there are those, again largely in less developed countries, where the economic costs or preference drawbacks of fertility regulation outweigh the potential gains. In both these cases, the determinants of fertility are largely independent of the preferences for children. "Demand models," with their emphasis on income and substitution effects, are not relevant. Although income might be a significant determinant of completed family size, its influence would be unintended and would work through improved nutrition and health, which would lead to increased fecundity and decreased infant mortality. Demand models tell a different story, typically suggesting that increases in income lead to an increase in the number of children demanded. For natural fertility societies, demand variables—correctly measured and interpreted—are insignificant.

At the other extreme are groups, largely in developed countries, that can be approximated by the perfect contraceptive society. In this case, births and infant mortality technology functions are not quantitatively important determinants of the level of fertility. The properly specified optimal solution function now contains the preference parameters related to children and may reflect endogenous tastes and household technology, including those aspects concerning child-rearing, as well as the budget constraint.

The general fertility model, which includes endogenous tastes and the births production function, has implications for a number of important demographic questions. We have already indicated its significance for specifying the optimal solution function in different societies for different time periods. It is of particular importance that the parameters of this function vary systematically in quantitative importance as one moves along the continuum from less to more developed economies and/or lower to higher socioeconomic classes within a society. Hence, elasticities of births and completed family size with respect to their arguments will vary systematically both across and within societies. We shall also indicate the model's implications for the analysis of the "demographic transition," long-run fertility swings, secular trends in fertility in both less developed countries and developed countries, and the welfare benefits of various types of fertility-control programs in different societies.

At various points we contrast our analysis with the "Chicago-Columbia" approach, by which we mean the line of inquiry exemplified in two recent special issues of the *Journal of Political Economy*, since published as an NBER volume.[1] That there is a distinctive Chicago-Columbia approach to the economics of fertility hardly requires demonstration. In a review of the volume that brings together the *JPE* work, Allen Kelley observes that "the papers are . . . largely of one voice, showing a common perspective to the analysis of economic problems and to a certain extent a mild intolerance of other approaches to viewing the world of social and economic behavior" (Kelley 1976, p. 517). As examples of spokesmen for the approach, one may cite T. W. Schultz (in his editor's introduction to the *JPE* volume), Michael Keeley (in a reply to a critique by Leibenstein), and T. P. Schultz (in several survey articles).[2] We shall draw particularly on the last two in comparing our framework with the Chicago-Columbia approach, because these articles provide valuable general discussions of that viewpoint.[3]

The Chicago-Columbia approach is most simply characterized by what it emphasizes and deemphasizes. Particular emphasis is placed on cost factors and on the opportunity cost of a wife's time; little or no attention is given to taste factors and to the births production function (the latter relates to what T. P. Schultz calls "supply" factors). T. P. Schultz asserts that "cross-sectional studies of individual countries at all levels of development have confirmed the qualitative predictions of this rudimentary demand theory of fertility" (T. P. Schultz 1976, p. 98).[4]

Our main reservation about this line of work is that its deemphasis of tastes and "supply" factors severely limits its empirical relevance. For developed countries the model is of limited application because it ignores preference variables. This is most strikingly illustrated by the failure of the Chicago-Columbia approach to advance an explanation for the recent fertility swing in the United States.[5] For less developed countries, fitting a "demand" model to data for households whose fertility is largely uncontrolled leads to unwarranted inferences about "demand" elasticities.

Furthermore, the subordination of taste considerations lends itself to dubious conclusions about economic welfare and public policy. Minimizing the importance of tastes makes it easier to draw unambiguous inferences about the desirability of policies aimed at reducing "unwanted" fertility, but the lack of attention to tastes make such inferences questionable. At the same time, the approach is unlikely to be helpful to those directing family planning programs, who must make choices between attempting to alter preferences (for example, by allocating resources to advertising the benefits of small families) and simply providing contraceptive information or cheaper services. Hence, we believe that both the analysis of fertility behavior and of the welfare effect of government programs requires a more balanced approach, one in which economic research on preferences and natural fertility takes equal place with the usual concerns of the Chicago-Columbia approach.

2.2 The Formal Model

In this section we develop a formal framework for analyzing marital fertility. We begin by summarizing the household production model, which provides the starting point for our analysis. In the three subsequent subsections we modify the household production model to incorporate a number of additional variables related to the determination of marital fertility and completed family size. In section 2.2.2 we incorporate the basic variables related to fertility into the household production model by adding two new "production" relations, a "births production function" and an infant mortality or "deaths function," and then describe two extensions of this model, one incorporating unperceived jointness (section 2.2.3) and the other interdependent preferences (section 2.2.4).

By unperceived jointness we mean a situation in which the family does not correctly recognize the relationship between its fecundity and its consumption or life-style decisions. For example, an increase in nonlabor income might cause an unintended and unanticipated increase in births through the following chain of causation: the increase in nonlabor income causes an increase in consumption of health care services or food, which leads to an improvement in health or nutrition; these in turn cause an increase in fecundity. The essence of unperceived jointness is that the decision to devote additional resources to improved health or nutrition rather than shelter or recreation is made without awareness of its implications for fertility.

By interdependent preferences we mean that the family's tastes are influenced by the consumption and family-size decisions of other families. In the "socialization" version of the interdependent preferences model the family's tastes are influenced by the observed behavior of other families in the society, perhaps those in a suitably restricted socioeconomic group. In the "intrafamily" version, a family's aspirations for both commodity consumption and family size are influenced by the consumption and family-size patterns the husband and the wife experienced in childhood and adolescence.

Our model provides a framework for analyzing a number of important aspects of fertility behavior, but it neglects a number of others. First, we deal exclusively with marital fertility. Second, we do not attempt to explain the determination of age at marriage. Third, our analysis is based on a single-period planning model in which the family makes a once-and-for-all decision about its consumption and fertility at the time of marriage. Those aspects of fertility behavior that are best understood in terms of a sequential decision-making model—for example, the timing and spacing of children—are beyond the scope of the analysis, although in principle it could be extended this way. Fourth, our model treats average fertility outcomes as if they were certain to be realized by the "representative family." That is, we ignore both the discreteness of children and the randomness of the births and deaths functions and focus on the mean experience of a group of identical families. In general, randomness and discreteness have implications for the average fertility of families who are not risk-neutral and whose behavior is therefore sensitive to the variance as well as to the mean outcome. Finally, we ignore the fact that children come in two sexes and that parents may have preferences for the sex composition of their families. Such preferences could be incorporated into a sequential model of fertility that recognized the role of uncertainty. In such a model one would expect sex preferences to influence family size, but such preferences cannot be incorporated into a one-period planning model in any straightforward way.[6]

2.2.1 The Household Production Model

In this section we introduce the standard household production model that serves as the basis for our subsequent discussion of fertility. The model is one in which the household purchases "goods" on the market and combines them with time in a "household production function" to produce "commodities."[7] These commodities, rather than the goods, are the arguments of the household's preference ordering; market goods and time are desired not for their own sake, but only as inputs into the production of "commodities." The n market goods are denoted by $X = (x_1, \dots x_n)$, and the m commodities by $Z = (z_1, \dots z_m)$, and the time allocation vector by t; the vector t records how much time each family member devotes to market work and to each household activity. Let R

denote the household's preference ordering over commodity vectors, and $U(Z)$ the corresponding utility function.[8]

We represent the household's technology by a production set, T. Thus, the "input-output" vector (Z,X,t) belongs to the set T, $(Z,X,t) \in T$, if and only if the commodity collection Z is producible from the goods collection X and the time-allocation vector t. We could distinguish those uses of time devoted to household production activities from those devoted to market work and include only the former as arguments of the household's technology, but it is harmless to include the entire vector, and we do so for notational convenience. Unless explicitly stated to the contrary, constant returns to scale and/or the absence of joint production are *not* assumed. If the household derives satisfaction or dissatisfaction from time spent at various household or market activities, the times devoted to these activities will appear as components of the vector Z as well as the vector t. Technically, this is a case of joint production, since, for example, time devoted to the activity "cooking" is both an input into the production of a "home cooked meal" and is itself one of the outputs of the activity "cooking"—an output that may yield a utility or disutility quite distinct from that associated with eating the meal itself. Because we have not ruled out joint production, there need not be a one-to-one correspondence between activities and commodities.

We let t_h denote the total time available to household member h, and t_{hs} the time which he (or she) allocates to activity s. Thus, the family's time constraint may be written as

$$\sum_{s=1}^{S} t_{hs} = \bar{t}_h \qquad h = 1, \ldots, H$$

where S is the total number of market and nonmarket activities and H the number of household members.

We distinguish between the set of market activities (M) and the set of household production or nonmarket activities (T). Thus, if w_h denotes the market wage rate of household member h, his earnings are given by $\sum_{s \epsilon M} w_h t_{hs}$ and the household's total earnings by $\sum_{h=1}^{H} \sum_{s \epsilon M} w_h t_{hs}$. We let μ denote the household's nonlabor income, and write its budget constraint in the form

$$\sum_{k=1}^{n} p_k x_k \leqq \mu + \sum_{h=1}^{H} \sum_{s \epsilon M} w_h t_{hs}.^{9}$$

"Optimal solution values" for the household's decision variables (Z,X,t) are found by maximizing the utility function $U(Z)$ subject to the constraints

$$(Z,X,t) \in T$$

$$\sum_{s=1}^{S} t_{hs} = \bar{t}_h \qquad h = 1, \ldots, H$$

$$\sum_{k=1}^{n} p_k x_k \leqq \mu + \sum_{h=1}^{H} \sum_{s \in M} w_h t_{hs}.$$

The optimal solution values are functions of the values of the variables the household takes as predetermined: goods prices, P; wage rates, w; nonlabor income, μ; and the household's technology, T. The "optimal solution" is optimal with respect to the household's own preferences, not necessarily with respect to any general social welfare criteria. The optimal solution function shows the relationship between the household's decision variables, (Z,X,t), and the parameters it takes as given, $(P,w,\mu;T)$. The optimal solution function is not a demand function in the conventional sense, nor does it treat commodity consumption as a function of commodity shadow prices. Indeed, commodity consumption and the optimal values of the other decision variables are functions of the predetermined variables: goods prices, wage rates, nonlabor income, and the parameters of the household's technology. Commodity shadow prices (i.e., the partial derivatives of the cost function with respect to commodities) have played an unduly prominent role in household production analysis. The difficulty with treating optimal commodity consumption as a function of commodity shadow prices is that commodity shadow prices reflect not only the constraints which the household faces, but also its preferences. With joint production, commodity shadow prices depend on the household's tastes as well as on goods prices and the household's technology. Our model of fertility builds on the household production model, but we reject the "commodity shadow price" version.[10]

2.2.2 The Simple Fertility Model

In this section we extend the standard household production model to include a number of variables related to fertility: children ever born (b), infant and child deaths (d), completed family size (N), frequency of coitus (a), the reproductive span of the household (Λ), the length of time over which each fertility control technique is practiced (θ) and the "intensity" with which each is practiced (τ), and a vector of "practices," such as lactation (l), which affect either the number of children born or their chances of survival.

To simplify the notation we shall not introduce subscripts to distinguish among fertility regulation techniques, but the framework we develop is well suited for discussing choices among techniques. For example, if one of the available techniques is a contraceptive pill that is to be taken daily, θ might represent the number of months during which it is taken and τ the ratio of the number of days on which the pill is taken to the number on which it is supposed to be taken.[11] Similarly, we do not use subscripts to distinguish among "practices"; formally, we interpret l as a vector, but we shall use "lactation" (i.e., the number of months of lactation following each birth) as an example of the type of variable we have in mind.

These variables are related to each other and the other variables in the household production model by two biological "production" relationships, a births function, B: $b = B(a,Z,X,l,\theta,\tau,\Lambda)$; and a deaths function, D: $d = D(b,Z,X,l)$; and by the identity defining completed family size: $N = b - d$.

The births function depends not only on frequency of coitus (a) and the household's fertility regulation practices (θ and τ), but also on a number of other variables that are likely to vary systematically from one society to another and from one socioeconomic group to another within a society. To take account of the role of factors such as health and nutrition in determining fecundity, we include the household's consumption of commodities (Z) and its purchase of goods (X) as arguments of the births function. Practices such as lactation that influence fecundity are also included; in the case of lactation, a longer interval of lactation following each birth will, ceteris paribus, imply fewer births, since lactation inhibits ovulation. The family's reproductive span, Λ, depends on age at marriage and age at the onset of permanent sterility. The latter is almost certainly endogenously determined by variables such as health and nutrition, but for simplicity we treat the reproductive span as exogenous.

The child and infant mortality function depends not only on the population at risk (b), but also on health and nutrition, which are reflected in the family's consumption of commodities and its purchases of goods. A variety of "practices" that influence deaths are captured by the vector l, although the components of l that influence deaths need not be the same as those that influence births. The length of the lactation interval, however, will appear in the mortality function because—in many societies, at least—a longer lactation interval is associated with lower infant mortality.

Both the births function and the deaths function represent biological "production" relationships. The existence of these biological relationships is quite distinct from the question whether families in either developed or underdeveloped countries perceive these relationships accurately. In this subsection we proceed on the assumption that families are fully aware of the fertility and mortality implications of their behavior. In the next subsection we drop this assumption of perfect knowledge and introduce the concept of unperceived jointness.

Preferences in the simple fertility model are relatively complicated. The utility function includes not only commodities (Z) and completed family size (N), but also infant mortality (d), frequency of intercourse (a), and the contraceptive variables (θ and τ). If frequency of intercourse (a) were not included in the utility function, then abstinence would be the dominant form of fertility regulation, since it is costless and completely effective. Similarly, if there were no disutility associated with infant and child mortality (d), then infanticide might be the second-choice technique, since it also provides an inexpensive and effective method for limiting completed family size. That these techniques do not play a prominent role in most societies clearly reflects preference drawbacks rather than economic costs. But it is not only these extreme techniques of population control that entail preference consequences or drawbacks; the use of any currently available fertility regulation technique (for a particular length of time and with a particular intensity) is likely to entail preference effects that may play an important role in determining not only their time span and intensity of use, but also the number of births and completed family size. We denote the utility function by $U(Z,N,d,a,l,\theta,\tau)$.[12]

The budget constraint must also be modified to allow for the cost of fertility regulation. We assume that its cost is a function of θ and τ alone and denote it by $\rho(\theta,\tau)$.[13]

The optimal solution to the simple fertility model is the set of values of the decision variables $(Z,X,t,b,N,a,l,\theta,\tau)$ that maximize the utility function $U(Z,N,d,a,l,\theta,\tau)$ subject to the constraints

$$(Z,X,t) \in T$$

$$\sum_{s=1}^{S} t_{hs} = \bar{t}_h \qquad h = 1,\ldots,H$$

$$\sum_{k=1}^{n} p_k x_k + \rho(\theta,\tau) \leqq \mu + \sum_{h=1}^{H} \sum_{s \in M} w_h t_{hs}$$

$$b = B(a,Z,X,l,\theta,\tau,\Lambda)$$

$$d = D(b,Z,X,l)$$

$$N = b - d.^{14}$$

The optimal solution values are functions of the variables the household takes as given: goods prices, P; wage rates, w; nonlabor income, μ; the household's technology, T; the births function, B; the deaths function, D; the cost function for fertility regulation, ρ; and the family's reproductive span, Λ.[15]

2.2.3 Unperceived Jointness

In this section we modify the simple fertility model by postulating that the household is not aware of all the ways its consumption and expenditure patterns affect fecundity and infant mortality. The resulting model is one in which consumption patterns affect realized fertility and mortality, but the effects are unintended. Consider, for example, a family that is not practicing fertility regulation: if it is unaware of the relationship between nutrition and fecundity, it will allocate its expenditure between food and other goods without taking account of the marginal impact of better nutrition on births. An increase in nonlabor income would lead to greater expenditures on food, and, ceteris paribus, through better nutrition to greater fecundity. But the effect on births would be an unintended consequence of the consumption pattern corresponding to a higher income; the household's allocation of expenditure between food and other goods had nothing to do with its desire for children. The family might regard the unintended increase in fertility as a blessing or a curse; in either case, however, the family could "do better" in terms of its own preferences if it knew the true relationship between nutrition and fecundity. If the family were aware of the true relationship it could allow for it in allocating its expenditure between food and other goods: a family that wanted more children would allocate more to food, while one that wanted fewer children would allocate less. We use the phrase "unperceived jointness" to describe a situation in which the family does not recognize the true relationship between its consumption pattern and its fertility or infant mortality.[16] In this section we formalize the concept of unperceived jointness and examine its implications for marital fertility and completed family size.

Although the definition of unperceived jointness does not formally presuppose a situation in which the family makes no deliberate use of fertility control, the concept is useful primarily in such cases. It is especially useful in the first two of the special cases we described briefly in section 2.1: that is, families who fail to recognize that their consumption and expenditure patterns have any effect on their fecundity and who do not employ deliberate fertility control techniques either because they expect to have fewer children than they desire or because, although they expect to have more children than they want, the economic costs and preference drawbacks of fertility regulation outweigh its advantages.

Unperceived jointness is a powerful concept with a wide range of potential applications to topics other than fertility. For example, health or various narrowly defined health states can be treated as commodities that are affected by many household activities, and it is plausible that the effects of many of these activities on health states are unknown to the household. The assumption that the household correctly perceives the relationship between diet and health is an uncomfortable one, especially in cases where the experts do not agree on the nature of the relationship or have learned of it only recently. Unperceived jointness allows us to recognize that health is related to many aspects of a family's consumption pattern and life-style without assuming that the household is fully aware of these relationships. Although we apply the concept of unperceived jointness only to the births production function and the infant mortality function, it could be applied to the household's knowledge of other aspects of its technology. In the fertility context, we could apply it to the length of the reproductive span, Λ, but for simplicity we shall continue to treat the reproductive span as exogenous.

Unperceived jointness does not imply complete ignorance; families may know a great deal about the effects of their behavior on fertility and infant mortality. Indeed, unperceived jointness is consistent with any assumption about the family's knowledge other than the traditional assumption of perfect knowledge. If we view the family's knowledge of the relationships governing fertility and mortality as a point on a continuum from complete ignorance to perfect knowledge, then unperceived jointness is present everywhere except at the polar case of perfect knowledge.[17]

We denote the perceived births function by $\hat{B}(a,Z,X,l,\theta,\tau,\Lambda)$ and the perceived deaths function by $\hat{D}(b,Z,X,l)$. The simplest specification of the perceived deaths function corresponds to the assumption of complete ignorance and is one in which the mortality rate is a constant, independent of the family's consumption and expenditure pattern (Z,X) and its practices (l): $\hat{D}(b,Z,X,l) = \delta\, b$. For example, the family might believe that one out of every four (or one out of every four hundred) of its children will die, but it does not believe that its behavior can alter this mortality ratio. The family's perception of the mortality rate might depend on the experience of other families in the society, or on that of other families of similar socioeconomic status.

The simplest specification of the perceived births function is also one of complete ignorance, one in which births are independent of the family's decision variables, at least when the family is not practicing any of the fertility control techniques specified by (θ,τ). This implies a perceived births function of the form $\hat{B}(a,Z,X,l, O,O,\Lambda) = \bar{B}$.[18] The family believes that (if it does not practice fertility regulation) its fertility will be exogenously determined and that $\bar{B}$ children will be born to it. The family's estimate of $\bar{B}$ might reflect its observations of the experience of other families in the society or that of other families of similar socioeconomic status.[19]

Completed family size is by definition the difference between births and deaths. In the polar case of complete ignorance, for a family not practicing fertility regulation, perceived completed family size is given by $(1 - \delta)B$. Actual births, deaths, and family size may depart from these expected levels and are determined by the actual births and deaths functions; hence, the actual values of these variables depend on the family's consumption pattern and on other family decision variables such as those grouped together as "practices" and on frequency of intercourse.

Beyond the simplest case of complete ignorance, we must face the question of how families form expectations and adjust the perceived births and deaths functions in the light of experience and observation. Similar problems, however, arise in any version of the household production model unless we assume that the household has perfect knowledge of its technology. If a family recognizes that its consumption and expenditure patterns affect its fertility, it seems plausible that it would systematically revise the perceived births function to reduce any gap between observed and expected fertility corresponding to any consumption pattern. But such revisions are not possible within the confines of a one-period planning model.[20]

With unperceived jointness there are two analogues of the "optimal solution." The first, the "optimal perceived solution," which we denote by the superscript p, is the vector of decision variables obtained by maximizing the utility function subject to the perceived constraints. The optimal perceived solution corresponds to the values of the births and deaths functions the household expects, not the levels that would be generated by substituting the household's consumption and expenditure patterns into the true births and deaths functions. The second, the "realized solution," which we denote by the superscript r, is the vector of decision variables obtained from the optimal perceived solution by replacing the perceived values for births, deaths, and completed family size by the values of these variables that would be generated by the true births and deaths functions, evaluated at the optimal perceived values of the other variables. In the case of goods purchases and the commodity consumption pattern, the realized solution coincides with the optimal perceived solution.[21] But the realized solution for births and deaths typically differs from the optimal perceived solution when there is unperceived jointness.

Formally, the optimal perceived solution to the model with unperceived jointness is the set of values of the decision variables $\{Z,X,t,b,d,N,a,l,\theta,\tau\}$ that maximize the utility function $U(Z,N,d,a,l,\theta,\tau)$ subject to the constraints

$$(Z,X,t) \in T$$

$$\sum_{s=1}^{S} t_{hs} = \bar{t}_h \qquad h = 1, \ldots, H$$

$$\sum_{k=1}^{n} p_k x_k + \rho(\theta,\tau) \leqq \mu + \sum_{h=1}^{H} \sum_{s \epsilon M} w_h t_{hs}$$

$$b = \hat{B}(a,Z,X,l,\theta,\tau,\Lambda)$$

$$d = \hat{D}(b,Z,X,l)$$

$$N = b - d.$$

We denote the optimal perceived solution values by $\{Z^p,X^p,t^p,b^p,d^p,N^p,a^p,l^p,\theta^p,\tau^p\}$; these values are functions of the variables the household takes as given: goods prices, P; wage rates, w; nonlabor income, μ; the household's technology, T; the perceived births function, $\hat{B}$; the perceived deaths function, $\hat{D}$; and the cost function for fertility regulation, ρ.

The realized solution coincides with the optimal perceived solution for the variables (Z,X,t,a,l,θ,τ), but the realized solution for the demographic variables (b,d,N) is determined by substituting the optimal perceived solution values of the other variables into the true births and deaths functions:

$$b^r = B(a^p,Z^p,X^p,l^p,\theta^p,\tau^p,\Lambda)$$

$$d^r = D(b^r,Z^p,X^p,l^p)$$

$$N^r = b^r - d^r.$$

A fulfilled-expectations equilibrium is a solution in which the realized values of b and d coincide with the optimal perceived values. This does not imply that in a fulfilled-expectations equilibrium the family knows the true births and deaths functions—only that its predictions of b and d are correct. It need not know the effects of changes in X or Z on births or deaths, and it may even believe that b and δ are exogenously given.[22] If births and deaths were truly exogenous, then equilibrium could be reached only through the revision of beliefs about the births and deaths functions. When they are not exogenous, the adjustment toward a fulfilled-expectations equilibrium involves both changes in perceptions and changes in behavior that change the realized levels of births and deaths. In equilibrium, observing the fertility and mortality experience of the family will not cause another family holding similar beliefs to revise its perceptions of these functions.[23]

2.2.4 Taste Formation

In this section we introduce endogenous tastes into our model of marital fertility. Within our one-period planning model, interdependent preferences—that is, preferences that depend on the consumption and family-size decision of other families—are the only admissible specification of endogenous tastes.[24] Such preferences are endogenous to the society, but not to the family itself. The model of interdependent preferences is greatly simplified when it is driven by the *past* rather than the current consumption and family-size decisions of other families; because the lagged specification is at least as plausible as the simultaneous one, we shall rely on it exclusively.[25]

Two versions of the lagged interdependent preferences model are of particular interest. The first is a model of "socialization," whose simplest specification is one in which each family's preferences depend on the average consumption and family size of all families in the previous generation or cohort. This specification can be modified by restricting the relevant group of families to those with a particular social or economic status, or by allowing consumption and family-size patterns in the more distant past to play a role in the formation of tastes. The second version, the "intrafamily" model, is one in which each family's preferences are determined by the consumption and family-size patterns the husband and wife experienced during their childhood and adolescence. The intrafamily version predicts that differences in consumption and family-size patterns within a group of families that are similar with respect to such economic variables as wage rates and nonlabor income as well as such variables as education, social status, and religion will be systematically related to differences in the consumption and family-size patterns experienced by husbands and wives during childhood and adolescence. The socialization version does not imply the existence of any systematic differences within such a group of similar families. The intrafamily specification is a version of interdependent preferences rather than habit formation, because tastes depend on the consumption and family-size decisions of the husband's parents and the wife's parents rather than on their own past consumption decisions. Within the context of lagged interdependent preferences, the socialization and the intrafamily specifications are competing hypotheses about whose past consumption and family-size patterns determine a family's tastes.

The socialization model of interdependent preferences is essentially that presented in Pollak (1976*b*) in a traditional demand analysis context. The intrafamily version has been put forward by Easterlin (1968, 1973) and by Wachter (1972*b*, 1975) as an explanation of the recent fertility and labor force participation rate swings in the United States. The intrafamily version is somewhat more complicated than the socialization model because its specification requires a notation that associates each family with the corresponding "parent families" in the previous generation. Rather than introduce such a notation, we shall discuss only the socialization specification.

We formalize interdependent preferences by postulating that each family's tastes depend on "normal levels" of commodity consumption (Z^*) and family size (N^*), and that these normal levels are related to the past consumption and family-size decisions of other families. Normal levels can sometimes be interpreted as "aspiration levels" or "bliss points," sometimes as "necessary" or "subsistence" levels. The essence is that the normal level of a variable is positively related to the family's preference for the commodity in question or for children, so that, ceteris paribus, one would expect an increase in the normal level of a variable to increase its level in the optimal solution.

We shall not specify an explicit form for the family's utility function, but we assume that its tastes for commodities and children are nonnegatively related to the corresponding normal levels.[26] Since the family's preferences depend on normal levels of consumption and family size, we denote its utility function by $U(Z,N,d,a,l,\theta,\tau;Z^*,N^*)$. The semicolon separating the normal levels of Z^* and N^* from the other variables is intended to indicate that this utility function corresponds to a preference ordering over the variables (Z,N,d,a,l,θ,τ), which depends on the value of the normal variables, not to a preference ordering over the extended set of variables $(Z,N,d,a,l,\theta,\tau,Z^*,N^*)$. A preference ordering over the variables (Z,N,d,a,l,θ,τ) that depends on the values of the normal variables is called a "conditional preference ordering," while a preference ordering over the extended set of variables is an "unconditional preference ordering."[27] The distinction between conditional and unconditional preferences plays a crucial role in the analysis of welfare implications in section 2.5.

From a formal standpoint, normal levels are simply parameters that influence preferences in a nonnegative way toward the variables in question. In some cases (e.g., the linear expenditure system) we can interpret them as "necessary" or "subsistence" levels, while in others (e.g., the additive quadratic utility function) they have plausible interpretations as "bliss points," "target levels," or "aspiration levels." However, there are some situations in which neither interpretation is appropriate.[28]

To complete the socialization version of the interdependent preferences model, we must specify how the normal levels N^* and Z^* are determined by past levels. We shall present only the simplest specification, one relating normal levels to average levels in the previous generation. That is, we let $\bar{Z}$ and $\bar{N}$ denote average levels of Z and N in the previous generation and postulate that Z^* and N^* are given by $Z^* = E^Z(\bar{Z})$ and $N^* = E^N(\bar{N})$. The short-run behavior implied by the interdependent preferences model differs from that implied by the model with constant tastes described in section 2.2.3 in that average past consumption and family size, $\bar{N}$ and $\bar{Z}$, operate through the normal levels N^* and Z^* to determine preferences. The analysis of the effects of changes in prices, wages, nonlabor income, or the household's technology presents no new issues. By hypothesis, an increase in a particular $\bar{z}_i$ increases z_i^*, and one would expect this to cause an increase in the optimal solution value of z_i; similarly, an increase in N will increase N^*, and one would expect a corresponding increase in the optimal solution level of N.

The "optimal solution" to the endogenous tastes model is a set of values of the decision variables $(Z,X,t,b,d,N,a,l,\theta,\tau)$ that maximizes the utility function $U(Z,N,d,a,l,\theta,\tau;Z^*,N^*)$ where

$$Z^* = E^Z(\bar{Z})$$
$$N^* = E^N(\bar{N}),$$

subject to the constraints

$$(Z,X,t) \in T$$
$$\sum_{s=1}^{S} t_{hs} = \bar{t}_h \qquad h = 1, \ldots, H$$
$$\sum_{k=1}^{n} p_k x_k + \rho(\theta,\tau) \leqq \mu + \sum_{h=1}^{H} \sum_{s \in M} w_h t_{hs}$$
$$b = B(a,Z,X,l,\theta,\tau,\Lambda)$$
$$d = D(b,Z,X,l)$$
$$N = b - d.$$

The optimal solution values are functions of the values of the variables the household takes as given: goods prices, P; wage rates, w; nonlabor income, μ; the household's technology, T; the births function, B; the deaths function, D; the cost function for fertility regulation, ρ; the variables that determine the normal values for commodities and family size, $\bar{Z}$ and $\bar{N}$; and the family's reproductive span, Λ.

2.3 Special Cases

The framework we have sketched views fertility as the outcome of maximizing a utility function subject to four constraints: the budget constraint, the household's technology, the births production function, and the infant mortality function. Needless to say, empirical application of such a model is constrained by the limited amount of available data. On certain assumptions, however, subcases of the general model can be identified, some of which are much simpler than the complete model. In section 2.3.1 we develop a classification scheme distinguishing four special cases of fertility determination. We show that under certain assumptions the preferences for children may play no role in explaining fertility; under others, the births production function and infant mortality function may play no essential role, and completed family size is governed largely or wholly by the utility function, budget constraint, and household technology—that is, by the variables traditionally emphasized in economic analyses of fertility. Section 2.3.2 takes up the empirical relevance of the proposed classification scheme. The evidence presented suggests that in the typical less developed country, observed fertility for the bulk of the population may depend on the simple model in which preferences for children play no essential role in determining completed family size, but that in developed countries the situation tends increasingly toward one in which preferences play a central role and the births production function and the infant mortality function play no essential role. In section 2.3.3 we develop some implications of this scheme for research on cross-sectional differentials and time-series trends in fertility.

2.3.1 Special Cases of the General Model

Two concepts, prominent in the demographic literature, are of central importance in the development of our classification scheme—desired fertility, b^d, and natural fertility, b^n.

The definition of desired fertility involves another notion common in the literature, that of the "perfect contraceptive society" (Bumpass and Westoff 1970). In terms of our framework this is a situation characterized by a contraceptive technology with no economic costs and free of preference drawbacks (that is, $\rho(\theta,\tau) = 0$ and $\frac{\partial U}{\partial \theta} = \frac{\partial U}{\partial \tau} = 0$). The term "perfect contraceptive technology" is sometimes used in the literature interchangeably with "perfect contraceptive society." We prefer the latter, because the former conveys the notion of a situation involving only technological aspects of fertility regulation, whereas clearly subjective preferences are also involved.

Desired fertility, b^d, is defined as the number of births a family would choose in a perfect contraceptive society. Desired fertility is independent of the births production function, but it does not depend solely on preferences: other constraints facing the household, its budget constraint, its technology, and its infant mortality function will all influence desired fertility. Although there is no real-world perfect contraceptive society, we believe there are families in a number of societies that effectively approximate such a situation in that further reductions in the economic costs and preference drawbacks of fertility control would have no effect on their fertility behavior.

Natural fertility, b^n, is defined as the number of births a family believes it would have if it made no deliberate attempt to influence its fertility. It is the value of the births function when its arguments are determined without regard to preferences concerning family size.

The natural fertility case thus assumes that unperceived jointness or social taboos or both essentially fix all the arguments of the births production function except the fertility control variables relating to contraception and induced abortion, which take on zero values. As in the case of the perfect contraceptive society, we do not argue that the pure case of natural fertility is often observed; instead, we argue that it is a useful empirical approximation.

Natural fertility, as we have defined it, is quite different from a biological maximum level of fertility. Natural fertility will almost certainly fall below the maximum value of the births function because a household's consumption pattern involves deficient health or nutrition or because there are social practices (e.g., with regard to nursing children) that restrict the output of children. In addition, natural fertility is influenced by many facets of the family's behavior. For example, the level of natural fertility may reflect such factors as observance of an intercourse taboo, coital frequency, and the consumption bundle chosen by the family. The central point, however, is that natural fertility is independent of the household's preferences for children; although its preferences for commodities and practices play a major role in determining the values of the arguments of the births production function, the relevant decisions are made without regard for their effect on fertility.

Both behavioral and biological factors shape natural fertility. The issue with regard to behavioral influences is whether the behavior is consciously motivated, at least in part, by considerations of its effect on fertility. If it is not, then such behavioral influences are consistent with natural fertility. The question of the household's motivation is clearly important for predicting the likely response to a policy intervention. If, for example, a family has no motivation to regulate its fertility, there is little reason to suppose that establishing a government family planning program would elicit a response from the population.[29]

We also assume for empirical purposes a constant level of infant mortality that is independent of preferences. This is more troublesome than the comparable assumption applied to the births function, because households are likely to realize that they have some control over infant mortality through their expenditures on children's food and health care. Our assumption is that the degree of social control over these variables is great enough that individual family discretion is not empirically important in altering fertility or completed family size. On this assumption, N^n, the natural level of completed family size, as well as b^n, natural fertility, is independent of family preferences.

The concepts of desired and natural fertility can be used to identify four special cases of fertility determination. Natural fertility may be greater than, less than, or equal to desired fertility; that is, a family's desires may range from more to fewer children than it thinks it could produce if its fertility were uncontrolled. An optimal solution for births below the family's perceived natural fertility ($b^o < b^n$) implies a motivation to practice deliberate fertility regulation. An optimal solution for births above the desired level ($b^o > b^d$) implies the existence of "excess" or "unwanted" fertility, as these terms are used in the demographic literature. Using these concepts of deliberate fertility control and excess fertility, households can be classified into four groups on the basis of the determinants of their fertility:

	Excess or Unwanted Fertility		*Practice of Deliberate Fertility Control*	
Group I	No	$b^o \leq b^d$	No	$b^o = b^n$
Group II	Yes	$b^o > b^d$	No	$b^o = b^n$
Group III	Yes	$b^o > b^d$	Yes	$b^o < b^n$
Group IV	No	$b^o = b^d$	Yes	$b^o < b^n$

For those in group I, natural fertility is less than or equal to desired fertility. In this "deficit fertility" situation there is no motivation to limit fertility, and hence actual fertility will depend on the determinants of natural fertility.

In contrast, all households in groups II, III, and IV have a motivation to regulate fertility because their natural (or "uncontrolled") fertility would result in a greater number of births than desired ($b^n > b^d$). Whether these families practice fertility control depends on the economic costs and preference drawbacks of control relative to its anticipated benefits.

For those in group II the economic costs and preference drawbacks of fertility control outweigh the benefits, and no deliberate control is practiced. For this group, then, as for group I, actual fertility equals natural fertility. Families in group II differ from those in group I, however, in that natural fertility is greater than desired fertility; hence, families in the two groups will respond differently to changes in the economic costs or preference drawbacks of fertility regulation.

Households in both group I and group II do not deliberately attempt to influence their fertility—group I, because of lack of motivation; group II, because the economic costs or preference drawbacks outweigh the incentive. In both cases, therefore, observed fertility behavior corresponds to the natural fertility level and is independent of preferences for births.

For group III the benefits of fertility regulation outweigh the economic costs and preference drawbacks, and these families practice fertility control. But the economic costs and preference drawbacks of fertility control are such that these families have "excess fertility" in the sense that the number of children called for by the optimal solution exceeds desired fertility. Hence, for families in group III: $b^n > b^o > b^d$. For this group, preferences for commodities and children and all of the constraints—the births production function, the infant mortality function, the budget constraint and the household's technology—enter into the determination of actual fertility. The identification of the factors that distinguish families in group III from those in group II is of substantial interest, since these are the factors that push households across the threshold of fertility regulation and cause them to adopt deliberate fertility control.

For group IV the economic costs and preference drawbacks of fertility control are so low relative to motivation for control that the group regulates its fertility to the point where actual births are equal to desired births. Thus, for group IV we have $b^n > b^o = b^d$. Strictly defined, no individual families are in group IV because no perfect contraceptive society exists. However, we believe that a sizable number of families in developed economies are close enough to this case that it provides a useful empirical approximation.[30] For such families the level of fertility is independent of the births production function.

A simple illustration may clarify our classification scheme. Consider a population of households identical in all respects except for nonlabor income and the preference drawbacks of fertility control. Suppose that there is only a single composite commodity, z, one unit of which is produced from each unit of market goods. Consider the indifference map of economic theory with b measured along the horizontal axis and z along the vertical axis. The curve labeled b^d in figure 2.1 is the "expansion path" or "income-consumption curve" of consumer demand theory,

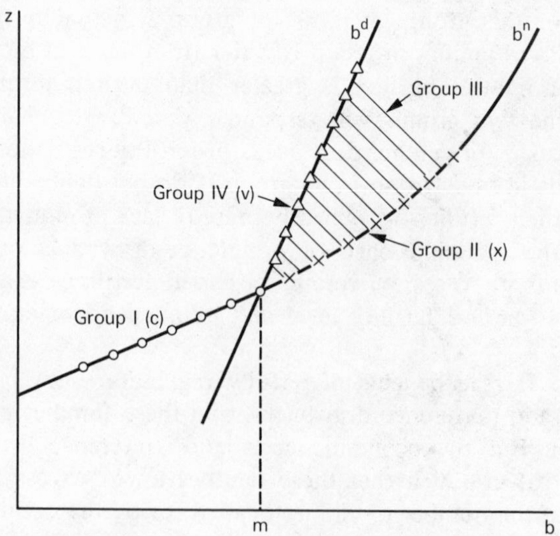

Fig. 2.1 Illustration of four-group classification scheme.

showing the amount of z and b that would be demanded as nonlabor income varied, given tastes and prices. Each point on the curve is obtained from the tangency of an indifference curve and perceived feasible set. One may think of the values of b for various assumed levels of nonlabor income, thus derived, as the "Engel curve" for births—that is, how births would change with the level of nonlabor income. As drawn, the curve shows the number of births increasing with nonlabor income, implying that births are a normal good.

Let us now consider how the ability of households to produce live births might vary with the level of nonlabor income if no deliberate attempt were made to regulate fertility. If nonlabor income were extremely low, then health and nutrition might be so poor that a household would be effectively sterile, that is, $b = 0$. Higher levels of nonlabor income (implying higher input values of health and nutrition in the births production function) would, up to some limit, imply increasing numbers of births. The b^n curve of figure 2.1 traces the path that the potential output of births is assumed to take as nonlabor income grows; that is, it shows how natural fertility might vary with income.

Consider now households whose income is so low as to place them to the left of point m. For these households, desired fertility, b^d, is greater than their reproductive ability, b^n. Hence they would have as many births as they could, and their actual fertility would correspond to natural fertility. These are our group I households; observations for this group would fall along the b^n curve, as shown by the "c" values in the figure.

All households to the right of point m are in an "excess supply" situation; their reproductive potential, b^n, exceeds their desired fertility, b^d. Differences in the actual fertility of these households would arise only from differences in their nonlabor income and the size of the drawbacks they attach to fertility control, because all other factors are assumed to be the same for all households. Households that perceive the drawbacks as so great that they do not practice deliberate fertility control will have observed fertility equal to natural fertility; such households are in our group II, and the observations for this group fall along the b^n curve, as illustrated by the "x" values in figure 2.1. For households who view the preference drawbacks as negligible, observed fertility will equal desired fertility; these households are in our group IV, and the observations for them all along the b^d curve (illustrated by the "v" values in fig. 2.1). Finally, households that practice some deliberate control, but for whom the drawbacks are so great as to result in some excess fertility, will fall in the shaded area between the b^d and b^n curves; these are the group III households.

For some populations the entire b^n curve could lie to the left of the b^d curve, in which case all households would fall in group I, with observed fertility equal to natural fertility. For other populations, the relevant part of the b^n curve might lie wholly to the right of the b^d curve, and if obstacles to fertility control were negligible, all households might fall in group IV, with observed fertility equal to desired fertility. Typically, however, one would expect most societies to include a distribution of households ranging from group I through group IV. When this is so, if one plotted the observations for the population as a whole, one would obtain a scatter of points corresponding to the c, x, and v values as well as some that fall in the shaded area.

If all fertility-determining functions were known, there would be no difficulty in explaining variations among households in observed fertility. When full information is lacking, we suggest using survey response data to divide the population into four groups based on the concepts of natural and desired fertility. For those falling in groups I and II a births production function can be estimated, reflecting the effect of income changes on natural fertility. For those in group IV, it is appropriate to ignore the births production function. For those in group III, we require a model involving preferences for children and fertility control as well as the births production function and infant mortality function.

2.3.2 Some Evidence

Within our general model of fertility determination we have identified four special cases. The empirical evidence currently available, although limited, suggests that it is analytically useful to emphasize these special cases.

The most important evidence relates to the distinction between socially controlled and family controlled fertility (groups I and II versus groups III and IV). For demographers and sociologists, the absence of deliberate family control of fertility is unlikely to raise serious questions, because most noneconomists think of premodern populations as primarily "natural fertility" regimes. Economists, however, are predisposed toward viewing behavior, including reproductive behavior, as a matter of conscious choice. For example, in work on agricultural production behavior in peasant societies, the trend of research has been toward establishing the applicability of rational decision-making models. Thus it has been shown that an unfavorable price movement for a product influences production decisions and causes a contraction in the acreage of the crop planted, in a manner consistent with the predictions of decision-making models (Behrman 1968). By the same token, one might suppose that a decrease in the returns from child labor might lead to curtailment of the output of children.

Reproductive behavior, however, differs from production behavior in an important respect. Babies, since they are a product of sexual intercourse, tend to be produced whether or not they are wanted, whereas rice and wheat do not. Hence, a decision to limit fertility typically requires conscious action, such as abstinence, contraception, or induced abortion. If reproductive behavior is a matter of deliberate choice, then one would expect to find evidence of deliberate practice of fertility control. In fact, the evidence points to the general absence, rather than presence, of deliberate fertility control in less developed countries.

The evidence available is of two types—survey data in which households report on their knowledge and use of fertility control, and census or other data on actual age-specific marital fertility rates.[31] The former come mostly from what are known as "KAP" surveys—surveys of the knowledge of, attitudes toward, and practice of fertility control—which have been conducted in a number of countries since World War II.[32] The other body of data relating to the presence or absence of consciously controlled fertility is quite different; here one draws inferences from the actual fertility behavior of the population, instead of relying on subjective responses. The procedure requires brief exposition, although the essential idea is a simple one.

If no conscious effort were made to limit family size, the age pattern of marital fertility would be governed largely by fecundity and would show a slow decline from ages 20–24 through 35–39, then drop sharply thereafter. If couples were consciously limiting family size, the age pattern of fertility would tend, as age rises, to diverge increasingly in a negative direction from the natural fertility pattern. This is because when a young couple is at the start of the family-building process, there is little incentive to regulate fertility, and hence actual fertility would tend to coincide with natural fertility. However, as a couple ages and family-size grows, approaching or exceeding the desired level, the incentive for deliberate action to restrict family size increases, and correspondingly so does the incentive to adopt deliberate control measures; if such measures are adopted, one would observe the gap between actual fertility and natural fertility increasing over time.

Building on this notion, deriving from Louis Henry's work, that deliberate control involves behavior affecting fertility that is modified as parity increases, Ansley Coale has recently developed a summary index of fertility control, "m," that measures the extent to which an observed age pattern of fertility departs from that believed to characterize a natural fertility regime. An important advantage of the Coale measure (defined in the note to table 2.2) is that it rests on observed behavior, not subjective responses to an interviewer. Moreover, Coale's index would reflect any technique of deliberate control, including abstinence, withdrawal, lactation practices, and induced abortion. In this respect, it avoids two possible problems in the survey data—the possibility that some techniques of deliberate control may have been omitted from the survey, and the possibility of misrepresentation in the responses.[33] A disadvantage is that the Coale measure, unlike survey data, would fail to register a growth in deliberate control if it occurred uniformly at all reproductive ages, for the measure is premised on the assumption that when deliberate control is common, the fertility of older married women is especially low relative to the fertility of younger women. Both a priori reasoning and experience suggest that this is usually true, but the full empirical significance of this qualification remains to be established.[34]

Clearly, one may have doubts about either body of evidence—household surveys of fertility control or inferences from observed fertility behavior—as an adequate indicator of the extent of deliberate fertility control. However, if the results from the two sources are mutually consistent, this would significantly enhance the credibility of each. In fact, as comparison of tables 2.1 and 2.2 shows, this proves true.

Both sets of data show quite limited practice of fertility control in most countries at a premodern or early modern stage of development. In table 2.1 the proportion of the population in such areas reporting that they have ever attempted to control fertility is often about 10% or less. In table 2.2 the index of fertility control, which can range from values about zero (virtual absence of fertility control) to about 2.0, is usually about 0.25 or less.[35] In contrast, in contemporary developed countries, both measures show substantial practice of deliberate control.[36]

The two sets of data also show similar results with regard to rural-urban differences in fertility control. Uniformly, the practice of fertility control is higher in urban than in rural areas.

Finally, for the one case, Taiwan, for which data were readily available for a comparison of the changes over time in the two measures, they show a quite similar trend. In figure 2.2, Coale's index of fertility control is plotted for three dates, 1956, 1965, and 1973. The 1956 value is just about zero, which means that the age pattern of fertility in Taiwan at that date was almost identical with that of a natural fertility regime. Subsequently the index rises sharply to 1965 and again to 1973, implying the rapid adoption and spread of deliberate control. For the last two dates we can compare this pattern with the results of KAP surveys. At each date the survey value is approximately one-half that of "m," and the trend (broken line) lies very close to that shown by the Coale index. Although this is a very simple comparison and the female populations covered by the two measures are not identical, the closeness of the trends indicated by the two measures is encouraging.

Thus we have two bodies of evidence that are mutually confirming—one drawn from personal reports on the knowledge and practice of fertility control and the other based on inferences from observed behavior. It appears that households are, in fact, behaving as they say they are. In most less developed countries, this means that a large proportion of

Table 2.1 **Percentage of Married Women of Reproductive Age Currently Using Contraception, Developed and Developing Countries, Recent Dates**

Country	Date	National	Rural	Urban
	A. Developed Countries			
Australia	1971	66		
Belgium	1966	76	70	77
Czechoslovakia	1970	66	59	69
Denmark	1970	67	64	69
England and Wales	1967	69		
Finland	1971	77	79	76
France	1972	64	59	65
Hungary	1966	64	64	65
Netherlands	1969	59	43	64
Poland	1972	57	51	62
Yugoslavia	1970	59	54	69
USA	1965	64		
	B. Developing Countries			
Africa				
Egypt	1975	21		
Ghana	1976	2		
Kenya	1971	2		
Mauritius	1971	25		
Morocco	1969	1		
Tunisia	1971	12		
Asia				
Bangladesh	1976	5		
India	1969	7–8		
Indonesia	1971	0.5		
Iran	1969	3		
Korea	1972	30		
Malaysia	1969	6		
Nepal	1971	3		
Pakistan	1968–69	6	4	10
Philippines	1972	8		
Taiwan	1971	44		
Thailand	1969–70		13	42
Turkey	1968	35	25	65
Latin America				
Colombia	1974	31	19[a]	35[a]
Costa Rica	1976	34		
Dominican Republic	1976	24		
Ecuador	1974	3		
El Salvador	1976	10		
Guatemala	1974	4		
Haiti	1976	5		
Mexico	1973	13		
Paraguay	1975	10		
Trinidad and Tobago	1971	44		

Source: Nortman (1977), tables 2 and 7.
[a]1969. Data are for those ever using contraception.

Table 2.2 **Coale Index of Fertility Control, *m*, for Females 20–49, Contemporary and Historical Western Populations and Asian Populations by Place of Residence, Specified Dates**

Population	Date	National *m*	Date	Rural *m*	Total Urban or Provincial Urban *m*	Large Cities or Capital *m*
A. Contemporary Western Populations						
Bulgaria	1956	1.67				
Denmark	1963	1.51				
Finland	1960	1.22				
Norway	1960	1.02				
Sweden	1963	1.33				
Australia	1961	1.20				
B. Historical Western Populations						
Bulgaria	1901–5	.02				
Denmark	ca. 1865	.26	ca. 1865	.24	.25	.56
Finland	1871–80	.24				
Norway	1871–75	—.05	1910–11	.31	.86	
Sweden	1751–1800	.23				
6 north French villages			17th–18th cent.	.00		
7 south and central French villages			17th–18th cent.	.02		
14 northwest French villages			17th–18th cent.	.03		
8 Germanic villages			17th–18th cent.	—.00		
1 Swedish village			1745–1820	.13		
Quebec			17th cent.	—.06		
C. Asian Populations						
Japan	1925	.21				
Korea	1961	.03	1960	.01	.36	
Malaysia	1957	.25				
Pakistan	1963–65	—.24				
Philippines	1963–67	.19	1963–67			.69
Sri Lanka	1953	.44				
Taiwan	1956	—.02	1961	.16	.29	.66
Thailand	1960	.11	1968–70	.15	.47	.58
Indonesia			1965–70	.17	.28	
Mysore, India			1952	.26	.16	.56
West Malaysia			1967	.27	.32	.97
China (rural)			1930	.06		
Comilla (Bangladesh)			1963–64	.13		
4 Japanese villages			17th–19th cent.	.18		
Hong Kong			1961			.61
Singapore			1957			.30

households are not deliberately regulating their fertility and thus fall in groups I and II of our classification scheme.

The discussion so far relates to evidence of the division of the population between groups I and II versus groups III and IV. There are no published data that permit the classification of a population into our four groups—a cross-classification based on the practice of fertility control and absence or presence of excess fertility—and hence judgments on empirical importance of the individual groups must be more tentative. However, in the case of Taiwan, for which the availability of unpublished data permit us to derive at least an illustrative distribution of the population among all four groups, the results suggest that all four groups were important in 1965.

The data contain various biases, such as inadequate recall and a tendency after the fact to adjust one's view of desired fertility to realized fertility. Nevertheless, the results shown in table 2.3 may provide a rough idea of orders of magnitude of the four groups at that time. In 1965, the population is divided fairly evenly among the four. For 30% (group I), the number of children was less than or equal to that desired, and consequently, there was no incentive to practice fertility control.[37] Another 26% (group II), although in an excess fertility situation, had not resorted to fertility control, presumably because the costs or preference drawbacks of such control exceeded its benefits. The total of these two groups together amounts to 56%, a majority of the population. The observed fertility behavior of this segment of the population reflects the operation of social controls but not of deliberate family control of fertility; its fertility behavior is independent of preferences for children. The remaining 44% of the population had resorted to deliberate control. This group was almost equally divided between those who had excess fertility (group III), 21%, and those who had not (group IV), 23%.

Source: A, unpublished data kindly provided by Ansley J. Coale; B and C, Knodel (1977, tables 1 and 2), except 1960 data for Korea, which were also provided by Coale.

Note: The index of fertility control, *m*, is calculated from a comparison of the age-specific marital fertility schedule in the subject population with that presumed to characterize a natural fertility regime according to the following formula:

$$r(a) = M \times n(a) \times e^{m \cdot v(a)},$$

where
- a stands for age (from 20–24 through 40–49)
- n(a) is an empirically derived natural fertility schedule
- r(a) is the marital fertility schedule of the subject populations
- M is a scale factor equal to the ratio of r(a) to n(a) at ages 20–24, and
- v(a) is an empirically derived function expressing the typical age pattern of voluntary control of fertility.

See Coale and Trussell (1974, p. 187) and Knodel (1977, n. 12).

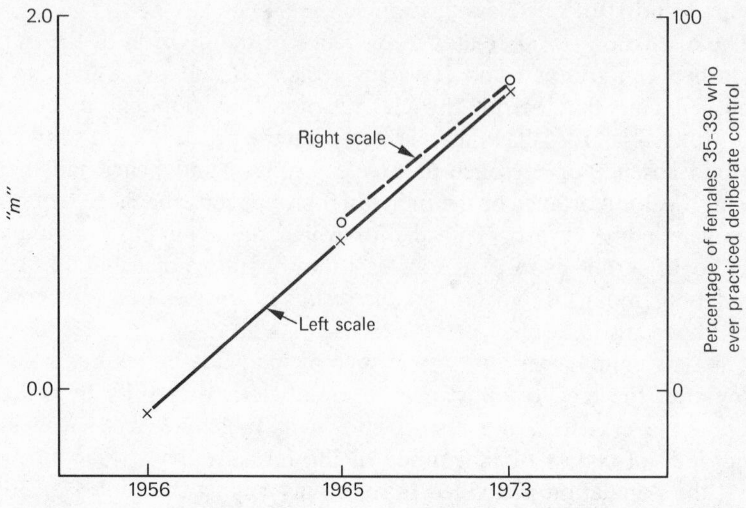

Fig. 2.2 Coale index of fertility control, "*m*", and survey responses on deliberate control, Taiwan, 1956–73. Index values from Knodel (1977, fig. 5). Survey data from KAP 1 and KAP 4 surveys (cf. table 2.3).

In sum, these data suggest that all four groups in our classification scheme may be empirically important at certain times and places. What stands out most clearly is the importance of social as opposed to deliberate family control of fertility in many less developed countries. Evidence of a pervasive lack of knowledge and use of deliberate fertility control relates especially to rural areas in less developed countries. Since the rural sector typically comprises such a large proportion of a less developed country's population, this means that the behavior over time of the national average of fertility may be largely dominated by the behavior of a natural fertility population. The evidence does not indicate a total absence of deliberate family control of fertility, but it does suggest that such control is usually very limited among premodern and early modern populations.

2.3.3 Research Implications

Our four-group classification scheme, to the extent it has empirical relevance, has important implications for research. First, it implies that for cross-sectional analyses the population should be subdivided based on survey questions regarding deliberate fertility control and excess fertility, and the resulting groups should be analyzed separately. For households in groups I and II, natural fertility models stressing the births production function and ignoring preferences for children are appropriate. For those in groups III and IV, preferences play a crucial role, and we view hypotheses regarding tastes as a high priority area for future research. Our viewpoint is illustrated below in regard to the analysis of fertility differentials and trends.

Fertility Differentials

Our classification scheme suggests that the cross-sectional pattern of fertility differentials by socioeconomic status for a national population is a weighted average of the patterns for the component groups. Pooling the data for all groups is unlikely to lead to correct identification of the underlying relationships. On the other hand, disaggregation of the data into the component groups and separate analysis of each should clarify the basic relationships.

Let us illustrate in terms of a hypothetical example. Suppose that for households in groups I and II, those whose behavior is governed by natural fertility conditions, there would typically be a mild positive relation between socioeconomic status and fertility around a fairly high

Table 2.3 Percentage Distribution by Practice of Fertility Control and Deficit or Excess Fertility, Wives Aged 35–39 of Unbroken Marriage, Taiwan, 1965

	Practice of Deliberate Fertility Control					
	Never Practiced			Ever Practiced		
	Total	Desired Family Size		Total	Desired Family Size	
Total		Greater Than or Equal to Actual (group I)	Less Than Actual (group II)		Less Than Actual (group III)	Equal to Actual (group IV)
100	56	30	26	44	21	23

Source: KAP 1 and KAP 4 surveys. We are grateful to Ming-cheng Chang, Ronald Freedman, and Albert Hermalin for making these data available to us and for help in interpreting them. The specific basis for classification is:

1. Excess fertility: the excess for each respondent of living children over the ideal number of living children.
2. Practice of fertility control: based on replies to the question whether the respondent "ever used any birth control."

Because our concern is with marital fertility, the data shown refer to wives, not to all women, and, in order to eliminate the effect on fertility of marital disruption, to wives whose marriage has not been broken. For those who are at an early stage of the reproduction process, one would expect that desired fertility would exceed natural fertility. Hence the data are for women aged 35–39 (the oldest age group available), whose fertility is virtually completed.

average level of fertility.[38] Such a pattern might result from the impact of higher income and better health working through the births function. This is illustrated by the groups I–II curve in figure 2.3. Assume further that for households approximating the conditions of a perfect contraceptive society (group IV) there would be a zero correlation between fertility and socioeconomic status around a low average level of fertility—perhaps because systematic variations in taste or cost factors offset a positive income effect. This pattern is suggested by some data on desired family size in the United States. This is shown by the group IV curve in figure 2.3. Finally, let us suppose that for households in group III the pattern of fertility differentials is dominated by differences in the adoption of fertility regulation practices, which are perceived by those in higher socioeconomic status groups to involve fewer preference drawbacks. Then for this group we have a relation between socioeconomic status and fertility given by the group III curve in figure 2.3.[39] The overall pattern of socioeconomic status-fertility differentials would in these circumstances be a weighted average of the patterns for the component groups. By appropriate variations in the underlying assumptions one could produce a great variety of fertility-socioeconomic status patterns.

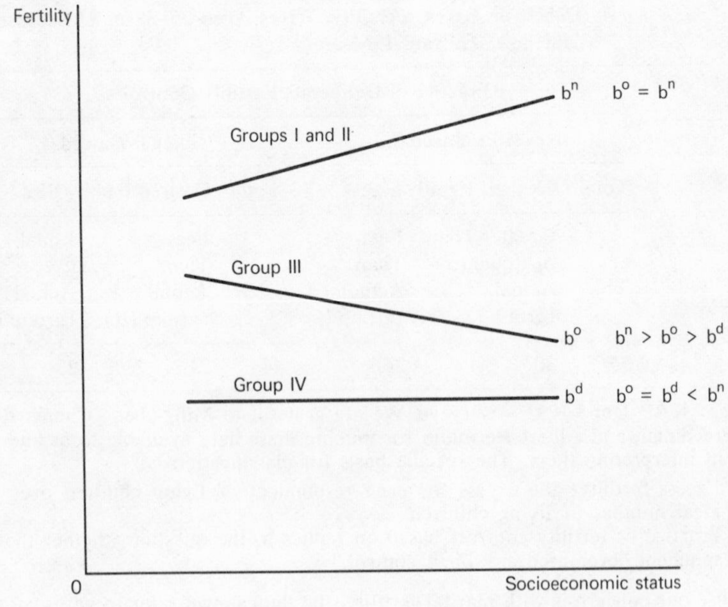

Fig. 2.3 Hypothetical fertility differentials by socioeconomic status.

Fertility Trends

In this area, the most important research questions relate to the demographic transition—the factors behind the shift from high to low fertility during socioeconomic development—and to the long-term outlook for fertility in now-developed countries.

Our classification scheme is compatible with, although it does not require, a view of the demographic transition as a shift from a primarily natural fertility regime (groups I and II) to one eventually largely comprising a "perfect contraceptive society" (group IV), an interpretation consonant with much of the demographic literature. An illustration is provided in figure 2.4, which shows some hypothetical trends during "modernization" (i.e., the transition from a premodern to a modern society) in the levels of natural fertility, desired fertility, and the optimal solution. In the diagram, the process of economic and social modernization is assumed to be correlated with increasing family income and corresponds to a movement to the right along the horizontal axis. The diagram represents only the general nature of the possible relationships during modernization; no implication is intended regarding specific magnitudes.

Natural fertility is assumed to increase during social and economic development, then to level off. This reflects the effect of, for example, increasing income on the health and nutrition of mothers and children, which operates through the births function to increase fertility. Desired family size is assumed to trend downward during the demographic transition, owing perhaps to a change in tastes or to a relative increase in the prices of the inputs required for child-rearing. As drawn, the diagram implies that in premodern societies natural fertility is less than desired fertility (that is, most households are in group I), but the analysis would be essentially the same if most households were in group II. The main point is that initially there is no deliberate practice of fertility regulation.

Consider the trend in the optimal solution implied by our assumptions about natural fertility and desired fertility. At points to the left of m, the optimal solution coincides with natural fertility: parents would have no motivation to practice fertility regulation even if it were free of economic costs and preference drawbacks. At points to the right of m, desired fertility is less than natural fertility, and families would practice fertility regulation if it were available without economic costs or preference drawbacks.

Since fertility control has economic costs and preference drawbacks, we anticipate that initially, as natural fertility edges above desired fertility, the benefits of fertility control would not be great enough to offset

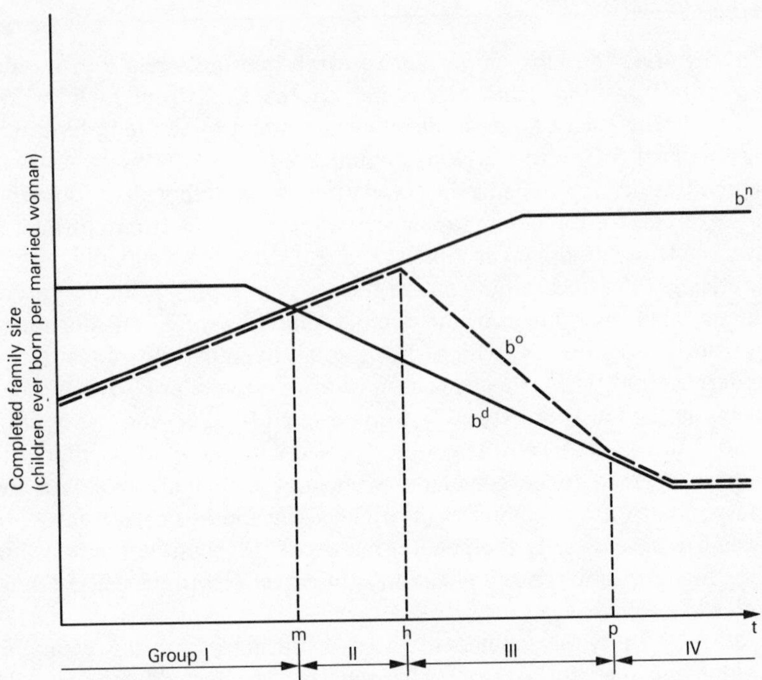

Fig. 2.4 Hypothetical trends in fertility variables associated with economic and social modernization.

its costs, and the optimal solution continues to coincide with natural fertility. As the movement to the right continues, excess fertility and the welfare loss to the family associated with it becomes larger, and a point is reached at which the benefit of fertility control exceeds its economic costs and preference drawbacks. At this point, the "threshold" of fertility regulation, labeled *h* in the diagram, the family adopts fertility control. Beyond *h*, the optimal solution no longer coincides with the natural fertility curve; instead, the optimal solution curve turns downward in the direction of the desired births curve, and, eventually, beyond point *p*, merges with it.

In terms of the previous classification of the population, the situation to the left of point *m* corresponds to a group I situation—no unwanted fertility and no practice of fertility control—as shown in the space beneath the diagram. Between points *m* and *h* there is a group II situation—excess fertility but no practice of fertility control. Between points *h* and *p* there is a group III situation, and to the right of point *p*, a group IV situation. Thus, one might think of the fertility transition as an evolution from a group I situation to a group IV situation. Actually, as we have seen, at any given time the households in a population are distributed among groups I through IV. More realistically, therefore, one might say that in the course of modernization a society gradually shifts from a predominantly group I (and/or group II) situation to a predominantly group IV situation. The main point is that there is a shift in the nature of fertility determination from one where natural fertility factors are largely or wholly dominant and preferences regarding fertility play virtually no role to one in which the influence of natural fertility disappears and conscious choice plays the dominant role.[40]

2.4 Research Implications

Although the four cases identified in section 2.3 depend on special assumptions, a number of other research implications follow from our general model. In this section we discuss the use of preferences as explanatory variables; some issues involving the births and household production functions; and the estimation of elasticities of births and family size with respect to income variables and the wife's wage rate. Our discussion does not depend on the special cases of section 2.3, although it is sometimes explicated more easily by reference to them. To bring out the distinctive features of our approach, we contrast it with the Chicago-Columbia view.

2.4.1 The Role of Preferences as Explanatory Variables

The arguments in section 2.3 regarding the prevalence of unperceived jointness and social taboos suggest that the role of preferences for children in determining observed fertility is smaller in less developed than in more developed countries. Hence, a section devoted to preferences must emphasize issues more relevant to the latter.

In the interplay between preferences and constraints, the Chicago-Columbia approach assumes that systematic variations in fertility are due largely if not entirely to differences in the constraints. Preferences are assumed to be constant across households in cross-sectional studies and over time. Partisans of the Chicago-Columbia approach are generally opposed to investigating taste formation. An example is provided by Michael and Becker (1973, p. 380): "For economists to rest a large part of their theory of choice on differences in tastes is disturbing since they admittedly have no useful theory of the formation of tastes." Going further, Keeley (1975, p. 462) argues that "the household production model lessens the reliance on tastes by incorporating socioeconomic variables in the technology of household production and thus provides a framework where the effects of socioeconomic variables on the shadow prices of home-produced commodities can be systematically analyzed."

A related view is that of T. P. Schultz, who asserts that "however conceptualized and quantified, the influence of these 'taste' factors can be properly assessed only *after* the tangible pecuniary returns have also been isolated and taken into account" (Schultz 1976, p. 95, n. 3; emphasis added). But unless one works exclusively with subsamples in which all households have identical tastes, the attempt to isolate "pecuniary returns" must fail. Since one cannot perform controlled experiments, there is no way to segregate the effects of price and income changes from the effects of habits or other types of endogenous taste formation if these phenomena are actually taking place. Hence, estimates of price and income effects obtained from a specification that presupposes fixed tastes are conditional on the maintained hypothesis of fixed tastes. In demand analysis, for example, introduction of habit-formation not only improves R^2 but also changes the estimates of price elasticities, income elasticities, and marginal budget shares.[41]

The notion that economists have an acceptable theory of systematic differences in household technology, but do not have a definitive theory of taste formation, is hardly a justification for excluding or neglecting hypotheses related to tastes.[42] Indeed, economists do not have very satisfactory theories of systematic differences in technologies available to firms in different regions, and the problems posed by household technologies are substantially more difficult because the outputs are often not measured directly. In any case, the testing of alternative models should be left to the empirical arena and not settled by a priori arguments about the proper scope of economics, demography, or other social sciences.

We advocate research on the effect of tastes along with other determinants of variations in fertility. For example, our own work suggests that models incorporating systematic changes in tastes are capable of providing an explanation of recent fertility swings in the United States and some other developed countries.[43] The Chicago-Columbia approach, on the other hand, has been unable to provide a satisfactory explanation of this experience. The Chicago-Columbia approach emphasizes that children are "time intensive in household production." Continuing advances in female education continue to raise the real wage of the wife and consequently the opportunity cost of child-rearing. In this framework, fertility in developed economies should then trend monotonically downward once a regime of low infant mortality is established. Important swings in fertility rates are not anticipated or explained.

In contrast, an endogenous preference mechanism leads to different implications for the long-term outlook in developed countries. Over the long term, it is possible that income growth may be fertility-neutral in the sense that shifts in the budget constraint favoring children are offset by an endogenous preference mechanism functioning as a lagged result of income growth that disfavors children. (This is suggested in fig. 2.4 by the leveling off of the b^d curve, once, say, a low infant mortality regime is established.) These two influences however, may differ in their timing effect and consequently generate longer-term fluctuations in fertility. In this view, recent observations of total fertility rates below the zero population growth level in the United States may be a low point on a long-swings cycle rather than the continuation of a secular decline owing, for example, to increasing female wage rates that increase the cost of child care.[44]

A framework that incorporates research on taste formation along with other social and economic variables will extend the range of empirical problems potentially amenable to treatment. In addition, it may forestall possibly biased results in analyses that omit taste consideration. For if preference variations enter into the determination of fertility variations along with variations in included variables such as wage rates, then failure to take simultaneous account of taste factors will lead to biased estimates of the effects of changes in the included variables.

2.4.2 The Technology of Child-rearing

Central to the Chicago-Columbia approach is the assumption that, as a technological datum, child-rearing is time intensive. Despite its importance, however, there has been little research on the technology of child-rearing. The lack of progress in this area may be due to two factors: the lack of measurable outputs that can be associated with child-rearing and the difficulties of distinguishing between the effects of technology and those of tastes in child-rearing behavior.

We would argue that while children today may be time intensive, especially in their early years, this results from the interplay of tastes, technology, and the budget constraint. There is little evidence to support the notion that the technology requires child-rearing to be time intensive, independent of prices and tastes.

An analysis of the child day-care industry could highlight some of these factors. Has the growth of day-care centers been solely due to a shift in techniques of child care resulting from an increase in the opportunity cost of the wife's time, or has the development of this industry also been due to a change in attitudes toward child-rearing and the role of women? Taking these factors into account, one could develop a number of scenarios in which child-rearing might cease to be a time-intensive activity for the household. For example, if the day-care industry were at an "infant" industry stage (no pun intended), its development, viewed as a dynamic process, could lead to a substantial reduction in the price of child care outside the home. This would lead to a substitution in favor of day-care centers and a decline in household time devoted to child care, but it would be independent of changes in the wife's wage rate. Similarly, a change in preferences in favor of day-care centers as a desirable way to rear children would lead to a decline in household time devoted to child-rearing, although the change might be unrelated to any changes in market prices or wage rates. In these situations it is far from certain that fertility rates would continue to decline, or even remain low, as income and female wages trended upward.

When dealing with the technology of child-rearing, the Chicago-Columbia school tends to treat commonly used socioeconomic variables such as education as proxies for inputs of the household technology. For example, Michael (1973) assumes that differences in education among individuals cause differences in household efficiency but have no effect on tastes. In this framework, the anticipated relationship between education and family size depends upon the relative gains in efficiency in consuming different "commodities" including children. Since the model does not lead to a priori restrictions on the sign of the coefficients, it cannot be separately identified from the preference effects that include education.[45] Is it not possible that education operates through both preferences and technology?

2.4.3 Births Production Function

Another important line of research suggested by our general model is the investigation of the births production function. This is especially important for less developed countries where observed behavior for a substantial share of the population is typically governed by a natural fertility regime. Research on the births production function might be of interest for developed countries, but it would be more difficult because of the smaller proportion of direct observations available.

Suppressing the fertility regulation variables θ and τ, the births production function used in section 2.2 is of the form $b = B(a,Z,X,l,\Lambda)$. Since observations on frequency of intercourse, a, are usually not available, and taking the reproductive period, Λ, as given in an analysis of marital fertility (i.e., focusing on women with the same age at marriage), one would focus on the second and third terms of the relationship, the vectors Z and l. A number of suggestions on relevant empirical variables are available in the literature. Perhaps best known is the line of research stimulated by Rose Frisch (1975), which hypothesizes a positive relation between nutrition and fertility. To date, the most thoroughgoing attempt to test this notion in a context of less developed countries is that of Anderson and McCabe, who find supporting evidence for a biological relationship between nutrition and fertility among younger women in Kinshasa, Zaire (Anderson and McCabe 1975). Another fundamental factor that often receives attention is health conditions. Romaniuc, for example, in a study of data for districts of the Congo, concluded: "the evidence points definitely to the existence of a sequence of events one would logically expect to occur. The birth rate is low because of the high incidence of sterility; the latter is caused by venereal disease, the incidence of which varies with the degree of sexual promiscuity" (Romaniuc 1968, p. 233). In Ceylon, malaria eradication appears to have had a positive effect on births (Barlow 1967). Among other factors (not necessarily independent) that figure in the literature as determinants of natural fertility are lactation practices (Jain and Sun 1972), cultural norms such as intercourse taboos (Leridon 1977), occupational circumstances (e.g., fishing or a nomadic life) (Chen et al. 1974; Romaniuc 1974; Henin 1972), and altitude above sea level (Heer 1967; James 1966).

What is needed in the study of the births production function is an approach analogous to that employed in studying mortality (Auster, Leveson, and Sarachek 1969). Such work would embrace a variety of input variables—nutrition, health, and others of the types just mentioned—that determine fertility as an output. This approach could ascertain the roles of these variables both singly and in conjunction with others as determinants of fertility variations.[46]

As has been noted, in the Chicago-Columbia approach, the prevailing view is that "demand" models of the type used for empirical research on developed countries are, with the addition of a child mortality function, a satisfactory point of departure for empirical research on less developed countries. (Advocates of a demand approach are not confined to those working in the Chicago-Columbia tradition.) When discussed —which is rarely—the need for research relating to the births production function is not emphasized. Thus, T. P. Schultz, in defending the demand model and the disregard of the births production function, argues that:

> If, as seems intuitively reasonable, exogenous differences in a woman's expected fecundity are not usually correlated with exogenous factors affecting her demand for births, proxies for exogenous biological fecundity may be omitted from the demand model of fertility determination and, if this is true, pose no estimation problems [Schultz 1976, p. 93].

We argue that the typical Chicago-Columbia demand model poses a serious misspecification for less developed economies and that Schultz's attempt at salvaging the model does not work.[47] Most troublesome for the demand model advocates is that the "demand" variables, properly interpreted, may simply not be relevant in many less developed countries, except for explaining family size *desires* as distinct from behavior. A prerequisite for a preference model is evidence that the deliberate practice of fertility control is linked to variations in observed fertility. In fact, as discussed above, evidence relating both to age patterns of fertility and to survey responses suggests an absence of deliberate control among much of the population in a typical less developed country.[48] Variables such as income that economists usually interpret as demand variables may, however, be significant in a statistical sense because of their effect on births through the births production function. The variables "fit," but for the wrong reasons. The Schultz argument that the explanatory variables in the demand and supply models are different, so that the demand variable coefficients are uncontaminated, is dubious for the same reason; a woman's fecundity is likely to be positively correlated with income, a factor that also affects her demand for children.

2.4.4 Estimating the Optimal Solution Functions

The empirical fertility literature focuses on estimating the effects on births and completed family size of certain key explanatory variables such as nonlabor income and the wife's wage rate. In the Chicago-Columbia approach, the problem is often treated as one of estimating elasticities (assumed to be constant), and these elasticities are assumed to correspond to the traditional income and substitution effects that would be present in a model in which preferences and the techniques of household production were unchanged.[49]

In our general model, the effects on births and completed family size of changes in nonlabor income and the wife's wage rate operate through at least three distinct lines of causation. Because we are not simply maximizing a utility function subject to a budget constraint, the optimal solution function is not directly comparable to a demand function.

To see this, consider the effect of an increase in the family's nonlabor income. First, the budget constraint shifts out so that the new budget line is parallel to the old one, indicating that the family faces a larger feasible set in the goods space, but that the relative prices of goods are unchanged. This is a possible analogue of the "income effect" of traditional demand theory, although it is not the only possible one. The outward shift in the budget set in the goods space implies a corresponding outward shift in the feasible set in the commodity space. If the household's technology exhibits constant returns to scale, then the new feasible set in the commodity space will be a radial blowup of the old feasible set. Second, if the household's preferences are not homothetic, it may choose to consume commodities in different proportions than before; if this is the case, and if the household's technology exhibits joint production, then the commodity shadow prices at the new equilibrium commodity consumption pattern will differ from those at the old equilibrium, and the change will correspond to a change in the technique of production used by the household. The change in the household's commodity consumption pattern may affect the household's fecundity, even though the household is unaware of the relationship between its consumption pattern and its fertility. Unperceived jointness may operate on the side of infant and child mortality as well as of fecundity, and their net effect will determine completed family size. Third, in the long run, the increase in nonlabor income may lead to an endogenous change in preferences. In the relative income model, for example, an increase in income will in the long run alter aspirations and lead to taste-induced changes in fertility and the participation rate of married women.[50]

In the general model, a change in nonlabor income will affect fertility through all three of the mechanisms described above. Disentangling these separate effects and estimating the underlying structural parameters is a difficult task given the usual limitations on data and our lack of a priori knowledge of technology and tastes. This lack of information, however, does not permit us to assume that induced changes in techniques of production or in tastes are quantitatively unimportant relative to the traditional income and substitution effects. Indeed, we believe the available data suggest that the effects that operate through changing techniques and changing tastes are significant, and that their relative importance varies systematically across societies and across groups within a given society. Our suggestion in section 2.3 that populations be divided into four groups whose fertility behavior should be analyzed separately is our response to this problem. Whether or not one adopts the assumptions necessary to classify populations strictly into these four special cases, the evidence on the practice of deliberate control suggests that for many less developed societies the response of births to changes in nonlabor income and wage rates will operate largely through unperceived effects of consumption patterns on the births and infant mortality functions and that preferences for children will not play a quantitatively important role. For developed economies, on the other hand, response to changes in nonlabor income and wage rates will reflect preferences for children (which may be endogenous) and the household's childrearing technology as well as the traditional income and substitution effects of the Chicago-Columbia school.

Regressing wage rates and nonlabor income on fertility does not yield sensible estimates of the impact of these variables. The bias would be greater in less developed than in more developed societies, and greater for lower than for higher socioeconomic groups within a society. One way to minimize these biases is to divide the population into groups on the basis of survey responses or income levels and to estimate the parameters separately for each group. In our four special cases, parameters related to preferences for children can be omitted for groups I and II, and those related to the births technology can be omitted for group IV.

2.5 Welfare Implications

Our emphasis on unperceived jointness and endogenous tastes requires substantial modifications in the usual formulation of welfare arguments. But even without unperceived jointness and endogenous tastes, our stress on the preference drawbacks as well as the economic costs of fertility regulation as a determinant of fertility control has important implications for evaluation of the welfare effects of policies aimed at reducing "excess" or "unwanted" fertility. These issues are taken up in order below.

2.5.1 Endogenous Preferences

Any type of endogenous tastes considerably complicates welfare analysis. In section 2.2 we discussed a model of interdependent preferences in which a family's tastes depend on the consumption and family-size decisions of others. More specifically, we assumed that each family's preference ordering over its decision variables—vectors of the form $(Z,X,b,d,N,a,l,\theta,\tau)$—depend on the "normal values" of Z and N, which we denote by Z^* and N^*. These normal values might depend on the consumption and family-size patterns it observes in the surrounding society (in the socialization version) or on the levels of Z and N experienced by the husband and wife in childhood (in the intrafamily version). In section 2.2 we described the preference ordering over the decision variables as "conditional" on the values of Z^* and N^* and indicated this by writing the utility function as $U(Z,N,d,a,l,\theta,\tau;Z^*,N^*)$, with the semicolon separating the normal levels Z^* and N^* from the other variables. We did this to distinguish between an "unconditional" preference ordering over the extended set of variables $(Z,N,d,a,l,\theta,\tau,Z^*,N^*)$ and a "conditional" preference ordering over the decision variables (Z,N,d,a,l,θ,τ) that depends on the levels of the normal variables Z^* and N^*.

A conditional preference ordering captures the notion that families with different consumption and family-size experiences may have different tastes and may make different decisions, but it does not permit us to compare situations that correspond to different normal values, Z^* and N^*.[51] Such comparisons must be based on the unconditional preference ordering over the extended set of variables $(Z,X,b,d,a,l,\theta,\tau,Z^*,N^*)$. To see this, suppose that preferences for children are determined by the number of children in the wife's family, independent of the commodity consumption pattern of that family, in the following very simple way: regardless of other considerations, the family attempts to have the same number of children as were present in the family in which the wife grew up, and it is unwilling to trade off children against commodities in attempting to accomplish this. In such a world, the size of the family in which the wife grew up uniquely determines the number of children she will have, but there is no way to use this information to compare the welfare level of women with one sibling with that of women with two siblings. Notice that the woman with one sibling is observed to choose two children rather than three, while the woman with two siblings is observed to choose three children rather than two.[52]

The welfare implications of a model of interdependent preferences must be derived from the unconditional preference ordering, but these preferences are not revealed by the family's choices of the decision variables. Thus the conceptual basis for welfare evaluation in such a model must be quite different from the "revealed preference" approach usually employed by economists. We see two possible bases for welfare evaluation with endogenous preferences. The first is based on direct comparisons of the well-being of different families as reflected by their responses to survey questions which ask them directly about their "happiness" or "well-being."[53] The second approach relies on a different type of interpersonal comparison. Sen (1973, p. 14) discusses this approach:

> If I say "I would prefer to be person *A* rather than person *B* in this situation," I am indulging in an interpersonal comparison. While we do not really have the opportunity (or perhaps the misfortune, as the case may be) of in fact becoming *A* or *B*, we can think quite systematically about such a choice, and indeed we seem to make such comparisons frequently.
>
> Representing (x,i) as being individual i (with his tastes and mental qualities as well) in social state x, a preference relation R defined over all such pairs provides an "ordinal" structure of interpersonal comparisons.

In the case of interdependent preferences, one would ask a family whether it would rather be in the position of family *A*, which experienced the consumption–family-size pattern α during adolescence, or of family *B* which experienced the consumption–family-size pattern β during adolescence, but it is possible that the family's choice between the alternatives (A,α) and (B,β) will depend on its own consumption–family-size experiences during adolescence. If individuals are unable to abstract from their own backgrounds and upbringing in making choices of this type, there is little chance of extracting an unconditional preference ordering from responses to such questions. If this is the case, welfare evaluations must rest on direct comparisons of "happiness" or "well-being" reflected either by responses to survey questions or by an appeal to general (and often questionable) assumptions about "human nature."[54]

2.5.2 Unperceived Jointness

Even without interdependent preferences, unperceived jointness complicates welfare evaluation. Economists are accustomed to asserting that if a family chooses alternative *A* when it could have chosen *B*, then *A* is at least as good as *B* according to the family's preferences.[55] The analogous correct version of this assertion is the following: If the family intends to choose *A* when it believes it could have chosen *B*, then *A* is at least as good as *B* (according to the family's preferences). Unperceived jointness breaks the automatic link between observed consumption and intended choice, since the family that intends to choose *A* may be observed with *A′* (e.g., a larger number of children, because of the effect of better nutrition on fertility). Similarly, with unperceived jointness the household's perception of the set of feasible alternatives may be quite different from the true feasible set, and inferences about preferences must be based on the perceived rather than the actual feasible set. These difficulties of inferring preferences from observed choices in the presence of unperceived jointness are not restricted to situations involving nutrition and fertility but apply equally to choices involving diet and health or transportation and safety, or any other context in which unperceived jointness is present.

Welfare inferences—even welfare inferences based on the family's preferences—are difficult to make in the unperceived jointness model because it is difficult to infer the family's preferences from its observed choices. This is clearly true in the short run, when the number of births or deaths realized by the family is different from the numbers it expected on the basis of the perceived births and deaths functions. But it is also true in the long run, when realized and perceived births and deaths coincide. The difficulty with revealed preference-type inferences based on the fulfilled expectations solution is that even in such an equilibrium the family's perception of its feasible set of alternatives is inaccurate.

2.5.3 Unwanted Fertility

We have defined "excess" or "unwanted" fertility as the difference between optimal and desired fertility; that is, $b^o - b^d$. We are concerned with two general causes of unwanted fertility, the economic costs and the preference drawbacks of fertility regulation.[56] A reduction in the economic costs of fertility regulation (e.g., a reduction in the price of condoms, diaphragms, or pills) represents a clear welfare gain to those whose excess fertility is reduced. The introduction of a new fertility-regulation technique (e.g., the pill) also represents a clear welfare gain for those who choose to use it. However, the welfare evaluation of a reduction in unwanted fertility due to an increase in the use of contraceptives because of a change in the family's attitudes toward their use is more complex. Evaluated in terms of the family's new preferences, the change is an improvement, but evaluated in terms of its old preferences it is not. Thus the evaluation of the welfare impact of a government program that operates by changing tastes so as to reduce the preference drawbacks of fertility regulation is necessarily ambiguous.[57]

The view is common in the demographic literature that reduction or elimination of unwanted fertility through public policy would increase welfare. The Chicago-Columbia version of the economics of fertility lends itself to this view because it minimizes the role of preferences in determining contraceptive usage and emphasizes the importance of access to information and efficient use of a contraceptive technique. Thus Becker (1960) attributed the high completed family size of poor families to contraceptive failure owing to inadequate information. Similarly, Michael and Willis (1976) show that in the United States higher levels of formal education are related to lower contraceptive failure rates. If this reflects the greater efficiency of these families in fertility regulation, then a decrease in excess fertility would imply an improvement in the welfare of a family.

We do not assert that government-sponsored programs to control fertility cannot be valuable. But we do insist on distinguishing between benefits that accrue to the families whose excess fertility is reduced and benefits that accrue to others in the society.[58] In evaluating the benefits to the families whose excess fertility is reduced, it is important to understand the mechanisms through which such programs operate. To the extent that such programs operate by changing the preferences of the families whose excess fertility is reduced, there is no clear way to determine whether the families in question have benefited.[59]

A government-sponsored program that reduced unwanted fertility by lowering the economic costs of fertility regulation clearly benefits families whose excess fertility is reduced, provided the costs of the program are paid by others (i.e., by other groups within the society or by outside groups such as the United Nations). If the costs of the program are paid by taxes levied in part on the group whose unwanted fertility is reduced, then the question whether their welfare is increased depends on the balance between the benefits of lower-cost fertility regulation and the costs in the form of higher taxes; there is no presumption that the benefits outweigh the costs.

The strongest case for economic benefits can be made on the grounds of market failure. The argument for the existence of market failure is generally based on the fact that information collection and dissemination is a public or quasi-public good. A governmental unit can internalize both the information costs and the direct costs of establishing a market, whereas individual families cannot. The information–market-failure argument for government intervention presupposes an absence of knowledge on the part of families that particular techniques of fertility regulation are available, a situation that is more likely to exist in less developed countries than in advanced industrial societies.[60]

When the reduction in excess fertility is the result of government proselytizing for the acceptability of contraception in order to reduce its preference drawbacks, we cannot infer that the reduction in excess fertility implies a welfare gain to the family. Even when the fertility control program is associated with a reduction in the economic costs of fertility regulation (e.g., by the free provision of fertility control devices and associated medical care not financed by taxes levied on those who practice fertility regulation), welfare gains cannot be inferred if tastes are changed at the same time.

In evaluating the welfare impact of family planning programs one must distinguish between developed and less developed countries. Preference drawbacks and economic costs underlie excess fertility in both areas, but economic costs are likely to be more significant in less developed countries, whereas preference drawbacks are likely to predominate in developed countries. Family planning programs designed to change preferences regarding the use of fertility regulation may be justified in terms of their benefit to society as a whole, but it is difficult to argue that such programs improve the welfare of the families whose tastes they change and whose excess fertility they thereby reduce. The benefits to families whose excess fertility is reduced by a government program that reduced the economic costs of fertility regulation are likely to be considerably smaller in developed countries than in less developed countries because the costs of access to information are typically much lower in developed countries. Most parents know of the existence, availability, and method of use of "reliable" techniques of fertility regulation (i.e., techniques with low theoretical failure rates). Many, however, continue to report unwanted fertility. Since the economic costs, including information access costs, are low in developed countries, the preference drawbacks must be decisive. Hence the main elements in unwanted fertility in developed countries appear to involve preference and motivation and not the economic costs or lack of information about fertility control.

2.6 Conclusion

Although there have been important advances in the analysis of fertility since the pathbreaking work of Becker (1960) and Leibenstein (1974*a*), the subject has become increasingly fettered by a narrowing view of the determinants of fertility. The framework laid out in this paper is intended to reverse this tendency by emphasizing a number of neglected determinants of fertility that deserve further exploration. Some of the principal views we have advanced are the following:

1. To come to grips with the variety of real-world fertility behavior, models of fertility determination must be expanded to include preferences and the biological production relationships. We propose a framework that includes such considerations in section 2.2, where we emphasize the role of "interdependent preferences" and the "births production function."

2. This model of section 2.2, although rich in analytical potential, is complicated, and practical application is limited by the lack of data. On fairly reasonable assumptions, however, special cases of the model can be distinguished, ranging from one in which fertility is independent of preferences for children to one in which the births production function becomes irrelevant and preferences for children—perhaps endogenously determined—play a crucial role. These special cases are discussed in section 2.3.1.

3. Evidence both from household surveys of fertility control practices and from census and other data relating to actual fertility behavior show that in many less developed countries deliberate efforts by individual families to regulate their fertility are rare. Hence the fertility of the bulk of the population is determined by its "natural fertility." For such countries, time-series and cross-sectional fertility variations may primarily reflect determinants of natural fertility rather than desired family size (see section 2.3.2).

4. Survey data make it possible to subdivide a population into those who practice deliberate fertility regulation and those who do not. We believe the analysis of fertility requires that these groups be treated in different ways. To explain the behavior of those who do not deliberately control their fertility, models stressing "natural fertility" and ignoring preferences for children are appropriate. For those who deliberately control their fertility, models emphasizing preferences for children and the effects of prices and income on desired family size are appropriate. Attempting to analyze the fertility behavior of an entire population without distinguishing between those who deliberately regulate their fertility and those who do not may result in biased estimates of the likely response of fertility to changes in incomes or to wider access to modern techniques of fertility regulation (sections 2.3.3, 2.3.4).

5. There is a need for further research in three relatively unexplored areas: preferences (sections 2.2.4, 2.4.1), the births production function (section 2.4.3), and unperceived jointness. Research on preferences could include both the endogenous formation of preferences for children and the role of the preference drawbacks of fertility regulation as a determinant of observed fertility. The investigation of the births production function should clarify the effect on fertility of practices such as lactation as well as such variables as health and nutrition. Of particular importance in evaluating the births production function is the role of

unperceived jointness. In this case the family does not fully incorporate into its behavior the relationship between its fecundity and its consumption decisions. Unperceived jointness is a pervasive problem in economics because individuals are often maximizing without taking account of the full interrelationships among constraints and between constraints and preferences.

6. Because our framework embraces a wider range of fertility determinants than the Chicago-Columbia approach, it is consistent with a greater variety of hypotheses regarding the factors that shape fertility trends and differentials. For example, it is consistent with an explanation of the demographic transition in which, in the early stages, an upsurge in fertility occurs owing to natural fertility factors. It is also consistent with the possibility that there will be substantial long-term fluctuations in fertility in developed countries rather than a monotonic downward trend. The framework also suggests a more cautious approach in evaluating the welfare effect of reducing "unwanted fertility," since its reduction may reflect a change in tastes (e.g., a reduced aversion toward the use of certain fertility regulation techniques) rather than a movement to higher indifference curves on an unchanging indifference map (section 2.5).

Notes

1. See Schultz (1974). No single designation for this approach is fully satisfactory. Here we adopt the term used by one of its advocates, Keeley (1975).

2. See Schultz (1974); Keeley (1975), Leibenstein (1974*b*), and Schultz (1976).

3. T. Paul Schultz's article, although published in 1976, was originally prepared for a 1973 conference. Inevitably, there are differences among members of a "school" on particular points, and injustice may be done to one or another individual in a general discussion. Moreover, there are indications that several of the leading workers may be venturing in directions we advocate. A recent paper by Michael and Willis, for example, departs strikingly from the usual Chicago-Columbia model, and introduces a "natural fertility" concept (Michael and Willis 1976). T. Paul Schultz has encouraged work on natural fertility at the Rand Corporation and has recently given more attention to "biological factors" in a discussion of the relation between infant mortality and fertility. Ben-Porath, whose identification with the Chicago-Columbia approach is in any event uncertain, has explored the issue of intergenerational taste influences (Ben-Porath 1975).

4. T. W. Schultz, on the other hand, is markedly restrained in commenting on the relevance of the Chicago-Columbia approach to less developed countries: "Turning to fertility behavior in low income countries the [Chicago-Columbia] household model as it now stands has not been developed to treat the particular classes of circumstances that constrain the household in these countries. These are countries in which illiteracy abounds, human time is cheap, and the income oppor-

tunities that women have outside the home are mainly not jobs in the labor market. Furthermore, infant mortality is high, life expectancy is low, debilitation during the adult years is substantial for reasons of inadequate nutrition and endemic diseases, and the availability of modern contraceptive techniques, including information about them, is, in general, wanting. These classes of circumstances are not yet at home in the household model" (Schultz 1974, p. 20).

5. This failure is admitted by both Keeley (1975, p. 466) and Schultz (1976, p. 94). Curiously, although the value of a relative income model in explaining this movement is generously acknowledged by these writers, they are not led to reconsider their general stance against research on preferences.

6. For a discussion of the role of sex preferences in determining family size, see Ben-Porath and Welch (1976).

7. The seminal paper in the household production literature is Becker (1965). In Lancaster's model (Lancaster 1966*a*,*b*, 1971) goods possess "characteristics" that are often identified with Becker's "commodities," and the "technology" is linear. Becker often uses fixed coefficient production functions as an expositional device, but linear technology is not an integral part of his model. For a recent sympathetic statement of the household production approach, see Michael and Becker (1973). For a discussion of some of its limitations, see Pollak and Wachter (1975).

8. It is customary to assume that the household's preferences over the commodity space are well behaved in the sense that they can be represented by a continuous utility function that is strictly quasi-concave and nondecreasing in its arguments. If the feasible set in the commodity space is convex, these assumptions guarantee that the utility maximizing collection of commodities is unique.

9. The "cost function," $C(P,w,Z;T)$, is defined as the minimum cost of producing the commodity bundle Z with the technology T at goods prices P and wage rates w. That is,

$$C(P,w,Z;T) = min \sum_{k=1}^{n} p_k x_k + \sum_{h=1}^{H} \sum_{s \epsilon T} w_h t_{hs},$$

subject to $(Z,X,T) \epsilon T$. We can use the cost function to translate the budget constraint from the goods space into the commodity space. The translation of the constraint is the requirement that $C(P,w,Z;T)$ not exceed the family's "full income" (i.e., the household's total earnings if it devoted all of its time to market work):

$$C(P,w,Z;T) \leq \mu + \sum_{h=1}^{H} w_h \bar{t}_h.$$

10. These issues are discussed in Pollak and Wachter (1975), where it is argued that joint production is pervasive in household production situations, especially when the role of time is recognized. For further discussion, see Barnett (1977) and the reply by Pollak and Wachter (1977).

11. Formally, it would be possible to treat the same fertility-regulation technique practiced with different intensities as different techniques. Our formulation is more consistent with ordinary usage and is capable of casting some light on the question why some population groups have higher "failure rates" than others using the same technique.

12. We take the family (more specifically, the parents) rather than the individual to be the basic unit of analysis. The assumption that the family (i.e., the husband and wife collectively) has well-defined preferences begs the issue of aggregating the separate preferences of the husband and wife into a collective preference ordering. Samuelson (1956) provides a classic statement of the problem; Nerlove

(1974, p. S 204) describes the resolution of these problems by postulating a "family utility function" as the "Samuelson finesse."

13. If the total cost of fertility can be decomposed into a fixed cost, $\rho_o(\tau)$, and a variable cost, $\rho_1(\tau)\theta$, the cost function takes the form

$$\rho(\theta,\tau) = \rho_o(\tau)k + \rho_1(\tau)\theta,$$

where

$$k = 0 \text{ if } \theta = 0 \text{ and } k = 1 \text{ if } \theta > 0.$$

The cost of fertility regulation might also depend on the fecundity of the family, which may in turn depend on its goods purchases and commodity consumption; abortion is an example of a technique whose cost depends on fecundity.

14. The earnings of children could be incorporated into the model either by expanding it to include an "earnings function" or by interpreting vector t to include the allocation of the time of children. We implicitly adopt the latter course to avoid additional notation.

15. Existence of a solution poses no real problems, but uniqueness is a different matter. We have not ruled out the possibility of multiple solutions. The usual uniqueness argument rests on the assumptions that feasible sets are convex and preferred sets are strictly convex. But some of our variables have no "natural" units of measurement, and there are no market units we could adopt by convention. For example, given any index of the intensity of use of a particular fertility regulation technique, any increasing transformation of that index would serve equally well. But such transformations can alter the convexity properties of feasible sets and preferred sets, so that the usual type of uniqueness argument cannot be made. Of course, the uniqueness of the solution cannot be altered by such transformations, and uniqueness is assured if there exist any units of measurement in which the feasible sets and the preferred sets are both convex and one or the other is strictly convex. Since we cannot establish uniqueness, we cannot guarantee that the optimal solutions are continuous in the variables the family takes as exogenous.

16. The term "unperceived jointness" is motivated by viewing the household as having a single production technology instead of three distinct technologies, one producing births, another infant mortality, and the third the other commodities. We call this single technology the household's "generalized technology." This treatment avoids treating births, deaths, and fertility regulation as distinct from the other commodities by extending the notion of commodities to include all of the arguments of the family's utility function; we refer to these variables as "generalized commodities." The generalized technology exhibits joint production because the same inputs affect the output of more than one generalized commodity: for example, purchased food inputs produce the generalized commodity "nutrition," which is desired for its own sake, but they also influence the output of the generalized commodities "births" and "deaths." The assumption that the family is not fully aware of the relationship between nutrition and births (or deaths) implies that the jointness in the household's generalized technology is at least in part "unperceived."

17. The polar cases here are the extreme points on the continuum from ignorance to knowledge; they do not coincide with the special cases of the classification scheme described in section 2.1. Indeed, that discussion assumed "complete ignorance" in order to define "natural fertility."

18. Since the family's reproductive span, Λ, is not a decision variable for the family, this constant specification is equivalent to $\hat{B}(a,Z,X,l,0,0,\Lambda) = \beta\Lambda$ where the family believes that the ratio β is not affected by its decisions. If the reproduc-

tive span were made a decision variable, then the two specifications would no longer be equivalent, and age at marriage would become a possible mechanism of conscious and deliberate fertility regulation.

19. For example, $\bar{B}$ might be equal to the average fertility of the most recent cohort to have completed its reproductive span, or a weighted average of the experience of such recent cohorts, perhaps restricted to families of similar socioeconomic status. A more complicated specification might make use of the experience of families who had not yet completed their reproductive spans. This would be legitimate even in our one-period planning model, but it would not be legitimate to use the family's own experience or that of other families of its cohort as a basis for prediction.

20. A one-period planning model cannot capture the behavior of a family that did not intend to practice fertility regulation, has more children than it expected, and then begins to practice fertility regulation. Inability to reflect this type of period behavior is a serious drawback of one-period planning models. Two points should be made. First, this defect is relevant only for families that have knowledge of fertility-regulation techniques they would utilize if they knew their true fecundity. Second, the difficulty of incorporating unperceived jointness into the one-period planning model is a point against the one-period planning model, not against unperceived jointness.

21. There is a conceptual difficulty here, again reflecting the confines of the one-period planning model. Presumably, the eventual allocation of expenditure among goods is determined by realized rather than perceived family size: a family that expects two children and has four will buy more "child goods" and fewer "adult goods" than it planned. One can imagine a two-period model in which the consumption pattern in period one determines realized family size, and realized family size determines the consumption pattern in period two. In a multiperiod model, births and mortality in each period would depend on consumption patterns in previous periods, and consumption patterns in each period would depend on actual family size and composition in that period.

22. Similarly, in a Cournot duopoly equilibrium each firm correctly predicts the output of the other firm without perceiving the reaction function that generates that output.

23. Notice that perceived and realized completed family size could be equal even if $b^p \neq b^r$ and $d^p \neq d^r$, if there are offsetting errors, but this is not a fulfilled-expectations equilibrium. We have defined an equilibrium in terms of births and deaths rather than completed family size because a divergence between perceived and realized births will cause a revision of expectations about the births function and a revision of plans.

24. It might be thought that a model of habit formation in which a family's own past consumption levels influenced its taste for goods would be appropriate, but such a specification cannot be developed within the structure of a one-period planning model. For the family's own past consumption experience to play a role, we need a sequential model in which the family makes decisions at more than a single decision point.

25. The simultaneous specification in which each family's preferences depend on everyone else's current decisions is analytically intractable because the preferences of each family in a particular cohort are determined by variables whose values depend on the behavior of all families in that cohort. In the lagged specification the preferences of each family in a particular cohort depend on the behavior of families in earlier cohorts, and hence the model has a recursive rather

than a simultaneous structure. With the lagged specification it is only in a "steady state" equilibrium that the full effects of interdependent preferences manifest themselves.

26. The notation of a nonnegative relationship between normal levels and preferences can be formalized as in Pollak (1977, n. 8).

27. This terminology is used in Pollak (1977) to distinguish preferences over goods (X) that depend on prices (P)—"conditional preferences"—from preferences over alternative goods-vector-price vector situations (X,P)—"unconditional preferences." The nomenclature is analogous to that used for conditional probability.

28. The "necessary" level interpretation works for the linear expenditure system, provided that certain parameters assume nonnegative values; but there is no a priori reason to believe that these parameters are nonnegative. For a discussion of both of these systems and references to the literature, see Pollak (1970, 1971).

29. A word is necessary also on the distinction between "socially controlled" and "family controlled" fertility. By "family controlled" or "family regulated" fertility we mean deliberate efforts by individual households to influence their fertility. From this point of view, natural fertility is socially controlled but not family controlled. For example, an intercourse taboo observed as a matter of custom is a social control that affects the level of natural fertility. It does not, however, imply controlled fertility in our sense, since observance of the taboo by individual households is not geared to family-size concerns. For a contrary view, see T. Paul Schultz (1976, p. 92). It should be noted also that while the present concept of natural fertility reflects social controls, such controls are only one of a number of societal conditions that affect natural fertility. War, for example, may reduce natural fertility by separating spouses, but it would not be viewed as a social control on fertility.

30. The focus of our approach is on groups or collections of families rather than on individual families or on society as a whole. This is to avoid both the problems associated with random or stochastic elements in the births and infant mortality functions and the discreteness of children. This allows us to interpret our model as applying to the mean experience of a group of identical families. We do not assume that all families in a particular society belong to the same group—quite to the contrary, important aspects of demographic behavior can be captured only by recognizing the changing balance among the groups we have described.

31. A possible third type of evidence comes from studies in which an attempt is made to formulate and test hypotheses that distinguish between "behavioral" and "biological" determinants of fertility. As explained in the preceding section, a finding in favor of behavioral influences does not necessarily imply controlled fertility in our sense, since the actual issue relates to whether the behavior is motivated by its possible fertility effect. On the other hand, a finding in favor of biological influences can be viewed as support for uncontrolled fertility in our sense. Without pretending to do a systematic survey, our impression is that the results of a number of these studies lean toward the importance of biological factors. (Cf., e.g., Anderson and McCabe [1977], Chowdhury et al. [1976], and Taylor et al. [1976].

32. A useful early summary report on some of these surveys is Mauldin (1965); a recent review is given in Nortman (1977).

33. Some surveys aim explicitly for comprehensive coverage of possible methods. For example, a recent survey in Nigeria asked specifically about traditional methods, the practice of abstinence, and possible use of extended lactation as ways of limiting family size (Caldwell and Igun 1972).

34. A useful discussion of some of the shortcomings of the Henry concept is given in David and Sanderson (1976, pp. 143 ff.).

35. The index value can actually take on mildly negative values. This is because the "standard" age pattern for a natural fertility regime is an average of schedules for ten cases, and a given situation might actually involve a relationship between the age-specific fertility of older and younger women that is higher than the standard natural fertility case.

36. See also Knodel (1977). Knodel's paper is especially pertinent to the present discussion, for it concludes, from calculations of m, that "modern family limitation (i.e., parity-specific fertility control) was largely absent prior to a secular fertility decline in both Europe and Asia" (Knodel 1977, abstract).

37. Some additional data may be noted bearing on the prevalence of "excess demand" situations. Survey data for rural Morocco (1966), West Malaysia (1967), and Kenya (1966) indicate that among wives 35–49 the proportion who want more children is substantial, ranging between about one-fourth and one-half. A recent survey in an area of rural Indonesia states that "despite relatively high levels of ideal family size (average 4.5) . . . , women in Mojalena give birth to an average of only 3.9 children; moreover, owing to high rates of mortality, completed family size averages 2.7 children" (Singarimbun and Manning 1976, p. 175). On the other hand, in Potharam (1964) the proportion was only a tenth or less. The Morocco data are from Lapham (1970); Kenya, from Heisel (1968); and West Malaysia, from Palmore (1969). The figures for Kenya include those for whom the "desire for children" was not ascertained or "up to God," a category that in rural Morocco accounted for only about 4–6% of the respondents. Indonesian data are from Singarimbun and Manning (1976); the Potharam data, from Peng (1965). See also Tabbarah (1971).

38. This is a pattern suggested by the data for rural Mysore (United Nations 1961, chap. 10) and more recently by work on Indonesia (Hull and Hull 1977) and Iran (Ajami 1976).

39. As drawn, this curve lies below that for groups I and II, but one can imagine conditions under which it might lie above it. Clearly, for all of the groups, identification of typical patterns is itself a research issue.

40. One might imagine a corresponding trend in fertility differentials by socioeconomic status as the nature of the underlying determinants changed. Suppose, for example, that the demographic transition involved simply a shift from an initial group I–group II situation through group III to a wholly group IV situation. Then the initial pattern of socioeconomic status–fertility differentials for the population as a whole might be given by the positively inclined b_n curve of figure 2.3 above, reflecting the effect of natural fertility factors. When the society was in the group III situation, the negatively inclined curve would prevail, and in group IV the horizontal curve. Thus one might hypothesize a trend in fertility differentials by socioeconomic status from positive through zero to negative and back to zero again. However, this is only one possibility. The point is that the expected pattern of fertility differentials would shift as the underlying determinants of fertility changed.

41. See, for example, Pollak and Wales (1969), Wales (1971), and Howe, Pollak, and Wales (1977).

42. Taste differences, like differences in technology, can be and often are used as a deus ex machina when other explanations fail. But the fact that specifications involving taste differences (or technological differences) can be misused is not a justification for ignoring them.

43. See, for example, Easterlin (1973) and Wachter (1975). For other work on taste formation in a time series context, see Leibenstein (1974*b*), Lee (1976, 1977), and Lindert (1978). For the application of the relative income model to the related question of labor force participation behavior, see Wachter (1972*b*, 1974).

44. See Easterlin (1973), Lee (1975 *a,b*), and Wachter (1972*b*, 1974).

45. Indeed, some empirical work suggests that the ceteris paribus relationship between education and family size is U-shaped. See, for example, Yoram Ben-Porath (1973).

46. Work at the level of intermediate variables, represented by what are known as "renewal models," seeks to account for fertility through factors such as age at sexual union, frequency of intercourse, probability of conception, length of the nonsusceptible period, and duration of reproductive union. So far as the present framework is concerned, this research is of interest primarily for the guidance it may provide into more fundamental causal factors at work. For example, if the nonsusceptible period (NSP) is an important source of fertility variation between two societies, one may be led to inquire into lactation practices, a seemingly important determinant of NSP and, in turn, into the determinants of these practices. However, the proximate components of fertility do not each depend uniquely on different causal factors—for example, a number of the intermediate variables might be affected by nutrition. An excellent concise presentation of renewal models is given by Keyfitz (1971). Economists who have followed this lead in recent work include Michael and Willis (1976), David and Sanderson (1976), and Crafts and Ireland (1976). Leridon (1977) has recently completed a valuable comprehensive survey of the field, which makes accessible in English the pioneering work of the French demographers, led by Henry and Bourgeois-Pichat.

47. We have avoided here the terminology of "demand" and "supply" models. As the optimal solution function illustrates, there are no demand and supply functions in the traditional sense.

48. If one disregards Puerto Rico and Chile, which are uncertain representatives of less developed countries' experience even for Latin America, the studies cited by Schultz as empirical support for the relevance of the Chicago-Columbia type of demand approach to less developed areas are: Egypt 1960, Philippines 1968, Thailand 1960, and Taiwan 1964–69. With the exception of Taiwan, the available evidence indicates extremely low levels of deliberate fertility control in these countries at the times studied. Table 2.3 shows very low indexes of fertility control for the Philippines and for Thailand. In Egypt in 1960 the proportion of married women of reproductive age who had practiced family planning was, in rural areas, 1.5%; semiurban, 12.0%; and urban, 17.0% (Mauldin 1965, p. 9). (The rural proportion of the population in 1960 in Egypt was 62.0%.) Even in regard to Taiwan, as shown in table 2.1 above, in 1965 less than half of married females aged 35–39 had practiced deliberate control. These observations suggest that in the studies cited by Schultz a substantial share of the population, and in some cases almost all the population, is in a natural fertility situation.

49. A good concise exposition is provided in Schultz's appendix (Schultz 1976).

50. See Easterlin (1968) and Wachter (1972*b*).

51. A similar point is made in Pollak (1976*b*) in the context of interdependent preferences, and in Pollak (1977) in the context of price-dependent preferences.

52. Our example assumes a lexicographic preference for family size, but this is not crucial. Notice that, because the relevant utility functions are conditional rather than unconditional, we could multiply the utility function of the woman with one sibling by 100 while leaving the conditional utility function of the woman with two siblings unchanged; such transformations have no effect on the behavior

implied by the utility functions, but the admissibility of such transformations shows that the level of utility cannot be used to compare the satisfaction or well-being in such cases.

53. See Easterlin (1975) for a survey of results of this type.

54. A third approach, based on the long-run behavior implied by the endogenous taste model, makes use of the "long-run" utility function. This approach was proposed by von Weiszäcker (1971) and criticized on conceptual and technical grounds by El-Safty (1976*a*,*b*), Hammond (1976), and Pollak (1976*a*).

55. Strictly speaking, the assertion in the text should refer to an individual rather than a family, but we assume that families, like individuals, have well-defined preferences.

56. There is a third source of excess fertility. No fertility regulation technique (excluding abstinence) is technically perfect even under ideal conditions. Associated with each method of fertility control is a minimum failure rate, termed the "theoretical" failure rate (Leridon 1977, p. 122).

57. A fertility control program which changes preferences for children may reduce fertility without reducing excess fertility. This is not an unlikely result.

58. Those whose fertility is unaffected might benefit from a reduction in the fertility of other groups in the society if the tax and transfer structure caused them to pay a portion of the cost of the unwanted children.

59. For a more detailed exposition of this argument, see Wachter (1972*a*).

60. Costs of fixed information and costs of access to fertility control may be sizable in many less developed countries today. Where modern medicine is not readily available, the costs of acquiring modern contraceptive techniques can be prohibitive. For example, parents in a rural village that has neither a doctor nor a clinic could not import modern contraceptive techniques and associated medical care except at a very high initial or fixed cost. For these families, the traditional methods of abstinence and withdrawal may be the only forms of regulation that can be adopted without violating the budget constraint. To the extent that excess fertility prevails, the fact that these methods are often not utilized attests to their significant preference drawbacks. As development occurs, an increasing proportion of households in less developed countries have the motivation to practice fertility control, but the economic costs are too high for modern techniques and the preference drawbacks too high for traditional fertility regulation. At this stage these areas offer at least the potential of large economic benefits if the government were to organize the necessary infrastructure for dispensing contraceptive information and techniques. The government is in effect capturing an externality by establishing a market for modern contraceptive devices.

Comment Harvey Leibenstein

This is an unusually stimulating paper on a very difficult subject. Its main features, as I see them, are as follows: (1) It emphasizes and employs a demographic view of economic development. (2) It contains a taste-shift factor that is unique for models of this type. (3) It develops

Harvey Leibenstein is Andelot Professor of Economics and Population at Harvard University.

an interesting concept in the notion of "unperceived jointness." (4) It separates the demand for children and the demand for controls. (5) In one sense the model is conventional in that it assumes the maximization of utility.

Among the clearly desirable features of the model are its introduction of the taste-shift factor and its use of a demand for controls equation.

It is very difficult to assess the purely demographic view of economic development. Demographic behavior appears to hang in a void unconnected to economic and social trends. An alternative that might have been considered is to connect the theory to reasonably uniform patterns of development of the type studied by Kuznets, Chenery, and others. For example, fairly specific things can be said about shifts of labor toward urban areas, increases in education, and shifts in broad occupational categories, which usually accompany economic development. A model more explicitly connected with persistent patterns of change would add a feeling of realism, but it is impossible to say at this point if it would have greater explanatory power.

An interesting feature of the model is its use of the concept of natural fertility within marriage as an anchoring point for the predevelopment situation. The difficulty with this approach is that it omits the marriage age as a control variable. The view I am espousing is that there are wide variety of social controls of population even in developing countries, and, furthermore, that the social controls are *substitutes* for private controls. The view emphasized is that we must not underestimate the significance of the *substitution* of some controls for others as part of the process of demographic change.

It may help to keep in mind the following list of *population* controls:

a. Nonmarriage of women—spinsterhood
b. Late marriage
c. Celibacy rules for some professions
d. Taboos on widow remarriage
e. Periods of noncohabitation
f. Infanticide
g. Neglect leading to infanticide
h. Long lactation periods
i. Ritual taboos on intercourse
j. Abortions
k. Contraceptive means
l. Outmigration

We should note that the word used is population rather than fertility. All population controls are to some degree substitutes for each other. Some of these controls are social controls, others are individual controls within the power of family members. But the individual controls are substitutes for social controls. Hence, if we consider only fertility within marriage, we may lose some sense of the capacity for substitution between various types of controls. While the use of the demand for fertility control in the Easterlin model strikes me as an excellent idea, in some contexts fertility controls are likely to be substitutes for existing population controls, and hence a sense of the degree of substitution may help us assess the *net* demand for some specific fertility controls.

The concept of unperceived jointness seems extremely useful and is likely to take care of observed anomalies in the analysis of specific situations. There is some danger in a concept of this sort, since it is unlikely to be observable, in that it may be tempting to use it as a rationalization of any deviation between the results of empirical research and the predictions from a specific model.

It is understandable that Easterlin, Pollak, and Wachter should use a utility-maximizing model, since this is the conventional approach among economists. But this seems to me to be a questionable procedure. First, it leaves out frequently observed characteristics of behavior—repetitive behavior and inertia. Second, and most important, it leaves out changes in degree of rationality as an explanatory factor. In criticizing the maximization assumption, a question that frequently arises is whether there is any alternative. In the pages that follow, I shall present the bare bones of a nonmaximizing model and suggest, albeit quickly and necessarily vaguely, how this model might be used to handle some of the concepts of the Easterlin/Pollak/Wachter model or related models. Below, a brief comparison is made between the standard theory and the one I propose, which I shall refer to as general X-efficiency theory. (For a detailed exposition of these ideas, see Leibenstein (1976, chaps. 5–10.)

Postulates and Basic Variables	*Conventional Microtheory*	*General X-Efficiency Theory*
1. Behavioral postulate	1. Maximization or minimization	1. Selective rationality
2. Units	2. Households and firms	2. Individuals
3. Efforts	3. Assumed given	3. Discretionary variable
4. Interpersonal interactions	4. None	4. Some
5. Inert areas	5. None	5. Important variable
6. Agent-principal relationship	6. Identity of interests	6. Differential interests
7. Motivation as an output	7. Assumed given	7. Significant variable

The basic assumption behind my theory is that people work out a compromise between the way they would like to behave, in the absence of constraints, and the way they would like to see themselves behave in terms of their standards of behavior, or superego. Under selective rationality, individuals do not pursue opportunities for gain to the maximum degree given the constraints, nor do they optimize the pursuit of information. In other words, they select the degree of constraint concern their personalities dictate.

The cost of ignoring constraints is a feeling of pressure. This pressure may be in part the result of ignoring consequences and one's desires to behave in accordance with one's internalized standards (superego). Thus, individuals "choose" a compromise position between *pressures* and *a degree of constraint concern* to operate at a psychologically comfortable level. This implies, first, that individuals do not necessarily or usually pursue gains to be obtained from an opportunity to a maximum degree; and, second, *maximizing behavior is a special case in this system.* The specific compromise an individual makes between the competing demands of his id (unconstrained desires), and his superego (standards), on the average, may be viewed as an index of his personality. If he yields too much to his superego, he will feel pressure to behave in terms of less constraint, and if he behaves with too little constraint he will feel the pressure of his conscience. Thus personality and context select, so to speak, the degree of rationality that will control an individual's decision-making (and performing) behavior. The context may contain strong countervailing pressures to increase the degree to which an individual approaches maximizing behavior.

Since motivation is extremely important in determining behavior, we have to take into account interpersonal interactions and especially peer group interactions that determine the system of approval and disapproval, which in its turn influences choices. At the same time, the distinction between principals and agent is extremely important in such contexts, since if effort is a variable there is no reason to presume that the interests of the agent and the principal are identical. Many choices are carried out by agents, but there is no reason to assume that the agent puts forth the same degree of effort that the principal would in similar circumstances.

An important element in our system of analysis is the concept of inert areas. As its name suggests, this is akin to the notion of inertia. Individuals are presumed to choose effort positions (a set of related effort options) in interpreting their jobs or roles in specific contexts. The basic idea is that once an effort position exists for some time period, an individual may not shift to a new position even though a gain may be achieved thereby, because the cost of moving from one effort position to another is larger than the perceived gain. Thus, individuals may find themselves stuck within inert areas even though, apart from the cost of moving, superior effort positions may exist even from the individual's viewpoint.

In what follows, the idea of inert areas will be used to examine some of the basic notions in the Easterlin/Pollak/Wachter paper in order to illustrate how they could fit into a nonmaximizing framework. Given the space constraints, we can only vaguely suggest how it all works out. Now inert areas are made up of two components: a segment that expresses some aspects of selective rationality (e.g., ignoring very careful calculation), and another segment that involves the cost of moving from one position to another.

Natural Fertility

We may visualize natural fertility as being based on routine behavior patterns utilizing a traditional mix of population controls. These routine behavior patterns are presumed to operate within an inert area. They do not change unless pressure is exerted beyond some minimum level. Thus, natural fertility would not be interpreted here to imply some maximal level of fertility, nor would it imply a complete lack of population controls, including nonmechanical means of contraception (e.g., coitus interruptus); rather, it would imply a situation before the introduction of modern contraceptive means. Thus a situation frequently found in developing countries before sustained fertility decline could be fitted into the natural fertility idea. The transition between the natural fertility state and the partially controlled state would then be observed as pressure increases sufficiently to induce some people to adopt additional controls.

Tastes

The concept of the transmission of taste from one generation to another can also be interpreted in terms of the inert area principle. Up to a point, the inherited taste pattern would persist, but as modernization creates pressures for new tastes and consequent consumption patterns that compete significantly with children, we would expect the old tastes to yield to some degree. Furthermore, we would expect the existing tastes at any one time to be the product of inherited tastes as well as peer-group influences, to the degree that peers adopt modern consumption standards. As fertility declines, a conflict is created between the inherited tastes and the peer group influences, and the rate at which there is a shift from one to the other would be determined by the size of the inert areas.

Techniques of Control

Like the above, techniques of control could also be interpreted through the inert area framework. Namely, the set of controls normally used would be surrounded by inert areas; but, as sufficient pressure is generated and new techniques are introduced, the new techniques gradually become part of the option set of the techniques available. Those with the narrowest inert areas are likely to become the initial adopters. (For an innovation adoption model along these lines, see Leibenstein [1976, pp. 234–39].) One could visualize a variety of stages between old techniques and new ones, representing different degrees of knowledge and confidence. We would not expect that the new techniques to become part of the demand for control until they become noticed, generally known, and tried.

Rationality Increase as a Factor in Fertility Determination

The existing theory does not allow for changes in degrees of rationality in determining eventual fertility decline. Clearly, if a maximizing model is used, this forecloses any increase in rationality. But the degree of rationality may depend on the diffusion of responsibility within which the nuclear family finds itself. Thus, if the nuclear family is part of an extended family in which there is considerable diffusion of responsibility for children and for economic well-being of household members, then there will be little pressure toward a high degree of rationality. As we obtain a shift toward the nuclear family as a separate independent unit and responsibility for economic welfare of the household becomes concentrated, then there is likely to be increased pressure for rational behavior. Exogenous influences, such as the gradual spread of secularization through modern education, will also result in an increase in rationality. In particular, as nuclear families become more responsible for their own welfare, the inert areas that surround their critical choice variables become narrower, and hence they respond to pressure with less inertia.

Comment Warren C. Sanderson

Economic theory teaches us that competition among producers usually benefits consumers. Competition among producers of economic models of fertility behavior is no different. Even though the market is dominated

Warren C. Sanderson is associated with the Department of Economics at Stanford University.

by two large producers, the Pennsylvania school and the "Chicago-Columbia" school, the contest to produce a model that more economists would buy has resulted not only in a substantial improvement in the models themselves, but in a number of valuable "spinoff" developments as well.[1] This essay by Easterlin, Pollak, and Wachter is the formal presentation of the 1976 Pennsylvania school model with a full description of all its novel features and a discussion of why it is superior to what the competition has to offer.

The paper focuses on three features of the new model: "endogenous preferences," supply side factors, and consideration of behavior under imperfect information. I shall comment briefly on each of the three.

"Endogenous preferences" is not a new feature of the 1976 Pennsylvania school model. Quite the contrary, it has been standard equipment on Pennsylvania school models since 1966.[2] What motivates its discussion in the paper, then, is not its novelty, but the manner in which the competition has reacted to its introduction. The members of the Chicago-Columbia school not only have refused to incorporate this feature into their own models, they have positively rejected it as being dangerous to the health of economic theory.

Before continuing the discussion of the "endogenous preferences" specification, it is useful to note that the contending models are not nearly so different as their producers might lead us to suppose. First of all, in the context of a single generation, preferences are just as *exogenous* in the 1976 Pennsylvania school model as they are in any of the Chicago-Columbia school models. Current preferences and behavior are not simultaneously determined in the models of either large producer.

There is a difference between the two types of models when dealing with fertility change over the course of several generations. In the Pennsylvania school models since 1966, preferences change generation by generation in a manner determined within the model. Until recently this stood in sharp contrast to the Chicago-Columbia school models, which maintained that preferences were invariant over time. With the publication of Stigler and Becker (1977) even this difference narrowed. Stigler and Becker argued that tastes are truly invariant, but that household production structures vary over time and space. Therefore consumers now seem to have a choice between a model that deals with intergenerational fertility changes within a framework in which preferences vary and the household production structure does not, and a framework in which the household production structure varies and preferences do not.

That preferences vary both across time and across cultures is plausible enough. Certainly, as the authors argue, this view should not be discarded on theoretical grounds. The same can be said, however, with regard to household production structures. Perhaps one day a combination model will be produced.

The second aspect of the 1976 Pennsylvania school model featured in the paper is concern with the biological aspects of fertility behavior. In section 2.2 a births function and a deaths function are introduced into a formal economic model of fertility, and in section 2.3 the concepts of natural fertility and the difference between desired and achieved fertility are incorporated into an economic framework. Again, the best context in which to understand these contributions is that of the competition between the two rival schools of economists. Scholars have produced substantial bodies of literature on the biological determinants of fertility and on the biological and behavioral correlates of infant mortality. These go far beyond anything found in this paper. One contribution of the 1976 model, then, is the integration of past demographic findings into an economic context. Demographers may find little new here, but in the competition between the two large producers, the Pennsylvania school has scored a success in aligning itself somewhat more closely with the results of previous demographic research.

In the same vein, section 2.3 can best be read as criticism of the competition for not incorporating the biological aspects of fertility behavior into their formal model. Without this perspective, a substantial portion of that section may seem rather puzzling. For example, a long argument is made to demonstrate that there are indeed some contemporary cultures in which the volitional practice of fertility control is virtually absent; but there are very few social scientists, if there are any at all, who would contest this point. The rationale of the argument becomes clear when it is viewed as a warning to economists not to use other models in those contexts where the biological aspects of fertility are likely to be important.

The third aspect of the 1976 Pennsylvania school model highlighted in the paper is the notion of behavior under imperfect information. Each couple is viewed as choosing a pattern of goods consumption, time allocation, fertility, and infant mortality that, subject to resource and technology constraints, maximizes their utility. The problem with adopting this view naively, as the authors point out, is that people are often ignorant of the consequences on fertility and infant mortality of various seemingly unrelated aspects of their behavior. To make their model more realistic, the authors suggest that couples be treated as if they maximized their utility subject to their resources, household technology, and possibly incorrect beliefs about the determinants of their experience of fertility and infant mortality. These couples are then assumed to maintain all other aspects of their behavior invariant even though the resulting family size is different from the one they anticipated.

This specification has two serious drawbacks. The first, mentioned by the authors in a note, is that consumption and time allocation should depend on actual family size as opposed to a hypothetical family size that never materializes. The second problem is more technical in nature. Since the family's consumption alternatives may depend on the earnings of children, it may not be possible to hold all other aspects of behavior constant when the actual family size is substantially below the anticipated one. In economic argot, the procedure proposed in the paper to deal with the problem of imperfect information is not guaranteed to result in feasible solutions. New models often have bugs in them, and I am confident that future technological advances will result in a preferable treatment of behavior under imperfect information.

My final comments concern the formal economic model presented in section 2.2 and its relationship to the arguments made in the other sections of the paper. It is important to note here that although the authors present an economic model of fertility behavior, they never use the model in the framework of a comparative statics analysis. This is a bit like creating an intriguing piece of machinery one never intends to use. The art in creating microeconomic behavioral models is in abstracting from all but the most important factors in a given problem so that the analysis of the model results in falsifiable implications. The model in section 2.2 is not constructed on this principle. Instead, it is specified so generally that in its present form it has no unambiguous implications when any of the exogenous variables are altered one at a time.

Since the model is consistent with almost any kind of behavior, it offers no guidance on what is plausible and what is not. For example, in section 2.3 there are three graphs concerning desired fertility—one in which it is drawn as an increasing function of nonlabor income, one in which it is drawn as invariant with respect to socioeconomic status, and one in which it is drawn as either a constant or a decreasing function of social and economic development. The model is certainly consistent with all three graphs. Indeed, the model is consistent with desired fertility being a *decreasing* function of nonlabor income (even if desired fertility is a "normal" good), a *sinosoidal* function of socioeconomic status, and an *inverted U-shaped* function of social and economic development. In other words, the model in section 2.2 has less substantive connection with what is said in the other parts of the paper than one might wish.

In conclusion, then, I reiterate that this paper is the product of a competitive struggle between two rival producers of economic models of fertility behavior. It contains not only explicit criticisms of alternative models, but numerous implicit criticisms. Although some of the arguments may seem either arcane or pointless to the nonspecialist, they are all aimed at perceived weaknesses in the Chicago-Columbia school's product lines.

Will the 1976 Pennsylvania school model come to dominate the market? It is not clear. After all, different people have different tastes/production functions (choose one or both) when it comes to the formulation and use of economic models of fertility behavior.

Notes

1. For example, Easterlin (1974), Sanderson (1974), and Stigler and Becker (1977).

2. Endogenous preferences were first introduced into the Pennsylvania school's models in Easterlin (1966).

References

Ajami, I. 1976. Differential fertility in peasant communities: A study of six Iranian villages. *Population Studies* 30 (November): 453–64.

Anderson, Barbara A., and McCabe, James L. 1977. Nutrition and the fertility of younger women in Kinshasa, Zaire. *Journal of Development Economics* 4 (December): 343–63.

Auster, Richard; Leveson, Irving; and Sarachek, Deborah. 1969. The production of health, an exploratory study. *Journal of Human Resources* 4 (fall): 411–36.

Barlow, Robin. 1967. The economic effects of malaria eradication. *American Economic Review* LVII (May): 130–48.

Barnett, William A. 1977. Pollak and Wachter on the household production function and its implications for the allocation of time. *Journal of Political Economy* 85 (October): 1073–82.

Becker, Gary S. 1960. An economic analysis of fertility. In *Demographic and economic change in developed countries*, ed. Universities-National Bureau Committee for Economic Research, pp. 209–31. Princeton: Princeton University Press.

———. 1965. A theory of the allocation of time. *Economic Journal* 75 (September): 493–517.

Behrman, Jere R. 1968. *Supply response in underdeveloped agriculture: A case study of four major annual crops in Thailand, 1937–1963.* Amsterdam: North Holland Publishing Co.

Ben-Porath, Yoram. 1973. Economic analysis of fertility in Israel: Point and counterpoint. *Journal of Political Economy* 81 (March/April): S202–33.

———. 1975. First generation effects on second generation fertility. *Demography* 12 (August): 397–405.

Ben-Porath, Yoram, and Welch, Finis. 1976. Do sex preferences *really* matter? *Quarterly Journal of Economics* 90 (May): 285–307.

Bumpass, Larry L., and Westoff, Charles F. 1970. The "perfect contraceptive" population. *Science* 169 (18 September): 1177–82.

Caldwell, J. C., and Igun, A. 1972. Anti-natal knowledge and practice in Nigeria. In *Population growth and economic development in Africa*, ed. S. H. Ominde and C. N. Ejiogu, pp. 67–76. London: Heinemann.

Chen, Lincoln C.; Ahmed, Shamsa; Gesche, Melita; and Moseley, W. Henry. 1974. A prospective study of birth interval dynamics in rural Bangladesh. *Population Studies* 28 (July): 277–97.

Chowdhury, A. K. M.; Khan, A. R.; and Chen, L. C. 1976. The effect of child mortality experience on subsequent fertility: Pakistan and Bangladesh. *Population Studies* 30 (July): 249–62.

Coale, Ansley J., and Trussell, T. James. 1974. Model fertility schedules: Variations in the age structure of childbearing in human populations. *Population Index* 40 (April): 185–258.

Crafts, N. F. R., and Ireland, N. J. 1976. Family limitation and the English demographic revolution: A simulation approach. *Journal of Economic History* 36 (September): 598–623.

David, Paul A., and Sanderson, Warren C. 1976. Contraceptive technology and family limiting behavior: Toward a quantitative history of the diffusion of contraceptive practices in America, 1850–1920. Unpublished manuscript.

Easterlin, Richard A. 1966. On the relation of economic factors to recent and projected fertility changes. *Demography* 3(1): 131–53.

———. 1968. *Population, labor force, and long swings in economic growth: The American experience*. New York: National Bureau of Economic Research.

———. 1973. Relative economic status and the American fertility swing. In *Family economic behavior: problems and prospects*, ed. Eleanor B. Sheldon. Philadelphia: J. B. Lippincott.

———. 1974. Does economic growth improve the human lot? In *Nations and households in economic growth: Essays in honor of Moses Abramovitz*, ed. Paul A. David and Melvin W. Reder. New York: Academic Press.

———. 1975. An economic framework for fertility analysis. *Studies in Family Planning* 6 (March): 54–63.

———. 1978. The economics and sociology of fertility: A synthesis. In *Historical studies of changing fertility*, ed. Charles Tilly. Princeton: Princeton University Press.

El-Safty, Ahman E. 1976*a*. Adaptive behavior, demand and preferences. *Journal of Economic Theory* 13 (October): 298–318.

———. 1976*b*. Adaptive behavior and the existence of Weiszäcker's long-run indifference curves. *Journal of Economic Theory* 13 (October): 319–28.

Frisch, Rose E. 1975. Demographic implications of the biological determinants of female fecundity. *Social Biology* 22 (spring): 17–22.

Hammond, Peter J. 1976. Endogenous tastes and stable long-run choice. *Journal of Economic Theory* 13 (October): 329–40.

Heer, David M. 1967. Fertility differences in Andean countries: A reply to W. H. James. *Population Studies* 21 (July): 71–73.

Heisel, Donald F. 1968. *Fertility limitation among women in rural Kenya.* Nairobi: University College, Institute for Development Studies. Discussion Paper 62.

Henin, R. A. 1972. The level and trend of fertility in the Sudan. In *Population growth and economic development in Africa*, ed. S. H. Ominde and C. N. Ejiogu. London: Heinemann.

Hossein, Askari, and Cummings, John Thomas. 1977. Estimating agricultural supply response with the Nerlove model: A survey. *International Economic Review* 18 (June): 257–92.

Howe, Howard; Pollak, Robert A.; and Wales, Terence J. 1977. Theory and time series estimation of the quadratic expenditure system. University of Pennsylvania Discussion Paper #388; *Econometrica*, forthcoming.

Hull, T. H., and Hull, V. J. 1977. The relation of economic class and fertility: An analysis of some Indonesian data. *Population Studies* 31 (March): 43–58.

Jain, Anrudh K., and Sun, T. H. 1972. Interrelationship between socio-demographic factors, lactation, and postpartum amenorrhea. *Demography India* 1 (October): 1–15.

James, William H. 1966. The effect of altitude on fertility in Andean countries. *Population Studies* 20 (July): 97–101.

Keeley, Michael. 1975. A comment on "An interpretation of the economic theory of fertility." *Journal of Economic Literature* 13 (June): 461–67.

Kelley, Allen C. 1976. Review of *Economics of the family: Marriage, children and human capital*, edited by Theodore W. Schultz. *Journal of Economic Literature* 14 (June): 516–20.

Keyfitz, Nathan. 1971. How birth control affects births. *Social Biology* 18 (June): 109–21.

Knodel, John. 1977. Family limitation and the fertility transition: Evidence from the age patterns of fertility in Europe and Asia. *Population Studies* 31 (July): 219–49.

Lancaster, Kelvin J. 1966*a*. Change and innovation in the technology of consumption. *American Economic Review* 56 (May): 14–23.

———. 1966*b*. A new approach to consumer theory. *Journal of Political Economy* 74: 132–57.

———. 1971. *Consumer demand: A new approach.* New York: Columbia University Press.

Lapham, Robert J. 1970. Morocco: Family planning attitudes, knowledge and practice in the Sais Plain. *Studies in Family Planning*, no. 58 (October), pp. 11–22.

Lee, Ronald D. 1976. Demographic forecasting and the Easterlin hypothesis. *Population and Development Review* 2 (September/December): 459–68.

———. 1977. *Fluctuations in U.S. fertility, age structure, and income.* Final Contract Report to NICHHD (August).

Leibenstein, Harvey. 1974*a*. *Economic backwardness and economic growth.* New York: John Wiley.

———. 1974*b*. An interpretation of the economic theory of fertility: Promising path or blind alley? *Journal of Economic Literature* 12 (June): 457–79.

———. 1976. *Beyond economic man.* Cambridge: Harvard University Press.

Leridon, Henri. 1977. *Human fertility: The basic components.* Translated by Judith F. Helzner. Chicago: University of Chicago Press.

Lindert, Peter. 1978. Fertility and scarcity in America. Princeton: Princeton University Press.

Mauldin, W. Parker. 1965. Fertility studies: Knowledge, attitude, and practice. *Studies in Family Planning*, no. 7 (June), pp. 1–10.

Michael, Robert T. 1973. Education in nonmarket production. *Journal of Political Economy* 81 (March/April): 306–27.

Michael, Robert T., and Becker, Gary S. 1973. On the new theory of consumer behavior. *Swedish Journal of Economics* 75 (December): 378–96.

Michael, Robert T., and Willis, Robert J. 1976. Contraception and fertility: Household production under uncertainty. In *Household production and consumption*, Conference on Research in Income and Wealth, pp. 27–94. New York: National Bureau of Economic Research.

Nerlove, Marc. 1974. Household and economy: Toward a new theory of population and economic growth. *Journal of Political Economy* 82 (March/April): S200–218.

Nortman, Dorothy. 1977. Changing contraceptive patterns: A global perspective. *Population Bulletin*, vol. 32, no. 3.

Palmore, James A. 1969. Malaysia: The west Malaysian family survey, 1966–67. *Studies in Family Planning* no. 40 (April): pp. 11–20.

Peng, J. Y. 1965. Thailand: Family growth in Pho-tharam District. *Studies in Family Planning* no. 8 (October), pp. 1–7.

Pollak, Robert A. 1970. Habit formation and dynamic demand functions. *Journal of Political Economy* 78 (July/August): 745–63.

———. 1971. Additive utility functions and linear Engel curves. *Review of Economic Studies* 38 (October): 401–14.

———. 1976*a*. Habit formation and long-run utility functions. *Journal of Economic Theory* 13 (October): 272–97.

———. 1976*b*. Interdependent preferences. *American Economic Review* 66 (June): 309–20.

———. 1977. Price dependent preferences. *American Economic Review* 65 (March): 64–75.

Pollak, Robert A., and Wachter, M. L. 1975. The relevance of the household production function and its implications for the allocation of time. *Journal of Political Economy* 83 (April): 255–77.

———. 1977. Reply: Pollak and Wachter on the household production function approach. *Journal of Political Economy* 85 (October): 1083–86. .

Pollak, Robert A., and Wales, T. J. 1969. Estimation of the linear expenditure system. *Econometrica* 37 (October): 611–28.

Romaniuc, A. 1968. Infertility in tropical Africa. In *The population of tropical Africa*, ed. J. C. Caldwell and C. Okonjo, pp. 214–24. Princeton: Princeton University Press.

———. 1974. Modernization and fertility: The case of the James Bay Indians. *Canadian Review of Sociology and Anthropology* 11 (no. 4): 344–59.

Samuelson, Paul A. 1956. Social indifference curves. *Quarterly Journal of Economics* 70 (February): 1–22.

Sanderson, Warren C. 1974. Does the theory of demand need the maximum principle? In *Nations and households in economic growth: Essays in honor of Moses Abramovitz*, ed. Paul A. David and Melvin W. Reder. New York: Academic Press.

Schultz, T. Paul. 1976. Determinants of fertility: A micro-economic model of choice. In *Economic factors in population growth*, ed. Ansley J. Coale, pp. 89–124. New York: Halsted Press.

Schultz, Theodore W., ed. 1974. *Economics of the family: Marriage, children and human capital*. Chicago and London: NBER.

Sen, Amartya. 1973. *On economic inequality*. Oxford: Oxford University Press.

Singarimbun, Masri, and Manning, Chris. 1976. Breastfeeding, amenorrhea, and abstinence in a Javanese village: A case study of Mojolama. *Studies in Family Planning* 7 (June): 175–79.

Stigler, George J., and Becker, Garry S. 1977 De gustibus non est disputandum. *American Economic Review* 67 (March): 76–90.

Tabbarah, Riad B. 1971. Toward a theory of demographic development. *Economic Development and Cultural Change* 19 (January): 257–77.

Taylor, C. E.; Newman, J. S.; and Kelly, Narindar U. 1976. The child survival hypothesis. *Population Studies* 30 (July): 263–78.

United Nations Department of Economic and Social Affairs. 1961. *The Mysore population study*. Population Studies no. 34. New York: United Nations.

von Weiszäcker, Carl Christian. 1971. Notes on endogenous change of tastes. *Journal of Economic Theory* 3 (December): 345–72.

Wachter, Michael L. 1972*a*. Government policy towards the fertility of the poor. Fels Center of Government Discussion Paper no. 19.

———. 1972*b*. A labor supply model for secondary workers. *Review of Economics and Statistics* 54 (May): 141–51.

———. 1974. A new approach to the equilibrium labor force. *Economica* 41 (February): 35–51.

———. 1975. A time series fertility equation: The potential for a baby boom in the 1980s. *International Economic Review* 16 (October): 609–24.

Wales, Terence J. 1971. A generalized linear expenditure model of the demand for non-durable goods in Canada. *Canadian Journal of Economics* 4 (November): 471–84.

3 Child Mortality and Fertility: Issues in the Demographic Transition of a Migrant Population

Yoram Ben-Porath

3.1 Introduction

The relationship between child mortality and fertility is central in explaining the transition of European populations from high to low levels of fertility. The recent decline in child mortality in several less developed countries has caused a renewed interest in this relationship, and several cross-sectional studies have tried to sharpen some of the issues concerning it.

Several cross-sectional studies have found statistically significant relationships between fertility and child mortality. Some interpret this evidence as indicating a fairly strong and rapid response that would not predict a long lag between turning points in aggregate fertility series after the onset of declining mortality (Schultz 1975). Others tend to view the evidence as showing modest to small response (Preston 1975*a*). As to the aggregate experience over time, there is no dispute concerning the long and variable (across individual countries) lag in the decline in fertility relative to the decline in mortality in Europe. As far as the less developed countries of today are concerned, while Taylor, Newman, and Kelly (1976) (and United Nations 1974) indicate a shorter lag than historically observed, Kuznets (1974), examining the aggregate

Yoram Ben-Porath is professor of economics at the Hebrew University of Jerusalem.

I thank W. Butz, J. DaVanzo, E. Van der Walle, S. Freund, S. Kuznets, J. P. Smith, and A. Williams for helpful comments on earlier drafts and the staff of the Demographic Section of the Central Bureau of Statistics of Israel for providing me with the data sources. I carry sole responsibility for the paper and the data. I draw here on my work at the Falk Institute for Economic Research in Israel. The paper was prepared under a grant from the Rockefeller Foundation to the Rand Corporation.

time series of LDCs, emphasizes the sluggishness in the response of fertility to the decline in child mortality.[1]

In this paper I consider the experience of the foreign-born population of Israel from this perspective. Immigration to Israel constituted a sharp change in conditions that is a dramatically speeded-up version of economic and social development for those immigrating from the less developed countries of Asia and Africa. There is no way to assess how much the responses to a shock like this can tell about processes of more continuous change—potentially this can either sharpen what is otherwise confounded with other things or bring out "anomalies" that would make it so unique as to be uninteresting.

In section 3.2 I briefly review some of the main issues in the child-mortality/fertility relationship, then in section 3.3 I present cross-sectional regression models based on the analysis of the experience of individual foreign-born women in Israel. In section 3.4, using mostly the same data, I infer what happened over time abroad and following immigration, then try to fit this together with the cross-sectional findings.

3.2 Some General Issues

Here let me summarize some of the main issues with respect to the mechanism relating fertility to child mortality (see also Schultz 1975; Preston 1975*a*).

3.2.1 Replacement versus Hoarding

The reaction of fertility to child mortality can take two forms: replacement, a sequential response to a death, and what is described as hedging or hoarding—the response to *expected* mortality. If mortality of offspring were only infant mortality, and if there were no fecundity constraints on the number of successful pregnancies, replacement would be the superior mode of response.

The need for hoarding arises when there is a danger of not attaining the desired number of surviving children of the right age and at the right time. Offspring who die as adults may not be replaced by the same mother because she is too old (or has died); or, even if they can be replaced, they would not be available as earners contributing to family income at the necessary time. Situations like this involve uncertainty concerning the number and age distribution of surviving children along the parental life cycle. Hoarding is a natural strategy to cope with the problem, particularly if one has a view of the demand for children as being of the "at least (so many children/sons)" type. It should, however, be stressed that hoarding implies not only a higher expected cost of surviving children, but also higher risk that disposable income will be "too low" for parental or per capita consumption if the number of surviving children is ex post facto "too large." (Such a risk may be more tolerable with higher income, and this may itself lead to a direct relationship between births and income, for a given level of expected child mortality.)

The distinction between replacement and hoarding is important for at least two reasons: (*a*) quantitatively, the effect on fertility of hoarding in order to achieve a given target is greater than that of replacement (O'Hara 1972*b*); (*b*) replacement is a quick response, and it is natural to expect replacement to generate a close, short-lagged, association between fertility and child mortality. Hoarding, based as it is on expectations, may respond sluggishly to child mortality, depending on the speed at which expected mortality is revised as actual mortality changes.

Classical demographic transition, reflecting a lag of several decades before the decline in aggregate child mortality is followed by a decline in aggregate fertility, would be consistent with the importance of hoarding, but the long lag in aggregate series could also result from a combination of replacement and some countervailing force.

The issue is whether hoarding can be quantitatively distinguished from replacement and, if not, what can be said about the likely dominant mechanism behind the coefficients estimated in cross-sectional studies. These obvious things have to be noted: (1) To the extent that expected mortality is shared by the observation analyzed, obviously it is not reflected in fertility differences and is thus silent. (2) To the extent that expected mortality is strongly correlated with experienced mortality (and any attempt to estimate expected mortality will have to rely heavily on experienced mortality), it cannot be distinguished from replacement. (3) Similarly, to the extent that variables other than experienced mortality affect expected mortality, if they also affect fertility directly, the effect of expected mortality would be confounded with these direct effects. (4) Hoarding may have its larger effect on age at marriage.

In a cross section of countries or regions or social classes, the sample observations are likely to differ in expected mortality, so that hoarding has a chance to contribute to the explanation of differential fertility. This contribution will, however, be empirically expressed through experienced mortality and other variables (schooling, income, etc.) in the fertility equation. The effect of hoarding is based on the reciprocal of surviving probability and should be larger than that of replacement; so in this type of data we should expect larger coefficients if hoarding is indeed important.

In a cross section of households in one country, all shared expectations are, of course, silenced. If people tend to infer from excessive experienced mortality that their future children are less likely to survive, then the estimated effect of experienced mortality includes some hoarding. Obviously, some of the differences in experienced mortality are systematic, depending on permanent health and environmental characteristics of parents and households. Such factors may operate for more than one generation and reinforce the correlation between expected and experienced mortality. The variables that enter the fertility equations for other reasons will carry some of these effects. In general the correlation between experienced and expected mortality is likely to diminish as the data are more disaggregated. It is also reasonable to expect that in studies where experienced mortality and, say, schooling are included—and particularly where the data are organized sequentially—the coefficient of experienced mortality expresses mostly a replacement mechanism. If hoarding is important, then in a cross section of countries the coefficients of mortality should be larger (in absolute terms) than those of the household studies; and in household studies the coefficient of experienced mortality should be greatly affected by introduction of those other variables. (For a recent attempt to identify hoarding by direct questions on expected mortality see Heer and Wu 1975.)

3.2.2 Rigid and Revised Targets

The simple way of looking at child mortality and fertility is to take a given objective in terms of desired number of children (or sons) and ask how many births are required to attain at least this number of surviving children (with a given level of certainty). The level of experienced or expected child mortality may also affect the target, and the relationship between fertility and child mortality is the net outcome of the effect of mortality on the desired number (or rather profile) of surviving children and the effect of mortality on the number of births necessary to reach the target.

The *experience* of child mortality by itself is analogous to a loss of real income. This loss is likely to increase with the age of the child at death. Targets would be revised according to the relevant income elasticities. The less income-elastic the demand for children (and the lower the income loss associated with the death), the more complete should replacement be. Less than full replacement may occur near the attainment of the (revised) desired number of surviving children, or, more likely, the revision may be distributed over the life cycle, letting the whole time profile of surviving children absorb the downward revision. Some evidence for that is provided in Rutstein (1974) and Ben-Porath (1976*b*).

Expected mortality affects the price of children and generates both an income and a substitution effect against surviving children. If children were to die only after the full parental expenditure on them has been made, then we could say that the elasticity of the number of births with respect to the survival rate (η_{ns}) equals $-(1 + \eta_{n\pi})$, where $\eta_{n\pi}$ is the demand elasticity for children. This would mean that if the demand for children has an elasticity larger than unity, the response of fertility to increased survival would be direct because the increased demand for survivors increases births by more than the decline in the number of births necessary for one survivor. If we remind ourselves, however, that most of child mortality is infant mortality and only a fraction γ of expenditures on children who would survive is spent on children who do not survive, then this equation becomes $\eta_{ns} = -(1 + \eta_{n\pi}\gamma)$, which implies that the elasticity of demand will have to be larger (in absolute terms) than $1/\gamma$ in order for fertility to respond favorably to increased survival (declining mortality). For reasonable values of γ, the demand for children is not likely to be elastic enough for this condition to be fulfilled. (Incidentally, this would mean that it is incorrect to infer from an inverse relationship between fertility and mortality that the demand for children is inelastic.)

All this rests on the premise that the demand for surviving children in fact will rise when child mortality declines, which is rather inescapable if expenditures on children are treated as an exogenous price.

However, this is not clear if, as argued by O'Hara (1972*a*) and others, there is a substitution from numbers of children to quality as mortality declines; or, as argued by Kuznets (1973, 1974), there is a shift from human lottery to human capital. Under certain conditions it is then possible, but not necessary, that the demand for *surviving* children will decline as mortality declines.[2] It may be reasonable to suggest that the revisions of desired number of surviving children that are related to changing expenditure patterns lag behind this more "technical" response.

The pure effects of the uncertainty associated with high child mortality are difficult to tackle. An attempt to guarantee a given number of survivors is associated, as already indicated, with greater risks concerning the consumption levels of the parents and the children, so that it may reduce the demand for children unless demand is indeed asymmetrically biased toward "at least" a given number of children. Note, however, that where high mortality prevails other risks are greater, so nothing firm can be said here.

3.2.3 Partial versus Global Effects

The discussion of the effects of infant or child mortality on fertility in most microdata (including this study) does not deal explicitly with some associated developments that may lead to quantitative discrepancies—perhaps even to the extent of a change in direction—between the temporal relationships and the partial cross-sectional estimates.

Although the trends of declining mortality do not occur uniformly along the age profile of mortality, the rapid declines in mortality that have occurred in LDCs in the last few decades have not been confined to children (Stolnitz 1974). The increase in parental life expectancy, unlike the increase in the survival of children, is on the whole likely to be pronatal. First, supply considerations: fewer mothers die when they are still in the childbearing period; fewer marriages are dissolved by the husband's death, and thus the loss of time between marriages and early cessation of pregnancies owing to widowhood are reduced (Ryder 1975). Parental health that improves with declining mortality may increase fecundity (see United Nations 1974; Stolnitz 1974; Sheps and Ridley 1965). Second, demand considerations: the discussion of old-age support is couched in terms of how many births are required to guarantee at least one son for the father when he is, say, 65. Whatever the merits of this, its implications for demand surely depend on the probability that the father will survive to age 65. As mortality declines, the probability that children will survive to a *given* parental age rises more than the probability that they will outlive their parents. As mortality declines, some parents may be afraid that they will survive their children. The issue is not just that of having one surviving supporter, but also that of spreading the heavier burden of support implied by the longer period among more children. This is a partial effect and is likely to be less important in the long run than the simultaneous decline in the desired number of surviving children and the rise in investment in human capital. But the timing of the responses may differ, and we cannot rule out the possibility that at some initial phase the positive effects on demand would stand out.

Beyond this, we have the obvious problem of the correlation between the decline in mortality and other aspects of economic and social change. Other variables may either strengthen or eliminate the effect of declining mortality on fertility, and the relationship between mortality and other variables relevant for fertility varies over time and place and may be different in cross-sectional data and time-series data.

3.2.4 Reverse Causality

The death of children is not necessarily given to the families but rather can be a result of behavior. Parents have discretion as to the amount of care they devote to protecting children from common causes of death, in particular gastrointestinal illnesses. The endogenous element in the decline in child mortality in Europe may have been substantial (Shorter 1975). In our data there is a strong relationship between child mortality and parental schooling. (We have examples of increased child mortality when women have left the house for work and delegated infant care to the older children.) In some cases infant mortality is just another way of regulating family size, where the control of the number of pregnancies is complicated. Thus, families who find themselves with more children than they want would let excess infants die off. Except for some cursory remarks, I shall not deal with this possibility here (see Kelley, this volume, chap. 7).

3.2.5 Behavior versus Physiology

In the economic-demographic literature there is a distinction between demand and supply factors in the explanation of fertility (see, e.g., Easterlin 1975). Sometimes biological or physiological factors are the dominant determinant of fertility—natural fertility being the effective constraint on the number of births. The postpartum sterility accompanying lactation reduces the number of possible pregnancies. Infant mortality and the interruption of breast-feeding raise the possible number of pregnancies and perhaps the number of live births (Knodel 1968; Jain et al. 1970). When fewer children are desired than would result from uncontrolled fertility, the explanation of fertility response to child mortality must be sought within a demand framework. In the gray area between supply and demand there are social customs that may act as constraints on individual behavior but that in the long run are themselves shaped by the needs of individuals. Breast-feeding customs may belong here, and thus the effect of mortality on fertility via lactation may in part depend on demand considerations. In general we can assume that in populations of low fertility demand considerations are dominant. It is hard to distinguish between supply and demand factors in populations that have high fertility.

But the issue is broader than that. The incidence of child mortality is likely to be correlated with nutrition and health of the mother, which in turn may affect fecundability. Age at menarche is associated with levels of nutrition, and certain diseases affect fecundity within marriage and pregnancy wastage. There is no reason to assume that there is some stable relationship between all these supply effects. It could well be that measures that result in a decline in child death rates directly affect fecundability in some situations more than others. As we will see later, this is an issue of some importance in the present context.

3.3 Micro Cross-sectional Data of the 1961 Census

The 1961 census of population in Israel included a 20% sample of households for which a detailed questionnaire on economic and demographic matters was completed. The unique feature of this population is that most of the adult women were foreign-born and that there is a large population of women who were married before immigration and had had some children abroad. Sample size is large enough to allow separate analyses by woman's country of birth, thus providing the opportunity to do a quasi-international study with a homogeneous body of data. The important pieces of information for our purposes are the number of births that took place in Israel (BIS), the number of births abroad (BAB) (before immigration), and the number of children born abroad who died before they were five years old (DAB). We know the woman's age when she immigrated and her age at the time of the census; there is no information on the age and sex of the children.

The population considered covers a broad spectrum of countries of origin. Immigration from Asia and Africa was mostly from the Arab countries of the Middle East and North Africa and from Turkey and Iran, with mean levels of completed fertility abroad of approximately six or seven children, of which approximately one out of three or four died by the age of 5. The immigrants classified here as European and American are mostly from Eastern and Central Europe, with completed fertility abroad of two or three children, of which one in seven or eight died by the age of 5. Large, though somewhat narrower, differences are also present in fertility in Israel after immigration.

We can get an initial impression of the mortality-fertility relationship by examining a cross-tabulation of births in Israel by age at immigration and the number of births and deaths that occurred abroad, distinguishing between immigrants from countries in Asia and Africa and those from countries in Europe and America (table 3.1). The number 0.933 in column 2 and row 2–1 means that women who were 25–29 of age when they immigrated and who had had two births abroad (BAB), had 0.933 more children in Israel (ΔBIS) if two of their children died abroad rather than one (2–1). What emerges from the table is the following: (*a*) women with a given number of births abroad (BAB) had more children in Israel if they had lost one or more of the children born abroad; (*b*) the response of fertility to child mortality is in some cases greater than unity, particularly among young women and at low birth orders; (*c*) the particular response to the death of one child tended to be lower for women who were past the mid-thirties when they immigrated; (*d*) given the woman's age at immigration, the response to a death is lower, the greater the number of births she had had before immigration; (*e*) the response to the second or third death of a child is often negative; (*f*) the response of women born in Asia or Africa (AA) is greater than that of women born in Europe or America (EA).

I am concerned mainly not with examining the determinants of desired fertility but rather with the effect of child mortality on fertility. Still, it is impossible to ignore the fact that joint determinants of both may create an inflated impression of the effect of one on the other (even if we go on ignoring the possible causality from fertility to mortality).

The equations estimated include schooling categories of the mother (dummy variables), place of birth of the mother (continent or country), and age variables (age at immigration and age at the time of the census).

The age variables are not attached to the occurrence of a vital event; absence of such information is a drawback of this body of data.

Deaths abroad (DAB) and births abroad (BAB) are introduced into two functional forms: a free-form discrete interaction model (model I; with separate dummy variable for each DAB BAB combination) and a restricted continuous interaction form (model II).[3]

There is no control for child mortality in Israel. The level has been very low, but it is quite clear that it is correlated with child mortality abroad, so that its absence can generate an upward bias in the coefficient of DAB.

In table 3.2, results of model I are presented for women who were 30–34 at immigration and above 40 in 1961, classified in two categories

Table 3.1 **Difference in Births in Israel (△BIS) between Women (aged 40+ in 1961) with Different Numbers of Deaths Abroad (△DAB), by Woman's Continent of Birth, Age at Immigration, and Births Abroad (BAB)**

Age at Immigration and △DAB	Births Abroad (BAB)						
	1	2	3	4	5	6	7
			Women Born in Asia-Africa				
20–24							
1–0		0.236					
2–1							
3⁺–2							
25–29							
1–0	1.031	1.829	1.316	0.222	0.590		
2–1		0.933	−0.116	0.401	−0.223		
3⁺–2				0.635	0.656		
30–34							
1–0	1.740	1.526	0.881	1.289	0.293	0.533	0.321
2–1		1.576	1.039	0.143	0.328	0.242	−0.170
3⁺–2			0.869	−1.106	0.769	−0.053	−0.377
35–39							
1–0	0.127	−0.698	0.662	0.573	0.539	0.234	0.084
2–1				0.701	0.254	0.333	0.033
3⁺–2				−0.167	0.725	0.228	−0.333
40–44							
1–0		1.967	0.079	0.354	0.174	−0.049	0.131
2–1					−0.085	0.656	−0.097
3⁺–2					1.985	−0.304	−0.025
45–49							
1–0			0.320	0.550	−0.261	0.939	0.021
2–1							−0.030
3⁺–2							

Table 3.1 (continued)

Age at Immigration and △DAB	Births Abroad (BAB) 1	2	3	4	5	6	7
	Women Born in Europe-America						
20–24							
1–0	1.490						
2–1							
3⁺–2							
25–29							
1–0	0.885	0.932	0.755				
2–1		0.852	−0.158				
3⁺–2							
30–34							
1–0	0.884	0.752	0.035	−0.653			
2–1			−0.804				
3⁺–2							
35–39							
1–0	0.602	0.438	0.182	−0.550			
2–1		0.457	0.117	0.145			
3⁺–2							
40–44							
1–0	0.167	0.094	−0.060	0.138	0.024		
2–1			0.143	−0.190	−0.087		
3⁺–2					0.105		
45–49							
1–0	0.092	−0.006	0.024	−0.044	0.083		
2–1		0.200	0.567	0.205			
3⁺–2							

Source: Based on unpublished CBS data from the 1961 Census of Population.
Note: Foreign-born women, married abroad, married once, and with at least one birth abroad.

by place of birth. There is some reduction in the estimated "effect" of mortality on fertility compared with the tabulations, but essentially the same picture remains true (in spite of the fact that women's education is correlated with fertility and child mortality).

The aggregation of all countries of origin by continent may be too crude given the heterogeneity of the individual countries. Looking now at all women who immigrated when they were ages 15–49 and running separate regressions for each country, pooled with dummy variables for each country and pooled without dummy variables, we see that the country differences turn out to be statistically significant.[4] Most of the country differences are captured by the dummy variables, though the contri-

Table 3.2 **Difference in Births in Israel (△BIS) between Women (aged 30–34 at Immigration and 40+ in 1961) with Different Numbers of Deaths Abroad (△DAB), by Continent of Birth and Births Abroad: Regression Results of an Interaction Model**

△DAB	Births Abroad (BAB)							
	1	2	3	4	5	6	7	8
			Women Born in Asia-Africa					
1–0	1.427	1.201	0.743	1.025	0.084	0.534	0.508	0.038
2–1		1.470	0.793	0.353	0.365		−0.067	0.094
3^{+}–2			1.006	−1.069	0.541		−0.682	−0.258
Mean DAB = 1.1		Mean BAB = 4.7		$R^2 = 0.327$			Observations 866	
			Women Born in Europe-America					
1–0	0.877	0.700	0.036	−0.623	0.100			
2–1		0.266	0.761	0.404	−0.504			
3^{+}–2			0.770	0.685	−0.238			
Mean DAB = 0.2		Mean BAB = 1.7		$R^2 = 0.158$			Observations 1,474	

Note: Foreign-born women, married abroad, married once, and with at least one birth abroad.

Other variables in the regression: woman's age at immigration, age in 1961, and years of schooling (six categories, dummy variables); and dummy variables for country of birth (seven countries in Asia-Africa, six in Europe-America).

The figures are differences in the coefficients of dummy variables. Where no figure appears, it is because at least one of the coefficients did not pass a critical (low) level of significance.

bution of separate coefficients by country is statistically significant. (This is based upon model II.)

Examining both the regression coefficients and the derivatives of BIS with respect to DAB, we find the following (table 3.3): (1) The responses to DAB and BAB are significant and in the expected direction in both continent groups (AA and EA). (2) There is a negative interaction between BAB and DAB that implies that the response of births in Israel to child mortality abroad is smaller, the greater the number of births abroad. (3) For any given BAB and DAB combination, the response to child deaths abroad is greater among AA women than among EA women, but, if we calculate the response close to the mean level of fertility (BAB = 4 for AA and BAB = 2 for EA), the response of EA women is slightly higher (because of the significant interaction between BAB and DAB). (4) The country dummy variables in the pooled regression indicate that women from Libya and Algeria and Tunisia have significantly higher fertility in Israel and women from Egypt significantly lower than would be indicated by their experience abroad, education, and age (there is some variation in EA as well). (5) The response to child deaths around mean fertility is in the range 0.3–0.5 in the individual AA countries and goes up to 0.6 in EA. All these magnitudes are somewhat higher in the regressions confined to women aged 30–34 at immigration and aged 40+ in 1961, ranging from 0.35 to 0.71 for AA and going up to 0.8 for EA (now shown). Model I, which (as in table 3.2) does not constrain the functional form of the interaction (see table 3.A.1) was run separately for each country and shows that the response to one death in the low birth orders is in some countries above one. (6) The magnitude of the coefficient of experienced mortality in the regressions for the continents is not larger than in regressions for individual countries.

What do these findings suggest? The similarity between magnitude in the pooled and country regressions may be interpreted to mean one of two things: (1) Hoarding is not that important; this is based on the conjecture that expected mortality should be more closely associated with experienced mortality across countries than across individuals in the same country. (2) Given that the dependent variable is fertility in Israel, in a regime of much lower and uniform child mortality, past experience has been discarded as a predictor of future survival.

That even the low fertility immigrants from Europe show a high response indicates that demand-based mechanisms are very important. It may still be true that supply mechanisms are important in the Asian and African populations, and this may explain the somewhat higher coefficient (per parity) in AA. The variation in coefficients among individual countries is not consistent with the U-shaped relationships observed by Preston (1975*b*) as one moves from what he describes as

Table 3.3 **Effect on Births in Israel (BIS) of Births Abroad (BAB) and Deaths Abroad (DAB): Regression Model II (Women Aged 15–49 at Immigration)**

Woman's Country and Continent of Birth	Regression Coefficients of[a]					Derivative of BIS with respect to DAB at $D_{AB} = 1$ and		R^2	Number of Observations
	DAB	DAB^2	DAB ×BAB	BAB	BAB^2	BAB = 2	DAB = 4		
Asia-Africa	0.921 2·0	0.004 0·7	−0.116 15·5	−0.329 35·9	0.013 4·1	0.697	0.465	0.485	74,426
Algeria and Tunisia	0.833 6·4	0.014 1·0	−0.116 4·9	−0.273 2·8	0.018 1·7	0.513	0.397	0.527	697
Egypt and Sudan	1.106 6·2	0.012 0·5	−0.155 4·4	−0.145 1·5	0.013 1·1	0.820	0.510	0.364	602
Iran	0.982 6·7	−0.011 0·5	−0.110 14·0	−0.547 5·0	0.025 2·1	0.740	0.520	0.459	619
Iraq	1.053 12·0	0.005 0·5	−0.130 8·7	−0.390 7·3	0.019 3·3	0.803	0.543	0.486	2,068
Libya	0.894 5·7	0.012 0·5	−0.117 3·9	−0.354 2·8	0.014 1·0	0.684	0.450	0.561	543
Morocco and Tangier	0.606 8·0	—[b]	−0.073 7·4	−0.067 1·3	−0.010 1·9	0.557	0.314	0.471	1,989
Yemen and Aden	0.777 6·8	−0.008 0·5	−0.080 3·1	−0.557 5·1	0.013 1·0	0.601	0.441	0.465	908

Table 3.3 (continued)

Woman's Country and Continent of Birth	Regression Coefficients of[a]					Derivative of BIS with respect to DAB at $D_{AB} = 1$ and		R^2	Number of Obser-vations
	DAB	DAB^2	DAB ×BAB	BAB	BAB^2	BAB = 2	DAB = 4		
Europe-America	0.674 22.8	0.061 5.9	−0.154 13.9	−0.372 16.9	0.051 13.3	0.488	0.184	0.316	9,117
Bulgaria	0.848 9.5	0.067 2.6	−0.191 5.2	−0.618 10.3	0.086 7.5	0.600	0.218	0.438	830
Germany and Austria	0.372 1.6	−0.107 0.6	−0.036 0.4	−0.275 2.5	0.038 2.3	0.086	−0.034	0.182	344
Hungary	0.494 2.9	0.271 2.9	−0.243 3.9	−0.159 1.5	0.036 2.1	0.550	0.064	0.364	372
Poland	0.696 14.6	0.064 3.1	−0.156 8.5	−0.453 12.9	0.058 9.8	0.512	0.300	0.295	3,564
Romania	0.559 8.4	0.027 0.8	−0.134 5.7	−0.235 5.6	0.040 5.2	0.345	0.077	0.293	2,536
Russia	0.859 11.0	0.055 2.4	−0.176 6.4	−0.412 6.9	0.052 4.8	0.617	0.265	0.400	1,471

Note: Foreign-born women, married abroad, married once, and with at least one birth abroad.

[a]Other variables in the regression are woman's age at immigration and in 1961, and years of schooling (six categories, dummy variables). The regressions for the continent totals include dummy variables for the individual countries.

[b]Variable excluded because the associated *F*-statistic was too low.

supply-dominated to imperfect demand control to efficient planning societies.

Why does the estimated response decline from full (or more) replacement as the number of births abroad rises? Women with births abroad consist of those who had fewer children than they would have liked (at that phase of their life cycle), those who had exactly the number of children they wanted, and those who had more children than they would have liked. The first group would want to replace deceased children fully and will do so unless there are constraints operating from the supply side (fecundity, health, etc.); if child death by itself relaxes a supply constraint (the lactation effect), those below desired fertility would respond fully. Those who are close to the optimum may revise the desired number of children downward (see section 3.1), and this may result in less than full replacement. Those who have more children than they want would not replace deceased children. When the data are controlled for some exogenous determinants of fertility and the women are grouped by the *actual* number of children, the proportion of those with excess fertility increases with the number of births. The random element in fertility should lower the estimated response. If those at low birth orders are not constrained in replacing deceased children, the major reason for lack of response is excess fertility, and thus the coefficient should decline with the number of children. Also, a greater number of births may already include a preimmigration response; in fact, the quicker the response, the less likely it is to be reflected in births in Israel.

This is also related to the age pattern of response. We observe that women who immigrated in their forties, particularly from EA, have a lower coefficient of BIS on DAB. This seems to contradict the hypothesis that women approaching the end of their childbearing period would be more responsive to child death. A reason for this could be that early child deaths have been replaced abroad. In another body of data where the birth order of the deceased children was known and the subsequent stopping probabilities and births intervals could be observed (for EA), I found a stronger response of older than of younger women (Ben-Porath 1976*b*).

Just in passing we can ask how these results fit the reverse causality —the view that more children die when there are more births. Given that births in Israel are subsequent to deaths abroad, they would be correlated according to this view only if people who expect to have higher future fertility (while in Israel) are particularly negligent with their earlier children (while abroad). This is, to say the least, unlikely.

There is another finding worth stressing: in the free-form interaction model (model I), cases with more than two deaths are often associated with *lower* births in Israel than cases with less (or no) child mortality. (This was also found in the Taiwanese data by Heer and Wu 1975.)

Let me suggest two possible explanations: a demand-based view suggests that those who experience child mortality beyond the common experience of their environment may "learn" from their experience and give up trying. There may, however, be a supply consideration. Generally, in discussing micro data there is a tendency to emphasize physiological and environmental factors that induce a *direct* relationship between child mortality and fertility. The termination of postpartum sterility is an explicitly causal factor. In addition, there may be a correlation across households between the ability to keep children alive and the ability to control family size. There may, however, be health and physiological factors that reduce both infant and prenatal mortality. The history of pregnancies terminated without the birth of a live child is not well documented and has been only sparsely researched, but there is evidence that (apart from stillbirths) a large proportion of pregnancies do not come to term, and it seems quite reasonable that there are physiological and environmental causes common to both prenatal and postnatal mortality.[5] This is in fact a major line that will be followed later—unfortunately, only speculatively.

3.4 Fertility and Mortality over Time

In this section I will try to infer the temporal aggregate movements in fertility and child mortality from more or less the same data. These developments fall into two phases: (*a*) changes that occurred in the country of birth; and (*b*) changes associated with immigration to Israel. I concentrate on the Asia-Africa immigrants, since the Second World War and its atrocities complicate a temporal analysis of the Europe-America immigrants.

3.4.1 Temporal Changes in Fertility and Mortality in the Countries of Birth

The main source used to trace the movements over time abroad is again the 1961 census of population of Israel.[6] Tabulations of fertility abroad and child mortality abroad by woman's age at immigration, period of immigration, or age at the time of the census (1961) can provide a basis for some inferences concerning temporal movements before immigration. The drawbacks of such a procedure are obvious; first, births in general and particularly births of children who did not survive are likely to be underreported, particularly by older women. This can reduce or even eliminate a downward trend in both fertility and child mortality; second, even if the data can give a reasonable picture of the immigrant population, it may not be a proper representation of the Jewish communities in the country of origin. In comparing immigrants of different periods it seems that individual choice and selection were less important in the period 1948–61 than in either prior or subsequent waves of immigration. In relative terms, emigration in this period involved whole communities, complete families, and greater predominance of Israel as a destination. But even here selectivity bias cannot be ruled out.

Let us now examine the evidence by period of immigration and age at immigration. By observing women of a given age at immigration we control the life-cycle phase; differences in period of immigration translate into year of birth. There is at least one other selectivity problem—we are dealing with women who were married abroad when they immigrated, married once, and were still married at the time of the census. Given the variance in the age of marriage and the close relationship between fertility and duration of marriage, women who were young and already married at the time of immigration have more children than would be representative of the cohort as a whole.

The data for immigrants from Asia and Africa taken as a group (tables 3.4 and 3.A.2–5) indicate that there has been a downward trend in child mortality abroad, and that this decline probably started sometime in the early 1940s. This is based on the following observations: holding age at immigration constant, the more recent immigrants report lower child mortality abroad than earlier immigrants. The differential is the greatest and extends over the longest period of some twenty years for women aged less than 25 when they immigrated: while those immigrating in the early 1940s report a loss of about one out of three or four children, those who immigrated in the late 1950s report a loss of one

Table 3.4 **Percentages of Children Who Died before Age 5 and Average Births Abroad, by Mother's Age at Immigration and Period of Immigration: Women Born in Asia and Africa**

Period of Immigration	Percentage of Children Who Died		Average Number of Births	
	20–24[a]	40–44	20–24	40–44
1956–61	12.5	22.3	1.7	6.1
1951–55	16.1	23.5	1.8	6.1
1946–50	24.8	27.1	1.5	5.6
1941–45	34.2	18.8	1.6	
1936–40	27.8	54.1	(2.3)	
1931–35	32.4	(25.0)	1.6	
1926–30	(24.5)[b]		(2.3)	
–1925	(40.0)		(1.5)	
Mean	20.2	24.8	1.7	5.9

Source: Tables 3.A.2–5.
[a]Mother's age at immigration.
[b]Parentheses indicate small numbers of observations.

child in eight. Among women who were older at immigration, the differentials between birth cohorts (or immigration cohorts) are smaller, reflecting the fact that more of their children were born when mortality was higher (there is always the possibility that the older women underreported child mortality and births).[7]

This description rests on an aggregation of immigrants from AA countries that differ from each other. Because of the small number of observations, we can get only a tentative picture of individual countries. The reported child death rate in Yemen and Aden is over 40%, and there seems to be no downward trend in it. The other Asian countries report rates half or somewhat less than half of this figure, and there seems to be a (somewhat blurred) moderate trend of decline. In North Africa, Egypt—with a Jewish community partly of European origin—has the lowest child mortality. Mortality in the other North African countries (Morocco and Tangier, Algeria and Tunisia, Libya) is higher than in the countries of the Middle East; the decline in the death rate in North Africa (with the possible exception of Libya but including Egypt) is steeper than in the Middle East. What is said here about *trends* in individual countries is partly based on the difference between countries in the cross-sectional variation of the child death rates by age at immigration, holding constant the *period* of immigration (1948–54, see table 3.A.6). Although in a single cross section age differentials confound life cycle with temporal variations, the differences between countries probably reflect differences in the time trends (the typical curve relating infant mortality to age of mother is J-shaped with a trough at the early twenties; see, e.g., Legg et al. 1969).

Let us turn now to the evidence on fertility. Looking first at the number of children born abroad (tables 3.4 and 3.A.2–5) by period of immigration and age at immigration, one can see a slight decline from the early to the late 1950s. The immigrants of the period before the 1950s often report lower fertility abroad than do those of recent periods. This could reflect a real increase in fertility abroad, but it could also be due to changes in the selection of immigrants from the original population and to a downward bias in reporting early fertility. A recent retrospective study of marriage cohorts also found that AA women who married before the late 1940s had lower fertility, with duration of marriage held constant, than those who married later (Central Bureau of Statistics 1976). In any case, there is little evidence in the by-continent aggregation of any tendency for fertility to decline to match the decline in mortality.

In individual countries, Iraq is the only one for which three five-year means show a consistent downward trend in fertility; in Libya and Algeria and Tunisia there is a tendency to decline over two five-year means.

Table 3.5 relates fertility and mortality levels across countries: Turkey, Syria and Lebanon, and Egypt are relatively low both in fertility and in mortality. The fertility ranking between the middle and the top mortality levels is ambiguous. Yemen, with at least twice the mortality of any other country, has a fertility level below that of Morocco and Algeria and Libya.

Note that intercountry differences in fertility are closely associated with women's age at marriage, as indicated by the percentage of women married abroad who married under 17 (table 3.5). The simple correlations across countries are 0.64 between number of children born and percentage deceased; 0.81 between number of children and age at marriage; and 0.59 between percentage deceased and age at marriage. I draw attention to this relationship because if there is a relationship between desired fertility and child mortality, to the extent that it operates via age at marriage, it *must* be a relationship between desired fertility and *expected*—as distinct from *experienced*—child mortality.

3.4.2 Changes in Fertility after Immigration: Aggregate Figures

Immigration was associated with a dramatic change in environment and conditions. The extent of the changes varied depending on where the immigrants came from and when they came. As already indicated, there were differences among the immigrants from Asia and Africa, and correspondingly this would mean that the impact of immigration could differ (the economic and social gap between the Jews coming from Alexandria or Baghdad and those coming from Yemen was no less

Table 3.5 **Fertility, Child Mortality, and Early Marriage: Selected Countries in Asia-Africa (Women Aged 40–44 at Immigration)**

Woman's Country of Birth	Number of Children Born Abroad	Children Who Died before Age 5 (%)	Women Married before Age 17 (%)
Algeria and Tunisia	6.2	32.0	27.4
Egypt and Sudan	4.1	17.3	18.9
Iran	5.9	21.4	48.5
Iraq	6.3	19.5	35.7
Libya	6.9	33.2	37.0
Morocco and Tangier	7.3	24.4	53.5
Syria and Lebanon	4.9	13.7	31.3
Turkey	3.8	13.5	14.1
Yemen and Aden	6.5	47.8	54.9

Source: Central Bureau of Statistics 1961, p. 54, table 20 (births abroad); p. 61, table 25 (child deaths); p. 10, table 5 (married young).
Note: Foreign-born women married abroad, married once, and with at least one birth abroad.

than the gap many of the immigrants faced by immigrating). Note also that the largest wave of immigration that occurred in 1948–51 (known as the period of mass immigration) was very large relative to the original population (population almost doubled in this short period) and constituted a large pressure on resources, so that immigration was not an immediate jump to the mean per capita income of a semideveloped country. For many of the immigrants, the initial period of residence in Israel was associated with poor housing conditions in camps of temporary huts and with significant unemployment. Others were settled on the land and got their income from public employment projects. It is impossible to judge their realized real income and, more important, their initial expectations concerning their future material well-being. Subsequent years have seen rising incomes, improved housing, increased labor force participation of women, and other corollaries of participation in a rapid development process. The issues that matter here are the differential timing in realization of the change in income, the change in price of children (and their schooling and health), and the timing of changes in the supply of births.

Total fertility for women born in Asia and Africa declined (except for a slight rise at the period of mass immigration when new immigrants with high fertility were added en masse to the small community of longer residence and low fertility) (see tables 3.A.7–8). Child mortality declined (see tables 3.10 and 3.A.10). It would be desirable to follow the changing behavior associated with immigration of women at different phases of their own and the family life cycle—unmarried, married abroad, married with children born abroad, and at various ages at immigration—but we do not have the means to follow in the necessary detail the process of adjusting to this sudden change.

Let us first consider women married before immigration (and in most cases with some children born abroad). We know the number of children by the woman's age in 1961 and also the number of children born abroad, so that we know how many were born in Israel and can calculate a rough measure of children born per year of residence in Israel. The birthrate abroad can be inferred from the difference in the number of children born to women of different ages who immigrated in a given period. If fertility abroad has tended to decline, these differences would give an *upward*-biased estimate of the birthrate abroad; and if fertility abroad has risen, these rates would give an underestimate. The rates will likewise be underestimated to the extent that older women underreport births.

Table 3.6 yields the following observations:

1. The total number of children born to women married abroad and aged j years in 1961 (the date of the census) is generally higher than

Table 3.6 **Births per Year, in Israel up to 1961, and Abroad, by Period of Immigration, Selected Countries (per 1,000 Women)**

Country of Birth and Period of Immigration	Age (i) in 1961 and (ii) at Immigration					Length of Period over Which Calculated
	25–29	30–34	35–39	40–44	45–49	
Asia-Africa						
1948–54						
i. Rate in Israel	349	340	283	217	113	10.6
ii. Rate abroad	210	240	230	170	90	10.0
1955+						
i. Rate in Israel	415	415	268	146	98	4.1
ii. Rate abroad	320	220	220	140		5.0
Algeria and Tunisia						
1948–54						
i. Rate in Israel	385	424	405	267	118	10.1
ii. Rate abroad	210	290	330	190	*180*	10.0
Egypt and Sudan						
1948–54						
i. Rate in Israel	280	220	180	90	40	10.0
ii. Rate abroad		140	*230*	170	200	10.0
1955+						
i. Rate in Israel	231	231	128	51	103	3.9
ii. Rate abroad	80	140	*220*	20		5.0
Iran						
1948–54						
i. Rate in Israel	395	346	296	148	128	10.2
ii. Rate abroad	230	310	260	120	*140*	10.0
Iraq						
1948–54						
i. Rate in Israel	343	295	246	197	98	10.2
ii. Rate abroad	200	130	240	*230*	120	10.0
Libya						
1948–54						
i. Rate in Israel	415	433	361	289	135	11.1
ii. Rate abroad	260	320	280	220	*150*	10.0
Morocco and Tangier						
1948–54						
i. Rate in Israel	346	365	336	207	89	10.1
ii. Rate abroad	260	340	320	170	10	10.0
1955+						
i. Rate in Israel	434	434	320	114	46	4.4
ii. Rate abroad	400	300	260	*140*		5.0
Turkey						
1948–54						
i. Rate in Israel	195	195	119	102	85	11.8
ii. Rate abroad	80	170	*160*	140	120	10.0

Table 3.6 (continued)

Country of Birth and Period of Immigration	Age (i) in 1961 and (ii) at Immigration 25–29	30–34	35–39	40–44	45–49	Length of Period over Which Calculated
Yemen and Aden						
1948–54						
i. Rate in Israel	362	379	336	250	172	11.6
ii. Rate abroad	240	250	230	220	120	10.0
Europe-America						
1948–54						
i. Rate in Israel	174	141	108	75	41	12.1
ii. Rate abroad	50	70	60	50	30	10.0
1955+						
i. Rate in Israel	227	131	65	65	33	3.0
ii. Rate abroad	140	80	20	40	—	10.0
Poland						
1948–54						
i. Rate in Israel	(161)	136	110	85	51	11.8
ii. Rate abroad	50	70	70	60	40	10.0
1955+						
i. Rate in Israel	169	141	56	56	56	3.5
ii. Rate abroad		100	20	40	0	5.0
Romania						
1948–54						
i. Rate in Israel	183	147	119	73	27	10.9
ii. Rate abroad	50	70	60	50	*40*	10.0
1955+						
i. Rate in Israel	199	199	132	66	66	1.5
ii. Rate abroad	120	60	20	—	0	5.0
Russia						
1948–54						
i. Rate in Israel		156	110	92	46	10.9
ii. Rate abroad		60	40	50	10	10.0
1955+						
i. Rate in Israel	221	147	110	74	74	2.7
ii. Rate abroad	120	80	0	20	—	5.0

Source: Appendix table 3.A.9 and Central Bureau of Statistics (1975, p. 4, table 1).

Note: i. Births per year of residence in Israel up to 1961, by mother's age in 1961, calculated by taking the difference between the total number of children and the number born abroad and dividing by average years of residence.

ii. Birthrates abroad calculated as one-tenth the difference between the number of children born abroad to women whose age at immigration differed by ten years.

Foreign-born women married abroad, married once, and with at least one birth abroad.

that born to women aged *j* years at immigration [compare lines i and ii in table 3.A.9].

2. Correspondingly, births per year of residence in Israel of foreign-born women married abroad is higher than births per year abroad, even for women coming from countries of very high fertility.

3. The increase in fertility (in Israel compared with abroad) is general (over countries) and substantial for women who were relatively young at the time of immigration.

4. There is a somewhat blurred picture as to the crossover age—the age at immigration at which women reduce rather than raise fertility after immigration. In table 3.6 the italic figures indicate the crossover ages. The younger crossover ages are found in the countries with the lowest child mortality (of those listed), Egypt and Turkey. The highest crossover age (and it is not clear that there is a crossover at all) is for Yemen and Aden and Libya, the countries with the highest rates of child mortality abroad.

5. There is some evidence (in a calculation similar to that of table 3.6, based on somewhat different tabulations) that immigrants from a given country who came after 1955 had more births per year by 1961 than those who came in 1948–54 (in table 3.6 this is so for Morocco and Tangier but not for Egypt and Sudan).

It can be argued that the phenomenon we point to, namely the increased fertility after immigration, reflects the fact that immigration is associated with postponed fertility, so that preimmigration fertility is depressed and postimmigration fertility exaggerated. The procedure used for estimating fertility rates abroad by taking *differences* in number of

Table 3.7 **Annual Percentage of Change in Total Fertility in Israel, Selected Periods of Immigration**

		Women Born in Asia-Africa		Women Born in Europe-America	
Period of Immigration	End Points for Calculated Change	Specified Period	All	Specified Period	All
-1947	1951–61	−4.1	−2.7	−2.2	−2.4
1948–54	1951–61	−3.4	−2.7	−1.8	−2.4
	1961–64	−3.6	−1.4	6.9	4.1
-1954	1964–71	−0.0	−1.6	6.3	1.6
1955–60	1968–71	−4.2	−1.6	7.2	3.6
1961–64	1969–74	−5.3	−2.5	−1.4	0.1

Source: Tables 3.A.7–8. Annual rates are calculated for end points of the designated period. In the case of the immigrants classified to subperiods, 1961 is the average for 1960, 1961, 1962.

children born abroad between women of different age at immigration is likely to avoid half of this problem. Fertility rates in Israel, however, could in principle reflect such possible postponement effects. We would get these results artificially if women were systematically classifying births abroad as if they occurred in Israel, but I do not see any reason to assume so. Dr. Van der Walle has raised the possibility that women who were older at immigration could have had lower marriage duration than the selected group of those who were already married when they immigrated at a younger age. This would indeed bias downward the estimated birthrates abroad. Given, however, that marriage abroad occurred at a very young age, this could apply only to the very young. Also, looking at the immigrants from all of Asia and Africa we can control for duration of marriage: In table 3.8 we first compare the total number of births abroad by duration of marriage for women married abroad, by age at immigration (lines 3), with the number of births (in Israel and abroad), by age in 1961 (lines 2). The latter figure is consistently and significantly higher and indicates that per year of marriage, fertility in Israel of AA women married abroad was significantly higher than it was abroad.[8]

Admitting the possible biases, and noting the unusual pattern of the implied birthrates by age, I still tend to regard the phenomenon described as a real one.

It is interesting to consider the women who married in Israel. The control for duration of marriage is admittedly imperfect (the five-year interval may be too crude); subject to this qualification, we see that in the first decade of marriage, the fertility of women who married in Israel (lines 1) in table 3.8 is *higher* than the fertility abroad of women of the same age (lines 3) and lower than fertility (including fertility in Israel) of those married abroad (lines 2).

We do not have an unbiased way of inferring the change in the marriage age after immigration. There is, however, enough indication to believe that the picture of rising age at marriage (table 3.A.11), though exaggerated, does point in the right direction. If this is so, we can summarize the picture in the following way: (*a*) foreign-born women who came to Israel unmarried curtailed early marriage and raised the average age at marriage; (*b*) within marriage, fertility is somewhat higher in the first few years than it was abroad for women who married abroad, and limitation of family size then sets in; (*c*) women who married abroad and immigrated to Israel relatively young increased the number of births immediately after immigration and then reduced fertility gradually; (*d*) women close to the end of the childbearing period tended to reduce fertility after immigration, though the evidence for this is somewhat ambiguous. The rates of decline of fertility of a given immigration co-

Table 3.8 **Average Number of Births, by Woman's Age, Place of Marriage, and Duration of Marriage (Women Born in Asia-Africa)**

		Duration of Marriage (Years)				
Age	Total	0–4	5–9	10–14	15–19	20–24
20–24						
1. Age in 1961: married in Israel	1.0	1.2	2.7			
2. Age in 1961: married abroad	2.9	1.8	3.2			
3. Age at immigration: married abroad	1.7	0.9	2.5			
25–29						
1. Age in 1961: married in Israel	2.5	1.4	2.9	3.7		
2. Age in 1961: married abroad	4.2	1.9	3.4	4.6		
3. Age at immigration: married abroad	3.0	1.0	2.7	4.2		
30–34						
1. Age in 1961: married in Israel	2.5	1.5	2.7	3.5		
2. Age in 1961: married abroad	5.2	1.8	3.3	4.7	6.2	
3. Age at immigration: married abroad	4.3	1.3	2.6	3.1	5.8	
35–39						
1. Age in 1961: married in Israel	2.2	1.0	2.6	2.8		
2. Age in 1961: married abroad	5.7		3.1	4.1	5.7	7.3
3. Age at immigration: married abroad	5.3	0.9	2.6	4.0	5.6	6.7

Source: Central Bureau of Statistics (1975, p. 38, table 14 [lines 1, 2], p. 57, table 22 [lines 3]).
Note: Women married once. Empty cells indicate no cases or too few cases. Lines 1, BIS, lines 2, BLS+BAB, lines 3, BAB.

hort will be above or below the rate of decline for the total depending on how recent was immigration compared with the recency of arrival of other immigrants (see table 3.7).

I have refrained so far from discussing the experience of the immigrants from Europe-America (mostly Europe). Fertility before immigration was much lower than in the countries of Asia-Africa. Child mortality was also lower, but by no means negligible. Those who immigrated in 1948–54 were mostly survivors of the holocaust. Their marital histories were disturbed and interrupted; child mortality was also a result of war and atrocities. Calculations analogous to those shown above indicate that EA women also experienced a rise in fertility after immigration. But fertility does not decline sharply. In the case of EA women there is more reason to believe that preimmigration fertility was abnormally low. There has been some decline in period fertility rates of European-born women in Israel and then some increase. On the whole, higher levels of fertility were sustained than those experienced abroad.

3.5 Can Things Be Fitted Together?

The cross-section microdata indicated a strong direct relationship between child mortality abroad and fertility in Israel. They also indicated that response in terms of fertility in Israel is weaker among those who immigrated with many children and those who immigrated relatively old and is often negative among those who lost many children. The significant direct relationship between child mortality and fertility leads us to expect a downward trend in fertility abroad, for those periods and countries where child mortality declined, and a decline in fertility after immigration as a consequence of the sharply reduced child mortality.

When the same data were aggregated in order to unravel the relationships, we observed a small and unstable decline in fertility accompanying decline in child deaths abroad. Subject to qualifications stemming from possible biases in the data, there is some possibility that fertility had even increased in the past. More interesting and clear is the finding that, after immigration, young foreign-born women who married abroad first increased fertility, then gradually reduced it; this was not always true if they immigrated in their late thirties or forties. Those who immigrated unmarried postponed marriage in Israel, started their married life with a high level of fertility, then reduced it after only a few years of marriage.

At this point it may be relevant to bring in the experience of Israel's Arab population. This group experienced very high and declining levels of infant and child mortality in the period of the British Mandate. The Arabs who lived in Israel also experienced rapidly declining mortality after 1948 (see table 3.9). The fertility of the Arab population has, however, increased from the British to the Israeli period and during the Israeli period. Moslems, who constitute approximately two-thirds of the Israeli Arabs, increased fertility steadily for several decades, from about 6 in the late 1920s, 7 in the mid-1930s and 1940s (Central Bureau for Medical Statistics 1945), to reach a peak of close to 10 in the mid-1960s; it is only in the last decade that they have reduced fertility. Among Christian Arabs the decline in fertility began earlier.

Even when one is dealing with a single group of people, so that there is no change in personal characteristics, immigration entails a dramatic change in environment, personal conditions, and expectations. But the response to the different aspects of the change may vary. If one looks only at the time series of total fertility in Israel of AA women, the trend is downward, as would be expected on the basis of several reasons, including lower child mortality. The surprise is in the initial increase in fertility immediately after immigration, and the questions are what could cause this burst and why is it so pronounced among the younger women.

Table 3.9 **Infant and Child Mortality of Non-Jews: Selected Years, 1924–42 (Palestine) and 1953–71 (Israel)**

	Infant Mortality		Child Mortality Age 0–4	
	Moslems	Christians	Moslems	Christians
1924–26	167.1	151.9		
1931–33	162.9	133.7	350.6	209.4
1940–42	139.7	100.1	302.6	150.9
1953	65.4	42.8		
1961	48.5	45.8		
1971	32.2	33.7		

Source: Schmelz (1974, p. 56, table A; p. 71, table 1).

Here I start speculating about health rather than behavior. Immigration meant a shift to a different public health system. This was very quickly reflected in low child mortality rates, but it presumably also affected the health of women in and out of pregnancy. The improvement in health services and nutrition could have some effect on fecundability, at least among the most undernourished immigrants (Yemen and Aden). There also seems to be room for an increase in the number of births out of a given number of pregnancies through a reduction in pregnancy wastage of various sorts (see Bierman et al. 1965). Some nutritional and behavioral habits that reduce prenatal wastage are transferable and are not predetermined by the mother's "permanent" characteristics. One hypothesis is that immigration was followed by a decline in both child mortality and prenatal wastage, so that initially the same number of pregnancies resulted in more live births. To the extent that women were previously constrained by the supply of births, one can see why the initial increase in supply would be welcome before desired family size is revised downward. But even if this was not the case, the downward adjustment in fertility that is supposed to reflect replacement would have required an even larger reduction in pregnancies to compensate for the increase in successful pregnancies, or for a means of inducing abortion, and one could see why this would not be instantaneous. Induced abortion has probably been the most important means of controlling family size in Israel, and it is also prevalent among AA women. (This may be the closest substitute for natural abortion, and it has the advantage over the then most popular preventative method that it does not depend on the husband.) There is, however, strong evidence on the nature of the pre- and postbirth mortality correlations that would support this particular emphasis.

Can this hypothesis account for the fact that the increase in fertility after immigration was marked in the young age groups and may not have occurred among older women of childbearing age? Two things might be at work here: Older women may have found it easier to reduce the frequency of pregnancy. On the other hand, for older women who arrived with a large stock of children who survive, the new realities of low child mortality would have much more immediate consequences in terms of family size. Younger women could borrow from the future by allowing themselves higher fertility as long as they were below their desired completed family size. Potentially, older women had more room for increase in successful pregnancies; the question is whether they would be responsive to the changed health regime.

What we are examining is the possibility that the health measures that affected mortality were associated with health developments that increased fertility; this possibility is consistent with the before-and-after immigration experience, with the experience of the Arab population, and perhaps with the experience of immigrants over time abroad. Although we do not have a direct test of this hypothesis, let us examine some child mortality data to see whether they can provide some support for it.

The decline in child mortality over time has the following features (table 3.10)[9]: (1) neonatal, postneonatal, and perinatal mortality all declined; (2) infant mortality declined relatively more than perinatal mortality; (3) within infant mortality the steepest decline in the period as a whole is in mortality after the first month of life (which declined to between one-quarter and one-fifth of its initial level). In the early 1950s, however—that is, immediately after mass immigration—the decline in perinatal mortality was as large as that in postneonatal mortality. This would be sympathetic (to use a weak term) to the speculation offered here. Comparing child mortality by mother's continent of birth in 1952 and 1960–63, we again observe that (4) the decline in postneonatal mortality is the most marked in both continent groups (table 3.A.10). Also, the only important differences *between* continents are in postneonatal mortality; (5) the decline in deaths from infectious diseases, pneumonia, and gastroenteritis is the main cause of the decline in infant mortality. The data by continent of birth do not reflect the early relative decline in perinatal mortality, which had already occurred by 1952, and the comparison between the continents does not provide support for this speculation.

Is there a demand-behavior explanation for the short-term rise in fertility and the subsequent decline? A reasonable speculation would be that a pronatal income effect precedes the adjustment in the elements of the economic changes in the life of parents and their aspirations for their children that generate antinatal substitution effects. As indicated, we do not have a well-defined picture of *actual* real income of immigrants immediately after immigration. If a direct income effect is to be

Table 3.10 Infant Mortality, Perinatal Mortality, and Late Fetal Deaths: 1948–70 (per 1,000 Live Births)

Year	Total (2)+(3) +(4) (1)	Infant Mortality 1–11 Months (2)	7–27 Days (3)	0–6 Days (4)	Late Fetal Deaths (5)	Perinatal Mortality (4)+(5) (6)
1948	36.3	—	—	—	14.9	—
1949	50.3	28.0	7.6	14.7	18.6	33.3
1950	45.6	22.9	7.9	14.8	17.3	32.1
1951	39.4	21.8	6.0	11.6	15.0	26.6
1952	38.7	22.8	5.4	10.5	15.7	26.2
1953	35.9	18.0	5.3	12.6	15.3	27.9
1954	34.4	17.9	4.8	11.7	14.1	25.8
1955	32.3	16.3	4.6	11.4	13.6	25.0
1960	27.2	10.7	3.3	13.2	13.0	26.2
1965	22.7	7.4	2.4	12.9	14.2	27.1
1970	18.9	5.4	1.9	11.6	10.3	21.9

Source: Central Bureau of Statistics (1974, p. 112, table 1).

invoked, it must rely on the revision of permanent income on the hopes that immigrants had for the new phase in their lives. Such an income effect would indeed be more powerful for younger than older women and would thus be consistent with the age patterns observed.

With respect to the Moslem population, we have a longer period of rising fertility and of rising incomes, and there is some indirect support to the lag in the emergence of fertility-reducing variables (see Ben-Porath 1972).

What implications does the temporal phenomenon have for the cross-sectional findings? In discussing the cross-sectional results I partly ignored the fact that we are relating fertility in Israel, occurring under conditions of much lower child mortality, to prior differences in child mortality and fertility abroad. There has been a downward *convergence* of child mortality in Israel. Thus, higher child mortality abroad is associated with steeper declines in child mortality: higher fertility in Israel, given the number of births abroad, means greater increase in fertility (in Israel compared with abroad). It is thus possible that what we have estimated is a mixture of the positive replacement effect of child deaths on fertility, with the positive effect on fertility of factors associated with the *decline* in child mortality. This could explain the presence of coefficients greater than unity in the Asia-Africa countries. The smaller response in the cross-sectional study observed for older women would again be consistent with the temporal finding that older women did not increase fertility after immigration. I should mention that a study based on another body of data in which behavior following each birth was analyzed according to whether or not the child survived resulted in somewhat smaller responses than those observed here (Ben-Porath 1976*b*).

3.6 Summary

This paper poses some of the issues relating to the relationship between child mortality and fertility, then examines the fertility-mortality relationship of mostly foreign-born women in Israel, women who immigrated from various countries in Asia, Africa, and Europe and continued childbearing in Israel. The marriage between questions of general interest and the experience of a very particular population, coupled with methodological problems, means not only that these findings do not settle the questions one started with, but that the road to generalizations may be obscured. There is, however, a potential gain from the diversity in background of immigrants, the nonmarginal nature of the changes associated with immigration, and the unusual configuration and timing of various corollaries of economic and social development, coupled with a uniform set of data.

Among the general issues I listed, in section 3.5 a major one is the distinction between response to the experience of child mortality (replacement) versus the response to expected mortality (hoarding). This distinction is important with respect to both the magnitude and the promptness of the responses. Some of the other issues are the distinction between behavioral and physiological mechanisms, the degree to which child mortality affects the desired number of surviving children, and the effect of other variables correlated with the decline in fertility affecting either the demand or the supply of births and children.

The cross-sectional phase of the study consists of regressions of fertility in Israel as a function of fertility and mortality abroad, and education and age variables. The regressions were run by separate countries of origin and pooled for Asia and Africa and Europe. Fairly sizable coefficients of child mortality on fertility were estimated. The presence of such effects among the immigrants from Europe suggests the importance of the behavioral mechanism. The strong effect among the high-fertility immigrants from Asia-Africa may be partly reflections of a supply mechanism.

That the coefficients in intercountry regressions were not higher than in the intracountry regressions is considered evidence against the hoarding hypothesis (based on the supposition that the intercountry differences in expected mortality are more strongly correlated with experienced mortality than the intracountry differences). The weakness in replacement among older women in this particular study (unlike another body of data describing Israeli women) is here taken to result from fairly quick replacement response abroad.

Viewing the same data for inferences concerning what happened over time, I concluded that (1) in the countries of origin there had been a decline in child mortality without appreciable decline in fertility; (2) immigration was followed quickly by drastically declining mortality, but fertility initially *rose* above its preimmigration levels; (3) beyond the initial stage, fertility of Israeli women married abroad declined, and there have been also postponed marriages of unmarried immigrants and decline in their fertility after the first years of marriage. The increase in fertility after immigration, as well as the rising fertility over time of Moslems (in the face of declining child mortality) suggests that the discrepancy between the cross-sectional and time-series relationships between fertility and mortality (i.e., the sluggish aggregate response compared with large cross-sectional coefficients) may arise from the operation of other variables in the two contexts rather than from the slow revisions of expectations concerning child mortality, as part of a hoarding mechanism.

In speculating about the nature of the phenomena that delay the effect of replacement, I mention the possibility that income effects (associated with immigration in the case of the Jews) may precede in time the adjustment in life-style and aspirations that generates the fertility-depressing substitution effects. Alternatively, it is being argued that correlated with the same factors that reduced fertility over time there were health developments that increased the supply of births, possibly by reducing various forms of pregnancy wastage.

To sustain the latter hypothesis we must argue that temporally, either in the before-and-after immigration comparison or in some phases of the temporal decline in child mortality, the factors that determine child mortality and those that determine prenatal death or involuntary sterility are correlated with one another more closely in the time series than in the cross section.

It is not clear how implications can be carried over from a case of a sudden change associated with immigration from a less developed to a semideveloped country to a process of gradual development. The experience of the Arab population in Israel is not inconsistent with the explanation presented here, so it may well be that in a more moderate way similar counteracting forces operate in a more usual less developed country setting.

Appendix

Table 3.A.1 **The Difference in Births in Israel (△BIS) between Women (aged 15–49 at Immigration) with Different Numbers of Deaths Abroad (△DAB), by Country of Birth and Births Abroad: Regression Results of an Interaction Model**

Age at Immigration and △DAB	Births Abroad (BAB)						R^2
	1	2	3	4	5	6+	
Women Born in Asia-Africa							
Algeria and Tunisia							0.545
1–0	2.054	0.703	0.563	0.669			
2–1		0.513	0.953	0.362	0.300		
3^{+}–2			−1.577	−1.519	−0.642	0.660	
Egypt and Sudan							0.394
1–0	2.572	1.484	−0.118	0.528			
2–1		1.816	0.413	1.322	0.532		
3^{+}–2			1.330	−2.263	−0.073	−0.587	
Iran							0.450
1–0	2.391	1.535	0.105	1.062			
2–1		−0.115	1.188	0.741	0.793		
3^{+}–2			−2.254	0.540	−0.237	−0.522	
Iraq							0.423
1–0	0.882	0.115	0.108	0.451			
2–1		0.697	0.916	0.112	0.339		
3^{+}–2			−2.178	−1.692	−0.511		
Libya							0.394
1–0	1.303	1.066	0.833	1.092			
2–1		0.143	0.741	−0.363	−1.036		
3^{+}–2			0.781	0.128	0.726	−1.086	
Morocco and Tangier							0.438
1–0	0.926	0.761	0.392	0.197			
2–1		−0.042	0.757	0.770	0.878		
3^{+}–2			−0.830	0.114	−0.060	−1.177	
Yemen and Aden							0.456
1–0	0.115	1.066	1.402	1.194			
2–1		1.089	−0.390	0.098	1.144		
3^{+}–2			−0.668	−0.647	−0.608	−0.157	

Table 3.A.1 (continued)

Age at Immigration and △DAB	Births Abroad (BAB)						R^2
	1	2	3	4	5	6+	
Women Born in Europe-America							
Bulgaria							0.466
1–0	1.112	0.441	1.056	0.567			
2–1		1.003	0.287	−0.092	0.102		
3^{+}–2			−1.065	−0.468	0	0.734	
Germany and Austria							0.193
1–0	0.455	−0.007	0.020	0.297			
2–1		−0.128	−0.593	0.044	−0.489		
3^{+}–2			0.581	−0.416	0.144	0.212	
Hungary							0.377
1–0	0.965	2.085	−0.092	−0.421			
2–1		−2.096	0.131	0.518	0.334		
3^{+}–2			3.673	2.231	−0.543	2.815	
Poland							0.310
1–0	0.870	0.575	0.058	0.042			
2–1		0.155	0.475	0.402	−0.199		
3^{+}–2			0.998	−0.096	−0.091	0.347	
Romania							0.297
1–0	0.598	0.336	0.153	−0.151			
2–1		0.739	−0.214	−0.053	0.057		
3^{+}–2			0.629	−0.068	−0.252	0.072	
Russia							0.398
1–0	0.732	0.546	0.397	0.466			
2–1		0.687	0.308	0.214	0.985		
3^{+}–2			−1.512	−0.231	−0.885	−1.012	

Note: Foreign-born women, married abroad, married once, and with at least one birth abroad. Other variables in the regression are woman's age at immigration, age in 1961, and years of schooling (six categories, dummy variables). The figures are differences in the coefficients of dummy variables. Where no figure appears it is because at least one of the coefficients did not pass a critical (low) level of significance.

Table 3.A.2 **Percentage of Children Who Died before Age 5, by Mother's Age at Immigration and Period of Immigration (Women Born in Asia-Africa)**

Age at Immigration	Period of Immigration								
	Total	1956–61	1951–55	1946–50	1941–45	1936–40	1931–35	1926–30	–1929
Number of Women	81,155	16,365	27,880	31,200	2,110	845	1,685	500	570
Total	23.5	19.2	21.0	28.0	30.0	30.1	28.3	33.3	39.0
0–19	22.9	13.5	15.4	28.0	32.6		21.3		35.0
20–24	20.2	12.5	16.1	24.8	34.2	27.8	32.4	(24.5)	(40.0)
25–29	22.9	19.5	19.4	30.4	30.6	19.5	25.5	(33.3)	(44.2)
30–34	21.2	15.8	19.3	25.8	28.3	(28.6)	26.1	(29.2)	(13.0)
35–39	22.2	18.0	18.6	27.8	39.6	25.6	28.4		
40–44	24.8	22.3	23.5	27.1	18.8	54.1	(25.0)		
45–49	25.6	20.0	25.7	29.1	14.9	(50.0)		58.8	
50+	29.4	24.8	26.3	30.3	36.6		(38.0)		

Source: Central Bureau of Statistics (1966, p. 56, table 21; p. 63, table 26).
Note: Foreign-born women, married abroad, married once, and with at least one birth abroad. Empty cells indicate too few cases or no cases. Parentheses indicate small number of cases.

Table 3.A.3 **Average Births Abroad, by Mother's Age at Immigration and Period of Immigration (Women Born in Asia-Africa)**

Age at Immigration	Period of Immigration								
	Total	1956–61	1951–55	1946–50	1941–45	1936–40	1931–35	1926–30	–1929
Number of Women	81,155	16,365	27,880	31,200	2,110	845	1,685	500	570
Total	3.6	4.1	4.0	3.6	2.6	2.7	2.3	2.1	1.7
0–19	0.7	0.6	0.8	0.7	0.6	0.6	0.9	0.5	(1.5)
20–24	1.7	1.7	1.8	1.5	1.6	(2.3)	1.6	(2.3)	(1.5)
25–29	3.0	3.2	3.1	2.8	2.3	(3.1)	2.0		
30–34	4.2	4.4	4.4	4.0	3.1		3.4		
35–39	5.3	5.5	5.5	5.0	(4.8)				
40–44	5.9	6.1	6.1	5.6					
45–49	6.1	6.0	6.6	5.7					
50+	6.0	5.5	6.4	6.2					

Source: Central Bureau of Statistics (1966, p. 56, table 21; p. 63, table 26).
Note: Foreign-born women, married abroad, married once, and with at least one birth abroad. Empty cells indicate too few cases or no cases. Parentheses indicate small number of cases.

Table 3.A.4 **Percentage of Children who Died before Age 5, by Mother's Age at Immigration and Period of Immigration (Women Born in Europe-America)**

Age at Immigration	Period of Immigration								
	Total	1956–61	1951–55	1946–50	1941–45	1936–40	1931–35	1926–30	–1929
Number of Women	120,285	21,340	10,670	60,815	2,745	8,360	12,555	1,325	2,475
Total	11.2	9.6	11.9	11.6	12.3	8.1	11.6	10.6	19.2
0–19	7.6			7.1			(22.2)		
20–24	8.4	(4.3)	(6.7)	7.1	(23.8)	22.0	12.7		15.1
25–29	9.1	4.7	13.1	8.5	(11.1)	9.4	10.8		18.4
30–34	9.7	3.8	9.6	12.1	15.2	6.0	8.8	11.1	25.0
35–39	11.2	4.9	13.2	14.7	16.7	8.5	12.2		14.0
40–44	11.7	11.0	12.3	12.4	12.6	7.0	13.0		(16.7)
45–49	13.1	15.7	13.4	12.0		7.0	16.3		(50.0)
50+	12.9	15.5	11.7	12.8	(6.5)	8.6	7.1		

Source: Central Bureau of Statistics (1966, p. 56, table 21; p. 63, table 26).
Note: Foreign-born women, married abroad, married once, and with at least one birth abroad. Empty cells indicate too few cases or no cases. Parentheses indicate small number of cases.

Table 3.A.5 **Average Births Abroad, by Mother's Age at Immigration and Period of Immigration (Women Born in Europe-America)**

Age at Immigration	Period of Immigration								
	Total	1956–61	1951–55	1946–50	1941–45	1936–40	1931–35	1926–30	–1929
Number of Women	120,285	21,340	10,690	60,815	2,745	8,360	12,555	1,325	2,475
Total	1.3	1.6	1.6	1.3	1.0	0.9	1.0	0.7	1.0
0–19	0.4	(0.2)	0.3	0.4	(0.1)	0.2	0.3		0.3
20–24	0.4	0.4	0.4	0.5	0.2	0.1	0.2	0.3	0.9
25–29	0.8	1.2	0.9	0.9	0.4	0.4	0.6	0.7	1.0
30–34	1.3	1.6	1.3	1.3	1.1	0.9	1.4	1.5	2.2
35–39	1.7	1.7	1.5	1.6	1.6	1.7	2.3		2.4
40–44	1.9	1.9	1.8	1.8	1.9	2.1	2.1		
45–49	1.9	1.6	1.6	2.0	(1.8)	2.5	3.9		
50+	2.5	2.0	2.4	2.8	(2.1)	2.9	(4.3)		

Source: Central Bureau of Statistics (1966, p. 56, table 21; p. 63, table 26).
Note: Foreign-born women, married abroad, married once, and with at least one birth abroad. Empty cells indicate too few cases or no cases. Parentheses indicate small number of cases.

Table 3.A.6 **Average Births Abroad and Percentage of Children Who Died before Age 5, by Mother's Age at Immigration, Period of Immigration, and Country of Birth**

	Period of Immigration							
	Average Number of Children				Percentage Who Died before Age 5			
Age at Immigration	All Periods	1946–50	1951–55	1956–61	All Periods	1946–50	1951–55	1956–61
Algeria, Tunisia	3.8				28			
0–14	0.7				18			
15–19	0.4	0.3	0.5		12	14	21	
20–24	1.1	1.0	1.1	1.3	22	32	15	15
25–29	2.5	2.6	2.6	2.4	21	32	14	18
30–34	4.0	3.9	4.2	3.7	21	22	26	13
35–39	5.9	5.5	5.3	5.0	27	36	23	22
40–44	6.1	6.2	6.0	6.3	32	35	32	30
45–49	6.6		7.1	6.0	33		38	26
50+	6.3		7.4	5.6	35		41	25
Egypt and Sudan	2.8				16			
0–14	1.5	1.7			9	12		
15–19	0.5	0.6		0.3	6	16		0
20–24	1.2	1.1	1.2	1.6	9	9	12	5
25–29	2.0	2.1	1.3	2.0	13	14	5	4
30–34	2.7	2.7	3.0	2.6	13	17	14	9
35–39	3.9	4.5	3.4	3.7	19	27	9	15
40–44	4.1	4.3	4.0	4.0	17	27	23	9
45–49	4.5	6.1		3.3	22	37		9
50+	4.2		4.2	4.0	21		10	20

Table 3.A.6 (continued)

Age at Immigration	Period of Immigration							
	Average Number of Children				Percentage Who Died before Age 5			
	All Periods	1946–50	1951–55	1956–61	All Periods	1946–50	1951–55	1956–61
Iran	3.6				22			
0–14	1.2	1.8			26	44		
15–19	0.7	0.6	0.6	0.7	23	24	28	7
20–24	1.7	2.0	1.5	1.5	16	23	9	4
25–29	3.2	3.2	3.0	3.5	20	20	18	25
30–34	4.8	5.1	4.5	4.7	22	27	18	17
35–39	5.7	5.0	6.2	5.8	22	26	21	18
40–44	5.9	5.6	5.5	7.1	21	17	19	30
45–49	7.1	6.6	7.3	7.1	25	22	27	24
50+	7.4	9.0	6.9	6.6	29	27	28	32
Iraq	3.9				18			
0–14	0.9	2.2	0.6		23	18	43	
15–19	0.7	0.7	0.9		17	15	13	
20–24	1.7	1.9	1.6	1.1	15	14	15	9
25–29	2.8	2.9	2.8		15	16	15	
30–34	3.9	4.4	3.9	1.7	15	13	14	36
35–39	5.1	6.1	4.9	3.7	15	19	13	
40–44	6.3	6.5	6.2		19	19	19	34
45–49	6.4	6.7	6.2		20	14	19	
50+	6.7	6.7	6.6		22	21	23	

Table 3.A.6 (continued)

Age at Immigration	Period of Immigration							
	Average Number of Children				Percentage Who Died before Age 5			
	All Periods	1946–50	1951–55	1956–61	All Periods	1946–50	1951–55	1956–61
Libya	4.0				30			
0–14	1.9				28			
15–19	0.5	0.5			24	30		
20–24	1.6	1.7	1.2		21	22	15	
25–29	3.1	3.2	2.9		26	28	21	
30–34	4.7	4.8	4.7		31	30	31	
35–39	6.0	6.3	5.3		31	35	23	
40–44	6.9	6.8	7.2		33	35	31	
45–49	7.7	7.2	8.1		29	24	36	
50+	6.4	6.9	5.8		36	40	31	
Morocco, Tangier	4.3				21			
0–14	2.5	2.4	3.0		16	14	20	
15–19	0.7	0.6	0.9	0.6	16	22	13	19
20–24	2.1	1.9	2.5	2.0	17	25	18	14
25–29	4.0	3.2	4.3	3.9	20	29	20	17
30–34	5.6	5.4	5.5	5.8	19	19	19	18
35–39	7.0	6.6	7.2	7.0	21	14	21	20
40–44	7.3	6.3	7.0	7.6	24	30	26	22
45–49	7.2	6.9	7.2	7.2	24	35	30	19
50+	6.4	7.9	5.8	6.6	30	41	29	30

Table 3.A.6 (continued)

Age at Immigration	Period of Immigration							
	Average Number of Children				Percentage Who Died before Age 5			
	All Periods	1946–50	1951–55	1956–61	All Periods	1946–50	1951–55	1956–61
Syria, Lebanon	3.2				14			
0–14								
15–19	0.4				11			
20–24	1.5				8			
25–29	2.2	2.4			13	8		
30–34	3.4	3.5			11	14		
35–39	4.8	5.1			17	9		
40–44	4.9	5.8	3.2		14	14	14	
45–49	5.9			5.4	14			5
50+	5.3		5.4	4.6	18		19	8
Turkey	2.4				18			
0–14	0.9	1.0			0	0		
15–19	0.4	0.4		0.2	33	40		0
20–24	0.9		1.5	0.9	18		36	8
25–29	1.3	1.2	1.7		17	9	17	
30–34	2.4	2.5		2.1	21	25		3
35–39	2.8	2.9		2.7	16	17		5
40–44	3.8	3.9		3.3	13	14		12
45–49	4.0	3.9	5.4	3.7	17	18	24	10
50+	3.8	3.6	3.0	4.6	22	19	27	22

Source: Unpublished Central Bureau of Statistics data from the 1961 Census of Population.

Table 3.A.7 Total Fertility of Jewish Women in Israel by Continent of Birth

Year	Asia-Africa	Europe-America	Israel	Year	Asia-Africa	Europe-America	Israel
1950	5.6	3.2	3.9	1963	4.6	2.4	2.5
1951	6.3	3.2	3.6	1964	4.6	2.6	2.8
1952	6.2	3.0	3.3	1965	4.6	2.6	2.9
1953	5.6	2.8	3.2	1966	4.5	2.5	2.8
1954	5.7	2.7	2.9	1967	4.2	2.4	2.7
1955	5.7	2.6	2.8	1968	4.3	2.6	2.9
1956	5.6	2.6	2.8	1969	4.2	2.7	2.9
1957	5.4	2.6	2.8	1970	4.1	2.8	3.1
1958	4.9	2.5	2.7	1971	4.1	2.9	3.2
1959	5.2	2.3	2.7	1972	3.8	2.7	2.9
1960	5.1	2.4	2.8	1973	3.7	2.7	3.0
1961	4.8	2.3	2.7	1974	3.7	2.8	3.1
1962	4.6	2.3	2.5				

Source: Central Bureau of Statistics, *Statistical Abstract*, various years.

Table 3.A.8 **Total Fertility by Continent of Birth and Period of Immigration**

	Asia-Africa					Europe-America				
Year	–1947	–1954	1948–54	1955–60	1961–64	–1947		1948–54	1955–60	1961–64
1951	5.1		6.9			3.50		2.80		
1954	4.3		6.0			2.80		2.50		
1960–62	3.4		4.9			2.60		2.35		
1963			4.5			2.70		2.36		
1964		4.27	4.4				2.44	2.89		
1965		4.24					2.49			
1966		4.17					2.50			
1967		3.88					2.39			
1968		4.07		4.49			2.58		2.54	
1969		4.09		4.21	5.12		2.79		2.62	2.82
1970		4.11		4.00	4.72		3.20		2.81	2.90
1971		4.26		3.96	4.59		3.80		3.28	2.97
1972					4.24					2.70
1973					4.00					2.61
1974					3.92					2.63

Source: Central Bureau of Statistics, *Statistical Abstract*, various years.

Table 3.A.9 **Births (up to 1961), by Period of Immigration, Selected Countries**

	Age (i) at Immigration and (ii) in 1961					
	20–24	25–29	30–34	35–39	40–44	45–49
Asia-Africa						
1948–54						
i. Births abroad	1.6	2.9	4.0	5.2	5.7	6.1
ii. Total births	3.6	4.4	5.2	5.6	6.4	6.3
Abroad	0.8	0.7	1.6	2.6	4.1	5.1
In Israel	2.8	3.7	3.6	3.0	2.3	1.2
1955+						
i. Births abroad	1.8	3.4	4.5	5.6	6.3	6.1
ii. Total births	2.7	3.8	5.4	5.9	6.4	6.7
Abroad	0.8	2.1	3.7	4.8	5.8	6.3
In Israel	1.9	1.7	1.7	1.1	0.6	0.4
Algeria and Tunisia						
1948–54						
i. Births abroad	1.1	2.5	4.0	5.8	5.9	7.6
ii. Total births		4.4	5.3	6.4	6.9	6.8
Abroad		0.5	1.0	2.3	4.2	5.6
In Israel		3.9	4.3	4.1	2.7	1.2
Egypt and Sudan						
1948–54						
i. Births abroad	1.1	1.9	2.5	4.2	4.2	(6.2)
ii. Total births			4.0	4.1	4.3	4.8
Abroad		(0.9)	1.2	1.9	2.5	3.9
In Israel		2.8	2.2	1.8	0.9	0.4
1955+						
i. Births abroad	1.6	2.0	2.7	3.8	3.9	3.3
ii. Total births	(1.8)	2.8	3.1	3.5	4.2	4.2
Abroad	(0.6)	1.9	2.2	3.0	4.0	3.8
In Israel	(1.2)	0.9	0.9	0.5	0.2	0.4
Iran						
1948–54						
i. Births abroad	1.7	3.1	4.8	5.7	5.6	7.1
ii. Total births		4.5	5.3	6.1	7.2	7.3
Abroad		0.5	1.8	3.1	4.7	6.0
In Israel		4.0	3.5	3.0	1.5	1.3
Iraq						
1948–54						
i. Births abroad	1.7	2.8	4.0	5.2	6.3	6.4
ii. Total births	(3.1)	4.3	4.8	5.3	6.0	6.3
Abroad		0.8	1.8	2.8	4.0	5.3
In Israel		3.5	3.0	2.5	2.0	1.0

Table 3.A.9 (continued)

	Age (i) at Immigration and (ii) in 1961					
	20–24	25–29	30–34	35–39	40–44	45–49
Libya						
1948–54						
i. Births abroad	1.6	3.2	4.8	6.0	7.0	7.5
ii. Total births		4.9	6.2	6.9	9.8	7.8
Abroad		0.3	1.4	2.9	4.6	6.3
In Israel		4.6	4.8	4.0	3.2	1.5
Morocco and Tangier						
1948–54						
i. Births abroad	2.2	3.9	5.6	7.1	7.3	7.2
ii. Total births	(4.2)	4.6	6.0	9.0	8.0	9.7
Abroad		1.1	2.3	3.6	5.9	6.8
In Israel		3.5	3.7	3.4	2.1	0.9
1955+						
i. Births abroad	2.1	4.1	5.6	6.9	7.6	9.1
ii. Total births	3.0	4.3	6.2	7.3	7.4	9.9
Abroad	0.8	2.4	4.3	5.9	6.9	7.7
In Israel	1.2	1.9	1.9	1.4	0.5	0.2
Turkey						
1948–54						
i. Births abroad	0.8	1.2	2.5	2.8	3.9	4.0
ii. Total births		2.7	3.3	3.4	3.9	3.7
Abroad		0.4	1.0	2.0	2.7	2.7
In Israel		2.3	2.3	1.4	1.2	1.0
Yemen and Aden						
1948–54						
i. Births abroad	1.8	3.3	4.3	5.6	6.5	6.8
ii. Total births	(3.8)	4.7	5.9	6.8	7.3	7.4
Abroad	0.7	0.5	1.5	2.9	4.4	5.4
In Israel		4.2	4.4	3.9	2.9	2.0
Europe-America						
1948–54						
i. Births Abroad	0.6	1.0	1.3	1.6	1.8	1.9
ii. Total births		2.3	2.2	2.2	2.1	2.0
Abroad		0.2	0.5	0.9	1.2	1.5
In Israel		2.1	1.7	1.3	0.9	0.5
1955+						
i. Births abroad	0.5	1.2	1.6	1.7	1.9	1.7
ii. Total births	1.0	1.5	1.9	1.9	2.0	1.9
Abroad	0.3	0.8	1.4	1.7	1.8	1.8
In Israel	0.7	0.7	0.5	0.2	0.2	0.1

Table 3.A.9 (continued)

	Age (i) at Immigration and (ii) in 1961					
	20–24	25–29	30–34	35–39	40–44	45–49
Poland						
1948–54						
i. Births abroad	0.6	1.0	1.3	1.7	1.9	2.1
ii. Total births		(2.0)	2.1	2.2	2.2	2.1
Abroad		(0.1)	0.5	0.9	1.2	1.5
In Israel		(1.9)	1.6	1.3	1.0	0.6
1955+						
i. Births abroad	0.7	1.3	1.8	1.9	2.1	2.1
ii. Total births	(1.2)	1.6	2.1	2.1	2.1	2.3
Abroad	(0.3)	1.0	1.6	1.9	1.9	2.1
In Israel	(0.9)	0.6	0.5	0.2	0.2	0.2
Romania						
1948–54						
i. Births abroad	0.4	0.8	1.1	1.4	1.6	1.8
ii. Total births		2.1	2.0	2.1	1.8	1.7
Abroad		0.1	0.4	0.8	1.0	1.4
In Israel		2.0	1.6	1.3	0.8	0.3
1955+						
i. Births abroad	(0.4)	1.0	1.3	1.4	1.3	1.3
ii. Total births	(1.0)	1.1	1.5	1.5	1.6	1.3
Abroad	(0.5)	0.8	1.2	1.3	1.5	1.2
In Israel	(0.5)	0.3	0.3	0.2	0.1	0.1
Russia						
1948–54						
i. Births abroad	0.7	1.1	1.3	1.5	1.8	1.6
ii. Total births			2.4	2.3	2.2	2.0
Abroad			0.7	1.1	1.2	1.5
In Israel			1.7	1.2	1.0	0.5
1955+						
i. Births abroad	0.8	1.4	1.8	1.8	1.9	1.5
ii. Total births		(1.5)	2.1	2.1	2.1	1.9
Abroad		(0.9)	1.7	1.8	1.9	1.7
In Israel		(0.6)	0.4	0.3	0.2	0.2

Source: Central Bureau of Statistics (1966, tables 12, 19, and 20).

Table 3.A.10 **Stillbirths and Infant Mortality Rates, by Mother's Continent of Birth: 1952 and 1960–63**

	Asia-Africa		Europe-America and Israel	
	1952	1960–63	1952	1960–63
Stillbirths	15.9	14.7	15.2	12.0
Perinatal mortality	26.3	26.5	25.9	26.2
Infant mortality	47.9	27.0	28.3	23.7
Neonatal mortality	17.0	14.6	15.5	16.9
Postneonatal mortality	30.9	12.4	12.8	6.8
Postneonatal mortality, by cause of death				
Infectious diseases	3.4	0.9	1.7	0.4
Pneumonia, bronchitis	6.5	3.2	3.0	1.6
Gastroenteritis	10.7	2.8	2.6	1.4
Malformations and diseases of early infancy	3.8	2.4	3.1	1.8
External causes	0.7	0.3	0.4	0.1
Other	5.0	2.8	2.7	1.6

Source: Peritz and Adler (1974, p. 41, table A).

Table 3.A.11 **Age at Marriage in Israel and Abroad (Women Born in Asia-Africa)**

Country of Birth	Percentage of Women Married before Age 17		Mean Age at Marriage	
	Abroad	Israel	Abroad	Israel
Algeria and Tunisia	27.4	15.9	20.7	27.1
Egypt and Sudan	18.9	13.7	21.8	22.0
Iran	48.5	18.9	18.4	21.4
Iraq	35.7	13.2	19.8	21.8
Libya	37.0	14.5	19.3	20.6
Morocco and Tangier	53.5	24.4	17.4	20.1
Syria and Lebanon	31.5	18.4	20.4	21.2
Turkey	14.1	20.0	23.1	21.4
Yemen and Aden	54.9	26.5	17.0	20.2

Source: Central Bureau of Statistics (1966, p. 10, table 5).
Note: Foreign-born women, married, divorced, or widowed.

Notes

1. One should note, of course, that even with full replacement, halving of (e.g.) 200 per 1,000 child death rate would reduce a 45 per 1,000 birthrate to just 40 per 1,000, and half replacement to 43 per 1,000.

2. Take a simple model where

$$(1) \qquad \max u[q(t,x)n, s] \quad s.t.\ \pi n x + s = y,$$

where t = indicator of survival
n = number of children
q = index of child quality
s = consumption of parents
y = full family income
x = inputs into children
π = the price of one unit of x.

Both optimum quality of children, q^*, and optimum expenditure on them, x^*, can be solved as a function of survival (t). The solution of equation 1 is:

$$(2) \qquad \eta_{nt} = -\eta_{q^*t} + \eta_{n\pi}-(\eta_{x^*t} - \eta_{q^*t}).$$

The first term represents a technical relationship—as children survive longer, parents have more child services ($\eta_{q^*t} > 0$) and need fewer children for a given volume of child services. The second term represents the effect of prices and expenditure. The term $\eta_{x^*t} - \eta_{q^*t}$ is equal to the elasticity with respect to survival of expenditure per unit of quality, $\eta_{(x^*/q^*)t}$. This term is likely to be positive and thus to contribute a downward slant to the fertility-survival relationships via the negative price elasticity (see also O'Hara 1972*a*). If expenditure were independent of survival, we would have the simple expression $\eta_{nt} = -(1 + \eta_{n\pi})\eta_{q^*t}$ which, like the analogous case of augmenting technical change, indicates that fertility will be directly associated with mortality if the demand for children is inelastic (see Ben-Porath and Welch 1975; Ben-Porath 1976*b*).

3. $\text{BIS} = \alpha_1\,\text{DAB} + \alpha_2\,(\text{DAB})^2 + \alpha_3\,\text{BAB} + \alpha_4\,(\text{BAB})^2 + \alpha_5\,(\text{BAB} \times \text{DAB}) + \beta\chi$

BIS the number of births that occurred in Israel.
BAB the number of births that occurred abroad.
DAB the number of deaths that occurred abroad.

$$\frac{\partial \text{BIS}}{\partial \text{DAB}} = \alpha_1 + 2\alpha_2\,\text{DAB} + \alpha_5\,\text{BAB}.$$

4.

	R^2	F	Degrees of Freedom
Women born in Asia-Africa			
Separate regressions for each country	0.515	6.4	68/7,339
Same slope, different intercept	0.486	32.6	6/7,407
Single regression	0.479		
Women born in Europe-America			
Separate regressions for each country	0.337	2.8	58/9,041
Same slope, different intercept	0.317	6.3	5/9,099
Single regression	0.315		

5. This possibility was suggested by Professors Davies and Halevi of the Department of Ecological Medicine, Hadassah Medical School, the Hebrew University.

6. See Schmelz (1971) for a valuable compendium on child mortality of Jews in the Diaspora and for a description and evaluation of the child mortality data in the 1961 census.

7. In retrospective data there are many problems associated both with the reported levels and with placing in time. In the Israeli census the distinction between children born abroad and children born in Israel is based on direct questions as to the number of children born in each place rather than an inference from matching birthrates of children and data of immigration. Age at immigration is determined by comparing year of birth and year of immigration.

8. The gross difference in fertility between women grouped by age in 1961 and grouped by age at immigration is larger than the difference when we also control for duration of marriage. Average marriage duration is longer for the grouping by age in 1961, compared with the age-at-immigration grouping. Because 1961 is approximately one decade after mass immigration, the women who married very young and immigrated soon after appear with long duration in 1961 and with short duration (and with younger age) when classified by age at immigration.

9. We use the following definitions: stillbirths, born dead after 28 weeks of gestation; neonatal mortality, deaths in the first month of life; and perinatal mortality, the sum of stillbirths and deaths in the first week of life. Rates are per 1,000 live births.

Comment Etienne van de Walle

That parents strive to replace their dead children is plausible on a priori grounds. Nevertheless, the replacement child has been an evasive entity in empirical research. The data presented by Professor Ben-Porath are therefore both tantalizing and suspect. Tantalizing, because the relationship between mortality and subsequent fertility appears very strong—too good to be true. Suspect, because retrospective data collected in censuses are tricky to handle and abound in statistical traps. Add the problem of assigning causality when a relationship is detected. Is higher mortality (abroad) causing higher fertility (in Israel), or is some common factor operating on both variables? Ben-Porath does a beautiful job of untangling the evidence as much as possible. I shall perfunctorily list a few rather unconvincing alternative explanations of his findings before turning to some wider implications of his results.

Is it possible that some factors account for both higher fertility and higher mortality? The most likely set of such factors would be education and related socioeconomic statuses, and education has been controlled for in the regressions. One might unearth a factor unrelated to education;

Etienne van de Walle is associated with the University of Pennsylvania.

one ideal (but implausible) culprit would be the existence of sects that prohibit both contraception and medical assistance. If some women belonged to such sects, they would have had higher mortality before arriving in Israel and also higher fertility since their arrival. A more likely factor affecting both fertility and mortality is the time of entry in Israel; women entering more recently would be likely to have been subjected to lesser infant mortality and to lesser fertility than those belonging to earlier cohorts.

Professor Ben-Porath discards the possibility of reverse causality; that is, of high fertility resulting in high infant mortality, because births in Israel are necessarily subsequent to deaths abroad. But the same women could have had high fertility—and as a result, high mortality—both abroad and in Israel. It is also possible that women prone to losing their children (perhaps because they have unusually short birth intervals) benefited from better medical care in Israel and that their children, who would otherwise have died abroad, survived in their new country. Similarly, better prenatal care may have insured live births to women who would otherwise have miscarried.

Granted, the above mechanisms cannot be expected to account fully for the relationship found between infant mortality and subsequent fertility. The demographic transition framework implied in the paper's title seems to demand that a reduction in infant mortality provoked a reduction in fertility. If high mortality explains high fertility, must we also conclude that a decline in mortality—or in the author's phrase, the "dramatically speeded-up version of economic and social development" resulting from immigration to Israel—caused a drop in fertility? Were women whose children were surviving resorting to the deliberate control of their fertility after (and perhaps because of) their arrival in Israel whereas high-mortality women were curtailing contraception? Paradoxically, it is among women born in Asia and Africa, among whom fertility was least controlled, that the so-called replacement of dead children is most marked. But the shape of the fertility curve in table 3.6, with its very high childbearing in the forties, does not suggest family limitation.

The issues are further confused by some evidence of a rise in the fertility of migrants in Israel. The evidence is not very clear on this. Ben-Porath compares the experience of married women in Israel with that of women of unknown marital status abroad (in table 3.6). But it is not surprising that fertility may have been rising; after all, a very large proportion of the migration was occurring in the 1950s, when fertility was peaking almost everywhere—the baby boom phenomenon. Whether these findings have wider implications for other places and other times is doubtful. But this unique body of data was well worth exploring for the questions it poses rather than for the answers it provides.

Comment Anne D. Williams

I wish to thank Professor Ben-Porath for an excellent paper. I am basically in agreement with his approach and findings, and I find it particularly intriguing to have access through the Israeli immigration experience to people with diverse origins and later common experience. The paper is a valuable contribution for the study of the response of fertility to infant mortality, yet tantalizing for the questions raised that cannot yet be answered.

To summarize briefly, Ben-Porath discusses the interaction of child mortality with fertility in considerable detail and sophistication and focuses in detail on the various mechanisms through which child mortality (assumed to be exogenous) can influence fertility. He then uses the 1961 Israeli census data to describe this response, first in terms of the cross section of household data, then with aggregate data showing some of the time trends. He finds substantial differences between the cross-sectional data and the time-trend evidence. The cross section shows a strong response of fertility to infant and child loss, particularly for young women at low parities who seem to have more than full replacement of child mortality. The results for individual countries of origin are very similar to the pooled results. The data which the author uses to measure time trends, however, present a completely different picture. Over time there has been continuing high fertility in the face of large declines in child mortality. He feels that this reflects rising levels of income over time, which not only reduce mortality but also stimulate fertility, for both biological and behavioral reasons.

I would like to comment in turn on each of these two basic findings.

Strong Cross-Sectional Response

Ben-Porath uses the sequential approach to fertility decisions that he and Finis Welch pioneered in the analysis of pregnancy histories (Ben-Porath and Welch 1972). Here he can observe each woman at only two points in the life cycle, first at immigration into Israel and later at the 1961 census. He thus has information on births up to the age of immigration, on how many of those births survived, and on the number of later births between immigration and 1961. The number of children born abroad who died is a good proxy for child mortality as of the time of immigration, because child mortality overwhelmingly takes place in the first year of life. He then explains fertility after immigration as a function of fertility and mortality experience before immigration, while

Anne D. Williams is assistant professor in the Department of Economics and a research associate of the Population Studies Center, University of Pennsylvania.

holding constant the effects of other variables such as age, country of origin, and education.

He is not able, however, to obtain data on proportion surviving among children born in Israel after immigration. I believe this missing information serves to bias upward the estimated response of fertility to child mortality. Even though mortality should have fallen after immigration to Israel, one would expect high correlations between mortality before immigration and mortality after immigration, because of family-specific factors that could be either biological or behavioral. Information on later deaths would reduce the size of the coefficients but would not completely detract from his conclusion of a strong cross-sectional response.

The result of a strong cross-sectional response comes through clearly in both the cross-tabulations and the regressions. Let me note that although my own work (Williams 1976) has relied exclusively on regression analysis, I must confess to a growing suspicion that use of continuous variables to measure mortality and fertility may lead to spurious results. This is because of the high intercorrelations of fertility, mortality, current age, age at immigration, and birth order. I understand the attempt to conserve parameters in the regressions of table 3.3, but I prefer the use of dummy variables as in table 3.2.

Finally, it would also be interesting to know whether there has been any change in the response of fertility to mortality over different immigration cohorts.

Time-Trend Results

Ben-Porath uses data on fertility of women at different ages and different times of immigration to construct a picture of the time path of fertility of an individual woman. From tables 3.6 through 3.8 he concludes that the individual woman has relatively low fertility abroad. Immediately after immigration she has higher fertility (relative to her age group), which then tapers off over time. He feels this increase could be both biological and behavioral in origin. If I read the tables correctly there may be another, though not mutually exclusive, explanation.

Table 3.6 is difficult to interpret, partly because it does not hold marriage duration constant. Table 3.8, however, does indicate a rise in fertility after immigration. Looking at women married 10–14 years, for example, we can compare the fertility of those immigrating at different times. The table shows that women aged 30–34 in 1961 who were married abroad had 4.7 children, some of whom were born abroad, and some in Israel (line 2 of the third panel). The next line gives the number of children born by age 30–34 to women who immigrated to Israel at that age. For those married 10–14 years, number of children was 3.1, all of whom had been born abroad. The inference is that fertility after immigration exceeds that before immigration, holding constant age and marriage duration.

However, it must be noted that women who were aged 30–34 at immigration are members of earlier cohorts than women age 30–34 in 1961. In fact, looking at the time patterns of immigration in tables 3.A.2–5, it seems quite possible that they were on average born ten years earlier than the women age 30–34 in 1961. Referring again to tables 3.A.2–5, it is clear that over the period described, immigrants of a given age have entered Israel with higher and higher fertility. For example, women who immigrated at age 30–34 in the early forties had 3.1 children, but those entering Israel at the same age in the late fifties had an average of 4.4 children.

Thus, although the phenomenon of rising fertility over time is clear, I am not convinced that there was a substantial rise in Israel after immigration. The women age 30–34 in 1961 are younger than those who immigrated at that age. Their higher fertility by age 30–34 may simply reflect higher fertility abroad before immigration. Over time there may have been a change in the composition of immigrants or change in the fertility abroad of a given population, owing to falling mortality and rising income. Thus the change in fertility behavior that Ben-Porath locates in Israel may in fact have taken place abroad. Then the Israeli experience would be one of continuously falling fertility, as migrants respond to the new environment.

It would be useful to compare women in 1961 of a given age and marriage duration with respect to their age at immigration and the extent of their fertility both before and after immigration.

Finally, in section 3.5 Ben-Porath discusses the nature of the increase in fertility owing to supply considerations. He emphasizes the importance of declines in fetal losses and child mortality for increasing the potential number of surviving children. In fact, there may also be a significant effect of improvements in nutrition and health on the ability to conceive (Frisch and McArthur 1974). Or there may be a decline in early fetal losses that is not apparent in the recorded data. French and Bierman (1962) and James (1970) estimate true spontaneous fetal loss rates of 250–500 per 1,000 conceptions in contrast with reported rates of 100–200. The effect on fertility of declines in malaria, in particular, may operate through this channel (Barlow 1967).

Conclusions

The answers to both my speculations appear, unfortunately, not to lie in the data source at hand. Ben-Porath has, however, described in another paper to which he refers here (Ben-Porath 1976), a 1971 fertility survey that asked about the timing of live births. His work with these data showed lower cross-sectional responses of fertility to mortality and a different response pattern by age of the woman. He was able to stratify by country of origin, but it was not clear to me whether the date of immigration had also been recorded in the survey. If it has, we can observe the timing of fertility in the years before and after immigration rather than having to rely on just the total number of children born abroad and in Israel to determine the time trends.

I think that Ben-Porath's thoughts about observing the details of a modern demographic transition in the Israeli experience are well founded. The data he has used so far have provided some tantalizing insights. Future data analysis should prove even more rewarding.

References

Barlow, Robin. 1967. The economic effects of malaria eradication. *American Economic Review* 57, no. 3 (May): 130–48.

Ben-Porath, Yoram. 1972. Fertility in Israel, an economist's interpretation: Differentials and trends, 1950–1970. In *Economic development and population growth in the Middle East*, ed. Charles A. Cooper and Sidney S. Alexander, pp. 501–39. New York: Elsevier.

———. 1976*a*. Fertility in Israel: A mini-survey and some new findings. In *Economic factors in population growth*, ed. Ansley Coale, pp. 136–72. London: Macmillan.

———. 1976*b*. Fertility response to child mortality: Micro data from Israel. *Journal of Political Economy* 84, no. 4, part 2 (August): S163–78.

Ben-Porath, Yoram, and Welch, Finis. 1972. *Uncertain quality: Sex of children and family size*. Report R-1117-NIH/RF. Santa Monica: Rand Corporation.

———. 1975. Child traits and the choice of family size. Unpublished MS Rand P-5556.

Bierman, Jessie M., et al. 1965. Analysis of the outcome of all pregnancies in a community: Kanai pregnancy study. *American Journal of Obstetrics and Gynecology* 91, no. 1 (January): 37–45.

Central Bureau for Medical Statistics. 1945. Statistical tables on the natality among the various sections of the population of Palestine. Pamphlet no. 3. Jerusalem: Hadassah Medical Organization.

Central Bureau of Statistics. 1966. *Marriage and fertility: Part II*. Census 1961 Publication no. 32. Jerusalem.

———. 1974. *Late fetal and infant deaths in Israel: 1948–1972*. Special Series no. 453. Jerusalem.

———. 1975. *Immigration to Israel: 1948–1972. Part II. Composition by period of immigration.* Special Series no. 489. Jerusalem.

———. 1976. The fertility of Jewish marriage cohorts in Israel: 1966–1974. *Monthly Bulletin of Statistics* 27, supplement to no. 6 (June): pp. 1–18.

Easterlin, Richard A. 1975. An economic framework for fertility analysis. *Studies in Family Planning* 1 (March): 54–63.

French, Fern E., and Bierman, Jessie M. 1962. Probabilities of fetal mortality. *Public Health Reports* 77 (October): 835–47.

Friedlander, D. 1973. The fertility of three Oriental migration groups in Israel: Stability and change. In *Papers in Jewish demography, 1969*, ed. U. O. Schmelz, P. Glikson, and S. Della Pergola, pp. 131–42. Jerusalem: Institute of Contemporary Jewry, Hebrew University.

Frisch, Rose E., and McArthur, Janet W. 1974. Menstrual cycles: Fatness as a determinant of minimum weight for height necessary for their maintenance or onset. *Science* 185 (13 September): 949–51.

Heer, D. M., and Wu, H. W. 1975. The separate effects of child loss, perception of child survival and community mortality level upon fertility and family planning in rural Taiwan with comparison data from urban Morocco. In *Seminar on infant mortality in relation to the level of fertility*. Paris: C.I.G.R.E.D.

Jain, A. K.; Hsu, T. C.; Freedman, R.; and Chang, M. C. 1970. Demographic aspects of lactation and post partum amenorrhea. *Demography* 7, no. 2 (May): 255–71.

James, W. H. 1970. The incidence of spontaneous abortion. *Population Studies* 24, no. 2 (July): 241–45.

Knodel, J. 1968. Infant mortality and fertility in three Bavarian villages: An analysis of family histories from the 19th century. *Population Studies* 12, no. 3 (November): 297–318.

Kuznets, Simon. 1973. *Population trends and modern economic growth.* Economic Growth Center Discussion Paper no. 191. New Haven: Yale University.

———. 1974. *Fertility differentials between less developed and developed regions: Components and implications.* Economic Growth Center Discussion Paper no. 217. New Haven: Yale University.

Legg, Susan; Davies, Michael A.; Prywes, Rachel; Sterk, Velimir V.; and Weiskopf, Pearl. 1969. The Jerusalem perinatal study. 2. Infants deaths 1964–1966: A cohort study of socioethnic factors in deaths from congenital malformations and from environmental and other causes. *Israel Journal of Medical Sciences* 5, no. 6 (December): 1107–16.

O'Hara, Donald J. 1972*a*. *Changes in mortality levels and family decisions regarding children.* R-914-RF. Santa Monica, Calif.: Rand Corporation.

———. 1972*b*. Mortality risks, sequential decisions on births and population growth. *Demography* 4, no. 3 (August): 285–98.

Peritz, E., and Adler, B. 1974. Linkage data on infant mortality in the Jewish population of Israel. In *Late fetal and infant deaths in Israel: 1948–1972*, pp. 37–42. Special Series no. 453. Jerusalem: Central Bureau of Statistics.

Preston, Samuel H. 1975*a*. Introduction. *Seminar on infant mortality in relation to the level of fertility*. Paris: C.I.C.R.E.D.

———. 1975*b*. Health programs and population growth. *Population and development review* 1, no. 2 (December): 189–99.

Rutstein, S. O. 1974. The influence of child mortality on fertility in Taiwan. *Studies in Family Planning* 5, no. 6 (June): 182–88.

Ryder, Norman B. 1975. Reproductive behaviour and the family life cycle. In *The population debate: Dimensions and perspectives.* Papers of the World Population Conference, Bucharest, vol. 2. Department of Economic and Social Affairs, Population Studies, no. 57. New York: United Nations.

Schmelz, U. O. 1971. *Infant and early childhood mortality among the Jews of the diaspora*. Jerusalem: Institute of Contemporary Jewry, Hebrew University.

———. 1974. Infant and early childhood mortality among the non-Jewish population of Palestine and Israel. In *Late fetal and infant deaths in Israel: 1948–1972*, pp. 55–84. Special Series no. 453. Jerusalem: Central Bureau of Statistics.

Schultz, T. Paul. 1969. An economic model of family planning and fertility. *Journal of Political Economy* 87 (March/April): 153–80.

———. 1976. Interrelationships between mortality and fertility. In *Population and development: The search for selective interventions*, ed. Ronald G. Ridker, pp. 239–89. Baltimore: Johns Hopkins University Press.

Sheps, M., and Ridley, J. C., eds. 1965. *Public health and population change*. Pittsburgh: University of Pittsburgh Press.

Shorter, Edward. 1975. *The making of the modern family*. New York: Basic Books.

Stolnitz, George J. 1974. International mortality trends: Some main facts and implications. U.N. World Population Conference, Bucharest, August 1974. Conference Background Paper E/CONF. 60/CBP/17.

Taylor, Carl E.; Newman, Jeanne S.; and Kelly, Narindar U. 1976. Interactions between health and population. *Studies in Family Planning* 7, no. 4 (April): 94–100.

United Nations. World Health Organization. 1974. Health trends and prospects in relation to population and development. World Populalation Conference, Bucharest, August 1974. Conference Background Paper E/CONF. 60/CBP/26.

Williams, Anne D. 1976. *Fertility and reproductive loss.* Ph.D. diss. University of Chicago.

4 An Economic Interpretation of the Decline in Fertiliiy in a Rapidly Developing Country: Consequences of Development and Family Planning

T. Paul Schultz

4.1 Introduction

Parents make sacrifices to rear children. And though some rewards of parenthood are virtually immediate, other benefits cannot be realized for years or even decades. In understanding the process by which reproductive goals change, therefore, the demand for children should be interpreted as in part a demand for a *durable* input that enters into many lifetime production and consumption possibilities.[1] Given the number of children parents want, their spacing undoubtedly confers on parents relative advantages that might be explained in terms of either their life-cycle production and investment environment or their anticipated psychological and economic "returns to scale" in rearing of children at different time intervals.[2] But as yet few theoretical insights have emerged to prescribe how circumstances, even under static conditions, affect a couple's desired regime of child-spacing. Clearly, it is still more difficult to deduce how parents adjust their flow of births over the course of time as environmental changes modify their reproductive goals.

As a first approximation, therefore, reproductive goals will be summarized in terms of a desired lifetime stock of children. Accepting this working hypothesis, economists have begun to explore parent-revealed

T. Paul Schultz is associated with Yale University.

This research was supported in part by AID contract otr-1432 and in part by Rockefeller Foundation grant RF 70051 to Yale's Economic Demography Program. In the acquisition of data for Taiwan, I am grateful for the help of A. I. Hermalin and of the University of Michigan and to T. H. Sun of the Taiwan Provincial Institute of Family Planning. The research assistance of N. Kwan, J. Oder, and S. Chun is much appreciated. I have benefited from the comments of B. Boulier, G. Fields, R. Freedman, J. McCabe, T. W. Schultz, R. B. Tabbarah, and F. Welch.

demands for lifetime stocks of children as though conditioned by traditional determinants of consumer and producer demand: input and output prices, income, technology, and tastes. Ignoring radically different strategies in the timing of births, demand for annual increments to the existing stock of children, or period-specific birthrates, should also be systematically related to revealed demand for a lifetime stock.[3] This paper explores empirically several aspects of the time dimension of the relationship between cohort fertility in Taiwan and the presumed determinants of lifetime reproductive goals, namely, the value of time of women and men proxied by their schooling, accumulated and recent experience of child mortality, and the availability of birth-control information and services. First, the accumulated stocks of births are analyzed by age of woman, and regional variation in this measure of cohort fertility is decomposed into effects operating through age at marriage and through birthrate per year of marriage. Second, the simplest possible stock-adjustment framework is fit to the data on reproductive stocks and flows in Taiwan to describe the dynamics of behavioral change in a population that has experienced disequilibrating demographic, social, and economic change for several decades.[4] Coefficients from stock and flow demand equations estimated for various years are then used to appraise whether in Taiwan these relationships are relatively constant across birth cohorts and over time.

Several qualifications and limitations to this investigation should be stressed at the outset, ones that cannot be corrected here for want of appropriate individual panel data or analytical tools to cope with the probable complexity of reproductive capabilities and preferences. The most serious limitation is the unit of analysis: large regional populations of women born in various time periods. These aggregates are the only units for which data are publicly available on both the stocks and flows of births in Taiwan. Investigation at the level of individuals is also imperative, permitting disaggregation by women's educational attainment, a factor that appears crucial for understanding the changing age pattern of reproductive behavior in contemporary Taiwan. Nonetheless, despite the well-known deficiencies of aggregate data, it may still be fruitful to estimate behavioral relationships at different levels of aggregation in order to document the value and limitations of each unit of analysis; to neglect widely available information on grounds of "principle" is hard to justify.

Aside from subjective preferences of parents for bearing their own children, social restrictions on their exchange in most cultures encourage parents to produce their own supply.[5] Variability in supply, or in the biological capacity to bear children, prevents some individuals in all populations from achieving their reproductive goals. Yet biological differences in the supply of births do not appear to exert a dominant effect on *aggregate* fertility except under extreme conditions of malnutrition and specific endemic disease, such as gonorrhea. It is assumed that in Taiwan recent regional differences in fertility are not substantially affected by such health and nutritional impairments to the aggregate supply of births.[6]

Most studies of the determinants of reproductive demands have dealt with high-income countries, and consequently *consumer* demand theory is emphasized. In low-income countries, children are more obviously a productive asset, at least at maturity if not always at birth (Mamdami 1973; Nag 1976). The theory of producer-derived demand for inputs might provide a framework better suited to explaining differences in fertility in developing countries. A standard model of investment behavior in a durable input assumes that demand is homogeneous of degree zero in all prices, holding constant the interest rate (Griliches 1960). But imposing this restriction appears inadvisable in this case, since a couple's demand for children is limited both because consumer benefits from children are probably satiable and because the cost of funds to invest in one's children is undoubtedly upward-sloping.[7] Producer-demand theory also relies on assumptions of constant returns to scale, competitive input and output markets, and (observable) financial markets for borrowing, none of which is appealing in the study of household demand for children.

It is still useful to explore the stylized dynamic framework of the stock-adjustment model that has been extensively used to study demand for durable producer inputs and durable consumer goods. The stock-adjustment model applied to reproductive behavior is not invoked here to prescribe the path of life-cycle accumulation against which reproductive performance of a cohort can be evaluated before it reaches the end of its potential childbearing period. This shortcoming is, of course, just another reflection of our inability to specify determinants of the spacing of births. Substantial differences remain to be explained across countries at one point in time, and among countries over time, in the relative distribution of births by age of mother.[8] However, subject to identification and estimation problems discussed in subsequent sections, information for women of a particular age can be used to infer the current speed with which the apparent gap between current stock and lifetime desired stock of children is being closed. If this response parameter is assumed constant across a society but possibly variable over time, such a parameter is estimable from interregional variation in age-specific reproductive behavior. Comparisons between stock and flow predictive equations may also help us understand how the demographic transition works its way through a population.

The paper is ordered as follows. Section 4.2 describes a few salient features of the situation in Taiwan for which a model is sought and relates the limitations of available data for testing an aggregate model. The stock-adjustment framework is adapted to reproductive behavior in the section 4.3, with discussion focused on the simplifying assumptions implied by this model and on the estimation problems. Regional variation in cohort stock fertility is decomposed in section 4.4 into marriage duration and marital fertility, to provide insight into the responsiveness to environmental change of fertility and social institutions such as marriage. The stock-adjustment model is estimated in section 4.5 and the results are discussed further in a concluding section.

4.2 Description of Taiwan and Available Data

4.2.1 Demographic Transition

Mortality declined in Taiwan, notably among adults, during the period of Japanese colonial administration of the island in 1895–1945 (Barclay 1954). Though the rise in per capita income among the Taiwanese in this interwar period was probably less than the substantial growth in agricultural productivity, food consumption by the Taiwanese increased (Ho 1966). The more dramatic second phase of mortality reduction occurred after the Second World War, with land reform and economic recovery. The greatest proportionate declines were achieved among infants and children, and, though the evidence is not firm, the rural public health program, universal education, and decreased income inequality may all have contributed to this achievement. Undoubtedly, the growth of income and personal consumption helped; since 1952 the rate of per capita economic growth has been high by world standards, particularly after 1962. Today the expectation of life at birth is 67 for men and 72 for women, not far short of that recorded in high-income countries.[9]

Though the demographic transition began building from the start of the century, the first indication of a decline in birthrates emerged in the late 1950s among older women, and then only after a moderate postwar baby boom had run its course. But in the subsequent span of twenty years, the total fertility rate—that is, the sum of annual age-specific birthrates—decreased by half (see appendix table 4.A.1). This was first caused by a reduction in the frequency of childbearing among women over the age of 30, and in the last decade the pattern of declining birthrates gradually spread to younger women. This was accompanied by a slow rise in the age at marriage (see appendix table 4.A.2), which can be traced irregularly back to the turn of the century (Goode 1970; Barclay 1954). As a consequence of the separation over time of the declines in death rates and birthrates, the annual rate of population growth in Taiwan increased from about 1% in the first two decades of this century, to 2.3% during the interwar period, and peaked at more than 3.5% during the 1950s. Population growth has begun to ease in recent years and was somewhat less than 2% per year in 1974 (appendix table 4.A.3).

4.2.2 Family Planning Program

Taiwan organized and executed one of the first, most extensively studied, and apparently most effective national family planning programs in the world. Starting in 1963 with a controlled social experiment in the city of Taichung to determine the acceptability and effectiveness of family-planning activity, in several years an islandwide program was expanded to every township and city precinct in the country (Freedman and Takeshita 1969). Analyses of regional birthrates and regional family planning activity find a strong negative partial association between the seemingly random allocation of family planning fieldworkers and the level and decline in birthrates of women over the age of 30 (Freedman and Takeshita 1969; Hermalin 1968, 1971; Schultz 1969*b*, 1971, 1974). The implied effect of program personnel on birthrates, however, diminishes from 1965 to 1968, and after about 1969 it becomes difficult to assess whether the accumulated activity of the program has continued to affect birthrates by a statistically significant amount (Schultz 1969*b*, 1971).

This finding can be explained in part as a natural cycle in the diffusion of an innovation; with the introduction of distinctly superior technology for birth control—the IUD and the pill—the period of disequilibrium behavior that follows is likely to be shortened by the subsidized dissemination of information, services, and supplies relevant to its adoption. But in contrast to the classical case of agricultural extension activities in a dynamic productive environment, there has been only one quantum advance in birth control technology, not a stream of improved inputs and combinations of inputs to enhance yields and lower costs. Hence, the family planning innovation cycle is likely to eventually meet with diminishing returns to scale (extension effort per woman of childbearing age) unless communication between generations is absent. This tendency is already evident from cross-sectional analyses of program inputs and birthrates after two years, even though the output of services and supplies distributed to the population exhibited a more nearly linear relationship for several years (Schultz 1969*b*, 1971).

Another partial explanation for the difficulty of assessing the regional effect of the family planning program after 1968 is the limitation of the small (361 subdivisions) units of analysis and the uncontrolled interregional flows of knowledge, services, and users (migration). The spillover of influence of local program activity beyond regional boundaries may have blurred the cross-sectional associations between treatments and outcomes after several years. A similar spillover effect was thought to have been a shortcoming of the Taichung City experimental design in 1963 (Freedman and Takeshita 1969).

Regardless, program activity in the initial years is unambiguously linked to lower birthrates among older women, and, as one might expect, the two classes of fieldworkers working for different government agencies appear to be substitutes for each other in bringing about this outcome (T. P. Schultz 1974). Some indications are found that those regions that were lagging in reducing their birthrates toward the levels predicted by an economic-demographic model estimated from initial period cross-sectional data were regions in which the family planning program had its greatest effect (T. P. Schultz 1974).

Possibly more important than narrowing unexplained interregional differences in reproductive performance, public support for the diffusion of modern means of birth control narrows socioeconomic class differences in contraceptive knowledge and use and thereby moderates class differentials in fertility that appear to especially penalize the upward mobility of the lower class during the transitionary period of rapid population growth (Nelson, Schultz, and Slighton 1971; Freedman and Berelson 1976). These changes in class differentials of contraceptive knowledge, use, and fertility are carefully documented in Taiwan during the 1960s and 1970s (Freedman et al. 1974), but it remains difficult to infer how much of this change is due to Taiwan's family planning program.

4.2.3 Education and Fertility

I should like to interpret educational attainment as a proxy for the "value of time" of men and women. It is appropriate, therefore, for me to marshal evidence of the relation between education and wage rates for men and women in Taiwan. But I have as yet found no primary data on this score and no published analysis of education's effect on earnings in Taiwan.[10] Though this probably reflects my inability to read the relevant Chinese literature, it does not diminish the obvious emphasis recently given to education by the government and the people of Taiwan. For example, from 1966 to 1974, the proportion of men age 20–24 with some junior high school increased 32%, from 0.44 to 0.58, while exposure to junior high school increased 125% among women of the same age, from 0.24 to 0.54. This increase in the proportion reaching junior high school in an eight-year period is all the more remarkable when one realizes that the size of the birth cohort to educate in that period also increased by about 80%.

Direct evidence is available, however, that educational attainment is associated with reproductive behavior in Taiwan, for whatever reason. Tables 4.1 and 4.2 report 1974 birthrates, calculated by date of occur-

Table 4.1 **1974 Birthrates by Age and Educational Attainment of Mother (Per 1,000, by Date of Occurrence)**

Educational level	15–19	20–24	25–29	30–34	35–39	40–44	45–49	Total Fertility Rate[a]
Illiterate and those without schooling	110.5	315.8	223.3	82.8	33.6	9.3	1.1	3,882
Literate without graduating from primary school	97.2	247.7	192.2	77.3	28.2	10.7	1.7	3,275
Primary school graduate without graduating from junior high or junior vocational school	48.7	244.3	235.7	95.3	34.6	9.7	1.7	3,350
Junior high graduate without graduating from senior high or senior vocational school	8.0	136.4	221.7	96.6	29.2	5.2	1.9	2,495
Senior high graduate without graduating from junior college or university	6.6	70.7	201.3	112.5	48.6	6.5	0.7	2,235
Junior college and university graduate, graduate school attended, graduate school graduate	11.7	37.7	163.3	101.7	41.1	8.4	1.3	1,826
All educational groups	32.2	183.3	219.0	91.2	32.7	9.3	1.4	2,846

[a]Total fertility rate is five times the sum of age-specific birthrates.

Source: *1974 Taiwan Demographic Factbook*, tables 4 and 48 for Taiwan area.

Table 4.2 **1974 Birthrates by Age and Educational Attainment of Father (per 1,000, by Date of Occurrence)**

Educational Level	15–19	20–24	25–29	30–34	35–39	40–44	45–49	50–54	55–59	60+	Total Fertility Rate[a]
Illiterate and those without schooling	5.3	72.4	188.7	180.6	79.9	31.5	14.2	4.2	1.5	0.3	2,893
Literate without graduating from primary school	13.2	67.7	220.0	155.2	67.1	31.8	20.5	8.9	3.9	0.8	2,946
Primary school graduate without graduating from junior high or junior vocational school	8.4	83.8	261.0	177.5	67.3	28.6	18.2	8.6	3.4	0.7	3,288
Junior high graduate without graduating from senior high or senior vocational school	2.2	55.4	231.5	169.0	59.6	43.0	33.4	12.8	4.7	0.9	3,063
Senior high graduate without graduating from junior college or university	2.1	24.3	174.2	151.7	49.9	46.4	34.1	11.8	4.8	0.5	2,499
Junior college and university graduate, graduate school attended, graduate school graduate	8.9	19.0	109.7	137.0	55.3	46.2	33.3	10.1	2.6	0.7	2,114
All educational groups	4.6	57.0	218.4	167.0	64.4	33.8	23.5	9.0	3.2	0.5	2,907

Source: *1974 Taiwan Demographic Factbook*, tables 4 and 47 for Taiwan area.
[a]Total fertility rate is defined as for women as five times the sum of the age-specific birthrates.

rence, for mothers and for fathers, by age and educational attainment. Three things may be noted. A sharp reduction in total fertility rates (i.e., sum of age-specific birthrates times five) occurs among women going beyond primary school. If the distribution of education must be summarized by a single measure, the distinctly nonlinear relationship with fertility is perhaps better represented by the proportion continuing to junior high school than by an average number of years of schooling (implying a linear relationship), or by another higher cutoff point such as college education, which is further from the mode of the educational attainment distribution.

The second observation drawn from table 4.1 is more tenuous, for here the cross section of age groups is used to infer the longitudinal pace of reproduction. In 1974, better educated women start having births at a later age than do less educated women, but they also appear to continue bearing children somewhat longer, into their thirties. This is a relatively new pattern in later age- and education-specific birthrates in Taiwan that was less evident in 1971 or 1966 (Anderson 1973; *Taiwan Demographic Factbook* 1974, p. 15; Freedman et al. 1976). To investigate these changing patterns of childbearing would require information on stocks and flows of births by educational group, which are not published. These changes in the timing of childbearing may explain why earlier analyses of cross-sectional changes in birthrates found that the negative effects of women's education on birthrates were attenuated after age 34 (T. P. Schultz 1974). The partial association between current births and sex-specific educational attainment may be seen more clearly when conditioned on the number of children already born to various educational groups.

The third regularity to note is the lesser, more ambiguous variation in birthrates with father's education (table 4.2) than with mother's education (table 4.1). From illiterates to those with higher education, mother's total fertility rates decline almost monotonically by 53%, whereas father's total fertility rates rise 13%, peaking among primary school graduates, and then fall 28% below the level of those men with no education. Since the correlation between husband's and wife's education is substantial in most societies, we should expect the partial effect of women's education, holding husband's education (and earnings) constant, to be even more negative, and conversely, the partial effect of men's education to be less negative and perhaps even positive. This result would be consistent with our expectation that the income effect of men's earnings will outweigh their price-of-time effect, but the price-of-time effect embodied in women's value of time (education) will outweigh the income effect, reducing reproductive demands as women's education rises (Willis 1974; Schultz 1976; Ben-Porath 1975).

Though the advance of women in secondary schooling relative to men has already been cited, table 4.3 presents the parallel data for literacy and higher education and extends the data series to earlier birth cohorts. Though women have gradually increased their literacy, as have men, the notable advance of women into secondary and higher education has occurred largely since 1950. It may be asked, How much of the decline in fertility has been due simply to the increased educational attainment of women? Partitioning the change in crude birthrates into changes in women's age composition, educational composition, and a residual change *within* age/education cells, it was found that 24% of the decline in age-specific rates from 1966 to 1974 was accounted for by change in the distribution of women by five educational classes (Freedman et al. 1976).

4.2.4 Child Mortality and the Demographic Transition

For reasons that may be intuitively plausible, if not derived from a simple formal model of reproductive behavior, fertility is generally higher in populations that experience higher child mortality rates. At the regional or individual level, differences in child mortality are observed to be directly associated with differences in fertility, moderating

Table 4.3 Educational Attainment at Ages 20 to 24, by Year of Birth and by Sex (Percentages)

Minimum Educational Level	1950–54	1942–46	1932–36	1922–26	1912–26
Literate					
Men	99	97	90	85	69
Women	96	82	66	46	26
With some junior high school					
Men	58	44	27	34	20
Women	54	24	11	11	6
With some higher education					
Men	16	10	5	7	6
Women	10	5	1	1	1

Source: 1950–54 birth cohort—*1974 Taiwan Demographic Factbook*, table 4. Earlier cohorts—1966 Taiwan census, vol. 2, no. 3, table 2.

Note: The 1950–54 birth cohort is observed in 1974, before all members may have attended a higher educational institution. The earlier cohorts are all observed as of 1966 (census), and it is therefore assumed that no differential mortality by educational level affects their enumerated composition at that later date. The emigration of close to a million Chinese from the mainland in the post–Second World War period notably augmented the male proportion with secondary and higher education in the cohort born between 1922 and 1926 and residing in Taiwan in 1966.

and sometimes reversing the cross-sectional pattern between mortality and size of surviving family. This evidence is strongly suggestive of a mechanism, probably both involuntary (biological) and voluntary (behavioral) in nature, that achieves some manner of population equilibrium given environmental health and economic constraints (Schultz 1967, 1976; Dumond 1975). But existing evidence does not explain how such modifications in fertility are accomplished, or how rapidly they occur as the regime of mortality changes. Knowledge of the mechanisms involved and of the lags in adjustment is essential to assessing the duration of the current phase of rapid population growth in low income countries and to appraising the gains and losses from policy interventions that seek to improve nutrition and health and thereby to reduce mortality more rapidly.

The data from Taiwan may be useful in exploring these questions; the Household Registry System appears to be a relatively accurate source of current information on fertility and mortality; the 1966 census retrospective information from women on their number of children ever born and the survival status of their offspring is internally consistent and plausible in all regions of the island. It is possible, then, in Taiwan to hold past child losses constant and examine how the recent regional variation in child mortality is associated with current fertility.

4.2.5 Overview of Available Data

The unit of analysis is a highly aggregated region of Taiwan: five major cities and sixteen counties. Only for these large subdivisions are the number of children ever born and the number of children living reported by region and age of woman (1966 census). The Household Registry System has published information since 1961 on births by age groups of mothers, and deaths by age of the deceased. A number of assumptions are made to estimate the stock of children ever born and the number living for earlier and later years, using as a benchmark the birth cohorts as enumerated in the 1966 census.[11]

The marital status of women is reported by age groups and distributed according to the year of first marriage (1966 census). The relationship between mean age of a cohort and mean age of first marriage is approximated within each region and used to interpolate regional estimates for the standardized five-year age groups for which fertility data are available. Births are not published, to my knowledge, by current age of woman and age of marriage.

Educational attainment of the population is available in various censuses by age and sex and has recently been published by the Household Registry System. Data on regional economic conditions are regrettably scarce for Taiwan. A Household Income and Expenditure Survey is tabulated by regions for the first time in 1970, but sampling variability may be a serious limitation of these data as well as the lack of disaggregation by age and educational attainment of household head. The unweighted means and standard deviations of variables used in later analyses are summarized in appendix table 4.A.4.

Since the regional observations for Taiwan coincide with five cities and sixteen less urbanized and rural areas, it could be anticipated that relationships noted between fertility and such conditioning variables as child mortality and schooling could simply reflect urban/rural differences. If, in fact, other environmental conditions called "modernization" or culturally induced "norms and tastes" were responsible for urban/ differences in fertility, then a causal role might be erroneously attributed to health and education. Unless a case is made for the exogeneity of observable variables that produce the conditions of "modernization, norms, or tastes," it is difficult to conclude that these alternative factors are better or worse at explaining fertility than child mortality and sex-specific schooling. It is of some interest, nonetheless, to determine how much of the partial association between fertility and specific characteristics such as child mortality and schooling is captured by the direct admission of different levels of fertility (stocks and flows) in urban and rural regions. To perform this test, an urban dummy variable is introduced into the explanatory model, even though we are unable at this time to pinpoint precisely what objective features of the urban and rural environment might be responsible for such shifts in behavior.

4.2.6 Conclusions

Taiwan was launched into the demographic transition by changes in social and economic organization first imposed by the Japanese, followed by heavy investments in the agricultural infrastructure (Barclay 1954; Ho 1966). Deeper structural change in the ownership of productive assets after the Second World War facilitated rapid industrialization and urbanization, while policies also promoted the rapid modernization of small-scale agriculture. Costly investments in education and public health accelerated the declining trend in death rates and possibly fostered labor mobility, both developments that are closely associated with modern economic growth and enhanced labor productivity. The remarkable pace of recent economic growth and fertility decline holds out the possibility that more could be learned from this unusual period that would have somewhat wider applicability and relevance for policy: What was the role of growth in economic product, investment in human capital, intervention to hasten the adoption of modern birth control technology, and the peculiar social and economic institutions of Taiwan? The available data, though exceptional with respect to aggregate demographic detail, limit the goals of this study to the examination of crude proxies for the level and composition of personal household income and relative prices. To refine further the questions that currently occupy economic demography, it may be necessary to analyze household economic information, which will almost certainly entail the use of sample surveys to collect time-budget data as well as income, wealth, and expenditure detail (see Kelley's chapter in this volume).

4.3 A Stock-Adjustment Model of Reproduction

My objective is to estimate an adaptive model of demand for a durable good—children—that might clarify the process by which reproductive behavior responds over time to disequilibriums caused by economic and demographic change. A framework to account for both stocks and flows of births may also provide a means for modeling the important component decisions that determine reproductive performance—the timing of marriage and the spacing of births. The standard variety of rigid stock-adjustment model is proposed as only a useful starting point for such exercises.

To simplify the task, I neglect certain aspects of the problem that might elicit different strategies of decision-making in forming a family. A couple's reproductive preferences are represented by a *single-valued indicator* of their desired lifetime stock of births. Several strong assumptions are implied. First, it is assumed that preferences among alternative family size outcomes greater or less than the single-valued goal do not influence reproductive outcomes. In fact, given the uncertainty that attaches to both the biological capacity to bear children and their subsequent survival and development, parents probably weigh the consequences of a wide range of family-size outcomes that are likely to occur with different probabilities conditional on their behavior (Schultz 1967). Some segments of society exceed their reproductive goals and others fall short of them, possibly because their preferences are asymmetric in the vicinity of their single most preferred family-size goal. Pioneering research on the measurement and interpretation of family-size preferences indicates that asymmetries in these preferences may be important for understanding differences in fertility in Taiwan, at least at the level of the individual survey respondent or across education classes (Coombs 1974, 1976; Coombs and Sun 1978). When regions are the unit of analysis within a single cultural area, this assumption may be somewhat less restrictive.

The second simplification is required to deal with child mortality. The frequency of child mortality is undoubtedly affected by the availability of household resources, by production and consumption technology, and by relative prices, and in some circumstances it may even reflect allocative decisions and preferences of household members, all of which are to some degree endogenous. Nonetheless, it is widely believed that regional and time-series variation in aggregate mortality rates is attributable primarily to climate, public investments, available drugs and medical knowledge, and modifications in social organization, not to household decision-making. Therefore, given the scarcity of predetermined factors that are thought to influence reproductive behavior, I shall treat child mortality here as exogenous to the fertility decision.[12]

The consequences of child mortality for reproductive goals and behavior are too complex for me to simply restate demands in terms of "surviving children."[13] In the long run, as the level of child mortality decreases the number of births needed to achieve a given number of survivors decreases, and the average cost of rearing a child to maturity decreases, while at the same time all investments in the human agent, including children, appreciate in value (Schultz 1976). Though an economist may aspire to sort out these offsetting supply, price, and also wealth and cross-substitution effects of mortality on the demand for births, the essential question for population growth is simply the overall magnitude and time path by which fertility adapts to change in mortality (see Ben-Porath's paper in this volume).

4.3.1 A Simple Framework for the Joint Analysis of Stocks and Flows

With these simplifications, I assume that parents, at a particular time t, desire a specific number of births, $C_t{}^*$, over their lifetime. Demand for this durable stock will depend upon what people expect of the future and, of course, on their own preferences. The formation of expectations must be expressed in terms of current or past conditioning variables. Psychological and economic aspects of habit persistence, perception, information-processing, and uncertainty are all cited as justifications for assuming the existence of distributed lags mediating the effect of stimuli on behavior (Nerlove 1958).

$$C_t{}^* = \alpha + \sum_{i=1}^{M} \sum_{j=1}^{n} \beta_{ij} Z_{i,\, t-j-1} + u_t, \tag{1}$$

where the Z_i's are M conditioning variables whose effect on C^* extend for n periods, α and β_{ij} $(i = 1, \ldots, M; j = 1, \ldots, n)$ are parameters, and u_t is a residual disturbance that represents the net effect of many omitted factors and any errors of approximation in the functional form of the relationship. Given the central role of multiplicative interactions between births, child survival rates, surviving offspring, and price effects reflected in the *relative* educational attainment of women to men, the dependent and independent variables in equation 1 are all expressed in (natural) logarithms, unless otherwise noted.[14]

Primarily for biological reasons, a lapse of time is required for the realization of desired increments to the existing stock of births, just as technological (and economic) factors introduce lags between capital investment decisions in plant and equipment and realized increases in productive capacity. Though the human gestation period is only three-fourths of one year, the median interbirth interval for couples who report they want an additional birth immediately varies from one to three years, depending on age of spouses and perhaps on their health and nutritional status.[15]

A conventional representation of the stock-adjustment process assumes that a proportion, $\delta(a)$, of the relative difference between desired stock and the actual stock is delivered in each time period. For the study of reproduction, a minimum lag of a year for conception and gestation seems appropriate.

$$C_t - C_{t-1} = \delta(a)(C^*_t - C_{t-1}) + f(a), \tag{2}$$

where $0 < \delta(a) < 1$, the index a being possibly related to a woman's age, for reasons of biological reproductive capacity and the desired relative distribution of births over the reproductive period, and $f(a)$ is an excess fertility function discussed below. Actually, the speed of reproductive adjustment is affected by many considerations, only the most obvious and perhaps not the most important of which is the biological constraint imposed by reproductive potential. Given a lifetime reproductive goal of three children, and a tendency to have one birth every third year after marriage before terminating childbearing, one might expect $\delta(a)$ to be about 0.1 at the start of marriage. The relationship may deviate from log-linearity when large increases are sought, and of course decreases in the stock are inadmissable. These shortcomings of the stock-adjustment framework for the study of reproductive behavior are analogous to widely recognized but frequently ignored defects of the framework for analysis of investment behavior. But more serious, in my judgment, is the inability to deal explicitly with the imperfect control a couple exercises over the accumulation of stocks.

Because of birth control failures, some women wanting no more children have births. Consequently, even when a cohort's average number of births equals or exceeds the average preferred number of births, some women may prefer more children and will therefore continue to try to have additional births. Table 4.4 shows this "excess" fertility by mother's education and age, as reported in a recent survey of Taiwan (Freedman et al. 1976). The precise behavior of $f(a)$ with respect to age is not clear, since the proportion of women wanting no more children (column 5 or 7) rises with age, whereas their current-period reproductive capacity decreases with age. To sort out the offsetting factors that underlie $f(a)$ requires individual survey data on preferences and reproductive performance, or substantially stronger assumptions (see Lee 1976). At

Table 4.4 **Actual and Preferred Number of Births of Wives in 1973, Proportion Currently Married in 1971, and Birthrate in 1974, by Age and Education**

Age and Education	(1) Sample Size Wives KAP-IV 1973	(2) Mean Live Births 1973	(3) Mean Preferred Number of Children 1973	(4) Differences Between Preferred and Actual (3) − (2)	(5) Proportion of Wives Wanting No More Children 1973	(6) Proportion Currently Married 1971	(7) Estimate Wanting No More Children[a] (5)·(6)	(8) Birth Probability or Rate 1974
Ages 20–24								
Illiterate	135	2.11	3.31	1.21	.341	.738	.252	.304
Some primary school	98	1.95	3.05	1.10	.398	.704[b]	.280	.250
Primary school graduate	729	1.61	3.03	1.42	.276	.545	.150	.249
Junior high graduate	88	1.30	2.63	1.33	.205	.338	.069	.133
Senior high graduate	79	.87	2.44	1.57	.165	.171	.028	.074
Total	1,129	1.62	2.99	1.37	.281	.480	.135	.193
Ages 25–29								
Illiterate	248	3.09	3.35	.26	.641	.939	.602	.217
Some primary school	127	3.06	3.24	.18	.654	.931[b]	.609	.192
Primary school graduate	792	2.73	3.12	.40	.562	.889	.500	.248
Junior high graduate	157	2.25	2.68	.43	.541	.811	.439	.219
Senior high graduate	149	1.52	2.42	.90	.389	.691	.269	.209
Total	1,473	2.65	3.05	.40	.563	.870	.490	.228
Ages 30–34								
Illiterate	509	4.06	3.61	− .45	.841	.948	.772	.078
Some primary school	164	3.86	3.38	− .48	.817	.958[b]	.783	.075
Primary school graduate	623	3.65	3.27	− .28	.830	.933	.774	.098
Junior high graduate	104	3.29	2.97	− .32	.856	.910	.779	.095

Table 4.4 (continued)

Age and Education	(1) Sample Size Wives KAP-IV 1973	(2) Mean Live Births 1973	(3) Mean Preferred Number of Children 1973	(4) Differences Between Preferred and Actual (3)−(2)	(5) Proportion of Wives Wanting No More Children 1973	(6) Proportion Currently Married 1971	(7) Estimate Wanting No More Children[a] (5)·(6)	(8) Birth Probability or Rate 1974
Senior high graduate	102	2.55	2.60	.05	.794	.848	.673	.112
Total	1,502	3.71	3.33	.38	.832	.935	.770	.091
Ages 35–39								
Illiterate	497	4.63	3.79	− .84	.918	.949	.871	.034
Some primary school	295	4.78	3.71	−1.07	.946	.953[b]	.902	.029
Primary school graduate	502	4.19	3.52	− .67	.902	.925	.834	.035
Junior high graduate	88	3.74	3.07	− .67	.932	.918	.856	.027
Senior high graduate	52	2.96	2.63	− .33	.827	.908	.751	.030
Total	1,434	4.39	3.60	− .79	.916	.938	.859	.032

Sources: Col. 1–5, R. Freedman et al (1976, table 10); KAP Survey IV (1973), Wives; col. 6, ibid., table 8; col. 8, ibid., table 7 and *Taiwan Demographic Factbook, 1974*, table 18, based on date of registration.

[a]This estimate is based on the extreme assumption that those women not currently married would want (more) children if they could become married.

[b]Categories called literate appear to refer to persons who are literate but not graduates of primary school.

the aggregate level of analysis undertaken here, $f(a)$ is simply interpreted as a margin of excess fertility that cannot now be statistically distinguished from $\delta(a)\alpha$.

The annual flow of births or the birth probability is defined,

$$B_t = e^{C_t} - e^{C_{t-1}}, \tag{3}$$

since the stock of births are expressed in logarithms. Substituting equation 1 into equation 2, a function for the growth of the stock of births is obtained.

$$C_t - C_{t-1} = \delta(a)\alpha + f(a) + \delta(a) \sum_{i=1}^{M} \sum_{j=1}^{n} \beta_{ij} Z_{i,\ t-j-1} - \delta(a) C_{t-1} + \delta(a) \mu_t. \tag{4}$$

If we collapse the expectation formation distributed lag into a discrete lag of τ years, say the mean length of the underlying distributed lag, then either the flow of births relative to prior stock as in equation 4 or the current period as in equation 5 below becomes a simple expression of prior stock and discretely lagged conditioning variables.

$$C_t = \delta(a)\alpha + f(a)\ \delta(a) \sum_{i=1}^{M} \beta_i Z_{i,\ t-\tau} + (1 - \delta(a)) C_{t-1} + \delta(a)\ \mu_t. \tag{5}$$

Either equation 5 or a comparable discretely lagged version of equation 4 yields identical parameter estimates and standard errors. The high collinearity between C_t and C_{t-1} yields, however, a higher R^2 in equation 5 and an "inflated" value of the t ratio for the coefficient on C_{t-1}. Hence, results are subsequently reported in terms of the flow equation 4.

Commonly $\delta(a)\beta_i$ is interpreted as a short-run (one year plus τ) demand elasticity with respect to Z_i, and β_i is the analogous long-run demand elasticity. This interpretation, however, is not appropriate here for the long run, since the value $\delta(a)$ is fixed only for a birth cohort five years in breadth. For example, if $\delta(a)$ was 0.1, and the coefficient estimated on $Z_{i,\ t-\tau}$ was 0.5, the short-run elasticity would be 0.5, and the five-year elasticity for a woman to pass through this segment of her life cycle cannot be readily inferred from information about an age cross section.

4.3.2 Estimation

Even when $\delta(a)$ is assumed constant, as may be tenable within a narrow age group, the estimation of equation 5 presents problems. Many of the omitted factors that account for the residual μ_t, in the desired stock equation 1, persist for an individual population over time or for a cohort as it ages. The disturbances are therefore likely to be positively serially correlated over time, at least toward the end of the childbearing period, and ordinary least-squares (OLS) estimates will be biased because C_{t-1} will tend to be positively correlated with $\delta(a)\mu_t$. Notably, the OLS estimates of $(1 - \delta(a))$ will tend to be biased upward (positively), and, conversely, estimates of $\delta(a)$ are biased downward (negatively) (Nerlove 1958; Griliches 1960, 1961).

This simultaneous equation bias can be eliminated if the prior stock is separately identified with additional information or, in this case, if one or more instruments are obtained that are independent of μ_t but are related to C_{t-1}. These instruments act as important identifying restrictions on this model of reproductive behavior; they determine the meaningfulness of the entire exercise.[16]

The lagged fertility stock variable can also be replaced by its determinants, and by repeating this substitution process until the start of the cohort's reproductive period we can eliminate all lagged values of C from the equation. This reduced form of the equation would require simplification to be empirically practical. In the case of conditioning factors, Z's, that did not change from the start, a single long-run response coefficient could be estimated. The response to accumulated cohort child mortality is less adequately incorporated into such a model, for in this case the dynamic path of adjustment to the timing of the child mortality may be important. But it seems a useful exercise, nonetheless, to compare the short-run response coefficients obtained from flow equation 5 with the long-run response coefficients obtained from even a simplified reduced-form stock equation. In the next section, I will discuss empirical specification of Z and the choice of identifying restrictions that permit one to estimate the stock and relative-flow equations.

4.4 Duration of Marriage and Marital Fertility Rate: Estimation of Reduced Forms

Reproductive behavior in Taiwan is first summarized by fitting reduced-form relationships for the stock of children ever born per woman by age as reported in the 1966 census. Within five-year birth cohorts a logarithmic specification is estimated from data for twenty-one administrative regions of the island.[17] The following cohort-specific explanatory variables are considered: (*a*) the reciprocal of the accumulated child survival rate; (*b*) the proportion of women with some junior high school education as a proxy for the value of a mother's time; (*c*) the proportion of men with the same level of schooling (of the same age)[18] as a proxy for male labor earnings; and (*d*) the man-months of family planning fieldworker activity in the region per woman of childbearing age—15 to 49. All but the family planning input variable are expressed in logarithms and derived directly from the 1966 census.

Since cohort fertility may vary because of variation in either the timing of marriage or the level of marital fertility, these multiplicative components are treated as dependent variables in subsequent parallel logarithmic regressions. The sum of the regression coefficients (or elasticities for those in logs) from the component equations equals the regression coefficient from the overall cohort fertility regression; the two-way decomposition of the logarithmic variance of fertility thus is straightforward.

If those married in a given cohort were married for the same number of years, on average, across regions, the readily observed proportion married at a specific age would be a reasonable proxy for the mean duration of marriage, except for a scale factor (constant) that would change with current age. The nearly universal exposure of Taiwanese women to marriage, however, makes this assumption unsatisfactory among older women when variation in the proportion ever married is relatively minor. For example, by age 35, 98% or more of Taiwanese women have been married.[19]

More satisfactory figures for age at marriage are obtained from 1966 census tabulations of married women by current age and age at marriage. How mean age at marriage is estimated from published data within regions is explained in the second part of Appendix B, and estimates of marital duration are reported in table 4.A.8.[20] The logarithm of cohort fertility is then linearly decomposed into two dependent variables: (1) the logarithm of the average years of exposure to marriage per woman, and (2) the logarithm of the residually defined annual marital fertility rate—namely, the number of children born divided by the years of marital exposure. Since fertility may vary over the life cycle, the level of marital fertility rates may be expected to reflect this, and the constant terms are likely to decrease among older age groups.[21]

4.4.1 Cohort Fertility

Among women over age 30, when childbearing is nearly completed, the proportion of women with some junior high school education is negatively associated with cohort fertility (table 4.5). The absolute value of the elasticity of fertility with respect to this measure of women's schooling increases in the cross section to age 44, then diminishes (later ages not shown). The partial association between men's schooling and reproductive performance is less uniform, though a positive partial association is evident between the ages 20–24 and 30–39. The hypothesis that in the postwar era the growth in men's schooling, and presumably income, is associated with increased demand for children is not rejected by these data.[22] After age 24 the women's education coefficient (elasticity) exceeds the men's in absolute value, and though the level of women's education is lower than the level of men's, it has recently been

Table 4.5 **Regressions on Cohort Fertility or Stocks: Logarithm of Children Ever Born per Woman by Age in 1966**

Age of Women	Constant Term	Cohort Child Mortality[a]	Proportion with Some Junior High School: Women	Proportion with Some Junior High School: Men	Family Planning up to 1965[b]	R^2 (SEE)[c]
15–19	−2.98 (6.83)	20.1 (1.75)	1.07 (1.50)	−1.61 (1.17)	−144.0 (1.09)	.3628 (.366)
20–24	−.613 (4.21)	22.1 (5.56)	−.269 (1.57)	.664 (2.33)	12.6 (.31)	.6789 (.111)
25–29	.562 (10.2)	5.94 (5.07)	−.0886 (1.54)	.0542 (.58)	9.21 (.64)	.8062 (.0403)
30–34	1.07 (32.7)	3.28 (5.90)	−.0992 (4.09)	.0686 (1.79)	−9.81 (1.11)	.8913 (.02410)
35–39	1.26 (32.4)	1.77 (3.87)	−.148 (6.29)	.103 (2.76)	−17.7 (1.69)	.8865 (.0289)
40–44	1.31 (26.7)	.680 (1.59)	−.168 (5.01)	.0761 (1.18)	−17.3 (1.31)	.8777 (.0366)
45–49	1.38 (20.8)	−.335 (.78)	−.118 (3.10)	−.0452 (.65)	−3.33 (.19)	.8422 (.0466)

Note: Numbers in parentheses beneath regression coefficients are *t* values. Observations are twenty-one major subdivisions of Taiwan for which data are published in the Taiwan 1966 census, vol. 2, nos. 2 and 3.
[a]Reciprocal of cohort's proportion of children ever born who are still living as reported in 1966 census.
[b]Man-months of family planning fieldworker effort expended in region through calendar year 1965, divided by the number of women in the region of childbearing age (i.e., 15–49).
[c]Standard error of regression estimate is reported in parentheses beneath R^2.

increasing at a much faster rate than has men's. Similar results are found for both sexes when other levels of educational attainment are used in place of junior high school.[23]

Child mortality is positively associated with cohort fertility among women under age 45; after age 20–24 the magnitude of the elasticity of fertility with respect to child mortality falls with age. The regression coefficient on child mortality changes to a negative sign among still older cohorts but loses statistical significance. Among women over age 39, interregional variation in cohort fertility is insufficient to "offset" variation in child mortality. In other words, since the child mortality elasticity is less than +1.0, areas of relatively high fertility report relatively high surviving fertility. Among younger women the reverse is noted; high-fertility areas are associated with relatively low surviving fertility, other things equal. Problems of measurement lead one to suspect that the coefficient on child mortality is biased in a positive direction, but the magnitude of this bias is likely to be substantial only for the younger women.[24]

4.4.2 The Timing of Marriage and Marital Fertility

In diverse premodern and preindustrial societies it is observed that the age at marriage is an important regulator of lifetime reproductive performance. To perpetuate society and maintain family lines in the face of heavy child mortality, couples are encouraged to marry and start bearing children at an early age. This institutionalized adaptation to the regionally *anticipated* level of mortality relieves individual couples of some of the burden of controlling their fertility within marriage in response to actual child mortality (Dumond 1975). A couple's fertility might then respond to whether it experienced above- or below-average child losses, but this latter within-marriage *lagged* response to child mortality might be difficult to distinguish with aggregate data.

The median age at marriage in Taiwan increased from about 18 at the turn of the century (Goode 1970) to 21 in 1940, and to about 25 today (cf. table 4.A.2). Assuming that contemporary birthrates for married women did not change, delaying marriage six years from age 18 to age 25 implies two fewer births per woman; compared with traditional cohort lifetime fertility of five or six births, this represents a reduction in cohort fertility of one-third. An understanding of the causes for this magnitude of secular change in the timing of marriage or even lesser differences across regions should be a help in explaining fertility declines.

The questions I want to explore are the extent to which age at marriage accounts for regional differences in cohort fertility, and whether these patterns of marriage are readily explained by conditioning economic and demographic variables that are thought to modify reproductive demands. In the traditional Chinese family the timing of the marriage decision is, for the most part, made by parents for their children, and relaxation of this control is a quite recent phenomenon (Wolf 1972). The age at marriage, therefore, is likely to reflect the parents' perception of the benefits and costs of earlier marriage, of which the interval to childbearing is probably important, as well as the time parents require to accumulate a girl's dowry. Conversely, the frequency within marriage and the lifetime number of births may reflect to a greater degree the perceptions and interests of the younger generation of parents. The economic incentives of a husband's and wife's value of time are more likely to make themselves evident in this later decision-making process, though admittedly the dividing line between generations and their respective interests is not always clear (Ben-Porath 1975).

The regressions on the estimated duration of marriage and marital fertility rate are shown in tables 4.6 and 4.7. The duration of marriage

Table 4.6 **Regressions on Duration of Marriage: Logarithm of the Average Years of Exposure to Marriage per Woman by Age in 1966**

Age of Women	Constant Term	Cohort Child Mortality[a]	Proportion with Some Junior High School: Women	Proportion with Some Junior High School: Men	Family Planning up to 1965[b]	R^2 (SEE)[c]
15–19[d]	−2.92 (6.00)	20.1 (1.57)	.775 (.98)	−1.48 (.97)	−137. (.93)	.3081 (.409)
20–24[d]	−.177 (.93)	25.0 (4.81)	−.356 (1.59)	.696 (1.86)	−7.68 (.15)	.6384 (.145)
25–29	1.37 (16.0)	6.11 (3.36)	.0676 (.76)	−.199 (1.37)	20.2 (.90)	.6146 (.0626)
30–34	2.19 (45.0)	2.18 (2.65)	−.0060 (.17)	−.0265 (.47)	6.92 (.53)	.5340 (.0357)
35–39	2.63 (79.1)	1.04 (2.66)	−.0065 (.32)	−.0162 (.51)	7.22 (.80)	.5287 (.0247)
40–44	2.95 (107.0)	.507 (2.11)	.0053 (.28)	−.0327 (.90)	4.90 (.66)	.4583 (.0205)
45–49	3.18 (126.0)	.315 (1.94)	.0124 (.86)	−.0353 (1.35)	4.41 (.68)	.4627 (.0177)

Note: Numbers in parentheses beneath regression coefficients are *t* values. Observations are twenty-one major subdivisions of Taiwan for which data are published in the Taiwan 1966 census, vol. 2, nos. 2 and 3.

[a]Reciprocal of cohort's proportion of children ever born who are still living as reported in 1966 census.

[b]Man-months of family planning fieldworker effort expended in region through calendar year 1965, divided by the number of women in the region of childbearing age (i.e., 15–49).

[c]Standard error of regression estimate is reported in parentheses beneath R^2.

[d]Marital duration calculated by indirect procedure for women less than 25 years old. See Appendix B. Regression coefficient for cohort child mortality is biased upward because of measurement error, particularly for younger women, as explained in text and note 25.

within an age group is associated with the regional incidence of child mortality among all cohorts of women over age 20. The regression coefficients from the marital-duration equation for women age 30–34 (table 4.6), imply that a decline in child mortality from 15% to 5%, as is recorded between women age 45–49 and 30–34, is associated with a compensating variation in age at marriage of nearly two years, other things unchanged. Though this estimate is probably biased upward because of problems of measurement,[25] the linkage between child mortality and the timing of marriage deserves further study to find out why it arises, how fast it responds to change, and whether economic and social policies can encourage this potentially important institutional response to diminished mortality.[26]

Table 4.7 **Regressions on Marital Fertility Rate: Logarithm of Children Ever Born per Year of Marital Exposure by Age in 1966**

Age of Women	Constant Term	Cohort Child Mortality[a]	Proportion with Some Junior High School: Women	Proportion with Some Junior High School: Men	Family Planning up to 1965[b]	R^2 (SEE)[c]
15–19[d]	−.0599	.0379	.290	−.126	−6.76	.4906
	(.58)	(.01)	(1.72)	(.39)	(.22)	(.0873)
20–24[d]	−.436	−2.91	.0863	.0325	20.2	.5352
	(7.62)	(1.86)	(1.28)	(.29)	(1.28)	(.0435)
25–29	−.805	−.169	−.156	.253	−11.0	.2315
	(10.8)	(.11)	(1.99)	(1.99)	(.56)	(.0548)
30–34	−1.12	1.09	−.0931	.0950	−16.7	.4839
	(20.5)	(1.19)	(2.32)	(1.50)	(1.14)	(.0399)
35–39	−1.38	.723	−.142	.119	−24.9	.6939
	(24.5)	(1.09)	(4.15)	(2.21)	(1.64)	(.0418)
40–44	−1.64	.172	−.173	.109	−22.1	.7785
	(26.5)	(.32)	(4.11)	(1.34)	(1.33)	(.0460)
45–49	−1.80	−.650	−.130	−.0099	−7.72	.7828
	(24.0)	(1.34)	(3.03)	(.13)	(.40)	(.0529)

Note: Numbers in parentheses beneath regression coefficients are *t* values. Observations are twenty-one major subdivisions of Taiwan for which data are published in the Taiwan 1966 census, vol. 2, nos. 2 and 3.

[a]Reciprocal of cohort's proportion of children ever born who are still living as reported in 1966 census.

[b]Man-months of family planning fieldworker effort expended in region through calendar year 1965, divided by the number of women in the region of childbearing age (i.e., 15–49).

[c]Standard error of regression estimate is reported in parentheses beneath R^2.

[d]Marital fertility rate calculated by indirect procedure for women less than 25 years old. See Appendix B. Regression coefficient for cohort child mortality is biased downward because of measurement error, particularly for younger women, as explained in text and note 25.

The proportions of men and women with junior high schooling are not consistently related to women's age at marriage, except perhaps among older women, namely those over age 44 in 1966 (table 4.6). In older groups (not shown), there is a slight tendency for women to marry earlier in regions where women had more access to secondary schooling; conversely, men's schooling is associated with somewhat later marriage among women, as is common today in high-income countries.

Marital fertility rates are not consistently associated at the regional level with child mortality (table 4.7), but a negative bias at younger ages is anticipated. The schooling variables, which are interpreted as the value of husband's and wife's time, account for much of the regional variation in later marital fertility rates; in other words, birth control within marriage is strongly affected by schooling in the anticipated manner, with women's schooling depressing fertility and men's schooling augmenting it.

When both men's and women's schooling increase by similar proportions, marital fertility rates decrease among women over age 34. But, given the actual proportionate changes in the past eight years (1966–74) in men's and women's schooling for those age 20–24 (table 4.3), the regression equations imply a 7% reduction in marital fertility rates for women age 25–29, 9% for age 30–34, 14% for age 35–39, and 19% for age 40–44. Since sex-specific levels of schooling are not notably associated with the regional pattern of marriage, the effect of the expansion of the educational system, and in particular the relative gains women have made in that system in the past twenty years, accounts for large decreases in cohort fertility between the ages of 35 and 49.

Two years after the start of the national family planning program there are already indications that local program activity is beginning to modify the regional pattern of completed fertility among older women (table 4.5). But for women 35 to 39 in 1966, only about 6% to 8% of their children were born in 1965 and 1966. Thus the impact of the program on their completed fertility must inherently be marginal, and naturally this effect operates through reducing marital birthrates (table 4.7).

4.4.3 Tentative Conclusions

Among younger women reaching their thirties in the later 1960s, regional variation in age at marriage appears to have overcompensated for remaining regional differences in child mortality. In regions with relatively high fertility and high child mortality, these younger cohorts are achieving traditional reproductive goals at an earlier age than did their parents' generation. If marital fertility is not excessively difficult or costly to control, these younger women seem likely to reduce their flow of additional births in the decade following the 1966 census.

Since a single cross section of a population by age provides no way to disentangle life-cycle effects from birth-cohort or time-series effects, the tendency for the elasticity of cohort fertility with respect to child mortality (table 4.5) to diminish with age admits to more than one interpretation.

Mortality in Taiwan appears to have declined most rapidly in two periods: during the first decade of this century and again from 1945 to 1955. For women over age 44, born before 1921, childbearing was largely completed during the second period. Moreover, many of the offspring of these older women may have died in the dislocation and conflict of the war years and their aftermath of epidemics. A smaller reproductive response relative to accumulated child losses among these older cohorts might be anticipated.

Alternatively, as a cohort advances through its life, the elasticity of fertility with respect to child mortality may be expected to decline, because offspring continue to die after their mother is unable to replace them with additional births. This gradual process should be increasingly noticeable after women reach 35 and average fecundity falls. The marked decline in reproductive response to child mortality with increased age can therefore be explained in terms of either life-cycle aging or changing historical events. It is also possible that errors in measuring child survival to a comparable age and the possible relationship between early childbearing and infant loss might exaggerate the positive association noted here between fertility and cohort child mortality, especially among younger women.

In sum, fitting a simple reduced-form equation for stocks of children confirms the commonly found positive relationship with child mortality, the negative relationship with women's schooling, and a slight indication that men's schooling is positively related to fertility. The family planning program inputs after two years are slightly related to lower completed fertility among women over age 29, which replicates earlier analyses of birthrates and family-planning activity at a lower level of disaggregation (Schultz 1969*b*). The regional cohort association with child mortality is primarily explained by the earlier age of marriage in high-mortality regions. On the other hand, the anticipated effects of regional sex-specific schooling levels on fertility is not achieved by variation in the timing of marriage, but by changes in the rate of births per year of marriage duration. The effect of women's schooling on marital fertility rates is negative and consistent across age groups, substantially exceeding the summation of positive men's schooling elasticities. The advance made by Taiwanese women, both absolutely and relative to men, in gaining access to secondary schooling in the postwar period can thus account for a substantial fraction of the contemporary decline in cohort fertility. If these cross-sectional relationships are stable over time, which will be investigated in the next section, they also imply that the recent decline in fertility will continue.

4.5 A Stock-Adjustment Model for Current Fertility in 1967

The flow of births in 1967 as a proportion of the prior stock of births in 1966 is the dependent variable in the simplified stock-adjustment equation 4. Both ordinary least-squares (OLS) and instrumental-variable (IV) techniques, the latter procedure being more appropriate if C_{t-1} is not independent of μ_t, are shown in table 4.8. In addition to the

Table 4.8 **Stock-Adjustment Equation: Relative Change in Children Ever Born, 1967**

Age of Women	Estimation Method[c]	Constant Term	Period Child Mortality[a] t-2	Proportion with Some Junior High School		Family Planning[b] t-1	Children Ever Born t-1	R^2 (SEE)
				Women	Men			
16–20	OLS[d]	.299 (2.07)	−1.07 (.64)	−.326 (3.46)	.358 (2.14)	34.3 (2.66)	−.110 (2.91)	.8301 (.0438)
	IV[d]	.938 (.93)	−6.83 (.73)	−.558 (1.44)	.541 (1.38)	52.1 (1.51)	−.075 (.26)	(.0707)
21–25	OLS	.187 (12.3)	−.0896 (.33)	−.0517 (4.44)	.0156 (.81)	7.04 (3.32)	−.162 (11.5)	.9557 (.00721)
	IV	.199 (8.78)	−.316 (.76)	−.0501 (4.07)	.00828 (.37)	6.49 (2.78)	−.146 (5.59)	(.00753)
26–30	OLS	.183 (10.6)	.307 (1.51)	−.0181 (2.38)	.00963 (.82)	−.819 (.56)	−.130 (4.20)	.6613 (.00500)
	IV	.216 (4.40)	.658 (1.25)	−.0225 (2.13)	.0110 (.81)	.142 (.07)	−.198 (2.02)	(.00575)
31–35	OLS	.0568 (1.54)	.288 (1.88)	−.00955 (2.40)	.0170 (3.52)	−2.73 (3.10)	−.0203 (.58)	.7387 (.00308)
	IV	.0286 (.47)	.186 (.80)	−.00791 (1.61)	.0167 (3.38)	−2.65 (2.93)	−.00660 (.11)	(.00314)
36–40	OLS	−.00589 (2.8)	.257 (3.82)	−.00134 (.53)	.00847 (3.34)	−1.81 (3.39)	.0110 (.65)	.8823 (.00174)
	IV	−.00937 (.29)	.249 (2.78)	−.00101 (.30)	.00829 (2.93)	−1.77 (3.03)	.0137 (.53)	(.00174)

Table 4.8 (continued)

Age of Women	Estimation Method[c]	Constant Term	Period Child Mortality[a] t-2	Proportion with Some Junior High School: Women	Proportion with Some Junior High School: Men	Family Planning[b] t-1	Children Ever Born t-1	R^2 (SEE)
41–45	OLS	.00678	.133	−.00175	.00419	−.779	−.00406	.7841
		(.74)	(4.92)	(1.24)	(2.38)	(2.72)	(.59)	(.00097)
	IV	−.00283	.121	−.00066	.00381	−.688	.00319	
		(.15)	(3.54)	(.28)	(1.96)	(2.06)	(.23)	(.00101)
46–50	OLS	.00435	.0179	−.00276	.000049	−.003	−.00315	.6573
		(3.07)	(3.71)	(1.38)	(.17)	(.062)	(3.13)	(.00019)
	IV	−.00105	.0210	.000189	.000223	.022	.000763	
		(.12)	(2.50)	(.24)	(.46)	(.25)	(.12)	(.00027)

Note: t or asymptotic t values are reported in parentheses beneath regression coefficients. Observations are twenty-one major subdivisions of Taiwan for which data are published in the Taiwan 1966 census, vol. 2, nos. 2 and 3. The dependent variable is the difference between the logarithms of children ever born to the cohort in t and t-1; that is, $\ln C_{t-1} - \ln C_t$, so that the regression coefficient on the lagged stock of children is an estimate of δ.

[a]Reciprocal of child survival rate derived from period age-specific death rates from birth to age 15, lagged two years, that is, for 1965. The choice of the two-year lag is discussed in T. P. Schultz (1974).

[b]Man-months of effort by family planning fieldworkers expended in region through 1967, divided by the number of women in the region of childbearing age (i.e., 15–49).

[c]R^2 is inappropriate basis for comparison with IV estimates.

[d]OLS: Ordinary least-squares estimates.

IV: Instrumental variable estimates where children ever born (1966) is treated as endogenous and cohort child mortality and pre-1966 family-planning inputs are the excluded instruments used to identify equation.

contemporaneous schooling variables for men and women, period-specific child mortality and accumulated family planning inputs are lagged two years and one year respectively. (See earlier work by T. P. Schultz [1969, 1974] for justification of lag structures.) The lagged stock of children ever born is identified by two instrumental variables: the cohort's prior child mortality experience, and family planning inputs prior to 1966. The reduced-form equation that implicitly accounts for the 1966 fertility stock is reported in table 4.5.

The stock-adjustment model revolves around the parameter $\delta(a)$, or minus the regression coefficient on the 1966 children ever born variable (C_{t-1}). The instrumental-variable estimates of this parameter in table 4.8 for the seven childbearing age groups are as follows: 0.07, 0.15, 0.20, 0.01, —0.01, —0.00, and —0.00. Given the low level and possibly unplanned nature of fertility in older ages, the implied lack of discernible compensatory adjustment in these age groups is not unanticipated. The moderate and statistically significant level of the estimates of $\delta(a)$ from age 21 to age 30 does not contradict the working hypothesis of the adjustment model over the prime childbearing years, but these single-year estimates for 1967 provide little support for the framework at younger and older ages.

In contrast to the earlier analysis of cohort marital fertility rates, the dynamic stock-adjustment model implied compensating higher current flow of births to women over 35 in regions where child mortality has recently been higher. When women are completing the formation of their families, their reproductive behavior is likely to be more sensitive to the survival or death of earlier children. This has been found empirically in numerous studies (T. P. Schultz 1974), and in this case the short-run response elasticity is about 0.2 from age 30 to age 39. The magnitude of this short-run response exceeds that which could be attributed to involuntary biological feedback mechanisms in a healthy population (Schultz 1976).

Women's schooling is associated with lower current flows of births among women up to age 35. For men's schooling, the positive relationship is also apparent from 31 to 45. The men's and women's schooling elasticities are of approximately the same magnitude among teen-age women, the women's elasticities exceed the men's during the twenties, and the reverse is true between the age 30 and age 44.

The intensity of family-planning activity by region is associated with a decreased flow of births among women 31 to 45, those ages where the family planning program is widely regarded to have made its major impact (Freedman and Takeshita 1969; Freedman and Berelson 1976; T. P. Schultz 1969*b*, 1974). A very different pattern of program effectiveness emerges among women 16 to 26, where the flow of births is higher in regions that are more intensively canvassed by the family planning program fieldworkers. This pattern of response among younger women in Taiwan, which I have noted before (Schultz 1969*b*, 1974), might be explained if the preferred path to obtain the desired lifetime stock of children were itself a function of birth control technology. It was hypothesized earlier that the delay of childbearing and the spacing of births may be a means of reducing the likelihood of excess fertility given the unreliability of traditional birth control measures. As modern methods of fertility control become more widely accessible and understood, birth intervals in Taiwan may increasingly conform to the pattern of most industrialized countries where married women frequently participate in the nonagricultural labor force. In some of these developed countries, the intervals between births have indeed declined in the twentieth century despite the reduction in completed cohort fertility. A corollary of this hypothesis is that birthrates in Taiwan during the 1970s may start to decline even before women reach age 30.

There are several methods for investigating the stability over time and the internal consistency of these estimated reproductive flow relationships and the reduced-form stock equations reported in the previous section. One approach is to use the 1966 stock equation estimates in table 4.5 to predict (average regional) cohort fertility in 1971, given the observed values of the conditioning variables observed in 1971. This exercise is reported in the upper panel of table 4.9. Apparently the 1966 relationship overpredicts declines in fertility in the youngest ages and in the later ones. But between the ages of 25 and 39 predicted declines parallel actual reductions in cohort fertility. The predicted declines among women reaching age 40–49 in 1971 exceed that which might have been achieved if they had given birth to no children in the period 1966–71. A margin of excess fertility implied by this exercise is not inconsistent with the evidence presented earlier in column 4 of table 4.4.

The predicted reductions in cohort fertility are decomposed into the changes attributable to changes in the four explanatory variables in the lower panel of table 4.9. The contribution of declining child mortality appears to be of increasing importance among younger women. The reversal in the effect of education between ages 35–39 and ages 30–34 is a reflection of the lower educational achievement in the younger age groups, who because of the war may have been denied educational opportunities compared with the older age groups; the older cohort also includes many better-educated immigrant mainland Chinese. The postwar advance of women in the schooling system appears linked to declines in fertility, but this effect cannot be realistically partialed out from the educational achievements of men, which appear to be offsetting. Taking the groups together, education's effect varies from cohort to cohort but promises to increase in magnitude in the next decade among women reaching age 35. Family planning inputs account for 28% to 66% of

Table 4.9 Actual and Predicted Change in Sample Mean of Children Ever Born, 1966 to 1971, Based on 1966 Stock Estimates

	Age of Women in 1966 and 1971					
	20–24	25–29	30–34	35–39	40–44	45–49
Relative changes in sample mean						
Actual	−.045	−.052	−.101	−.101	−.054	−.027
Predicted	−.120	−.036	−.109	−.144	−.135	−.062
Shares of predicted change						
Child mortality	−1.67	−1.31	−.40	−.25	−.17	+.21
Women's schooling	−.86	−158	−.22	+.07	−.18	−.173
Men's schooling	+.98	+57	+.08	−.18	+.01	−.20
Family planning	+.55	+132	−.146	−.62	−66	−.28
Men's schooling	+.98	+57	+.08	−.18	+.01	−.20
Total	−100	−100	−100	−100	−100	−100

Source: "Actual" cohort fertility based on projections as described in Appendix B; "predicted" based on regressions coefficients in table 4.5, sample means of conditioning variables in table 4.A.4, and projections of child mortality described in Appendix B.

the predicted declines in cohort fertility after age 30. Although these point estimates of the effect of family planning activity are not precise (i.e., large standard errors are associated with these coefficients), they are nonetheless large in magnitude. As a first approximation, this exercise suggests that about half of the decline in fertility among women over age 30 occurring in the period 1966 to 1971 could be attributed to reductions in child mortality and changes in educational attainment, whereas the remainder is associated with family planning.

Another way to test the stability of the 1966 stock-equation estimates is to reestimate these equations in 1971 as shown in table 4.10. Several changes may be noted between the 1966 and the 1971 coefficients. The elasticity of fertility with respect to child mortality has increased and become more statistically significant after age 25; educational elasticities of both men and women increased in later ages; the coefficients on family planning inputs are more statistically significant and of roughly similar magnitude, as in 1966, though the level of accumulated inputs increased fourfold over this five-year period. Overall, the vector of coefficients for the equation based on 1966 and 1971 data are not dissimilar. Applying the *F*-ratio test to the linear restriction of coefficient equality across years, one cannot reject the hypothesis of equality in any of the six age groups at the 10% level.[27]

Accounting for changes in stocks is predictably more difficult than explaining variation in levels. Reproductive behavior for a cohort ap-

Table 4.10 **Reduced-Form Stock Equation for Children Ever Born, 1971**

Age of Women	Constant Term	Cohort Child Mortality[a]	Proportion with Some Junior High School: Women	Proportion with Some Junior High School: Men	Family Planning up to 1970[b]	R^2 (SEE)[c]
20–24	−.664	21.8	.197	−.374	4.92	.5805
	(3.31)	(3.63)	(.85)	(.96)	(.17)	(.123)
25–29	.539	6.99	−.0979	.0722	4.61	.6900
	(5.97)	(3.33)	(1.02)	(.43)	(.34)	(.0539)
30–34	1.03	4.45	−.127	.107	−7.82	.7906
	(15.1)	(3.48)	(2.12)	(1.01)	(.78)	(.0378)
35–39	1.28	4.40	−.127	.127	−18.5	.7854
	(18.6)	(3.89)	(3.58)	(2.16)	(1.66)	(.0397)
40–44	1.35	2.62	−.141	.108	−14.7	.8021
	(18.8)	(3.03)	(4.79)	(2.24)	(1.25)	(.0427)
45–49	1.35	.847	−.165	.0839	−8.39	.8534
	(19.8)	(1.39)	(5.69)	(1.51)	(.72)	(.0405)
50–54	1.35	−.620	−.122	−.0200	11.4	.7923
	(15.3)	(.96)	(3.44)	(.29)	(.75)	(.0534)

Note: Numbers in parentheses beneath regression coefficients are *t* values. Observations are twenty-one major subdivisions of Taiwan for which data are published in the Taiwan 1966 census, vol. 2, nos. 2 and 3.

[a]Reciprocal of cohort's proportion of children ever born who are still living as reported in 1966 census.

[b]Man-months of family planning fieldworker effort expended in region through calendar year 1965, divided by the number of women in the region of childbearing age (i.e., 15–49).

[c]Standard error of regression estimate is reported in parentheses beneath R^2.

proaching the end of its childbearing period may be predicted with a reasonably stable equation, but year-to-year flows of births are more volatile and possibly sensitive to the excessively rigid specification of the stock-adjustment hypothesis and the functional forms adopted here. To test the stability of the stock-adjustment equation, birth cohorts are followed for eight years, 1967 to 1974 (see Appendix B), and since each year's cross section of birthrates is in some sense a new observation conditioned by changing stocks and environmental variables,[28] the time series of cross sections are therefore pooled. A sample of 168 observations for each birth cohort is thereby obtained, though the value $\delta(a)$ is now undoubtedly changing as the cohort progresses eight years through its life cycle, and its estimate should thus be interpreted with caution. Another problem with pooling time series is the tendency for birthrates to decline for a cohort after age 25 and, for most regions, within age groups over time, contributing to a pronounced secular decline in the time series on relative changes in a cohort's stock of children. This tendency may produce a misleading association with other strongly trended variables, notably the past accumulated inputs of family planning in a region. In table 4.11 I have chosen to introduce a linear trend in time as one method for emphasizing the cross-sectional variation about the time trend, and not the smooth time trends in variable levels.[29] These estimates are consistent, based on instrumental variables as in table 4.8 to identify the influence of the lagged-stock variable.[30]

Coefficients in table 4.11 should be compared with an analogous average of the age-specific equations in table 4.8. The signs and magnitudes of the coefficients in the two tables are not notably dissimilar, though some changes are according to expectation. The average effect of family-planning inputs has diminished, as expected given the nature of innovational diffusion cycles, though the allowance of a linear trend in time may understate the program's role in the secular downtrend of birthrates. The effect of child mortality, which is also strongly trended downward, appears somewhat larger in the entire period 1967–74 than it was in 1967, but a stable elasticity of about 0.2 to 0.3 is still evident after a woman reaches age 30. The elasticity of relative increments to the stock of births with respect to the proportion of women with junior high school is negative at all ages, but the magnitude of the elasticity is less than men's schooling for women between about the ages of 30 and 40. This is again consistent with other indications that men's schooling proxies an income effect that extends the years of childbearing until the woman is in her mid- to late thirties, whereas women's schooling *conditional on the current stock* of children exerts a dampening effect on the flow of births throughout the life cycle. The magnitudes of the adjustment coefficient are better behaved, except for a slight rise in level for the oldest birth cohort. A strict interpretation of the stock-adjustment hypothesis implies reproductive goals in the range of 5–6 births, which exceeds survey responses, perhaps because of our inability to explicitly identify the role of contraceptive failures. Overall, however, these pooled results for the stock-adjustment equation are more stable than we might have anticipated given the rudimentary nature of the working hypothesis and the limitations of the aggregate data. There is clearly an important systematic element of feedback from past stocks to current flows of births that should in the future be modeled with greater realism and examined in individual survey data.

A possible shortcoming of analyses of regional data such as are used in this study is that explanatory variables may not account for fertility differences *within* urban and rural environments but may only reflect urban/rural differences in amenities that approximately parallel reproduction without causing differences. As expected, a city/noncity dummy variable, defined as equal to one for the five major cities and zero for

Table 4.11 Stock-Adjustment Equation: Relative Change in Stock of Children Ever Born, 1967–74

Instrumental Variable Estimates[d]	Constant Term	Period Child Mortality[a] t-2	Proportion with Some Junior High School		Family Planning to t-1[b]	Calendar Year –1900[d]	Children Ever Born t-1[e]	SEE[c]
			Women	Men				
Age of Women								
Age 15–19 in 1966 and age 22–27 in 1974	—.853 (.94)	.710 (1.18)	—.0629 (3.27)	.0317 (.95)	.146 (.08)	.0136 (1.10)	—.221 (10.0)	.0255
Age 20–24 in 1966 and age 28–32 in 1974	.960 (3.19)	—.142 (.61)	—.0337 (6.81)	.00752 (.85)	.086 (.16)	—.0108 (2.49)	—.148 (6.85)	.00831
Age 25–29 in 1966 and age 33–37 in 1974	.782 (5.35)	.122 (.64)	—.00657 (1.57)	.00307 (.52)	—.191 (.40)	—.00970 (3.97)	—.0510 (1.54)	.00700
Age 30–34 in 1966 and age 38–42 in 1974	.211 (5.31)	.335 (2.78)	—.00794 (3.31)	.0123 (5.00)	—.505 (1.88)	—.00224 (2.63)	—.0329 (1.39)	.00402
Age 35–39 in 1966 and age 43–47 in 1974	.0375 (2.10)	.261 (3.91)	—.00486 (2.38)	.00701 (4.09)	—.616 (4.14)	—.00007 (.18)	—.00224 (1.51)	.00223
Age 40–44 in 1966 and age 48–52 in 1974	.0369 (1.88)	.192 (2.47)	—.0102 (2.13)	.00572 (2.29)	—.361 (2.04)	.00064 (1.30)	—.0617 (2.06)	.00215

Note: Asymptotic *t* values reported in parentheses beneath regression coefficients. See note e for definition of dependent variable and note f for identifying instruments.

[a]Reciprocal of child-survival rate derived from age specific death rates from birth to age 15 two years before in 1965. The choice of the two-year lag is discussed in T. P. Schultz 1974.

[b]Family-planning inputs per woman summed to the prior year as an accumulative stock of nondepreciating knowledge.

[c]R^2 is inappropriate basis for comparison with IV estimates.

[d]Linear time trend introduced by the variable of the last two digits to the calendar year; i.e., 66, 67, etc.

[e]The dependent variable in this equation is the first difference of the logarithms of children ever born—i.e., $ln\ C_{t-1} - ln\ C_t$—so that the regression coefficient on lagged children is an estimate of δ.

[f]The identifying excluded exogenous variables are the cohort's child mortality to *t*-2, and family planning inputs summed to *t*-2.

the other sixteen regions of Taiwan, is found to be strongly negatively correlated across our sample with reproductive stocks among older women, the simple correlation being on the order of —0.6 to —0.8 in both 1966 and 1971; the city dummy variable is less highly correlated with birth flows in 1967 among older women, namely —0.2 to —0.3. Including this city dummy variable in the birth-stock equation often significantly increases the explanatory power of the equation, particularly for older women (see appendix tables 4.A.9 and 4.A.11), whereas it is not important in partially explaining regional differences in the flow of births (table 4.A.10). The only variable whose coefficient is notably altered by this modification in model specification is that of family planning inputs in the stock equation, where the previously noted partial association is largely subsumed by the city/noncity distinction. The apparent diminution of the effect of family planning on accumulated reproductive performance is not confined, however, in the temporally better-specified birth-flow equation for 1967. Quite the contrary. Overall, it does not appear that child mortality and schooling patterns are only a proxy for "urbanization" and capture this alleged modernizing influence on reproductive goals and performance. Urban/rural differences in completed fertility remain, however, a spur to further research into reproductively relevant characteristics of urban life or those who choose it. In 1971, women by age 40 still had 10% fewer children if they lived in the five major cities of Taiwan rather than elsewhere on the island (table 4.A.11), after controlling for important associations with child mortality and sex-specific schooling. It is not difficult to think of many omitted variables, particularly lagged conditions and ethnic diversity in these large populations, that might account for this residual urban/rural variation in past reproductive performance. On the other hand, somewhat unexpectedly, one finds that flows of births in 1967 conditioned on prior reproductive performance do not differ substantially across city and noncity regional populations in Taiwan, holding constant the same four seemingly crude proxies for child mortality, educational status of women and men, and prior family planning.

4.6 Concluding Notes and Qualifications

How should disequilibrium be characterized, and how should behavior be modeled as it adapts to unexpected changes in conditioning variables? Theories of fertility, particularly in developing areas, are moving beyond the widely replicated exercises of accounting for differences in lifetime stocks of births, toward simplified explanations of how current reproductive behavior is conditioned by past accumulated reproductive performance and other variables. The past matters for present behavior and future goals, as in most areas of household behavior where the life-cycle durability of decisions is inescapable.

But past outcomes and current behavior cannot be realistically assumed to be statistically independent. The identification quandary arises for lack of time-independent variables that conveniently perturb a behavioral relation in one period but leave it untouched in the succeeding period. These exogenous variables are hard to come by, and to measure, in the household sector, and those used in the last section of this paper, though tenable, can easily be criticized for belonging in the current-period distributed lag function. Moreover, the stock-adjustment framework is only the simplest way to deal with a most complex process. With more and better data for cohorts over time, more elaborate frameworks may add much to our understanding of reproductive behavior.[31]

Another problem arises in part because I have worked with aggregate data. The lack of information on individual preferences, or at least the distinction whether or not parents want more births, limits how one can treat the unreliability of birth control and resulting margins of "excess fertility." Though these subjective variables add richness to a model (Lee 1976), they also extract their claims, for to close the system they too require explanation in terms of environmentally given conditioning variables.

A third area that requires more explicit study is the age of marriage. The timing of marriage has many implications for the allocation and accumulation of resources in the household sector and the transfer of resources between generations. Its effects on fertility are unmistakable. As a starting point, decomposition of cohort fertility into an age at marriage and a marital fertility rate may help to sort out sources of fertility change over time and to clarify how social institutions respond to environmental constraints. Though the required data are available in virtually every census and survey, analysis of age at marriage remains uncommon using cross-sectional data. I have encountered few econometric studies of the causes of time-series change in age at marriage within communities or over generations within families, though much thinking has gone into the problem (Goode 1970).

The hypothesis has been advanced that education's effect on a considerable range of household behavior can best be understood in terms of its influence on the marginal productivity of labor, and hence on the opportunity value of time (T. W. Schultz 1974). But education surely has other consequences for behavior, and abstracting a single "price of time" may mislead if it is not recognized that time is not homogeneous and perfectly substitutable over an individual's diurnal, seasonal, and life cycles. The "value of time" hypothesis predicts that better-educated women allocate more time and interest to market-oriented activities and less time to child-rearing. How can one get directly at the mechanisms by which education influences fertility? Can a variety of subtler predictions be advanced as to how education affects the value of time and thereby the mix of inputs used in a variety of household activities, as well as demands for final family outputs, such as children? Are there other aspects of the husband's and wife's economic contribution to the family that can be quantified and related to schooling? What are the consequences of physical wealth on the household's choices? Does wealth augment the strength of its owner's "time-value" based viewpoint in the allocation of family resources, or does it increase the demand for all normal goods, particularly leisure, without introducing an offsetting price-of-time effect? In particular, does material wealth increase fertility, even if it enters the family from the mother's side? What are the limits to the family in terms of its ability to pool economic resources, and how do they change with development? Modern economic growth places a premium on regional and occupational mobility that seems designed to erode the economic foundation of the extended family.

Finally, the intertemporal transfer of resources is at the very heart of the nuclear family and its relations with previous and succeeding generations. It might be postulated that the increase by half in life expectancy in many low-income countries in the last three decades would have reduced the rate of social time preference, with predictable consequences for savings and investment behavior. The mortality reduction should also enhance the returns on human capital relative to physical capital, shifting the balance in family portfolios. Conversely, if income streams can be purchased more cheaply in terms of physical assets due to rapid economic development such as in Taiwan, will household resources allocated to enlarging the subsequent generation diminish? The testing of many of these propositions and obtaining a consistent set of assumptions that account for related facets of household behavior could make the "value of time" hypothesis pivotal for the study of the household sector in low-income economies.

Appendix A. Additional Statistical Tables

Table 4.A.1 Age-specific Annual Birthrates for Taiwan: 1949–74 (Births per 1,000 Women of Childbearing Age)

Births Registered in Year[a]	Total Fertility Rate[b]	Number of Births per 1,000 Women of Specific Ages[c]						
		15–19	20–24	25–29	30–34	35–39	40–44	45–49
1949	5,900	61	241	290	263	186	111	27
1950	6,030	61	246	297	269	191	112	30
1951	7,040	68	287	349	311	226	132	35
1952	6,615	53	272	342	294	220	113	29
1953	6,470	48	265	336	292	218	108	27
1954	6,425	48	263	334	292	218	104	26
1955	6,530	50	273	341	295	219	103	25
1956	6,505	51	264	340	296	222	105	23
1957	6,000	45	249	325	275	197	92	17
1958	6,055	43	248	336	281	199	90	14
1959	5,990	46	258	334	270	190	86	14
1960	5,750	48	253	333	255	169	79	13
1961	5,585	45	248	342	246	156	71	10
1962	5,465	45	255	338	235	145	65	10
1963	5,350	41	252	337	231	139	60	10
1964	5,100	37	254	335	214	120	52	8
1965	4,825	36	261	326	195	100	41	6
1966	4,815	40	274	326	188	91	38	6
1967	4,220	39	250	295	158	70	28	4
1968	4,325	41	256	309	161	68	26	4
1969	4,120	40	245	298	151	63	23	4
1970	4,000	40	238	293	147	59	20	3
1971	3,705	36	224	277	134	51	16	3
1972	3,365	35	208	257	117	41	13	2
1973	3,210	33	203	250	105	37	12	2
1974	3,045	34	197	235	96	35	10	2

Source: 1949–64, *Demographic Fact Book 1964*.
1964–74, *Demographic Fact Book 1974*.

[a]Births are attributed to the year in which they are registered.

[b]The total fertility rate is five times the sum of the age-specific birthrates. Perhaps because of rounding, the totals do not always add up.

[c]Births by age of mother divided by the midyear estimate of the number of women of that age.

Table 4.A.2 **Percentage of Women Ever Married in Taiwan by Age, 1940–74**

Period and Source	Percentage of Age Group						
	15–19	20–24	25–29	30–34	35–39	40–44	45–49
1940 census	29.5	84.4	95.9	98.3	98.8	99.2	99.4
1956 census	11.5	70.6	95.2	97.9	98.5	98.7	99.0
1966 census	8.6	59.5	92.9	98.1	98.9	99.1	99.1
1970 census	7.2	49.7	91.3	97.8	98.8	98.8	98.8
1974 Household Registry	5.8	44.1	84.9	95.4	97.0	97.6	97.4

Sources: 1940 census, table 13, p. 54.
1956 census, table 17, p. 265.
1966 census, vol. 2, no. 3, table 2, p. 125.
1970 census, extract, table 9, p. 135.
1974 *Taiwan Demographic Factbook*, table 9, p. 366.

Table 4.A.3 **Selected Demographic Time Series for Taiwan, 1906–74**

Period	Natural Rate of Population Increase (% per Year)	Crude Vital Rates (per 1,000 Population)		Infant Death (per 1,000 Live Births)	Life Expectancy (Years at Birth)	
		Birth	Death		Male	Female
1906–20	1.02[a]	42	31	172	25–30	
1921–40	2.32[a]	45	22	155	35–45	
1947–49	2.5	40	15	—[b]	—[b]	—[b]
1950–54	3.58	45.9	10.1	37	56.1	60.2
1955–59	3.49	42.9	8.0	37	60.5	65.9
1960–64	3.08	37.2	6.4	30	62.7	68.0
1965–69	2.44	29.7	5.3	22	64.4	70.0
1970–74	2.01	24.8	4.8	16	66.5	71.8

Sources: 1906–40, Barclay 1954, pp. 13, 161, 241.
1947–49, *1959–1961 Household Registry Statistics of Taiwan*, table 1.
1950–64, *1972 Demographic Factbook, Taiwan*, table 1, *1970 Demographic Factbook*, table 15.
1965–74, *1974 Taiwan Demographic Factbook*, tables 61, 74, 76.

[a]Taiwanese geometric rate of growth between censuses (Barclay 1954, p. 13).
[b]Not available.

Table 4.A.4 Means and Standard Deviations of Variables Used in Regressions on Fertility

Variable	Age Group of Women						
	15–19	20–24	25–29	30–34	35–39	40–44	45–49
Children ever born 1966: C_{66}	.0622 (.0285)	.853 (.157)	2.50 (.204)	3.95 (.253)	4.93 (.366)	5.44 (.483)	5.65 (.558)
Log (C_{66})	−2.86 (.410)	−.174 (.175)	.912 (.0818)	1.37 (.0653)	1.59 (.0766)	1.69 (.0934)	1.73 (.105)
Log (C_{67}/C_{66})	.781 (.0920)	.296 (.0297)	.105 (.00743)	.0362 (.00522)	.0137 (.00440)	.00431 (.00181)	.00056 (.00028)
Log (reciprocal of cohort child survival 1966)	.0238 (.00817)	.0262 (.00718)	.0352 (.00931)	.0514 (.0120)	.0744 (.0164)	.110 (.0221)	.152 (.0277)
Log of child death rate 1965[a]	.0521 (.0112)	Not age-specific variable; i.e., identical for all age groups					
Log (proportion of women with junior high school)	−1.16 (.339)	−1.55 (.355)	−2.19 (.442)	−2.42 (.477)	−2.36 (.511)	−2.50 (.586)	−2.89 (.713)
Log (proportion of men with senior high school)	−.692 (.184)	−.870 (.217)	−1.25 (.259)	−1.39 (.300)	−1.14 (.314)	−1.15 (.301)	−1.43 (.386)
Family planning per woman to 1965	.00161 (.00063)	Not age-specific variable, i.e., identical for all ages					
Family planning per woman in 1966	.00268 (.00081)	Not age-specific variable, i.e., identical for all ages					

Note: The standard deviations of the variables are reported in parentheses beneath the means. Values are unweighted over sample of twenty-one regions.

[a]The natural logarithm of the reciprocal of the product of the age-specific rates within the region from birth to age 15.

Table 4.A.5 **Initial Estimate of Marital Fertility Rate by Age of Woman Used to Calculate Beta**

Age of Woman	Initial Relative Value of Fertility	Age of Woman	Initial Relative Value of Fertility
14 or less	0		
15	.100	35	.125
16	.200	36	.100
17	.250	37	.090
18	.300	38	.080
19	.350	39	.070
20	.400	40	.060
21	.425	41	.050
22	.450	42	.040
23	.425	43	.025
24	.400	44	.010
25	.375	45	.007
26	.350	46	.005
27	.325	47	.003
28	.300	48	.002
29	.275	49	.001
30	.250	50 and over	0
31	.225		
32	.200		
33	.175		
34	.150		

Table 4.A.6 **Initial Proportions of Children Living by Current Age and by Age of Mother in 1966**

Age Group of Mothers	Age of Children						
	0	1–4	5–9	10–14	15–19	20–24	25 and over
15–19	.545	.455	0	0	0	0	0
20–24	.313	.624	.063	0	0	0	0
25–29	.149	.525	.305	.021	0	0	0
30–34	.066	.321	.414	.186	.013	0	0
35–39	.033	.148	.319	.341	.150	.009	0
40–44	.014	.064	.166	.295	.316	.137	.008
45–49	.004	.023	.074	.161	.289	.307	.142
50–54	0	0	.025	.073	.162	.291	.449

Table 4.A.7 **Form of Age at Marriage Tabulations in Taiwan 1966 Census**

Age at First Marriage	Current Age of Married Women				
	12–24	25–34	35–44	45–54	55 and over
12–14	X	X	X	X	X
15–19	X	X	X	X	X
20–24	X	X	X	X	X
25–29		X	X	X	X
30–34		X	X	X	X
35–44			X		
35–54				X	
55 and over					X

Source: 1966 Taiwan census, vol. 3, table 6.

Table 4.A.8 **Logarithms of Estimated Marital Duration in Years and Marital Fertility Rate per Year**

Region	Current Age of Women					
	15–19		20–24		25–29	
	Duration	Rate	Duration	Rate	Duration	Rate
Taipei Hsien	−2.10382	−0.37907	0.55780	−0.60008	1.72252	−0.81382
Ilan Hsien	−2.32702	−0.31383	0.45386	−0.56378	1.82714	0.88363
Taoynan Hsien	−2.19788	−0.30315	0.52947	−0.59850	1.75780	−0.81288
Hsinchu Hsien	−2.53190	−0.44011	0.27596	−0.53876	1.52539	−0.62567
Miaoli Hsien	−2.95563	−0.37978	0.15718	−0.51614	1.69647	−0.81278
Taichung Hsien	−2.79355	−0.32774	0.22025	−0.55726	1.72383	−0.83792
Changhwa Hsien	−3.20471	−0.38523	0.09867	−0.55769	1.76350	−0.89020
Nantou Hsien	−2.57412	−0.39012	0.42442	−0.61280	1.75533	−0.82081
Yunlin Hsien	−3.05406	−0.34214	0.42273	−0.06939	1.76606	−0.81746
Chiayi Hsien	−2.79355	−0.41044	0.36615	−0.59859	1.71474	−0.78803
Tainan Hsien	−2.85851	−0.39600	0.33541	0.56633	1.71127	−0.77974
Kaohsiung Hsien	−2.40954	−0.33907	0.48844	−0.60049	1.69939	−0.77058
Pingtung Hsien	−2.36250	−0.33907	0.54631	−0.64095	1.73837	−0.78945
Taitung Hsien	−1.46114	−0.43598	0.93131	−0.69679	1.87130	−0.77446
Hualien Hsien	−1.80229	−0.40681	0.76965	−0.62858	1.89169	−0.84556
Penghu Hsien	−2.22124	−0.40681	0.51707	−0.67512	1.68380	−0.72545
Taipei City	−2.87916	−0.14497	0.10938	−0.50213	1.58571	−0.86141
Keelung City	−2.31328	−0.29855	0.58543	−0.54755	1.74900	−0.80420
Taichung City	−2.97814	−0.07310	0.21069	−0.47258	1.63904	−0.80583
Tainan City	−2.58319	−0.06786	0.15804	−0.53521	1.59571	−0.82723
Kaohsiung City	−2.58319	−0.19582	0.46793	−0.63304	1.61767	−0.78990

Current Age of Women							
30–34		35–39		40–44		45–49	
Duration	Rate	Duration	Rate	Duration	Rate	Duration	Rate
2.36912	−1.01742	2.75858	−1.20307	3.03816	−1.43261	3.25641	−1.64611
2.42640	−1.01091	2.79850	−1.16805	3.06907	−1.32586	3.28181	−1.51797
2.38573	−0.99612	2.76848	−1.15355	3.04460	−1.34002	3.26075	−1.52457
2.25035	−0.86078	2.66619	−1.06082	2.95903	−1.25094	3.18525	−1.44524
2.35351	−0.96674	2.74529	−1.10062	3.02657	−1.25766	3.24586	−1.43801
2.37108	−0.98711	2.76076	−1.14050	3.04046	−1.30656	3.25878	−1.47185
2.39278	−1.01548	2.77602	−1.16066	3.05240	−1.31516	3.26870	−1.48560
2.38276	−1.00161	2.76533	−1.15637	3.04136	−1.31001	3.25744	−1.48560
2.39439	−1.00955	2.77728	−1.16172	3.05348	−1.30157	3.26967	−1.43490
2.36939	−0.98332	2.76169	−1.14882	3.04272	−1.31312	3.26185	−1.45404
2.36981	−0.99729	2.76347	−1.15425	3.04519	−1.31108	3.26475	−1.44204
2.35495	−0.97507	2.74756	−1.13297	3.02875	−1.30340	3.24798	−1.49287
2.36853	−0.98359	2.75209	−1.13727	3.02864	−1.30868	3.24504	−1.46783
2.43966	−0.94375	2.79982	−1.09924	3.06405	−1.28396	3.27285	−1.49504
2.45088	−0.98566	2.80739	−1.14138	3.06966	−1.30299	3.27724	−1.50264
2.34374	−0.89526	2.73788	−1.02009	3.01985	−1.21238	3.23956	−1.40605
2.30452	−1.09198	2.71839	−1.32313	3.01025	−1.56729	3.23589	−1.77588
2.38227	−1.01284	2.76695	−1.23370	3.04407	−1.42552	3.26083	−1.73593
2.33181	−1.02575	2.73715	−1.22409	3.02477	−1.42552	3.24787	−1.59262
2.31230	−1.04113	2.72546	−1.23271	3.01696	−1.42930	3.24239	−1.58972
2.31519	−1.05075	2.72211	−1.25518	3.01052	−1.45753	3.23410	−1.64437

Table 4.A.9 **Regressions on Cohort Fertility or Stocks: Logarithm of Children Ever Born per Woman by Age in 1966 (Including Urban-Rural Component)**

Age of Women	Constant Term	Cohort Child Mortality[a]	Proportion with Some Junior High School: Women	Proportion with Some Junior High School: Men	Family Planning up to 1965[b]	Urban-Rural Variable[d]	R^2 (SEE)[c]
15–19	−2.53	21.5	1.41	−1.57	−125.0	−.343	.4022
	(3.99)	(1.86)	(1.79)	(1.14)	(.94)	(.99)	(.3665)
20–24	−.551	22.1	−.232	.662	14.2	−.035	.6812
	(2.30)	(5.40)	(1.11)	(2.25)	(.34)	(.33)	(.1138)
25–29	.722	5.83	−.079	.155	16.0	−.0826	.8534
	(8.23)	(5.53)	(1.52)	(1.62)	(1.21)	(2.20)	(.0362)
30–34	1.19	3.32	−.0681	.0952	−1.65	−.0592	.9297
	(25.0)	(7.18)	(2.97)	(2.87)	(.21)	(2.86)	(.0200)
35–39	1.37	1.76	−.0973	.0959	−7.33	−.0691	.9339
	(29.8)	(4.89)	(4.01)	(3.25)	(.83)	(3.28)	(.0027)
40–44	1.42	.704	−.124	.0805	−6.59	−.0759	.9180
	(24.3)	(1.94)	(3.82)	(1.48)	(.56)	(2.72)	(.0309)
45–49	1.45	−.237	−.0998	−.0193	4.45	−.0599	.8612
	(17.5)	(.56)	(2.57)	(.28)	(.25)	(1.43)	(.0452)

Note: Numbers in parentheses beneath regression coefficients are *t* values. Observations are twenty-one major subdivisions of Taiwan for which data are published in the Taiwan 1966 census, vol. 2, Nos. 2 and 3.

[a]Reciprocal of cohort's proportion of children ever born who are still living as reported in 1966 census.

[b]Man-months of family planning fieldworker effort expended in region through calendar year 1965, divided by the number of women in the region of childbearing age (i.e., 15–49).

[c]Standard error of regression estimate is reported in parentheses beneath R^2.

[d]Urban-rural variable equals 1 for five cities (Tainan, Taipei, Keelung, Taichung, and Kaohsiung), 0 for seventeen rural areas.

Table 4.A.10 Stock-Adjustment Equation: Relative Change in Children Ever Born, 1967 (Including Urban-Rural Component)

Age of Women	Estimation Method[d]	Constant Term	Period Child Mortality[a] (*t*-2)	Proportion with Some Junior High School		Family Planning[b] (*t*-1)	Children Ever Born (*t*-1)	Urban-Rural Variable	R^2 (SEE)[c]
				Women	Men				
16–20	OLS[d]	.308 (1.99)	−1.07 (.62)	−.315 (2.83)	.354 (2.05)	34.7 (2.57)	−.111 (2.82)	−.00902 (.21)	.8306 (.0453)
	IV[d]	.818 (1.33)	−5.87 (.99)	−.536 (1.81)	.515 (1.66)	4.85 (1.94)	.0456 (.25)	.0137 (.20)	(.0661)
21–25	OLS	.180 (9.23)	−.0818 (.30)	−.0558 (4.06)	.0157 (.80)	6.81 (3.09)	−.162 (11.3)	.00421 (.60)	.9568 (.00737)
	IV	.190 (7.57)	−.282 (.70)	−.0545 (3.81)	.00923 (.41)	6.31 (2.64)	−.148 (5.83)	.00434 (.60)	(.00763)
26–30	OLS	.185 (7.53)	.312 (1.46)	−.0182 (2.30)	.0107 (.76)	−.731 (.45)	−.132 (3.87)	−.000884 (.15)	.6618 (.00517)
	IV	.240 (4.21)	.749 (1.61)	−.0238 (2.19)	.0191 (1.01)	.921 (.37)	−.222 (2.46)	−.00620 (.72)	(.00633)
31–35	OLS	.0416 (.92)	.253 (1.52)	−.00993 (2.42)	.0159 (3.01)	−2.96 (3.02)	−.00962 (.24)	.00223 (.60)	.7452 (.00315)
	IV	.0594 (.84)	.311 (1.28)	−.0106 (2.31)	.0164 (2.98)	−2.93 (2.95)	−.0254 (.41)	.00157 (.37)	(.00317)
36–40	OLS	−.0344 (1.38)	.215 (3.25)	−.00139 (.59)	.00746 (3.10)	−2.02 (3.99)	.0293 (1.59)	.00343 (1.87)	.9059 (.00161)
	IV	−.0244 (.60)	.236 (2.50)	−.00202 (.65)	.00792 (2.79)	−2.07 (3.92)	.0219 (.73)	.00303 (1.36)	(.00162)

Table 4.A.10 (continued)

Age of Women	Estimation Method[d]	Constant Term	Period Child Mortality[a] (t-2)	Proportion with Some Junior High School		Family Planning[b] (t-1)	Children Ever Born (t-1)	Urban-Rural Variable	R^2 (SEE)[c]
				Women	Men				
41–45	OLS	.00589	.133	—.00174	.00415	—.789	—.00354	.000138	.7843
		(.50)	(4.71)	(1.19)	(2.24)	(2.57)	(.43)	(.13)	(.00101)
	IV	—.00125	.126	—.00115	.00385	—.769	.00148	.000474	
		(.05)	(3.39)	(.46)	(1.79)	(2.40)	(.08)	(.30)	(.00102)
46–50	OLS	.00420	.0181	—.000274	.000036	—.00700	—.00308	.000035	.6581
		(2.47)	(3.54)	(1.32)	(.12)	(.12)	(2.73)	(.18)	(.00195)
	IV	—.00516	.0247	.000274	.000126	—.0170	.00329	.000463	
		(.27)	(1.54)	(.28)	(.22)	(.15)	(.25)	(.50)	(.000352)

Note: Numbers in parentheses beneath regression coefficients are t values. Observations are twenty-one major subdivisions of Taiwan for which data are published in the Taiwan 1966 census, vol. 2, nos. 2 and 3.

[a]Reciprocal of cohort's proportion of children ever born who are still living as reported in 1966 census.

[b]Man-months of family planning fieldworker effort expended in region through calendar year 1965, divided by the number of women in the region of childbearing age (i.e., 15–49).

[c]Standard error of regression estimate is reported in parentheses beneath R^2 for OLS estimates, whereas R^2 is inappropriate for comparisons with IV estimates.

[d]OLS: Ordinary least-squares estimates.

IV: Instrumental variable estimates where children ever born (1966) is treated as endogenous and cohort child mortality and pre-1966 family-planning inputs are the excluded instruments used to identify equation.

Table 4.A.11 Reduced-Form Stock Equation for Children Ever Born, 1971 (Including Urban-Rural Component)

Age of Women	Constant Term	Cohort Child Mortality[a]	Proportion with Some Junior High School		Family Planning up to 1970[b]	Urban-Rural Variable[d]	R^2 (SEE)[c]
			Women	Men			
20–24	−.582 (2.49)	20.9 (3.34)	.271 (1.05)	−.347 (.87)	11.1 (.36)	−.0707 (.71)	.5942 (.1244)
25–29	.556 (5.11)	6.83 (3.06)	−.0850 (.79)	.0753 (.43)	6.28 (.41)	0.0139 (.29)	.6917 (.0555)
30–34	1.10 (14.3)	3.82 (3.06)	−.106 (1.85)	.153 (1.50)	−.617 (.06)	−.0584 (1.79)	.8274 (.0355)
35–39	1.36 (17.7)	3.74 (3.40)	−.0865 (2.22)	.145 (2.63)	−8.09 (.70)	−.0680 (1.93)	.8280 (.0367)
40–44	1.47 (23.1)	2.06 (3.10)	−.0725 (2.50)	.117 (3.24)	−.686 (.07)	−.104 (3.66)	.8955 (.03203)
45–49	1.47 (23.0)	.534 (1.10)	−.104 (3.53)	.0860 (1.98)	3.92 (.40)	−.0978 (3.33)	.9158 (.0317)
50–54	1.46 (14.5)	−.640 (1.07)	−.0871 (2.33)	.00916 (.14)	17.8 (1.23)	−.0875 (1.92)	.8331 (.04942)

Note: Numbers in parentheses beneath regression coefficients are t values. Observations are twenty-one major subdivisions of Taiwan for which data are published in the Taiwan 1966 census, vol. 2, nos. 2 and 3.

[a]Reciprocal of cohort's proportion of children ever born who are still living as reported in 1966 census.

[b]Man-months of family planning fieldworker effort expended in region through calendar year 1965, divided by the number of women in the region of childbearing age (i.e., 15–49).

[c]Standard error of regression estimate is reported in parentheses beneath R^2.

[d]Urban-rural variable equals 1 for five cities (Tainan, Taipei, Keelung, Taichung, and Kaohsiung), 0 for seventeen rural areas.

Appendix B. Procedures for Regional Cohort Projections

Consistent Estimates of Birth Stocks and Flows

First, the proportion married by single year of age j, in the ith region is defined

$$_{j+1}m_{ji}(66) = (p_{ji}(66) - s_{ji}(66))/p_{ji}(66),$$
$$i = 1, \ldots, 21$$
$$j = 15, \ldots, 49$$

where p refers to all women and s to those single or never married according to the 1966 census (vol. 3, table 2).

In years after 1966, information is annually published from the Household Registry on proportion of the population ever married by five-year age groups. Using the individual year population totals for each subsequent year, t, a predicted proportion married is calculated; for example, for age 15 to age 19:

$$_{19}M_{15,i}(t) = \left[\sum_{j=15}^{19} p_{ji}(t) * m_{ji}(66) \right] \sum_{j=15}^{19} p_{ji}(t).$$

I then define alpha (α) as a marriage deflator for each region, each year, and the seven five-year age intervals for which Household Registry data are available:

$$_{19}\alpha_{15,i}(t) = {}_{19}M_{15,i}(t)/{}_{19}m_{15,i}(66),$$

where $_{19}m_{15,i}(t)$ is the actual proportion of women between the ages of 15 and 19 registered as ever married in year t. If the age weights had not relatively changed, and age-specific marital rates declined over time, the α's would presumably increase and exceed unity after 1966. The estimated proportion of women married by single year of age, in calendar year t, can then be expressed for, say, age 18 as follows:

$$_{19}m_{18,i}(t) = {}_{19}m_{18,i}(66)/{}_{19}\alpha_{15}(t)$$

The second step is to estimate birthrates for women by individual ages, though birthrates are reported from the Household Registry only by five-year intervals. Using initial arbitrary estimates of marital fertility reported in table 4.A.5, denoted F_j, that are not untenable at the national level for the base year 1966, a similar procedure of deflation is performed to obtain estimates of individual-year birthrates that are roughly consistent with the changing age composition of regional populations, marriage patterns, and age-aggregated birthrates as recorded in the household registration system by date of registration. The base-year estimate of the birthrate would become:

$$_{19}B_{15,i}(t) = \left[\sum_{j=15}^{19} p_{ji}(t) *_{j+1}m_{j,i}(t) * F_j \right] \sum_{j=15}^{19} p_{ji}(t),$$

and a birthrate deflator for the seven age intervals is defined as beta (β),

$$_{19}\beta_{15,i}(t) = {}_{19}B_{15,i}(t)/{}_{19}b_{15,i}(t),$$

where $_{19}b_{15}(t)$ is the registered birthrate for women of ages 15 to 19 in region i in calendar year t. Similarly, a final estimate of the birthrate for women of individual ages is obtained:

$$_{19}b_{18,i}(t) = [F_{18} *_{j+1}m_{j,i}(t)]/{}_{19}\beta_{15,i}(t).$$

Women are then followed by individual years in the 1966 census age distribution, attributing to them their estimated birthrates in subsequent years, in addition to the number of children already born as reported in the 1966 census. These single-year-of-birth cohorts are summed into five-year age groups each calendar year, and observations are constructed to follow through time the aging regional cohort, neglecting the effects of internal migration. Thus the 35- to 39-year-old women in region 2 (Ilan Hsien) had 5.11 children on average in 1966 and in 1971 were estimated at age 40–44 to have 5.34 children ever born. In contrast, those women age 35–39 in 1971 had on average only 4.63 children ever born.

Survival of Cohort's Living Children

The mortality rates for each region and year are read or calculated for infants and children age 1–4, 5–9, and 10–14. Based on national levels of age-specific mortality between 1965 and 1970, the mortality rates for children age 15–19, 20–24, and 25 and over are arbitrarily assumed to be proportional to the death rate for children 10–14 in the region, where the factors of proportionality are 1.73, 2.55, and 2.90, respectively. Mortality among older offspring is relatively low and intrinsically of less interest to us here because an increasing proportion of their mothers are no longer of childbearing age.

To project the cohort's living offspring forward to the next period, age-specific survival rates are applied to the age distribution of the initial living children. The total number of living children for the seven standard (five-year) age intervals of women is obtained by region from the 1966 census (vol. 3). Initially, I assume the proportion of those living children in each current age group is as arbitrarily reported in table 4.A.6, chosen to be roughly consistent with national birthrates in the early 1960s. But if absolute differences in infant mortality remain substantial by region, as in Taiwan in the 1960s, it seems appropriate to use regional Household Registry birthrates in 1966 to estimate directly the number of infants (age 0) by region and age of mother, and use the relative proportions in table 4.A.6 to distribute only living children age 1 and over. For example, women 20–24 in region 1 (Taipei Hsien) registered a birthrate of 0.287 in 1966 and reported in the census 0.938 children living. Ignoring infant mortality, the rest of children living, 0.651, are distributed between the age groups 1–4 and 5–9 in proportion to their cell values in table 4.A.6, or 90.8% and 9.2%, respectively.[32] Clearly, further refinements and more extensive checks for consistency could be introduced by using information on registered birthrates and death rates in prior years (Maurer and Schultz 1972, p. 8), but these errors need not jeopardize our objective of obtaining estimates of cohort accumulative fertility and surviving offspring.[33]

Overall, the procedures described above should not introduce relatively large errors unless the census and registry systems are incompatible. The least satisfactory assumption is probably that embodied in the uniform age-specific marital fertility schedule. There has been much change in age-specific marital birthrates in recent years in Taiwan. As the age at marriage has increased, the marital birthrate has increased among those who still married early, between the ages of 15 and 19 (Anderson 1973). This may have been partially due to changes in the age composition of married women in this interval (becoming older), but it would also be consistent with a selectivity process by which those getting married are increasingly fecund, either because they were pregnant before marriage (perhaps unusually fecund for their age) or inclined to start their childbearing immediately, and hence marrying at an atypically young age. Whatever the cause, these changes in marital fertility rates are not allowed to modify the relative shape of the schedule but only displace the schedule up and down uniformly over the five-year age intervals. This, in fact, may be a poor approximation for how marital fertility schedules have been changing in different regions of Taiwan. However, since our primary interest attaches to the behavior of older women, I hope this defect in my calculations will not be a serious shortcoming for this analysis.

Estimates of Duration of Marriage

The 1966 census is tabulated by region, for women by five current age intervals, and for those ever married by several age intervals of first marriage (see table 4.A.7). Neglecting the intervals between dissolution of marriages and remarriage, on which there is no information, these census tabulations can be used to approximate the average number of years elapsed since first marriage for each current five-year age group of women.

There are three distinct issues: (1) estimating the mean current age in the age intervals reported; (2) estimating the mean age at first marriage in the age at marriage intervals; and (3) interpolating age at marriage for the standard five-year age intervals to complement other published data. In the first case, the mean age within current age intervals can be directly calculated for ever-married women at the regional level from single-year age distributions by marital status (vol. 3, table 2). In the second case, two procedures are used. Among women age 25 or more, most of the cohort is married. An estimate of the average age at marriage (AM) for those married at each current age is calculated as follows:

$$AM_j = \left(\sum_{k=1}^{n} m_{jk} \cdot AM_{jk} \right) \sum_{k=1}^{n} m_{jk}, \qquad \begin{array}{l} j = 1, \ldots, 5 \\ k = 1, \ldots, n \end{array}$$

where the regional subscript is suppressed, j refers to current age interval, and k refers to age-at-marriage interval. A relation over age cohorts between AM and current age would be affected by the tendency of older groups to have had more years to get married, increasing with age the average reported age at marriage, other things being equal. Also, there is some evidence that the median age at marriage has decreased among more recent birth cohorts during the twentieth century (Goode 1970; Barclay 1954). Linear regressions are fit within regions to the four current age groups over age 24, with the mean age at marriage expressed in either arithmetic or logarithmic form as a function of the current mean age and an intercept. The arithmetic form accounted satisfactorily for the secular upward trend in age at marriage and was used to interpolate values for five-year intervals over age 25—that is, coefficients of determination were between 0.8 and 0.9.

For younger women a different approach was needed, given the form of the age at marriage tabulations (see table 4.A.7). The working assumption is that cross-sectional differences in the proportion married at different single ages represents the marrying fraction of a stable "synthetic" cohort that begins to marry at age 12. For women currently aged 15 to 19, for example, the average duration of marriage is then approximated as

$$_{19}D_{15} = \sum_{l=15}^{19} \sum_{i=12}^{l} (m_j - m_{j-1})^* p_l^* (l - i))/ \sum_{l=15}^{19} p_l,$$

where the regional subscript is suppressed, and m_j and p_j refer to single-year married proportions and female populations of exactly age j. For women currently 20–24, the summations over the l index run from age 20 to age 24.

To determine if the first method of direct observation yields results similar to those of the second, comparisons are possible only over the entire current age interval from 15 to 24 and later age groups. The two resulting estimates of marriage duration for age 15–24 are correlated at 0.99 over the 21 regions. At later ages the two approaches are, as one might anticipate, less highly correlated.

The first direct interpolation method is used to obtain the estimates of the average duration of marriage or years of exposure since first marriage for the age cohorts older than 24 in 1966. The second synthetic cross-sectional method is used to obtain the duration estimates for the two younger birth cohorts in 1966. The natural logarithm of this marital duration variable is reported in table 4.A.8 by region along with the logarithm of the cohort's birthrate per year of exposure to marriage. The sum of these logarithmic variables is, of course, the logarithm of the cohort's average number of births per woman.

Notes

1. The services produced by the numerical stock of children enter into many family consumption and production activities. The output of these activities depends on associated expenditures of time and goods, some of which directly enhance the value of the child services, such as the children's schooling and health. Unfortunately, the final outputs of these family activities are not generally observed or ascribed market prices. Therefore the dimension of demands for child services that is used here is simply the number of children born or surviving to a specified mature age. See Becker (1960); Willis (1974); DeTray (1974); Becker and Lewis (1974).

2. See Zajonc (1976) for review of evidence and a stylized interpretation of intelligence differences by birth order and number of siblings. Lindert (1974) presents new evidence on this pattern and provides an explanation in terms of a mother's allocation of time among children.

3. Economic models of fertility have usually been formulated in terms of a single period-static choice problem in which parents demand the optimal lifetime stock of children for their income, relative prices, and technology (Becker 1960; Willis 1974). Empirical tests of this framework have examined reproductive stocks or flows as though one were proportional to the other. Easterlin (1968) and others have stressed a dynamic mechanism by which fertility is adjusted in response to the gap between actual and anticipated income. Linking cohort income deviations to relative cohort size, Lee (1975) has proposed to complete the demographic feedback loop. But in the context of low-income countries or in Europe during its demographic transition, there is surprisingly little exploration of adaptive behavioral models. Indeed, the period of demographic transition is interpreted by some as convincing evidence that no generalizations are applicable beyond an ethnic/cultural region (Coale 1969, 1973). Given the nature of the data available and the sophistication of its analysis to date for evidence of multicausal relations, such a broad conclusion may be premature.

4. The desirability of incorporating stocks in the interpretation of reproductive flows was appropriately stressed by Tobin (1974). Though he is not responsible for this application of the stock-adjustment framework, his comments stimulated my search for the stock data analyzed in this paper.

5. Children are generally viewed by society as irreversible commitments by parents, and markets to exchange children are not condoned except in placing orphans or unwanted illegitimate offspring. But in Taiwan exceptional arrangements historically evolved for combining adoption and marriage to provide parents with the opportunity to "adopt out" girls and even boys into uxorilocal marriages. It was common for a couple to adopt a baby girl who was later to marry their son in a "sim-pua" form of marriage. This arrangement permitted a poor couple to avoid the economic sacrifice of rearing a girl to marriageable age and assured the adopting couple a loyal and servile daughter-in-law (Wolf 1972, chap. 11). More than half of the marriages in the Taipei area before 1925 did not require the transfer of a young woman into her spouse's household (Wolf 1972, p. 171). Adoptions are today 50% more common for girls than for boys and equaled about 3% of the births in 1970–72. There are other reflections of the lesser demand for girls (p. 60) including the reported historical practice of infanticide among girls (p. 54). Contemporary analysis of birthrates reveals a greater reproductive replacement response when a male infant dies than when a female infant dies (Schultz 1969), and preferences for male offspring are well documented in contemporary Taiwan surveys (Coombs and Sun 1978).

6. See Tabbarah (1971) and Easterlin (1975). In fact, difference in health conditions may affect the rate with which cohorts achieve their lifetime reproductive goals, but this effect is thought to be secondary to demand factors. To the extent that health-related supply limitations were positively associated with child mortality rates, the estimated partial association between child mortality and fertility would be biased in a negative direction by the omission of supply limitations or their determinants. There are still instances in which far less healthy and more malnourished populations, such as exist in sub-Saharan Africa and Bangladesh, might display regional differences in fertility that are attributable to differences in reproductive capacity or supply (Mosley and Chen 1976). See also Easterlin, Pollak, and Wachter's chapter in this volume.

7. Children as a producer durable expand the household's budget constraint (see Kelley's chapter in this volume), but not indefinitely, given imperfectly elastic supplies of contemporary inputs. For example, a small farmer might be able to borrow to buy additional land for his sons to farm, but the capital market may not view sons as the least risky form of collateral and might thus require an increasing risk premium on such a loan.

8. See United Nations (1965) for evidence of dissimilar age patterns of births across countries and over time. As yet no characterization of optimal child-spacing strategies has gained wide acceptance, though models are implicit in several studies (Sanderson and Willis 1971; Heckman and Willis 1975).

9. Barclay (1954, pp. 154–65) suggests life expectancy increasing from 25–29 about the turn of the century to 40–45 by 1936–40, but surprisingly little reduction occurred in infant mortality. Infant mortality declined from levels of 160 per 1,000 about 1940 to 32 by 1960 and 14 in 1974. (*Taiwan Demographic Factbook* 1974). Though some understatement of mortality exists and some transfer of infant deaths to the second year of life probably persists in the registry, these errors are unlikely to alter the noted trends or undermine confidence in interregional variation in registered vital rates (*Taiwan Demographic Factbook* 1964).

10. I have since found a reference by Chien-shen Shih (1976, p. 296) to a mimeographed study, "Rates of Return to Education in Taiwan, Republic of China, July 1972," prepared by K. G. Gannicott for the Ministry of Education. Gannicott's estimates of the social rate of return to education, as cited by Shih, are 27, 12, 13, 13, and 18% per annum for primary, junior high, senior high, senior vocational, and university education, respectively. It is unclear whether returns are calculated separately for men and women or what secular growth in real labor incomes is assumed that adjusts upward the cross-sectional age differences to obtain a synthetic estimate of longitudinal (cohort) returns to education.

11. These assumptions are discussed in the Appendix B; except for a variety of smoothing procedures to interpolate values for individual years, the primary assumption is that internal migration is not selective with respect to women according to their fertility, and that age-specific mortality does not differ with the child's mother's age.

12. In 1950, for example, multiplying out age-specific survival rates for Taiwan, the life table probability for a live birth to reach age 15 was 0.84, and having reached age 15 the chance of reaching age 30 was 0.95. In 1960 these survival rates had increased to 0.93 and 0.97 respectively, and by 1974 they stood at 0.96 and 0.98. See *Taiwan Demographic Factbook* for 1964, table 11, and 1974, table 34.

13. An obvious approach for dealing with child mortality is to choose a threshold age at which to measure "surviving children"; an age before which most child mortality occurs and beyond which survival prospects are favorable (see note 12).

Though arbitrary, this procedure appears at first to be an improvement over assuming that parents formulate their reproductive goals in terms of live births, valuing all the same regardless of survival status (see O'Hara 1972 on problems of evaluation and summation). But if we assume a multiplicative model of demand for births, and child-survival rates are an explanatory argument, we can rearrange terms and directly test the hypothesis whether demand for "surviving children" is indeed perfectly inelastic with respect to child mortality. However, imposing the "surviving child" hypothesis on the demand equation not only loses information, it makes it more difficult to interpret parameter estimates across birth cohorts of women for whom child survival is inherently observed to different threshold ages.

The equation estimated later in table 4.5 can be written

$$ln\ CEB = \alpha + \beta ln\,(CEB/CA) + \gamma ln\ SF + \delta ln\ SM$$
$$+ \epsilon FP + \mu,$$

where *CEB* is the number of children ever born per woman, *CA* is the number of those children still living per woman, *SF* and *SM* are the proportions of women and men with some junior high schooling, *FP* is family-planning inputs per woman, μ is a normally distributed constant variance disturbance, and α, β, γ, δ, and ϵ are estimated response elasticities. Rewritten in terms of the number of living children per woman, one has

$$ln\ CA = \alpha\,\beta + (\frac{\beta - 1}{\beta}) ln\ (CEB) + \frac{\gamma}{\beta} ln\ SF + \frac{\delta}{\beta}$$
$$ln\ SM + \frac{\epsilon}{\beta} FP + \mu/\beta.$$

But, if estimated in this form, the high definitional collinearity of *CA* and *CEB* makes interpretation difficult, as would the admission of errors in measuring cohort fertility. The "surviving child" hypothesis could be rigidly tested in this context by determining if the coefficient on *CEB* were actually zero, that is, $\beta = 1$.

14. The measures of education and the inverse of the child-survival rate (based on either cohort experience or recent period-specific rates) are essentially proportions and are not unreasonably specified in the double logarithmic or constant elasticity form. Family planning effort, on the other hand, is an absolute measure of inputs up to the previous calendar year per potential recipient, and in this case the exponential functional form has the appeal of permitting the elasticity to rise or, more likely, fall with the scale of inputs. The predictive power of the cohort-fertility equation was also increased slightly when family planning inputs were specified in a form that required the fertility response to inputs to approach an asymptotic limit, such as $1/(1 + FP)$.

15. Stochastic models of the biological components to their interbirth interval are compatible with the distributed-lag framework, modified to allow the lag structure to be unimodal and skewed to the right, such as the log normal in excess of the minimum gestation period. See Sheps and Menken (1973) and Potter (1975).

16. Another estimation approach was explored for three age groups (30–44). An iterative maximum likelihood procedure would choose a value of δ, obtain OLS estimates of β where the dependent variables is $C_t - \delta C_{t-1}$, and iterate on δ to maximize the predicted fit for C_t. Similar parameter estimates were obtained, but *t* ratios were generally increased, particularly for women's schooling and child mortality.

17. Barclay (1954, pp. 248–54), in his classic study of Taiwan up to 1945, disparages the idea that there is little variation in the prewar high fertility level between rural and urban areas. He notes further that "it has not been possible to find any evidence of association between fertility and other recorded types of behavior of rural Taiwanese by Districts" (townships), whereas "the strongest spatial pattern of fertility was the sectional one, viewed in prefectual units" (counties examined here). This puzzles him, since Taiwan was recently settled and did not appear to have evolved distinct regional cultural traditions. Earlier, however, Barclay did note that the prefectual spatial arrangement of mortality and fertility is "somewhat the same." Though Barclay does not indicate what recorded types of behavior he investigated, it seems unlikely that he looked at child mortality, women's schooling, or women's labor force activity outside of agriculture.

18. The husbands of a cohort of women are, on average, older. But without information from the census on exactly how much older, the educational attainment of men of the same age has been used here. The estimated relationship should not be greatly confounded by this relatively uniform error in measurement. The tendency would be for the estimated coefficient to be biased toward zero from that for actual husbands who are older and less well educated than the age group used here.

19. Cohort fertility can also be decomposed into the proportion married and the number of children born per married woman. Since it is uncommon to find census tabulations by age at marriage and current age and common to encounter tabulations by marital status and age, it is worth noting that this less satisfactory decomposition reveals roughly the same results as does the duration-of-marriage decomposition (tables 4.6, 4.7). Particularly among the younger women for whom the proportion married appears a reasonable proxy for marital duration, the associations with child mortality are notable. Similarly, the education variables are more important in the regressions on children born per married women.

20. Divorce is rare though not absent in Taiwan, but remarriage appears to occur promptly (Barclay 1954, chap. 8). Presumably an increasing share of the time since first marriage is spent without a husband as the cohort ages, owing to widowhood. This effect may be impounded in the fertility regression constant term among older women. Regional and time series variation in marriage proportions and the frequency of divorce has been attributed to sex ratio differences in Taiwan (Goode 1970, pp. 289–316), but this endogenous aspect of the problem is not treated here.

21. Standardizing these marital fertility rates according to a given reproductive schedule is not necessary. There is obviously a parallel between this form of cohort fertility decomposition and the procedures adopted in the Princeton European Fertility Study (Coale 1969, 1973). Since their methodology relies on regional period-specific births and indirectly standardizes these for age and marital status composition of the population, a Hutterite fertility schedule is used to weight the age distribution. In Taiwan there is little evidence in cohort data of the tradeoff found by Demeny (1968) in marriage and marital fertility indexes, but further research on this issue is needed.

22. Though our expectation is that income from the husband's earnings increases the demand for children, other things equal, this result does not follow from the simple demand theoretical framework without additional assumptions (T. P. Schultz 1974). Therefore a two-tailed t-test of significance seems appropriate in evaluating the male schooling regression coefficients.

23. The proportions literate, with primary school (or more), and with senior high school (or more) were used in place of the proportion with some junior high

school (or more) as measures of schooling/wage rates. They were slightly less successful in explaining fertility, but similar age patterns of regression coefficients were obtained.

24. Since it is likely that higher fertility is associated with earlier childbearing, the children of mothers' of a given age may be somewhat older, on average, in regions where fertility is higher. With older children, child survival would be lower, even if age-specific death rates are uniform across regions. This inability to measure child mortality to the same age level imparts an upward bias to the estimated elasticity of cohort fertility with respect to cohort child mortality. In addition, some evidence suggests that child mortality is greater among the offspring of very young mothers (see also note 25). There are clearly many difficulties to disentangling life-cycle relationships among age at marriage, fertility, and child mortality, and this investigation deals only with a few preliminary indications of such relations.

25. As indicated in note 24, the relationship between marriage duration and child mortality is undoubtedly overstated (positively), since women who married earlier had their children earlier, on average. Their children were therefore older at the time of the census and had experienced more mortality risks. This effect, however, diminishes markedly as the cohort of women age and their youngest children outgrow the period of heaviest mortality. But earlier-born children were also exposed to the earlier and undoubtedly higher infant and childhood death rates. This time-series effect and the duration effect would both tend to bias upward the partial association between marriage duration and child mortality. Techniques proposed by Brass, Sullivan, and Trussell to estimate life-table mortality rates from retrospective survey information on child-survival rates should help to mitigate the bias arising from the greater age of offspring of mothers that married at a younger age.

26. Coale (1973, p. 57) is convinced that the timing of marriage, at least in Europe, does not respond to reproductive goals, and he thereby directs his attention to changes in marital fertility as a precursor to the demographic transition. "Few couples marry at 25 instead of 24 because of a calculation that they will have one birth less; whereas the practice of contraception or abortion is directly aimed at fewer births." Both components of cohort fertility may bear further examination by behavioral scientists to better understand the demographic transition, even in the European setting.

27. The F-statistics with 5 and 37 degrees of freedom are 0.98, 0.45, 0.52, 1.55, 1.59 and 0.95 for the age groups 20–24, 25–29, 30–34, 35–39, 40–44, and 45–49, respectively. At the 10% confidence level, one could reject the hypothesis of coefficient equality if the $F(5,37)$ exceeded 2.01.

28. Child mortality is observed in each year in each region through the age of 15. The measure of schooling of men and women—that is, the proportion with some junior high school—is interpolated between the 1966 census and tabulations published from the Household Registry system in the Factbooks of 1973/1974. These changes would primarily reflect cohort migration among regions. Family planning inputs are accumulated per potential recipient. A slightly better fit to the data is obtained if the family planning inputs are transformed to $1/(1+FP)$, which implies more sharply diminishing returns to scale approaching an asymptotic limit as past inputs accumulate. The easier to interpret linear exponential specification is retained in tables 4.8 and 4.11, however.

29. Another procedure is to include a vector of dummy variables for all but one calendar year to account for yearly changes in flows, without restricting the trend

to be linear. This more flexible procedure reduces degrees of freedom but implies similar results.

30. As in table 4.8, the two variables used to identify the lagged endogenous stock variable are the cohort's child mortality experience, lagged two years, and family planning inputs, lagged two years. Note that the cohort's child mortality is derived initially from different data than the period-specific child mortality level that enters directly into the stock-adjustment equation. The former is based primarily on retrospective child survival as reported in the 1966 census and adjusted over time by period-specific death rates, as discussed in the Appendix B. The latter period-specific variable is obtained from the region's age-specific death rates (for all cohorts) two years before the dependent variable birthrate.

31. One step would be to estimate continuous distributed lag structures rather than the discrete two-year lag in mortality and the one-year lag in family planning inputs. Another step would be to model the innovation (birth control technology) adoption mechanism along the lines proposed by Welch (1970), allowing for more flexible substitution possibilities between classes of family planning workers (Schultz 1969*b*) and interaction effects between women's (and men's?) schooling and the application of family planning extension activity. When I explored such interaction effects in the context of the stock-adjustment equation (tables 4.8, 4.11), the interaction coefficients were positive (as expected if women's schooling substitutes for extension effort in diffusing modern birth control technology), but not quite statistically significant from age 35 to age 44. The coefficients (and their t ratios) for the cross-product terms were for age 35–39, 29.3 (1.00), age 40–44, 20.0 (1.33).

32. The convention is followed of subjecting the calendar year's registered births to mortality of that year on 31 December before obtaining the population of living children for the next year. Hence, the census at the end of November 1966 is taken as a year-end population total, in which the births are assumed to occur on the last day of the accounting period. The 1967 year-end total of one-year-olds will then be the 1966 registered births diminished by the 1967 infant mortality rates. The small error in measurement introduced by this convention in the initial year, therefore, will not be cumulative, though it will overrepresent infants in these demographic accounts.

33. Methods could be applied at the regional level based only on current-period fertility and mortality schedules by age. (See p. 8 of Maurer and Schultz 1972.) Using more information about recent levels of birthrates and death rates seems superior, though perhaps more complicated.

Comment Ronald Freedman

As usual, T. Paul Schultz has prepared a stimulating paper. He has anticipated in one way or another most of the questions that might be raised about his models and their empirical test, but discussion of some of these problems may nevertheless be worthwhile, since a number of points are debatable.

Ronald Freedman is professor of sociology and associate director of the Population Studies Center, University of Michigan.

The stock-adjustment concept, as I understand it, is the economist's version of the demographer's cohort analysis, in which current and prospective reproductive experience is examined in the light of past performance of the cohort. This becomes especially useful when (*a*) the experience to date is broken down into different attained parities and progression ratios, preferably by parity, computed from year to year; and (*b*) for explanatory purposes significant social or economic subgroups are examined for differential cumulative experience to date and differential progression ratios. This requires a great deal of data. However, a similar problem confronts attempts to make the stock and flow concept applicable to meaningful subgroups.

As the stock and flow model is set forth, it involves making certain assumptions that Schultz acknowledges might be problematic. I want to discuss a few of these.

One assumption is that a constant proportion of the relative difference between desired stock and the actual stock is delivered in each time period across population categories. But a number of component elements enter into the timing of the adjustment flow of births. Among these are spacing of births, age at marriage, and the preferred number of children. We know that there is a strong relation between education and first use of contraception for spacing. (See my table C4.1.) This will tend to slow the absolute pace at which the better educated have children once they marry.

Second, we also know that the proportion married at each age (especially at the younger ages) is strongly related to education (see table C4.5). If one measures the pace at which different educational strata move toward their reproductive goals from similar ages, as this model does, then late age at marriage also contributes to a slower rate of movement toward the reproductive goal of the better educated. Working in an opposite direction is the fact that preferred number of children is less for the better educated (see Schultz's table 4.3), so any given absolute pace of movement toward the observed goal means a faster rate of attainment of the additional stock wanted for the better educated. In the same direction, there will be small effects making for faster movement at higher educational levels because the better educated have higher fecundity (Jain 1968) and make somewhat less use of breast-feeding (Jain et al. 1970).

All these phenomena are changing over time. These observations illustrate how a set of specific mechanisms that affect the timing of fertility are changing differentially between educational strata and also between rural and urban strata (and five of the twenty-one regional units in this analysis are Taiwan's five largest cities). A model that does not take this into account is likely to miss essential elements of the dynamics that Schultz is valiantly trying to represent in the aggregate. The

Table C4.1 **Percentage of Wives Who Have Ever Used Contraception and Percentage of All Wives and of All Users Who First Used Contraception for Spacing Purposes, by Wife's Education and by Marriage Duration: Taiwan, 1973 (KAP-IV)**

Wife's Education	% Ever Using Contra- ception	% of All Wives First Using for Spacing	% of Users First Using for Spacing	N Total	N Users
Marriage duration 0–4 years					
None	20.7	12.4	60.0	145	30
Some primary school	25.4	12.7	(50.0)	71	18
Primary graduate	30.7	21.8	71.2	815	250
Junior high graduate	54.8	39.7	72.5	146	80
Senior high graduate or more	65.0	56.4	86.7	197	128
Total	36.8	27.2	73.9	1,374	506
Marriage duration 5–9 years					
None	62.5	17.2	27.5	355	222
Some primary school	61.8	19.8	32.1	131	81
Primary graduate	71.9	27.5	38.2	841	605
Junior high graduate	83.9	45.0	53.6	149	125
Senior high graduate or more	92.4	51.9	56.1	106	98
Total	71.5	27.8	38.9	1,582	1,131
Marriage duration 10–14 years					
None	76.7	11.4	14.9	489	375
Some primary school	86.0	16.6	19.3	157	135
Primary graduate	85.8	21.5	25.1	599	514
Junior high graduate	92.3	31.9	34.5	91	84
Senior high graduate or more	92.9	51.8	55.8	56	52
Total	83.3	19.3	23.2	1,392	1,160
Marriage duration 15 years or more					
None	80.7	5.4	6.6	503	406
Some primary school	85.4	7.3	8.5	247	211
Primary graduate	83.1	10.9	13.2	402	334
Junior high graduate	79.2	18.9	23.8	53	42
Senior high graduate or more	100.0	53.8	53.8	26	26
Total	82.8	9.2	11.1	1,231	1,019
Total	68.4	21.4	31.3	5,579	3,816

problem here is perhaps similar to the one Simon Kuznets addresses in his paper (chap. 8): aggregation that summarizes components or processes that are themselves moving differentially and in opposing directions in a rapidly changing reproductive regime may miss some essentials, both for prediction and for understanding.

Schultz deals explicitly with some of these problems when he argues that, while an assumption such as we have just discussed may not be justified at the individual or social strata level, it can be sustained for the interregional analysis he is carrying out. I have two observations:

1. Five of the twenty-one regions he deals with are Taiwan's five largest cities, and we know they are different from the other sixteen units with respect to many characteristics, including the use of contraception, the use of contraception for spacing births, and age at marriage. Apart from the large number of development variables not explicitly treated, there is a marked bimodality with respect to education. For example, among women 25–29 in 1966, the proportions who were junior high school graduates or more were 28% for Taipei, 15–18% for the four other large cities, and less than 10% for fourteen of the other sixteen units. Schultz deals mainly with only two predictor variables, mortality and education. It seems plausible that their relationships with fertility and nuptiality may be a function of some of the large number of other variables in which the five big cities differ from the other sixteen areas.

2. It is not necessarily desirable that using these particular regional units washes out some specific relationships involving specific social strata because they are not differential between regions, even though it simplifies the equations. It can, and in some cases does, lead to omission of important relationships that are pertinent to population dynamics in Taiwan but that do not emerge on an interregional basis. Although the analysis is in terms of the twenty-one regions, the inferences made, and some of the public policy discussion, appear to lose this strict reference and move to the individual or social stratum level.

A second basic assumption of the model is that preferences as to number of children are distinctive single values and that "preferences among alternative outcomes greater or less than the single valued goal are assumed not to influence reproductive behavior." (All quotations are from Schultz's paper.) Schultz properly acknowledges that "parents . . . probably weigh a range of family size outcomes that are likely to occur with different probabilities" and that "asymmetries in these preferences may be important for understanding differences in fertility in Taiwan at least at the level of individual survey respondent or across educational lines." However, he adds that "when the regions are the units of analysis within a single cultural area, the assumption may be somewhat less restrictive."

In this connection he cites the work of my colleagues L. Coombs and T. H. Sun, who have demonstrated the empirical utility of what they call IN, a scale that measures the underlying preference structure for number and sex of children—a structure that lies behind the usual single-valued preference statement on surveys. I think it is worthwhile for the conference to have a few tables illustrating this work. My table C4.2, for example, indicates within educational strata the variation in the

Table C4.2 Educational Level Differences in the Relationship of IN Values to Selected First Preferences: Taiwan, 1973

First Preference for Number of Children and Wife's Education	Percentage Distribution in IN Scale				
	IN1–3	IN4	IN5	IN6–7	(N)
First choice = 2 children					
No education	31	58	8	3	(116)
Primary school	37	57	6	0	(518)
Junior high	37	57	3	0	(150)
Senior high and over	49	47	4	0	(216)
First choice = 3 children					
No education	5	23	38	24	(547)
Primary school	10	30	48	13	(1,430)
Junior high	13	42	43	2	(231)
Senior high and over	23	46	29	2	(157)
First choice = 4 children					
No education	0	10	38	52	(642)
Primary school	1	12	45	42	(1,057)
Junior high	0	21	52	12	(70)
Senior high and over	4	20	64	12	(25)
Total	12	28	36	25	(5,463)

Source: Coombs and Sun (1976).

underlying preference structure or bias for smaller or larger numbers of children for persons who have expressed the same first preference. My table C4.3 shows that these variations in the underlying structure or IN scale are associated with behavioral differences in contraceptive use after adjusting for the effects of first preference and for whether the wife said she wanted more children. Finally, my table C4.4 shows the variation in preference structure with the rural-urban categories for persons having the same first preference. This is particularly relevant to Schultz's paper because it indicates the distinctive variation in the preference structure of the five large cities among the twenty-one regions. The assumption that the asymmetry is not pertinent to the regional variation may not be applicable.

I turn now to some comments on the specifications and empirical aspects of the model:

1. First of all, that five of the twenty-one regions are Taiwan's five largest cities and that the other sixteen include all the smaller towns and the rural areas leads to questions about a model that involves just two explanatory variables—education and mortality. The five cities are different from the other sixteen units with reference to a long list of development and demographic variables. It seems likely that these other

differences that do not enter the model directly would affect the relationships Schultz measures. While he fully acknowledges this complexity and the need for further detail in specification, I think the point needs to be stressed, especially since he makes rather emphatic statements about the connection between mortality and nuptiality that I think are debatable.

2. Let us turn to that issue. Based on the analysis represented in his tables 4.6–8, Schultz finds the support for the interesting and important idea that there is a linkage between prior mortality declines and later age at marriage, "which deserves further study to find out why it arises, how it responds to change and whether social and economic policies can facilitate this important institutional response to declining mortality." It was this kind of statement that I had in mind when I said that findings based on a rather specific and limited set of regional variations were followed by inferences and policy speculations that transcend regional

Table C4.3 **Relation of IN Values to Use of Birth Control, with Adjustments for First Preference and Marriage Duration (Wives 20–39 Years)**

	Percentage Ever Using Contraception			Percentage Currently Using Contraception			Percentage Ever Using Abortion			
	Actual	Adjusted		Actual	Adjusted		Actual	Adjusted		
IN Values		A1[a]	A2[b]		A1	A2		A1	A2	N
20–29 years										
1–3	67	65	67	50	48	50	16	16	17	401
4	58	57	57	43	42	42	13	12	12	844
5	49	51	51	34	36	36	10	9	9	910
6–7	51	43	42	28	31	29	8	9	8	416
Total	54			39			11			2,571
30–39 years										
1–3	87	88	89	76	74	75	29	30	32	240
4	84	84	85	72	71	71	30	30	30	691
5	84	83	83	70	69	69	30	29	29	1,028
6–7	76	78	77	65	67	66	23	25	24	927
Total	82			69			28			2,886
20–39 years										
1–3	75	75	79	60	60	66	21	23	25	641
4	70	70	71	56	57	58	19	21	22	1,536
5	67	67	66	53	53	54	20	20	20	1,940
6–7	65	64	61	53	53	48	18	18	16	1,346
Total	68			55			20			5,463

Source: Coombs and Sun (1976).
[a]Adjusted in multiple classification analysis for first preference for number of children.
[b]Adjusted for first preference and marriage duration.

Table C4.4 **Distribution of !N (Number Preference Scale) by First Preference, for Five Large Cities and Other Regions: Taiwan, 1973**

First Preference and Type of Place	IN: 1–3 Small Families	4	5	6–7 Large Families	N
2 Preferred					
Five large cities	50	45	4	0	454
Other places[a]	30	62	7	1	554
(Rural townships)	26	60	11	2	211
3 Preferred					
Five large cities	13	33	44	10	714
Other places	8	30	47	15	1,662
(Rural townships)	6	29	46	20	764
4 Preferred					
Five large cities	1	15	42	42	390
Other places	1	11	42	46	1,418
(Rural townships)	0	12	36	52	758

Source: Data from unpublished work by L. C. Coombs and T. H. Sun.
[a]Includes smaller cities, and urban and rural townships.

differences. But I also have some questions about the relationship itself.

In the first place, one plausible explanation of the relation is that mortality decline and later age at marriage are both responses to a broad range of other development changes that differentiate the regions, particularly the large cities from the other places. Second, I have a question on a technical point. The measure of mortality used in tables 4.6 and 4.8 are simply the survival rates for the children ever born to the women in each age group, that is, the ratio of surviving children to those ever born. You may remember that in tables 4.6 and 4.8 the relationship between mortality and nuptiality or marriage duration is very strong in the younger ages and rapidly diminishes with the age of the women. My question is, To what extent is this a simple result of the fact that the mortality measure is sensitive to the differential exposure to mortality of the children that is related to marital duration?

In the young age groups, variations of a year or so in the age at marriage will result in large variations in marriage duration and, therefore, in the period of risk of child mortality. In older cohorts a variation of a year or so in marriage age makes much less difference. To what extent is the strong relation in the young ages a result of a mortality measure that has a built-in nuptiality component, producing as an artifact a strong correlation with nuptiality? This problem does not arise in tables

4.9 and 4.10, where the mortality measure is directly based on age-specific death rates and where the results in the relation to fertility are therefore rather different. Schultz acknowledges this problem in a footnote, but, in view of the importance he attaches to the relation of nuptiality and mortality, the nature of this effect needs empirical clarification. On the other hand, in tables 4.7 and 4.8, on the basis of the regional units, Schultz finds very little relation between education and age at marriage or percentage married at even the younger ages. This is inconsistent with the cross-sectional data for strata that show very strong educational differentials in the percentage married, especially at the younger ages. This relationship, which has prevailed for quite a few years, is illustrated in my table C4.5 for 1966.

Perceptions that mortality of children is still relevant for childbearing were still fairly common in Taiwan as recently as 1973. Responses to this question: "People used to think families should have a large number of children because some would die; do you think this is still important these days?" are indicated in my table C4.6. About 10% answered "very important" and 27% more said "fairly important"; only 19% said "not important at all." The number of children preferred varied by half a child between those considering mortality very important and those considering it not important at all, even after adjusting for the effects of education, type of residence, and marital duration.

Table C4.5 Proportions of Women Married by Age and by Education: Taiwan, 1966

Age and Educational Status	Percentage Married	Age and Educational Status	Percentage Married
15–19		*25–29*	
Illiterate	17.0	Illiterate	92.6
Literate	13.7	Literate	93.1
Primary school graduate	8.3	Primary school graduate	88.6
Junior high graduate	3.6	Junior high graduate	81.0
Senior high graduate	4.0	Senior high graduate	69.7
Total	8.7	Total	88.6
20–24		*35–39*	
Illiterate	74.1	Illiterate	94.2
Literate	70.9	Literate	93.0
Primary school graduate	59.3	Primary school graduate	91.5
Junior high graduate	40.0	Junior high graduate	91.5
Senior high graduate	24.5	Senior high graduate	90.5
Total	57.4	Total	92.3

Source: Table II-1, *1966 Demographic Factbook, Republic of China,* Department of Civil Affairs, Taiwan Provincial Government, October 1967.

Table C4.6 **Importance Attached to High Mortality of Children as Reason for Having Large Families—Proportions Giving Various Responses and Preferred Numbers of Children Related to These Responses: Taiwan, 1973**

	% Distribution of Responses	Mean Preferred Number of Children	
		Unadjusted	Adjusted[c]
Response:[a]			
Very important	10.2	3.54	3.48
Fairly important	26.8	3.51	3.44
Not too important	43.7	3.15	3.18
Not important at all	18.8	2.95	3.02
Total percentage[b]	100.0		
N	5,588		

[a]The question asked was: "People used to think families should have a large number of children because some would die; do you think this is still important these days? Would you say, Very important, Fairly important, Not too important, or Not important at all?"
[b]Includes 0.6 no answer.
[c]Adjusted for wife's education, marriage duration, and type of place of residence.

A third basic aspect of the model specification interprets women's education as a proxy for value of time—a common procedure in economic models of reproductive behavior. I wonder if this is meaningful with respect to marital fertility in societies like Taiwan, in which few wives work in the modern sector. For example, Eva Mueller (unpublished manuscript), analyzing Taiwan survey data for 1969–70 found that only about 7% of the married women 22–42 years old were working away from home full time, and an additional 3% worked away from home part time. Among these, almost half were wives of farmers who often worked as agricultural laborers for other local farmers. In addition, about 42% had worked at some time in the preceding year on a family farm or in some other family enterprise. But that kind of work has been found to have little relationship to fertility either in Taiwan or elsewhere.

The role of education as an indicator of value of time in relation to nuptiality is much more plausible and much more consistent with the micro data than the relationship to marital fertility. A large number of Taiwanese women do work in the modern sector during the period before marriage. They often state their reason as saving toward a trousseau and household furnishings for when they do marry. A recent issue of the *Wall Street Journal* called attention to a current labor shortage in Taiwan. This is in the face of a large potential reservoir of well-educated young married women who might be expected to work under the value-of-time interpretation. Apparently, so far the normative and cultural restraints are more important than the demands of the labor market.

I suspect that one reason why Taiwan fertility has not fallen even more rapidly to date and why the strong preference for sons remains an important barrier to more rapid fertility decline is that the institutional restraints on paid work by wives means that their educational attainment has not been translated into valued time that is redeemable in the modern labor market. A change in that situation might help to erode the institutional basis for the strong preference for sons. In the meantime, however, for married women education is not plausibly interpreted primarily in terms of value of time.

An additional factor bearing on the value-of-time hypothesis is that large numbers of Taiwanese couples of childbearing age are living with parents or married siblings who could provide child care even if the wife worked away from home. As of 1973, somewhat more than half of the wives 20–39 were living in such extended households (Freedman et al. 1978). In addition, 12% of the husbands' parents were living with one of his married brothers in the same town, and visiting relationships to couples living in nuclear households are reported as very frequent and offer the possibility of child care. In a large proportion of these cases the couple is also making financial contributions to the husband's parents.

Schultz has quite properly called for additional research to get at the meaning of the relation between education and fertility. In such a situation as Taiwan's, the value-of-time interpretation seems a little strained for marital fertility but not for nuptiality, as I have indicated. In passing I suggest several other possibilities: education in Taiwan, as elsewhere, leads to nonwork activities and interests outside the home; education and its close connection to mass media access exposes the individuals to the Western role model of the small family and later marriage. Jack Caldwell (1976) has advanced the view that this Western (rather than modern) model has a powerful direct effect that is additional to development per se in Africa and elsewhere.

Schultz calls attention to the possible continuing role of parental mate selection, at least on nuptiality. I can supply some data on this point. As of 1973, 50% of the Taiwanese wives 20–39 years old said that their marriages had been arranged by their parents, 31% by parents and the couple together, and only 18% by the couple alone. Those whose marriages were arranged did marry earlier than others and were more poorly educated. There is also a carryover relation to preferred family size after marriage. Those whose marriages were arranged wanted about 12% more children than other couples, even after adjusting for the effects of wife's education and degree of urbanization of place of residence.

Schultz specifies that a necessary assumption in the empirical work is that migrants between the regions should not be different from the nonmigrants with respect to fertility. I think one might add that they also should not differ in the rate at which they reach their reproductive goals. As of 1973, in the sixteen regions that do not include the five largest cities the cumulative fertility of migrants was about 10% less than that of nonmigrants for the age groups 30–34 and 35–39, and in these age groups the migrants had a larger proportion of couples originally using contraception to space their children. (A migrant is here defined as a person who has moved between townships, which are subcategories of the regions; so these are not necessarily all interregional migrants in terms of the Schultz model.)

M. C. Chang (1976) also shows that, among migrants from rural areas to large cities, both preferred and actual fertility tend to be lower for migrants than for nonmigrants at the place of destination (as well as at place of origin) after adjustment for effect of age and duration of marriage. Chang's analysis is based on a definition of migration as involving a move from place of birth to current place of residence.

Schultz uses one of his regression equations and micro data for 1966–74 to estimate reductions in marital fertility attributable to education ranging from 7% to 18% as one moves from ages 25–29 to ages 40–44. This can be compared with total declines in marital fertility at these ages ranging from about 25% at ages 25–29 to 75% at ages 40–44. This averages out to be about 25% of the total marital fertility decline as attributable to education changes and 75% to changes within education categories—closely comparable to the finding Schultz cited from work based on analyses of the vital statistics. It is important to keep in mind that the decline in fertility within educational strata is three times as great as the decline attributable to structural changes in the educational distribution. This, together with the rapidity of the decline, is one plausible argument for rapid diffusion of birth control consistent with program effort effects during this period in Taiwan, involving women of low educational status at least as much as those of high educational status. It also indicates an important phenomenon affecting fertility that is not so well represented by macro data at the regional level.

In this connection, a fact Schultz mentions—that well-educated women were having their children later into the thirties in 1974 than the less well educated—is not a result of any known new trend toward postponement of births for those well educated. It results instead from the fact that, while age-specific birthrates declined for all educational strata between 1966 and 1974, the much greater decline in this period for the poorly educated at the older ages (over 30) means that the differentials in period rates by education were reversed from a high negative relation in 1966 to a modest positive relation by 1974.

In his comments on the final stock-adjustment model (table 4.9), Schultz finds that inputs of the family planning program are uniquely positively correlated to fertility at ages 15–19 and 20–24, and the expected negative correlation appears at older ages. He offers a possible interpretation of the peculiar relationship at younger ages that would be plausible if "the preferred path to obtain the desired stock of children were itself a function of birth control technology." I interpret Schultz to mean here that these young women either married early or had their babies early in order to attain desired family size very quickly and then stopped childbearing with the aid of birth control. He draws as a possible parallel the shorter birth interval in the twentieth century, along with lower fertility in some Western countries. I do not find this interpretation highly plausible.

The married women at ages 15–19 and 20–24 have been increasingly the select group who did not postpone marriage. They are significantly less well educated than those who did not marry young, and a substantial proportion, especially of those 15–19, were premaritally pregnant. In 1966, for example, only 9% of the women 15–19 were married and, among these, 32% were less than primary school graduates and only 8% had more than a primary education. Among those 20–24 years old in 1966, 58% were married and, among these, 37% were less than primary school graduates and only 12% had more than a primary education. A further consideration is that during this period around 1966 the family planning program was primarily directed to and accepted by couples with at least two living children. This is not the kind of group background from which one would expect the rational reproductive regime I understand Schultz to be describing. They are more plausibly the backward, rather than a vanguard, group in areas of rapid transition.

Finally, setting aside the specifics, the general objective Schultz sets forth is certainly desirable. We do need better models and more appropriate data to permit us to relate dynamic changes in the reproductive system to dynamic changes in the social and economic system. As he indicates for developing countries, this requires dealing with relationships under conditions of disequilibrium. In these circumstances, I think it is particularly important to have, as part of the enterprise, initial disaggregation of important variables that are subparts of the model when we have reason to believe that elements in such subsystems are changing at differential rates for different strata of the population. This, as I have tried to indicate, is probably the case with respect to the dependent variable in the stock-adjustment model—the rate at which major groups of families are moving from the existing number of children ever born to their eventual goals.

Fertility is part of a very complex biosocial system. Demographers have made some progress in taking elements of this system apart and measuring their dynamic components. We have done less well in putting the parts back together into models that represent the functioning whole or in relating the reproductive system to the social and economic determinants on a cohort basis. Economists are more skilled, and I think more interested, in building models, especially at the macro level or with macro units. Demographers tend to be more concerned with empirical specifics, with data at the social and demographic stratum level. The broad goal Schultz sets forth requires both kinds of materials. Otherwise an effort that is conceptually of great interest is limited because everything in the system is represented by a few variables whose interpretation then becomes problematic. Looking to the future and recognizing the value of the objective, I wonder if the model need lead to the use of the kinds of regional units employed, which are awkward for reasons I have tried to indicate.

This brings me back to my opening comments. Are we really much further ahead with a translation of cohort fertility analysis into the stock-adjustment model at the regional level? Could we not apply the concept to time series of surveys providing data to relate to ongoing cohort analyses of major strata? Then such matters as reproductive preferences and many other variables could be obtained from the surveys. As I understand it, the stock-adjustment model is often used with reference to a sample of firms; then why not deal with samples of individuals aggregated into the social units that are socially and economically meaningful, rather than into geographical-administrative units that blur some important aspects of the dynamics of reproduction?

Comment Riad B. Tabbarah

In the field of the economics of fertility as it stands today, it is important to differentiate between theoretical validity and technical sophistication. While theory can stand on its own, the value of the techniques in the application of theory depends not only on the inherent quality and consistency of the techniques, but also on the validity of the theory itself. The criticisms I shall present of Schultz's paper and, particularly, of some of its conclusions, relate to the theoretical basis to which the techniques were applied and not, generally speaking, to the techniques

Riad B. Tabbarah is Chief of the Population Division, United Nations Economic Commission for Western Asia (ECWA). The views expressed in this comment are those of the author and not necessarily those of ECWA.

themselves. Let me hasten to add that this theoretical shortcoming, which Schultz readily admits in the introduction to his paper, is to some extent an unfortunate characteristic of the field he was asked to deal with.

Children are a peculiar commodity, unlike any other for which economic demand theory has been formulated (Leibenstein 1974). The tools developed in conjunction with demand theory therefore need to be adapted and supplemented for the analysis of the demand for children. This is admittedly a very difficult task—one that perhaps requires more time than has already passed since the field of the economics of fertility has become popular among economists and that certainly requires more concentrated effort. The temptation, therefore, has been very strong among many economists to adapt the problem to their tools rather than fit their tools to the new problem. Beginning with Becker in 1960, economists have assumed children to be a consumer durable, a commodity for which their tools of analysis were highly developed. Schultz assumes at the outset that "the demand for children [is] in part a demand for a *durable input* that enters into many lifetime production and consumption possibilities." Reproductive goals are then "summarized in terms of a desired lifetime stock of children." While this represents, perhaps, a greater degree of sophistication than Becker's assumption, it remains basically an attempt at adapting the problem to the tools and not the other way around.

Schultz readily admits that the theory of demand is not workable because consumer benefits from children are satiable and because the cost of funds to invest in children is upward-sloping. But there are more fundamental reasons why the theory of demand is not applicable in the case of children, and these have to do with the tools underlying the theory.

Let me take one example—the cost of children. What is important here, it seems, is the cost of a child relative to the income of the parents. One may argue that, to the extent that the items of expenditure on the child in the household budget remain basically the same with development, this relationship should remain fairly constant: as the income of the head of the family rises, his expenditure on, say, food, housing, and clothing for himself will increase in approximately the same proportion as that spent on the other members of the family. With development, however, new items of expenditure on children emerge (notably education), and this tends to make the burden of dependency relatively higher, if, of course, a significant cost is attached to education.

But more important than the relative *cost of a child* is, perhaps, the relative *cost of children*. In societies at the very early stages of development, a child becomes financially independent of his household (and may become a contributor to its income, but this will be neglected here) at a relatively early age—say nine years. If we assume that, given the relatively low fecundity and high infant mortality in these societies, a child surviving to maturity is born every three years to given parents, then by the time the fourth child is born the first one becomes financially independent, by the time the fifth child is born the second becomes financially independent, and so on, so that the burden of support of children of this household is limited to three children no matter how many it eventually produces. By extending the period of support and reducing the potential interval between surviving children (because of increased fecundity), the spread of education—and hence development—increases the *cost of children* to parents relative to their income in a very significant fashion. Thus, in a developed country, if parents were to have, say, eight children spaced two years apart and to be supported to the age of 17 years, they would at a given moment in their life, be supporting all eight children at the same time. Therefore, even when education is free, the relative cost of children increases immensely by the mere increase in the average schooling period.

This observation has obvious implications for, say, the budget line in an indifference curve analysis. In a society at the early stages of development, the budget line might slope downward from the *Y*-axis (representing all other goods) to the point corresponding to two or three children and then become horizontal to the *X*-axis (representing number of children). More popularly stated, if parents in these very underdeveloped societies can afford two or three children, they can afford "as many as God wills."

As we have already learned from various authors (Leibenstein 1957; Easterlin 1969), a socioeconomic theory of fertility must take into account, inter alia, the utility and disutility of children, the adequacy of income given conventional standards (Tabbarah 1972), the cost of a child also given conventional standards, and the cost of children as explained earlier. The effect of a given variable on the demand for children (that is, on desired family size) can then be assessed in terms of its effect on these components of household decision-making. For example, educational attainment tends to reduce the desire for children because, among other things, it increases the disutility of children by opening up competing alternatives, increases the cost of a child because it represents a new item of expenditure, increases the cost of children because of the resulting increase in the period of support, and perhaps also has straining effects on the adequacy of income. Schultz's models interpret educational attainment as a proxy for the value of time of men and women, and he finds that, as such, educational attainment is negatively associated with the desire for children. His conclusion is therefore probably correct. But is the explanation of it an adequate one? Or is this explanation so partial that it is of limited significance? Schultz himself wonders whether one can sustain the economists' broad and powerful hypothesis that the productive "value-of-time" is the driving force behind education's effect on diverse forms of household behavior and whether there are other aspects of the husband's and wife's economic contribution to the family that can be quantified and related to schooling. The answer to the first question is probably no, and to the second is probably yes. But what is more important is that this wondering reflects the limitation of the theoretical base on which the quantitative model is built.

A socioeconomic theory of fertility must also take into account the fecundity constraint (or supply constraint), which is most evident in countries and among groups at the early stages of demographic development. In these circumstances, at least a large majority of couples are unable to achieve their desired number of children in their completed family. This is due not only to a relatively low fecundity (caused by malnutrition, infections associated with childbearing, and the prevalence of certain diseases), and to high infant and child mortality, but also to a relatively high number of children desired. Since Schultz, in drawing conclusions from his models, takes fertility as a proxy for the desired number of children—that is, for the demand for children—the existence of this constraint could considerably weaken the validity of his conclusions. Although Schultz is aware of the difficulty this constraint might introduce in his models, he nevertheless assumes it away on the grounds that it is only significant "under extreme conditions of malnutrition and specific endemic disease, e.g., gonorrhea"—conditions that presumably did not exist in Taiwan, the country to which his models are applied. I find this assumption not completely tenable. Because I have been responsible for pointing out this fecundity constraint (Tabbarah 1964) and have since presented a model of demographic development based on it (Tabbarah 1971), I should perhaps explain in some detail why I believe Schultz's assumption is not necessarily justified.

The model I am referring to identifies four stages of demographic development: the first stage is where the desire for children is relatively high because of prevailing social and economic conditions and where the maximum attainable number of children is relatively low because of both low fecundity and high infant and child mortality. At this stage, a large proportion of couples are unable to attain their desired number of children and therefore aim at maximum reproduction. Because their reproductive aims are unattainable, they are often expressed in terms of "as many as God wills" or "as many as possible," and their knowledge of methods of fertility regulation is limited.

The second stage is reached when the desired number of children becomes more or less equal to the maximum attainable number owing both to a decline in the desired number caused by improved social and economic conditions and to an increase in the maximum attainable number mainly owing to the improved health of parents (i.e., higher fecundity) and of children (i.e., reduced infant and child mortality). At this stage, a large proportion of couples are able to just attain their reproductive goals, with a proportion able to exceed them and another proportion unable to attain them.

At the third stage of demographic development, the desired number of children becomes lower than the maximum attainable number for the large majority of couples, creating a potential need for fertility regulation and the use of contraceptive methods. During this stage, however, lags in the decline of fertility tend to appear because of the lack of family planning programs and inadequate societal knowledge of contraception, and because of underestimation by couples of the extent of the decline in mortality and other such factors, thus resulting in a significant proportion of unwanted births (Tabbarah 1976).

Finally, at the fourth stage of demographic development, which is characteristic of the developed countries, a situation is reached where the desired number of children is relatively low and easy to achieve, and is actually achieved by most couples. (It must be noted that the population of a given country might be, at any given point, at more than one stage of demographic development. See Tabbarah [1978]. See also the model presented in this volume by Easterlin, Pollak, and Wachter.)

Now Schultz maintains that "fertility is generally higher in populations that experience higher child mortality rates" and that "this evidence is strongly suggestive of a mechanism, probably both involuntary (biological) and voluntary (behavioral) in nature, that achieves some manner of population equilibrium given environmental health and economic constraints." But if the model of demographic development is basically correct, then it is clear that the relationship between fertility and child mortality is not as simple as stated here. At the first stage of demographic development fertility might be low and child mortality high, while only at the second and third stages would the positive relationship between fertility and child mortality begin to appear.

What is more important for the present purpose, if such a relationship (a positive association between fertility and child mortality) was actually observed in Taiwan when making regional comparisons, as Schultz indicates, then one might draw the conclusion that the various regions of Taiwan were, in 1966, at the second and third stages of demographic development. If this is true, it follows that a significant proportion of couples, at least in some regions, were not achieving their desired number of children; and their fertility therefore could not be taken as proxy for their desire for children (i.e., demand for children), as Schultz does throughout the paper. In fact, the situation is more serious than this, since women up to the age of 60 and over in 1966 enter into the analysis. Many of these women had their main reproductive years sometime in the 1940s or earlier, a time when Taiwan was undoubtedly at an early stage of demographic development, where no positive relationship existed between fertility and desired number of children. Schultz's findings actually show that the positive relationship between fertility and child mortality is strong only for the younger age groups; after age 40 the elasticity of fertility with respect to child mortality becomes almost nil, and the association eventually becomes negative but loses statistical significance. Schultz's explanation of this is that, "as a cohort advances through its life, the elasticity of fertility with respect to child mortality may be expected to decline, because offspring continue to die after their mother is unable to replace them with additional births." But considering the low mortality rates of children after age 15 or 20 when mothers reach the end of their reproductive years, the fact that even at younger ages mothers may not replace lost offspring, and the very significant decline and eventual disappearance of association between fertility and child mortality, this explanation cannot be readily accepted. The existence of a fecundity constraint among the older age groups during their reproductive years seems to offer a much more powerful explanation; and if this is so, fertility, at least for these women, would not reflect their desired family size and may not, therefore, be taken as proxy for their demand for children.

In conclusion, quantitative models like the ones used by Schultz, which are intended as applications of a given theory, are necessarily *associative*. The conclusions derived from them as to the causal relationship between variables can be made only on the basis of the causal model on which they are based, since correlation by itself does not mean causation. Thus, if the causal theory is weak or untenable, then the quantitative associative model based on it is itself necessarily weak, no matter how internally consistent or sophisticated it is. Considering the inadequacy of the traditional tools of economic theory in analyzing the demand for children, it is difficult to develop quantitative associative models based on them that could satisfactorily explain the mechanism of household decision-making with regard to desired family size. This does not mean that associative models, such as the ones Schultz presents, should not be developed; imperfect as they may be, they generate information that itself can be valuable for the eventual development of new tools and an appropriate causal theory. From this perspective, Schultz's paper serves the purpose for which it was written—to shed light on certain important associative relationships between fertility and some social and economic variables.

References

Anderson, J. E. 1973. The effects of marital fertility, nuptiality and educational attainment on fertility change in Taiwan, 1966–1971. Taiwan Population Studies Working Paper no. 25, University of Michigan. (See also *Studies in Family Planning* 6 [March 1975]: 3.)

Barclay, G. W. 1954. *Colonial development and population in Taiwan.* Princeton: Princeton University Press. Reissued Port Washington, N.Y.: Kennikat Press, 1972.

Becker, G. S. 1960. An economic analysis of fertility. In *Demographic and economic change in developed countries.* Universities-National Bureau Conference 11. Princeton: Princeton University Press.

Becker, G. S., and Lewis, H. G. 1974. Interaction between quantity and quality of children. In *Economics of the family*, ed. T. W. Schultz. Chicago: University of Chicago Press.

Ben-Porath, Y. 1975. Fertility and economic growth: Some micro-economic aspects. Discussion Paper 756, Falk Institute for Economic Research, Jerusalem.

Ben-Porath, Y., and Welch, F. 1972. *Chance, child traits, and choice of family size.* Report R-1117. Santa Monica: Rand Corporation.

Caldwell, John C. 1976. Towards a restatement of demographic transition theory. *Population and Development Review* 2, nos. 3 and 4 (September/December): 321–66.

Chang, M. C. 1976. Migration and fertility. Paper presented at a seminar at the University of Pennsylvania.

Coale, A. J. 1969. The decline of fertility in Europe from the French Revolution to World War II. In *Fertility and family planning*, ed. S. J. Behrman, L. Corsa, and R. Freedman. Ann Arbor: University of Michigan Press.

———. 1973. The demographic transition reconsidered. Paper presented at the International Population Conference of the IUSSP, Liège, Belgium.

Coombs, L. C. 1974. The measurement of family size preferences and subsequent fertility. *Demography* 11, no. 4 (Nov.): 587–611.

———. 1976. Are cross cultural preference comparisons possible? A measurement-theoretic approach. IUSSP Paper no. 5. Liège, Belgium.

Coombs, Lolagene C., and Sun, Te-hsiung. 1978. Family composition preferences in a developing culture: The case of Taiwan, 1973. *Population Studies* 32, no. 1 (March): 43–64.

Demeny, Paul. 1968. Early fertility decline in Austria-Hungary: A lesson in demographic transition. *Daedalus* 97 (spring): 502–22.

DeTray, D. N. 1974. Child quality and the demand for children. In *Economics of the family*, ed. T. W. Schultz. Chicago: University of Chicago Press.

Dumond, D. E. 1975. The limitation of human population: A natural history. *Science* 187 (28 February): 713–21.

Easterlin, R. A. 1968. *Population, labor force and long swings in economic growth.* New York: National Bureau of Economic Research.

———. 1969. Toward a socio-economic theory of fertility: A survey of recent research on economic factors in American fertility. In *Fertility and family planning: A world view*, ed. S. J. Behrman et al. Ann Arbor: University of Michigan Press.

———. 1975. An economic framework for fertility analysis. *Studies in Family Planning* 6, no. 3 (March): 54–63.

Freedman, Ronald. 1963. Norms for family size in underdeveloped countries. *Proceedings of the Royal Statistical Society*, ser. B, 159: 220–45.

Freedman, Ronald, and Berelson, B. 1976. The record of family planning programs. *Studies in Family Planning* 7, no. 1 (January): 1–40.

Freedman, Ronald; Coombs, L. C.; and Chang, M. C. 1972. Trends in family size preferences and practice of family planning: Taiwan, 1965–1970. *Studies in Family Planning* 3, no. 12 (December): 281–96.

Freedman, Ronald; Coombs, L. C.; Chang, M. C.; and Sun, T. H. 1974. Trends in fertility, family size preferences, and practice of family planning: Taiwan 1965–1973. *Studies in Family Planning* 5, no. 9 (September): 270–88.

Freedman, Ronald; Moots, Baron; Sun, Te-hsiung; and Weinberger, Mary Beth. 1978. Household composition and extended kinship in Taiwan. *Population Studies* 32, no. 1 (March): 65–80.

Freedman, Ronald, and Takeshita, J. Y. 1969. *Family planning in Taiwan: an experiment in social change.* Princeton: Princeton University Press.

Freedman, Ronald; Weinberger, M. B.; Fan, T. H.; and Wei, S. P. 1976. Recent trends in fertility and in the effects of education on fertility in Taiwan, 1961–1974. Taiwan Population Studies Working Paper no. 31, Ann Arbor.

Goode, W. J. 1970. *World revolution and family patterns.* New York: Free Press.

Griliches, Zvi. 1960. The demand for a durable input: Farm tractors in the United States, 1921–1957. In *The demand for durable goods*, ed. A. C. Harberger. Chicago: University of Chicago Press.

———. 1961. A note on serial correlation bias in estimates of distributed lags. *Econometrica* 29 (January): 1.

Heckman, J. J., and Willis, R. J. 1975. Estimation of a stochastic model of reproduction: An econometric approach. In *Household production and consumption*, ed. N. E. Terleckyi. Studies in Income and Wealth, no. 40. New York: National Bureau of Economic Research.

Hermalin, A. I. 1968. Taiwan: An area analysis of the effects of acceptance on fertility. *Studies in Family Planning* no. 33 (August), pp. 7–11.

———. 1971. Appraising the effects of a family planning program through an areal analysis. Taiwan Population Studies Working Paper no. 14. University of Michigan.

———. 1975. Empirical research in Taiwan on factors underlying differences in fertility. In *Economic aspects of population growth*, ed. A. J. Coale. New York: International Economics Assn., Halsted Press.

Ho, Yhi-min. 1966. *Agricultural development of Taiwan, 1903–1960.* Kingsport, Tenn.: Vanderbilt University Press.

Institute of Economics, Academia Sinica. 1976. *Conference on population and economic development in Taiwan*, 29 December 1975–2 January 1976, Taipei, Taiwan.

Jain, Anrudh K. 1968. Fecundity components in Taiwan: Application of a stochastic model of reproduction. Ph.D. diss., University of Michigan.

Jain, Anrudh K.; Hsu, T. C.; Freedman, R.; and Chang, M. C. 1970. Demographic aspects of lactation and postpartum amenorrhea. *Demography* 7, no. 2 (May): 255–71.

Lang, Olga. 1950. *Chinese family and society.* New Haven: Yale University Press.

Lee, R. D. 1975. Fertility, age structure and income in the United States, 1947–1974. Paper presented at Econometrics Society Third World Congress, Toronto, August.

———. 1976. Marital fertility in the U.S.: 1949–1974. University of Michigan. Mimeographed.

Leibenstein, Harvey. 1957. *Economic backwardness and economic growth.* New York: John Wiley.

———. 1974. An interpretation of the economic theory of fertility. *Journal of Economic Literature* 12 (June): 457–79.

Levy, Marion. 1949. *The family revolution in modern China.* Cambridge: Harvard University Press.

Lindert, P. H. 1974. Fertility and the microeconomics of inequality. Discussion paper, University of Wisconsin, Madison.

Liu, P. K. C. 1967. *The uses of household registration records in measuring the fertility level in Taiwan.* Economic Papers no. 2. Taipei, Taiwan: Institute of Economics, Academica Sinica.

Mamdami, Mahmood. 1973. *The myth of population control.* New York: Monthly Review Press.

Maurer, K., and Schultz, T. P. 1972. *A population projection model.* Report R-953. Santa Monica: Rand Corporation.

Mosley, W. H., and Chen, L. 1976. Health and human reproduction in developing countries. Johns Hopkins University. Mimeographed.

Mueller, Eva. 1972. Economic motives for family limitation: A study conducted in Taiwan. *Population Studies* 27, no. 3 (November): 383–403.

Nag, Moni. 1976. The economic view of children in agricultural societies: A review and a proposal. In *Culture, natality, and family planning*, ed. J. F. Marshall and S. Polgar, pp. 3–23. Monograph 21. Chapel Hill: University of North Carolina, Carolina Population Center.

Nelson, R. R.; Schultz, T. P.; and Slighton, R. L. 1971. *Structural change in a developing country*. Princeton: Princeton University Press.

Nerlove, Marc. 1958. *Distributed lags and demand analysis of agricultural and other commodities*. USDA Agricultural Handbook no. 141. Washington, D.C.: GPO.

———. 1971. A note on error-components models. *Econometrica* 79, no. 1 (March): 383–96.

———. 1972. On lags and economic behavior. *Econometrics* 40, no. 1 (March): 221–51.

Nerlove, Marc, and Schultz, T. P. 1970. *Love and life between the censuses: A model of family decision making in Puerto Rico, 1950–1960*. Report RM-6322. Santa Monica: Rand Corporation.

O'Hara, D. J. 1972. *Changes in mortality levels and family decisions regarding children*. Report R-914. Santa Monica: Rand Corporation.

Potter, R. C. 1975. Changes of natural fertility and contraceptive equivalents. *Social Forces* 54, no. 1 (September): 36–51.

Rutstein, S. O. 1974. The influence of child mortality on fertility in Taiwan. *Studies in Family Planning* 5, no. 6 (June): 182–89.

Sanderson, Warren, and Willis, R. J. 1971. Economic models of fertility: Some examples and implications. New York: National Bureau of Economic Research. Mimeographed.

Schultz, T. P. 1967. *A family planning hypothesis: Some empirical evidence from Puerto Rico*. Report RM-5405. Santa Monica: Rand Corporation.

———. 1969*a*. An economic model of family planning and fertility. *Journal of Political Economy* 77, no. 2 (March/April): 153–80.

———. 1969*b*. *The effectiveness of family planning in Taiwan*. Report P-4069. Santa Monica: Rand Corporation.

———. 1971. Evaluation of population policies. Report R-643. Santa Monica: Rand Corporation.

———. 1974. Birth rate changes over space and time: A study of Taiwan. In *Economics of the family*, ed. T. W. Schultz. Chicago: University of Chicago Press. (Also Report R-1079, Rand Corporation.)

———. 1976. Interrelationships between mortality and fertility. In *Population and development: The search for selective interventions*, ed. R. G. Ridker. Baltimore: Johns Hopkins University Press.

Schultz, T. W., ed. 1974. *Economics of the family*. Chicago: University of Chicago Press.

Sheps, M. C., and Menken, J. A. 1973. *Mathematical models of conception and birth*. Chicago: University of Chicago Press.

Shih, Chien-sheng. 1976. The contribution of education to economic development in Taiwan. In *Conference on population and economic development in Taiwan*, pp. 287–314. Taipei, Taiwan: Institute of Economics, Academica Sinica.

Sun, T. H. 1976. The prospects for population growth: Socio-economic implications for Taiwan. In *Conference on population and economic development in Taiwan*. Taipei, Taiwan: Institute of Economics, Academia Sinica.

Tabbarah, Riad. 1964. Birth control and population policy. *Population Studies* 18 (November): 187–96.

———. 1971. Toward a theory of demographic development. *Economic Development and Cultural Change* 19 (January): 257–76.

———. 1972. The adequacy of income: A social dimension in economic development. *Journal of Development Studies* 9, no. 3 (April): 57–75.

———. 1976. Population education as a component of development policy. *Studies in Family Planning* 7, no. 7 (July): 197–201.

———. 1978. Fertility behaviour in demographic development. United Nations Economic Commission for Western Asia (ECWA), *The Population Framework*, Beirut: ECWA.

Taiwan. 1966*a*. *Report of the Taiwan and Fukien area population and housing census of 1966*. Vol. 2. Taiwan Province, no. 2. *Marriage status of the population and women's fertility*.

Taiwan, 1966*b*. *Report of the Taiwan and Fukien area population and housing census of 1966*. Vol. 2. *Taiwan Province*, no. 3. *The level of education of the population*.

Taiwan demographic factbook. 1961–74. Various years. Department of Civil Affairs and Ministry of Interior, Taiwan Provincial Government, Taiwan.

Taiwan Department of Budget, Accounting, and Statistics. 1966–74. *Report of the survey of family income and expenditure*. Various years. Taiwan Provincial Government, Taiwan.

Taiwan Provincial Institute of Family Planning. 1969–75. *Family planning reference book*. Vols. 1–13. Taichung, Taiwan.

Tobin, James. 1974. Comment. In *Economics of the family*, ed. T. W. Schultz. Chicago: University of Chicago Press.

United Nations, Department of Economic and Social Affairs. 1953. *The determinants and consequences of population trends.* Population Study no. 17. New York.

———. 1965. *Population Bulletin*, no. 7. *Fertility*. New York.

Welch, F. 1970. Education in production. *Journal of Political Economy* 78, no. 1 (January/February): 35–59.

Williams, A. D. 1976. Fertility and reproductive loss. Ph.D. diss. University of Chicago.

Willis, R. J. 1974. Economic theory of fertility behavior. In *Economics of the family*, ed. T. W. Schultz. Chicago: University of Chicago Press.

Wolf, A. P. 1968. Adopt a daughter-in-law, marry a sister: A Chinese solution to the problem of the incest taboo. *American Anthropologist* 70, no. 5 (October): 864–74.

Wolf, Margery. 1972. *Women and the family in rural Taiwan.* Stanford: Stanford University Press.

Zajonc, R. B. 1976. Family configuration and intelligence. *Science* 192 (16 April): 227–36.

5

Causes and Consequences of Mortality Declines in Less Developed Countries during the Twentieth Century

Samuel H. Preston

Only a few countries of Africa, Asia, and Latin America can supply suitable data for estimating mortality levels in 1900. Many more can supply such data for 1940 or 1950. Without exception, the estimated levels of mortality prevailing in those years are higher than current levels. For those countries that can provide data at both earlier points, most improvement as indexed by life expectancy at birth has been achieved since 1940. It appears from fragmentary records that life expectancy at birth during 1935–39 was about 30 years in Africa and Asia and 40 years in Latin America. The respective levels in 1965–70 were on the order of 43, 50, and 60 (World Health Organization 1974*b*; United Nations, Population Division 1973).

The magnitude and the demographic character of this improvement have been documented in a number of excellent reviews, and for this reason they need not detain us here (United Nations 1963, 1973, 1974; Stolnitz 1974; Arriaga 1970; World Health Organization 1974*b*). These works suggest that the mortality improvements, when measured by the absolute decline in age-specific death rates, have tended to be largest at ages under 5 (especially infancy) and above 40. The proportionate declines, on the other hand, have been largest in the older childhood ages. Life expectancy gains for females have been larger than those for males. It is likely that gains have been more rapid in urban than in rural areas. In these matters, mortality experience in less developed countries

Samuel H. Preston is associated with the University of Washington.

The author is grateful to Avery Guest, James McCann, Peter Newman, and Masanori Hashimoto for comments and suggestions and to William Grady and Thomas Revis for research assistance. This research was aided by National Institutes of Health Center Grant 1POL HD 09397–01.

(LDCs) has roughly recapitulated that in more developed countries (MDCs). Life expectancy differences between MDCs and LDCs have narrowed, although the lagging pace of improvement in Africa has produced greater dispersion within LDCs themselves. The decadal rate of mortality decline in many LDCs surpasses that ever observed in populations of the now-developed world.

This paper has two purposes: to identify the factors responsible for these mortality improvements in LDCs and provide estimates of their relative importance; and to begin tracing the effect of these improvements on demographic and economic processes. Less developed countries are defined regionally to comprise Africa, Latin America, and Asia except Japan. Data on mainland China, North Korea, and what was formerly North Vietnam are not available, and for all practical purposes these countries are also excluded from the set under review. Conclusions reached about the importance of various factors in the mortality decline do not appear to conflict with the impressions of informed observers of these matters in China (Wegman, Lin, and Purcell 1973).

5.1 Causes of Declining Mortality

There is much more consensus on the fact of mortality decline in LDCs than on its causes. Considerable dispute remains about whether the decline has been principally a by-product of social and economic development as reflected in private standards of nutrition, housing, clothing, transportation, water supply, medical care, and so on or whether it was primarily produced by social policy measures with an unprecedented scope or efficacy. A third possibility is that technical changes reduced the relative costs of good health. This possibility is usually subsumed within the social policy position because it is clear to most observers that the major technical changes that have occurred—immunization against a host of infectious diseases, vector eradication, chemotherapy —had to be embodied in social programs in order to affect the mortality of the masses in LDCs. Demographers have almost unanimously favored the social policy–technical change interpretation of mortality decline (Davis 1956; Coale and Hoover 1958; United Nations, Population Division 1974; Stolnitz 1974). As evidence, they have principally cited the unprecedented rate of mortality reduction in many LDCs and certain dramatic examples of obviously effective government intervention, most notably in Sri Lanka and Mauritius. Many specialists in international health (Fredericksen 1961, 1966*a*,*b*; Marshall, Brown, and Goodrich 1971), medical historians focusing on primarily Western populations (McKeown and Record 1962; McKeown 1965), and some economists (Sharpston 1976) have opposed this interpretation, usually claiming that social interventions have been largely ineffective or insufficiently widespread.

Kuznets (1975) and Coale and Hoover (1958) have argued that, in one sense, the distinction between economic development and public health interventions creates a false dichotomy. Development itself strengthens the nation-state, improves communications among nations and hence facilitates the transfer of medical technology, and routinizes scientific advance. While this position is unassailable, it leaves unanswered the question whether the mortality decline was a product of changes in private consumption or of public programs and technical change, regardless of whether the latter were in turn produced by economic development in its broadest sense. Even if public programs and technical changes were merely intervening variables in the relation between mortality and development, the importance of their role remains to be identified.

5.1.1 Effect of Private Income Levels on Mortality

That mortality rates are sensitive to private living standards, independent of the national level of economic development, scarcely needs documentation. Studies of mortality differentials among individuals by social or economic class in countries as disparate as India and the United States consistently reveal lower mortality rates among the upper classes (Kitagawa and Hauser 1973; Vaidyanathan 1972). The role of private living standards in creating the pattern of international mortality differentials is more difficult to assess. Richer countries not only have richer people but, in general, have larger and more effective social programs.

Some indication of the importance of private living standards for international mortality differences may be gained by examining the importance of income distribution as a factor in those differences. The international relation between national income per capita and life expectancy is decidedly nonlinear, with life expectancy showing strongly diminishing returns to increases in income (Preston 1975*a*; Vallin 1968). It is reasonable to expect that mortality also responds nonlinearly to individual income levels, in which case the distribution of income within a nation should influence its aggregate level of mortality. In particular, suppose that the relation between individual income and life expectancy is log linear:[1]

$$e^o_{0i} = a + b \ln Y_i,$$

where e^o_{0i} = life expectancy at birth in income group i
Y_i = level of income received by group i
a, b = constants.

If the national level of life expectancy is simply the aggregate of these individual-level relations, with no contribution from the *national* level of income except insofar as it reflects individual incomes, then the life expectancy for the population, $e^o{}_{0p}$, will be equal to

$$e^o{}_{0p} = f[\sum_i (a + b \ln Y_i)]$$
$$= a + b \ln Y + b \times f \times \sum_i \ln (S_i/f),$$

where $Y =$ mean level of income in the population
$S_i =$ share of total national income earned by group i
$f =$ share of total population represented by group i, assumed to be constant among the groups.

Life expectancy will be a function of mean national income, Y, and of the distribution of income as represented by the term $\sum_i \ln(S_i/f)$. This term, which is related to the entropy measure of income distribution, ranges from 0 if income is perfectly evenly distributed to $(-\infty)$ if one group has no income. Strictly speaking, the weights that permit subgroup life expectancies to aggregate into population life expectancy are provided by births rather than by population size, but the two will be very highly correlated.

To examine the importance of private incomes for national life expectancy, the value of this income distribution measure was computed for fifty-two populations on which income shares were estimated in 5% population segments. The values and sources can be found in appendix table 5.A.2, along with values of $e^o{}_0$ and Y. The importance of private incomes can be inferred from the consistency of coefficients on Y and on the income distribution measure. If national life expectancy is simply a function of private income levels, the coefficients on $\sum_i \ln(S_i/.05)$ should be 0.05 of the coefficient on Y. If national income contributes independently of private income, the ratio should be less than 0.05. The equation as estimated by ordinary least squares on the fifty-two observations is

$$e^o{}_0 = 19.105 + \underset{(.859)}{6.984} \ln \overline{Y} + \underset{(.237)}{.375} \sum_i \ln(S_i/.05)$$

$$R^2 = .651$$

$$\overline{R}^2 = .644.$$

The coefficient of the income distribution term is in fact 0.0536 of that of national income, suggesting that relations between mortality and income at the national level are indeed dominated by relations between mortality and income at the individual level. This result should be treated with great caution because of inaccuracy and incomparability in the measure of income distribution and because the log-linear functional form probably simplifies a more complex relationship. Furthermore, the standard error of the income distributional coefficient is large enough to prevent rejection of the hypothesis that the true coefficient is zero. Nevertheless, one direct implication of the result is that the mortality risks facing a family earning $10,000 per year or $100 per year are not strongly influenced by the prevailing level of average income in the nation in which they reside.

The suggestion that private incomes are very influential in determining national levels of life expectancy at a moment in time does not imply, of course, that changes in private incomes have been the dominant factor in mortality changes during this century. The actual changes in income may have been too small, in conjunction with the sensitivity of mortality to income, to account for the observed mortality changes. Before trying to establish the role played by changes in private living standards in LDC mortality declines, it is useful to make an assessment of the causes of death responsible for those declines.

5.1.2 Causes of Death Responsible for Mortality Declines

Interpretation of mortality declines in LDCs would depend on whether the cause of death responsible for the majority of declines were, for example, smallpox, diarrheal disease, or malaria, since it is clear that death rates from these causes are fundamentally responsive to different influences. Unfortunately, the causes of death responsible for mortality change in LDCs have never been documented on a broad scale. A large part of the reason is that most LDCs still cannot supply national-level data on cause patterns, and data for those that can undoubtedly reflect inaccurate diagnoses and incomplete coverage. Problems are magnified when attention is turned to the patterns of earlier years. Nevertheless, it is possible to piece together a picture that provides some useful clues about the order of magnitude of the causes responsible.

First, it is clear that, in high-mortality populations, infectious and parasitic diseases bear almost exclusive responsibility for shortening life below the modern Western standards of 69 years for a male and 75 for a female. Life tables by cause of death have been constructed for 165 populations at varying levels of mortality (Preston, Keyfitz, and Schoen 1972). When the aggregate of infectious and parasitic diseases were hypothetically eliminated from those life tables and life expectancy was recalculated, the common result was to produce a life expectancy between 65 and 70 for males and between 70 and 75 for females, regardless of a population's initial mortality level (Preston, Keyfitz, and Schoen 1973). In 1920, Chilean males would hypothetically have gone from a life expectancy of 28.47 to one of 65.68 and females from 29.85 to 69.76. In Taiwan, males would have enjoyed a life expectancy of

72.27 years instead of 26.68, and females 76.00 instead of 29.18 (Preston, Keyfitz, and Schoen 1972, pp. 150–51, 702–3).[2]

Despite the appeal of life table measures, they are an unnecessarily awkward vehicle for discussing causes of death because the causes are nonadditive in their effect on life table parameters. This problem is averted by the use of age-standardized death rates. Models have been constructed to represent the typical cause-of-death structure for populations at various levels of mortality as indexed by the age-standardized crude death rate from all causes combined (Preston and Nelson 1974). Of the 165 populations supplying data for these models, only 41 were from Africa, Asia, or Latin America, and of these 5 were for Japan and 3 for the Jewish population of Israel. Nevertheless, the results suggest that cause-of-death structures, controlling mortality level, vary less between MDCs and LDCs than they do among regional groups within MDCs. Lower cardiovascular mortality and higher mortality from diarrheal diseases and maternal causes in LDCs represent their only significant divergence from MDC patterns (Preston and Nelson 1974, p. 37). John Gordon, one of the leading epidemiologists whose work focuses on developing countries, states that "infectious disease in the tropics and in some other preindustrial areas is too often viewed elsewhere as a collection of odd processes peculiar to those regions. Such diseases as schistosomiasis, filariasis, paragonimiasis, and all the others do exist. The plight of children, however, [who account for the bulk of annual deaths in LDCs] is the result of the everyday infections of the intestinal and respiratory tracts and with the communicable diseases specific to early life everywhere" (Gordon 1969, p. 218). Even among adults, the exotic tropical diseases are typically much more important sources of morbidity than of mortality.

Thus, there is some justification for allowing LDC cause-of-death patterns to be represented by relationships calculated on the basis of a data set that includes both MDCs and LDCs. The typical cause structures pertaining to populations with age-standardized crude death rates of 0.035 and 0.020 are presented in table 5.1.[3] These are roughly the levels that probably best characterize the average mortality situation in LDCs in 1900 and 1970, since they correspond to life expectancies at birth of 27.5 and 50.[4]

What is perhaps surprising about the table is that the specific "name" infectious and parasitic diseases (the first two listed) account for only an estimated 26.1% of mortality change. More important than all of these diseases combined—tuberculosis, typhoid, typhus, cholera, measles, diphtheria, whooping cough, malaria—is the category of respiratory diseases, which comprises a wide assortment of respiratory difficulties that are concentrated largely in infancy and old age. To be sure, some of the deaths in this category are improperly assigned complications of

Table 5.1 "Normal" Cause-of-Death Patterns at Standardized Crude Death Rates of 35/1,000 and 20/1,000 and Cause-Patterns of Change

Cause of Death	Model Value (Mean, Male and Female) of Age-Standardized Crude Death Rate from Cause at Age-Standardized Crude Death Rate from all Causes Combined of		Percentage of Decline Attributable to Cause
	35/1,000	20/1,000	
Respiratory tuberculosis	3.85	1.42	9.5
Other infectious and parasitic diseases	4.00	1.51	16.6
Influenza/pneumonia/bronchitis	7.85	2.87	33.2
Diarrheal disease	2.32	1.34	6.5
Maternal causes	.27	.14	0.9
Certain diseases of infancy	1.37	.88	3.3
Violence	.89	.78	0.7
All other and unknown	15.45	11.06	29.3
Total			100.0

Source: Preston and Nelson (1974).

specific infectious diseases. After undergoing a careful review of the initial medical certification in 1962–64, death certificates assigned to influenza/pneumonia/bronchitis in ten cities in Latin America, San Francisco, and Bristol, England, suffered a net loss of 1.0% of the original deaths assigned at ages 15–74, while the total of specific infectious and parasitic diseases increased by 5% (Puffer and Griffith 1967, pp. 230, 235). In a similar study of deaths before age 5 in thirteen Latin American and two North American areas between 1968 and 1972, respiratory diseases forfeited 22% of their originally assigned deaths, while the specific infectious diseases gained 23% (Puffer and Serrano 1973, pp. 332, 342). Corresponding adjustment of figures in table 5.1 would equalize the contribution of the specific infectious diseases and of the respiratory diseases to mortality decline at about 28–30%. Nevertheless, the "name" infectious diseases remain relatively submerged compared with popular accounts of their role, a point also stressed by McDermott (1966). Part of the reason for overemphasis on the role of the "name" diseases in mortality decline is probably their preeminent importance in the relatively small-scale English decline from 1851 to 1901, as has been elegantly documented in a widely cited paper by McKeown and Record (1962).

Some indication of whether the patterns depicted in table 5.1 provide a suitable representation for LDCs can be gained by examining the few LDC records that are available. In so doing, it is useful to provide more detail on specific members of the infectious and parasitic set. Mortality changes during long periods will be considered in order to avoid sampling periods during which specific public health interventions may have badly distorted the cause pattern of change.

Table 5.2 presents crude death rates from certain diseases of infectious origin for five populations of LDCs in the early twentieth century and for a more recent year. By and large, they support the previous estimate of the relative importance of respiratory tuberculosis and diarrheal diseases. Influenza/pneumonia/bronchitis is somewhat less important a source of decline than depicted in table 5.1, but the reason is probably that by the latter date each of the four populations supplying information on this cause achieved a mortality level far superior to the 20/1,000 age-standardized rate assumed in table 5.1. This cause is generally a more important source of mortality decline in movements between high and intermediate levels than between intermediate and low ones (Preston and Nelson 1974, pp. 31–33). As a very shaky generalization based on these undoubtedly unrepresentative populations, it may not be too far off the mark to assign 2% of the twentieth-century mortality decline in LDCs as a whole to smallpox, 2% to whooping cough, and 1% each to typhoid, typhus, measles, cholera, and plague (the latter estimate accounting for the disease's heavy concentration in India), and 0.5% to diphtheria. The epidemic nature of typhoid, cholera, and plague add even more uncertainty to these figures.

But the major uncertainty relates to the role of malaria. If estimates for British Guiana and India are to be believed, malaria by itself has accounted for 18–35% of large-scale mortality declines, equaling or exceeding the contribution we have estimated for all infectious and parasitic diseases combined. It should be noted that both estimates are based upon assignment to malaria of an arbitrary portion of deaths originally ascribed to "fever." A less arbitrary approach was pursued by Newman (1965, 1970), who had access to regional mortality data before and after an eradication campaign in Sri Lanka, as well as to regional data on malarial endemicity. Newman estimates by indirect techniques that the malaria eradication campaign in 1946 reduced Sri Lanka's crude death rate (CDR) by 4.2/1,000 between 1936–45 and 1946–60 (1970, p. 157). The relative contribution of such a decline to the total mortality reduction depends, of course, on the size of the latter. Had it been experienced by one of the populations in table 5.2, where the average drop in CDR was 26/1,000, it would account for about 16% of the mortality reduction. As a component of the smaller decline during the shorter period considered by Newman in Sri Lanka, it represented 42%. Simple inspection of time-series data on crude death rates suggests that virtually complete malaria eradication reduced the crude death rate by

Table 5.2 **Crude Death Rates (per 1,000) by Cause in Certain LDCs in the Early Part of the Century and Recently**

Cause of Death	Chile, 1920[a]	Chile, 1971[b]	% of Decline	Taiwan, 1920[c]	Taiwan, 1966[d]	% of Decline
Typhoid	.665	.007	2.9	.045	0	.2
Typhus	.439	0	2.0	n.a.	—	—
Malaria	.026	0	0	2.123	0	7.7
Smallpox	.008	0	0	.065	0	.3
Measles	.697	.061	2.8	.358	.039	1.2
Whooping cough	.789	.006	3.5	.046	.004	.2
Diphtheria	.062	.006	.2	.013	.004	0
Influenza/pneumonia/ bronchitis	4.527	1.355	14.1	8.231	.613	27.8
Respiratory tuberculosis	2.404	.209	9.8	1.813	.333	5.4
Diarrhea, dysentery, cholera nostras	2.120	.397	7.7	1.691	.215	5.4
Cholera	n.a.	—	—	.452	0	1.6
Total	30.85	8.389		32.686	5.246	

[a]Chile, Oficina Central de Estadistica, *Annuario Estadistico*, vol. 1 (1920).

[b]World Health Organization, *World Health Statistics Annual*, vol. 1 (1972).

[c]Taiwan, Jinki Dotai Tokei, *Sotoku Kanbo Chosaka* (1920).

[d]United Nations, *Demographic Yearbook* (1967), table 24.

[e]Pani (1917, pp. 192–99).

[f]Mandle (1970, p. 303).

[g]United Nations, *Demographic Yearbook* (1973), table 33.

[h]Compiled from material in Davis (1951, pp. 33–53). The 8.7 malaria estimate assumes that one-third of fever deaths are due to malaria. All estimates are highly suspect because of very deficient coding. Data on cholera, plague, and smallpox are probably most accurate because they were most consistently "notifiable" causes of death at the provincial level. Coale and Hoover (1958, p. 67), using a completely different technique, estimate the pre–spraying program level of malaria death rates in India to be about 6/1,000, including deaths indirectly attributable to the disease.

[i]Crude death rate from United Nations, Population Division, *Selected World Demographic Indicators by Countries, 1950–2000* (1975), p. 125. Average, 1960 and 1965. Distribution of deaths by cause from United Nations, *Demographic Yearbook* (1967), table 24. Data are for medically certified deaths in Poona and Bombay corporations and deaths in public hospitals in Rajasthan. The World Health Organization provides some confirmation of the virtual eradication of malaria from India by noting a hundredfold decline in reported cases between 1952 and 1972. World Health Organization, *Fifth Report on the World Health Situation*, Official Records no. 225 (1975), p. 142.

[j]Bunle (1954).

[k]Deaths under age 2 only.

[l]Malaria and undefined fevers.

[m]Pneumonia and bronchitis.

[n]Tuberculosis, all forms.

Table 5.2 (continued)

Cause of Death	Mexico City, 1904–12[e]	Mexico, 1922–25[j]	Mexico, 1972[b]	% of Difference, Mexico City–Mexico	% of Decline, Mexico
Typhoid	.068	.341	.065	0	1.7
Typhus	1.363	.040	.001	4.1	.2
Malaria	.076	1.471	.001	.2	9.0
Smallpox	.733	.826	0	2.2	5.0
Measles	.290	.427	.219	.2	1.3
Whooping cough	.284	.938	.080	.6	5.2
Diphtheria	.169	.062	.002	.5	.4
Influenza/pneumonia/ bronchitis	7.838	3.213	1.664	18.6	9.4
Respiratory tuberculosis	2.485	.653	.152	7.0	3.1
Diarrhea, dysentery, cholera nostras	9.785	1.861[k]	1.337	25.4	—
Cholera	n.a.	n.a.	—	—	—
Total	42.314	25.489	9.081		

Cause of Death	British Guiana, 1911–20[f]	Guyana, 1967[g]	% of Decline	India, 1898–1907[h]	India, 1963[i]	% of Difference
Typhoid	n.a.	—	—	n.a.	—	—
Typhus	n.a.	—	—	n.a.	—	—
Malaria	4.185[l]	0	18.1	6.0–8.7	0	24.3–35.2
Smallpox	n.a.	—	—	.27	.08	.8
Measles	n.a.	—	—	n.a.	—	—
Whooping cough	n.a.	—	—	n.a.	—	—
Diphtheria	n.a.	—	—	n.a.	—	—
Influenza/pneumonia/ bronchitis	3.680[m]	.055	15.7	n.a.	—	—
Respiratory tuberculosis	1.432[n]	.024	6.1	n.a.	—	—
Diarrhea, dysentery, cholera nostras	2.780	.026	11.9	1.96	.14	7.4
Cholera	n.a.	—	—	1.66	1.18	1.9
Plague	n.a.	—	—	1.82	0	7.3
Total	30.049	6.987		43.5	18.8	

about 3/1,000 in Guatemala (Meegama 1967, pp. 231–33), by 5–9 points in Mauritius (Titmuss and Abel-Smith 1968, pp. 49–50), and by 2–3/1,000 in Venezuela (Pampana 1954, p. 504).

The importance of malaria reduction as a source of declining mortality in a country obviously depends upon initial endemicity and the success of antimalarial campaigns. Southern Africa, southern Latin America, and northern Asia were never seriously afflicted with the disease; malaria in tropical Africa is highly endemic but, with few exceptions, it has not been successfully attacked (World Health Organization 1975*a*). A valuable compilation by Faust (1941, p. 12) suggests that recorded crude death rates from malaria in Mexico, Central America, and the West Indies during the 1930s, before any inroads had been made against the disease in rural areas, was 1.66/1,000. But he considers this "a figure probably far too low." The recorded CDR from malaria in cities of Burma in 1939 was 2.14 (Simmons et al. 1944, p. 11). The preprogram malarial CDR in Venezuela was 1.73/1,000 (Pampana 1954, p. 504). But recorded levels are often greatly in error. Newman calculates for Ceylon that each death assigned to malaria represented approximately four deaths that were directly or indirectly caused by it. But such an inflation factor is simply not tenable in Guatemala or Venezuela, where contemporaneous declines in crude death rates and malarial crude death rates suggest that a 2:1 ratio is the most that could have been sustained. Part of the inflation factor reflects malaria's role as "the great debilitator," but another part may be spurious. Spraying with residual insecticides reduces not only malaria but other vector-borne diseases such as yellow fever, typhus, and especially diarrheal disease. As Newman points out, an indirect approach that bases estimates on relations between regional changes in aggregate mortality and changes in spleen rates may well overascribe mortality decline to malaria reductions (but not to insecticide campaigns themselves). Finally, there is an often-quoted estimate, the basis of which is unknown, that worldwide malarial deaths have declined from 2.5 million per year to less than 1 million (*Lancet* 1970, p. 599), figures suggesting for LDCs a decline in crude death rates on the order of 1/1,000. The 2.5 million estimate evidently first appears in Pampana and Russell (1955) and presumably applies to 1955. Russell put the figure at at least 3 million for 1943 (1943, p. 601).

There is obviously much work to be done on this issue. In the present state of semi-ignorance, it seems judicious to adopt a range of CDR declines of 2–5/1,000, within which the twentieth-century LDC mortality decline attributable to antimalarial programs seems to have a better than even chance of falling. Sri Lanka, the best-documented case, falls within this range, and Sri Lanka was apparently intermediate in terms of initial endemicity, although the program there probably enjoyed unusual success and malaria reduction may not be solely responsible for the mortality decline produced by insecticide spraying. The range is also consistent with the apparently widespread malarial CDR declines of 1.5–2.0/1,000 and with inflation factors of 1.4–2.5.

These assorted scraps of information are pieced together in table 5.3, where diseases that seem in the main to be responsible for mortality declines in LDCs between 1900 and 1970 are classified into three groups according to their dominant mode of transmission. An estimate—obvi-

Table 5.3 **Diseases Responsible for LDC Mortality Declines and Methods That Have Been Used against Them**

Dominant Mode of Transmission	Diseases	Approximate Percentage of Mortality Decline in LDCs, 1900–1970, Accounted for by Disease	Principal Methods of Prevention Deployed[a]	Principal Methods of Treatment Deployed[a]
Airborne	Influenza/Pneumonia/Bronchitis	30		Antibiotics
	Respiratory tuberculosis	10	Immunization; identification and isolation	Chemotherapy
	Smallpox	2	Immunization	Chemotherapy
	Measles	1	Immunization	Antibiotics
	Diphtheria / Whooping cough	2	Immunization	Antibiotics
		45		
Water-, food-, and fecesborne	Diarrhea, enteritis, gastroenteritis	7	Purification and increased supply of water; sewage disposal; personal sanitation	Rehydration
	Typhoid	1	Purification and increased supply of water; sewage disposal; personal sanitation; partially effective vaccine	Rehydration, antibiotics
	Cholera	1	Purification and increased supply of water; sewage disposal; personal sanitation; partially effective vaccine; quarantine	Rehydration
		9		
Insectborne	Malaria	13–33	Insecticides, drainage, larvicides	Quinine drugs
	Typhus	1	Insecticides, partially effective vaccines	Antibiotics
	Plague	1	Insecticides, rat control, quarantine	
		15–35		

[a]Major sources: Paul (1964); Morley (1973); Hinman (1966).

ously highly tentative but nevertheless the first that appears to have been offered—of the relative importance of the various diseases in the decline is also supplied. The category totals are somewhat more robust than the figures for individual diseases because diagnostic confusions, disease interactions, and program externalities are more likely to occur within groups than between groups. Since progress was very slow between 1900 and 1935, the listing may serve as an adequate representation of declines between 1935 and 1970 as well. Finally, some indication of the public health and medical instruments that have been deployed against the various diseases is also provided. The modes of transmission that are listed are not mutually exclusive or exhaustive, but the classification is not seriously distortive.

5.1.3 Influences Operating on the Various Causes of Death

Mortality from every disease listed in table 5.3 would be expected to decline when personal living standards rise. Of the many linkages, probably the most important are those between nutritional status and influenza/pneumonia/bronchitis, diarrheal disease, and respiratory tuberculosis. The mechanisms of effect are not well known, but it appears that protein malnutrition impairs the production of circulating antibodies in response to bacterial and viral antigens and that undernutrition can produce atrophy of the organs responsible for the immune response (World Health Organization 1972, pp. 24–25). There is no question of the importance of poor nutrition as a factor underlying high mortality rates in LDCs. The PAHO study of child mortality in thirteen Latin American projects found that immaturity or malnutrition was an associated or underlying cause of 57% of the deaths before age 5 (World Health Organization 1974*a*, p. 279). Immaturity is in turn a frequent product of maternal malnourishment (Mata et al. 1972). The problem is apparently equally severe in Africa, although the data are much more fragmentary (Bailey 1975). Diet supplementation programs in Peru (Baertl et al. 1970) and Guatemala (Ascoli et al. 1967; Scrimshaw 1970) significantly reduced child mortality in test populations, but, oddly, without having substantial effects on indexes of child physical development. Despite the improvement, mortality and morbidity in the Guatemalan villages remained "shockingly high," which was attributed to irregular participation in the feeding program and to the continued heavy burden of infection to which the children were subject (Scrimshaw 1970, pp. 1689–90).

But nutritional status is not exclusively determined by diet, nor is diet determined only by the availability of calories or protein. There is now extensive evidence that infectious diseases themselves are an extremely important source of malnourishment, independent of the child's nutritional state at the time of attack (Mata et al. 1972; Scrimshaw 1970; World Health Organization 1972, p. 27). Infection increases metabolic demands and often reduces the absorption of nutrients and increases their excretion. Nutritional intake can also be reduced by nausea or through customs denying food to the sick. Infections among pregnant women can reduce birthweights and, among new mothers, milk secretion (Mata et al. 1972; Bailey 1975). Gordon (1969, p. 218) suggests that diet fails by far to explain all the prevalent malnourishment in LDCs. The frequency of inappropriate nutritional practices despite adequate food supplies does not require emphasis (Bailey 1975; Food and Agriculture Organization 1975). The importance of nutritional practices is indicated by the reported reversal of expected social class differences in infant mortality in Chile, a condition attributed to earlier weaning among children of upper-class women (Plank and Milanesi 1973). The point is simply that, even if nutritional status were the only influence on mortality from a disease, mortality declines from that cause do not necessarily imply that an improvement in food supplies has occurred. Nutritional practices and exogenous declines in the incidence of other infections must also be considered candidates for explanation. The "subsistence level" of food production is obviously fictitious if it is presumed to represent a fixed requirement that is independent of the state of prophylactic or nutritional arts.

Despite the undoubted influence of nutritional intake and other components of general living standards on mortality, it is clear from table 5.3 that many other influences have also been at work. Obvious as it may be, it is easy to forget that death from an infectious disease involves an encounter between a pathogenic organism and a vulnerable human host. The rate of death can be altered by changing the rate or terms of the encounter without any prior change in the host. It is not possible and is probably not necessary to document individually the preventive and curative measures that have been utilized for this purpose. With the exception of influenza/pneumonia/bronchitis, it seems likely that preventive measures have been more effective than curative ones.

That preventive measures have been widely deployed in each of the three categories can be demonstrated relatively easily. At the end of 1964, 1.935 billion persons lived in areas that were originally malarious. Of these, 41% were living in areas from which malaria had been eradicated; 16% were living in areas where incidence was very low and was being controlled by case detection and treatment; 24% were living in areas protected by extensive mosquito control measures; and 19% were living in areas without specific antimalarial measures, most of these in tropical Africa (World Health Organization 1975*a*). The cost of programs producing virtually complete eradication has been estimated at 10–30 cents per capita per year, with programs probably extending over a two- to three-year period and a continuing annual cost of 5 cents per capita required for surveillance thereafter (Pampana and Russell 1955, table 1, provides the most complete cost compilation).

India has vaccinated 170 million persons against tuberculosis and in 1968 alone vaccinated 83 million against smallpox (World Health Organization 1975*b*, p. 142). It has finally succeeded in eliminating smallpox completely, as has every other country. Colombia dispensed 5.9 million vaccinations in 1972, one-third of the population size; Egypt vaccinated 15 million persons against cholera in the same year and 25 million against smallpox in 1970. All primary-school entrants in the Philippines are vaccinated against tuberculosis. Barbados has compulsory immunization against diphtheria, polio, smallpox, and tetanus upon school entrance (World Health Organization 1975). An expert committee assembled by WHO estimated that 80% of the 70 million children reaching age one in LDCs each year could be immunized against measles, polio, tuberculosis, pertussis, tetanus, diphtheria, and smallpox at a cost, exclusive of personnel, of $37.5–$60 million, or $0.67–$1.07 apiece (World Health Organization, 1975*c*, p. 2).

Conditions of water supply and sewage disposal have also been markedly improved, despite continued abysmal conditions in many areas. Many of the improvements were normal and integral parts of economic expansion and hence cannot be specifically interpreted as public health interventions of an unprecedented sort. WHO surveys of government officials in 1962 and 1970 indicated that the proportion of LDC urban populations served by house connections to public water supply increased from 0.33 to 0.50 during this eight-year period for the seventy-five countries that replied in both years (World Health Organization 1973, p. 726). No rural population comparisons could be made, but in 1970 only 12% of rural LDC populations had "reasonable access" to community water supply (public fountain or standpipe within 200 meters of a house). The figure was only 6% in India (World Health Organization 1973, pp. 727, 729). New urban house connections were estimated to cost an average of $35 per capita, and providing rural residents with easy access to safe water to cost $12 per capita. In 1970, 69% of LDC urban populations had sewage disposal facilities (27% were connected to public sewerage and 42% had private household systems). New connections to urban public sewerage cost an average of $29 per head. Only 8% of the rural population was judged to have adequate sewage disposal, although the average cost of providing such facilities was estimated at only $4 per capita (World Health Organization 1973, pp. 732–33, 738–43). No trends in sewage facilities could be established, but improvement is probably fairly rapid in urban areas and slow in rural areas. Clearly, the initial cost of such programs is considerably higher than that for programs of vector control and immunization. Water supply improvements were among the very first changes to modify mortality patterns in European countries in the mid-nineteenth century. But they are lagging relative to other improvements in LDCs. This may explain why diarrheal disease remains relatively more prominent as a contributor to total mortality in LDCs than it was in European countries at the same general mortality level (Preston and Nelson 1974).

With the exception of water and sewerage improvements and smallpox vaccination, the techniques of preventive and curative health care that have been widely deployed in LDCs are twentieth-century products. Virtually all were facilitated by ultimate acceptance of the revolutionary germ theory of disease at the turn of the century. Even smallpox eradication has benefited from technical improvements such as freeze-dried vaccine and the forked needle (Foege et al. 1975). The next section attempts to identify the relative importance of these technical improvements, as typically embodied in government health programs enjoying some measure of external assistance or support, in LDC mortality improvements during the last three decades.

5.1.4 Structural Changes in Relations between Mortality and Other Development Indexes

That mortality reductions have not merely been residual by-products of socioeconomic development is best illustrated by showing that major structural changes have occurred in the relationship between mortality and other indexes of development. Important technical changes and exogenous increases in government health commitment or foreign health assistance should result in a shift in the average level of life expectancy that corresponds to a particular level of other development indicators. Preston (1975*a*) suggested that such a change had occurred in the relation between mortality and national income, and this section will attempt to supplement that observation by introducing new variables and a larger sample of countries. Data have been gathered on national levels of life expectancy, per capita income (in 1970 U.S. dollars), daily calorie consumption, and literacy for thirty-six nations in or about 1940, including seventeen LDCs and several others that today would be classified as LDCs if 1940 conditions had persisted. The LDC estimates of life expectancy are based largely upon indirect demographic techniques such as intercensal survival analysis rather than upon vital statistics. Data on these same variables have been generated for 120 nations in or around 1970. The data and sources are presented in appendix tables 5.A.1 and 5.A.2.

A preliminary indication that structural changes have occurred is presented in table 5.4. Countries are cross-classified by level of per capita national income (in 1970 U.S. dollars) and by daily calorie consumption per head. Complete information was available for only twenty-nine countries in 1940. Nevertheless, it is clear that, within every

Table 5.4 **Mean Life Expectancy at Birth of Countries in Various Ranges of National Income and Calorie Consumption, 1940 and 1970**

Daily Calories Per Capita	National Income per Capita in 1970 U.S. Dollars <150	150–299	300–699	700+	
<2,100	42.7 (17)	51.5 (8)	53.3 (5)	69.5 (1)	47.5 (31)
	38.3 (5)	36.0 (1)	(0)	(0)	37.9 (6)
2,100–2,399	42.6 (16)	49.9 (14)	56.2 (7)	71.4 (2)	49.1 (39)
	40.0 (1)	43.9 (2)	46.1 (1)	(0)	43.4 (4)
2,400–2,899	45.4 (1)	57.9 (8)	61.3 (10)	68.0 (7)	61.4 (26)
	(0)	44.1 (2)	50.4 (4)	59.6 (2)	51.1 (8)
2,900+	(0)	(0)	(0)	71.6 (24)	71.6 (24)
	(0)	(0)	58.7 (2)	65.2 (9)	64.0 (11)
	42.7 (34)	52.4 (30)	57.8 (22)	70.8 (34)	55.9 (120)
	38.6 (6)	42.4 (5)	52.2 (7)	64.1 (11)	52.2 (29)

Source: Appendix tables 5.A.1 and 5.A.2.
Note: 1970 countries appear in the top rows, 1940 countries in the bottom rows. The number of countries is shown in parentheses.

one of the nine cells where both 1940 and 1970 populations appear, average life expectancy was higher at the later date. The average intra-cell gain is 8.7 years of life expectancy.

A somewhat more precise indication of the magnitude of structural changes can be obtained by regressing life expectancy on income, calories, and literacy separately for 1940 and 1970 observations. Because of nonlinearities expected on obvious inductive and deductive grounds, natural logarithms of calorie consumption and income are used as regressors. Daily calorie consumption is measured from 1,500, approximately the average level required to meet minimum daily metabolic demands. Literacy, a personal dichotomous variable, cannot act nonlinearly at the individual level, since it takes on only two values. Barring spillover effects whose existence in income relations was called into question in section A, the proportion literate should be linearly related to life expectancy at the aggregate level. No claim is made that the resulting equations are perfectly specified, but simply that the socioeconomic variables included are the only ones available in the 1930s. It seems unlikely that relations between terms omitted and terms present would have changed in such as way as to influence the outcomes described below.

The equations as estimated by ordinary least squares are the following:[5]

$$1970\text{:}\quad e^o_0 = \underset{(7.4090)}{17.1464} + \underset{(.6524)}{4.2488} \times 1n\overline{Y} + \underset{(.0212)}{.2086} \times LIT + \underset{(1.3492)}{.3170} \times 1n\,CAL$$

$$N = 120,\ R^2 = .860 \qquad R^2 = .858$$

$$1940\text{:}\quad e^o_0 = \underset{(18.5102)}{-13.1035} + \underset{(2.3860)}{5.4352} \times 1n\overline{Y} + \underset{(.0626)}{.1654} \times LIT + \underset{(3.7176)}{2.9470} \times 1n\,CAL$$

$$N = 36,\ R^2 = .856 \qquad R^2 = .845,$$

where e^o_0 = life expectancy at birth, average male and female
$\overline{Y}$ = national income per capita, 1970 U.S. dollars
LIT = percentage literate of the adult population
CAL = excess of daily calorie consumption per capita over 1,500.

Coefficients of all three variables in both equations are properly signed. The explanatory power of the regression equations is virtually identical for the two years. Income and literacy terms are highly significant in both periods and retain approximately the same magnitude. This stability was unexpected because of the high degree of colinearity among regressors. The coefficients indicate that a 10 percentage point increase in literacy is associated at both points with a gain in life expectancy of approximately 2 years, and that a 10% gain in national income by itself increases life expectancy by approximately one-half year. Coefficients of the calorie term decrease over time but are insignificant in both periods. It is very unlikely that the availability of calories for daily consumption has no influence on mortality. The calorie variable is probably subject to greater measurement error than the other two, and the influence of calorie availability is probably being reflected through them. The constant term increases by about 30 years between 1940 and 1970, although by itself this change is not readily interpreted, since the zero-points on variables are well below the range of observed experience. The hazards of extrapolation are shown by the negative (though insignificant) intercept for 1940.[6]

The substantive significance of the structural shift, as reflected primarily in the intercept, is probably best illustrated in the following way. Each of the 120 countries in 1970, including 94 LDCs, can supply estimates for each of the three regressors. It is therefore possible to estimate what life expectancy would be for every country at its current developmental level if no structural change had occurred in the relation between mortality and socioeconomic development. This estimate is simply obtained by substituting values of the three regressors for 1970 into the 1940 regression equation. Differences between actual life expectancy and that predicted if 1940 relations had continued to prevail indicate the amount of change in life expectancy attributable to the structural shift. A weighted average of such differences will indicate the importance of the shift for LDCs as a whole.[7] Results of this exercise are presented in table 5.5.

Estimates presented in this table indicate that life expectancy for LDCs as a unit (exclusive of China, North Korea, and North Vietnam) would have been 8.66 years lower in 1970–75 if life expectancy had continued to be related to other development indexes as it was in 1940. Excluding South Vietnam, where special factors were obviously distorting life expectancy, the figure is 8.84. This is an estimate of the amount of increase in life expectancy that is attributable to factors exogenous to national levels of income, literacy, and calorie consumption.[8] What fraction of the total gain in life expectancy during the period this 8.84-year structural shift represents is difficult to assess. WHO estimates that life expectancy in LDCs was 32 years in 1935–39 (30 in Africa and Asia and 40 in Latin America) and 49.6 years in 1965–70 (World Health Organization 1974, p. 23). The earlier figure is based on very little information, but if we accept it, the implication is that the structural change accounts for about half (50.2%) of the total gain in life expectancy during these nearly equivalent 30-year periods. This estimate is lower than the 79.5% (9.7/12.2) figures estimated for MDCs and LDCs combined by Preston (1975, p. 238) not so much because the estimated Δe^o_0 attributed to structural shifts differ (the difference is in fact only 0.86 years) but because the estimated gains in life expectancy differ (12.2 years for the world as a whole between 1938 and 1963 by Preston versus 17.6 years for LDCs between 1935–39 and 1965–70 by WHO). Part of the discrepancy in the estimates probably results from differences in the universe covered. Because MDCs had achieved by 1940 levels of developmental indicators high enough that relatively little gain in life expectancy was to be expected from advances in living standards, it is likely that exogenous factors represented a larger fraction of the gains that occurred there than they did in LDCs. Another part may reflect differences in the periods covered, since the present estimate pertains to a somewhat later period. Suggestions that the pace of mor-

Table 5.5 **Life Expectancy in 1970–75 and Life Expectancy Predicted if 1940 Relations between Life Expectancy and Levels of Literacy, Income, and Calorie Consumption Had Continued to Prevail**

Africa	Predicted e^0_0*	Actual e^0_0	Difference	*Latin America*	Predicted e^0_0*	Actual e^0_0	Difference	*Asia*	Predicted e^0_0*	Actual e^0_0	Difference
Algeria	41.42	53.20	11.78	Argentina	61.84	68.20	6.36	Afghanistan	30.16	40.30	10.14
Angola	37.32	38.50	1.18	Bolivia	39.49	46.80	7.31	Bangladesh	31.49	35.80	4.31
Botswana	34.13	43.50	9.37	Brazil	50.85	61.40	10.55	Burma	41.23	50.00	8.77
Burundi	40.39	39.00	−1.39	Chile	56.62	62.60	5.98	Cyprus	56.21	71.40	15.19
Central				Colombia	51.36	60.90	9.54	India	40.11	49.50	9.39
African Rep.	35.16	41.00	5.84	Costa Rica	56.07	68.20	12.13	Indonesia	39.54	47.50	7.96
Chad	30.29	38.50	8.21	Dominican Rep.	48.38	57.80	9.42	Iran	43.23	51.00	7.77
Congo	42.47	43.50	1.03	Ecuador	47.14	59.60	12.46	Iraq	42.57	52.70	10.13
Dahomey	33.60	41.00	7.40	El Salvador	45.09	57.80	12.71	Israel	63.10	71.00	7.90
Egypt	41.95	52.40	10.45	Guatemala	43.86	52.90	9.04	Jordan	43.59	53.20	9.61
Ethiopia	30.39	38.00	7.61	Guyana	51.21	67.90	16.69	Khmer Rep.	47.19	45.40	−1.79
Gabon	41.65	41.00	−.65	Haiti	29.48	50.00	20.52	Korea, Rep. of	52.20	60.60	8.40
Gambia	33.47	40.00	6.53	Honduras	44.10	53.50	9.40	Laos	32.95	40.40	7.45
Ghana	43.10	43.50	.40	Jamaica	54.93	69.50	14.57	Lebanon	55.11	63.20	8.09
Guinea	30.43	41.00	10.57	Mexico	55.24	63.20	7.96	Malaysia	50.43	59.40	8.97
Ivory Coast	41.97	43.50	1.53	Nicaragua	48.51	52.90	4.39	Nepal	31.63	43.60	11.97
Kenya	37.37	50.00	12.63	Panama	55.47	66.50	11.03	Pakistan	37.05	49.80	12.75
Liberia	35.68	43.50	7.82	Paraguay	47.84	61.90	14.06	Philippines	47.95	58.40	10.45
Libyan Arab Rep.	52.23	52.90	.67	Peru	46.72	55.70	8.98	Saudi Arabia	42.56	45.30	2.74
Madagascar	39.55	43.50	3.95	Puerto Rico	59.60	72.10	12.50	Singapore	55.22	69.50	14.28
Malawi	33.05	41.00	7.95	Trinidad				Sri Lanka	46.86	67.80	20.94
Mali	28.99	38.00	9.01	and Tobago	54.17	69.50	15.23	Syria	44.14	54.00	9.86
Malta	58.07	70.80	12.73	Uruguay	59.54	69.80	10.26	Taiwan	54.32	69.40	15.08
Maritius	49.47	65.50	16.03	Venezuela	55.14	64.70	9.56	Thailand	48.09	58.00	9.91
Mauritania	33.50	38.50	5.00					Turkey	49.03	56.90	7.87

Table 5.5 (continued)

Africa	Predicted e^0_0*	Actual e^0_0	Difference	*Latin America*	Predicted e^0_0*	Actual e^0_0	Difference	*Asia*	Predicted e^0_0*	Actual e^0_0	Difference
Morocco	39.92	52.90	12.98	Mean difference, Latin America			= 10.90	Vietnam, Rep. of	49.08	40.50	−8.58
Mozambique	38.98	43.50	4.52					Yemen	31.53	44.80	13.27
Niger	30.20	38.50	8.30	1970 population-weighted mean difference, Latin America			= 9.54	Yemen, P.D.R.	31.79	44.80	13.01
Nigeria	37.52	41.00	3.48								
Rhodesia	38.39	51.50	13.11								
Rwanda	29.66	41.00	11.34								
Senegal	36.25	40.00	3.75								
Sierra Leone	35.25	43.50	8.25								
Somalia	28.37	41.00	12.63								
South Africa	50.59	51.50	.91								
Sudan	34.70	48.60	13.90								
Togo	33.93	41.00	7.07								
Tunisia	42.32	54.10	11.78								
Uganda	37.62	50.00	12.38								
Cameroon	45.40	41.00	−4.40								
Tanzania	32.00	44.50	12.50								
Upper Volta	28.92	38.00	9.08								
Zaire	37.16	43.50	6.34								
Zambia	45.02	44.50	−.52								
Mean difference, Africa			= 7.05	Mean, all LDCs			= 8.61	Mean difference, Asia			= 9.14
1970 population-weighted mean difference, Africa			= 7.22	1970 Population-weighted mean, all LDCs			= 8.66	1970 population-weighted mean difference, Africa			= 8.90

*Based on substitution of 1970 values of literacy, income, and calorie consumption into 1940 regression relating e^0_0 to these variables.

tality decline in LDCs has slowed in the past decade (Hansluwka 1975; World Bank 1975) imply that the shift in the mortality/development relation may have essentially ended by the early 1960s, while gains in living standards continue to exert an influence on mortality. In any case, the estimated amount of the structural shift is consistent between the two estimates at about 9 years of life expectancy at birth.

The structural shift has evidently been least pronounced for African countries and most pronounced for Latin America. Africa has unquestionably experienced the least penetration by modern public health measures of any region. The problem is not simply poverty but also a widely dispersed population that increases program costs (World Health Organization 1975*b*, p. 17). Several of the African countries have lower life expectancies in 1970–75 than could have been expected based on 1940 relations. The apparent advantage enjoyed by Latin American countries may be due to their special relations with the United States. The United States has been by far the largest bilateral donor in international health aid, and the bulk of aid appears to go to Latin American countries, either directly or through the Pan American Health Organization (World Bank 1975, pp. 68–69). It is worth noting that, of the ninety-four LDCs, Sri Lanka and Mauritius are two of the four whose estimated structural changes are largest. It is unfortunate that so much attention has focused on these unusual cases.

Attributing to all countries the relations prevailing in countries for which data are available is always risky. The preceding analysis of change can be complemented by one that focuses exclusively on the cases that can be documented. Each of the thirty-six countries providing data in 1940 can also supply data in 1970. According to the previous formulation, we should expect Δe^o_0 to be linearly related to $\Delta 1nY$, $\Delta 1n$ CAL, and ΔLIT, with a relatively large positive intercept reflecting the structural shift. In the first specification of the model, we add three terms believed to reflect factors responsible for a portion of the structural shift. The first (MAL) is an estimate of the degree of malarial endemicity in 1940, which is a proxy for the effect of antimalarial programs on Δe^o_0. Each of the thirty-six countries with endemic malaria has had a major antimalarial campaign. It is hoped that the coefficient of this term will provide a clearer indication of the effect of antimalarial activities on gains in life expectancy than was previously available. The second (AID) is an estimate of the average annual per capita nonmilitary aid in United States dollars received from bilateral and multilateral donors between 1954 and 1972. The third (WAT) is an estimate of per capita aid received for water and sewerage projects between 1965 and 1970 (U.S. dollars). The latter two variables are assumed to be proxies for the amount of total per capita health aid received between 1940 and 1970. Their values are generally highest for the Latin American countries. Values of these variables are presented in appendix table 5.A.3.

The estimated equation with all six terms present is the following:[9]

$$\Delta e^o_0 = \underset{(2.8468)}{6.5212} + \underset{(2.4111)}{3.4500} \times \Delta \ln \bar{Y} + \underset{(.0927)}{.0354} \times \Delta LIT$$

$$+ \underset{(4.9362)}{.5605} \times \Delta \ln CAL$$

$$+ \underset{(.9411)}{3.1328} \times MAL + \underset{(.2376)}{.1460} \times AID + \underset{(.3668)}{.1955} \times WAT$$

$$R^2 = .595$$

$$\bar{R}^2 = .506.$$

Each of the coefficients has the expected positive sign. The coefficient of income remains similar in absolute value to that estimated in the cross-sectional regressions, but that of literacy declines by a factor of five and calories remain an insubstantial factor. Receipt of external aid contributes positively but insignificantly to mortality improvement. The most interesting result refers to the constant term. For a country essentially free of malaria in 1940 ($MAL = 0$), it is estimated that life expectancy would have increased by 6.52 years in the absence of socioeconomic development and external aid during the three decades. For a country in which malaria was highly endemic ($MAL = 3$), the corresponding gain is 15.92 years, of which 9.40 is attributable to factors associated with malarial endemicity. The average life expectancy for the seventeen LDCs was 39.29 in 1940 and 59.42 in 1970, giving an average gain of 20.13 years. The average malaria endemicity score for these seventeen was 2.59. Of the total gain in e^o_0, 8.11 years (3.1328×2.59), or 40%, is attributable to factors associated with malarial endemicity, and the constant term of 6.5 years, or 23%, represents other exogenous factors. The sum of 72% is considerably higher than that implied by the previous procedure. The external aid terms contribute an additional 1.13 years, or 5.6%.[10]

Whether or not antimalarial programs themselves produced the gain of 8.11 years attributed to malarial endemicity remains in serious doubt. The malaria score is correlated with life expectancy in 1940 at —.873. It is thus acting as a proxy for the initial level of mortality from a host of potentially eliminable infectious and parasitic diseases. When the initial level of life expectancy is entered as an independent variable, the magnitude of the structural change remains roughly the same but the portion attributable to the malarial term declines to zero:

$$\Delta e^o_0 = \underset{(8.5108)}{31.4722} + \underset{(2.0533)}{3.6048} \times \Delta \ln Y + \underset{(.0790)}{.0430} \times \Delta LIT$$
$$- \underset{(4.2327)}{.9865} \times \Delta CAL$$
$$- \underset{(1.3059)}{.0211} \times MAL + \underset{(.2036)}{.0750} \times AID + \underset{(.3139)}{.2939} \times WAT$$
$$- \underset{(.1328)}{.4063} \times e^o_0(1940)$$

$$R^2 = .720$$
$$R^2 = .643.$$

Other coefficients are not affected in such a way as to substantially alter interpretations, but the coefficient of malarial endemicity becomes effectively zero. The amount of structural change for the seventeen LDCs, the gain that is not accounted for by changes in Y, LIT, or CAL, is 16.46 years of life, or 81.8% of the average gain during the period.[11] The estimated structural change is close to that estimated directly above, but malaria's role in it is now negligible. When malarial endemicity is operationalized as a series of dummy variables, none of the dummy coefficients is significant, and the relation between mortality change and endemicity is nonmonotonic. Other functional forms and variable operationalizations should be investigated; at the moment all we can conclude is that the longitudinal analysis provides no better fix on malaria's role than the largely inconclusive cause-of-death analysis.

Two estimates have been advanced of the fraction of LDC gains in life expectancy between 1940 and 1970 that are attributable to structural change. The first estimate of one-half was based on a regression-decomposition technique that assumed all nations had relations between mortality and development indexes in 1940 identical to those prevailing in nations that could supply data for that year. The second estimate of approximately 80% was based solely upon examination of trends in the latter group. There is an important technical reason to favor the former estimate, namely, that measurement error is likely to be a more important source of distortion in longitudinal than in cross-sectional data. Measurement error biases coefficients toward zero. If random measurement error were all that was reflected in our measured changes in income, literacy, and calorie consumption, then the entire change in life expectancy would be absorbed in the constant term and attributed to structural change, regardless of the actual importance of these factors. Development levels are undoubtedly better measured than development rates, giving greater stability to the analysis based on a comparison of cross sections. There are, however, indications that a fraction of the gain larger than one-half would be attributed to structural shifts if analysis had focused more narrowly on the period between 1940 and 1960.

The estimate of one-half is roughly consistent with the preceding cause-of-death analysis. Influenza/pneumonia/bronchitis has accounted for perhaps a third of the mortality decline. No effective preventive measures have been deployed against these diseases, the effectiveness of immunization being minimal, and there are suggestions that antibiotics, sulfa drugs, and curative services are not widely enough available in LDCs to have substantially altered the disease picture (Sharpston 1976; Bryant 1969, pp. 314–23). Diarrheal diseases probably account for another 9% or so of the decline, and the principal method of control has been improvements in water supply and sewerage that, because of their expense, are closely associated with economic development.[12] It is likely that social and economic development—especially as reflected in water systems, nutrition, housing, and personal sanitary knowledge—have operated largely through these diseases. In the case of other diseases it appears that programs of a narrowly public health nature that have embodied inexpensive new techniques, especially vector control and immunization, have been the decisive forces in mortality reductions.

5.1.5 The Role of MDCs in LDC Gains

Many have argued that MDCs have played a decisive role in the mortality declines experienced by LDCs, although the case has not been well documented. Certain of the influences are clear enough. Sulfa drugs, antibiotics, and most vaccines and insecticides, including DDT, have been developed in laboratories within MDCs. MDCs contributed 5,764 technical assistance workers in health services to LDCs in 1968 (Organization for Economic Cooperation and Development, n.d., pp. 276–77). Governmental health agencies were often created under colonial auspices. The role of external financing has also been stressed, but the accounts have focused on the dramatic examples in relatively small countries where international campaigns have often been undertaken largely for their demonstration value.

Health assistance in the developing world began with the work of medical missionaries, who were established in the Philippines in 1577 and in China by 1835 (Maramag 1965; Bowers 1973).[13] The early efforts of colonial governments were designed primarily to protect the colonials from epidemic diseases (Beck 1970). Correspondingly, cooperative international health efforts principally attempted to protect Europe and North America from imported cholera, plague, and yellow fever (Howard-Jones 1974). An evolving social conscience in the interwar years led to greater concern with the health of the native population itself and to the establishment of local medical colleges (Beck 1970). The most effective international efforts of the period were undoubtedly those of the Rockefeller Foundation, which led a successful campaign to eradicate yellow fever from Latin American cities in 1916–23, repelled the invasion of *Anopheles gambiae* into Brazil in 1938, financed medical schools around the world, and was "probably the largest single factor in improving the public health education of the world up to the creation of the WHO" (Goodman 1971, pp. 381, 266, 377–82). Its antimalarial activities began in 1915 and included demonstrations of the superior cost effectiveness of vector control compared with treatment and the feasibility of complete eradication. The antimalarial activities were considered by Russell, one of the world's leading malariologists, to be of fundamental importance in ultimate control of the disease. "In instance after instance the foundation provided the catalyst, or the inexpensive mainspring, or the seed money that resulted in control of the disease" (Russell 1968, p. 644).

The total amount of money appropriated by the Rockefeller Foundation from 1914 to 1954 for antimalarial activities, exclusive of salaries and overhead was only $5 million (Russell 1968, p. 644). This is a vivid illustration that contributions to mortality change are inaccurately reflected on financial ledgers. International aid for health purposes is a small part of total health expenditures in LDCs and probably always has been. But its cost effectiveness has certainly far surpassed the average for internally financed appropriations, which are too often focused on expensive curative services in urban areas.[14]

Only crude indications are available of the relative magnitudes of internal and external sources of health expenditures in LDCs. In 1970, government health expenditures were estimated for LDCs containing 1.89 billion people. Total government expenditure on health in these areas came to $7.67 billion, or about $4 per capita.[15] Private health expenditures in LDCs are probably slightly larger than public expenditures, judging from comparisons that can be made in seven countries.[16] Addition of private and public expenditure in countries not represented would bring the total annual expenditure perhaps to the range of $20–30 billion.

In contrast, the largest single source of international assistance for health, the World Health Organization, dispersed only $115 million in 1972, a figure that includes family planning activities and some dispersals to MDCs (World Bank 1975, pp. 68–69). The annual budget of the World Health Organization in 1970 was less than that of Massachusetts General Hospital! (Goodman 1971, p. 223). Of its regular budget, the United States contributed 31% and the USSR 13%, with no other country making a contribution larger than 7% (Goodman 1971, p. 220). The second largest source of international assistance in 1972, USAID, contributed $42 million. All together, the ten largest multilateral or bilateral sources of health aid contributed $300.7 million in international assistance for health programs in 1972 (World Bank 1975, p. 68), probably between 1% and 2% of total health expenditures in LDCs. To this should be added a portion of the $79 million in loans and credits made by the World Bank for water supply and sewerage construction in that year (World Bank 1975, p. 48).

It seems very likely, then, that total external health aid received by LDCs is less than 3% of their total health expenditures. The figure may have been somewhat higher earlier in the postwar period. The cumulative United States contribution to antimalarial activities through national research and international assistance has been estimated to be about one-half billion dollars (Russell 1968), but the annual contribution has declined drastically (Weller 1974; World Health Organization 1975*a*). But even the cumulative total is a paltry figure compared with annual expenditures in LDCs themselves. MDC contributions to mortality declines in LDCs have not been primarily financial; according to the estimates of the preceding section, the financial contributions are associated with an increase in e^0_0 of about one year in the seventeen LDCs between 1940 and 1970. Instead, they seem to have consisted of the development of low-cost health measures exploitable on a massive scale, demonstration of their effectiveness in relatively small areas, training and provision of personnel, and occasionally the initiation of large-scale programs whose major cost was often absorbed by the recipient country.[17] When action appeared to be remarkably cost effective and timely, such as a campaign to eradicate smallpox from West and Central Africa, the entire burden of effort was occasionally absorbed by an MDC (Foege et al. 1975).

5.2 Consequences of Mortality Reductions

In this section we can do no more than begin to sketch in the major influences of these mortality declines on populations of the less developed world, since these declines affect virtually every aspect of individual and collective life in a manner that undoubtedly varies with a host of initial conditions present in the population. It is probably wise to begin with the most concrete and least variable effects, the demographic ones.

Other things remaining the same, mortality declines increase the rate of population growth. The initial effect obviously is to increase the crude rate of natural increase by the absolute amount of the decline in the crude death rate. To a close approximation, the long-run effect of a permanent decline is to increase the rate of natural increase by the average (unweighted) decline in age-specific death rates between age zero and the mean age of childbearing (Preston 1974). This effect is almost fully realized within two generations. In neither case is the growth response strongly conditioned by the prevailing level of fertility. Not a shred of doubt remains that the vast majority of the acceleration in world population growth during the twentieth century is attributable to mortality decline rather than to a rise in fertility.

It is important to recognize that changes in rates of population growth typically have very different effects on demographic, economic, and social processes depending on their source. Coale and Hoover (1958) in their classic study were careful to point out that they were studying the economic implications of variation in fertility, but the study has often been misinterpreted as suggesting the deleterious effects of rapid population growth per se. Application of a modified Coale-Hoover model by Barlow (1967, 1968) demonstrated much more ambiguous economic effects when the source of growth acceleration was mortality decline. Loose discussions of relations between population and economic growth are usually aimed implicitly at the fertility component, even though it is mortality variation that has been the root of trends in population growth.

The fundamental reason why effects differ is a difference in the ages of persons affected. Changes in fertility initially affect only the number of zero-year-olds, and permanent changes permanently affect the age distribution of the population. Mortality changes typically affect all ages, and age distributional changes are relatively minor (Coale 1956; Stolnitz 1956). Such as they are, the short-run age distributional changes induced by mortality decline typically increase the proportion of the population at ages below 5 or 10 and above 40 and decrease the proportion at other ages. The pertinent index is the age-specific death rate, μ_x. When this declines by more than the population-weighted average, the proportion of the population in the immediately succeeding ages will rise. Since mortality declines have tended to be largest in absolute (but not proportional) terms at the extremes of life, the dependency burden initially rises. The long-run effect of a permanent decline in mortality is typically to increase the proportion of the population at ages below 20 and above 75. The pertinent age-specific index here is the cumulative change (unweighted) in age-specific death rates since age zero relative to an appropriately defined average (Preston 1974). The long-run effect on the dependency burden is also positive. With the gross reproduction rate fixed at 2.5, a rise in female life expectancy from 30 to 50 to 70 years in stable populations characterized by "West" mortality patterns increases the ratio of those outside of labor force age (15–64) to those within from 0.635 to 0.764 to 0.847 (Coale and Demeny 1966, pp. 82, 98, 114). All of this increase is sustained in the ages below 15. These changes are not trivial, but they are rather small relative to those induced by movements of fertility within its observed range.

It follows from this discussion and the formal analysis that supports it that if all ages experience an identical decline in death rates (usually termed a "neutral" decline), the age composition of the population will be unaffected in both the short run and the long run. The probability of survival from age x *to* age $x + n$ is equal to $\exp\{-\int_x^{x+n} \mu(t)dt\}$, where $\mu(t)$ is the death rate at exact age t. A decline in mortality by amount k at all ages will raise all n-year survival probabilities by the factor, $\exp\{kn\}$. Since the population at each age grows by the same factor (including infants via the greater survivorship of prospective parents), the proportionate age distribution is unaffected. Barring behavioral changes, a decline that is neutrally distributed among population subgroups, however defined (e.g., occupational or educational groups), will not affect population composition. The point is worth emphasis: it is *differential* mortality change that affects population composition. A change that is equally shared affects only size and growth. To the degree that typical mortality changes have been differentially distributed, the first-order changes induced in population composition have been economically unfavorable. Not only have the very young and the very old profited disproportionately, but so have women and unskilled or semiskilled workers.[18] Unlike programs of human resource development, which usually aim directly at an upgrading of population composition in ways that relate to production, programs of mortality decline have typically increased population size and reduced, at least initially, the desirability of its configuration.

Although mortality and fertility variation have very different effects on population composition, the mechanism by which they influence population size is the same in the long run: changes in the annual number of births. The principal long-run effect of mortality decline on population size arises not from the greater survivorship of persons who would have been born in any event, but from the larger number of births that are produced. To see this clearly, suppose that a neutral mortality change occurs to an initially stable population such that all ages experience a permanent reduction in death rates of .02. If age-specific fertility rates remain unchanged, the rate of population growth will increase by .02 and the rate of increase in the annual number of births will also rise by .02. Consider the number of 20-year-olds in the population 60 years after the mortality decline. The original number born into this cohort will be larger as a result of the mortality decline by $[e^{.02(40)} - 1] = 123\%$, whereas their improved survivorship after birth will have increased their numbers by $[e^{.02(20)} - 1] = 49\%$, a growth factor less than half as large. More than half the members of the cohort would not have been born had mortality not declined. This fraction continues to grow over time, but the improved survivorship factor does not. Stated more vividly, any LDC child "saved" from death today adds only one to the population size for a time. But the progeny of that child will ultimately be infinite in numbers if current rates of mortality and fertility are maintained by all generations. The prevailing practice in health economics of ignoring the offspring of the population "saved" seriously misrepresents the effect of health programs on populations (see reviews in Weisbrod 1975 and Klarman 1967).

5.2.1 Economic and Behavioral Responses

In discussing aggregate economic and behavioral responses to mortality decline, it is useful to recognize that all of the responses must make themselves felt through one of four indexes. This follows directly from a formal identity:

$$CDR = CBR + CRNM - R_p + R_{pc},$$

where CDR, CBR, $CRNM$ = crude rates of death, birth, and net migration

R_p, R_{pc} = proportionate rate of growth of total production and of production per capita.

When the crude death rate declines, one of the terms on the right side must change to keep the identity in balance. The first three terms on the right side—birthrates, migration rates, and the economic growth rate—primarily reflect behavioral adjustments to mortality change. The fourth—the growth rate of output per capita—is basically a default option, inevitably activated if none of the other three terms change. If none of the four terms on the right can change, or change for very long, the decline in CDR cannot be sustained. This is the basic Malthusian model, in which the "passion between the sexes" placed a floor on the crude birthrate, a subsistence level of production bounded R_{pc} from below, migration was defined as impossible, and slow technical change and rapidly diminishing returns to labor constrained R_p from above.

As an identity, any term in it could be isolated on one side of the equation and the others forced to "respond" to its changes. The justification for isolating the CDR is provided in the first part of the paper: a substantial fraction of changes in CDR have been induced by factors independent of any term on the right side, and it is reasonable to view them as being forced to respond to it. To the extent that declines in CDR have been produced by increases in rates of growth of production per head, the equation as presented is misleading.[19]

In most of the remainder of this section we will consider the various ways populations appear to have responded to mortality declines, taking each of the possibilities in turn. The review attempts to be positive and historical rather than normative.

Declines in Crude Birthrates

There are a multitude of ways that changes in mortality can induce changes in fertility. Three of the effects are quasi-biological. Declines in mortality change the age structure in such a way as to reduce the proportion of the population in the childbearing years and to reduce crude birthrates if age-specific fertility rates remain constant. Using the earlier example, gains in female life expectancy from 30 to 50 to 70 years, with age-specific fertility held constant at a level that produces a gross reproduction rate of 2.5, changes the crude birthrate from 38.78/1,000 to 37.12 to 35.99. The decline in the crude death rate over this range is from 33.34 to 5.78, so that the decline in the birthrate compensates for 10.1% of the decline in crude death rates through this age-structural route (Coale and Demeny 1966).

A second biological mechanism operates through breast-feeding. Breast-feeding inhibits ovulation, particularly in poorly nourished populations. Survival of the previous birth, by extending lactation, tends to delay the arrival of the next birth. Estimates of the average amount of net delay range as high as 12–13 months in Senegal, Bangladesh, and certain preindustrial European populations, although an estimate of about 7 months is probably more representative of poor agrarian populations (see the review in Preston 1975*b*). Since average interbirth intervals in such populations average about 30–35 months, the compensating variation in fertility to a change of infant mortality rates can be as high as 35% but is more likely to be in the area of 20%. That is, if all a woman's children die in infancy, her average interbirth intervals will be shorter by 20% and she will have approximately 20% more births over her reproductive life than if all had survived. In urban Latin American settings, where breast-feeding is usually short if it occurs at all, the compensating variation from this source is negligible (Rutstein and Medica 1975).

A third quasi-biological influence operates in the opposite direction but is probably fairly weak. Mortality declines make it more likely that marriages will survive through the end of the partners' reproductive periods. In areas such as India where sanctions against widow remarriage are strong, reductions in the incidence of widowhood probably exert an upward pressure on fertility. Arriaga (1967) has argued that this mechanism is responsible for substantial postwar increases in child-woman ratios in certain Latin American populations. However, his argument neglects the age-structural changes that are directly produced by mortality declines. The maximum effect of mortality changes on a woman's completed fertility can be estimated by assuming that no remarriage is possible and that childbearing occurs at a constant rate throughout her reproductive life up to the death of her husband or for 25 years, whichever comes first. Then her completed fertility is simply proportional to the expected number of years lived by the husband in the first 25 years of marriage. Assuming that males are age 20 at marriage, this expectation goes from 20.97 years in a population with a male life expectancy at birth of 30.08 to 24.49 when life expectancy is 68.56

(Coale and Demeny 1966, pp. 7, 23). Fertility would increase by 16.8%, or by perhaps 6 points, while the death rate would decline by perhaps 25 points. Complete prohibition of widow remarriage could thus boost the growth acceleration induced by mortality decline by some 25%, making it roughly equivalent to but opposite in sign from the lactational effect. However, it does not appear that taboos on widow remarriage are sufficiently widespread outside of India to have anywhere near this effect.

In addition to the three quasi-biological links, there are many possible behavioral ones. Since these are the subject of another conference paper (chap. 3), they will not be reviewed here (see also O'Hara 1975). Suffice it to say that the magnitude of one relationship has now been investigated rather carefully in a variety of populations in Asia and Latin America, as well as in preindustrial Europe. It has repeatedly been shown that, among women of a particular parity, those who had experienced one additional child death subsequently bore, on average, far fewer than one additional birth. Furthermore, some of the additional childbearing that did occur could be traced indirectly to the biological link identified above. The studies have attempted to control other characteristics of women believed to influence fertility (see studies by Chowdhury, Khan, and Chen; Heer and Wu; Rutstein and Medica; and Knodel in Committee for . . . Demography 1975). The largest "replacement" effect was 0.28 identified in Taiwan by Heer and Wu. It may be that the dead children were replaced in advance, but the simple demography of death makes this an inefficient reproductive strategy. The large majority of children who die before adulthood do so in the first two or three years of life, and their death can be observed and reacted to by parents during their own reproductive period.

The apparent failure of parents in many LDCs to behave as though they were pursuing a single reproductive target framed in terms of surviving children should not be surprising. It is clear that many of the social norms and sanctions that regulate reproductive behavior in LDCs refer to age at entry into union, frequency of intercourse, postnatal abstinence, number of partners, lactation, remarriage, and so on, rather than specifically to the number of children born or surviving (Polgar 1972). It is not necessary to reject the view that reproducers are goal-directed, but only to recognize that social norms and expectations have established other goals than "the" number of children. These norms and expectations are not responsive to an individual's experience with child death, although they may be responsive to aggregate mortality rates. Such conditioning is in fact the basis of functionalist theories of fertility. Davis (1955) has repeatedly argued that high-mortality populations must adopt a set of institutions and customs producing high fertility or else face extinction. The major adaptive institution he points to is the extended family, which encourages early entry into union by arranging marriages and stimulates fertility by removing many of the child-rearing costs from the parents. The expected positive effect of family extension on fertility has not been observed in most empirical studies at the household level (see the review in Burch and Gendell 1970). More to the point, it is not clear how the group-selection processes that are supposed to have created such institutions in the first place would operate to change them when mortality conditions relax.

There is one aggregate-level linkage between death rates and birthrates that deserves mention because of its apparent importance in preindustrial Europe. In a spatially limited system where land is the basis of wealth and accession to land the prerequisite for marriage, the rate of marriage and hence childbearing will depend upon the rate at which land becomes available, hence on mortality. Exogenous declines in mortality will, more or less automatically, reduce fertility by slowing the turnover of land and delaying marriage. Such a system was apparently an important feature of demographic-economic relations in Western Europe from 1600 to 1800 and may account for the generally late age at marriage in these populations (Habakkuk 1971; Wrigley 1969; see Eversley 1957 for a vivid numerical description of the expected responses to an epidemic). More important, economic historians have suggested that this mechanism, the "European marriage pattern," was a fundamental basis of the industrial revolution since it facilitated capital accumulation by severing the link between the level of mortality and the rate of growth of income per capita (Wrigley 1969; Habakkuk 1971). How important this mechanism is in contemporary less developed countries is unclear. Increased rates of population growth have been accompanied by declining proportions married throughout much of Asia since 1960 or so (Smith 1976). However, many other modernizing influences have also been at work. In Asia, at least, the prevalence of an extended family system in rural areas reduces the dependence of marriage on individual acquisition of land and presumably attenuates the link between population pressure and individuals' marital behavior. In urban areas, however, a "suitable" job may come to play an analogous, though no doubt less decisive, role.

That the sum of responses of fertility to mortality declines in LDCs has been quantitatively weak is shown clearly in the history of population growth rates. Durand (1967, p. 7) puts the annual rate of population growth for LDCs at 0.3% for 1850–1900 and 2.1% for 1950–65. He further suggests that, with few exceptions, birthrates have not declined. The United Nations Population Division "estimates and conjectures" that CDRs in LDCs were 38/1,000 in 1850–1900 and 17/1,000 in 1960–70, whereas CBRs were 40/1,000 and 41/1,000 in the two periods (United Nations 1971, p. 7). These figures suggest no compensating variation in fertility whatever, although mortality declines may have reduced the increase in fertility that would otherwise have occurred. It is true that several of the postulated relations should operate with a lag, and widespread (but small) declines in fertility since 1970 in LDCs might be partially attributed to prior mortality decline. But the evidence is that changes in birthrates have not been a major mechanism of adjustment to date.

Declines in Crude Rates of Net Migration

An increase in out-migration for the world as a whole is clearly impossible, and it has been scarcely more of an option for LDCs as a bloc. Perceived cultural, economic, and political difficulties attendant upon migration from LDCs to MDCs have resulted in MDC immigration quotas that are fixed at a point where they represent a tiny fraction of annual natural increase in LDCs. International migration among LDCs faces similar obstacles (see the discussion in Myrdal 1968, pp. 1459–62). In this matter the present LDC situation is again markedly at variance with that of European populations in the eighteenth and nineteenth centuries, when a substantial amount of population increase was drained off via overseas or transcontinental migration. Friedlander (1969) stresses the importance of this "safety valve" for delaying fertility reductions in England and Sweden. My calculations indicate that 15–25% of persons born in Sweden in the middle decades of the nineteenth century died outside its borders.

When subnational territories are considered, the migration response probably becomes more consequential, because the export of population growth from one area to another faces fewer legal, cultural, and institutional impediments. In Indonesia, the Philippines, and Ceylon, government programs have attempted to redistribute population from dense, rapidly growing areas to sparsely populated ones, although relative to natural increase the movements have been small (Myrdal 1968, pp. 2139–49). How important mortality declines in rural areas have been for rural-urban migration in LDCs has simply not been identified, to my knowledge. The region with apparently the sharpest mortality decline since 1900, Latin America, has also had the most rapid rural to urban migration (United Nations 1971). But both regional peculiarities may have been caused by its more rapid economic growth. Unlike the European situation, net rural-urban migration is not required to maintain constant proportions in the two sectors. Rural birthrates are higher, but so in general are rural death rates. Rates of natural increase are not widely disparate (Davis 1973). It has often been suggested that, in Asia at least, a large fraction of rural natural increase (which accounts for the large bulk of the annual volume) simply cannot be exported to urban areas because the cities cannot create enough new jobs. Even if these predictions prove pessimistic, it remains that, for national aggregates, changes in net migration rates have not been and will not be an important response to mortality decline.

Increases in Growth Rates of Total Production

The effect of population growth on economic growth is obviously a topic whose scope and complexity are too vast to be adequately reviewed here. While the effects of changes in death rates on output are difficult to partial out (see Denison 1962 for one attempt), economic history and economic theory are quite consistent with the view that R_p has been the principal respondent to changes in CDR.

A decline in CDR generally increases the growth rate of the labor force in roughly equal measure. As noted above, the labor force growth rate is typically incremented in the short run by a slightly smaller amount than the population growth rate. But even after accounting for this tendency, if we accept standard estimates of the elasticity of production with respect to changes in the quantity of labor input on the order of 0.5 to 0.8, more than half of the "response" can be accounted for without any change in other inputs or in technology.

There are reasons to believe that other inputs have typically changed in a reinforcing fashion. In some instances (South America, Southern Africa, and much of Asia) the growing population has had access to unutilized land not markedly inferior to that already under production (Myrdal 1968). According to D. Gale Johnson (1974, p. 89), between 1935–39 and 1960 approximately 75% of the increased grain output in developing countries resulted from expansion of the planted area. In some cases the mortality reduction campaigns themselves have liberated large areas of previously inhospitable territory. Taylor and Hall (1967) cite examples of such effects from antimalarial programs in Nepal, Sri Lanka, Sardinia, and Mexico (see also Sorkin 1975). Schultz (1964, pp. 63–70) shows that the response is also present when mortality changes in the opposite direction. An estimated 8% fall in the Indian labor force resulting from the 1918–19 influenza epidemic was accompanied by a reduction of 3.8% in acreage sown.

Expansion of land use obviously cannot continue indefinitely, and to the (apparently minor) degree that fixed factors are important in production, the particular effect of accelerated population growth on per capita production will be negative. For most purposes it is more important to know the effects of mortality decline on the capital supply. With one possibly important exception, the effects should not be radically different from those of increased fertility. The age distributional effects are similar in nature, though muted in the case of mortality change. When mortality declines, the proportion of the population in a stage of dissaving increases—permanently. Households face an increased dependency burden and governments a greater press of immediate consumption demands. Business optimism regarding future demand for their products rises with the growth rate of potential consumers. Business profits and internally financed investments may increase as the labor supply curve shifts outward, unless the shift also reduces consumers' purchasing power. These effects have been reviewed elsewhere in conjunction with fertility effects, and it is not profitable to reconsider them here.

The one possibly important difference is that members of a lower-mortality population can look forward to longer lives in which to reap the benefits of personal investment. There is no such effect when fertility is the source of growth acceleration. The present value of investments with a long gestation period, such as extended schooling, retirement equities, or children, necessarily rises when mortality rates fall. Mushkin (1964), Schultz (1975), and others have suggested that such effects may represent an important economic benefit of reduced mortality.

It seems indisputable that such effects operate, and are probably reinforced by the increased proportion of the population who are in the investment stage. Nevertheless, it appears that the effects are relatively small and can be easily overwhelmed by minor variations in discount rates. To illustrate, define the present value of an investment in the standard manner prior to a change in mortality:

$$P.V. = \int_0^\infty p(a) \left[\frac{B(a) - C(a)}{e^{ra}} \right] da,$$

where $p(a)$ = the probability that the investor will survive a years from the time of investment according to the mortality schedule in effect prior to the mortality decline

$B(a), C(a)$ = benefits and costs of the investment realized or incurred in year a

r = subjective rate of discount, continuously applied.

Now superimpose a neutral mortality decline of 0.01 per year, equivalent to a reduction in the CDR of 10/1,000, that is, a large decline. This is the average reduction in age-specific death rates between ages 15 and 50 when male life expectancy at birth increases from 30.1 to 51.8 years (Coale and Demeny 1966, pp. 7, 16). The new present value is

$$P.V.' = \int_0^\infty p(a)\, e^{.01a} \left[\frac{B(a) - C(a)}{e^{ra}} \right] da$$

$$= \int_0^\infty p(a) \left[\frac{B(a) - C(a)}{e^{(r-.01)a}} \right] da.$$

That is, such a major change in mortality conditions has the same effect on present value as reducing the discount rate by only 0.01 and retaining the initial mortality conditions. In view of the wide variation that seems to prevail in discount rates, as partially reflected in the common analytic practice of applying several that differ by 0.05 or even more, it is readily seen that mortality prospects are a relatively minor influence on present value.

As a more concrete illustration, we will compute the internal rate of return on investment in schooling and show how it is affected by empirically observed variation in mortality. We have chosen Mexico for the illustration because Carnoy (1967) provides all of the necessary information except life tables.[20] We will compute the internal rate of return for a 15-year-old male who has completed grade 8 from his subsequent completion of grades 9, 10, and 11. Three mortality schedules are used: the male life table of Mexico, 1921, having a life expectancy at birth of 33.66 years (Arriaga 1968); the male life table of Mexico, 1966, having a life expectancy at birth of 59.49 years (Keyfitz and Flieger 1971); and immortality. Results are shown in table 5.6.

It is clear from this table that the increment to the private or social rate of return that results from replacing an e^o_0 of 33.7 by immortality is only 1.5 points. This is approximately the difference it makes to use continuous rather than once-a-year compoundings. The reason for the weak effect is simply that mortality rates in young and middle adulthood are not high enough even in very high mortality populations to substantially alter expected payoffs. The large variability in rates experienced in childhood do not figure in the calculation, and the large variability at older ages is heavily discounted.

The effect of mortality variation would be somewhat stronger if individuals were predominantly risk-aversive and made decisions on the basis of the entire distribution of expected outcomes rather than simply on the basis of the mean. Higher mortality adds greater variability to the distribution of expected outcomes as well as reducing the mean. It increases the chance that zero or negative returns will accrue to investment, and this increase is faster than is the reduction in mean. Nevertheless, for the bulk of investors—those in early and middle adulthood

Table 5.6 **Internal Rate of Return from Completing Grades 9, 10, and 11 in Mexico, 1963, under Varying Assumptions about Mortality**

Assumption	Private Rate of Return	Social Rate of Return
Mexican life table of 1921	12.8	9.9
Mexican life table of 1966	13.9	10.9
Immortality	14.3	11.4

Sources: Carnoy (1967); Keyfitz and Flieger (1971); Arriaga (1968).

—it does not appear that even very radical mortality change could exert much influence on perceived investment profitability.

On balance, it does not appear that the effects of population growth acceleration on capital formation when mortality is the source should be markedly different *in nature* from the effects when fertility is the source. The Coale-Hoover model postulates a less-than-proportionate increase in capital supply when the population grows faster via higher fertility, and this feature is retained when the effects of mortality change are simulated (Barlow 1967, 1968). Largely for this reason, Barlow concludes that the antimalarial campaign in Ceylon ultimately had negative effects on per capita income growth, even after the improved health of the labor force is accounted for. Confidence in this conclusion depends on one's confidence in the savings-investment assumptions of the Coale-Hoover model.

It is also possible that mortality reductions foster economies of scale in production and an intensification of individual work effort. Again, the subject is very complex, and in most respects the analysis of mortality variation need not differ from that of fertility variation. A postulated difference is that mortality control programs have an important demonstration effect (Mushkin 1964; Fein 1964; Malenbaum 1970; and others). That is, they demonstrate that individuals can control their own destiny through the rational application of science and technology. They attest to the power of man in contrast to that of the supernatural and hence spark work effort and a stronger motivation toward self-fulfillment. Malenbaum (1970) argues that this is the basis of observed associations between mortality rates and labor productivity, but there are surely other mechanisms that offer more plausible interpretations. The contention has not been put to a rigorous test. It seems inconsistent with observations that poor illiterate farmers in LDCs have always responded quickly to new and profitable opportunities and technologies (Johnson 1974). A sense of personal control over the environment is one of the strongest components of "modern" attitudes (Sack 1974, p. 90). But the importance of mortality declines in the development of this attitude and the influence of the attitude on output remain to be demonstrated, important as the issue may be.

Changes in Growth Rates of Production per Capita

With constant technology and no changes in nonlabor factors of production, it is reasonable to expect that a CDR decline of 10/1,000 would raise the growth rate of total production only by 0.6–0.7% or so. If no birthrate or migration adjustments were forthcoming, the rate of growth of per capita income would decline by 0.3–0.4%. This is not a large amount relative to prevailing growth rates, and it is not surprising that the mortality declines have left no unmistakable imprint on per capita national economic growth rates.

Nevertheless, there are circumstances where the mortality decline has apparently had a decisive negative effect on economic well-being. Perhaps the most vivid account is offered by William Allan (1965, especially chap. 21). Allan outlines a cycle of land degeneration in East Africa that was, he argues, initiated by a mortality reduction. Population pressure at the kin-group level led to land subdivision and fragmentation, since landowners were expected to share their holdings with needy kin. Subdivision led in turn to a shortening of the fallow period and to soil depletion and erosion. Declining yields led to accelerated shortening of the fallow and to ultimate soil exhaustion. "Perhaps the greatest 'sin' of the suzerain powers was the saving of life, the lives of millions of men who under the old conditions would have died in early childhood, or in later life, of famine, disease, and violence" (Allan 1965, p. 338). Ultimately the response was out-migration, but not before a stage of economic misery was encountered. The initial stages of intensified land use are those described by Boserup (1965), but the outcome is very different. Instead of self-sustaining growth supported by a newly developed work ethic, the result was simply impoverishment. Obviously, some soils can support extreme intensification and multiple cropping and others cannot. Population pressure by itself is clearly not sufficient for sustained technological change, nor does it appear to be necessary once the possibilities of trade are opened up.

It is clear that general statements cannot be made about how populations have reacted or will react to exogenous mortality declines. The reaction will depend on a wide variety of initial conditions. In agrarian populations it appears that the most important conditioning factors are type of soil, land tenancy and kinship-marriage systems, density, possibilities for out-migration, savings and investment relationships, and the saliency of surviving-children goals. A great deal of work in recent economic and demographic history remains to be done before the quantitative details of the outline sketched in these sections can be confidently filled in.

Appendix

Table 5.A.1 Estimates of National Indexes about 1940

Country	Life Expectancy at Birth	Year of Estimate	Source	Daily Calories per Capita Available at Retail Level	Year of Estimate	Source: (6) Unless Noted
Australia	66.09	(40)	(2)	3,128	(40)	
Belgium	59.08	(38–40)	(3)	2,885	(40)	
Canada	64.62	(40–42)	(1)	3,109	(40)	
Czechoslovakia	56.79	(37)	(1)	2,761	(40)	
Chile	38.10	(40)	(4)	2,481	(40)	
Colombia	36.04	(38)	(4)	1,860	(38)	(7)
Denmark	66.31	(40)	(2)	3,249	(40)	
Egypt	38.60	(36–38)	(1)	2,199	(40)	
Finland	57.39[a]	(40)	(1)	2,950	(40)	
Greece	54.37	(40)	(1)	2,523	(40)	
Guatemala	30.40	(40)	(4)	—	—	
Honduras	37.50	(40)	(4)	2,079	(40)	
Hungary	56.57	(41)	(1)	2,815	(40)	
India	32.27	(41)	(5)	2,021	(40)	
Ireland	60.02	(40)	(1)	3,184	(40)	
Japan	49.12	(39–41)	(3)	2,268	(40)	
Korea	48.90	(38)	(1)	1,904	(40)	
Luxembourg	60.07	(38–42)	(3)	2,820	(34–38)	(8)
Mexico	38.80	(40)	(4)	1,909	(40)	
Netherlands	65.43	(40)	(2)	2,958	(40)	
New Zealand	67.00	(36)	(2)	3,281	(40)	
Nicaragua	34.50	(40)	(4)	—	—	
Panama	42.40	(40)	(4)	—	—	
Peru	36.50	(40)	(4)	2,090	(40)	
Philippines	46.26	(38)	(1)	2,021	(40)	
Portugal	51.06	(40)	(2)	2,461	(40)	
Puerto Rico	46.09	(39–41)	(1)	2,219	(40)	
Spain	50.18	(40)	(1)	2,788	(40)	
Sweden	66.64	(40)	(1)	3,052	(40)	
Switzerland	64.88	(40)	(2)	3,049	(40)	
Taiwan	47.80	(41)	(1)	2,153	(40)	
Thailand	40.02	(37–38)	(1)	2,173	(40)	
Turkey	33.91	(35–45)	(15)	2,619	(40)	
United Kingdom	61.64	(40)	(2)	3,005	(40)	
United States	63.74	(39–41)	(1)	3,249	(40)	
Venezuela	39.91	(41)	(1)	—	—	

National Income per Capita in 1970 U.S. Dollars	Year of Estimate	Source: (9) Unless Noted	Percentage Illiterate	Age Range	Year of Estimate	Source: (10) Unless Noted	Population in Thousands (1940)(13)
1,128	(38–40)		2.5	—	(40)	(14)	7,039
715	(38–39)		4.5	—	(40)	(14)	8,301
1,041	(38–40)		3.16	10+	(40)		11,682
438	(38)		3.6	—	(37)	(14)	14,429
371	(38–40)		28.2	10+	(40)		5,063
190	(38–40)		44.10	10+	(38)		8,702
971	(38–40)		1.5	—	(40)	(14)	3,832
167	(39)		84.9	10+	(37)		16,008
419	(39)		8.8	—	(40)	(14)	3,698
187	(38)		34.4	—	(40)	(14)	7,319
78	(40)		65.4	7+	(40)		2,201
109	(41–42)		66.35	10+	(45)		1,146
318	(38–40)		6.0	10+	(41)		9,344
67	(38–39)		86.5	10+	(41)	(10,11)[b]	316,004
665	(40)		1.5	—	(40)	(14)	2,993
260	(39)		—	—	—		71,400
—	—		68.6	10+	(30)		21,817
795	(39)		4.4	—	(40)	(14)	292
138	(40)		51.5	10+	(40)		19,815
889	(38)		1.5	—	(40)	(14)	8,879
1,055	(38–40)		1.5	—	(40)	(14)	1,573
105	(40)		63.0	7+	(40)	(12)	825
374	(40)		35.25	10+	(40)		620
89	(40)	(16)	56.35	10+	(40)		7,033
113	(38)		37.75	10+	(48)		15,814
—	—		48.7	10+	(40)		7,696
413	(38–40)		31.5	10+	(40)		1,880
361	(40)	(16)	23.2	10+	(40)		25,757
1,091	(40)		0.1	10+	(30)		6,356
1,246	(40)		1.5	—	(40)	(14)	4,234
—	—		78.7	5+	(40)		6,163
128	(39)	(11)	46.25	10+	(47)		14,755
212	(39)		79.1	10+	(35)		17,620
1,334	(38–40)		1.5	—	(40)	(14)	41,862
1,549	(40)		4.2	10+	(40)	(13)	132,594
291	(40)		56.50	10+	(41)		3,803

Table 5.A.1 (continued)

Sources:
1. United Nations, *Statistical Yearbook* (1967).
2. Preston, Keyfitz, and Schoen (1972).
3. Keyfitz and Fleiger (1968).
4. Arriaga (1968).
5. Estimated by Davis (1951, pp. 62–63).
6. Estimates prepared by the Food and Agriculture Organization of the United Nations, cited in "Food, Income, and Mortality," *Population Index* 13, no. 2 (April 1947): 96–103.
7. United Nations, *Statistical Yearbook* (1951).
8. United Nations, Food and Agriculture Organization, *Production Yearbook* (1958).
9. Estimates prepared by the Technical Group, U.S. Bureau of the Budget; cited in "Food, Income, and Mortality," *Population Index* 13, no. 2 (April 1947): 96–103. All figures have been converted to 1970 U.S. dollars by application of the consumer price index from U.S. Bureau of the Census, *Statistical Abstract of the United States*, various issues.
10. United Nations, *Statistical Yearbook* (1949–50).
11. United Nations, *Statistical Yearbook* (1955).
12. United Nations Educational, Scientific and Cultural Organization, *Basic facts and figures: Illiteracy, libraries, museums, books, newspapers, newsprint, film and radios* (Paris, 1952).
13. United Nations, *Demographic Yearbook* (1960).
14. Banks (1971).
15. Calculated by author from estimates of e_5^0 presented in Shorter (1968). The Coale-Demeny "South" model mortality pattern was assumed to apply.
16. United Nations, *National Income Statistics of Various Countries, 1938–1948* (Lake Success, N.Y., 1950).

[a]Average 1936–40 and 1941–50.
[b]Interpolated from data for 1931 and 1951.

Table 5.A.2 National Indexes about 1970

	Life Expectancy at Birth 1970–75 (1)	Percentage Illiterate of the Adult Population (2)	Year of Esti-mate (2)	1970 National Income per Capita (1970 U.S. $) (3)	1970 Daily Calories Available for Consumption, per Capita (4)	1970 Population (in 1,000s) (1)	Index of Income Inequality (5)	Year of Esti-mate	Coverage
Africa									
Algeria	53.2	52.5	1971	295	1,710	14,330	—		
Angola	38.5	87.5	1973*	280	1,910	5,670	—		
Botswana	43.5	87.0	1971	132	2,040	617	—		
Burundi	39.0	35.0	1974*	68	2,330	3,350	—		
Central African Rep.	41.0	82.0	1975*	122	2,170	1,612	—		
Chad	38.5	90.0	1975*	70	2,060	3,640	—		
Congo	43.5	65.0	1970*	281	2,160	1,191	—		
Dahomey	41.0	80.0	1975*	81	2,250	2,686	—		
Egypt	52.4	62.0	1975*	202	2,360	33,329	−6.5660	1965	Nat. Household
Ethiopia	38.0	93.0	1975*	72	2,150	24,855	—		
Gabon	41.0	88.0	1974*	468	2,210	500	−17.2442	1960	Nat. Population
Gambia	40.0	90.0	1971*	99	2,370	463	—		
Ghana	43.5	56.5	1971	236	2,200	8,628	—		
Guinea	41.0	92.5	1971*	79	2,040	3,291	—		
Ivory Coast	43.5	80.0	1973*	325	2,490	4,310	−9.8088	1970	Nat. Income Recip.
Kenya	50.0	75.0	1975*	130	2,350	11,247	−13.1644	1969	Nat. Income Recip.
Liberia	43.5	88.0	1970	181	2,040	1,523	—		
Libyan Arab Rep.	52.9	68.0	1974*	1,450	2,540	1,938	—		
Madagascar	43.5	60.0	1975*	123	2,350	6,932	−9.8964	1960	Nat. Population
Malawi	41.0	75.0	1976*	68	2,150	4,360	−7.0502	1969	Nat. Household
Mali	38.0	90.0	1972	50	2,170	5,047	—		

Table 5.A.2 (continued)

	Life Expectancy at Birth 1970–75 (1)	Percentage Illiterate of the Adult Population (2)	Year of Esti-mate (2)	1970 National Income per Capita (1970 U.S. $) (3)	1970 Daily Calories Available for Consumption, per Capita (4)	1970 Population (in 1,000s) (1)	Index of Income Inequality (5)	Year of Esti-mate	Coverage
Mauritius	65.5	20.0	1974*	223	2,370	824	—		
Mauritania	38.5	95.0	1972*	147	2,060	1,162	—		
Morocco	52.9	78.6	1971	225	2,400	15,126	—		
Mozambique	43.5	80.0	1972	228	2,190	8,234	—		
Niger	38.5	94.0	1973*	70	2,180	4,016	—		
Nigeria	41.0	74.0	1973	135	2,290	55,073	—		
Rhodesia	51.5	95.0	1972	257	2,550	5,308	−14.8362	1968	Nat. Income Recip.
Rwanda	41.0	90.0	1973*	57	2,160	3,679	—		
Senegal	40.0	95.0	1971*	201	2,300	3,925	−12.1394	1960	Nat. Population
Sierra Leone	43.5	90.0	1974*	150	2,240	2,644	—		
Somalia	41.0	95.0	1974*	85	1,770	2,789	—		
South Africa	51.5	56.0	1974*	680	2,730	21,500	−14.3543	1965	Nat. Population
Sudan	48.6	80.0	1973	109	2,130	15,695			
Togo	41.0	90.0	1976*	125	2,160	1,960			
Tunisia	54.1	60.0	1972	257	2,060	5,137	−9.7467	1961	Nat. Population
Uganda	50.0	70.0	1976*	127	2,230	9,806			
United Rep. of the Cameroon	41.0	35.0	1976*	183	2,230	5,836	—		
United Rep. of Tanzania	44.5	71.0	1967	94	1,700	13,273	−8.1535	1967	Nat. Household
Upper Volta	38.0	90.0	1972	62	1,940	5,384	—		
Zaire	43.5	65.0	1971	118	2,040	21,638	—		
Zambia	44.5	52.7	1969	345	2,040	4,295	—		

Table 5.A.2 (continued)

	Life Expectancy at Birth 1970–75 (1)	Percentage Illiterate of the Adult Population (2)	Year of Esti-mate (2)	1970 National Income per Capita (1970 U.S. $) (3)	1970 Daily Calories Available for Consumption, per Capita (4)	1970 Population (in 1,000s) (1)	Index of Income Inequality (5)	Year of Esti-mate	Coverage
Asia									
Afghanistan	40.3	92.5	1973	83	1,950	16,978	—		
Bangladesh	35.8	90.0	1973	111	1,860	67,692	−3.5534	1967	Nat. Household
Burma	50.0	30.0	1974*	73	2,230	27,748	—		
Cyprus	71.4	18.0	1973	688	2,460	633	−3.3164	1966	Urban Household
India	49.5	40.0	1971	93	2,060	543,132	−7.6103	1968	Nat. Household
Indonesia	47.5	40.0	1971	98	1,920	119,467	—		
Iran	51.0	65.5	1974	352	2,080	28,359	−8.2776	1968	Urban Household
Iraq	52.7	70.0	1974*	311	2,250	9,356	—		
Israel	71.0	12.8	1974*	1,654	2,970	2,958	−3.1183	1970	Urban Household
Japan	73.3	2.0	1975*	1,636	2,310	104,331	−3.3217	1963	Nat. Household
Jordan	53.2	62.5	1972*	260	2,470	2,280	—		
Khmer Rep.	45.4	15.0	1973	123	2,410	7,060	—		
Korea, Rep. of	60.6	8.5	1970	252	2,420	30,721	−2.2963	1971	Nat. Household
Laos	40.4	75.0	1970*	71	2,080	2,962	—		
Lebanon	63.2	14.0	1975*	521	2,380	2,469	—		
Malaysia	59.4	24.0	1970	295	2,400	10,466	−10.0406	1970	Nat. Household
Nepal	43.6	86.0	1971	80	2,050	11,232	—		
Pakistan	49.8	83.0	1973	164	2,280	60,449	—		
Philippines	58.4	16.5	1970	225	1,920	37,604	−8.6939	1971	Nat. Household
Saudi Arabia	45.3	75.0	1973*	495	1,920	7,740	—		
Singapore	69.5	24.5	1974	918	2,080	2,075	—		

Table 5.A.2 (continued)

	Life Expectancy at Birth 1970–75 (1)	Percentage Illiterate of the Adult Population (2)	Year of Esti-mate (2)	1970 National Income per Capita (1970 U.S. $) (3)	1970 Daily Calories Available for Consumption, per Capita (4)	1970 Population (in 1,000s) (1)	Index of Income Inequality (5)	Year of Esti-mate	Coverage
Asia (continued)									
Sri Lanka	67.8	22.0	1971	160	2,240	12,514	−4.4313	1970	Nat. Household
Syria	54.0	60.0	1970	258	2,530	6,247	—		
Taiwan	69.4(7)	5.0(6)	1965	295(7)	2,662(7)	14,334	−3.6354	1964	Nat. Household
Thailand	58.0	18.0	1970	167	2,330	35,745	−8.3579	1962	Nat. Household
Turkey	56.9	44.0	1970	348	2,770	35,232	−11.6389	1968	Nat. Household
Vietnam, Rep. of	40.5	23.0	1971	232	2,340	17,952	−3.8293	1964	Rural Household
Yemen	44.8	82.5	1975*	77	1,970	5,767	—		
Yemen, P.D.R.	44.8	90.0	1970*	96	2,020	1,436	—		
Latin America									
Argentina	68.2	8.0	1973*	1,065	3,150	23,748	−6.2544	1961	Nat. Household
Bolivia	46.8	58.5	1973	191	1,840	4,780	—		
Brazil	61.4	33.0	1970	376	2,600	95,204	−17.7304	1970	Nat. Household
Chile	62.6	12.0	1970	618	2,460	9,369	−8.4001	1968	Nat. Household
Colombia	60.9	21.5	1973	358	2,250	22,075	−10.6656	1970	Nat. Economic Active Population
Costa Rica	68.2	10.0	1973	522	2,470	1,737	−6.4897	1971	Nat. Household
Dominican Rep.	57.8	32.0	1970	334	2,060	4,343	—		
Ecuador	59.6	30.0	1970	255	2,040	6,031	−17.3614	1970	Nat. Economic Active Population
El Salvador	57.8	40.0	1971	283	1,890	3,516	−8.1625	1969	Nat. Population
Guatemala	52.9	62.0	1974*	343	2,120	5,298	−2.8074	1966	Rural Household

Table 5.A.2 (continued)

	Life Expectancy at Birth 1970–75 (1)	Percentage Illiterate of the Adult Population (2)	Year of Esti- mate (2)	1970 National Income per Capita (1970 U.S. $) (3)	1970 Daily Calories Available for Consumption, per Capita (4)	1970 Population (in 1,000s) (1)	Index of Income Inequality (5)	Year of Esti- mate	Coverage
Latin America (continued)									
Guyana	67.9	14.0	1974*	319	2,080	709	—		
Haiti	50.0	90.0	1974*	100	1,720	4,325	—		
Honduras	53.5	53.0	1974*	259	2,180	2,553	−14.9221	1968	Nat. Household
Jamaica	69.5	18.0	1970	600	2,300	1,882	—		
Mexico	63.2	24.0	1970	655	2,560	50,313	—		
Nicaragua	52.9	47.0	1971	423	2,380	1,970	—		
Panama	66.5	21.5	1973	646	2,520	1,458	−11.2564	1969	Nat. Economic Active Population
Paraguay	61.9	38.0	1973	230	2,800	2,301	—		
Peru	55.7	44.3	1970	293	2,310	13,248	−14.7827	1971	Nat. Economic Active Population
Trinidad and Tobago	69.5	30.4	1970	732	2,360	955	—		
Uruguay	69.8	9.0	1975*	799	2,860	2,955	−6.8128	1967	Nat. Household
Venezuela	64.7	35.2	1971	954	2,460	10,559	−10.5676	1962	Nat. Household
North America									
Canada	72.4	1.0	1975*	3,369	3,190	21,406	−4.0518	1965	Nat. Household
United States	71.3	1.0	1969	4,289	3,270	204,879	−6.6384	1966	Nat. Household
Puerto Rico	72.1	27.9	1970	1,744	2,450	2,743	—		

Table 5.A.2 (continued)

	Life Expectancy at Birth 1970–75 (1)	Percentage Illiterate of the Adult Population (2)	Year of Esti-mate (2)	1970 National Income per Capita (1970 U.S. $) (3)	1970 Daily Calories Available for Consumption, per Capita (4)	1970 Population (in 1,000s) (1)	Index of Income Inequality (5)	Year of Esti-mate	Coverage
Europe									
Austria	71.2	1.0	1974*	1,730	3,340	7,447			
Belgium	72.9	2.0	1975*	2,421	3,390	9,638			
Bulgaria	71.8	5.0	1975*	2,726	3,300	8,490	−1.5225	1962	Nat. Workers
Czechoslovakia	69.3	0.0	1974*	3,013	3,190	14,339	−1.1290	1964	Nat. Workers
Denmark	73.9	1.0	1974*	2,898	3,230	4,929	−4.9775	1966	Nat. Income Recip.
Finland	70.4	0.0	1975*	1,998	3,020	4,606	−9.8462	1962	Nat. Income Recip.
France	72.6	3.0	1975*	2,550	3,210	50,670	−11.4365	1962	Nat. Household
Germany, W.	70.6	1.0	1970*	2,752	3,230	60,700	−7.5125	1964	Nat. Income Recip.
Greece	71.8	15.6	1971	1,051	2,900	8,793	—		
Hungary	69.5	2.0	1975*	2,244	3,180	10,338	−2.1548	1969	Nat. Population
Ireland	71.8	1.0	1974*	1,244	3,420	2,954	—		
Italy	72.0	7.0	1975*	1,591	3,170	53,565	—		
Luxembourg	70.8	2.0	1975*	2,613	3,390	339	—		
Malta	70.8	12.0	1974*	721	2,680	326	—		
Netherlands	73.8	2.0	1973*	2,232	3,290	13,032	—		
Norway	74.5	0.0	1974*	2,458	2,920	3,877	—		
Poland	70.1	2.2	1970	5,766	3,270	32,473	−2.2046	1964	Nat. Workers
Portugal	68.0	45.0	1970*	684	2,890	8,628	—		
Spain	72.1	19.9	1970	884	2,620	33,779	−5.1072	1965	Nat. Household
Sweden	73.3	0.1	1975*	3,724	2,800	8,043	−6.1269	1963	Nat. Income Recip.
Switzerland	72.4	0.0	1973*	2,963	3,250	6,267	—		
United Kingdom	72.3	10.0	1975*	1,990	3,140	55,480	−4.0915	1968	Nat. Household

Table 5.A.2 (continued)

	Life Expectancy at Birth 1970–75 (1)	Percentage Illiterate of the Adult Population (2)	Year of Esti- mate (2)	1970 National Income per Capita (1970 U.S. $) (3)	1970 Daily Calories Available for Consumption, per Capita (4)	1970 Population (in 1,000s) (1)	Index of Income Inequality (5)	Year of Esti- mate	Coverage
Oceania									
Australia	72.4	1.5	1975*	2,633	3,050	12,552	−3.6895	1968	Nat. Household
New Zealand	72.0	2.0	1975*	2,008	3,330	2,820	—		

Sources: (1) United Nations, *Selected World Demographic Indicators by Countries 1950–2000* (Population Division, Department of Economic and Social Affairs of the United Nations, 1975).

(2) Unstarred: United Nations Educational, Scientific, and Cultural Organization, *Statistical Yearbook, 1973* (Paris, 1974), table 1.4; starred: United States, State Department, *Background Notes*, individual country volumes, various years 1970–76.

(3) United Nations, *Statistical Yearbook, 1974*, tables 181, 188.

(4) United Nations, Food and Agriculture Organization, *The State of Food and Agriculture 1974: World Review* (Rome, 1975).

(5) Jain, Shail, "Size Distribution of Income" (International Bank for Reconstruction and Development, Bank Staff Working Paper no. 190, November, 1974).

(6) Kenneth Clark et al., *Area Handbook for the Republic of China* (Washington, D.C.: Department of the Army, 1969), p. viii.

(7) Taiwan, Council for International Economic Cooperation and Development, *Taiwan Statistical Data Book* (1972). All figures refer to 1970.

Table 5.A.3 **National Indexes Used in Analysis of Mortality Change, 1940–70**

	Malaria Endemicity in 1943[a] (1)	Annual Average International Economic Aid Received 1954–72[b c] (2)	External Assistance Received for Community Water Supply and Sewage Disposal Projects 1966–70[b] (3)
Australia	1	—0	0
Belgium	0	—0	0
Canada	0	—0	0
Chile	1	13.29	.14
Colombia	3	5.13	2.30
Czechoslovakia	0	—0	0
Denmark	0	—0	0
Egypt	2	7.61	.18
Finland	0	—0	0
Greece	2	19.55(4)	0
Guatemala	3	3.35[d]	3.45
Honduras	3	4.05[d]	.90
Hungary	0	—0	0
India	3	1.71	0
Ireland	0	—0	0
Japan	1	—0	0
Korea (South)	1	10.15	.52
Luxembourg	0	—0	0
Mexico	3	1.50	.34
Netherlands	0	—0	0
New Zealand	0	—0	0
Nicaragua	3	5.78[d]	3.40
Panama	3	10.79	19.48
Peru	2	4.13	3.55
Philippines	3	2.02	.58
Portugal	1	—0	0
Puerto Rico	2	—0	0
Spain	1	9.22(4)	0
Sweden	0	—0	0
Switzerland	0	—0	0
Taiwan	3	7.09	0
Thailand	3	1.63	.09
Turkey	3	—0	0
United Kingdom	0	—0	0
United States	0	—0	0
Venezuela	3	2.82	3.71

Sources: (1) Shattuk (1951, p. 4; 1943 map prepared by U.S. Army Medical Intelligence Branch); Faust (1941); Boyd (1949).
(2) United Nations, *Statistical Yearbook* (1958–74).
(3) World Health Organization, *World Health Statistics Report* (1973), vol. 26, no. 11.
(4) Organization for Economic Cooperation and Development, *Development Cooperation: Efforts and Policies of the Members of the Development Assistance Committee, 1973 Review* (Paris, 1973).

Notes

1. The zero-order correlation between e^o_0 and the natural log of national income per capita for the 120 countries in appendix table 5.A.2 is 0.859; the correlation between e^o_0 and national income itself is only 0.693.

2. Causes eliminated include influenza/pneumonia/bronchitis, diarrheal disease, and maternal mortality, and also a proportion of "other and unknown causes" equal by age to the proportion of known causes assigned to infectious diseases at that age.

3. The age distribution used for direct standardization is that of a female "West" stable population with $e^o_0 = 65$ and $r = .01$ (Coale and Demeny 1966).

4. WHO in conjunction with the United Nations Population Division has estimated that life expectancy for LDCs as a whole was 49.6 in 1965–70 (World Health Organization 1974*b*, p. 23). Life expectancy in 1900 is the author's guess based upon life tables calculated by Arriaga for Latin America and on life tables for India, Taiwan, and Japan around the turn of the century. Corresponding ASCDRs were computed by the author based on relationships between the two mortality measures in the set of 165 populations employed by Preston and Nelson (1974).

5. Pairwise deletion was employed for missing data in the 1940 regressions. That is, results are based upon correlation matrices computed exclusively on the basis of data that were available. *N* is taken as 28, the number of cases for which observations were complete. One observation was missing on literacy, three on national income, and four on calorie consumption. For no country was more than one piece of information missing. The data on LDCs were considered too valuable to sacrifice all information because one piece was missing. Standard errors are shown in parentheses.

6. Several alternative specifications of these equations were employed, but results were not appreciably altered. These included polynomial representations of income and calories and measurement of *CAL* from different base points. The R^2's for equations including first- and second-degree terms for *Y* and *CAL* were lower than those for the specification presented in the text despite the addition of two variables. The use of other base points for *CAL* left R^2 unaffected to four decimals. Population-weighted regressions were rejected on the grounds that they gave too much weight to India, where measurement of variables was believed to be unusually poor, especially in 1940.

7. There are of course many ways to attribute differences to changes in values of variables and to changes in coefficients, none of them clearly preferable. In this instance we are constrained by the unavailability of data for most LDCs in 1940. Substitution of 1970 values of the regressors into the 1970 equation will not, of

---

[a]0 = virtually none; 1 = low; 2 = moderate; 3 = high.

[b]Current U.S. dollars per capita.

[c]Includes net official flow of external resources to individual countries from developed market economies and multilateral agencies and bilateral commitments of capital by centrally planned economies. "Military expenditures and contributions are excluded as far as possible."

[d]Information not available for 1966 through 1968.

[e]Information for 1970–72 from source 4.

course, usually yield the correct 1970 life expectancy for a country. But the predictions must be very nearly correct in the aggregate, since the regression plane must pass through the mean of the variables and since 94 of the 120 observations are LDCs.

8. This figure is close to the 9.7 estimate derived by Preston (1975*a*, p. 238), who considered only income and used cruder, regional income distributions of 1963 to evaluate changes between 1938 and 1963.

9. Once again, pairwise deletion is employed for cases of missing data.

10. The mean values of *AID* and *WAT* for the 17 LDCs were 4.77 and 2.21, respectively.

11. $16.46 = 31.47 - .0211(2.59) - .4063(39.39) + .0750(4.77) + .2939(2.21)$. Of the 16.46 year gain, 1.01 years is attributed to external aid.

12. A large majority of countries in the WHO survey listed lack of financing as the principal barrier to expanded water supply and sewerage systems (World Health Organization 1973).

13. For an account of the impact of the Catholic diocese of Oklahoma on mortality in a Maya village, see Early 1970. The experience was probably repeated hundreds of times.

14. For ample documentation, see World Bank (1975) and Bryant (1969).

15. Compiled from United Nations, *Statistical Yearbook*, 1974, table 197. Figures refer to thirty-nine LDCs.

16. WHO has compiled estimates of private consumption expenditures on health care in certain LDCs (World Health Organization 1970). The percentage of total private consumption that is spent on health can be compared with the proportion of GNP represented by government health expenditure, a procedure that reduces incomparabilities resulting from differences in the years of estimate. The percentages are the following (private consumption appearing first): Sierre Leone, 2.9 and 0.9; Jordan, 0.6 and 2.8; Thailand, 3.6 and 1.2; the Philippines, 1.7 and 0.5; Malaysia, 2.4 and 2.5; Panama, 4.0 and 2.2; Jamaica, 1.1 and 2.7. Government health expenditures are from World Bank (1975, annex 3).

17. WHO, for example, does not absorb any materials costs but views its role exclusively as providing technical, advisory, and educational assistance (Goodman 1971, pp. 203–4). Dispute over the provisions of assistance for material led to the "resignation" from WHO of Soviet-bloc countries between 1949 and 1955.

18. The class distribution of gains in mortality is not well documented. There was a sharp contraction of age-standardized mortality ratios for various classes in England during the twentieth century (Antonovsky 1967, p. 63). Even constant ratios would entail reductions in absolute differences, which is the pertinent index when population composition is considered.

19. This is a less serious problem than it might at first appear. The coefficients of $1nY$ presented earlier range from 3.6 to 7.0 (the latter observed when no other term except income distribution is present in the cross-sectional analysis). A 1-point increase in the rate of per capita economic growth would thus be associated with at most a gain in life expectancy of 0.07 years. A gain in $e^o{}_0$ of 2 years is roughly associated with a drop in CDR of 0.0015. Thus, a 0.01 gain in the rate of economic growth would be expected to reduce the CDR by at most 0.07 $(.0015/2) = 0.000053$, or by 0.53% of the change in R_{pc}.

20. Earnings differentials were obtained from a 1963 survey of 4,000 urban wage earners. Adjusted earnings differentials presented in Carnoy's (1967) table 3 are employed. Retirement was assumed to occur at age 65. The continuously compounded rate of return was calculated using the formula presented in the text, with

P.V. set equal to zero. For calculation of social costs, the average annual public expenditure per student by grade is added to direct personal outlays and income forgone.

Comment J. D. Durand

I will attempt to fit some of Preston's findings with regard to the determinants of mortality, and related results in Ronald Lee's paper (chap. 9), into a sketch of salient features of the evolution of determinants of the overall levels and trends of mortality during recent centuries and decades.

Results of recent work in this field at the University of Pennsylvania suggest that the typical form of the trend of expectation of life in countries making the transition from premodern to modern regimes of mortality may be represented by an essentially logistic curve, which can be divided into fairly distinct phases as follows:

0—pretransitional phase, in which expectation of life fluctuates around a nearly constant long-term level;

1—initial phase of transition, in which expectation of life increases irregularly at a relatively slow long-term average rate;

2—"takeoff" phase, in which expectation of life rises at a steady, rapid rate;

3—final phase, in which expectation of life rises slowly and appears to be approaching a ceiling at a high level.

I will attempt to draw a tentative general sketch of principal causal factors that have contributed to the increases in expectation of life (e) during each of these phases of the transition, in terms of the following simplified formula: $e = f(y, k, s, n, \ldots)$ where y stands for income per head, k for knowledge of the causes of disease and death and methods of prevention and treatment (including what the layman knows as well as what the physician knows), s for social action in the broad field of health protection, and n for natural factors.

This is not a comprehensive formulation of the determinants of mortality. Preston shows that the distribution of income and nutrition are influential; among other factors that may have played significant roles in the gains of life expectancy during modern times are the advance of popular education and the decline of fertility; no doubt urbanization has influenced the trends in various countries, and other factors could be

J. D. Durand is professor of economics and sociology and a research associate of the Population Studies Center, University of Pennsylvania.

mentioned. However, probably the greater part of the increases in expectation of life in most parts of the world during the last two centuries can be attributed to the growth of *y*, the advances of *k* and *s*, and some favorable changes in *n*. I do not presume that the effects of these factors have been simply additive. It is not to belittle the value of Preston's regression models to postulate, for example, that the effects of given changes in each and all of the factors have varied with the levels of *e*, as is shown vividly by the smallness of recent gains of life expectancy in countries where the highest levels have been achieved.

Pretransitional Regimes

Lee's study of preindustrial England provides a most valuable example of conditions and factors of mortality in a pretransitional state. In this case, we may disregard factors *k* and *s*, assuming that they were constant in effect, at least up to the eighteenth century. From the thirteenth to the eighteenth century, there were important variations of mortality in England, both long-term and short-term, and Lee finds that these were due mainly to noneconomic factors; that is, presumably natural factors in the main. The identification of these natural factors remains an unsolved puzzle. Lee says, "they may have been climatic, or the by-product of independent epidemiological changes, or the result of voyages of exploration."[1] As regards climate, Le Roy Ladurie's work is rather discouraging to hopes of finding in its variations a satisfactory explanation for the long swings in mortality, but the question of its influence on the hazards of disease as well as on agriculture has by no means yet been disposed of. There were also important long- and short-term ups and downs of *y*, represented in Lee's analysis by indicators of wages and prices, and he finds that their influence on mortality was not negligible, although it was less potent than the influence of *n*. One of the most interesting features is the low ceiling over *e*. Apparently even the wealth of kings and dukes would not purchase more than about 25 to 35 years of life expectancy, depending on the conditions of *n*. The ceiling is much higher today, but it is still firm. Unlimited growth of national income per head seems unlikely under present conditions to bring expectation of life for the two sexes much above 75 years.

England's economic situation during the centuries shortly before the industrial revolution was relatively favorable compared with that of most other countries, as Lee points out. Both *e* and *y* were probably considerably lower in most of the rest of the world, and it is likely that the influence of changes of *y* over time may have been stronger elsewhere than it was in England. Lee suggests this with reference to Goubert's observations on mortality in Beauvais during the seventeenth and eighteenth centuries. However, I would hypothesize that *n* was a major factor in both temporal variations and international differences in mortality under the pretransitional regimes throughout the world.

Preston (1975) gives a chart of the changing relation between *e* and *y* in international cross sections about 1900, 1930, and 1960. If data were available to draw such a chart with reference to conditions around 1750 and earlier dates, I presume that the correlation between *e* and *y* would be seen to have been weaker, the curve representing the relation between the two variables would exhibit a less steep positive slope, and it would shift erratically up and down from one date to another under the influence of changing natural factors. A major feature of the transition to modern regimes of mortality has been progressive neutralization of the influences of *n* as a result of the growth of *y* and advances of *k* and *s*.

First Phase of the Transition

Although it is not easy to define the date of beginning of the mortality transition in any country, the secular trend of slowly rising expectation of life identified with the first phase of the transition was clearly general in Western Europe during the nineteenth century, and indications of accelerating rates of population growth suggest that it was also widespread in Eastern Europe, North Africa, and Latin America. The trend of mortality in the United States before the closing decades of the nineteenth century remains an unresolved question.

In the countries in the vanguard of industrial development during the nineteenth century, the growth of income per head was undoubtedly a major factor contributing to the decline of mortality in this first phase, but the effect of increasing *y* was reinforced by advances in *k* and *s*. Under the heading of *k*, in addition to the important innovation of smallpox vaccination, I surmise that increasing understanding of the importance of hygiene and proper feeding of children, linked with the advance of popular education in the industrializing countries, played an influential part. Under *s* were such social actions as protection of water supplies, urban sewerage, swamp drainage, quarantine practices, restriction of child labor, and regulation of conditions of women's employment. Such health-protective social actions were not confined to the wealthiest countries; Sanchez-Albornoz (1974) traces their development in Latin American cities during the nineteenth century.

With regard to the historical antecedents of Preston's (1975) chart of changing relations between *e* and *y* during the twentieth century, I postulate, although I cannot provide statistical proof, that the developments related to the first phase of the mortality transition during the nineteenth century had the following effects: making the correlation between *e* and *y* stronger than it had been under the pretransitional regimes; gradually shifting upward the curve of *e* values corresponding to given levels of *y*; and making the slope of the curve steeper—that is, widening the differences in *e* between richer and poorer nations.

Second Phase of the Transition

The decided quickening of the rate of gain in life expectancy that marks the beginning of the second phase of the transition took place in the 1890s or about a decade earlier or later in the more developed countries of Europe and America. It seems clear that this turn of the trend was primarily a result of the first revolution in death-control technology produced by the validation and wide acceptance of the germ theory of disease. The effect of this was not limited to the new techniques of immunization and therapy for particular diseases that began to be invented late in the nineteenth century. Meanwhile, increasing income and health-protective social actions continued to contribute to gains in *e*, and it seems a reasonable hypothesis that the tightening control of fertility may also have contributed to the quickening reduction in child mortality.

The less developed countries in Latin America, Asia, and Africa were slow to get much benefit from the advances in *k* at this stage. They were handicapped in applying the new knowledge by low income, low levels of popular education, small resources at the disposal of the governments, and perhaps colonial administrations' lack of interest in taking very costly actions to protect the health of the indigenous people. So the beginnings of the second phase of the transition were delayed in most of these countries until after World War I, and in many until the 1940s or 1950s. As a result, the differences in life expectancy between more and less developed countries widened during the early decades of the present century, and the slope of the curve of *e* in relation to *y* grew steeper as it shifted upward more rapidly in the higher than in the lower brackets of per capita income.

It might be tempting to infer that countries had to reach some threshold of income and development in other respects to be eligible for rapid progress in the reduction of mortality under the conditions of this period. But some observations imply that if this were true, the level of the threshold was not high enough to explain fully why so many less developed countries were so long retarded in entering the second phase of the mortality transition:

1. The case of the eastern and southern European countries: Although they were considerably less developed than the northwestern European countries, they were quick to join their richer neighbors in the sharp acceleration of gains in *e* around the turn of the century or shortly afterward. In spite of handicaps in income, education, and other

aspects of development, the countries in eastern and southern Europe generally managed to keep pace with those of northwestern Europe in rates of gain in life expectancy until about the 1940s, when they began to overtake the lead of the latter.

2. The case of Cuba: In a new study of the trend of mortality in Cuba since the late nineteenth century, Diaz Briquets (1977) shows that a spectacular reduction of mortality was achieved there during the few years of United States military occupation following the Spanish-American War, by a campaign of sanitary reforms and mosquito control instigated and aided by the army of occupation. He estimates that the crude annual death rate in the city of Havana dropped from a prewar average of 32 per 1,000 in 1891–95 to 20 in 1903–7, and a large decrease was achieved in the rest of the country also, in the face of general poverty and illiteracy.

3. The case of Taiwan under Japanese rule during early years of this century is another precocious example of the effective transfer of k and s from a more developed to a less developed country (Barclay 1954). This is even more remarkable than the Cuban case, because when the Japanese arrived Taiwan was a good deal less developed than Cuba, and the Japanese themselves had not yet reached a very high level of either e or y.

4. A decided upturn of the trend of e took place during the 1920s in a number of less developed countries (Cuba, Japan, Taiwan, and others). Diaz Briquets (1977) observes that this seems to have been especially characteristic of countries where export industries were dominant, and he suggests that an economic boom in such countries in the 1920s owing to expanding demand and rising prices for their exports might account for their having entered the second phase of the mortality transition earlier than other less developed countries did. The interest of their more developed trading partners in making these countries healthy places to do business with and in may also have been a factor.

The relevance of the trend of income to the life expectancy gains in less developed countries is illustrated in reverse by the example of Cuba in the 1930s and early 1940s, when the misfortunes of the international market for sugar cast Cuba into economic doldrums. Diaz finds that the decline of mortality in Cuba was checked and probably temporarily reversed during this period, and that worsening nutrition and diminishing public and private expenditures on health services were important factors.

A second revolution in the technology of disease control began about 1935 and progressed rapidly during the 1940s and 1950s, with major advances of k especially in the fields of immunization, chemotherapy, and chemical control of disease vectors. This time, the less developed countries were the principal beneficiaries. Although measures of trends in *e* since 1940 are lacking for many of these countries, especially among those at the lowest levels of development, it is apparent that substantial gains since that time have been practically universal in the less developed regions of the world. Preston's findings suggest that 50% to 80% of the gains between 1940 and 1970 in less developed countries may be attributable to *k* and *s* factors, but advances on these fronts have not gone so far as to make economic factors irrelevant. Gains in *e* since the 1940s have been less spectacular in the least developed countries, particularly in Africa, than in those that were somewhat more developed, and Preston finds a positive association between rates of increase in *e* and *y* among less developed countries.

A tendency toward slackening rates of gain in *e* in less developed countries is apparent in the 1960s and 1970s. While this might be due partly to slowing economic growth, Preston links it with a diminishing rate of "structural change," that is, slowdown of the advance of *k* and *s*. He observes that only a few innovations of major importance to health technology have been made during the last decade. The implication is that upward shifting of *e* in relation to *y* may be drawing to an end and that *e* gains in less developed countries henceforth may depend mainly on their ability to move up on the scales of *y* and related social developments. This has been suggested in a number of recent studies. However, there may still be a good deal of scope for raising *e* in less developed countries where it remains relatively low, through the pursuit of *s* actions to take fuller advantage of existing *k* at their present levels of *y*. To cite once again the example of Cuba: the series of Cuban life tables compiled by Diaz Briquets (1977) shows expectation of life at birth for the two sexes increasing from 58.8 years in 1953 to 72.1 in 1971 (70.6 for males, 73.9 for females). The 1971 figure compares favorably with that of the United States, especially for males. Diaz presumes that most of the gain in Cuba since 1953 has taken place since the establishment of the socialist government, and he attributes the high rate of gain since that time mainly to more equal distribution of income and government policies aimed at equalizing access to health services for all categories of the population.

Although the less developed countries were the main beneficiaries of the new advances in *k* since the 1930s, the more developed countries also benefited to an important extent. Examination of the trends in a number of more developed countries shows that the 1940s were a bumper decade for gains in life expectancy. Preston's analysis indicates that a major share of the gains in more developed as well as less developed countries since 1930 has been due to the upward shifting of the curve of *e* in relation to *y* and other indicators of development, which may be attributed to the advances of *k* and *s*.

Third Phase of the Transition

In more developed countries, the rates of gain in *e* have slowed conspicuously since the 1950s, and in many of them hardly any gains have been registered during the past ten years. The same tendency is noticeable in recent statistics from some less developed countries that have attained levels of *e* comparable to those of more developed countries. This feature is commonly interpreted as meaning that the expectation of life in countries where it is now highest is approaching a ceiling that cannot be surpassed by increasing income or by other means unless a new revolution in medical technology is achieved—a revolution that would make possible important gains in control over the so-called degenerative diseases. If this interpretation is correct and if the less developed countries where *e* is still well below such a ceiling manage to continue progress in reducing their mortality rates through economic development and fuller application of the present medical knowledge, the time may come when levels of mortality will be nearly equalized among countries around the world. The advances of *k* and *s* would then have neutralized, to a large extent, the influence of *y* as well as that of *n*.

An interesting aspect of the recent trends in countries where *e* is high is that they seem to be leveling off at considerably different values of *e*. If they are coming up against a ceiling, the level of the ceiling seems not to be the same in all countries. In the United States, for example, *e* seems to be stagnating some four or five years below the level achieved in the Scandinavian countries. On the surface, these differences do not seem very consistently related to per capita income. I mentioned earlier that Cuba's estimated expectation of life in 1971 compared favorably with that of the United States. The position of Puerto Rico and Hong Kong is similar, although they are far below the United States in per capita income. Perhaps a part of the explanation for such anomalies might be found in factors associated with advanced economic development that are unfavorable to health and longevity. I think it would be interesting to make a systematic study of factors related to the different levels of *e*, and of mortality rates for sex and age groups, causes of death, and so forth, at which the trends seem recently to have been stalling in many countries. The distribution of income, governmental action in fields of health care, environmental pollution, diets, and behavioral patterns relevant to health are among the factors that might usefully be examined.

Note

1. McNeill (1976) argues that major factors in the long-range trends of mortality and population growth in Europe between the fourteenth and eighteenth centuries were new diseases resulting from increased contacts with the Orient during the Mongol conquests and a subsequent gradual adaptation to these diseases, as well as variations of climate.

Comment Victor R. Fuchs

The paper by Preston has two principal purposes: to explain the increase in life expectancy in the less developed countries over the past several decades and to consider the effect of this increase on population size, output, and output per capita. The bulk of the paper is concerned with the first question, and I shall limit my comment to that. Furthermore, I shall examine only one aspect of Preston's multifaceted discussion—the attempt to partition the gain in life expectancy into the portion attributable to increased per capita income and the portion due to a structural shift in the relationship between life expectancy and per capita income.

Using the data Preston provides, I have run regressions of life expectancy (*LE*) on the natural logarithm of per capita income (*LnY*) for four separate groups of countries: LDCs in 1940 (*L40*), MDCs in 1940 (*M40*), LDCs in 1970 (*L70*), and MDCs in 1970 (*M70*).[1] The results are presented in table C5.1. I have also plotted the predicted (from the regressions) relationship between life expectancy and per capita income for each group in figure C5.1. The curves are plotted over the range of per capita income actually observed for each group.

Table C5.1 **Results of Regressing Life Expectancy on Logarithm of per Capita Income across Less Developed and More Developed Countries in 1940 and 1970**

$LE = a + b \ln Y$	L40	M40	L70	M70
b	4.99	6.65	7.82	.13
σ_b	(1.95)	(1.21)	(1.10)	(.85)
a	13.3	17.1	12.5	70.8
σ_a	(10.0)	(8.0)	(6.7)	(6.6)
R^2	.27	.68	.77	−.08
N	16	15	16	15

Inspection of figure C5.1 suggests that the structural relation between life expectancy and per capita income in the LDCs in 1940 was different from that in the MDCs in the same year. Given the level of income, life expectancy seems to have been appreciably higher in the MDCs. It is therefore inappropriate to pool the two groups of countries, as Preston does, without allowing for differences in structure. It should also be

Victor R. Fuchs is professor of economics at Stanford University and is a research associate of the National Bureau of Economic Research.

The author acknowledges the financial support of the Robert Wood Johnson Foundation, the research assistance of Sean Becketti, and the helpful comments of Robert J. Willis.

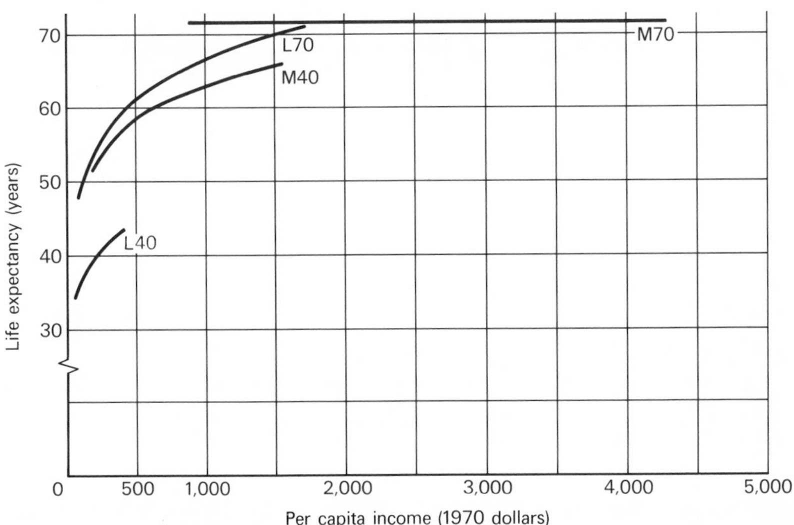

Fig. C5.1 The relationship between life expectancy and per capita income across less developed and more developed countries in 1940 and 1970.

noted that in the MDCs in 1970, the relationship between life expectancy and per capita income has disappeared, a phenomenon I have called attention to before (Fuchs 1965, 1974). There can be no question, therefore, of attempting to assess shifts in the function between the MDCs in 1940 and 1970 or between the LDCs and MDCs in 1970.

I have run regressions that pool LDCs and MDCs in 1940 and LDCs in 1940 and 1970 with dummy variables inserted to allow for differences in intercepts and slopes. These results are reported in table C5.2.

The first regressions (part A) constrain the slopes of the pooled groups to be equal but allow the intercepts to vary. We see that the shift coefficients are large and highly significant in both cases. This means that, compared with the LDCs in 1940, both the MDCs in 1940 and the LDCs in 1970 had substantially higher life expectancy for any given level of per capita income. The second set of regressions (part B) constrains the intercepts to be equal and allows the slopes to vary within each pair of groups. We now find that the slopes do differ significantly. The third set of regressions (part C) allows both the intercepts and the slopes to vary, and with this specification none of the interactions are statistically significant.

If one does not demand statistical significance, it is possible to answer Preston's question fairly unambiguously along the following lines. The mean life expectancy of the LDCs rose from 38.8 years in 1940 to 59.6

Table C5.2 **Pooled Regression Results with Interactions**

	L40 + M40	L40 + L70
A. $LE = a + b\,ln\,Y + c$ Intercept		
b	5.83	6.83
σ_b	(1.14)	(1.04)
c	−13.4	−14.6
σ_c	(2.10)	(1.70)
a	22.4	18.4
σ_a	(7.54)	(6.34)
$\bar{R}^2$	.91	.89
N	31	32
B. $LE = a + b\,ln\,Y + d$ Slope		
b	7.00	7.77
σ_b	(1.00)	(.95)
d	−2.29	−2.69
σ_d	(.35)	(.30)
a	14.7	12.8
σ_a	(6.50)	(5.74)
$\bar{R}^2$	.91	.90
N	31	32
C. $LE = a + b\,ln\,Y + c$ Intercept $+ d$ Slope		
b	6.65	7.82
σ_b	(1.63)	(1.27)
c	−3.79	.78
σ_c	(13.60)	(11.80)
d	−1.66	−2.83
σ_d	(2.31)	(2.15)
a	17.1	12.5
σ_a	(10.7)	(7.73)
$\bar{R}^2$	.91	.90
N	31	32

years in 1970, a rate of increase of 1.4% per annum (see table C5.3).[2] Over that same period the mean per capita income (in 1970 dollars) rose from $194 to $560. We can estimate what the change in life expectancy would have been as a result of income change alone by moving along either the 1940 predicted relation or the 1970 predicted relation. The former tells us that life expectancy would have changed from 39.6 years to 44.8 years, an increase of 0.4% per annum. If we calculate the change along the 1970 curve, we get a predicted increase of 0.5% per annum, from 53.7 years to 62.0 years.

Alternatively, we can look at the implied rates of change attributable to structural shift by comparing predicted life expectancies at the same per capita income in the two years. At $194 the implied change is 1.0% per annum; at $560 it is 1.1% per annum. Thus, either approach indicates that about one-third of the observed change in life expectancy in

Table C5.3 **Life Expectancy in Less Developed Countries in 1940 and 1970: Actual and Predicted Changes**

	Mean Life Expectancy (Years)
Actual 1940 (A40)	38.78
Actual 1970 (A70)	59.59
Predicted 1940 (P40:40) (from L40 regression)	39.56
Predicted 1970 (P70:40) (from L40 regression)	44.85
Predicted 1940 (P40:70) (from L70 regression)	53.68
Predicted 1970 (P70:70) (from L70 regression)	61.97
	Rates of Change (Percentage per Annum)
A40 to A70	1.4
P40:40 to P70:40	0.4
P40:70 to P70:70	0.5
P40:40 to P40:70	1.0
P70:40 to P70:70	1.1

the LDCs between 1940 and 1970 can be attributed to the growth of per capita income, and about two-thirds to a shift in the life expectancy–income relationship. Preston presents one estimate of 50% due to structural change and another of 80% due to that source. The results presented here are quite consistent with those estimates.

Notes

1. The LDCs are all in Asia, Africa, and Latin America, and all had life expectancies below 50 years in 1940. The MDCs are all in Europe, North America, and Australia, and all had life expectancies above 50 years in 1940.

2. The change is expressed in percentage per annum in order to minimize the problem of interaction between shifts in the function and movements along the function.

Comment Richard W. Parks

Preston presents an interesting regression test of the relative importance of private and national income in determining life expectancies. In light of the Kuznets and Fishlow discussions of interaction between the income distribution and the age distribution of the population, it may be useful to point out a possible bias in the Preston regression in section 5.1.1.

The income distribution as commonly measured does not correct for the age distribution of the population. Thus, in a hypothetical world with *no* differences among individuals in their lifetime income streams, we will observe considerable income inequality as conventionally measured if individuals follow the usual life-cycle pattern of earning and saving followed by retirement. For the determination of the effect of income on life expectancy, it appears that a permanent income rather than a measured income concept makes more sense, but given the data available to him, Preston relies on the distribution of measured income.

Preston's distribution measure, which I shall call $D = \Sigma\, 1n(S_i/.05)$, takes values ranging from $-\infty$ to 0 on a scale representing increasing equality. Thus we can represent the partial relationship between life expectancy e^o_o, and D as shown in figure C5.2.

We expect a positive association. Suppose we start at point *A* with given (unequal) distribution and low life expectancy. If incomes were to become more equal (in a life-cycle sense), we would expect to find a new point at *B* showing greater equality and higher life expectancy. However, even with the pattern of life-cycle income corresponding with point *B*, there is likely to be an effect on the measured income distribu-

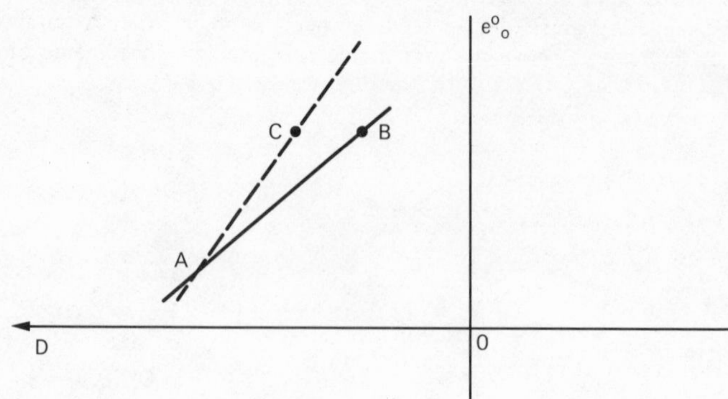

Fig. C5.2

Richard W. Parks is associated with the Department of Economics, University of Washington.

tion arising from the altered life expectancy. An increase in the share of population in nonproductive years, for example, older age groups, will have the effect of increasing the observed inequality. The observation based on measured income will be at point *C*, giving an upward bias to the slope coefficient. Since the crucial test of the relative importance of national and private incomes in the determination of life expectancy depends on the size of the slope coefficient, the upward bias would tend to suggest the absence of an effect for national income even when it was in fact important.

References

Allan, William. 1965. *The African husbandman*. London: Oliver and Boyd.

Antonovsky, Aaron. 1967. Social class, life expectancy, and overall mortality. *Milbank Memorial Fund Quarterly* 45: 31–73.

Arriaga, Eduardo. 1967. The effect of a decline in mortality on the gross reproduction rate. *Milbank Memorial Fund Quarterly* 45: 333–52.

———. 1968. *New life tables for Latin American populations*. Berkeley: Institute of International Studies, University of California.

———. 1970. *Mortality decline and its demographic effects in Latin America*. Berkeley: Institute of International Studies, University of California.

Ascoli, Werner; Guzman, Miguel A.; Scrimshaw, Nevin S.; and Gordon, John E. 1967. Nutrition and infection field study in Guatemalan villages, 1959–1964. IV. Deaths of infants and preschool children. *Archives of Environmental Health* 15 (October): 439–49.

Baertl, Juan M.; Morales, Enrique; Verastegui, Gustavo; and Graham, George. 1970. Diet supplementation for entire communities: Growth and mortality of children. *American Journal of Clinical Nutrition* 23(6): 707–15.

Bailey, K. V. 1975. Malnutrition in the African region. *Chronicle of the World Health Organization* 29: 354–64.

Banks, Arthur. 1971. *Cross-polity time-series data*. Cambridge: MIT Press.

Barclay, George W. 1954. *Colonial development and population in Taiwan*. Princeton: Princeton University Press.

Barlow, Robin. 1967. The economic effects of malaria eradication. *American Economic Review* 57(2): 130–48.

———. 1968. *The economic effects of malaria eradication*. Economic Research Series no. 15. Ann Arbor: University of Michigan School of Public Health.

Beck, Ann. 1970. *A history of the British medical administration of East Africa, 1900–1950*. Cambridge: Harvard University Press.

Boserup, Ester. 1965. *The conditions of agricultural growth: The economics of agrarian change under population pressure*. Chicago: Aldine.

Bowers, John. 1973. The history of public health in China to 1937. In *Public Health in the People's Republic of China*, ed. Myron E. Wegman, Tsung-Yi Lin, and Elizabeth F. Purcell, pp. 26–45. New York: Josiah Macy, Jr., Foundation.

Boyd, M. F. 1949. *Malariology*. Vols. 1 and 2. Philadelphia: W. B. Saunders.

Bryant, John. 1969. *Health and the developing world*. Ithaca: Cornell University Press.

Bunle, Henri. 1954. *Le mouvement naturel de la population dans le monde de 1906 à 1936*. Paris: Institut d'études demographiques.

Burch, Thomas K., and Gendell, Murray. 1970. Extended family structure and fertility: Some methodological and conceptual issues. *Journal of Marriage and the Family* 32(2): 227–36.

Carnoy, Martin. 1967. Rates of return to schooling in Latin America. *Journal of Human Resources* 2(3): 359–74.

Coale, Ansley J. 1956. The effects of changes in mortality and fertility on age composition. *Milbank Memorial Fund Quarterly* 34: 79–114.

Coale, Ansley J., and Demeny, Paul. 1966. *Regional model life tables and stable populations*. Princeton: Princeton University Press.

Coale, Ansley J., and Hoover, Edgar M. 1958. *Population growth and economic development in low-income countries*. Princeton: Princeton University Press.

Committee for International Coordination of National Research in Demography. 1975. *Seminar on infant mortality in relation to level of fertility*. Paris.

Davis, Kingsley. 1951. *The population of India and Pakistan*. Princeton: Princeton University Press.

———. 1955. Institutional patterns favoring high fertility in underdeveloped areas. *Eugenics Quarterly* 2: 33–39.

———. 1956. The amazing decline of mortality in underdeveloped areas. *American Economic Review* 46 (May): 305–18.

———. 1973. Cities and mortality. *Proceedings*, International Population Conference, Liège, Belgium, 3: 259–81.

Denison. Edward F. 1962. *The sources of economic growth in the United States and the alternatives before us*. New York: Committee for Economic Development.

Diaz Briquets, Sergio. 1977. Mortality in Cuba: Trends and determinants, 1880 to 1971. Ph.D. diss., University of Pennsylvania.

Durand, John R. 1967. A long-range view of world population growth. *Annals of the American Academy of Arts and Sciences* 369: 1–8.

Early, John. 1970. The structure and change of mortality in a Maya community. *Milbank Memorial Fund Quarterly* 48: 179–201.

Eversley, D. E. C. 1957. A survey of population in an area of Worcestershire from 1660 to 1850 on the basis of parish registers. *Population Studies* 10: 253–79.

Faust, Ernest Carroll. 1941. The distribution of malaria in North America, Mexico, Central America, and the West Indies. In *A symposium on human malaria*, ed. F. R. Moulton, pp. 8–18. Washington, D.C.: American Association for the Advancement of Science.

Fein, Rashi. 1964. Health programs and economic development. In *The economics of health and medical care. Proceedings of the conference on the economics of health and medical care, May 10–12, 1962*, ed. H. E. Klarman. Ann Arbor: Bureau of Public Health Economics and Department of Economics, University of Michigan.

Foege, William H.; Millar, J. D.; and Henderson, D. A. 1975. Smallpox eradication in West and Central Africa. *Bulletin of the World Health Organization* 52: 209–22.

Food and Agriculture Organization of the United Nations. 1975. *Population, food supply, and agricultural development*. Rome: FAO.

Fredericksen, Harald. 1961. Determinants and consequences of mortality trends in Ceylon. *Public Health Reports* 76 (August): 659–63.

———. 1966*a*. Determinants and consequences of mortality and fertility trends. *Public Health Reports* 81 (August): 715–27.

———. 1966*b*. Dynamic equilibrium of economic and demographic transition. *Economic Development and Cultural Change* 14 (April): 316–22.

Friedlander, Dov. 1969. Demographic responses and population change. *Demography* 6(4): 359–82.

Fuchs, V. R. 1965. Some economic aspects of mortality in the United States. National Bureau of Economic Research Study Paper.

———. 1974. Some economic aspects of mortality in developed countries. In *The economics of health and medical care*, ed. Mark Perlman, pp. 174–93. Proceedings of a conference held by the International Economic Association at Tokyo. London: Macmillan.

Goodman, Neville M. 1971. *International health organizations and their work*. Edinburgh: Churchill Livingstone.

Gordon, John. 1969. Social implications of nutrition and disease. *Archives of Environmental Health* 18(2): 216–34.

Habakkuk, H. J. 1971. *Population growth and economic development*. New York: Humanities Press.

Hansluwka, Harald. 1975. Health, population, and socio-economic development. In *Population growth and economic development in the Third World*, ed. Léon Tabah, 1: 191–250. Dolhain, Belgium: Ordina.

Hinman, E. Harold. 1966. *World eradication of infectious diseases.* Springfield, Ill.: Charles C. Thomas.

Howard-Jones, N. 1974. The scientific background of the International Sanitary Conferences, 1851–1938. *Chronicle of the World Health Organization* 28(10): 455–70.

Johnson, D. Gale. 1974. Population, food, and economic adjustment. *American Statistician* 28(3): 89–93.

Keyfitz, Nathan, and Fleiger, Wilhelm. 1968. *World population: An analysis of vital data.* Chicago: University of Chicago Press.

———. 1971. *Population: Facts and methods of demography*. San Francisco: W. H. Freeman and Company.

Kitagawa, E. M., and Hauser, P. M. 1973. *Differential mortality in the United States: A study in socioeconomic epidemiology*. Cambridge: Harvard University Press.

Klarman, Herbert E. 1967. Present status of cost-benefit analysis in the health field. *American Journal of Public Health* 57(11): 1948–53.

Kuznets, Simon. 1975. Population trends and modern economic growth: Notes towards an historical perspective. In *The population debate: Dimensions and perspectives*, 1: 425–33. Papers of the World Population Conference, Bucharest: New York: United Nations.

Lancet. 1970. Strategy of malaria eradication: A turning point? *Lancet* editorial. 1970 (21 March): 598–600.

McDermott, W. 1966. Modern medicine and the demographic-disease pattern of overly traditional societies: A technological misfit. *Journal of Medical Education* 41(9): 138–62.

McKeown, Thomas. 1965. Medicine and world population. In *Public health and population change*, ed. Mindel C. Sheps and Jeanne Clare Ridley. Pittsburgh: University of Pittsburgh Press.

McKeown, Thomas, and Record, R. G. 1962. Reasons for the decline of mortality in England and Wales during the 19th century. *Population Studies* 16: 94–122.

McNeill, William H. 1976. *Plagues and peoples.* Garden City, N.Y.: Anchor Press/Doubleday.

Malenbaum, Wilfred. 1970. Health and productivity in poor areas. In *Empirical studies in health economics*, ed. Herbert E. Klarman, pp. 31–57. Baltimore: Johns Hopkins University Press.

Mandle, Jay R. 1970. The decline in mortality in British Guiana, 1911–1960. *Demography* 7, no. 3 (August): 303.

Maramag, Ileana. 1965. The cost of public health programs in the Philippines. *Journal of the American Medical Women's Association* 20 (September): 848–57.

Marshall, Carter L.; Brown, Roy E.; and Goodrich, Charles H. 1971. Improved nutrition vs. public health services as major determinants of world population growth. *Clinical Pediatrics* 10 (July): 363–68.

Mata, Leonardo, et al. 1972. Influence of recurrent infections on nutrition and growth of children in Guatemala. *American Journal of Clinical Nutrition* 25 (November): 1267–75.

Meegama, S. A. 1967. Malaria eradication and its effect on mortality levels. *Population Studies* 26(3): 207–38.

Morley, David. 1973. *Paediatric priorities in the developing world.* London: Butterworth's.

Mushkin, Selma J. 1962. Health as an investment. *Journal of Political Economy* 70 (part 2, supplement): 129–57.

———. 1964. Health programming in developing nations. *International Development Review* 6(1): 7–12.

Myrdal, Gunnar. 1968. *Asian drama: An inquiry into the poverty of nations.* Vols. 1–3. New York: Random House.

Newman, P. 1965. *Malaria eradication and population growth: With special reference to Ceylon and British Guiana.* Research Series no. 10. Ann Arbor, Michigan: Bureau of Public Health Economics, School of Public Health, University of Michigan.

———. 1970. Malaria control and population growth. *Journal of Development Studies* 6: 133–58.

O'Hara, Donald J. 1975. Microeconomic aspects of the demographic transition. *Journal of Political Economy* 83(6): 1203–15.

Organization for Economic Cooperation and Development. N.d. *Resources for the developing world: The flow of financial resources to less developed countries, 1962–1968.* Paris: OECD.

Pampana, E. J. 1954. Effect of malaria control on birth and death rates. *Proceedings of the World Population Conference, 1954,* Rome, pp. 497–508. New York: United Nations.

Pampana, E. J., and Russell, Paul F. 1955. Malaria: A world problem. *Chronicle of the World Health Organization* 9(2–3): 33–100.

Pani, Alberto. 1917. *Hygiene in Mexico.* New York: G. P. Putnam's Sons.

Paul, Hugh H. 1964. *The control of diseases.* 2d ed. Baltimore: Williams and Wilkins.

Plank, S. J., and Milanesi, M. L. 1973. Infant feeding and infant mortality in rural Chile. *Bulletin of the World Health Organization* 48: 203–10.

Polgar, Steven. 1972. Population history and population policies from an anthropological perspective. *Current Anthropology* 13(2): 203–11.

Preston, S. H. 1974. Effect of mortality change on stable population parameters. *Demography* 11(1): 119–30.

———. 1975*a*. The changing relation between mortality and level of economic development. *Population Studies* 29(2): 231–48.

———. 1975*b*. Introduction. In *Seminar on infant mortality in relation to the level of fertility*, pp. 10–22. Paris: Committee for International Coordination of National Research in Demography.

Preston, S. H.; Keyfitz, N.; and Schoen, R. 1972. *Causes of death: Life tables for national populations.* New York: Seminar Press.

———. 1973. Cause-of-death life tables: Application of a new technique to worldwide data. *Transactions of the Society of Actuaries* 25 (December): 83–109.

Preston, S. H., and Nelson, V. E. 1974. Structure and change in causes of death: An international summary. *Population Studies* 28(1): 19–51.

Puffer, R. R., and Griffith, G. W. 1967. *Patterns of urban mortality.* Scientific Publication no. 151. Washington, D.C.: Pan American Health Organization.

Puffer, R. R., and Serrano, C. V. 1973. *Patterns of mortality in childhood.* Scientific Publication no. 262. Washington, D.C.: Pan American Health Organization.

Russell, Paul F. 1943. Malaria and its influence on world health. *Bulletin of the New York Academy of Medicine, September*, pp. 599–630.

———. 1968. The United States and malaria: Debits and credits. *Bulletin of the New York Academy of Medicine* 44(6): 623–53.

Rutstein, Shea, and Medica, Vilma. 1975. The effect of infant and child mortality in Latin America. In *Seminar on infant mortality in relation to the level of fertility*, pp. 225–46. Paris: Committee for International Coordination of National Research in Demography.

Sack, Richard. 1974. The impact of education on individual modernity in Tunisia. In *Education and individual modernity in developing countries,* ed. Alex Inkeles and Donald B. Holsinger, pp. 89–116. Leiden: E. J. Brill.

Sanchez-Albornoz, Nicholas. 1974. *The population of Latin America: A history*. Berkeley: University of California Press.

Schultz, Theodore. 1964. *Transforming traditional agriculture.* New Haven: Yale University Press.

Schultz, T. Paul. 1976. Interrelationships between mortality and fertility. In *Population and development: The search for selective interventions*, ed. Ronald G. Ridker, pp. 239–89. Baltimore: Johns Hopkins University Press.

Scrimshaw, Nevin S. 1970. Synergism of malnutrition and infection. *Journal of the American Medical Association* 212(10): 1685–92.

Sharpston, Michael J. 1976. Health and the human environment. *Finance and Development* 13(1): 24–28.

Shattuk, George. 1951. *Diseases of the tropics.* New York: Appleton-Century-Crofts.

Shorter, Frederick. 1968. Information on fertility, mortality, and population growth in Turkey. *Population Index* 34(1): 5.

Simmons, James Stevens; Whayne, Tom F.; Anderson, Gaylord West; Horack, Harold MacLachian; and collaborators. 1944. *Global epidemiology: A geography of diseases and sanitation.* Vol. 1. Philadelphia: J. B. Lippincott.

Smith, Peter C. 1976. Asian nuptiality in transition. Paper presented at the Seventh Summer Seminar in Population, East-West Population Institute, Honolulu.

Sorkin, Alan L. 1975. *Health economics: An introduction.* Lexington, Mass.: D. C. Heath, Lexington Books.

Stolnitz, George J. 1956. Mortality declines and age distribution. *Milbank Memorial Fund Quarterly* 34: 178–215.

———. 1974. International mortality trends: Some main facts and implications. Background Paper for United Nations World Population Conference E/CONF.60/CBP/17, Bucharest.

Taylor, Carl E., and Hall, Marie-Francoise. 1967. Health population and economic development. *Science* 157 (August): 651–57.

Titmuss, Richard M., and Abel-Smith, Brian. 1968. *Social policies and population growth in Mauritius.* London: Frank Cass.

United Nations, Population Branch. 1963. Population bulletin of the United Nations no. 6 (with special reference to the situation and recent trends of mortality in the world). New York.

United Nations, Department of Economic and Social Affairs. 1971. *The world population situation in 1970.* Population Study no. 49. New York.

———. 1973. *The determinants and consequences of population trends.* Vol. 1. New York: United Nations.

United Nations, Population Division. 1974. Recent population trends and future prospects. World Population Conference Paper E/CONF. 60/3.

Vaidyanathan, K. E. 1972. Some indices of differential mortality in India. In *Studies on mortality in India*, ed. K. E. Vaidyanathan. Gandhigram: Institute of Rural Health and Family Planning.

Vallin, J. 1968. La mortalité dans les pays du Tiers Monde: Evolution et perspectives. *Population* 23: 845–68.

Wegman, Myron E.; Lin, Tsung-yi; and Purcell, Elizabeth F., eds. 1973. *Public health in the People's Republic of China.* New York: Josiah Macy, Jr., Foundation.

Weisbrod, Burton A. 1975. Research in health economics: A survey. *International Journal of Health Services* 5(4): 643–61.

Weller, T. H. 1974. World health in a changing world. *Journal of Tropical Medicine* 77(4), suppl. 54: 54–61.

World Bank. 1975. *Health: Sector policy paper*. Washington, D. C.

World Health Organization. 1970. Special subject: Health expenditure. In *World health statistics annual, 1966–1967* 3: 236–45.

———. 1972. *Human development and public health*. Technical Report Series no. 485. Geneva: WHO.

———. 1973. Community water supply and sewage disposal in developing countries. *World Health Statistics Report* 26(11): 720–83.

———. 1974*a*. Childhood mortality in the Americas. *Chronicle of the World Health Organization* 28: 276–82.

———. 1974*b*. Health trends and prospects, 1950–2000. *World Health Statistics Report* 27(10): 672–706.

———. 1975*a*. The malaria situation in 1974. *Chronicle of the World Health Organization* 29: 474–81.

———. 1975*b*. *Fifth report on the world health situation*. Official Records of the World Health Organization, no. 225. Geneva: WHO.

———. 1975*c*. *First WHO seminar on expansion of the use of immunization in developing countries*. Offset Publication no. 16. Geneva: WHO.

———. 1976. Smallpox eradication in 1975. *Chronicle of the World Health Organization* 30: 152–57.

Wrigley, E. A. 1969. *Population and history*. New York: McGraw-Hill.

6 Internal Migration in Developing Countries: A Survey

Michael P. Todaro

6.1 Migration and Development: Some Critical Issues

As recently as a decade ago, internal migration in general and rural-urban migration in particular were viewed favorably in the economic development literature. Rapid internal migration was thought to be a desirable process by which surplus rural labor was withdrawn from traditional agriculture to provide cheap manpower to fuel a growing modern industrial complex (Lewis 1954; Fei and Ranis 1961). The process was deemed socially beneficial (at least on the basis of historical evidence; Kuznets 1964, 1971), since human resources were being shifted from locations where their marginal social products were often assumed to be zero to places where these marginal products were not only positive but also rapidly growing as a result of capital accumulation and technological progress.

Herrick (1965) reflected the prevailing view about the desirability of internal migration when he asserted that "in the absence of any movement, when rural fertility exceeds urban fertility, the agricultural labor force will grow faster than industrial employment. Movement from the country to the towns, which is necessary if strictly balanced growth of the two parts of the labor force is to occur, becomes even more important if an increase in the industrial sector is among the goals of the developing economy." Only a few years later, however, Jolly (1970)

Michael P. Todaro is professor of economics at New York University and senior associate with the Population Council, New York. This paper is a condensed and updated version of a book entitled *Internal Migration in Developing Nations: A Review of Theory, Evidence, Methodology and Research Priorities*, prepared for the International Labor Organization and published by the ILO in Geneva in 1976. The author gratefully acknowledges ILO permission to reproduce portions of the book.

seemed to be echoing a changing perception of the migration issue among economists when he noted that "far from being concerned with measures to stem the flow, the major interests of these economists [those who stressed the importance of labor transfer] was with policies that would *release* labour to *increase* the flow. Indeed, one of the reasons given for trying to increase productivity in the agricultural sector was to release *sufficient* labour for urban industrialization. How irrelevant most of this concern looks today!"

Numerous studies have now documented the fact that throughout the developing world rates of rural-urban migration continue to exceed rates of urban job creation and to greatly surpass the capacity of both industry and urban social services to absorb this labor effectively. No longer is rapid migration viewed by economists as an unambiguously beneficial process necessary to solve problems of growing urban labor demand. On the contrary, migration today is being increasingly viewed as the major contributing factor to the ubiquitous phenomenon of urban surplus labor and as a force that continues to exacerbate already serious urban unemployment problems caused by growing economic and structural imbalances between urban and rural areas.

Migration exacerbates these rural-urban structural imbalances in two major direct ways. First, on the supply side, internal migration disproportionately increases the growth rate of urban job-seekers relative to urban population growth, which itself is at historically unprecedented levels, because of the high proportions of well-educated young people who dominate the migrant stream. Their presence tends to swell the growth of urban labor supply while depleting the rural countryside of valuable human capital. Second, on the demand side, most urban job creation is more difficult and costly to accomplish than rural employment creation because of the need for substantial complementary resource inputs for most modern-sector industrial jobs. For example, an ILO (International Labor Office) estimate of investment costs per worker in Egypt in 1969 showed a cost of $5,070 for an industrial job compared with $616 for an agricultural job (ILO 1969). Moreover, the pressures of rising urban wages and compulsory employee fringe benefits in combination with the unavailability of "appropriate" (usually more labor-intensive) production technologies means that a rising share of modern-sector output growth is accounted for by increases in labor productivity. Together, this rapid supply increase and lagging demand growth tend to convert a short-run problem of manpower imbalances into a long-run situation of chronic and rising urban surplus labor.

But the influence of migration on the development process is much more pervasive than its obvious accentuation of urban unemployment and underemployment. In fact, the significance of the migration phenomenon in most developing countries is not necessarily in the process itself or even in its effect on the sectoral allocation of human resources. It is in the context of its implications for economic growth in general and for the "character" of that growth, particularly its distributional manifestations, that migration research has assumed growing importance in recent years.

We must recognize at the outset, therefore, that migration substantially in excess of new job opportunities is both a symptom of and a factor contributing to Third World underdevelopment. Understanding the causes, determinants, and consequences of internal migration is thus central to a better understanding of the nature and character of the development process. It is also essential for formulating appropriate policies to influence this process in socially desirable ways. A simple yet crucial step in underlining the centrality of the migration phenomenon is to recognize that any economic and social policy that affects rural and urban real incomes will directly or indirectly influence the migration process. This process in turn will itself tend to alter the pattern of sectoral and geographic economic activity, income distribution, and population growth. Since all economic policies have direct and indirect effects on the level and growth of either urban or rural incomes or of both, they *all* will have a tendency to influence the nature and magnitude of the migration stream. Although some policies may have a more direct and immediate effect (e.g., wages and income policies, employment promotion programs), there are many others that, though less obvious, may in the long run be no less important. Included among these policies, for example, would be alterations in the system of land tenure, commodity pricing, rural credit allocation, taxation, export promotion, import substitution, commercial and exchange rate policies, the geographic distribution of social services, the nature of public investment programs, attitudes toward private foreign investors, the organization of population and family planning programs, the structure, content, and orientation of the educational system, the structure and functioning of urban labor markets, and the nature of public policies toward international technological transfer and the spatial allocation of new industries. There is thus a clear need to recognize the central importance of internal migration and to integrate the two-way relationship between migration and population distribution on the one hand and economic variables on the other into a more comprehensive analytical framework designed to improve development policy.

In addition, we need to understand better not only why people move and what factors are most important in their decision-making, but also the *consequences* of internal migration for rural and urban economic and social development. If all development policies affect and are affected by migration, which are the most significant and why? What are the policy options and trade-offs among different and sometimes competing objectives (e.g., curtailing internal migration and expanding educational opportunities in rural areas)? In short, unless we are able to begin to *quantify* the relative effect of different economic policies on the nature, character, and magnitude of such migration and to ascertain what factors influence a person's decision to move in different countries and regions, we will be unable to formulate policies to deal effectively with the dual problems of rapid urban population growth and rising urban marginalism.

My broad objectives in this paper are threefold: first, to examine the literature on migration models and the role of internal migration in the process of economic development; second, to identify what has been empirically tested and where, giving special emphasis to a number of recently concluded econometric country studies; and, third, building on this background to identify the major priority questions in migration research that still remain to be answered and to suggest appropriate methods for dealing with these questions.

6.2 Toward an Empirically Testable Economic Theory of Rural-Urban Migration

The evidence of the 1960s and early 1970s, when many developing nations witnessed a substantial migration of their rural populations into urban areas in spite of rising levels of urban unemployment and underemployment, calls into question the validity of the traditional Lewis type of two-sector models of labor transfer and economic development. In a series of articles, I and others have attempted to fill this gap in migration theory by developing a model of rural-urban migration that tries to explain the apparently paradoxical relationship (at least in terms of traditional neoclassical economics) of accelerated rural-urban migration in the context of continuously rising urban unemployment.[1] We therefore begin by examining the basic nature of the Todaro model, then look at later modifications, criticisms, and extensions.

6.2.1 The Todaro Migration Model

Starting from the assumption that migration is based primarily on privately rational economic calculations despite the existence of high urban unemployment, the Todaro model postulates that migration proceeds in response to urban-rural differences in *expected rather than actual earnings*. The fundamental premise is that as decision-makers migrants consider the various labor-market opportunities available to them as, say, between the rural and urban sectors, choosing the one that maximizes their "expected" gains from migration. Expected gains are measured by the *difference in real incomes between rural and urban work opportunities* and the *probability of a new migrant's obtaining an urban job.* A schematic framework describing the multiplicity of factors affecting the migration decision is portrayed in figure 6.1. While the factors illustrated in figure 6.1 include both economic and noneconomic variables, the economic ones are assumed to predominate.

The "thought process" of the Todaro model can be explained as follows. Suppose the average unskilled or semiskilled rural worker has a choice between being a farm laborer (or working his own land) for an annual average real income of, say, 50 units per year, and migrating to the city where a worker with his skill or educational background can obtain wage employment yielding an annual real income of, say, 100 units. The more traditional economic models of migration that place exclusive emphasis on the income differential factor as the determinant of the decision to migrate would indicate a clear choice in this situation. The worker should seek the higher-paying urban job. It is important to recognize, however, that these migration models were developed largely in the context of advanced industrial economies and, as such, implicitly assumed the existence of full or near-full employment in urban areas. In a full-employment environment the decision to migrate can in fact be predicated solely on securing the highest-paying job wherever it becomes available, other factors being held constant. Simple economic theory would then indicate that such migration should lead to a reduction in wage differentials through geographic changes in supply and demand, both in areas of out-migration (where incomes rise) and in points of in-migration (where they fall).

Unfortunately, such an analysis is not very realistic in the context of the institutional and economic framework of most Third World nations. First of all, these countries are beset by a chronic and serious problem of urban surplus labor, so that many migrants cannot expect to secure high-paying urban jobs immediately upon arrival. In fact, it is much more likely that upon entering the urban labor market many migrants will either become totally unemployed or will seek casual and part-time employment in the urban traditional sector for some time.[2]

Consequently, in his decision to migrate the individual must in effect balance the probabilities and risks of being unemployed or underemployed for a considerable period of time against the positive urban-rural real-income differential. That it is possible for our hypothetical migrant to earn twice as much annual real income in an urban area as in his rural environment may be of little consequence if his actual *probability* of securing the higher-paying job within a year is one chance in five. In such a situation the migrant's actual probability of being successful in securing the higher-paying urban job is 20%, so that his "expected" urban income for the one-year period is in fact 20 units, not the 100 units that a migrant in a full-employment urban environment might expect to receive. Thus, with a one-period time horizon and a probabil-

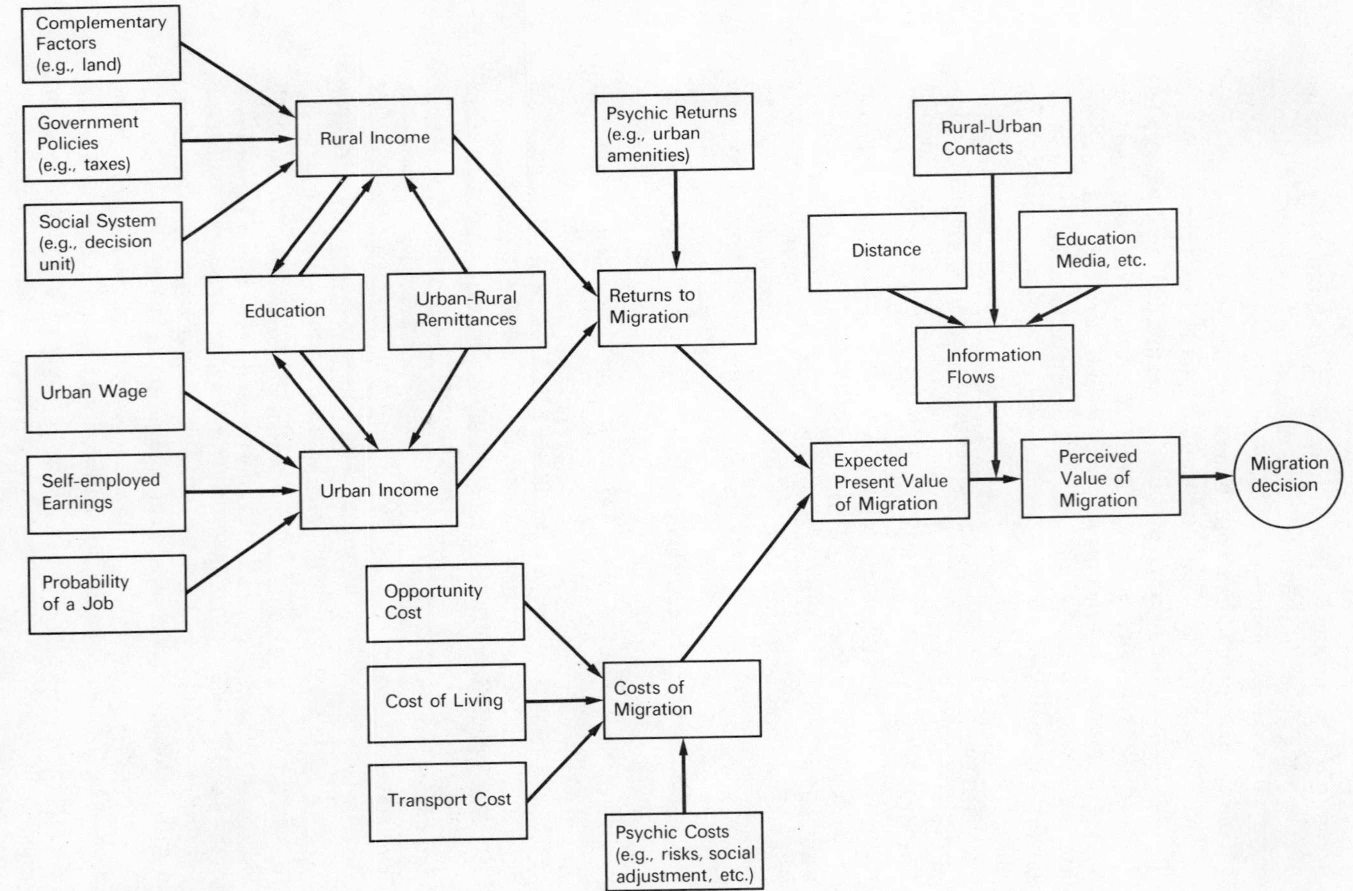

Fig. 6.1 A framework for the analysis of the migration decision.

ity of success of 20% it would be irrational for this migrant to seek an urban job even though the differential between urban and rural earnings capacity is 100%. On the other hand, if the probability of success were, say, 60%, so that the expected urban income is 60 units, it would be entirely rational for such a migrant with his one-period time horizon to try his luck in the urban job "lottery" even though urban unemployment may be extremely high.[3]

Returning now to the more realistic situation of longer time horizons for potential migrants, especially considering that the vast majority are between the ages of 15 and 24, I argue that the decision to migrate should be represented on the basis of a "permanent income" calculation. If the migrant anticipates a relatively low probability of finding regular wage employment in the initial period but expects this probability to increase over time as he is able to broaden his urban contacts, then it would still be rational for him to migrate even though expected urban income during the initial period or periods might be lower than expected rural income.[4] As long as the *present value* of the net stream of expected urban income over the migrant's planning horizon exceeds that of the expected rural income, the decision to migrate is economically justified. This, in essence, is the "thought process" that is schematically depicted in figure 6.1.

Rather than wage adjustments bringing about an equilibrium between urban and rural incomes, as would be the case in a competitive model, I argue that rural-urban migration itself must act as the ultimate equilibrating force. With urban wages assumed to be inflexible in a downward direction, rural and urban "expected" incomes can be equalized only by falling urban job probabilities resulting from rising urban unemployment. For example, if average rural wages are 60 units and urban wages are *institutionally* set at a level of 120 units, then in a one-period model a 50% urban unemployment rate would be necessary to vitiate the private profitability of further migration. Since expected incomes are defined in terms of *both* wages *and* employment probabilities, I argue that it is not only possible but likely to have continued migration in spite of the existence of sizable rates of urban unemployment. In the above numerical example, migration would continue even if the urban unemployment rate were 30 or 40%.

6.2.2 A Mathematical Formulation

Consider the following mathematical formulation. Individuals are assumed to base their decision to migrate on considerations of income maximization and what they perceive to be their expected income streams in urban and rural areas. It is further assumed that the individual who chooses to migrate is attempting to achieve the prevailing average income for this level of education or skill attainment in the urban center of his choice. Nevertheless, he is assumed to be aware of his limited chances of immediately securing wage employment and of the likelihood that he will be unemployed or underemployed for a certain period of time. It follows that the migrant's expected income stream is determined both by the prevailing income in the modern sector and the probability of being employed there rather than being underemployed in the traditional or "enforced" sector or totally unemployed.

If we let $V(0)$ be the discounted present value of the expected "net" urban-rural income stream over the migrant's time horizon; Y_u, $r(t)$ the average real incomes of individuals employed in the urban and the rural economy; n the number of time periods in the migrant's planning horizon; and i the discount rate reflecting the migrant's degree of time preference, then the decision to migrate or not will depend on whether

$$V(0) = \sum_{t=0}^{n} [p(t)Y_u(t) - Y_r(t)]\, e^{-it}dt - C(0)$$

is positive or negative, where

$C(0)$ represents the cost of migration, and

$p(t)$ is the probability that a migrant will have secured an urban job at the average income level in period t.[5]

In any one time period, the probability of being employed in the modern sector, $p(t)$, will be directly related to the probability π of having been selected in that or any previous period from a given stock of unemployed or underemployed job seekers. If we assume that for most migrants (with similar demographic and educational characteristics) the selection procedure is random, then the probability of having a job in the modern sector within x periods after migration, $p(x)$, is:

$$p(1) = \pi(1)$$

$$\text{and } p(2) = \pi(1) + [1 - \pi(1)]\,\pi(2)$$

$$\text{so that } p(x) = p(x-1) + [1 - p(x-1)]\,\pi(x)$$

$$\text{or } p(x) = \pi(1) + \sum_{t=2}^{x} \pi(t) \prod_{s=1}^{t-1} [1 - \pi(s)],$$

$$\text{where } \prod_{i=1}^{n} a_i = a_1 \times a_2 \times a_3 \times \ldots a_{n-1} \times a_n$$

and $\Pi(t)$ equals the ratio of new job openings relative to the number of accumulated job aspirants in period t.

It follows from this probability formulation that for any given level of $Y_u(t)$ and $Y_r(t)$, the longer the migrant has been in the city the higher his probability p of having a job and the higher, therefore, his expected income in that period.

Formulating the probability variable in this way has two advantages: (1) it avoids the "all or nothing" problem of having to assume that the migrant either earns the average income or earns nothing in the periods immediately following migration: consequently, it reflects the fact that many underemployed migrants will be able to generate some income in the urban traditional sector while searching for a regular job;[6] and (2) it modifies somewhat the assumption of random selection, since the probability of a migrant's having been selected varies directly with the time he has been in the city. This permits adjustments for the fact that longer-term migrants usually have more contacts and better information systems so that their expected incomes should be higher than those of newly arrived migrants with similar demographic characteristics and skills (Todaro 1969, p. 142, n.8).

Suppose we now incorporate this behavioristic theory of migration into a simple aggregate dynamic equilibrium model of urban labor demand and supply in the following manner. The rural labor force L_R is assumed to grow at a natural rate, r, less the rate of migration to urban areas, m, or

$$\dot{L}_R = (r - m)\, L_R, \tag{1}$$

where L_R is the time derivative of L_R.

The urban labor force L_u also grows at a rate, r, plus the migration from the rural areas

$$\dot{L}_u = rL_u + mL_R, \tag{2}$$

or, substituting $M = mL_R$, where M represents the actual amount of rural-urban migration, equation 2 can be written as

$$\dot{L}_u = rL_u + M. \tag{2'}$$

The growth of urban employment opportunities (the demand for urban labor) is assumed to be constant at a rate, g, so that

$$\dot{E}_u = gE_u, \tag{3}$$

where E_u is the level of urban modern sector employment.

So far the model is quite standard. The major innovation is a migration function in which the rate of rural-urban migration, $m \left(= \frac{M}{L_R}\right)$, is a function primarily of (1) the *probability* that an urban laborer can successfully find a modern-sector job, which in its most elementary form can be written as some simple (positive) monotonic function of the current urban employment rate $\left(\frac{E_u}{L_u}\right)$ or a negative function of the urban unemployment rate, $\frac{L_u - E_u}{L_u}$, and (2) the *urban-rural income differential*, which can be expressed as a ratio $\frac{Y_u}{Y_R} = W$, where $W > 1$ and is assumed to be fixed as a result of an institutionally determined urban wage and a given rural average product. Migration will also be related to (3) *other* factors, Z, like distance, personal contacts, urban amenities, and so forth, which also exert some influence on the migrant's perception of the relative "costs" and "benefits" of origin and destination opportunities. The basic Todaro migration equation can therefore be written as:

(4)
$$m = F\left(\frac{E_u}{L_u}, W, Z\right),$$

$$\text{where } F'\left(\frac{E_u}{L_u}\right) > 0;\ F'(W) > 0 \text{ and } F'(Z) \gtrless 0.$$

Holding W and Z constant, the function F can be simplified to read:

(5)
$$F\left(\frac{E_u}{L_u}, W, Z\right) = f\left(\frac{E_u}{L_u}\right),$$

$$\text{where } f' \geq 0 \text{ for all values of } \frac{E_u}{L_u} \text{ between zero and one.}$$

Substituting equations 4 and 5 into equation 2 yields the basic differential equation for urban labor force growth in the Todaro model, namely,

(6)
$$\frac{\dot{L}_u}{L_u} = r + \frac{L_R}{L_u} f\left(\frac{E_u}{L_u}\right).$$

By then comparing the time path of this equation with the growth rate of urban employment, we can analyze the dynamic process of rural-urban migration and urban unemployment under differing assumptions about population and employment growth rates (see Todaro 1969 and 1971*b*, appendix).

The main attribute of this mathematical model, however, is its rigorous demonstration that migration in excess of the growth of urban job opportunities not only is privately rational from the point of view of maximizing individual income but will continue to exist so long as the "expected" urban-rural real income differential remains positive. For any given relative real wage differential ($W > 1$), there will exist some urban unemployment rate that will finally equilibrate urban and rural "expected" incomes. But if the relative wage differential continues to grow (as it has in most developing nations), and if real urban wages are inflexible downward (as they have proved to be throughout the Third World), the rising rates of urban unemployment may never actually be able to exert their ultimate equilibrating influence on migration streams. On the contrary, continued and even accelerated rates of rural-urban migration will continue to exist simultaneously with these ever-higher levels of urban unemployment.

In summary, there are four essential features of the basic Todaro migration model:

1. *migration is stimulated primarily by rational economic considerations* of relative benefits and costs, mostly financial, but also psychological;

2. *the decision to migrate depends on "expected" rather than actual urban-rural real wage differentials* where the "expected" differential is determined by the interaction of two variables—the actual urban-rural wage differential *and* the probability of successfully obtaining employment in the urban modern sector;

3. *the probability of obtaining an urban job is inversely related to the urban unemployment rate*; and

4. *migration rates in excess of urban job opportunity growth rates are not only possible but rational and likely* in the face of continued positive urban-rural *expected* income differentials. High rates of urban unemployment are therefore inevitable outcomes of the serious *imbalances* of economic opportunities between urban and rural areas of most underdeveloped countries.

6.2.3 Modifications of the Basic Todaro Model

There have been a number of important modifications of the basic Todaro migration model since it first appeared as a Ph.D. dissertation in 1967. Many of these modifications were designed to introduce certain elements of reality into the migration process, elements that were assumed away or not taken into explicit account in the original Todaro model. But the basic features of the model remain intact, and they provide the framework for most contemporary econometric migration studies (see section 6.3 below). Among the major modifications of the original model, the following are perhaps among the most significant.

Harris and Todaro (1970)

First, I and my colleague John Harris utilized and extended the basic Todaro framework to construct a two-sector internal trade model of migration and unemployment that permitted explicit attention to the impact of migration on rural incomes, urban and rural output, and total social welfare (Harris and Todaro 1970). The two sectors are the permanent urban and the rural; for analytical purposes they are distinguished from the viewpoint of production and incomes. Thus it is assumed that the rural sector specializes in the production of agricultural goods, part of which are traded to the urban sector in return for the manufactured goods in which that sector specializes. It is assumed further that the rural sector has a choice of using all available labor to produce agricultural goods, some of which are traded for urban manufactured goods, or using only part of its labor to produce food while "exporting" the remaining labor to the urban sector (through migration) in return for wages paid in the form of manufactured goods. Thus it is assumed that the typical migrant retains his ties to the rural sector. The income he earns is assumed for analytical purposes to accrue to the rural sector. Such an assumption is clearly more valid for most African countries than it is for Asia or Latin America, where migrant ties to the rural sector are less pronounced.

Although these assumptions about intersectoral linkages enable Harris and Todaro to assess the welfare and distributional consequences of migration, they are not necessary for demonstrating the private rationality of continued migration in the face of rising urban unemployment. The crucial assumption for this proposition is once again my hypothesis that rural-urban migration will continue so long as the "expected" urban real income (the wage times the probability of finding a job) exceeds real agricultural income at the margin—that is, potential rural migrants behave as maximizers of expected utility.

The complete Harris-Todaro model, then, represents a simple extension of traditional two-sector neoclassical trade models. Thus there are variable proportions agricultural and manufacturing production technologies for the rural and urban sectors, neoclassical behavioral rules for the determination of levels of factor use and output in each sector, and a traditional trade-theory mechanism for determining the terms of trade between agricultural and manufactured goods. But it is the migration equation that represents the unique, most innovative feature of the overall model.

Harris and Todaro then utilize their internal trade with migration model to draw out a number of policy implications for developing countries. First, they evaluate the welfare effects (in terms of lost or gained output in each sector) of alternative urban employment policies —for example, uniform or sector-specific wage subsidies, urban demand expansion, and migration restriction (see Bhagwati and Srinivasan 1974, below, for a critique of some of this analysis). Second, and more important, they draw attention to the critical importance of urban wage determination, commodity pricing policies, and rural development programs on relative output levels, the terms of trade, and intersectoral labor allocation between sectors as a result of induced migration. Perhaps most important, the Harris-Todaro model shows that accelerated urban employment creation may actually increase levels of unemployment (see

Todaro 1976*b* and below for a new theoretical specification and empirical formulation of this concept of induced migration). Finally, they demonstrate the conditions under which coercive restraints on migration can actually *reduce* the level of rural welfare.

The mathematics of the Harris-Todaro model can be written as follows. Letting W_R and W_u respectively represent nominal agricultural and urban wage rates, E_u the number of urban jobs, and L_u the urban labor force, expected urban income, $E(W_u)$, can be written as:

$$E(W_u) = W_u \frac{E_u}{L_u}. \tag{7}$$

Expected rural income, $E(W_R)$, is simply W_R. The amount of rural-urban migration, $M = L_u$, is once again a function of the urban-rural expected wage differential, that is,

$$M = \dot{L}_u = f(E(W_u) - E(W_R)). \tag{8}$$

The rural-urban equilibrium expected wage condition is then

$$E(W_u) = E(W_R), \tag{9}$$

which becomes

$$W_u \times \frac{E_u}{L_u} = W_R, \tag{10}$$

so that the Harris-Todaro model predicts as a first approximation an "equilibrium" urban *un*employment rate given by:

$$1 - \frac{E_u}{L_u} = 1 - \frac{W_R}{W_u}. \tag{11}$$

This prediction should not be taken literally; it is intended only to illustrate an inverse relationship between equilibrium unemployment rates and urban-rural expected wage differentials.

While the combined Todaro/Harris-Todaro theoretical model does capture many of the most important labor market interactions between rural and urban sectors from the viewpoint of internal migration analysis, from an empirical or econometric estimation viewpoint the basic model clearly requires further modification and extension. The following are examples of such modifications and extensions.[7]

Johnson (1971)

Johnson (1971) was one of the first to modify theoretically the basic Todaro/Harris-Todaro model by explicitly introducing variables for the rate of labor turnover and the possibility of the urban employed sharing their income with the unemployed through some form of extended family network. Thus Johnson defines the actual income in urban areas as

$(1-\alpha)\ W_u + \alpha W_u n$ for the employed and $\alpha W_u n$ for the unemployed, where W_u is the urban wage rate, n is the urban employment rate, and $\alpha(<1)$ is the proportion of the total wage bill that is shared with the unemployed (Johnson 1971, p. 22). Therefore, if p is the probability that an individual will be employed at a point in time, urban expected income at that time can be represented as:

$$E(Y_u) = (1-\alpha)\ W_u p + \alpha W_u n. \tag{12}$$

Johnson also introduces into Todaro's basic job probability formulation a variable to reflect the rate of labor turnover in the urban modern sector. Rather than new job creation being simple $g \times E_u$ (which assumes no labor turnover), the rate of new urban "hires" can be represented by

$$\dot{E}_u = g \times E_u + \beta E_u, \tag{13}$$

where β is the rate of job turnover.

Although β is probably much lower in developing nations than in developed countries owing to the scarcity of urban-sector job opportunities and the fact that most people who quit do so only with the knowledge that another job awaits them, Johnson's introduction of a labor turnover variable does bring the probability formula of the simple Todaro model a bit closer to reality.

Bhagwati and Srinivasan (1974)

Bhagwati and Srinivasan (1974) provide an extensive yet, on the whole, positive critique of the Harris-Todaro model, identifying some of its major policy conclusions, especially those relating to the migration and employment effect of various wage and production subsidy programs in both rural and urban areas. In particular, they point out that the Harris-Todaro conclusion that a (second-best) combination of an urban wage subsidy with physical migration restriction would be necessary to achieve economywide production efficiency is not correct since a best solution can be realized by a variety of different tax or subsidy schemes, without the necessity of physical restrictions on internal migration.

Cordon and Findlay (1975)

Cordon and Findlay (1975) further extend the Harris-Todaro model by introducing intersectoral capital mobility between the rural and urban sectors in response to differentials in the return on capital. They also examine the comparative static effects of economic growth in both the original Harris-Todaro model and the modified model with perfect capital mobility and with commodity prices determined externally in an open economy framework. They then explore the policy implications of the modified model and reach a number of conclusions that both support and modify those derived by Harris and Todaro.

Fields (1975)

One of the most extensive and useful modifications of the basic Harris-Todaro framework is that provided by Fields (1975). Fields uses the Harris-Todaro framework of quantity rather than wage adjustments as the principal equilibrating force in urban labor markets to consider four additional factors in the determination of equilibrium levels of urban unemployment in developing countries: (1) a more generalized description of the urban job search process in which a rural resident may have some positive probability of finding an urban job without first migrating to the city; (2) the existence of underemployment in the urban traditional or "informal" sector in which workers are not barred from searching for a modern sector job although their probability of success is lower than that of an unemployed worker who engages in full-time job search; (3) the likelihood that educated workers will be given preferential treatment in modern-sector job hiring; and (4) the recognition of labor turnover in a multiperiod urban framework and the likelihood of differential attitudes toward risk aversion among different migrants. He shows that each of these realistic extensions implies a *lower* equilibrium urban unemployment rate than that "predicted" by the simple Harris-Todaro expected wage gap model.

On the basis of his analysis, Fields suggests three additional policy variables beyond those suggested by Harris and Todaro and Bhagwati and Srinivasan that may have an important effect on the volume of unemployment and underemployment in LDCs (p. 185). These include (1) the establishment of rural and urban labor exchanges designed to minimize the need for migrants to engage in costly (private and social) job search and thus to reduce the size of the urban informal sector, lower open unemployment, and raise national output; and (2) the (somewhat curious) recommendation that "overeducation of the labour force might have the beneficial effect of both lessening urban unemployment and increasing national income in both the rural and the urban areas" (p. 185). This paradox arises because more highly educated workers are selected first, thus reducing the probability that less-educated workers will successfully secure a modern sector job and thereby, through lower induced migration, reducing the number of potential migrants by more than the number of jobs taken by the better educated (via the Todaro induced-migration multiplier). Unfortunately, Fields does not take into account the "social costs" of overeducation, especially in terms of foregone job opportunities. The variables also include (3) the suggestion that it is *job hiring* rather than *number* of jobs that primarily influence worker's locational decisions. Fields shows, therefore, that "a small increase in the number of jobs has a much larger proportional effect on job hiring and induces substantial rural-urban migration and increases the rate of unemployment. Thus migration can be stemmed simply by not growing so fast" (p. 186). This last policy conclusion echoes the one in my original 1969 article but does not emphasize, as that article did, the concomitant importance of generating a more rapid rate of *rural* employment and output growth.

Conclusions

In spite of many significant modifications of the basic Todaro/Harris-Todaro model, it remains that its fundamental contribution—the idea that migration proceeds primarily in response to differences in "expected" urban and rural real incomes and that as a result of this the observed accelerated rates of internal LDC migration in the context of rising urban unemployment are not only a plausible phenomenon but in fact are entirely rational from the private "expected" income-maximization viewpoint of individual migrants—remains widely accepted as the "received theory" in the literature on migration and economic development (Fields 1975, p. 167; Jolly et al. 1973, pp. 13–16; Meier 1976, IV.C.1). This general acceptance at the "theoretical" level is reflected at the empirical level also by the widespread utilization of econometric migration functions that give explicit recognition to the "expected" income differential as one of the most important explanatory variables in the migration decision-making process. In the next section we look at this growing body of quantitative migration literature for a wide range of developing nations.

6.3 A Summary Review of Quantitative Migration Studies

Having set forth the general theoretical framework, we can now review and summarize the results of some completed migration studies. My main objective in this section is to determine what now seems to be known about migrant characteristics and the migration process in developing nations. This will allow us in the final section to delineate questions and issues that remain unanswered and therefore to suggest the most promising areas for future migration research.

6.3.1 Summary Results of the Nonrigorous Descriptive Literature

Our best sources of information on the range of *descriptive* migration literature for developing countries are the earlier comprehensive surveys by Brigg (1971, 1973), Carynnyk-Sinclair (1974), and, most recently, those of Connell et al. (1975) and Lipton (1976). Descriptive literature on economic, sociological, and demographic migration for a wide range of countries in Latin America, Asia, and Africa was examined by Brigg,

Carynnyk-Sinclair, Connell, and Lipton, and on the basis of these and other surveys (e.g., Byerlee 1974) the following generalizations can be made.

Who Migrates?

As I pointed out earlier, migrants typically do *not* represent a random sample of the overall population. On the contrary, they tend to be disproportionately young, better educated, less risk-averse, and more achievement-oriented and to have better personal contacts in destination areas than the general population in the region of out-migration.[8] In Africa, the problem of migrant "school leavers" is widespread (Byerlee 1974; Caldwell 1969; Rempel 1971). Although many migrants are unskilled, landless peasants, especially in Asia (Lipton 1976), many others possess job-transferable skills, have increasingly more years of schooling, and have some regular source of financial support for the period immediately following migration (Todaro 1971*a*; Barnum and Sabot 1975*b*; Schultz 1975). Although single men still appear to dominate the migration streams in Africa and Asia (Connell et al. 1975), married men (many accompanied by their families) and single women are now more prevalent in Latin American migration patterns (Brigg 1971; Herrick 1971).

Why Do People Migrate?

The overwhelming conclusion of almost all migration studies, both descriptive and econometric, is that people migrate primarily for economic reasons. The greater the difference in economic opportunities between urban and rural regions, the greater the flow of migrants from rural to urban areas. While distance is usually a significant intervening obstacle, its negative influence can be largely offset by sizable income differentials, especially for the more educated migrants (Barnum and Sabot 1975*b*; Schultz 1975; Lipton 1976).

In addition to the primary economic motive, people migrate (1) to improve their education or skill level (also ultimately an economic motive); (2) to escape social and cultural imprisonment in homogeneous rural areas; (3) to escape rural violence (Colombia) and political instability; and (4) to join family and friends who have previously migrated to urban areas. Few studies seem to support the often-heard hypothesis that migrants are attracted to cities in search of better entertainment or "bright lights."

What Are the Economic Effects of Migration on Source and Destination Areas?

The quantitative evidence necessary to begin to answer this most crucial of all questions is almost nonexistent in both the descriptive literature and most econometric studies. It is thus a major priority for future research. While there is no absence of hypotheses and conjectures about the relationship between migration and, say, rural development, such hypotheses are yet to be supported by anything more than casual empirical evidence (e.g., see Lipton 1976). As I pointed out earlier, internal migration was traditionally viewed as socially beneficent. Workers were shifted from low-productivity, labor-surplus source regions to high-productivity, labor-scarce destination areas. Seasonal migrants were able to supplement their incomes by short-term "circular" migration in accordance with seasonal variations in labor requirements (Elkan 1960, 1967). If real wages were imbalanced between two locations, the neoclassical price-adjustment model dictated that in-migration would work to restore the balance by raising rural average incomes and lowering urban wages.

More recently, internal migration has been viewed less sanguinely, especially with regard to its effects on rural productivity *and* income distribution (Lipton 1976). Rural-urban migration also appears to be accelerating in spite of rising levels of urban unemployment and growing numbers of "urban surplus" workers (Sabot 1975*b*). Rather than adjusting downward to rising unemployment, however, urban wage levels continue to rise, mostly as a result of institutional rather than competitive economic forces (see, for example, House and Rempel 1976 for evidence from Kenya). While most studies show that individual migrants appear to be behaving in a privately rational manner, many observers now believe that internal migration adversely affects the welfare of source areas (primarily rural) (see Lipton 1976; Connell et al. 1975; Schultz 1976; for a counterargument, however, see Griffen 1976). On the other hand, such migration seems to be contributing little, if anything, to expanded social welfare in destination areas (mostly urban) (Harris and Sabot 1976; Todaro 1976*c*). But, in spite of the growing acceptance of this "new view" of the contemporary relationship between internal migration and rural and urban development, little empirical evidence to convincingly support or refute this view can be gleaned from the descriptive migration studies reviewed in the Brigg, Sinclair, Connell, and Lipton surveys or in other descriptive studies. Clearly, more carefully designed econometric studies are required to test alternative hypotheses about the "net" social effects of internal migration on both source and destination areas.

We turn finally to the limited but growing number of technically sophisticated econometric migration studies that have recently begun to emerge to see if anything more can be learned.

6.3.2 A Survey of Recent Econometric Migration Literature

Yap (1975) has provided one of the most extensive reviews of the limited but growing econometric literature on internal migration in developing countries. The econometric studies examined by Yap cover Ghana (Beals, Levy, and Moses 1967), Kenya (Huntington 1974), and Tanzania (Barnum and Sabot 1975*b*) in Africa; Colombia (Schultz 1971), Brazil (Sahota 1968), and Venezuela (Levy and Wadycki 1972, 1973, 1974) in Latin America; Taiwan (Speare 1971) and India (Greenwood 1971*a*,*b*) in Asia; and Egypt (Greenwood 1969) in the Near East. More recently, the following studies (not included in the Yap survey) have been completed: Kenya (Knowles and Anker 1975; House and Rempel 1976); Tunisia (Hay 1974); Venezuela (Schultz 1975); Costa Rica (Carvajal and Geithman 1974); and Peru (Falaris 1976).

All the above are cross-sectional studies, although Barnum and Sabot utilize both cross-sectional and time-series data. Most explain point-to-point migration, usually between states or regions, although the studies by Barnum and Sabot, Huntington, Knowles and Anker, and House and Rempel deal specifically with rural-urban migration. All except the Taiwan and Tunisia studies consider aggregate flows between areas, and most utilized census data (again with the notable exceptions of Barnum and Sabot, Huntington, Knowles and Anker, and Hay). Most deal with male migration only.

With the exception of Hay's microprobability function for Tunisia explained earlier, all are "macro" migration functions. They typically are specified in logarithmic form, the basic general formulation being:

$$\frac{M_{ij}}{P_i} = f(Y_i, Y_j; U_i, U_j; Z_i, Z_j; d_{ij}; C_{ij}), \qquad \begin{array}{l} i = 1, \ldots, n \\ j = 1, \ldots, n \end{array}$$

where, as before,

$\frac{M_{ij}}{P_i} =$ rate of migration from i to j expressed in terms of the population in i

$Y =$ wage or income levels

$U =$ unemployment rates

$Z =$ degree of urbanization

$d_{ij} =$ distance between i and j, and

$C_{ij} =$ friends and relatives of residents of i in destination, j.

A capsule description including regression results for the studies of Tanzania, Venezuela, India, and Kenya is given in table 6.1.

The following is a summary of the major findings of these studies.

The Importance of Income and Employment Differentials

As might be expected, all of the above-cited econometric work demonstrates once again the overwhelming importance of economic variables in explaining migratory movements. Differences in average income or

Table 6.1 **Partial Income Elasticities, Migration Functions for Men: Selected LDCs**

	Kenya Huntington (1974)	Tanzania Barnum and Sabot (1975*a*)[b]	Venezuela Levy and Wadycki (1972)	India Greenwood (1971*a*)[c]	Venezuela Schultz (1975)[d]
Dependent variable[a]	$\frac{M_{ij}}{P_i P_j}$	$\frac{M_{ij}}{P_i}$	$\frac{M_{ij}}{P_i}$	M_{ij}	$\frac{P_{ij}}{P_{ii}}$
Destination wage (W_j) Wage (W_j)	+6.79* (4.61)	+1.26*	+0.94* (2.59)	+0.56* (2.02)	1.83* (4.33)
Origin wage	−1.15* (2.69)	−0.56	−0.85* (2.32)	−1.24* (4.48)	−.857* (1.96)

Sources: Schultz (1975, table 5*a*); Yap (1975, table 3).
$*p \leq .05$.
[a]Definitions: M_{ij} : Migration from place i to j.
P_i, P_j: Population in place i, k, respectively.
[b]Barnum and Sabot estimated a linear function, using lifetime earnings, undiscounted. The elasticities are calculated at the mean of the variables, using the income coefficients, .0024 (destination income), and −.0070 (origin income).
[c]Greenwood's dependent variable is M_{ij}, rather than M_{ij}/P_i. However, the income coefficients would not change if his model were reestimated, using the rate M_{ij}/P_j; for P_i, included on the right side of the equation, has a coefficient of approximately one. In other words, the income coefficient, α, is the same for $M_{ij} = Y \ \ Z^{\beta} X \ \ P$ and $M_{ij}/P_{ij} = Y \ \ Z^{\beta} X$
[d]Schultz's dependent variable estimated by OLS in his polytomous logistic model is the natural logarithm of the *ratio* of the migration probability or the gross migration rate $\left(\frac{M_{ij}}{\sum_{j=1} M_{ij}}\right)$ to nonmigrants, P_{ii}, used as the "numeraires."

wage levels between two places invariably turn up among the most important explanatory factors. When income levels are included as separate variables, migration is positively associated with the urban wage and negatively related to the rural wage. When urban-rural differentials are combined into a single variable, the rate of migration increases with the size of the differential.

The Importance of Job Probabilities and Urban Unemployment Rates

Perhaps even more important from a theoretical as well as a practical viewpoint is the finding in the studies by Levy and Wadycki, Carvajal and Geithman, and especially Barnum and Sabot, Knowles and Anker, Fields, Sapir, House and Rempel, and Schultz (for more educated migrants) that *the job probability variable appears to have "independent" statistical significance and to add to the overall explanatory power of the regressions when isolated from the relative or absolute income differential variable* (Levy and Wadycki 1972, p. 79; Carvajal and Geithman

1974, p. 121, n.13; Barnum and Sabot 1975*a*, pp. 17–18; Knowles and Anker 1975, pp. 17–21; Schultz 1975, tables 5*c*, 5*d*; House and Rempel 1976, p. 11; Sapir 1977; Fields 1979). Thus, for example, Barnum and Sabot, in the first really comprehensive and significant test of the Todaro hypothesis based on a carefully designed sample survey, find that "the addition to the explaines sum of squares in moving from the specification without probability to the specification including probability as a separate variable is significant at a 99 percent confidence level" (Barnum and Sabot 1975*a*, p. 22).[9] Moreover, when the wage and probability variables are combined to form an "expected" wage variable, the result is a definite improvement over the nominal wage rate in terms of the amount of variation explained. Levy and Wadycki obtained similar results for Venezuela (1972, p. 79), as did House and Rempel for Kenya (1976, pp. 11, 19), Sapir for Yugoslavia (1977, pp. 14–20), and Fields for Colombia (1979).

These studies provide preliminary support for the Todaro hypothesis of the importance of the "expected" wage in migration, at least for Tanzania, Kenya, Yugoslavia, Colombia, and Venezuela—the only countries where to my knowledge econometric studies have given explicit attention to a separate probability variable.[10] It should also be pointed out, however, that Hay, in his study of migration in Tunisia, also confirmed the statistical significance of urban "expected" incomes, except that in Tunisia "urban earnings functions" in combination with proxy variables for urban expected income levels (schooling and level of skills) had to be utilized owing to the absence of actual urban income and employment rate data.[11]

Urban Employment Expansion, Wage Differentials, Job Probabilities, and Induced Migration

Job Expansion and Induced Migration. An important hypothesis implicit in the original Todaro model and spelled out mathematically in the Harris-Todaro model concerns the "elasticity" of migration (the induced migration) response to changes in urban-rural wage differentials and urban employment probabilities. Todaro (1976*b*) has recently refined the concept and derived two simple formulas based on readily available migration, employment, and labor force statistics for estimating the conditions under which an autonomous increase in urban job creation designed to lower both levels and rates of urban unemployment may in fact lead to *increased* levels and rates of urban unemployment. The outcome is shown to depend on two "threshold" values of the elasticities of migration with respect to urban job probabilities—a threshold level related to the *amount* of unemployment and one related to the *rate* of urban unemployment. Using secondary data for fourteen Third World nations, I have estimated both threshold elasticities to be mostly in the range +0.20 to +0.60, although the unemployment *rate* threshold elasticity is always higher than the unemployment level elasticity (Todaro 1976*b*, table 1).

In this latest paper, I argue that if the actual econometrically estimated migration—job probability elasticity is higher than either or both of these threshold values, an expansion of urban employment opportunities can be expected, through the mechanism of higher job probabilities inducing additional migration, to lead to either a higher level, a higher rate, or *both* a higher level and a higher rate of urban unemployment. For example, in Tanzania, Barnum and Sabot estimate a migration elasticity with respect to job probabilities of +0.65 (1975*a*, regression no. 8, p. 21), well above the "threshold" level of +0.25 calculated by Todaro (1976*b*, table 1). Thus, as a first approximation, we may conclude that, ceteris paribus, an autonomous expansion of urban employment growth in Tanzania would likely lead not only to higher levels but also to higher rates of urban unemployment.

Equations 14 and 15 and the illustrative computations reported in Todaro (1976*b*), therefore, offer LDC policy-makers a simple and convenient methodology using readily available data, for estimating, *as a first approximation*, the unemployment implications of policies designed to stimulate urban employment. Sapir has applied the formulation to the Yugoslavian economy and found it to be an accurate predictor (1977, p. 16).

Wage Differentials and Induced Migration. With regard to the influence of changing urban and rural wage levels on migration rates—that is, the migration elasticity with regard to urban and rural wage levels—the rate studies by Huntington, Knowles and Anker and by House and Rempel for Kenya, and by Greenwood for India, as well as that of Barnum and Sabot for Tanzania and those Levy and Wadycki and of Schultz for Venezuela provide some initial evidence of the possible values of these differential elasticities. First, with regard to the relative importance of urban job probabilities compared with urban wage rates, the Tanzania study estimates that a given percentage increase in urban wages will induce *twice* as much rural-urban migration as the same percentage increase in employment (Barnum and Sabot 1975*a*, table 4, regression 7), while the earlier Venezuela study predicts roughly the same effect for *interstate* migration (Levy and Wadycki 1972, table 1). Schultz, however, finds employment rate elasticities of migration more significant than wage elasticities for migrants with some secondary and higher education (1975, tables 5*c*, 5*d*).

Table 6.1 provides illustrative data from the five studies cited above for destination and origin income elasticities of migration. In the two rural-urban studies (Huntington 1974; Barnum and Sabot 1975*a*), the urban wage elasticities are higher than the rural elasticities, indicating that rural incomes will have to rise faster than urban incomes simply to offset the migration effects of a given increase in urban incomes.[12] Levy and Wadycki's interstate regressions for Venezuela show little difference between origin and destination income elasticities, while Greenwood's results for India show that origin wages are twice as important as destination wages—the reverse of the Barnum and Sabot study for Tanzania and the Schultz results for Venezuela.[13]

Conclusions. Although this information provides us with the beginnings of a policy-relevant econometric approach to migration analysis, it is only a start. A major priority for future research focused on rural-urban migration and based on carefully collected field survey information along the lines suggested in section 6.3 is therefore a more scrupulous and detailed estimation of income and employment elasticities of migration for different countries at different points in time. From the policy point of view, a knowledge of such migration elasticities would go a very long way toward improving the empirical base from which effective wage employment and income policies designed to induce a more socially efficient spatial allocation of human resources can be formulated.

Differential Responsiveness of Population Subgroups and the Effects of Personal Contacts and Distance

The econometric literature in general supports most of the conclusions of the descriptive literature with regard to the differential responses of population subgroups to migration opportunities. More important, however, it provides quantitative estimates of the relative significance of these differential responses. The results can be summarized as follows:

1. At the time of migration, most migrants tend to be both younger and better educated than those who do not move. Even when age is controlled for, migration and education are positively correlated.

2. In Africa and South Asia, men predominate, although female migration is increasing, while in the more urbanized countries of Latin America there is a growing excess of women over men in the migration stream.

3. In each of the above cases—age, education, sex—economic motivations are paramount in the migration decision.

4. The relative abundance of urban services and amenities do not seem to exert an independent positive effect on migration. The evidence on this point, however, is very tentative and fuzzy, since none of the current econometric studies measures a migrant's utilization of urban services. Additionally, one must be careful when including an urban amenity variable to avoid difficulties of multicolinearity with other independent variables in the regression equation (e.g., wage levels, degree

of urbanization, population size, level of employment).

5. Almost all studies show a positive correlation between migration rates (or propensities to migrate, in the Tunisia study) and urban or state destination contacts in the form of friends and relatives. Such contacts can provide important information on job openings as well as lowering the effective costs of the job search by offering costless or low-cost accommodations to the migrant (Fields 1975). When contact variables are dropped from regression equations, however, the destination income elasticities remain significant and are reduced in size only slightly. Thus, the presence of friends and relatives, though representing positive factors in a migrant's decision to move, are not substitutes for economic incentives.

6. Finally, the negative effect of distance on migration, as predicted by traditional "gravity" models (Schultz 1976), is pronounced in most studies. Migrants tend to move to cities and towns in their own state or region, but they will move longer distances if the destination wages and employment opportunities are considerably higher (House and Rempel 1976, p. 14). More highly educated migrants are therefore likely to travel longer distances than those with less education.

Economic Benefits

With regard to the employment experience of migrants on arrival, their income gains, and their economic status relative to those born in urban areas, the following seems to summarize the evidence to date.

Private Returns. Migrants on the whole do appear to have increased their private (and/or household) welfare as a result of migration in spite of high and rising levels of unemployment (Yap 1975; Lipton 1976; Carvajal and Geithman 1974; Barnum and Sabot 1975*b*). By and large, many seem to have realized their private expected gains, although the proportion of "successful" migration appears to decline over time (Lipton 1976). A number find regular employment soon after arrival, and most seem to definitely improve their economic status over time. Quite a few start out in the informal sector before moving to formal-sector employment (Hay 1974). Many share their benefits with rural relatives through cash remittances (Connell et al. 1975; Johnson and Whitelaw 1972; Harris and Todaro 1970; Adepoju 1974; Sakdejeyont 1973).[14] As Yap notes, however, "the proportion who have difficulty in finding work is probably greater than the reported number. The surveys use retrospective information, and the failures who left the area would not be included in the surveys" (Yap 1975, p. 39).

Education and Income. The studies reported here all strongly support the hypothesis that the incomes of migrants are highly correlated with education and skill level while being little associated with their status as migrants. To the extent, therefore, that migrants are more educated and have better skills than the average urban native, their incomes will be higher and their unemployment rates lower than urban nonmigrants.

6.4 Looking toward the Future: Priorities for Migration Research

Having carefully reviewed both the theoretical structure of existing migration models and the empirical information generated by the available descriptive and econometric literature, we are now in a better position to answer the question, "What do we still need to know about the internal migration process and its effect on economic development?" The delineation of this "knowledge gap" enables us to formulate a list of research priorities that then provide the foundation for a comprehensive worldwide research program focused on the causes and consequences of internal migration.[15] The following is such a suggested list.

6.4.1 Migration and Development: Research Priorities

Although our general knowledge base on the characteristics of migrants and the migration process, especially the paramount nature of economic factors in the migrant's decision-making, is now well established, the literature on internal migration is just beginning to explore, albeit rather unsystematically, some of the really interesting and crucial issues surrounding the migration problem. The major "knowledge gaps" that remain to be carefully and systematically researched therefore include the following seven elements.

1. *Migrant Perceptions, Expectations, and Experiences*

How are migrant perceptions about job opportunities in potential destination areas formulated? Have their subjective perceptions been confirmed by experience and, if not, how can the information system about destination job opportunities be improved?[16]

2. *Characteristics of Nonmigrants, Potential Migrants, and Return Migrants*

We know little about the job histories of return migrants and only slightly more about why certain people or groups of people *do not* migrate. Better information generated by initial rural sample surveys followed up by urban "tracer" surveys would widen the net of migration studies to identify not only actual migrants but also nonmigrants, potential migrants, and return migrants. Comparative information on all four categories could greatly broaden our knowledge base about migrant and nonmigrant characteristics and the principal factors that influence mobility decisions.

3. *Importance of Job Probabilities and Expected Incomes*

In situations where there are positive income differentials between potential destination and source areas and an excess supply of labor in the destination area, does a separate probability variable related to destination unemployment (or, better, surplus labor) rates help to explain differentials in migration rates? In such situations, what are the "private," as compared with the "social," returns to migration? In short, do "expected" income differentials along the lines suggested in the Todaro models explain variations in migration rates and patterns better than simple "nominal" differentials? This crucial question needs to be researched carefully in future econometric studies.

4. *Wage and Job Probability Elasticities, Induced Migration, and Urban Unemployment*

Perhaps the most important parameters in need of careful estimation in future econometric migration studies, at least from a policy perspective, are the partial wage and job probability elasticities of migration. By generating empirical evidence on the relative size of the destination (urban) and source (rural) wage elasticities as well as the (mainly) destination job-probability elasticity both for individual countries and for a cross section of countries, general conclusions can be reached about the relative importance of wage and job creation policies in affecting the size and redirecting the flow of migration into more socially desirable patterns. The linkage between migration policy and general development policy can best be revealed by knowledge of how diverse development policies directly or indirectly affect urban and rural real incomes and job opportunities and therefore influence the magnitude and spatial distribution of national and regional populations. Such a formulation of the migration question underlines the important two-way linkages between demographic and economic variables as expressed, for example, in the ILO Bachue and other demographic-economic models (see, for example, Wery, Rodgers, and Hopkins 1974).

5. *The Short-term and Long-term Social and Economic Effect of Migration on Source and Destination Areas*

A major and persistent knowledge gap in internal migration studies in developing countries is the lack of detailed assessments of the social *consequences* of migration for both sending and receiving areas. In the case of internal rural-urban migration, the consequences of urban migration for rural source areas in terms of household income, productivity, and opportunity costs for different rural subgroups (e.g., educated and uneducated, small landholders, landless laborers, and peasant farmers as well as medium to large-scale landholders) needs to be carefully assessed.[17] On the other side of the coin, the consequences of internal migration for urban unemployment, the provision of housing, sanitation, health facilities, and other social services, the social, political, and psychic problems associated with urban congestion and slum development, and, finally, the relative effect of all these on the welfare of migrants as well as on urban-born residents needs to be carefully and systematically examined. In both cases, better knowledge of the flow of private transfer payments in the form of the inflow and outflow of cash remittances will give us a better picture of both the short- and long-run distributional effect of migration in terms of rural and urban household incomes. This is probably one of the most important areas for future research.

6. *The Relationship between Education and Migration*

Although it is well known that more education increases an individual's propensity to migrate, we are still unclear as to how much of this increased propensity can be explained *solely* by economic factors (i.e., more highly educated migrants have higher expected urban incomes owing both to higher wages and to greater employment probabilities—as demonstrated, for example, in Barnum and Sabot 1975*a*, table 1)—and how much is due to the effect of education on a rural individual's "world outlook." In other words, does education exert a noneconomic *independent* effect on propensities to migrate? It may do this, for example, by altering a rural individual's overall utility function so that his "psychic" benefit/cost calculation of the private returns to migration works to reinforce his "economic" benefit/cost calculations. Those with more education, therefore, may have an "acquired" personality factor that causes them to respond disproportionately to noneconomic as well as to economic incentives to migrate. Carefully designed survey questionnaires and well-structured econometric models can help us separate out these different effects of education.

7. *Migration, Income Distribution, and Population Growth*

The relationship between migration and income distribution on the one hand and migration and fertility on the other is probably among the least explored, yet potentially most significant areas of migration analysis within the broader context of economic and social development. Migration can have a direct effect on social welfare by altering the pattern of rural income distribution (Lipton 1976) and thereby indirectly affecting the level of national fertility and future population growth (Kuznets 1964). Although the effect of migration on the spatial distribution of existing populations is a crucial issue, its influence on future population growth remains unexplored. There are a number of reasons, however, why we might expect migration to influence the geographical pattern and rate of population growth. First, migration affects the pattern of income distribution in rural and urban areas, and income distribution is thought to be an important determinant of aggregate population growth (Rich 1973). In general, for any level of per capita GNP, countries with a more egalitarian distribution of income tend to have lower fertility rates (Repetto 1974), mainly as a result of the widened range of choice that higher incomes more equitably distributed bring to peasant families (Kuznets 1964).

Unfortunately, in spite of some valuable recent descriptive studies such as those of Connell et al. and Lipton, cited earlier, the relationship between migration and rural (as well as urban) income distribution is little understood. While migration may improve the private or even the household economic status of individual migrants (Griffen 1976), it is not clear what its "net" effects are on *aggregate* rural incomes and production. Since migration is selective of the younger, more able-bodied, better educated rural dweller, on balance the rural sector as a whole may stagnate as a result of the rapid depletion of its most dynamic human resources (Schuh 1976). While individual families may be made better off, the sector as a whole may be made worse off. As a result, high rural fertility rates may be indirectly reinforced by the out-migration of the most talented elements. On the other hand, if economic incentives and higher income-earning opportunities were promoted in rural areas, there might be the fourfold beneficial effect of lower rates of out-migration, less urban unemployment, higher rural incomes, and potentially lower levels of rural fertility.[18]

All of this obviously is very speculative ad hoc theorizing. But I hope it does suggest that a broader perspective on the relationship between migration, income distribution, and population growth is in order. Future theoretical and empirical research on migration should begin to focus explicitly on this relationship as well as on the other issues outlined above.

Notes

1. See, for example, Todaro (1968, 1969, 1971*b*, 1976*a*), and Harris and Todaro (1970).

2. For an empirical verification of this hypothesis, see, among other studies, Hay (1974, table 4.7, p. 78) for Tunisia and Carvajal and Geithman (1974, p. 110) for Costa Rica.

3. Clearly, the final decision will be influenced by migrant attitudes toward risk and uncertainty. Different migrants might react differently to the *same* expected urban income depending on whether the probability of success is high or low; that is, a 90% chance of 100 urban income units might be perceived as more desirable than, say, a 50% chance of earning 180 units. We will explore this issue further

in section 6.3 when we analyze various econometric migration studies.

4. The Hay (1974), Barnum and Sabot (1975*b*), and Oberai (1975) studies, among others, provide evidence that migrant urban incomes tend to rise rapidly over time, especially during the first few years after moving.

5. Clearly, the present value equation should be disaggregated further by age, education, and sex as well as by regions of origin and destination, since both wage levels and job probabilities are likely to vary for migrants with differing demographic and educational characteristics (see below).

6. A number of critics seem to have misread my original article by asserting that I failed to take into account the existence of an urban "traditional" or "informal" sector by assuming that a migrant would be either employed in the modern sector or openly unemployed. But see Todaro (1969, p. 139, n. 3; 1972, pp. 49–51). Admittedly, however, there is some ambiguity, and the implications of informal activities were not fully drawn out (see Fields 1975).

7. For a more detailed discussion of theoretical modifications see Todaro (1976*c*, pp. 32–46).

8. For historical evidence of this point from developed countries, see Kuznets (1964).

9. In his study of Kenyan migration, Rempel (1971) set out to test the Todaro model and found no independent significance for the expected "wage" differential, or for that matter for the urban wage per se, which in some regressions even had a negative sign! But, as pointed out earlier, Rempel's study surveyed only urban migrants, did not deal effectively with estimations of rural or urban incomes, had a statistically inadequate specification of the job probability variable, and in general suffered from a number of other methodological weaknesses. To this extent it was not a real test of the Todaro model. However, the more recent paper by House and Rempel (1976) as well as that by Knowles and Anker (1975), based on a more thorough sample survey of 1,074 Kenyan households in seven of Kenya's eight provinces, provide detailed support for the expected-income hypothesis.

10. Schultz's later (1975) study of Venezuela using the same 1961 census data as Levy and Wadycki finds the probability variable significant only for more educated migrants, while Falaris's study of Peru, which also includes an employment rate variable, reveals insignificant coefficients with the wrong sign. Falaris, however, points out that his results are flawed by census data measurement problems as well as simultaneity difficulties.

11. In their study of Soviet rural-urban migration, Stuart and Gregory use the "tightness of the urban labour market" as a proxy variable for urban job probabilities and find it to be an "important explanatory variable" (Stuart and Gregory 1974, p. 24).

12. Not much credence should be placed on Huntington's urban and rural elasticity parameters, since they are derived from Rempel's income data, which, as we have seen above, are deficient from a number of viewpoints. See, however, Knowles and Anker and House and Rempel for more credible results for Kenya.

13. The Schultz and the Levy and Wadycki studies illustrate one of the main problems of current econometric migration research—the limited comparability of results, even those using the same data base, because of different definitions and specifications of dependent (but also independent) variables. Clearly, the standardization of these definitions and the adoption of more comparable measurement and estimation procedures is a prerequisite for meaningful cross-country as well as intracountry comparisons.

14. A number of investigators, however, report substantial reverse (rural-urban) remittances (Connell et al. 1975), and in some cases it is argued that total rural

out-remittances plus migrant's education costs greatly exceed in-remittances (Essang and Mabawonky 1974).

15. Two major cross-country migration research projects are currently being carried out by the Population and Employment Division of the International Labor Organization and the Employment and Rural Development Division, Development Economics Department, of the World Bank.

16. Gugler (1974) argues for the use of employment exchanges and recruiting offices in rural areas along the lines of the Mexican *bracero* program to improve migrant information systems (see also Fields 1975, p. 185, for a similar proposal).

17. For suggestions of research priorities linking internal migration to rural productivity and inequality see Lipton (1976) and Schuh (1976).

18. For a survey of the literature on labor policy and fertility in developing countries, see Ridker and Nordberg (1976).

Comment Gary S. Fields

All of us who study labor market and population problems in less developed countries and their interaction via migration are indebted to Michael Todaro for the intellectual guidance he has provided over the last decade. Before he arrived on the academic scene, it was widely thought that urban unemployment in poor countries could be alleviated or even eliminated if governments could only channel enough resources and incentives to create more urban jobs. Todaro showed the futility of this kind of strategy, pointing out that more urban jobs would accelerate rural-to-urban migration and result in more rather than less unemployment. Todaro's call for development strategies emphasizing rural growth has been heeded and is now widely accepted. I cannot begin to estimate the impact of this shift on the economic well-being of the poor throughout the world.

I also owe Todaro a personal debt. When I first arrived in Kenya in 1970 to begin to study economic development, Todaro had just left. The halls of the Institute for Development Studies at the University of Nairobi (and, I am told, the inner channels of the Kenyan government as well) were alive with the excitement his ideas had generated. His influence on academicians and policy-makers was evident. As a young graduate student, Todaro's influence gave me hope that some day I too might be able to contribute to the economic betterment of the poor around me, whose plight I was just then beginning to grasp.

It is a privilege to discuss Todaro's paper. The material is presented clearly, succinctly, and fairly. Todaro claims credit where he has earned

Gary S. Fields is associate professor at Cornell University. At the time this comment was written, he was associated with Yale University.

it, gives credit where it is due, and withholds credit where it is not due. On the whole, the resulting document is an accurate survey, valuable both to practitioners in the field and to newcomers.

The survey is organized into three sections: toward a testable theory; review of empirical findings; and major unresolved questions. My remarks are organized accordingly.

Toward a Migration Theory

Section 6.2 contains a valuable summary of the Todaro model in its several variants and a number of subsequent modifications. Particularly apt is the summary of the four essential features of this class of models and the assessment of the current state of thinking. The reader is thereby introduced to the main ideas in their original and current developments. On the whole, I am in agreement with the points made in this section.

The expected-income hypothesis (alternative versions of which are set forth in Todaro (1969) and Harris and Todaro (1970) admits of two interpretations. Some, apparently including Todaro himself, see it as a *literal* representation of the functioning of labor markets in LDCs, or at least as a tolerably close first approximation. Others prefer to regard the expected-income hypothesis as the *central characteristic* of a suitably embellished model. I myself prefer the latter interpretation.

In a recent paper (Fields 1975) to which Todaro makes several references in his survey, I addressed the apparent discrepancies between some of the Todaro model's assumptions and predictions, on the one hand, and real-world complexities and data, on the other. Specifically, I dealt with the gap between LDC unemployment rates and the rates predicted by a literal interpretation of the Harris-Todaro model (Harris and Todaro 1970). I hoped to show that the disparity could be reconciled within the Harris-Todaro framework, appropriately augmented. As I concluded from my analysis (Fields 1975, p. 184): "These extensions permit us to retain the quite plausible notion, as set forth by Harris and Todaro, that the voluntary movement of workers between geographical areas is the primary equilibrating force in the labor markets of LDCs, while at the same time having a theory which is not contradicted by the facts." Thus, I interpreted the Harris-Todaro model as being incomplete, not incorrect. For empirical research, it is crucial to work with as complete a model as is practicable. I will say more on this below.

Let me mention some other, less fundamental points where I differ with Todaro:

1. I am puzzled by Todaro's claim in note 6 that he took into account the urban "traditional" sector in his 1969 paper. The footnote to which he refers (1969, p. 139, n. 3) shows his awareness of the existence of

this sector, but this awareness is not carried over into the formal analytics. I suppose we have a semantic disagreement over what it means to take something into account.

2. In his 1969 paper and again in this paper, Todaro claims that the rising probability of employment is consistent with longer-term migrants having better contacts and information. I think he is a bit misleading on this point. In his model the rising probability of employment is the result of a cumulative job search process with infinite job fixity in which the transition probability π is constant. The rising probability of being employed refers to the *state* probability. It does *not*, as Todaro suggests, result from the *transition* probability increasing with length of time in the city due to better contacts (i.e., rising $\pi^i(t)$ at time t for migrant cohort i).

Review of Quantitative Studies

Section 6.3 reviews the major empirical findings from the migration literature. He brings together the results of a large number of studies, including several that are as yet unpublished. I found his distinction between "nonrigorous descriptive" studies as opposed to "econometric studies" a bit artificial and the choice of terminology rather unfortunate, but his conclusions generally are clearly reasoned and are well documented where possible. Where studies of only a few countries support a given conclusion, this lack of solid support is duly noted. As a survey, then, this section is a fine capsule summary of the existing literature.

In this section, I wish Todaro had adopted a more critical stance in evaluating the various studies. Strong and weak studies are given equal weight. The studies differ greatly, however, in conceptual clarity, data suitability, statistical method, and sophistication in interpreting the findings. In some respects, therefore, the evidence is weaker than Todaro implies.

I would also like to have seen a prescriptive statement of how to go about conducting empirical migration research relevant to the Todaro model. As my own past research on migration in the United States has shown (Fields 1976), even if one takes the view that economic factors are primarily responsible for migration behavior, *which* economic variables are included and *how* they are specified makes a great difference in the explanatory power of the economic model. My colleague T. Paul Schultz has recently undertaken an extensive formal analysis of this question (Schultz 1976). I raise this point because I find it very difficult to ascertain what Todaro would regard as an appropriate "test" of "the Todaro model." Does statistical significance of an unemployment rate variable in a migration function constitute sufficient supporting evidence? Or does verification of the theory demand more, such as observing the same elasticity of migration with respect to employment probability as with respect to the wage rate? I looked in vain through Todaro's survey and his other writings for guidance on just how literally to take the model, on which propositions are critical and which result from a specific mathematical formulation, and on what evidence would be conclusive in supporting or refuting these propositions. I await a statement from Todaro clarifying his position on these issues.

Another concern I have is with Todaro's skeptical conclusion about the consequences of rural-urban migration. Todaro states his own position clearly: "migration substantially in excess of new job opportunities is both a symptom of and a factor contributing to Third World underdevelopment." Symptom, yes. But contributing factor? I am unconvinced and truly agnostic. These are contentious issues. As Todaro makes clear in section 6.3.1, the evidence is speculative and inconclusive. I would have liked to have seen more discussion of the positions on both sides.

One other point bothers me. In section 6.3.2 Todaro describes a procedure he has devised in his most recent work (1976*b*) for estimating the elasticities of migration with respect to urban employment opportunities and rural-urban wage differentials. Todaro contends that the suggested procedure, although not ideal, is useful "as a first approximation" to the magnitudes in question. Frankly, I doubt the validity of this approximation. We should note that the formulas upon which the estimated elasticities are based are derived from the literal Todaro model of 1969. Consequently, these estimates make no allowance for labor force heterogeneity, job search by currently employed persons, or the other real-world complications recognized earlier in the survey. Thus, Todaro does what he cautioned us against earlier: he takes his own theoretical model literally in empirical work. Indeed, the Harris-Todaro model, taken literally, gives an equilibrium urban unemployment rate of one minus the rural-urban wage ratio, or roughly ⅔, well outside the range of tolerance as a "first approximation," which is why we need an enriched model in the Harris-Todaro tradition. Might not Todaro's recent calculations of the employment and wage elasticities be in error by a similar amount? This is more than an academic point, since there are evident dangers in basing policy on parameter estimates as imprecise as these seem to be.

Priorities for Migration Research

The list of research issues posed by Todaro in section 6.4 contains the major unanswered questions, including those for which tentative answers are available for only a small number of countries. If we had answers to all these questions, we would have a much better understanding of the migration process and a much better sense of what policy direction to move in.

Of the topics mentioned on Todaro's list, in my judgment two merit highest priority. One is the empirical validation of the expected-income model in predicting migration patterns. The conceptual propositions set forth by Todaro (1969) and Harris and Todaro (1970) some seven or eight years ago have not received sufficient empirical documentation in many areas. More diligent empirical research lies ahead.

The other high-priority research need is for studies of the consequences of migration for the migrants themselves and for the economies of the sending and receiving areas. I welcome the concern voiced by Todaro and others for the income distributional effects of migration as well as the overall efficiency effects. In bringing these concerns to bear, though, let me voice a general caveat. It is quite possible that overall income distribution may improve with migration even though both the urban and rural distributions appear to worsen; this would follow if, as seems to be the case, migrants were in relatively favorable positions in the rural areas before their move but enter the urban labor market at a relative disadvantage, at least in the short run. The caveat, then, is that income distribution concerns must reflect changes in the entire economy, using tools of analysis that are sensitive to changing numbers of persons in the urban and rural sectors of a dual economy. The usual measures of income distribution within the urban and rural sectors taken separately may not suffice.

In sum, Michael Todaro has prepared a valuable synthesis of the conceptual framework and empirical research on migration in less developed countries. The paper stands as an authoritative statement of where the migration field is and where it is going. The careful reader will observe not only how much is known about this important facet of economic development but also how little. As yet unanswered are key questions such as the role of migration in promoting or impeding economic growth and alleviating poverty and the extent of responsiveness of LDC workers to differential employment and earnings opportunities in present and alternative locations. Much remains to be done.

Comment Robert J. Willis

More than anyone else, Michael Todaro is responsible for the currently prevailing explanation of the coexistence of high urban unemployment rates and substantial inflows of rural migrants to urban areas in the

Robert J. Willis is professor of economics at the State University of New York at Stony Brook and is a research associate of the National Bureau of Economic Research. At the time of the conference he was associated with Stanford University.

Third World. This explanation, embodied in the Todaro and Harris-Todaro models, has led to a radical shift in the opinion of most economists concerning the desirability of rural-to-urban migration in the developing countries and of policies designed to generate growth in urban employment opportunities.

Traditionally, migration is viewed as one among a number of economic mechanisms that reallocate resources from uses with relatively low value to those with higher value, thereby promoting economic efficiency and growth. Rural-to-urban migration clearly played this role in the economic development of the Western countries and was expected by many economists to play a similar role in the Third World. Today, however, Todaro argues that such migration is viewed as "*the* major contributing factor to the ubiquitous phenomenon of urban surplus labor and as a force that continues to exacerbate already serious urban unemployment problems caused by growing economic and structural imbalances between urban and rural areas" (Todaro, section 6.1, my emphasis). The basis for this judgment is provided by what has come to be known as the "Todaro hypothesis." In this paper Todaro reviews his theory, recent extensions and modifications of it, and the empirical evidence that has been brought to bear on internal migration in the less developed countries.

In important respects, the Todaro model is more a model of how labor markets operate in LDCs than it is a model of migration as such. In particular, the spatial aspects of the model do not seem crucial. For example, Mincer[1] uses a very similar model to analyze the employment and unemployment effects of minimum wage laws in the United States. He divides the economy into "covered" and "uncovered" sectors that parallel Todaro's urban and rural sectors, except that Mincer's sectors are defined according to statute while Todaro's are defined spatially. Of course the key feature that distinguishes the sectors in each model is the assumption that wage rates are fixed exogenously in one sector and are free to fluctuate with supply and demand in the other sector. Both Mincer and Todaro close the model by assuming that excess supplies of labor in the "covered" sector are probabilistically rationed and that individual supply conditions are governed by a comparison of expected wages in the two sectors.

It is interesting to note that Mincer finds that an increase in the minimum wage causes labor to leave the covered sector in the United States, while Todaro argues that policies designed to raise modern-sector wages above the competitive level are a major cause of labor inflow into urban areas in LDCs. In their respective contexts, as Mincer notes, both arguments may be correct. In particular, increases in the covered-sector wage are more likely to generate inflows of labor to the covered sector, the more rapid the growth of labor demand in that sector. Rapid demand growth may be more characteristic of the covered sector in developing countries than it is in the United States.

Two assumptions—exogenous (or downwardly rigid) modern-sector wages and probabilistic job rationing—are chiefly responsible for Todaro's conclusion that privately rational decisions to migrate to urban areas generate important social losses through urban unemployment or underemployment. Given the importance of these assumptions, Todaro devotes surprisingly little attention in this survey to their empirical validity or theoretical justification.

Consider first the question of rigid wages. Although he asserts that real urban wages have proved to be inflexible downward throughout the Third World, Todaro offers no evidence for this assertion. Nor does he elaborate on the sources of rigidity or define the scope of the "covered sector" in terms of the industries and occupational or skill categories for which the rigidity holds. My concern here is not that Todaro may be wrong in his assertion that wage rigidities are extremely important in LDCs. Rather, it seems to me that empirical tests of the Todaro model and discussions of its policy implications could benefit substantially from a more careful and precise consideration of these issues. For example, it is clear that a uniform minimum wage law impinges most severely on the least skilled workers, while artificially high wages for government bureaucrats are likely to affect the best educated portion of the population. In the former case, the achievement of market equilibrium is likely to involve the migration of unskilled workers from rural areas. In the latter case, equilibrium will probably not induce substantial rural-to-urban migration. Rather, the clearing mechanism more likely involves excessive investment in higher education by the urban middle class and the creation of an underemployed intelligentsia.

From a policy perspective, one of the most important contributions of Todaro's model is to remind us that artificially elevated wages may involve two sources of welfare loss. The first, most familiar source of loss is the misallocation of resources between the covered and uncovered sector caused by the distortion of the wage structure. Note that this distortion implies that the modern sector work force is smaller than optimal regardless of whether the high wage causes a net inflow or outflow of labor to the urban area. If there is a net inflow, the rural labor force is also smaller than optimal.

A second loss, emphasized in the Todaro model, arises because the use of time by unemployed or underemployed workers waiting to be selected for a high wage in the job lottery is socially unproductive. This type of loss is better known in other areas of economics as rent dissipation, a phenomenon that arises when property rights in a scarce resource are not well defined. The difference between the wage of a worker in the modern sector and his alternative wage is a rent to his job, which is an artificially scarce resource. If the worker "owned" his job, he would sell the right to occupy it to another individual for an amount equal to the present discounted value of this rent. Clearly, an organized market in job rights would eliminate the second type of inefficiency by eliminating unemployment as a market-clearing device. It is also clear that, apart from wealth effects, the same allocation of labor would be achieved whether the "owner" of the job were the employee, the employer, a foreman, a union, a government official, or such.

The job lottery assumed by Todaro results in at least a partial dissipation of scarcity rents on modern-sector jobs (if workers are risk-neutral and in perfectly elastic supply to the modern sector, the dissipation will be complete). The essence of the Todaro hypothesis seems, therefore, to be a contention that none of the economic or political actors mentioned above has managed to acquire sufficient control of the disposition of rights to modern-sector jobs to be able to capture the profits from such rights. While organized markets in job rights are doubtless rarely observed, I suspect that nepotism, bribery, union entry fees, and a myriad of similar practices are not unknown as job allocation mechanisms in LDCs. To the extent that such practices enable scarcity rents on modern-sector jobs to be captured, the existence and growth of a high-wage modern sector will fail to explain the high levels of urban unemployment in LDCs.

As a final comment, I must express my puzzlement about the failure of Todaro and others to explore the feasibility of policies to deal directly with rigid modern-sector wages. If feasible, elimination of such rigidities would surely represent a first best solution to the problems stressed by Todaro of misallocation of labor between urban and rural sectors and the social losses caused by unemployment or underemployment. Even if rigidities ultimately prove immune to policy, serious research on this issue may be useful in clarifying the workings of the urban labor market in LDCs and the nature of social, economic, and political constraints on its operation.

Note

1. Jacob Mincer, "Unemployment effects of minimum wages," *Journal of Political Economy* 84, no. 4, part 2 (August 1976): S87–104.

References

Adepoju, A. 1974. Rural-urban socio-economic links: The example of migrants in southwest Nigeria. In *Modern migrations in western Africa*, ed. J. Arnin. London: Oxford University Press.

Barnum, H. N., and Sabot, R. H. 1975*a*. Education, employment probabilities and rural-urban migration in Tanzania. Paper presented at 1975 World Congress Econometric Society.

———. 1975*b*. *Migration, education and urban surplus labor*. Paris: OECD Development Center, Employment Series.

Beals, R. E.; Levy, M. B.; and Moses, L. N. 1967. Rationality and migration in Ghana. *Review of Economics and Statistics* 49(4): 480–86.

Bhagwati, J., and Srinivasan, T. 1974. On reanalyzing the Harris-Todaro model: Rankings in the case of sector specific Stidky wages. *American Economic Review* 64: 502–8.

Brigg, P. 1971. Migration to urban areas. International Bank for Reconstruction and Development Staff Working Paper no. 107.

———. 1973. Some economic interpretations of case studies of urban migration in developing countries. IBRD Staff Working Paper no. 151.

Byerlee, D. 1974. Rural-urban migration in Africa: Theory, policy and research implications. *International Migration Review* 8, no. 4: 543–66.

Caldwell, J. C. 1969. *African rural-urban migration*. Canberra: Australian National University Press.

Carvajal, M. J., and Geithman, D. T. 1974. An economic analysis of migration in Costa Rica. *Economic Development and Cultural Change* 23(1): 105–22.

Carynnyk-Sinclair, N. 1974. Rural to urban migration in developing countries, 1950–70: A survey of the literature. ILO Working Paper WEP-2-19.

Connell, J.; Dasgupta, B.; Laishley, R.; and Lipton, M. 1975. Migration from rural areas: The evidence from village studies. University of Sussex, Institute of Development Studies, Discussion Paper no. 39.

Cordon, W. M., and Findlay, R. 1975. Urban unemployment, intersectoral capital mobility and development policy. *Economica* 42:165, 59–78.

Elkan, W. 1960. *Migrants and proletarians*. London and New York: Oxford University Press.

———. 1967. Circular migration and the growth of towns in East Africa. *International Labour Review* 96(6): 581–89.

Essang, S. M., and Mabawonky, A. F. 1974. Determinants and impact of rural-urban migration: A case study of selected communities in western Nigeria. Department of Agricultural Economics, Michigan State University, African Rural Employment Program, no. 10.

Falaris, E. M. 1976. The determinants of internal migration in Peru: An economic analysis. University of Minnesota, Department of Economics (mimeographed).

Fei, J. C. H., and Ranis, G. 1961. A theory of economic development. *American Economic Review* 51: 533–65.

Fields, G. 1975. Rural-urban migration, urban unemployment and underemployment, and job search activity in LDC's. *Journal of Development Economics* 2(2): 165–88.

———. 1976. Labor force migration, unemployment, and job turnover. *Review of Economics and Statistics* 58 (November): 407–15.

———. 1979. Lifetime migration in Colombia: Tests of the expected income hypothesis. *Population and Development Review*, vol. 5 (June).

Greenwood, M. 1969. The determinants of labor migration in Egypt. *Journal of Regional Science* 9(2): 283–90.

———. 1971*a*. An analysis of the determinants of internal labor mobility in India. *Annals of Regional Science* 5(1): 137–51.

———. 1971*b*. A regression analysis of migration to urban areas of a less-developed country: The case of India. *Journal of Regional Science* 11(2): 253–62.

Griffen, K. 1976. The impact of migration from rural areas: Comments on Michael Lipton's paper. Paper presented at Research Workshop on Rural-Urban Labor Market Interactions, International Bank for Reconstruction and Development, Washington, D.C.

Gugler, J. 1974. Migrating to urban centers of unemployment in tropical Africa. Paper presented at Eighth World Congress of Sociology, Toronto.

Harris, J., and Sabot, R. 1976. Urban unemployment in LDC's: Towards a more general search model. Paper presented at Research Workshop on Rural-Urban Labor Market Interactions, International Bank for Reconstruction and Development, Washington, D.C.

Harris, J., and Todaro, M. 1970. Migration, unemployment, and development: A two-sector analysis. *American Economic Review* 60(1): 126–42.

Hay, M. J. 1974. An economic analysis of rural-urban migration in Tunisia. Ph.D. diss., University of Minnesota.

Herrick, B. 1965. *Urban migration and economic development in Chile.* Cambridge: Massachusetts Institute of Technology Press.

———. 1971. Urbanization and urban migration in Latin America: An economist's view. In *Latin American urban research*, ed. F. Rabinovitz and R. Trueblood, vol. 1. Beverly Hills, Calif.: Sage Publications.

House, W. J., and Rempel, H. 1976. Labour market pressure and wage determination in less developed countries: The case of Kenya. Department of Economics, University of Nairobi (mimeographed).

Huntington, H. 1974. An empirical study of ethnic linkages in Kenyan rural-urban migration. Ph.D. diss., SUNY/Binghamton.

International Labour Office. 1969. *Employment policy in Africa*. Report IV(1). Third Accra: Africa Regional Conference.

Johnson, G. 1971. The structure of rural-urban migration models. *East African Economic Review* 3: 21–28.

Johnson, G., and Whitelaw, W. E. 1972. Urban-rural income transfers in Kenya: An estimated remittance function. Institute of Development Studies, University of Nairobi, Kenya (mimeographed).

Jolly, R. 1970. Rural-urban migration: Dimensions, causes, issues and policies. Conference on Prospects for Employment Opportunities in the Nineteen Seventies, Cambridge University.

Jolly, R.; De Kadt, E.; Singer, H.; and Wilson, F. 1973. *Third World Employment and Strategy*. Middlesex: Penguin Education.

Knowles, J. C., and Anker, R. 1975. Economic determinants of demographic behaviour in Kenya. ILO, Population and Employment, Working Paper no. 28.

Kuznets, S. 1964. Introduction: Population redistribution, migration and economic growth. In *Population redistribution and economic growth, United States, 1870–1950*, ed. H. T. Eldridge and D. S. Thomas. Philadelphia: American Philosophical Society.

———. 1971. *Economic growth of nations*. Cambridge: Harvard University Press.

Levy, M., and Wadycki, W. 1972. A comparison of young and middle-aged migration in Venezuela. *Annals of Regional Science* 6(2): 73–85.

———. 1973. The influence of family and friends on geographic labor mobility: An international comparison. *Review of Economics and Statistics* 55(2): 198–203.

———. 1974. What is the opportunity cost of moving? Reconsideration of the effects of distance on migration. *Economic Development and Cultural Change* 22(2): 198–214.

Lewis, W. A. 1954. Economic development with unlimited supplies of labour. *Manchester School of Economics and Social Studies* 20: 139–92.

Lipton, M. 1976. Migration from rural areas of poor countries: The impact on rural productivity and income distribution. Paper presented at Research Workshop on Rural Labor Market Interactions, International Bank for Reconstruction and Development, Washington, D.C.

Meier, G. M. 1976. *Leading issues in economic development*. 3d ed. London: Oxford Press.

Oberai, A. S. 1975. An analysis of migration to Greater Khartoum (Sudan). ILO-WEP, Population and Employment, Working Paper no. 19.

Rempel, H. 1971. Labor migration into urban centers and urban unemployment in Kenya. Ph.D. diss., University of Wisconsin.

Repetto, R. 1974. The interaction of fertility and the size distribution of income. Research Paper no. 8, Center for Population Studies, Harvard University.

Rich, W. 1973. *Smaller families through social and economic progress.* Washington, D.C.: Overseas Development Council.

Ridker, R. G., and Nordberg, O. S. 1976. Labour policy and fertility in developing countries. ILO, Population and Employment, Working Paper no. 30.

Sabot, R. H. 1975. The meaning and measurement of urban surplus labor. International Bank for Reconstruction and Development (mimeographed).

Sahota, G. S. 1968. An economic analysis of internal migration in Brazil. *Journal of Political Economy* 76(2): 218–45.

Sakdejeyont, Y. 1973. *Village life near Bankok.* Kyoto: Center for Southeast Asian Studies, Kyoto University.

Sapir, A. 1977. The Todaro hypothesis for internal migration: A case study for Yugoslavia 1954–1972. Department of Political Economy, Johns Hopkins University (mimeographed).

Schuh, G. E. 1976. Out-migration, rural productivity and the distribution of income. Paper presented at Research Workshop on Rural-Urban Labor Market Interactions, International Bank for Reconstruction and Development, Washington, D.C.

Schultz, T. P. 1971. Rural-urban migration in Columbia. *Review of Economics and Statistics* 53(2): 157–63.

———. 1975. The determinants of internal migration in Venezuela: An application of the polytomous logistic model. Paper presented at Econometric Society World Congress, Toronto.

———. 1976. Notes on the estimation of migration decision functions. Paper presented at Research Workshop on Rural-Urban Labor Market Interactions, International Bank for Reconstruction and Development, Washington, D.C.

Speare, A., Jr. 1971. A cost-benefit model of rural to urban migration in Taiwan. *Population Studies* 25(1): 117–30.

Stuart, R. C., and Gregory, P. R. 1974. A model of Soviet rural-urban migration. University of Texas, Austin (mimeographed).

Todaro, M. P. 1968. An analysis of industrialization, employment and unemployment in LDC's. *Yale Economic Essays* 8(2): 329–402.

———. 1969. A model of labor migration and urban unemployment in less developed countries. *American Economic Review* 59(1): 138–48.

———. 1971*a*. Education and rural-urban migration: Theoretical constructs and empirical evidence from Kenya. Paper presented at a Conference on Urban Unemployment in Africa, Institute for Development Studies, University of Sussex.

———. 1971*b*. Income expectations, rural-urban migration and employment in Africa. *International Labour Review* 104(5): 387–414.

———. 1976*a*. Rural-urban migration, unemployment and job probabilities: Recent theoretical and empirical research. In *Economic factors in population growth*, ed. Ansley J. Coale, pp. 367–86. Proceedings of an International Economics Association conference at Valescure, France. London: Macmillan.

———. 1976*b*. Urban job expansion, induced migration and rising unemployment: A formulation and simplified empirical test for LDC's. *Journal of Development Economics* 3(3): 211–25.

———. 1976*c*. *Internal migration in developing countries.* Geneva: International Labor Organization.

Wery, R.; Rodgers, G. B.; and Hopkins, M. D. 1974. A population and employment model for the Philippines. ILO-WEP 2-21, Working Paper no. 5.

Yap, L. 1975. Urban task force paper. International Bank for Reconstruction and Development (mimeographed).

7 Interactions of Economic and Demographic Household Behavior

Allen C. Kelley

7.1 Introduction

In the past decade there has been a notable increase in research studies by economists in the area of population-economic relationships. On the one hand, Malthusian demographics,[1] which emphasized biological drives in explaining family size, has given way to attempts to make population an endogenous rather than an exogenous variable in studies of economic growth and household behavior. For example, the "new home economics," pioneered by Gary Becker's seminal paper delivered at the 1960 NBER Conference on Demographic and Economic Change in Developed Countries, has convinced many social scientists that the decision to bear children may be productively analyzed in the context of rational decision-makers applying the calculus of cost-benefit analysis.[2] On the other hand, economists are beginning to question the theoretical and empirical foundations of some long-held economic-demographic connections highlighted in studies of economic development and to make needed refinements based on alternative analytical frameworks.[3] One of these connections relates to the effect of higher dependency rates

Allen C. Kelley is chairman of economics and associate director, Center for Demographic Studies, Duke University.

The author is grateful for the significant contributions of Caroline Swartz to every stage of this project, for the research assistance of April Brazell and Kevin Sparks, and for the comments on an earlier version of this research by Richard Blandy, Bruce Bolnick, Gary Fields, Tom Kniesner, Margie McElroy, Marc Nerlove, Peter Peek, Sol Polachek, Alan Powell, Gerry Rodgers, T. Dudley Wallace, and T. Paul Schultz. An early version of this study appeared as a working paper in the International Labor Office World Unemployment Program series. Financial support of the research provided by the Ford Foundation and the International Labor Organization is gratefully acknowledged.

on economic development, and in particular the effect of larger family sizes on the household's rate and composition of saving and labor force participation.[4]

In most models where these economic-demographic connections have been explicitly investigated, children are assumed (1) to make rather mechanically determined consumption demands (through adult-equivalency weights) on the household's resources; (2) to have an adverse (or possibly neutral) effect on the household's work force participation; and (3) to be "financed" by drawing down on the household's level of saving.[5] These models and assumptions are increasingly being questioned. The effect of children on the household's rate of asset accumulation is an empirical issue. For example, children may increase or decrease the market or home work activity of parents, and children may contribute directly to this activity. Likewise, children may make large consumption demands or relatively small ones, given the scale economies present in certain types of household consumption. Children may stimulate or deter the rate of asset accumulation, depending on the nature of the household's saving motivations and on whether the saving measure is broadened to include human-capital investments as well as financial saving. In summary, the influence of alternative family sizes and structures on basic household economic decisions—saving, consumption, income generation—is a very complex matter. The influences are likely to vary in direction and magnitude over time and across countries. We must be reluctant to accept simple generalizations of the adverse influence of large families until household behavior has been subjected to much closer analytical and empirical scrutiny. Lamentably, a careful assessment of the current state of the art in understanding the effect of population growth on the economy conforms to Simon Kuznets's analysis of this issue expressed at the 1960 NBER conference: "We have no tested, or even approximate, empirical coefficients with which to weight the various positive and negative aspects of population growth. While we may be able to distinguish the advantages and disadvantages, we rarely know the character of the function that relates them to different magnitudes of population growth."[6]

In this paper we develop several empirical models of the household that highlight the effect of alternative family sizes and structures on saving and income and that in turn examine the effect of selected economic influences on the family-size decision. Microeconomic and microdemographic data on urban Kenya are utilized to evaluate these models. We find that many of the traditionally held adverse effects of family size and structure on household saving and income simply do not hold in Kenya.[7] Moreover, some effects of children that are seldom considered in economic-demographic household modeling turn out to be relatively important there.

We cannot generalize from our results. While the basic models employed in this paper may be broadly applicable, their particular parameters may change from setting to setting and over time. Until these types of empirical paradigms are forthcoming in sufficient volume for several countries, using microeconomic and microdemographic data from low-income as well as high-income countries, there will be little solid basis for identifying the effects of alternative household sizes and structures on household behavior, and population's effect on economic development.

7.2 Models of Household Behavior

The primary dimensions of household behavior to be modeled are saving, income, and family size, all hypothesized to represent interrelated decisions. In exploring the various empirical and demographic specifications of such a model, the sets of equations describing household behavior will be modified in two general directions. First, the concept of household saving and investment will be expanded from the traditional financial concept to include the household's expenditures on children's education. This framework requires the construction of a different measure of saving that includes human-capital investments. Second, the occurrence of child deaths can itself be treated as endogenous, not so much in a decision-making, behavioral perspective, but rather because certain household attributes (e.g., children ever born and income) that may influence child mortality are in part within the control of the household's decisions.

Section 7.2.1 presents the "basic disaggregated model" where child deaths are taken to be exogenous, where saving is defined to exclude human capital investments, and where the effect of children by sex on saving is explicitly examined. This basic model is then extended to include investment in children's education (section 7.2.2) and endogenous child deaths (section 7.2.3). For ease of exposition the models are presented in explicit form, and the variables are specified to conform to Kenyan data-file restrictions.

7.2.1 The Basic Disaggregated Model

The basic structural model is presented in equations 1–4. Expectations on the direction of the partial effect of the various independent variables are indicated by superscript signs; a question mark appears where the causal influences flow in both directions and the net influence is therefore uncertain.

$$(1) \qquad S = a_0 + a_1 Y^{+} + a_2 C^{-}{}_{fh} + a_3 C^{-}{}_{mh} + a_4 C^{-}{}_{a} + a_5 A^{+}{}_{m} + a_6 A^{2-}{}_{m} + a_7 (1/U)^{?}$$

(2) $$Y = b_0 + b_1 C^{?}{}_{fh} + b_2 C^{?}{}_{mh} + b_3 C^{?}{}_{a} + b_4 A^{+}{}_{m} + b_5 A^{2-}{}_{m} + b_6 E^{+}{}_{mp} + b_7 E^{+}{}_{ms} + b_8 E^{+}{}_{fp} + b_9 E^{+}{}_{fs} + b_{10} T^{?}{}_{k} + b_{11} T^{?}{}_{l}$$

(3) $$C_{eb} = c_0 + c_1 Y^{+} + c_2 (1 - e^{-c_3 A_f}) + c_4 E^{-}{}_{mp} + c_5 E^{-}{}_{ms} + c_6 E^{-}{}_{fp} + c_7 E^{-}{}_{fs} + c_8 C^{+}{}_{d}$$

(4) $$C_{eb} = C_{mh} + C_{fh}\ C_a + C_d,$$

where $S =$ household savings in Kenyan shillings
$Y =$ household income from all sources in Kenyan shillings
$C_{eb} =$ number of children ever born
$C_a =$ number of children living away from the household
$C_{ih} =$ number of children living at home ($i = m =$ male; $i = f =$ female)
$A_i =$ age of adult ($i = m =$ male household head; $i = f =$ wife)
$E_{ip} =$ primary level is the highest educational attainment of the household member (=1; 0 otherwise); $i = m =$ male; $i = f =$ female
$E_{is} =$ secondary level is the highest educational attainment of the household member (=1; 0 otherwise); $i = m =$ male; $i = f =$ female
$U =$ number of years the household head has lived in the urban area
$T_k =$ household head is a member of the Kikuyu tribe (=1; 0 otherwise)
$T_l =$ household head is a member of the Luo tribe (=1; 0 otherwise).

This model has three endogenous variables of primary interest: saving (S), income (Y), and children ever born (C_{eb}); and three endogenous variables of secondary interest: the number of children living away from home (C_a), the number of male children living at home (C_{mh}), and the number of female children living at home (C_{fh}).[8]

Since the primary emphasis of this model is to isolate some of the interactions of key economic and demographic variables, the demographic specifications are extensive, including (1) the number of children in the household ($C_{fh} + C_{mh}$), (2) the sex composition of the children (C_{fh}, C_{mh}), and (3) the household's structure in terms of the number of children living at home and the number living away from home ($C_{fh} + C_{mh}$, C_a). A justification of these choices of demographic influences is considered below in the equation-by-equation discussion of the model. It is sufficient to note here only that the traditional roles of male and female children are quite different in the Kenyan household. Moreover, the household's asset accumulation and labor force participation decisions (captured in Y) are plausibly influenced by the number of children outside the household who may potentially remit income to the primary household unit or who may be attending boarding school.

The Basic Disaggregated Model's Key Decisions: Saving, Income, and Children Ever Born

Saving. As in most models of saving, the primary economic influence is captured by the positive effect of income,[9] and the primary demographic influence is represented by a life-cycle plan measured by the household head's age.[10] There are reasons to expect a somewhat smaller life-cycle influence in developing than in the developed countries, as well as the possibility of a somewhat different life-cycle plan. These reasons relate to the importance of the extended family where children serve as a source of income security (particularly in old age) and to the frequently held proposition that individuals' planning horizons are relatively short in low-income countries.[11] The first observation suggests not that the life-cycle saving plan is unimportant, but rather that the pattern of life-cycle saving may be different in developing countries. That is, the household may substitute investments in children (both quantity and quality) and in the extended family for financial saving. If this were the case, the life-cycle financial plan would call for a decline in saving as the household head approaches retirement. This represents the age when the returns on previous child and extended family investments would begin to be realized.

The hypothesized influence of children on household saving is negative, although there are possible differential effects depending on the child's sex and whether the child lives at home. The overall negative influences are several: children may represent a form of future security and thus substitute for current financial saving; children will increase consumption expenditures, although scale economies in consumption will attenuate this effect; and large families provide greater security against uncertainty in earning power.[12] Whether boys have a greater or smaller negative effect on saving than girls is largely an empirical issue, depending on differential consumption requirements and on differential family investment levels in children. The latter influence will be sensitive to the relative rate of return of investing (e.g., educational expenditures) in boys versus girls. In some low-income settings, boys represent a more attractive investment than girls since boys are charged with providing financial security for their parents in old age. In Kenya, however, girls provide the household with a bride-price varying, in part, with the quality (e.g., educational status) of the girl. This bride-price phenomenon is plausibly explained by the high value of women in rural production, where they are not only responsible for child care and household upkeep, but are also farm laborers. Finally, children away from home will lower current household saving to the extent that these children, as well as those at home, represent potential or actual remitters of income, that is, to the extent that these children are an income-yielding asset.[13] The negative effect of C_a on saving may be larger than that of C_{mn} or C_{fn} since children away from home are likely to supplement current income, while children at home are not yet in a position to do so. Children away from home may also induce a reduction in financial saving if these children are at school, and if as a result the household is shifting its resources from financial toward human-capital investments.

A final determinant of saving that is included in the model is urbanization, measured by the length of time the household has lived in the urban area. This variable might be taken as a proxy for the degree of household ties to the extended rural family, an influence that can be expected to exert a negative influence on household saving.[14] The urban area also provides wider outlets for saving, as well as some "forced" saving (e.g., employer retirement plans). For both of these reasons, urbanization should exert a positive influence on saving. Attenuating this influence might be the desire and ability of the household to increase its consumption owing to the desire to maintain a socially determined economic standing (i.e., the influence of the relative-income hypothesis),[15] as well as the wider opportunities for consumption afforded by the urban area. These various influences that flow in opposite directions result in an ambiguous prediction on the effect of urbanization on household saving. Irrespective of the direction of influence, however, the marginal effect of urbanization is likely to decline with the length of time the household is in the urban area. A nonlinear relationship, captured by the inverse of urbanization, is therefore postulated.

Income. The family decision that explains the household's income is the level and the nature of the labor force participation of the various family members. Ideally, a detailed household model would examine the determinants of this labor force participation as well as the determinants of nonlabor income. In the interests of simplicity of model construction, we have elected to explore a subset of this set of decisions and to focus on the determinants of total household income.

The two major determinants of household income incorporated in most models of this type are age and education. Age reflects the possibility of a life-cycle earnings pattern whereby earnings reach a peak and may decline at later stages of employment, depending in part on the type of employment. If skills and education are important attributes of the job, earnings may actually increase throughout the life cycle; that is, human-capital skills may appreciate in value and improve with use. The opposite argument might apply to manual employment, where the capital stock (in this case the physical capital stock of the worker) depreciates with use. Earnings, in part reflecting labor productivity, would decline as a result. Since this latter type of employment is most prevalent in Kenya, we hypothesize that $\partial Y/\partial A_m > 0$ and $\partial Y/\partial A^2{}_m < 0$.

Education will exert a positive effect on income. This effect can be expected to be relatively large in the low-income setting where educational skills are relatively scarce.[16] In Kenya the value of education to economic advancement is widely known. The government has been committed to greatly expanding the educational opportunities of its population. There has been an emphasis on primary and intermediate schooling, and the supply of workers with secondary and college-level skills is still relatively small. As a result, the differential effect on income of secondary over primary education can be expected to be large. The model incorporates both the male household head's and the wife's education levels to reveal any differential effects of education that may occur in Kenya.[17]

Children may exert either a negative or a positive effect on income and work force participation. On the one hand, the presence of children in the household deters the labor force participation of the mother, although this effect may be small in the low-income setting where substitutes for the services of the mother in the home are more readily available.[18] On the other hand, children may add directly to the family's income;[19] they may also induce adult family earners to work harder and longer to support the added consumption.[20]

Sex-specific child effects on family income will vary from country to country, depending on the relative value of boys versus girls in terms of the household's commitment to investment in child-related human capital and depending on the possible existence of sex bias in employment. For example, if male children represent the primary form of security for the household in old age, there may be a greater allocation of educational expenditures to boys than to girls. Work force participation to provide the income for this investment may well be stimulated by the presence of male children. Moreover, mothers may directly assume some of the responsibility for educating and training their daughters. As a result, the mother's work force participation may be particularly deterred by the presence of daughters. Alternatively, daughters may themselves assist in housework and child care, permitting mothers to participate in the market work force. Finally, boys may find it easier to obtain market employment and to contribute to household earnings. Whether there are in fact differences in family income owing to the sex composition of the children cannot be assessed on a priori grounds and is therefore an empirical issue.

The effect on family income of children away from home is ambiguous. On the one hand, their separation from the household will result in a smaller contribution to the household's earnings derived from the child's direct labor. On the other hand, they may represent an income-earning asset that reduces the need for the household to earn, given the commitment of children to care for their parents in old age.

The Kikuyu and Luo tribes, both politically powerful and economically active, may possess different income-earning levels and opportunities than other Kenyans. This possibility may be associated with the particularly strong value they place on investment in education; it may be associated with differential access to capital markets or possibly greater awareness of opportunities for investment in income-generating activities; and so forth. They may also have greater preferences for work over leisure.[21] Hard evidence that systematically documents any difference in economic behavior among tribes is almost nonexistent, although speculation is abundant. Given this lack of evidence, and given the inadequate analytical underpinnings predicting the nature of any tribal differences, we remain agnostic in our speculations and are content to explore the presence of a tribal influence empirically, but without any a priori expectation of the direction of the influence.

Children Ever Born. Families are assumed to strive for a number of surviving children, which is the net income of the number of children ever born (C_{eb}) and the number of child deaths (C_d). In the present version of the household model, the number of child deaths is taken to be exogenous; a later version will explore an endogenous specification of this variable. Because families attempt to meet their target number of surviving children, child deaths, other things being equal, will exert a positive influence on the number of children ever born.[22] Indeed, given a positive probability of child deaths, there may be overreplacement of children who have died; that is, the estimated parameter of C_d may exceed unity. On the other hand, if the household is unwilling or unable to replace a deceased child with another live birth, then the estimated parameter c_8 in the C_{eb} equation will be less than unity.[23]

The relationship between female age and number of children ever born is well established in the demographic literature. This is largely based on the relationship of age and biological fecundity. Fecundity is greatest in the early years of marriage, diminishes in middle age, and reaches zero when sterility occurs.[24] This relationship is captured in our model by a hypothesized nonlinear relationship in parameters.

The effect of income on the number of children ever born is somewhat complex.[25] This relationship has been most extensively exposed in writings on the "new home economics" by economists who effectively employ standard techniques of price theory to the family-size decision.[26] Children are assumed to be consumer durables, providing child services that are a normal good (i.e., the income elasticity of demand is positive) and that require direct costs (e.g., food and clothing) and indirect costs (e.g., the parents' time) to acquire and enjoy. Through the standard income effect, an increase in income will increase the household's demand for child services. On the other hand, this increased income may be associated with (and caused by) a higher value of the parents' time. This higher value of time, in turn, will exert a negative price-substitution effect; that is, children will be more expensive to raise and enjoy in terms of the opportunity cost of the parents' time. It is often assumed that the negative substitution effect outweighs the positive income effect.[27] The relation of income and children ever born is, of course, an empirical issue. Indeed, in the developing economy where there are relatively more low-cost alternatives to the parents' time in child-rearing, the positive income effect could well dominate.

The positive income effect on the demand for child services has come under attack from authors who have questioned the ability to separate the income effects from the price effects. It has been alleged that society establishes "norms" or social pressures that result in higher costs for children of parents in higher status groups. As a result, larger incomes do not necessarily raise the utility of children. Operationally, greater utility can be derived only from child expenditure levels that are larger than those of the parents' "peer" group. Thus, the price of a given level of utility from children would increase with the family's normal income, since this income simultaneously implies a corresponding higher-status peer-group level. These arguments, if empirically important, would attenuate the positive income effect.[28]

If one extends the conception of the value of child services from that of a consumer durable to that of a producer durable, where children are expected to contribute directly to income as well as to remit earnings to their parents in old age, then the income effect may be even more powerful. Some authors have hypothesized that in a developing economy, given the high value of children for direct production, income security, and current utility, there may be an excess demand for children; supply factors may in fact constrain family size.[29] These supply factors relate in part to the health of parents, which affects fertility and child mortality. Higher incomes and education will result in lower child deaths and will provide the ability to acquire better health and nutrition, conducive to larger family sizes. For these supply-oriented reasons, increased income in low-income societies may also result in larger family sizes over those income ranges up to a threshold subsistence consumption level.

The effect of education on the number of children ever born is, like the effect of income, quite complex. More highly educated parents command higher income. This particular association between education and income may be quantitatively important in developing countries, where skilled and educated manpower is relatively scarce. However, in our model, this education-income effect is captured in equation 2, and thus the influence of education in the children-ever-born equation represents influences other than the income effect of education.[30] More highly educated parents also command higher wages, and thus the opportunity cost of producing and consuming child services increases with education levels. Because wages increase more than proportionately to increases in education in Kenya, we would expect the negative price-substitution effect of education on children ever born to be higher for E_{is} than for E_{ip}. Moreover, since the burden of child care rests largely on the mother, we would expect $E_{mp} > E_{fp}$ and $E_{ms} > E_{fs}$.

Several other linkages have been highlighted in the literature. First, Robert T. Michael (1973, p. 173) has shown using American data that "more educated couples use contraceptive techniques more extensively, approve of their use more thoroughly, and adopt contraception at an earlier birth interval. Consequently, more educated couples are . . . less likely to have 'excess fertility' or 'unwanted' births." He also demonstrates that more highly educated parents employ relatively more efficient and effective contraceptive techniques, other things equal.[31] Second, in less developed countries where supply factors may constrain family size, more education may serve to release these supply constraints. According to Encarnacion (1973), below some threshold level more education results in better knowledge of health practices, enabling women to have more children and enabling families to avert some child deaths.

Finally, a few economists and many sociologists have associated higher levels of education with systematic changes in preferences away from child services and toward competing goods and services, and away from numbers of children and toward fewer but higher-quality children. It is held that more highly educated parents have a greater preference for better educated children, other things equal. Moreover, better educated parents may also have longer time horizons, influencing their preferences toward consumer durables, on the one hand, and toward more durable (e.g., higher-quality) child services on the other. Unfortunately, neither economists nor other behavioral scientists have developed an acceptable theory of taste formation. Thus, while education may indeed affect tastes in some unspecified manner, to date it has not proved feasible to identify this influence empirically.[32]

In summary, with the possible exception of the influence of education at very low income levels on the knowledge of health practices, the effect of education on the number of children ever born is expected to be negative.

Children at Home and away from Home: Closing the Basic Disaggregated Model

There are a priori reasons to expect that household saving behavior will be different depending on whether children are older and outside the household or whether the family is supporting and investing in children within the home. In the present version of the basic model, the location of children is taken to be endogenous. This specification can be justified in econometric terms, since one would expect that the error term in the children-ever-born equation would itself be related to and explained by family size, the sum of children living at home and away from home. A somewhat improved model specification is therefore expected by the endogenous treatment of C_a, C_{mh}, and C_{fh}. It should be noted, however, that we are not particularly interested in explaining these child-location and child-sex relationships from a behavioral or an analytical perspective. The method of estimating C_a, C_{mh}, and C_{fh} is discussed below in section 7.4.2.

7.2.2 The Basic Disaggregated Model Modified: The Decision on Investment in Child Education

The basic model considers only household capital accumulation in the traditional forms of financial saving: housing, pension-fund contributions, savings accounts, bonds, stocks, and so forth. This may represent an overly restrictive and unrealistic model of the typical household in a less developed country, where the investment in human capital, and notably in the education of children, may represent a major saving motivation and a direct outlet for household investment funds. This follows for several reasons. First, as already discussed, children may represent a producer as well as a consumer durable. They may provide for parents in their old age; they may also contribute to the household's current income. The level of this earned and/or remitted income from children is related to the value the market places on the labor services of the child; this in turn is positively associated with the child's education.[33] Second, the value of education itself is relatively large in low-income countries, where educational skills are scarce. Third, children may represent a safer and less expensive outlet for investment funds than many forms of financial assets, where underdeveloped capital markets may result in expensive information and search costs, infeasibly large or "lumpy" investments, and higher investment risks given the uncertainties of investing in new enterprises in the early stages of economic development.

Finally, in Kenya a large share of the costs of education has in the past been privately assumed. Unlike higher-income countries where this form of "saving" is in large part involuntary through compulsory education, and where schools are financed largely through taxation, in Kenya education has been voluntary and school fees have constituted a notable source of educational finances. School fees on the order of 10% of household income have not been uncommon. Given the financial burden of school fees, members of the extended family have traditionally assumed some role in amassing the savings necessary to underwrite the education of promising children.[34] In 1974 the government of Kenya removed fees for the first four years of schooling (standards 1–4); the fees for the upper elementary levels were also lowered and standardized. However, the data analyzed in the current study apply to the period of higher school fees. Moreover, there are still substantial private educational costs, particularly at the secondary and university levels.

Turning to the determinants of investment in children, we will consider four variables: income, number of children, education of the father and mother, and tribe. These variables, together with our expectations on the signs of the estimated parameters, are summarized in equation 5.

$$I_e = f_0 + f_1 Y^{+} + f_2 C^{+}{}_{mh} + f_3 C^{+}{}_{fh} + f_4 E^{?}{}_{mp} + f_5 E^{?}{}_{ms} + f_6 E^{?}{}_{fp} + f_7 E^{?}{}_{fs} + f_8 T^{?}{}_{k} + f_9 T^{?}{}_{l}. \tag{5}$$

Both as a normal consumption good and as a form of saving, educational expenditures will be positively associated with income. Similarly, investment in education will be directly related to the number of children, although this relationship may be somewhat complex. Other demographic factors such as child parity, intelligence, and sex may also have an effect on the household's educational investments. Indeed, a case can be made whereby the level of educational expenditures on children is relatively insensitive to the number of children in the household.[35] If, for example, educational investments in children are viewed largely as an augmentation of a producer durable, this investment will compete with other forms of financial investment by the household. The level of income may be the single most important factor determining the level of total saving. Other factors may then enter to largely explain the composition of that saving, as well as the composition of consumption.[36] If this is the case, the number of children may represent a relatively unimportant determinant of total educational expenditures.[37] Other factors could well dominate: the availability of "promising" (e.g., relatively bright) children, the number of boys (if they in fact possess a higher rate of return on educational expenditures), child parity (if custom and tradition allot the duty of supporting the parents according to parity), and so forth. In our model, while we hypothesize a positive effect of number of children on educational expenditures, this may not be a particularly strong relationship. Moreover, it is possible that educational expenditure on boys will exceed that on girls.[38]

The effect of the household head's education on investment in education is also complex. On the one hand, there may be a positive relationship to the extent that the household head's preferences for education as a consumption good are directly associated with his own education. On the other hand, there may be a negative relationship to the extent that the household head's own education may have been in part financed by the extended family. As a result, the commitment to repay this family debt through remittances is likely to be directly related to the level of his own education.[39] The effect of the mother's education on child-investment expenditures is also complicated. Like her husband, she may have a preference for investing in her children's education that is positively associated with her own educational level. On the other hand, since she is responsible not only for child-rearing, but also for the education of the children, her own education may substitute for or be a complement of child-investment expenditures. The relative strengths of these various influences is not known with sufficient precision to permit a prediction of the direction of the effect of the mother's education on child-education expenditures.

It is widely asserted in studies of Kenya that there are differences by tribe in preference for education.[40] There is almost no concrete evidence that isolates these differences. We include tribe as a possible variable explaining educational expenditures but remain agnostic on the direction or magnitude of the effect.

7.2.3 The Basic Disaggregated Model Modified: Child Deaths Endogenous

Models that seek to explain the household's family-size decision typically formulate this goal in terms of the number of surviving children. A child death, other things equal, will exert a positive influence on the number of children ever born. There have been several successful empirical models that have estimated this effect of child mortality.[41] Seldom, however, have researchers also attempted to identify the factors that explain child mortality and to include child mortality as an endogenous variable in the children-ever-born equation.[42] Such an endogenous specification of child mortality is formulated in this section as a modification of our basic model of household behavior.

While a child death is not a behavioral phenomenon in the sense that the family "plans" to implement a number of child deaths, it is plausible that child deaths are influenced by several household-specific variables, some of which are to a certain extent within the household's control. These variables, together with expectations on the signs of the estimated parameters, are indicated in equation 6.

$$(6) \quad C_d = g_0 + g_1 Y^- + g_2 C^+{}_{eb} + g_3 A^-{}_f + g_4 A^{2+}{}_f + g_5 E^-{}_{fp} + g_6 E^-{}_{fs}.$$

We expect child deaths to decline both with the household's income and with the level of mother's education. Higher income provides more resources for better diet and health care for mothers and children. Additionally, higher levels of education provide knowledge of the dietary and health factors conducive to child survival.[43]

When deaths are included as an endogenous variable in the equation for children ever born, the influence of education on children ever born should decrease (given the removal of the negative effect of education on deaths); similarly, the influence of income on children ever born should increase (given the removal of the negative effect of income on deaths).

The effect of age on child deaths is straightforward. Since we are considering only child deaths related to children who are brought to term and excluding miscarriages, we expect the incidence of child deaths to decline with the age of the mother. This is due to the greater ability of older mothers to care for children. On the other hand, there are biological reasons to expect that child mortality will increase with age. In particular, the incidence of congenital malformation and genetic disease increases with age and parity; this increase is particularly rapid after approximately age thirty-five.[44] The net result is expected to be an increasing prevalence of child mortality by the age of the mother, especially toward the end of the childbearing cycle.

Finally, since the exposure to the risk of child deaths increases with the number of children in the family, we expect a positive sign on the estimated parameter of the variable children ever born.

7.3 Data, Variable Definitions, and Values

7.3.1 The Data

The data used in the empirical analysis below pertain to three urban areas of Kenya: Nairobi, Kisumu, and Mombasa. These data were collected from December 1968 to October 1969 by the Central Bureau of Statistics, an organization that has been responsible for many household surveys and that has a permanent staff of trained and experienced enumerators, statistical analysts, and data processors.

The sample frame was confined almost exclusively to African households. Through disproportionate stratified sampling, more households were selected from the upper- and middle-income strata than from the lower-income stratum. The final sample included 1,146 households. Most of these represented "complex" households, where there were more than two adults or where there were children who belonged to different adults outside the household. Unfortunately, both parents of the children were not identified in the survey. Since the present research focuses on the determinants of family size, as well as the effect of family size on other household decisions, it was therefore necessary to include in the sample only households with two married adults, where there were no "other" household members besides the children of the household head. This reduced the sample to 401 households.

This sample of households may exhibit somewhat weaker ties to the extended family than the complex households. However, an analysis of the expenditures of the subsample indicates that this group does indeed remit some income outside the household, presumably to the extended family. Thus the households in our subsample should not be interpreted as being nuclear in the behavioral sense of having no economic ties to the extended family.[45]

7.3.2 Variable Definitions and Values

Table 7.1 presents the means and standard deviations of the continuous variables used in the empirical analysis, and the relative frequency distribution of the classificatory variables.

Income (Y) refers to total household income earned (not received) during the period and includes the basic salary, bonuses, overtime, housing allowances, net business profits, receipts from the sale of own produce, and income from rents, pensions, and transfers.[46] This definition and measurement includes elements of both transitory and permanent income. Distinguishing between these two types of income would enrich the analysis both analytically and empirically, but for two reasons the costs of separating income components appears to exceed the benefits, given the present research objectives. First, those techniques that have been employed using cross-sectional data to measure permanent income have reduced estimation efficiency and are deficient analytically and statistically in other dimensions.[47] Second, the combination of the two income components employed in the present research identifies typical household income variation, assuming that the share of the household's transitory and permanent income does not change over time and that these classes of income are not differently distributed among households over time.

Financial Saving (S) is measured as the difference between earned income and actual household consumption.[48] This saving definition has two primary difficulties: the treatment of cash remittances outside the household and the treatment of consumer durables. Both are household expenditures; however, both also incorporate an element of saving. Remittances are used by the extended household for various purposes, including the financing of current consumption, investment in housing, and payment of school fees. That share of remittances that results in some form of saving or capital formation should presumably be classified as saving to the remitting household. However, no concrete information is available on the use of remittances by the extended household.[49] Based on data on average saving pertaining to the rural households (where the urban household income is largely remitted), 20% of the remittances are assumed to represent saving.

Table 7.1 **Means and Standard Deviations of Variables Employed in the Regression Models**

Variable Name	Variable Symbol	Mean	Standard Deviation	Percentage in Indicated Categories
Income (Kenyan shillings)	Y	719.5	794.4	
Financial saving (excluding education)	S	7.1	544.8	
Total saving (including education)	S^*	36.4	550.2	
Investment in education	I_e	29.3	57.4	
Children ever born	C_{eb}	4.1	2.8	
0				8.0
1				12.0
2				13.0
3				14.0
4				12.5
5				11.0
6+				29.5
Surviving children	C_s	3.7	2.59	
Child deaths	C_d	.4	.8	
0				76.8
1				13.2
2				7.2
3+				2.8
Children away from home	C_a	.6	1.3	
0				76.1
1				7.7
2				6.5
3+				9.7
Male children at home	C_{mh}	1.6	1.4	
Female children at home	C_{fh}	1.5	1.6	
Age of household head	A_m	36.4	9.0	
(Age) of household head	$A_m{}^2$	1,407.0	736.8	
Age of wife	A_f	27.9	7.4	
(Age) of wife	$A_f{}^2$	830.3	470.5	
Education of household head				
Less than completed primary				37.2
Completed primary	E_p			36.4
Some secondary or university	E_s			26.4
Education of wife				
Less than completed primary				57.9
Completed primary	E_{pf}			37.4
Some secondary or university	E_{sf}			4.7
Tribal status				
Kikuyu	T_k			17.7
Luo	T_l			24.9
Binary variable for age of wife	D			
$D = 0$ if $A_f \leq 29$				63.8

Table 7.1 (continued)

Variable Name	Variable Symbol	Mean	Standard Deviation	Percentage in Indicated Categories
$D = 1$ if $A_f > 29$				36.2
$D \cdot A_f$		12.8	17.4	
Urbanization	$1/U$	.2	.2	

*Significant at least at the .05 level.

Consumer durables are considered as current consumption. There is no feasible way to estimate the rate of depreciation of the household's stock of consumer durables. The treatment of consumer durables as current consumption, while not entirely satisfactory, is widely employed in these types of household studies, given the above-mentioned data constraints.[50]

Total Saving (S^*), which combines financial saving with human capital investments in education (school fees, school uniforms, books), broadens the concept of household capital accumulation and is justified by considering educational expenditures as in part an investment in a producer durable. While the analytical distinction between education as current or future consumption and as investment in an income-earning asset has been clearly delineated by Theodore Schultz and others, empirical estimates of the share of education which is consumption and that which is investment have been meager. This study will therefore examine the two extreme cases: one in which education is entirely a consumption good (whether current or future consumption); and one in which education is entirely a producer durable. In advanced countries, the consumer durable motivation plausibly dominates. In lower-income countries, educational expenditures are also likely to be influenced by investment motivations. Education, especially more advanced levels such as high school and college, is a luxury good, given the closeness of many households to a subsistence level of consumption. Moreover, the rate of return on education is high, making it an attractive form of investment.[51]

Measured financial saving in Kenya is small, 7 shillings per household per period, or about 1% of average household income. As in most household surveys of this type, saving is likely to be underestimated. When human capital investments are added, the saving figure rises to 36 shillings, or 5% of average household income. In both measures the variation is large. This variation is explained in part by real factors and in part by notable measurement errors common both to the measurement of saving and to any measure formed as a residual of two large elements.

Education (E_{ip}, E_{is}) is classified into three categories: less than completed primary education, completed primary education (E_{ip}), and some secondary or university education (E_{is}). Kenyan education is divided into three levels: primary (standards 1–8), secondary (forms I–VI), and university. There is at present an insufficient supply of secondary and university facilities, given the fee schedule. As a result, students can advance to higher education levels solely by passing various standardized examinations. Only a small fraction of college-age students are admitted to the university. Because there were only seven households in our sample that had a member with any university education, considerations of statistical estimation reliability dictated that we collapse the secondary and university levels into a single category.[52]

7.4 Econometric Considerations

The models considered in this study are interactive in nature; that is, they represent a household paradigm where key decisions are simultaneously made.[53] Two-stage least-squares regression analysis is therefore employed throughout.

7.4.1 Nonlinear Estimation

The basic disaggregated model of household behavior summarized in equations 1–3 is nonlinear in the parameters. This results from the nonlinear association between the variables children ever born and age of mother. To estimate this model, nonlinear regression procedures were employed. After some experience with these procedures, it was decided that the benefits of the precision of nonlinear estimation were far outweighed by the costs, especially by comparison with a simpler and almost as satisfactory estimation method whereby the nonlinear relationship was linearly transformed into two straight-line segments.[54]

Our a priori expectations with respect to the nonlinear association between children ever born and age of mother are presented by the solid line in figure 7.1. Initial estimates that employed nonlinear regression procedures in fact provided estimates of this relationship that conformed to these expectations. Namely, completed family size is reached rather rapidly after childbearing begins and approaches an upper limit in the middle to later years of life, owing to the onset of female sterility. A linear approximation to this hypothesis is presented by the two broken line segments in the figure.

The linear approximation is obtained by defining a dummy variable D that takes on a value of zero below a specified age A^*_f and a value of unity thereafter. The regression equation represented by figure 7.1 would therefore be written as $C_{eb} = \alpha + \beta D + \gamma A_f + \delta A_f \times D + \epsilon$. The line segment to the left of A^*_f has an intercept of α and a slope of

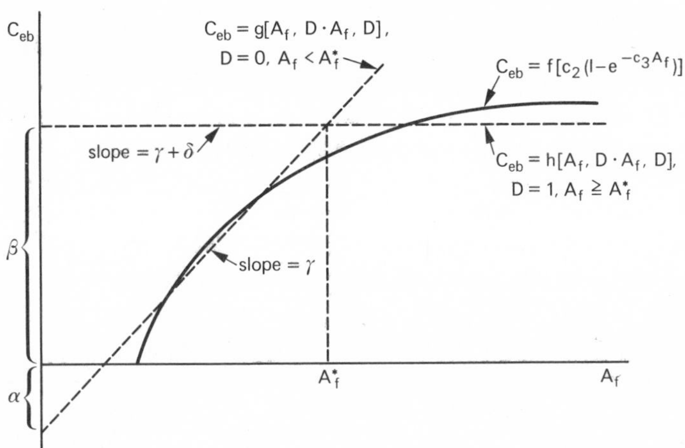

Fig. 7.1

γ. To the right of A^*_f, the intercept is the sum of α and β, and the slope is the sum of γ and δ. In practice, the estimate of A^*_f is given either on a priori grounds or is obtained by experimentation. In the present study, given our a priori expectations on the nature of the function, the value of A^*_f was obtained where the slope of the second line segment was flat, that is, where the sum of the estimates of γ and δ most clearly approximated zero.[55]

7.4.2 Categorical Variables, C_d and C_a, and the Estimation of C_{mh} and C_{fh}

Least-squares estimation procedures assume that the error terms of the estimated regression line are normally distributed.[56] This is not the case where the dependent variable is dichotomous or where it is categorical with limited variation. Examples of these types of variables in our model include children away from home (C_a) and child deaths (C_d). For C_a, the percentages of households who had zero, one, two, and three or more children away from home are 76.1, 7.7, 6.5, and 9.7 respectively; for C_d the corresponding percentages are 76.8, 13.2, 7.2, and 2.8. Since with ordinary least-squares procedures there are no constraints on the estimated values of C_a and C_d, the resulting estimates can be wide of the mark.

In the case of C_d, we have elected to explore two separate models: one in which C_d is endogenous and one in which C_d is exogenous. This treatment can be justified by our uncertainty about how this variable should be treated in our model. While child deaths may not be behaviorally determined and thus should not be taken as endogenous, they are indeed influenced by variables such as education and income over which the household has some control. It would therefore be instructive to ascertain the extent to which the estimates of equation 3, children ever born, are sensitive to whether C_d is treated as exogenous or endogenous. In the latter case, however, the model must be interpreted with some care, given the econometric considerations noted above.

C_a, while appropriately treated as endogenous, partakes of the same types of estimation difficulties as C_d. Moreover, the two endogenous variables that measure the household's sex composition, C_{hm} and C_{fh}, cannot be estimated with a standard regression framework since the variation in these variables is not systematically explained by household characteristics. We will therefore estimate C_a, C_{mh}, and C_{fh} by an alternative procedure that is consistent with both the basic model specification and the econometric requirements of obtaining asymptotically unbiased estimates in a household model of the type considered in this study. In particular, we assume that the ratio of C_a, C_{mh}, and C_{fh} to surviving children for each household can be treated as exogenous. We first compute C_{eb}, which is estimated for each household from a regression where C_{eb} is regressed on the exogenous variables in the system. This C_{eb} is then netted of C_d or C_d (depending on whether C_d is taken as endogenous or exogenous) and divided into three parts for each household, using the ratios noted above. This provides the resulting values for C_a, C_{mh}, and C_{fh} that are used where these variables appear in the household equations.

7.4.3 Heteroskedasticity

It is plausible that there is less variation in saving for low-income families than for high-income families, since the ability to save at low incomes is constrained by subsistence needs. The saving equations were therefore examined for heteroskedasticity using the Goldfeld-Quandt test. In all cases heteroskedasticity was found and was corrected by standard econometric procedures.[57]

7.5 The Results

An examination of the results using the basic disaggregated model reveals that while the model in general conforms to a priori expectations, there are virtually no effects on household saving and income owing to the sex composition of the household's children[58] or to the proportion of the family living within the household. This result implies that we can notably simplify the modeling of the household's demographic structure by aggregating these sex- and location-specific influences into either children ever born (C_{eb}) or surviving children (C_s), whichever is appropriate to the relationship being examined. This is done in what we denote as the "compact" model. For expositional convenience, only the compact model is analyzed in this section. The results of the disaggregated model are presented in appendix tables 7.A.1 and 7.A.2.

7.5.1 The Compact Model

The results are presented in table 7.2. The analysis will focus first on the version of this model where child deaths are treated as exogenous.

Child Deaths Exogenous

As expected, income is the primary determinant of saving. The marginal propensity to save is 0.110. Life-cycle factors (measured by age) do not appear to be important in explaining Kenyan household saving. This is not surprising given the discussion above in section 7.2.1. The most interesting result pertains to the effect of children on saving. Contrary to most theoretical discussions of household behavior, in our model children do *not* exert a direct negative effect on financial saving (S). However, a consideration of the total savings measure (S^*) provides some evidence that children may stimulate asset accumulation when the savings measure is broadened to include human-capital formation.[59] Here the marginal propensity to save is slightly higher, 0.139 compared with 0.110.

Support for a life-cycle pattern is also absent in the income equation, where neither of the age terms is significant. Tribal effects, held by many to be an important determinant of household income, do not emerge as a significant factor from the data employed in this study. It should be noted, however, that owing to the selectivity of rural-urban migration, where the better educated individuals of relatively higher socioeconomic status tend to migrate, tribal differences may as a result be difficult to observe in our particular sample. An interesting finding in the income equation is the large influence of education. While the effect of education on income has been shown to be high in studies of Africa and of Kenya, confirmation of this result using microeconomic data where some control has been obtained for related variables has not been fully explored.[60] Our results show that by comparison with the noneducated household head, primary education contributes 144 shillings per period; secondary education contributes 910 shillings (see above, table 7.2). Moreover, female education exerts about the same effect as male education. Given the mean household income level of 719 shillings per period in the sample, the distribution of educational endowments clearly constitutes one of the more important factors explaining the distribution of income in Kenyan urban society. Finally, it is of considerable importance to observe that surviving children exert a positive influence on household income. Whether this influence is direct, through the con-

Table 7.2 Regression Results for Compact Model of Household Saving, Income, Children Ever Born, and Child Deaths Using 2SLS

	Constant	Y	C_{eb}	C_s	C_d
Financial saving (S)[a]					
C_d exogenous	−263.26	.110*		7.46	
	(−1.09)	(2.13)		(.33)	
C_d endogenous	−241.01	.105*		10.61	
	(−.99)	(2.02)		(.48)	
Total saving (S^*)[a]					
C_d exogenous	−286.74	.139*		16.86	
	(−1.20)	(2.72)		(.76)	
C_d endogenous	−260.28	.132*		20.59	
	(−1.09)	(2.59)		(.94)	
Income (Y)					
C_d exogenous	−50.69			133.42*	
	(−.08)			(2.88)	
C_d endogenous	−134.72			123.66*	
	(−.23)			(2.72)	
Children ever born (C_{eb})					
C_d exogenous	−2.18*	.003*			1.08*
	(1.92)	(2.35)			(5.91)
C_d endogenous	−3.04*	.001			2.66*
	(−2.86)	(.84)			(2.30)
Child deaths (C_d)	−.16	−.0003*	.125*		
	(−.26)	(−2.36)	(2.26)		

[a]The heteroskedasticity correction divided each variable by $Y^{.39}$.
*Significant at least at the .05 level.
†Jointly significant at least at the .05 level.
§Jointly significant at least at the .05 level.

tribution of child labor in the marketplace and through remittances, or indirect, by encouraging or permitting parents to work more in market employment, cannot be adequately isolated in our data set.

The children-ever-born equation provides several interesting results. Child services are normal goods; that is, they are positively and strongly related to family income.[61] Indeed, family size increases by one child for every increase in income of 333 shillings. This result is at variance with some of the "new home economics" studies that show a negative effect of income on family size. However, unlike some of these studies, we have been able to control for the interaction of the household size and income relationships through a model that highlights interactive decision-making. Finally, children may be more valuable in low-income societies, where they are not only a consumer durable but a producer durable as well.

Child deaths and age of the mother enter the C_{eb} equation in the expected manner. Families aspire to surviving children; indeed, they

A_m	A_m^2	A_f	A_f^2	D	$D \cdot A_f$	E_{mp}	E_{ms}
7.26	−.089						
(.57)	(−.67)						
6.07	−.080						
(.48)	(−.61)						
7.33	−.095						
(.58)	(−.73)						
5.91	−.084						
(.47)	(−.64)						
2.33	−.108					144.84†§	910.67*†§
(.07)	(−.31)					(1.54)	(7.83)
7.15	−.149					145.44†§	918.27*†§
(.22)	(−.44)					(1.56)	(7.99)
		.167*		6.27*	−.173*	−.32	−2.82*
		(3.09)		(1.74)	(1.94)	(−.67)	(−1.83)
		.193*†		3.63†	−.123†	.27	−.27
		(4.14)		(.96)	(−1.38)	(.50)	(−.14)
		.02	−.0003				
		(.38)	(−.52)				

appear to approximately replace those children who have died, given their expectation of a positive infant and child mortality rate.[62] (Although the parameter on C_d exceeds unity, tests indicate that it is statistically different from unity only at the 0.25 level.)

We anticipated that the effect of increased education levels would diminish family size. While the signs on the education variables are generally negative, the estimated parameters are not statistically different from zero for primary education levels. Moreover, primary education exerts a smaller influence on children ever born than secondary education, and the negative effect of female secondary education is larger than that of male secondary education. These are quite plausible results. The mother assumes the primary role in child-rearing in Kenya. The opportunity cost of the mother's time in household production rises rapidly and nonlinearly with education levels. The latter, of course, is partially a proxy for the price of children. The full effect of changing educational standards on family size must also take into account the indirect effects

Table 7.2 (continued)

	E_{fp}	E_{fs}	T_k	T_l	I/U
Financial saving (S)[a]					
C_d exogenous					66.13
					(.82)
C_d endogenous					66.78
					(.83)
Total saving (S*)[a]					
C_d exogenous					79.88
					(1.01)
C_d endogenous					80.66
					(1.01)
Income (Y)					
C_d exogenous	119.03§	973.63*§	−105.93	−83.22	
	(1.34)	(5.42)	(1.14)	(−.99)	
C_d endogenous	120.23§	965.27*§	−106.56	−80.42	
	(1.37)	(5.44)	(−1.16)	(−.97)	
Children ever born (C_{eb})					
C_d exogenous	−.29	−3.88*			
	(−.70)	(−2.72)			
C_d endogenous	−.03†	−1.92†			
	(−.08)	(−1.20)			
Child deaths (C_d)	−.05	.18			
	(−.51)	(.68)			

of education on income, and of income on children ever born. These relationships are explored in detail in section 7.5.2.

Child Deaths Endogenous

The model that treats child deaths as an endogenous variable provides several interesting results. While for the statistical reasons discussed in section 7.4.2 we must be guarded in interpreting the C_d endogenous model, nevertheless the findings at least suggest some possible influences taking place within the family decision-making process.

The influence of family size and structure on financial saving (S) and total saving (S*) is the same in this model as in the one where child deaths were taken as exogenous. Thus the main finding of the present study, which relates to the interrelationships of family size and structure on saving, is preserved.

As in the case of the child-deaths exogenous model, when child deaths are endogenous surviving children exert a positive influence on household income. This influence is quantitatively large. Each additional child results in a direct increase in income of 123 shillings. While our discussion above clearly allows for this possibility, these results are at variance with the negative relationship postulated (and sometimes found) in the "new home economics" studies pertaining to high-income countries. The factors in the low-income setting that might account for this difference are (1) the possibility that children may be treated as producer as well as consumer durables, thereby directly contributing to income; (2) the lower educational requirements of children, permitting them to contribute to both market and home production; (3) the facilitation of the mother's market employment through providing assistance in home production (particularly babysitting); and (4) the absence of strictly enforced child labor laws.

Turning to the child-deaths equation, we find that income exerts a statistically significant negative effect. Child deaths are also directly related to exposure to the risk of death, as revealed in the significant positive parameter on the C_{eb} variable. Finally, child deaths are not influenced by the level of education. Presumably, the influence of education on mortality is less through "knowledge" of better nutrition and health and more through its effect on income, the latter providing the means for acquiring the inputs of better nutrition and health.

An examination of the C_{eb} equation where child deaths are endogenous provides more insight into this relationship. Specifically, education no longer enters directly as a statistically significant determinant of family size; moreover, even the direction of the relationship for E_{mp} has changed. Apparently the influence of education on family size is partially indirect, through its effect on the incidence of child deaths. This is an interesting finding, since education is an omnibus variable in family-formation studies. This variable has been taken as a proxy for tastes, the costs of children, and contraceptive efficiency. Our results provide some clarification of the specific interpretation of the education variable in the Kenyan case. Increased education is likely to provide more knowledge of, receptivity toward adopting, and ability to adopt better health practices, dietary standards, and procedures for child care.

An evaluation of the C_d endogenous model must be tempered by the existence of an implausibly large estimated parameter on the C_d term in the C_{eb} equation. Possibly more sophisticated statistical procedures would improve the results. On the other hand, the results of the C_d equation itself are plausible, the estimated parameters in the Y, S, and S^* equations are stable with respect to the C_d endogenous specification, and with only one exception, those parameter changes that have occurred in the C_{eb} equation broadly conform to a priori expectations. As a result, while we remain guarded in interpreting the C_d endogenous model results, we are mildly encouraged by the performance of this model and are optimistic that future research with endogenous mortality specifications will make more headway in untangling the nature of the complex family decision-making process.

7.5.2 An Alternative Conceptualization of Household Decision-making Behavior

Our conceptualization of the household views families as making several key decisions simultaneously. For example, the household's decision regarding family size, as well as its decision regarding the amount of labor services it supplies to the market (determining a large share of household income) are made jointly. This is not the only conceptualization possible. If instead the family size decision is either an overriding one in the sense that it is made first and without regard to decisions relating to labor force participation, or if economic factors do not enter the decision-making process relating to family size (e.g., if a naive Malthusian approach to family size determination is postulated), then a recursive decision-making conceptualization of the household may be more appropriate. With our simultaneous, decision-making framework, 2SLS provides consistent or unbiased (in the probability limit) estimates of the various parameters. If OLS procedures are employed, the resulting estimates would be inconsistent or biased. However, if a recursive decision-making framework is hypothesized, then OLS estimates would not be biased.

It is therefore useful to compare the OLS with the 2SLS estimates to identify the extent to which the key results are sensitive to the particular estimation method and to the particular conceptualization of household decision-making. This exercise has other benefits. When our results are compared with a limited number of others beginning to emerge in this literature, a pattern of biases may begin to emerge that will be useful to appraising a wide range of models of household behavior.[63]

Table 7.3 **Regression Results for Compact Model of Household Saving, Income, Children Ever Born, and Child Deaths Using OLS**

	Constant	Y	C_{eb}	C_s	C_d
Financial saving (S)[a]	−328.29*	.221*		−6.56	
	(−1.77)	(6.77)		(−.98)	
Total saving (S^*)[a]	−384.95*	.257*		−3.58	
	(−2.12)	(8.03)		(−.55)	
Income (Y)	−1017.14*			21.14	
	(−2.30)			(1.47)	
Children ever born (C_{eb})	−3.79*	.0002			1.03*
	(5.94)	(.97)			(7.82)
Child deaths (C_d)	.001	−.0001*	.127*		
	(.001)	(−2.04)	(7.58)		

[a]The heteroskedasticity correction divided each variable by $Y^{.39}$ (see section 7.4.3).
*Significant at least at the .05 level.

Accordingly, we have estimated both the compact and the disaggregated models using OLS procedures. The compact model OLS results are presented in table 7.3; the disaggregated model results are presented in appendix table 7.A.2. Only the compact model results will be analyzed here, and then only the major differences between these results and those provided in table 7.2.

The main finding of the study is upheld: children do not exert an influence on the household's saving level. However, in the OLS version the parameter on C_s is negative; it is positive in the 2SLS formulation. The major difference detected in the saving and income equations is the exceptionally large estimated marginal propensity to save in the OLS models, ranging from 0.221 to 0.257. This somewhat diminishes the credibility of the OLS model, although one might justify the larger than expected coefficient by arguing that the income measure includes notable transitory as well as permanent components, and thus a high saving propensity is plausible.

In the income equation there is a notable change in the interpretation of children's role in the household. In the OLS formulation, the parameter on C_s—while positive—is not significant. Thus children do not exert as strong a positive influence on income as they do in the 2SLS rendering of the household.

The major change in the models occurs in the children-ever-born equation. Income is not significant in the OLS model and, surprisingly, education exerts a much weaker negative influence on family size. Three of the four education terms have positive signs, and the negative effect of female education declines from —3.88 in the child-deaths exogenous

A_m	$A_m{}^2$	A_f	$A_f{}^2$	D	$D \cdot A_f$	E_{mp}	E_{ms}
8.47	—.079						
(.91)	(—.72)						
10.68	—.102						
(1.18)	(—.95)						
57.82*	—.586*					151.73*	998.10*
(2.56)	(—2.16)					(1.73)	(9.65)
		.265*		6.81*	—.207	.28	.45
		(11.40)		(2.60)	(—3.24)	(.93)	(1.15)
		.004	—.0001				
		(.12)	(—.28)				

Table 7.3 (continued)

	E_{fp}	E_{fs}	T_k	T_l	I/U	R^2
Financial saving (S)[a]					39.79	
					(.55)	.13
Total saving (S^*)[a]					48.76	
					(.69)	.17
Income (Y)	132.82	877.47*	−113.12	−51.03		
	(1.61)	(5.37)	(−1.31)	(−.66)		.41
Children ever born (C_{eb})	.06	−1.20*				
	(.22)	(−2.03)				.45
Child deaths (C_d)	−.12	−.04				
	(−1.42)	(−.22)				.18

model (2SLS) to −1.20 in the OLS formulation. Sign reversals are not uncommon between 2SLS and OLS models, especially where there are notable elements of colinearity between independent variables. Indeed, there are at least two other studies, which use Puerto Rican and Chilean data, that find that the positive effect of income on children ever born diminishes or even turns negative when one moves from 2SLS to OLS estimates.[64] This finding is consistent with our results where the estimated coefficient on income declines from 0.003 to 0.0002. The influence of education in the OLS model is less plausible than that of the 2SLS framework, given our interpretation of this variable, given the insignificant income effect in the OLS formation, and given the findings of others.[65]

There are at least two possible interpretations that might be offered in analyzing the differences between the OLS and 2SLS models. First, since economic factors (the income and price variables) do not enter as significantly in the OLS formulation, then the Malthusian conceptualization where biological factors explain family size, or the Easterlin framework where supply factors dominate at low-income levels, may appropriately explain urban Kenyan behavior.[66] Second, the OLS results are implausible and are due to the statistical biases inherent in using OLS estimators when one examines a simultaneous decision-making model of household behavior. We lean toward the latter interpretation, given (1) the large number of studies that have shown the education variable to exert a negative influence on family size; (2) the consistency of our results with the pattern of parameter changes beginning to emerge in the literature where both OLS and 2SLS results are presented; and (3) the somewhat lower marginal propensities to save found in other studies of saving. Moreover, if supply factors were constraining, we might expect to find a positive education effect at primary, but not at secondary, levels.[67] We thus concur with T. Paul Schultz that "simultaneous-equations techniques are needed if one is to obtain a deeper and more reliable understanding of the effects of population policies on reproductive behavior."[68]

7.5.3 The Effect of Education on Household Demographic and Economic Behavior

The primary objective of this study has been to assess the effect of alternative family sizes and structures on household saving behavior. While in the previous sections we have shown that the direct effects of family size on household saving are negligible, there are indirect effects that must also be taken into account. For example, since family size (C_{eb}) is itself endogenous in the model, the full examination of changes in saving caused by changes in family size can be analyzed only through an examination of the effects of changes in one of the model's exogenous variables. The most interesting variable for this purpose is education.

Tables 7.4 and 7.5 present the effects on the endogenous variables owing to changes in the husband's and the wife's levels of education. There are two ways of presenting these effects. The first is to calculate the "total" effect. If we designate V_j as the endogenous variable of interest, then the total effect represents dV_j/dE_i, which holds constant all exogenous variables other than E_i and allows the remaining endogenous variables ($V_i, i \neq j$) to adjust to the change in E_i. This formulation provides no information on the specific way these endogenous responses are changing but gives only the total net effect of changes in V_j owing to changes in education. This total effect is calculated by computing the relevant reduced-form parameters using the estimated parameters of the structural system. All endogenous-variable interactions are therefore incorporated in the estimate of the total effect.[69]

To gain more information on the indirect effects, we can calculate $\partial V_j/\partial E_i$. Here all exogenous variables other than E_i are held constant, as well as all endogenous variables other than the one of specific interest. Since the variable of interest may be influenced by rapid changes in some of the other endogenous variables, the sum of the indirect effects will *not* necessarily equal the total effect. These indirect effects, then, are obtained from the chain rule where, for example, $\partial S/\partial E_i$ via income (Y) equals $(\partial S/\partial Y)(\partial Y/\partial E_i)$. The first term in the product is obtained from the estimated parameters in the structural equations, and the second term is obtained from the estimated parameters in the reduced-form equations.

Several interesting findings emerge from an examination of the results presented in tables 7.4 and 7.5. First, and most important, the indirect effects of children through the income and children-ever-born equations do not alter our basic conclusion that Kenyan household saving is virtually invariant to the number of children in the family. Thus, for example, if the male household head's or the wife's education were to

Table 7.4 **Changes in Saving, Income, Children Ever Born, and Child Deaths Resulting from Changes in Male Education Levels**

Variable and Model	Illiteracy to Primary Education					Primary to Secondary Education				
	Total Effect	Indirect Effects				Total Effect	Indirect Effects			
		Y	C_{eb}	C_s	C_d		Y	C_{eb}	C_s	C_d
Financial saving (S)										
C_d exogenous	22.76	15.77		.88		88.81	88.75		3.06	
C_d endogenous	29.95	14.74		1.66		86.94	84.71		4.59	
Total saving (S^*)										
C_d exogenous	31.05	19.93		1.99		113.76	112.15		6.91	
C_d endogenous	42.17	18.53		3.21		111.07	106.50		8.92	
Income (Y)										
C_d exogenous	185.98			15.74		793.38			54.71	
C_d endogenous	222.38			19.29		803.19			53.55	
Children ever born (C_{eb})										
C_d exogenous	.31	.43				.20	2.42			
C_d endogenous	.64	.14			−.61	.05	.81			−.46
Child deaths (C_d)	.02	−.04	−.01			−.2	−.24	.03		

Table 7.5 **Changes in Saving, Income, Children Ever Born, and Child Deaths Resulting from Changes in Female Education Levels**

Variable and Model	Illiteracy to Primary Education					Primary to Secondary Education				
	Total Effect	Indirect Effects				Total Effect	Indirect Effects			
		Y	C_{eb}	C_s	C_d		Y	C_{eb}	C_s	C_d
Financial saving (S)										
C_d exogenous	17.78	14.13		1.07		66.41	77.56		−7.71	
C_d endogenous	12.08	13.95		1.52		63.59	74.16		−10.54	
Total saving (S^*)										
C_d exogenous	24.04	17.85		2.41		74.64	98.01		−16.74	
C_d endogenous	15.02	17.53		2.68		72.22	93.24		−20.24	
Income (Y)										
C_d exogenous	147.28			19.08		688.22			−132.49	
C_d endogenous	117.39			16.08		713.29			−121.56	
Children ever born (C_{eb})										
C_d exogenous	.21	.39				−1.25	2.11			
C_d endogenus	−.12	.13			.01	−1.17	.71			−.28
Child deaths (C_d)	−.09	−.04	.02			−.11	−.29	−.14		

increase from prmary to secondary level, total financial saving in the C_d exogenous model would increase by 88.8 and 66.4 shillings, respectively. Almost all of this increase is explained by the influence of education on income (88.8 and 77.6 shillings); the direct effect of education through children ever born is negligible, as well as the net effects of the interactions between income and children ever born (not shown). Similar results are obtained when we consider the broader definition of saving and also in both saving equations in the models where child deaths are endogenous.

Second, education itself exerts a powerful influence on household saving through its effect on earnings. These results must be qualified, however. They represent partial equilibrium influences only—that is, the effect on a single household in isolation. If we were instead considering a macroeconomic counterfactual experiment whereby education levels were being notably advanced for the entire urban population, the results would have to be modified. A notable increase in education standards for the entire population would likely drive down the rate of return to education itself and as a result would diminish the income effect revealed at the partial equilibrium level.

Third, turning to the family-size equations and concentrating on the C_d exogenous model, we see that the total effects of increases in male education and of increases in female primary education are moderate. (The results of the experiment of changing the female's education from the primary to the secondary level will be discussed below.) These findings are due in part to the opposing income and substitution effects. The income effect appears to consistently dominate the price-substitution effect.[70] Higher male education levels are therefore likely to *increase* family size in urban Kenya. This is also true of an increase in the prevalence of primary education among women. Note that while the direct effect of education in our structural equation estimates is for the most part negative, representing the price-substitution effect owing largely to the increased opportunity costs of child-rearing at higher education levels, there are also powerful and more than offsetting indirect effects. In particular, increased education raises family income. Since the demand for child services increases with income, education also exerts a strong and dominant positive influence on family size. This result is in contrast with the findings of several "new home economics" studies for high-income countries and indeed with the usual assumption employed in the analysis of the Chicago model of fertility. However, our findings are entirely plausible given the institutional setting and the stage of economic development in the low-income country. In this setting, the return to education is unusually high, resulting in exceptionally large income effects. At the same time, increased costs of child-rearing associated with higher education (i.e., the higher opportunity costs of the mother's time) are relatively low given the greater compatability of female work force participation and child-rearing. This is particularly true for the types of jobs available to women who possess only a primary education. Older children tend younger children; moreover, the extended family itself provides child-care services. If policy-makers are concerned, for example, about the pronatal effect of providing more education, then additional policies must be simultaneously implemented that effectively raise the cost of child-rearing. These policies might, for example, raise the opportunity cost to the female in terms of foregone earnings due to child-rearing. Compulsory education of children would be one such policy; implementation of child labor laws would be another. Both policies would increase the costs of children and, as a by-product, lower the rate of return to education as the greater supply of educated manpower is forthcoming.

Fourth, the effect of education on children ever born varies with the level of female education. An increase in female education from the primary to the secondary level dramatically *reduces* family size. This is in contrast to the *increase* in family size resulting from an improvement in female education from illiteracy to the primary level. The explanation for this relationship has been provided above. Namely, the opportunity costs in terms of market employment increase rather dramatically with higher education levels. Jobs that take advantage of higher education levels are less compatible with child-rearing than jobs that require only a primary education.[71] Government employment is an example of the former; domestic service is an example of the latter. These findings suggest that if reducing the birthrate is one of the objectives of policy, then distributing education toward female secondary education is likely to have a greater desired influence than a policy that is neutral toward education levels and toward the sex of the recipient.

Fifth, one of the beneficial effects of increased education is to reduce child mortality.[72] Currently the average number of child deaths per household is 0.40. An increase in female education from illiteracy to the primary level would reduce child deaths by 0.09, or 23% of the existing rate. This is a major reduction. It is interesting to note, however, that a comparable increase in male education levels has little influence on child mortality. Thus, in this education range, the greatest benefit of raising the education level comes through an investment in female, rather than male, education. Presumably much of the mortality reduction derives from the effect of education on the wife's *knowledge* about improved child-care practices: medical information, nutrition information, and so forth. We infer this because the negative income effect is relatively small. A quite different finding is obtained when one examines the effect of increasing male and female education from the primary to the secondary level. Here the dominant influence occurs through the income effect.

This likely represents a reduction of child mortality deriving from the *ability* to obtain better medical care, better food and shelter, and so forth. Given the greater importance of the male household head's earning power and the larger effect of education in raising male versus female earnings, the child-mortality-reducing effects are greater for male than for female education in the higher education levels. It is interesting that increasing both male and female education to the completed secondary level would reduce child mortality to the very low rates found in high-income countries. However, since such an increase in the education level is typically found only at rather advanced levels of economic development, our results, albeit founded on cross-sectional information, take on increased plausibility.

7.6 Conclusions

This study has employed microeconomic data from urban Kenya to examine the interactions of several key household decisions: saving, investment in education, family size, labor force participation (income), and child deaths. The underlying hypothesis is that these decisions are made simultaneously, and that the direct and indirect effects of key economic influences and outcomes cannot be revealed on a priori grounds. Several interesting results have been obtained.

First, the number of children does not influence the rate of household financial saving. Second, the number of children has an effect on the composition of saving if this definition is expanded to include human capital formation and specifically expenditures on education. Third, a simultaneous-equation model of the household appears to give a more plausible representation of behavior than a recursive decision-making framework. Fourth, additional insight into household decision-making can be obtained in models that consider child deaths an endogenous variable in the analysis.

Finally, the broad conceptualization of a household in which family size is determined in the context of a cost-benefit framework appears promising for urban Kenya. However, contrary to the usual model where children are considered only as consumer durables, there is some evidence that children may also serve as producer durables in the low-income setting. Moreover, in contrast to the usual assumption and finding of the "new home economics" model, we find that the income effects of an increase in education may in some instances outweigh the price-substitution effects, resulting in an increase in family size with increasing education levels.

Appendix

Table 7.A.1 Results of Disaggregated Model of Household Saving, Income, Children Ever Born, and Child Deaths Using 2SLS

	Constant	Y	C_{mh}	C_{fh}	C_a	C_d
Financial saving (S)[a]						
C_d exogenous	−219.88	.083*	−4.55	.97	−2.24	
	(−1.06)	(2.10)	(−.33)	(.07)	(−.17)	
C_d endogenous	−164.35	.073*	7.21	6.41	3.74	
	(−.73)	(1.78)	(.47)	(.40)	(.23)	
Total saving (S^*)[a]						
C_d exogenous	−262.44	.109*	−.88	2.46	−1.97	
	(−1.27)	(2.78)	(−.06)	(.18)	(−.15)	
C_d endogenous	−174.78	.094*	13.57	11.20	7.59	
	(−.78)	(2.31)	(.89)	(.71)	(.48)	
Income (Y)						
C_d exogenous	−835.64*		10.22	63.43*	29.45	
	(−1.81)		(.35)	(2.18)	(.96)	
C_d endogenous	−607.70		35.66	81.50*	47.04	
	(−1.17)		(1.05)	(2.34)	(1.31)	
Children ever born (C_{cb})						
C_d exogenous	−2.18*	.0034*				1.08*
	(−1.92)	(2.35)				(5.91)
C_d endogenous	−3.04*	.0014				2.66*
	(−2.86)	(.84)		C_{eb}		(2.30)
Child deaths (C_d)	−.16	−.0003*		.125*		
	(−.26)	(−2.36)		(2.26)		

[a]The heteroskedasticity correction divided each variable by $Y^{.39}$ (see section 7.4.3).
*Significant at least at the .05 level.
§Jointly significant at least at the .05 level.
†Jointly significant at least at the .05 level.

Table 7.A.1 (continued)

	A_m	A_m^2	A_f	A_f^2	D
Financial saving (S)[a]					
C_d exogenous	5.36	−.058			
	(.51)	(−.47)			
C_d endogenous	2.45	−.034			
	(.21)	(−.27)			
Total saving(S^*)[a]					
C_d exogenous	7.23	−.077			
	(.69)	(−.63)			
C_d endogenous	2.54	−.038			
	(.22)	(−.30)			
Income (Y)					
C_d exogenous	48.71*	−.496*			
	(2.07)	(−1.78)			
C_d endogenous	36.13	−.384			
	(1.34)	(−1.24)			
Children ever born (C_{cb})					
C_d exogenous			.17§*		6.27§*
			(3.09)		(1.74)
C_d endogenous			.193§*		3.63§
			(4.14)		(.96)
Child deaths (C_d)			.02	−.0003	
			(.381)	(−.52)	

$D{\cdot}A_f$	E_{mp}	E_{ms}	E_{fp}	E_{fs}	T_k	T_l	I/U
							60.21
							(.75)
							61.09
							(.76)
							65.92
							(.83)
							67.30
							(.85)
	150.41§*	999.14§*	125.86§†	884.35§†*	−119.36	−59.36	
	(1.69)	(9.55)	(1.51)	(5.36)	(−1.37)	(−.76)	
	143.42§*	973.63§*	120.99§†	907.31§†*	−120.80	−67.65	
	(1.60)	(9.04)	(1.43)	(5.39)	(−1.37)	(−.85)	
−.17§*	−.32	−2.81*	−.29	−3.88*			
(−1.94)	(−.67)	(−1.83)	(−.70)	(−2.72)			
−.123§	.27	−.27	−.03	−1.92			
(−1.43)	(.50)	(−.14)	(−.08)	(−1.20)			
	−.05	.18					
	(−.51)	(.68)					

Table 7.A.2 Results of Disaggregated Model of Household Saving, Income, Children Ever Born, and Child Deaths Using OLS

	Constant	Y	C_{mh}	C_{hf}	C_a	C_d
Financial saving (S)[a]	−328.14* (−1.76)	.22* (6.71)	−5.87 (−.53)	−6.90 (−.68)	−7.01 (−.63)	
Total saving (S^*)[a]	−385.17* (−2.11)	.26* (7.96)	−1.74 (−.16)	−4.79 (−.48)	−4.17 (−.38)	
Income (Y)	−1002.03* (−2.26)		5.99 (.25)	37.86* (1.76)	12.99 (.50)	
Children ever born (C_{eb})	−3.79* (−5.94)	.0002 (.97)				1.03* (7.82)
				C_{eb}		
Child deaths (C_d)	.07 (.16)	−.0001 (−.80)		.13* (7.67)		

	A_m	A_m^2	A_f	A_f^2	D	$D \cdot A_f$
Financial saving (S)[a]	8.44 (.91)	−.078 (−.71)				
Total saving (S^*)[a]	10.66 (1.17)	−.10 (−.94)				
Income (Y)	57.17* (2.52)	−.58* (−2.12)				
Children ever born (C_{eb})			.27* (11.40)		6.81* (2.60)	−.21* (−3.24)
Child deaths (C_d)			.005 (.15)	−.0002 (−.42)		

[a]The heteroskedasticity correction divided each variable by $Y^{.39}$ (see section 7.4.3).
*Significant at least at the .05 level.

E_{mp}	E_{ms}	E_{fp}	E_{fs}	T_k	T_l	I/U	R^2
						39.94 (.55)	.13
						49.04 (.69)	.17
148.42* (1.69)	998.60* (9.61)	131.56 (1.60)	873.38* (5.33)	−112.95 (−1.31)	−50.16 (−.65)		.42
.28 (.93)	.45 (1.15)	.06 (.22)	−1.20* (−2.08)				.45
−.17* (−1.82)	−.30* (−2.49)						.19

Notes

1. Malthus (1970).

2. Becker (1960). See T. W. Schultz (1974); Easterlin (1971); and Leibenstein (1975).

3. Easterlin (1967, 1975); Kelley (1972, 1974); Leibenstein (1957, 1975*a*); and Simon (1976).

4. Bilsborrow (1975); Kelley (1973, 1976); and Kelley and Lillydahl (1976).

5. In aggregate model-building, these assumptions are reflected in varying degrees in the works of Barlow (1967); Barlow and Davies (1974); Coale and Hoover (1958); Denton and Spencer (1974); Enke (1971); and McFarland, Bennett, and Brown (1973).

6. Kuznets (1960, p. 339).

7. Peek (1974) has identified a negative dependency rate effect on saving using grouped Philippine data. However, in his model income is exogenous. Moreover, he is justifiably cautious in analyzing the results, given the somewhat tenuous quality of the data he used (p. 21). See also Leff (1969).

8. The manner in which C_a, C_{mh}, and C_{fh} are estimated is discussed in section 7.4.2.

9. The most appropriate analytical measure of this influence would be some form of permanent income. Friedman (1957) hypothesizes that households consume virtually none of their increases in transitory income; thus the marginal propensity to save out of transitory income is very high, approaching unity. This result has been widely confirmed in studies of developing countries. See Betancourt (1971); Friend and Taubman (1966); Gupta (1970); Ramanathan (1968); and Williamson (1968).

The present study uses current income, and thus the estimated saving parameter can be expected to be higher than if only permanent income were used. While it would be desirable to separate the permanent versus the transitory influence of income on saving, this is difficult using cross-sectional data. In addition, it is somewhat beyond the scope of the present study, which focuses on the influence of demographic factors on saving and income.

10. The Modigliani-Brumberg (1954) life-cycle model hypothesizes that individuals plan no net lifetime saving, leave no bequests, and allocate their consumption evenly over their lifetimes. This results in low or negative saving in early and possibly late life-cycle stages. Alternative life-cycle predictions are possible, depending on the assumptions of life-cycle consumption behavior and on the temporal pattern of income. Empirical studies include those by Gupta (1971); Kelley and Williamson (1968); Landsberger (1970); and Leff (1969). A detailed discussion of the life-cycle model is provided by Kelley (1968).

11. Mikesell and Zinser (1973) have observed that long-run planning horizons may not represent the appropriate time frame in developing countries where households, small businesses, and small farmers are subject to severe fluctuations in income, family size, weather, and so forth.

12. A more detailed discussion and bibliography relating to the saving, family-size relationships is found in Kelley (1976). See also Coale and Hoover (1958, pp. 139–273); Demeny (1967); Eizenga (1961); Goldsmith, Brady, and Mendershausen (1956); Henderson (1949–50); and Leff (1969).

13. An analysis of the saving, extended-family relationships in Kenya is provided by Lillydahl (1976, chap. 3).

14. See Kamarck (1967, pp. 64–68); Lillydahl (1976, chap. 3); and Snyder (1971, 1974*b*, pp. 139–51). Williamson (1961, p. 46) has emphasized this aspect

of economic development to explain in part the growth of government expenditure: "[With urbanization] disappears the informal security of the family and village. Urban populations must be supplied with formal social security, unemployment insurance, a complex cosmopolitan political machinery, and formal protection to replace the family and village functions."

15. Duesenberry (1949).

16. Fields (1974); International Labor Office (1971); and Thias and Carnoy (1972).

17. A historical account of the role of education in Kenya is provided by Forrester (1962). See also Castle (1966, pp. 103–11); Lillydahl (1976, chap. 2); Ministry of Education (1971–75); and Raju (1973).

While a comparison in Kenya of the education levels of males and females yields results consistent with Becker's hypothesis of positive assortive mating (Becker 1973), it is also clear that there may be enough variation in household education levels of mates to identify differential effects of education. Of the 401 households studied in the empirical analysis below, 240 couples had the same educational level. Males tended to marry women of the same or a somewhat lower educational stuatus. Only 8 males married women who had higher educational status.

18. This negative effect has been highlighted for advanced countries, especially in studies pertaining to the United States. See Bowen and Finegan (1969); Cain (1966); and Sweet (1970).

19. Peek (1976); Rosenzweig and Evenson (1975). For an examination of the positive and negative effects of children on female work force participation in low-income countries, see Kelley and deSilva (1976); Peek (1975); and Rosenzweig (1975).

20. This possibility has been stressed by Easterlin (1967, p. 104): "Population pressure arising from mortality reduction may provide the spur to work harder, search information, increase capital formation, and try new methods." See also Adams (1971, p. 472) and Scully (1962). Perrella's (1970) study of American moonlighting rates confirms the influence of family size on the propensity of the household head to hold multiple jobs. Finally, Simon's (1971) study of the relationship of family size and income arrives at an intermediate position: "The effect of incremental children on the parents' labor is not important" (p. 7). Here the negative influence of children on the mother's work force activity is roughly outweighed by an increase in the father's work force participation.

21. Forrester (1962, p. 123) presents evidence of significant differences in tribal consumption patterns in East Africa. For example, she shows that tribal values (after controlling for income) appear to influence the type of house furnishings, the preferences for clothing, and the extent of investment in higher education, saving, and landownership.

22. Ben-Porath and Welch (1972); DeTray (1973); and T. Paul Schultz (1974, pp. 15–19).

23. Less than complete replacement appears to be the more likely behavioral response of households to child mortality, according to a review of the literature by Preston (1975).

24. T. Paul Schultz (1974, pp. 4–7).

25. The complexity and specific nature of the income-fertility relationship is well documented in the writings of Simon (1969, 1974).

26. Early contributions to this literature are provided by Becker (1960) and by Mincer (1963). Later extensions and more detailed expositions are offered by Becker and Lewis (1973); DeTray (1973); Michael (1973); T. W. Schultz (1973);

T. Paul Schultz (1974); and Willis (1973). For critical reviews, see Leibenstein (1974, 1975*b*); the comment by Keeley (1975); Namboodiri (1975); Perlman (1975); and Pollak and Wachter (1975).

27. The strength of the income effect depends on the origins of the increase in income. If this increase derives from an increase in the father's wage rate, and if children consume relatively little of the father's time, then the negative price effect will be small. If this increase derives from an increase in the mother's wage rate, and if she spends a large amount of time caring for and enjoying children, then the negative effect could be large. If the increase derives from nonlabor income, there will be no negative price effect. Michael (1971, p. 126) summarizes the usual assumptions employed: "It is usually assumed that the production of childservices is positively related to the opportunity cost of the wife's time. It is also generally assumed that the production of childservices uses relatively little of the husband's time, so the relative price of childservices is negatively related to his opportunity cost of time."

The effect of increased wage rates of husbands versus wives may also affect the quality versus quantity decision in terms of the family's production of child services: "If we assume that the husband's time is used relatively more extensively in the production of child quality, increases in his time value, holding income fixed, induce substitution toward quantity of children and away from higher quality children, while through substitution in consumption the demand for childservices rises. So the model predicts a positive effect of his time value on quantity of children and the effect on quality of children depends on the strength of the effects of substitution in production (away from quality) and in consumption (toward more childservices and therefore toward higher quality)" Michael (1971, p. 127). See also Becker and Lewis (1973) and DeTray (1973).

28. A critical evaluation of this approach is provided by Cain and Weininger (1973). Support for this approach can be found in Blake (1968). Duesenberry, who has analyzed in depth the relative-income hypothesis in explaining aggregate consumption levels, has supported this relative income approach to explain the consumption of child services. He has observed: "Economics is all about how people make choices. Sociology is all about why they don't have choices to make" Duesenberry (1960, p. 233). See also Anker (1974); Easterlin (1969, 1971, 1975); Freedman (1963); Leibenstein (1974, 1975*a*); Ryder (1973); and Turchi (1975).

29. Encarnacion (1973, p. 3) has provided evidence based on Philippine experience that "there is a threshold level of family income such that below this level, the effect of more income is to increase fertility. Above this level, . . . the marginal effect of income on fertility is negative." A similar argument is made with respect to education levels. Both education and income affect nutrition, the ability to acquire health services, and knowledge of health services. See also Bourgeois-Pichat (1967) and Easterlin (1975).

30. Even though education is included in the income determination equation, it should be noted that education itself may be a better proxy for permanent income than the current income measure, and that children ever born in probably much more influenced (in its positive effects) by permanent income than by measured income. This is especially so if children are young at the time of data-gathering. Lifetime labor force participation of the mother and hence her earnings in a permanent sense should be strongly positively related to her schooling. But if children are young, she most likely shows zero present labor force participation. Studies showing a negative influence of education on fertility for less-developed countries are numerous: Anker (1975); Caldwell (1967); Dandekar (1967); Matsunaga (1967); Morrison (1957); Stycos (1967); and Yaukey (1971).

31. For Kenya, see Heisel (1968).

32. Economists' methodological stance with respect to incorporating taste changes in models of fertility (or in any other models) is well articulated by Michael (1973, p. 134) and T. Paul Schultz (1974, pp. 7–9). For empirical attempts to isolate taste influences, see Griliches (1973); and Gronau (1973*a,b*).

33. A detailed study of the rates of return to education in Kenya has been made by Thias and Carnoy (1972). See also Fields (1974).

34. "Owing to the high demand of Africans for education, the Kikuyu father will sell his land, or the Luo will sell his cattle, to educate his children" Forrester (1962, p. 139). "But an African has many people who can help him pay a school bill—wives, brothers, sisters, even cousins" Fisher (1969, p. 157). A primary motivation for remitting income outside the household has been identified as that of underwriting school fees. Johnson and Whitelaw (1974).

35. This hypothesis is at variance with the assumptions underlying most educational projection models, as well as the macroeconomic-demographic paradigms. In these studies, educational expenditures are taken to be examples of "population sensitive" forms of investments, typically competing with other forms of private and public investment. See Coale and Hoover (1958); McFarland, Bennett, and Brown (1973); and Denton and Spencer (1974).

36. This "strong separability" assumption is frequently employed in Engle curve analysis. See Houthakker and Prais (1955).

37. This may be particularly true where the extended family institution is strong, since in this setting there are opportunities for investing in the children of relatives, a reasonably close (although not perfect) substitute for investment in the household's own children. See Lillydahl (1976, chap. 6); Massell and Heyer (1969, p. 226).

38. Whereas in Kenya boys are traditionally assigned the role of caring for their parents in old age, girls—given their high value in Kenyan society owing to their extensive role in market and farm production as well as other household activities—command "bride-prices." These prices are directly related to the bride's level of education. An interesting research issue relates to the relative rate of return on educating boys versus girls. This depends, in part, on the influence of education on bride-prices, the expected remittances from boys of varying degrees of education, and the time path of the benefits and costs of the educational expenditures.

39. In Kenya a primary motivation for remitting income outside the household is to educate the children of the extended family. See Johnson and Whitelaw (1974); and Lillydahl (1976, chap. 6).

40. Forrester (1962); Fisher (1969).

41. T. Paul Schultz (1969, 1971*b*, 1973); Ben-Porath and Welch (1972); DaVanzo (1970); Schultz and DaVanzo (1970); Heer and Smith (1969); and Knodel (1968). For a recent survey of the literature for low-income countries, see Preston (1975).

42. Most studies of microdemographic behavior have been carried out using data from advanced countries. Child mortality is relatively low, and thus, for econometric reasons, it may be infeasible (if not unimportant) to explore an endogenous specification of child mortality in the household's children-ever-born equation.

43. Encarnacion (1973).

44. See Brass (1970); Kessner et al. (1973); and Shapiro, Schlesinger, and Nesbitt (1968).

45. A detailed study of the relationship of Kenyan household structure and alternative indexes of the extended family is currently being undertaken with Carolina Swartz of Duke University.

46. The measure also includes severance pay and compensation, income from casual employment, remittances received, other income, cash gifts, expense and travel allowance, value of rations received, and value of uniforms received. Cash receipts not earned during the period are excluded. Examples include salary advances, cash loans, loans repaid to the household, withdrawals from savings, and new credit.

47. A discussion of the possibilities and problems of estimating permanent income from cross-sectional data is provided by Betancourt (1971); Simon and Aigner (1970); Ramanathan (1968); and Watts (1960).

48. Total household consumption includes all cash expenditures, credit expenditures, in-kind expenditures, trade union dues, rent, contributions to health insurance and social security, electricity payments, water payments, waste disposal payments, insurance subscriptions, home-repair expenses, payments of interest on mortgages and housing loans, as well as food, clothing, and purchases of consumer durables.

49. Johnson and Whitelaw (1974).

50. Increases and decreases of household indebtedness are ignored, a procedure consistent with our treatment of consumer durables. Borrowing and debt repayment do not change the household's net asset position, but rather change the composition of the assets and liabilities. Moreover, if payment on debts were considered as expenditures, and borrowing as income, then the purchase of consumer durables on credit in contrast to outright cash purchase would result in different measured saving levels. This is considered an arbitrary and inappropriate distinction.

51. An early conceptualization of the human capital model is provided by T. W. Schultz (1961). Recent studies that have examined rates of return to education and lifetime allocation decisions as related to education include the works of Ben-Porath (1967, 1970) and of Johnson (1970). For Kenya, see Fields (1974) and Thias and Carnoy (1972).

52. The alternative of excluding households that had a member with university education seemed less satisfactory on methodological grounds.

53. Useful summaries of opposing views on the merits of simultaneous versus recursive models of various aspects of household decision making are provided by Rodgers (1974, pp. 3–9) and Peek (1974, p.11). See also Rosenzweig (1975), and Rosenzweig and Evenson (1975).

54. Nonlinear estimation requires extensive experimentation with alternative starting values of the various parameters and a testing of the sensitivity of the final parameter estimates to alternative starting values. The infeasibility of the current estimation scheme derived in large part from the interactive nature of the model. The nonlinear term appeared not only in the children-ever-born structural equation, but in the reduced-form equation of *each* of the endogenous variables that were estimated.

55. It has been pointed out to me by Marc Nerlove that this regression specification is not quite correct. To insure that the ends of the lines meet at A^*, it is necessary to incorporate the constraint $\beta + \delta A^*_f = 0$. The equation then becomes $C_{eb} = \alpha + \gamma A_f + \delta D(A_f - A^*_f) + \epsilon$. We checked our unconstrained regression results to ascertain the extent to which the constraint was in fact met. Fortunately it was met almost precisely, and thus the models were not reestimated.

56. I benefited from the advice of my colleague T. Dudley Wallace on the econometric issues raised in this section.

57. Goldfeld and Quandt (1965). The appropriate transformation of the variables was obtained by estimating the equation $\log |\epsilon| = \gamma \log Y$. Each term in the equation was then divided by $Y^{y/2}$ to correct for heteroskedasticity. This in theory reduced the variance of the error term from $\sigma^2 Y^y$ to σ^2.

58. There is one exception to this statement. Female children at home exert a significant positive effect on income, likely representing the contribution of young girls assuming some of the mother's domestic responsibilities and releasing the mother to engage in market employment.

59. A side equation, not integral to the household model under consideration, was run to explain the household's investment in education. In both models (child deaths exogenous and endogenous) the estimate of the C_s parameter was positive, statistically different from zero at least at the .05 level, and small, ranging from 6.3 to 8.9 shillings.

The child deaths exogenous model is as follows:

$$\underset{}{I_e} = \underset{(-3.83)}{-26.74} + \underset{(1.63)}{.05Y} + \underset{(1.70)}{6.29C_s} - \underset{(-.29)}{2.38E_{mp}} - \underset{(-.31)}{9.63E_{ms}} + \underset{(.28)}{2.01E_{fp}} - \underset{(-1.85)}{60.16E_{fs}}$$

$$- \underset{(-.07)}{.53T_k} + \underset{(.79)}{4.98T_l}.$$

The child deaths endogenous model is as follows:

$$I_e = \underset{(-3.97)}{-28.04} + \underset{(.99)}{.028Y} + \underset{(2.66)}{8.93C_s} + \underset{(.20)}{1.60E_{mp}} + \underset{(.45)}{12.80E_{ms}} + \underset{(.68)}{4.84E_{fp}} - \underset{(-1.26)}{37.62E_{fs}}$$

$$- \underset{(-.46)}{3.38T_k} + \underset{(.49)}{3.09T_l}.$$

This model was reestimated using only households that had children, thereby permitting a slightly improved interpretation of the parameter on C_s. The results were virtually identical to those obtained above and are therefore not presented here.

60. An examination of the returns to education is provided by Thias and Carnoy (1972).

61. An extensive survey of the analytical and empirical relationships between income and fertility has been provided by Simon (1974). See also Chang (1976).

62. The findings on whether the household completely replaces or overreplaces a child who has died are mixed. See Fredericksen (1966); Heer (1969); Heer and Smith (1968, 1969); Preston (1975); and T. Paul Schultz (1969).

63. DaVanzo (1970); Harman (1971). Nerlove and Schultz (1970); T. Paul Schultz (1971*a*).

64. DeVanzo (1970); Nerlove and Schultz (1970).

65. The effect may be negative given the higher costs of child-rearing associated with higher education levels (the higher opportunity costs of the mother's time, and the higher costs due to social norms dictating more "expensive" or higher-quality children), and the greater contraceptive efficiency. Higher education levels also bring about higher income, the positive influence of which may dominate the negative "price" effects. Given the insignificance of the estimated parameter on the income term in our model, we might infer that the income effect is relatively low, and thus the negative price effects might well dominate.

66. Easterlin (1975).

67. Encarnacion (1973).

68. T. Paul Schultz (1971*b*, p. 1).

69. Let V be a matrix of endogenous variables, X a matrix of exogenous variables, and E a matrix of error terms. Our model can therefore be written in the form $V\Gamma + X\beta = E$, where Γ and β are the estimated or implied parameters of the endogenous and exogenous variables, respectively. These parameters are obtained from the structural equations. The corresponding reduced-form parameters can be found by expressing the endogenous variables as a function of the exogenous variables. Thus, $V = X(-\beta\Gamma^{-1}) + E\Gamma^{-1}$. The relevant parameters, then, are $\Pi = -\beta\Gamma^{-1}$.

70. Knowles and Anker (1975), who have employed single-equation OLS models using microeconomic household data to investigate various aspects of Kenyan household behavior, find that neither income nor the wife's education has a statistically significant effect on fertility. Only urban residence (here defined as whether the household is urban or rural) has an (negative) effect. Their model is formulated differently from ours, however, since in their framework income is exogenous. It is seen in our study that the endogenicity of income makes a considerable difference in the results.

71. This result has been found directly in a study of Brazilian urban households while the impact of female employment by occupation was examined in detail. While employment per se did not deter having large families, that specific type of employment which was incompatible with child-rearing did indeed exert a negative influence on family size (Kelley and deSilva 1976).

72. For a similar result using a different data file and estimation procedures, see Knowles and Anker (1975).

Comment Warren C. Robinson

Professor Kelley's paper addresses two questions, which it argues are closely related: the influence of fertility on household savings and income; and the influence of economic factors on the family-size decision. The thrust of the answer to the first question is to refute once again the Coale-Hoover hypothesis that the higher the fertility rate the lower the savings rate. His interest in the other characteristics of household behavior—family size, labor force participation, and so on—leads him to adopt a deterministic, human-capital approach to the second question. It seems to me that within such a model, within such a conceptual understanding of the household, the original question regarding the savings rate is irrelevant.

Let me begin by agreeing with Kelley's rejection of the "orthodox" assumptions of economic-demographic models regarding the savings rate. There is growing evidence for questioning all three. For example, not all members of the household share equally in consumption, and this

Warren C. Robinson is professor of economics and director of the Population Issues Research Program at the Pennsylvania State University.

is a more subtle differentiation than can be handled by equivalent adult consumer weightings. Adult males get first priority, children next, adult females after that in some cultures; in other cultures there is a clear bias in division of consumables toward male children and against female children; in many others it has been found that high-parity children suffer a systematic deprivation as opposed to their older siblings. And so on. The notion that there is some linear relationship between family size and consumption needs, or that available consumables are divided in a more or less equitable way among all household members is almost certainly not right. The household is a small society with a power structure, and with rights and obligations distributed in unequal ways and with a systematic exploitation of some members by others. Children may be exploited by parents and, almost certainly, females are exploited by males insofar as they bear most of the costs of childbearing, get few of the benefits, and have little say in the decision process. One can argue that these arrangements, including the exploitations, are functional to the extent that under hard, subsistence agricultural conditions they do result in perpetuating the household through time as an economic, social, and demographic entity.

The second assumption of these models is equally dubious. In most developing countries children become economically active at early ages, and even before they do they are not a barrier to female work force participation. In very few parts of the world is child-care viewed as a full-time job or are children thought of as remaining useless and helpless until they turn 16 or 18.

Finally, it seems to me that the notion that spending on consumption for children may be at the expense of savings, and hence asset accumulation misses the whole point. Children *are* a form of asset accumulation in many developing societies. If the primary resource of the household is its own labor services and there is a positive relationship between the volume of these labor services and the household's income potential, then, far from competing with the growth of productive capacity and income potential, a larger family size may contribute to it. The distribution of such increases in income within the family may be highly exploitative, but that is beside the point. What I am suggesting can be put in the following way. Under conditions in which the only way to increase output and income is to increase the labor input, a large family may actually increase the savings potential of the household, not decrease it. This all changes quickly once we move into a world with child labor laws, compulsory schooling, in nonagriculture urban settings, with changed household production function and distributive rules.

But if this view is accepted the search for a link between family size and savings is pointless, for family size itself is a part of gross investment by the household. Very low financial savings coupled with large number of children is merely an indicator of the asset portfolio held by the household, and rising financial savings coupled with falling family size indicates only a changing portfolio. Children cannot be a drain on savings if they are part of savings. This is what I meant by the irrelevance of Kelley's first question once a human-capital model is adopted.

As regards the savings ratio, the basic model takes into account only financial savings. This is modified to take into account investment in child quality, namely, educational expenditures. But, if there is anything to the human-capital approach, then spending on quantity of children as well as quality should be considered savings also. If couples are considered to demand children when quality (or price) has started going up, then surely they must be demanding them when price (or quality) is lower and quantity is greater. Indeed, the very low financial savings rate the data present suggests that most of the family savings are taking the form of investment in children (quality and quantity).

Finally, the nature of the subsample troubles me. The group analyzed covered 401 urban Kenyan households in which only two married adults and the children of the head of the household were present. All "complex" households—the other two-thirds of the overall sample—were excluded. But, if the "complex" household is the norm, does not this partitioning of the data introduce possible bias in the income or savings reported? Are not these households more likely to be sending cash remittances to other households, which are notoriously elusive for survey instruments to catch? Again, financial savings may be understated on this count.

Turning now to the economic variables effect on fertility, I wonder if there is any evidence that urban Kenyans actually plan their fertility as carefully as this model assumes. The mean children ever born is 4.1 in a sample in which 64% of the women are 29 years old or younger. Also, 40% report 5 or more children, close to the 36% over 29 years of age. Completed family size for this group almost certainly would be 6 plus, and if this is not natural fertility, it is at least high fertility for an urban sample. Without some information on knowledge, attitudes, and practices of contraception, I do not think we can assume that a deterministic model of fertility applies. Both on conceptual grounds, as developed by Easterlin, Leibenstein, and others, and also on empirical grounds as revealed in several recent surveys, including those of Simon, T. W. Schultz, and Ann Williams, there is abundant room for skepticism about the usefulness of the same model with the same assumptions in both developed, literate contracepting populations and less-developed populations with excess demand for children.

As regards the type of model, it is a simultaneous equations approach implying a series of interrelated simultaneously determined decisions within the household. Kelley argues that to use a "recursive" model rather than a simultaneous one is equivalent to saying that one decision comes first—family size, say—and that the others—labor force activity, savings versus consumption—follow from this. This he identifies with a naive Malthusian (biological) no-decision model or, alternately, with Easterlin's hypothesis about a supply constraint at very low levels of income making the fertility decision primary. He rejects this approach and his own OLS results in favor of the more comfortable 2SLS simultaneous model.

I have no quarrel with this operational judgment, but I do feel that there are substantial grounds for rejecting the notion that completed family size (or children ever born), quality of children, female labor force participation, and other asset acquisitions are decided in one single simultaneous decision process when the household is formed. The real system is recursive and sequential. The decision shortly after marriage is not Will we have zero to six children? but Will we have a child, and if so when? That decision is made simultaneously with a host of other decisions, including wives' immediate labor force plans, the vacation next year, buying or renting a house, and so on. The outcome of these decisions is in turn the input for a later round of decisions centering on a possible second child. And so on. Presumably the system grows smaller through time as some fairly permanent decisions are made—a home is purchased, the wife makes a considerable investment in acquiring special labor market skills, and so forth. Such a sequential model can also be explicitly stochastic by allowing for such factors as contraceptive failure, tastes for children (or other goods) that change with socioeconomic status, and objective changes in external labor market conditions. The deterministic, simultaneous equations model assumes not only rationality but unchanging utility functions, perfect foresight, and no genuinely stochastic elements. These conceptual matters have been treated at length by Namboodiri, Turchi, Simon, Leibenstein, and others.

I am fully aware that an approach such as I am suggesting would not be possible using Kelley's data set. He has undoubtedly done the best he could using a thin data base and a highly simplified model. His discussion of the variables and his econometric manipulations of the data are full of insight and skill, and the paper is a contribution to our understanding of African demographic-economic interrelationships.

Comment Julian L. Simon

General

The context of Allen Kelley's paper is the nonagreement of population theory with the empirical data on the relationship between per capita income and population growth from additional children (Kuznets 1967; Easterlin 1978; Chesnais and Sauvy 1973). The data show no negative effect, though existing theory does.

More specifically, one of the strands in Malthus's theorizing is that the resource stock—that is, land—is fixed in the short run. An additional child therefore causes no *immediate* increase in total income, and hence average income immediately falls proportionately when a child is born. "The constant effort of population . . . increases the number of people before the means of subsistence are increased. The food, therefore, which before supported eleven million, must now be divided among eleven million and a half" (Malthus 1817, p. 11). This proposition, zero short-run elasticity of family income with respect to children, is the secondary element in Kelley's study. The main topic of Kelley's paper is the Coale-Hoover idea of a negative savings effect of additional dependents.

So among the questions Kelley addresses are two of the central concerns of economic population theory: the response of family income with respect to fertility and the effect of fertility on savings.

Kelley's study is well and ingeniously done, up to the limits of the data. And its presentation is even better—clear, well organized, and sensible. Confidence in the results is increased by their insensitivity to making the child mortality rate endogenous or exogenous, and to the aggregation experiments. The difference between the OLS and 2SLS results is gratifying rather than worrisome and confirms an important piece of technical knowledge, that simultaneous-equation estimation is more appropriate in studying this question.

Kelley's Findings

I am prepared to agree with Kelley that fertility does not depress total saving. The past evidence on this matter has been mixed, and people's predisposition to think that fertility depresses savings may have been part of a general prejudice against poor people's economic rationality and ability to save. Not only laymen but also economists believe that the poor are unable to save. For example, in a comment on Leff's work on dependency and saving, Gupta wrote, "When income levels are as low as in these two [low-income] groups, there is no margin left for

Julian L. Simon is professor of economics and business administration, University of Illinois, Urbana.

savings" (1971, p. 471). Similar views were asserted in the past by such writers as Arthur Lewis, E. M. Bernstein, J. M. Keynes, and Ragnar Nurkse (summarized by Panikar 1961). But the data do not confirm this view.

The biggest body of data on household saving and income is from India. And many village surveys of Indians, summarized in a fascinating article by Panikar, then discussed at length by Hoselitz (1964), show that poor Indian farmers save very respectable proportions of their incomes—cash savings of perhaps 12% gross and 8% net. And when nonmonetary saving is included—as it should be—"the gross saving-income ratio among rural households would rise to 20% or so." The savings ratios of poor farmers, then, are not significantly lower than for the better-off farmers in the world.

Nevertheless, the Kenya data leave me with qualms about Kelley's finding on savings and fertility. It is hard to know whether the lack of effect of children on savings indicates real neutrality or errors in measurement. Such measurement error arises, as Kelley notes, both from the usual problems of measuring savings and from the fact that saving is here estimated by the arithmetic difference between two large magnitudes, income and expenditure, both measured with error.

The dimensions of the observations also give grounds for worry. The mean income of a family in the subsample Kelley reports on is 719 shillings. Mean financial saving is only 7 shillings, 1% of income. But Kelley estimates a marginal propensity to save (financially) as 11%. This means that if the representative household's income goes up by just 10%—from 719 shillings to 790 shillings—total saving would *double* (to 14 shillings). And if the representative household's income falls by only 10%—from 719 to 647 shillings—saving would fall to zero. Such a violent response of saving to income, over the very range of experience that Kelley focuses on, gives one pause. An observed marginal propensity to save ten times as large as the average propensity to save suggests a major difficulty in permanent-income measurement as well as errors in measurement of current income.

In brief, Kelley's finding that fertility does not depress saving makes sense and is consistent with other work. But reservations about the data sap this finding's strength.

On children and total income, now: Kelley's finding that additional children increase the work done by parents makes sense. If anything, Kelley qualifies his finding too much. It is true that he cannot distinguish between remittances and household earnings. But he can buttress his findings with the findings of others. Long ago Chayanov (1966), using Russian peasant data, and a flock of recent writers using data from the United States and Israel (summarized in Simon 1977, chap. 3), have found a large positive effect of children on the hours worked by the father and a positive effect of older children on the hours worked by the mother. A positive effect of fertility on average hours of work also appears in a cross-national study done by Pilarski (1976). And Scully (1962) showed higher physical and money output per acre of Irish farmers per unit of land input with more children. So Kelley might be more assertive in interpreting the increased income that accompanies more children as showing that children do indeed lead to more work.

My main technical suggestion for the study as a whole is to check whether the results are sensitive to the *sample*. It was sound workmanship for Kelley to restrict the main subsample to families with two married adults, because the status of adults—that is, the identification of which adults are parents of whom—is not given in the data. But this subsample made up only 29% of Kelley's original sample.

Kelley should be able to make good guesses about the status of the third (or even fourth) adult in many families. For example, a woman more than fifteen years older than the other two married people surely is a mother of one of them. It would be interesting to rerun the data with the original subsample augmented in this and other fashions to see whether the effects of children on income and savings are thereby altered. If there is no change, we would have still greater confidence in the results. And if there *is* a difference, these results might be the more valid because they cover more people. And Kelley would learn something about the effects of extended families and of having in-laws in the home.

A related technical suggestion for his further work is that Kelley split his observations into those with wife's age 29 or less and those with wife's age 30 or greater. This would avoid the nonlinear estimation problem and would enable him to check for interactions between wife's age and other variables—interactions that are not unlikely. Insensitivity of results to such a splitting of the observations would strengthen the results, in my judgment, at almost zero cost.

Now a question: An increment of woman's education causes about the same increase in income as a similar increment of men's education, in Kelley's results. This suggests that women work as much as men. Does this, in turn, suggest that children have no negative effect on labor force participation? If this result is reliable, it is startling.

Where Do We Go from Here?

If we accept the findings of Kelley and others that explode myths about family savings and income responses to fertility, where do we stand with respect to understanding the effect of population growth on income? By themselves these corrections to the received theory provide only a very partial reconciliation of theory and empirical reality. Even if income and saving are not reduced, the family data still imply less education and physical capital bestowed on *each* additional child. If we are to reconcile theory with the aggregate data on the relationship of population growth to per capita income, *we must go beyond the individual household and ask about an increase in the number of households, and investigate the macroresponses to fertility*. For some examples:

1. The fertility-induced reduction in investment in educational expenditures per child by the *government* is far less than the household reduction suggested by Kelley's data, as shown in cross-national studies by Simon and Pilarski (forthcoming) and by Anker (1978).

2. We must know more about economies and diseconomies of scale. It is easy to speculate about the congestion effects in this room of doubling the participants at this conference. But we must also learn more about how increased population density increases the infrastructure available to all. For example, increased population density has a very strong effect on the stock of roads, as is shown in Glover and Simon (1975).

3. Last, and perhaps most important, we must know more about the effects of more households and individuals on our stock of knowledge, as was emphasized by Kuznets at the NBER conference in 1960. And please note that the knowledge in question is not just the knowledge created by scientific geniuses. Rather, much of the relevant new knowledge is created by people who are neither well educated nor well paid —the dispatcher who develops a slightly better way of deploying the taxis in his ten-taxi fleet, the shipper who discovers that garbage cans make excellent cheap containers for many items, the supermarket manager who finds a way to display more merchandise in a given space, the supermarket clerk who finds a quicker way to stamp the prices on cans, the market researcher in the supermarket chain who experiments and finds more efficient and cheaper means of advertising the store's prices and sale items, and so on.

I will end with what I hope is an inspirational message, and what I am sure is a pat on the back for economics as a science.

The great strength of economics is its insistence on, and its capacity for, dealing with the *indirect* and *delayed* effects of system changes. This is one of economics' main improvements over untutored common sense. Our stock in trade is the human and institutional responses to such changes in circumstances. Population economics is a subject in which the indirect and delayed effects are particularly crucial, and leaving them out of the reckoning can lead to absolutely wrong conclusions.

Let's consider some examples, starting with Kelley's work:

1. *Saving*. A baby immediately needs milk and diapers and a costly priestly ceremony. All other expenditures are fixed in the very short run, so these new expenditures must come out of savings. But economics points to a longer-run delayed phenomenon, gradual substitution among

expenditures. And indeed this is what Kelley finds, in contrast to casual observation.

2. *Total income*. The amount of income-producing labor is fixed in the very short run, and hence total income does not immediately respond to an additional child. This is obvious to laymen. But the labor-leisure tradeoff depends on tastes, and these tastes are a function of per capita income, as Chayanov showed theoretically and empirically. Kelley once again confirms this indirect long-run effect, which differs from the short-run direct effect.

Now let us consider some examples of delayed and indirect effects that economics has not yet given enough attention to in the context of population:

3. *Natural Resources*. Malthus slipped up on the fixity of land, and Jevons (1865) on the fixity of the coal supply. The difficulty here is largely definitional. In the short run the relevant quantity is the known well-defined material stock. But in the longer run, substitution and invention render a physical definition meaningless. Does the concept of oil include shale oil? Oil from coal? Oil made with solar energy? It is true in the short run that resources are limited. But in the long run we create resources and actually reduce scarcity, as is shown by the long-run downward trends in resource prices (Barnett and Morse 1963). But this Resources-for-the-Future idea has yet to be integrated into formal economic thinking about population.

4. *Physical capital*. In the short run physical capital is fixed in supply. But in the longer run it is a function of profit. And population size influences sales and profits. Nor is additional investment always at the expense of consumption or other investment. So the long-run effect of population on the stock of physical capital, in contrast to the short-run effect, might well be positive.

5. *Knowledge*. Not in the short run, but in the long run additional children create new knowledge. They do so both because of additional demand for output and because of the additional supply of minds. We must stretch our science's capacity to the utmost to determine the nature and magnitude of this very important but very long-run phenomenon.

We must also come up with more new hypotheses about the long-run macroeffects of increased population. For example, is there a positive effect on mental agility and one's stock of information from having contacts with more people?

My pat on the back for economics is that—though perhaps not as quickly as one might have hoped—it has taken up and emphasized the indirect and delayed effects of population growth, as is seen in Kelley's paper. My message is that we must continue to do this with even more vigor and resourcefulness until we are able to improve our theory of population and our statistical data on population growth and economic growth to the point where we can consider them satisfactorily reconciled. At that time we may well see that the same increment of population growth that has a negative effect on income in the short run has a positive effect in some long-run future. Our judgment about whether population growth's overall effect is positive or negative thus depends on the discount factor with which we choose to weight the long-run relative to the short-run futures of our society.

Comment Paul Demeny

The subject of Professor Kelley's paper is economic and demographic household behavior in the urban population of Kenya. Surely, as any tourist who ever descended on Nairobi could confirm, this is a theme admirably suited for dissection at a conference on population and economic change in developing countries. In Nairobi, the visitor sees a city in the throes of rapid development—a picture of life rich in sharp contrasts of poverty and affluence, tradition and modernity, tribalism and Western mores, disorganization and upward social mobility. He sees the ubiquitous signs of class conflict; the clash of the young and the old; and environmental decay next to manifestations of some of the best urban planning anywhere in the developing world. What is below the surface is bound to be even more exciting. An anatomy of household behavior, organized around its crucial demographic components, should provide important insights into the dynamics of the development process in contemporary urban Kenya. It would be, of course, unreasonable to expect Kelley's equations somehow to capture all the essential features of the ongoing socioeconomic transformation that is behind the picture even the most unperceptive tourist will not fail to see—unless his gaze is totally riveted on giraffes. Scientific understanding progresses by disciplining one's curiosity and proceeding with rigorous analysis of a manageable segment of life.

Unhappily, the slice of life examined by the paper under discussion is much too thin to be justified by this principle. In the familiar fashion of the art, Kelley does deliver numerous propositions on economic-demographic interactions supported by whole tablefuls of quantitative findings. But these propositions and findings are singularly uninteresting and implausible. Let me pick some representative examples. "An increase in female education," we learn, "from illiteracy to the primary level would reduce child deaths by 0.09." "Each additional child results

Paul Demeny is director of the Center for Policy Studies, the Population Council.

in a direct increase in income of 123 shillings." "If the male household head's . . . education were to increase from primary to secondary level, total financial savings . . . would increase by 88.8 . . . shillings." "An increase in female education of the same sort dramatically reduces family size." We are also told why, in simple declarative sentences. "The opportunity costs, in terms of market employment, increase rather dramatically with higher education levels." The findings, of course, make eminent econometric sense as they follow logically from the data, the model, and its specifications. But it seems to me that the model is far too anemic to inspire much confidence in the substance of such statements, let alone to support the policy suggestions the paper sparingly but bravely spells out. We are dealing with a conflict-free society of unchanging tastes whose past is neatly captured by the reciprocal of something called U, the number of years the household head has lived in the urban area. What about its future? Can the model provide a prediction on the expected pattern of fertility change in urban Kenya and on the mechanisms that are likely to govern the process? The model specifies the variable children ever born in terms of income and educational attainment and, trivially, of age. Interpreting these as proxies for the true causal variables enables Kelley to make numerical propositions on what will happen under certain specified conditions; but, plainly, the ability of the model to grasp the essence of the relevant aspects of the developmental process is severely limited, hence the findings command little interest. It is hardly surprising that we are warned not to generalize from the results presented in the paper and are admonished that model parameters are apt to change from setting to setting and, more ominously, over time. One can surmise that a series of similar studies for urban Kenya are in order. But, by the time a pattern of change for the parameter values has emerged—and there is no reason to expect that such a pattern will lend itself to any useful interpretation—one hopes the problem that sparked the investigation to begin with will have long lost its significance.

There is, of course, a possibility that that has already happened, at least if one takes at face value Kelley's argument on the need for his analysis. That argument focuses on the issue of the influence of demographic variables on the rate and composition of household savings. Kelley posits an adverse effect of fertility on savings (in first-approximation financial savings) as the kingpin of the dominant models of economic-demographic development, but he claims that these models are "increasingly being questioned." Such a claim amounts to a vast understatement. A stress on the significance of household savings, to my knowledge, disappeared from the literature years ago, and for excellent reasons. Once Kelley found that the average yearly level of household saving was 7 shillings in his Kenya sample—barely 1% of total income

—perhaps simply reporting that result would have made his recapitulation of the verdict just as effective. Kelley's extension of the concept of saving to include saving for human-capital investment is salutory but far too narrow. What really matters to society on that score is the quality of children and, in particular, their economic abilities—entrepreneurship, diligence, honesty, ability to cooperate with their fellowmen, and so forth. These characteristics of crucial importance for development are manufactured primarily in the family unit rather than in the schools. Neither can they be captured by the kind of survey techniques Kelley has access to.

Let me conclude my remarks by venturing a somewhat fanciful report on the state of the field to which this conference is addressed. On the fringes of the social sciences there once lived a primitive tribe called demographers. They had a happy time in a hunting-gathering existence, picking up and consuming raw bits and pieces of data that they called names like "birthrates," "death rates," "rates of dependency," and "gross reproduction." To diversify their diet, they enjoyed digging up old chestnuts that their ancestors had buried many years before and chewing on them. Must infant mortality fall for birth control to be practiced? Is it true that affluent people have low fertility, and why? Keen to make sense of their small world, the demographers looked about in wonder and tried to explain puzzling changes in the objects of their curiosity. Some came to attribute magic properties to some happenings beyond their ken, developing strange beliefs such as that industrialization makes the birthrate drop or that education makes gross reproduction wilt. Others concluded that hospital beds per 1,000 population or telephones per capita have equally remarkable clout.

These happy and imaginative—if somewhat childlike—people were one day invaded by a bunch of warlike neighboring tribesmen who got tired of watching their neighbors' bumbling ways. Equipped with their superior bronze-age technology, the invaders had little trouble taking over the demographers' territory; and for a while they had great fun renaming the trees and the fruits in a logical and elegant fashion and driving out superstition about causes and effects. Education, they held, for example, demonstrably does have that wilting effect on birthrates; but it must be first tidily measured, labeled, and subscripted and seen as a proxy for other things, such as the value of mother's time. Such discoveries and the accompanying tidying-up were quite plausibly the dawn of a new era, with continuing rapid technological progress in store and full enlightenment within sight. As often happens, however, the conquerors liked the pickings on the new land, and soon they settled down, gathering and consuming the same fruits as their former neighbors who, subjugated and docile, still lived on the same territory. A not unpleasant symbiosis had developed. Even though things became a bit crowded sometimes, there were plenty of data to pick from to keep everyone well fed and satisfied. Also, new data kept growing, the ground having been fertilized by increasingly benevolent weather, bringing a steady rain of dollars. The demographers and the now-settled warriors happily shared a seemingly inexhaustible supply of married women 25–29, or of other more or less interesting age intervals, whose fertility rates needed to be urgently explained; and there was a rich storehouse of variables to help the explaining. Lacking in new challenges, sloth overcame the conquerors. The promise of a golden age faded, and a bastard bronze age began.

The parable should not be labored further. The main point I am trying to make is not that the theoretical and methodological advances made in the eighteen years since the predecessor of this conference met in Princeton in 1958 are insignificant. Certainly, the superior power of the models of household demographic decisions borrowed from the theory of consumers' behavior—in contrast, say, to regression analyses of piles of socioeconomic and demographic data relating to country units —is beyond dispute. Still, the new micromodels of demographic behavior remain patently inadequate to the task, drained as they are of sociological content and institutional, historical, and psychological substance. To this basic complaint another should be added, although blandly and without elaboration. Even within the narrow confines of the model, the grasp on behavioral variables and processes that can be gotten by using the kind of data that are now the staple of studies on developing countries—census data and survey data collected through remote control, as it were—has now run into rapidly diminishing returns. I know that many people are highly optimistic about the prospective yield of further exploitation of the standard survey methodology and the resultant better microlevel data. Certainly the sponsors of the World Fertility Survey must be among them. But the available evidence supporting optimism on that score does not strike me as persuasive.

If the complaints just registered have any merit, some serious soul-searching is in order for the field. The analytical approach exemplified by the paper under discussion now seems to claim a disproportionate share of the attention, the time, and the brains of the best practitioners of economic demographic studies. The opportunity costs are potentially important. I suspect, for instance, that I could have been a far more enthusiastic discussant at this conference if I had a chance to comment on a work by Professor Kelley that picked up some of the demographically relevant themes of his recent remarkable book on dualistic economic development. Paradoxically, since that economists' invasion the parochial and narrowly conceptualized traditional concerns of demographers seem to hold greater sway over the field than ever before. This conference bears the general title Population and Economic Change in Developing Countries. Perhaps it has a subtitle I am unaware of, making it a more specialized affair than this general label indicates. Or perhaps the National Bureau intends to organize another conference without waiting until 1994—another eighteen years—to explore important areas and issues of the economics of population not covered in this conference. Certainly, even the program of the 1958 NBER conference—although focused on the less obvious and less pervasive population problems of the *developed* countries—had a more catholic formulation than the present one. Then there were papers on macroeconomic aspects of population growth; on the effect of demographic change on aggregate demand, price level, aggregate employment, and labor supply; on population and resources; on the influence of population on the demand for food; on sectoral effects such as the demand for services. Forays into general equilibrium analysis were not off limits. In contrast, a detached observer, listening to our discussions, would have a very lopsided appreciation of economists' potential contribution to a scientific analysis of demographic aspects of development. Examples of subjects that were given short shrift form a long litany: from welfare economics to the economics of international trade; from externalities theory to the economics of public goods; from resource economics to the economics of development proper. It is unfortunate that little of that potential is captured by the present program; and it is even more so if the bias correctly reflects the actual distribution of ongoing academic research in economic demography. Arguably, what the field needs is another invasion by a marauding tribe of economists, equipped with new ideas and new analytical tools.

References

Adams, N. A. 1971. Dependency rates and savings rates: Comment. *American Economic Review* 59 (June): 472.

Anker, Richard. 1974. The effect of group level variables on fertility in a rural Indian sample. World Employment Program (mimeographed). Geneva: International Labor Organization.

———. 1975. An analysis of fertility differentials in developing countries. World Employment Program (mimeographed). Geneva: International Labor Organization.

———. 1978. An analysis of fertility differentials in developing countries. *Review of Economics and Statistics* (February): 58–69.

Barlow, Robin. 1967. The economic effects of malaria eradication. *American Economic Review* 57 (May): 130–57.

Barlow, Robin, and Davies, Gordon. 1974. Policy analysis with a disaggregated economic-demographic model. *Journal of Public Economics* 3 (February): 43–70.

Barnett, Harold J., and Morse, Chandler. 1963. *Scarcity and growth: The economics of natural resource availability*. Baltimore: Johns Hopkins University Press.

Becker, Gary S. 1960. An economic analysis of fertility. *Demographic and Economic Change in Developed Countries*. Universities–National Bureau Conference Series. Princeton: Princeton University Press.

———. 1973. A theory of marriage: Part I. *Journal of Political Economy* 81 (July/August): 813–46.

Becker, Gary S., and Lewis, H. Gregg. 1973. On the interaction between the quantity and quality of children. *Journal of Political Economy* 81, part 2 (March/April): S279–88.

Ben-Porath, Yoram. 1967. The production of human capital and the life cycle of earnings. *Journal of Political Economy* 75 (August): 352–65.

———. 1970. The production of human capital over time. In *Education, income, and human capital*, ed. W. Lee Hansen. Studies in Income and Wealth, vol. 35. New York: Columbia University Press (for National Bureau of Economic Research).

Ben-Porath, Yoram, and Welch, Finis. 1972. *Chance, child traits, and the choice of family size*. Santa Monica, Calif.: Rand Corporation.

Betancourt, R. R. 1971. The normal income hypothesis in Chile. *Journal of the American Statistical Association* 66 (June): 258–63.

Bilsborrow, Richard E. 1975. A critical review of the concept and measurement of economic dependency (mimeographed). Chapel Hill: University of North Carolina.

Blake, J. 1968. Are babies consumer durables? Critique of the economic theory of reproductive motivation. *Population Studies* 22: 5–25.

Bourgeois-Pichat, Jean. 1967. Social and biological determinants of human fertility in non-industrial societies. *Proceedings of the American Philosophical Society* 3 (June): 160–63.

Bowen, W. G., and Finegan, T. Aldrich. 1969. *The economics of labor force participation*. Princeton: Princeton University Press.

Brass, W., ed. 1970. *Biological aspects of demography*. London: Taylor and Francis.

Cain, Glen G. 1966. *Married women in the labor force*. Chicago: University of Chicago Press.

Cain, Glen G., and Weininger, A. 1973. Economic determinants of fertility: Results using cross-sectional aggregate data. *Demography* 10 (May): 205–24.

Caldwell, J. C. 1967. Fertility attitudes in three economically contrasting rural regions of Ghana. *Economic Development and Cultural Change* 15 (January): 217–38.

Castle, Edgar B. 1966. *Growing up in East Africa.* London: Oxford University Press.

Chang, Cheng-tung. 1976. Desired fertility, income and the valuation of children. World Employment Program (mimeographed). Geneva: International Labor Organization.

Chayanov, A. V. 1966. *The theory of peasant economy*, ed. D. Thorner et al. Homewood, Ill.: Richard Irwin.

Chesnais, Jean-Claude, and Sauvy, Alfred. 1973. Progrès économique et accroissement de la population: Une expérience commentée. *Population* 28: 843–57.

Coale, Ansley, and Hoover, F. M. 1958. *Population growth and economic development in low-income countries.* Princeton: Princeton University Press.

Dandekar, Kumudini. 1967. Effect of education on fertility. *World Population Conference.* Vol. 4. New York: United Nations.

DaVanzo, J. 1970. *The determinants of family formation in Chile, 1960.* Santa Monica, Calif.: Rand Corporation.

Demeny, P. 1967. Demographic aspects of saving, investment, employment and productivity. *World Population Conference 1965.* New York: United Nations.

Denton, Frank T., and Spencer, Byron G. 1974. Some government budget consequences of population change (mimeographed). Hamilton, Ont.: Department of Economics, McMaster University.

DeTray, N. Dennis. 1973. Child quality and the demand for children. *Journal of Political Economy* 81, part 2 (March/April): S70–95.

Duesenberry, James. 1949. *Income, savings, and the theory of consumer behavior.* Cambridge: Harvard University Press.

———. 1960. Comment on "An economic analysis of fertility" by Gary S. Becker. In *Demographic and economic change in developed countries.* Universities-National Bureau Conference Series. Princeton: Princeton University Press.

Easterlin, Richard A. 1967. The effects of population growth on the economic development of developing countries. *Annals of the American Academy of Political and Social Science* 364 (January): 98–108.

———. 1968. *Population, labor force, and long swings in economic growth.* New York: National Bureau of Economic Research.

———. 1969. Towards a socio-economic theory of fertility: A survey of recent research on economic factors in American fertility. In *Fertility and family planning: A world view*, ed. S. J. Behrman, Leslie Corsa, Jr., and Ronald Freedman. Ann Arbor: University of Michigan Press.

———. 1971. Does human fertility adjust to the environment? *American Economic Review* 61 (May): 399–407.

———. 1975. An economic framework for fertility analysis. *Studies in Family Planning* 6 (March): 54–63.

———. 1978. Effects of population growth on the economic development of developing countries. In *Social demography*, ed. T. Ford and Gidejong. Englewood Cliffs, N.J.: Prentice-Hall. Originally published in *Annals of the American Academy of Political and Social Science*, January 1967.

Eizenga, W. 1961. *Demographic factors and saving.* Amsterdam: North Holland Publishing Company.

Encarnacion, J. 1973. Family income, education level, labor force participation, and fertility (mimeographed). Manila: University of the Philippines.

Enke, S. 1971. *Description of the economic-demographic model.* Santa Barbara, Calif.: General Electric Company, Tempo Center for Advanced Studies.

Fields, Gary. 1974. The allocation of resources to education in less developed countries. *Journal of Public Economics* 3 (May): 133–43.

Fisher, Allan C., Jr. 1969. Kenya says harambee! *National Geographic* 35 (February): 154–65.

Forrester, Marion. 1962. *Kenya today: Social prerequisites for economic development.* The Hague: International Institute of Social Studies.

Frederiksen, Harold. 1966. Determinants and consequences of mortality and fertility trends. *Public Health Reports* 81 (August): 715–27.

Freedman, Deborah S. 1963. The relation of economic status to fertility. *American Economic Review* 53 (June): 414–26.

Friedman, Milton. 1957. *A theory of the consumption function.* Princeton: Princeton University Press.

Friend, I., and Taubman, P. 1966. The aggregate propensity to save: Some concepts and their application to international data. *Review of Economics and Statistics* 48 (May): 113–23.

Glover, Donald, and Simon, Julian L. 1975. The effects of population density upon infra-structure: The case of road building. *Economic Development and Cultural Change* 23: 453–68.

Goldfeld, S. M., and Quandt, Richard E. 1965. Some tests for homoskedasticity. *Journal of the American Statistical Association* 60 (June): 539–47.

Goldsmith, Raymond; Brady, Dorothy; and Mendershausen, Horst. 1956. *A study of saving in the United States.* Princeton: Princeton University Press.

Griliches, Zvi. 1973. Errors in variables and other unobservables. (mimeographed). Cambridge: Harvard University.

Gronau, Reuben. 1973*a*. The effect of children on the housewife's value of time. *Journal of Political Economy* 81, part 2 (March/April): S168–99.

———. 1973*b*. The intra-family allocation of time: The value of the housewives' time. *American Economic Review* 63 (September): 634–51.

Gupta, K. L. 1970. Personal saving in developing nations: Further evidence. *Economic Record* 46 (June): 243–49.

———. 1971. Dependency rates and savings rates: Comment. *American Economic Review* 69 (June): 469–71.

Harman, Alvin J. 1971. Interrelationships between procreation and other family decisionmaking (mimeographed). Santa Monica, Calif.: Rand Corporation.

Heer, David. 1969. Economic development and fertility. *Demography* 3 153–80.

Heer, David, and Smith, D. 1968. Mortality level, desired family size, and population increase. *Demography* 5: 104–21.

———. 1969. Mortality level, desired family size, and population increase: Further variations on a basic model. *Demography* 6: 141–49.

Heisel, Donald. 1968. Attitudes and practices of contraception in Kenya. *Demography* 5: 632–41.

Henderson, A. M. 1949–50. The cost of a family. *Review of Economic Studies* 17: 127–48.

Hoselitz, Bert F. 1964. Capital formation and credit in Indian agricultural society. In *Capital, saving, and credit in peasant societies*, ed. R. Firth and B. S. Yamey. Chicago: Aldine.

Houthakker, H. S., and Prais, S. J. 1955. *The analysis of family budgets.* Cambridge: at the University Press.

International Labor Office. 1971. *Employment, incomes and equality.* Geneva: Imprimeries Populaires.

Jevons, W. Stanley. 1865. *The coal question.* Cambridge: Macmillan.

Johnson, G. E., and Whitelaw, W. E. 1974. Urban-rural income transfers in Kenya: An estimated remittances function. *Economic Development and Cultural Change* 22 (June): 473–79.

Johnson, Thomas. 1970. Returns from investment in human capital. *American Economic Review* 60 (September): 546–60.

Kamarck, Andrew M. 1967. *The economics of African development.* New York: Praeger.

Keeley, Michael C. 1975. A comment on "An interpretation of the economic theory of fertility." *Journal of Economic Literature* 13 (June): 461–68.

Kelley, Allen C. 1968. Demographic change and economic growth. *Explorations in Entrepreneurial History* 5 (spring/summer): 115–85.

———. 1972. Demographic changes and American economic development: Past, present and future. *Economic Aspects of Population Change*, ed. Elliot R. Morse and Ritchie H. Reed. Washington, D.C.: Commission on Population Growth and the American Future.

———. 1973. Population growth, the dependency rate, and the pace of economic development. *Population Studies* 27 (November) 406–20.

———. 1974. The role of population in models of economic growth. *American Economic Review* 64 (May): 39–44.

———. 1976. Savings, demographic change and economic development. *Economic Development and Cultural Change*.

Kelley, Allen C., and deSilva, Lea. 1976. The role of children in household decision making in low income countries (mimeographed). Durham, N.C.: Duke University.

Kelley, Allen C., and Lillydahl, Jane. 1976. A reexamination of the concept of economic dependency (mimeographed). Durham, N.C.: Duke University.

Kelley, Allen C., and Williamson, J. G. 1968. Household saving behavior in developing economies: The Indonesian case. *Economic Development and Cultural Change* 16 (April): 358–402.

Kessner, D. U.; Singer, J.; Kalk, C. E.; and Schlesinger, E. R. 1973. Infant death: An analysis of maternal risk and health care. In *Contrasts in health status*, vol. 1. Washington, D.C.: Institute of Medicine, National Academy of Sciences.

Knodel, J. 1968. Infant mortality and fertility in three Bavarian villages. *Population Studies* 22 (November): 297–318.

Knowles, James C., and Anker, Richard. 1975. Economic determinants of demographic behavior in Kenya. World Employment Project (mimeographed). Geneva: International Labor Organization.

Kuznets, Simon. 1960. Population change and aggregate output. In *Demographic and economic change in developed countries*. Princeton: Princeton University Press.

———. 1967. Population and economic growth. *American Philosophical Society Proceedings* 3: 170–93.

Landsberger, Michael. 1970. The life-cycle hypothesis: A reinterpretation and empirical test. *American Economic Review* 60 (March): 175–83.

Leff, N. H. 1969. Dependency rates and saving rates. *American Economic Review* 59 (December): 886–96.

Leibenstein, Harvey. 1957. *Economic backwardness and economic growth: Studies in the theory of economic development*. New York: Wiley and Sons.

———. 1974. An interpretation of the economic theory of fertility. *Journal of Economic Literature* 12 (June): 457–79.

———. 1975*a*. The economic theory of fertility decline. *Quarterly Journal of Economics* 89 (February): 1–31.

———. 1975*b*. On the economic theory of fertility: A reply to Keeley. *Journal of Economic Literature* 13 (June): 469–71.

Lillydahl, Jane. 1976. Economic and demographic influences on household saving in urban Kenya. Ph.D. diss., Duke University.

McFarland, William E.; Bennett, James P.; and Brown, Richard. 1973. *Description of the TEMPO II budget allocation and human resources model*. Santa Barbara, Calif.: General Electric Company, Tempo Center for Advanced Studies.

Malthus, Thomas R. 1817. *An essay on the principle of population*. 5th ed. Reprinted 1963. Homewood, Ill.: Richard Irwin.

Malthus, T. R. 1970. *An essay on the principle of population and a summary view of the principle of population*. Baltimore: Penguin (originally published in 1798).

Massell, Benton F., and Heyer, Judith. 1969. Household expenditure in Nairobi: A statistical analysis of consumer behavior. *Economic Development and Cultural Change* 17 (January): 212–34.

Matsunaga, Ei. 1967. Measures affecting population trends and possible genetic consequences. In *World Population Conference*, vol. 2. New York: United Nations.

Michael, Robert T. 1971. Dimensions of household fertility: An economic analysis. *American Statistical Association Proceedings*, pp. 126–36.

———. 1973. Education and the derived demand for children. *Journal of Political Economy* 81, part 2 (March/April): S128–64.

Mikesell, Raymond, and Zinser, James. 1973. Nature of savings functions. *Journal of Economic Literature* II (March): 1–20.

Mincer, Jacob. 1963. Market prices, opportunity costs, and income effects. In *Measurement in economics: Studies in mathematical economics and econometrics in memory of Yehuda Grunfeld*, ed. Carl Crist et al. Stanford: Stanford University Press.

Ministry of Education. 1971–75. *Ministry of Education annual reports* (1970–74). Nairobi: Government Printer.

Modigliani, F., and Brumberg, R. 1954. Utility analysis and the consumption function: An interpretation of cross-section data. In *Post-Keynesian economics*, ed. K. Kurihara. New Brunswick: Rutgers University Press.

Morrison, William A. 1957. Attitudes of females toward family planning in a Maharashtrian village. *Milbank Memorial Fund Quarterly* 35 (January): 67–81.

Namboodiri, N. Krishnan. 1975. Review of *Economics of the family: Marriage, children and human capital*, ed. T. W. Schultz. *Demography* 12 (August): 561–69.

Nerlove, Marc, and Schultz, T. Paul. 1970. *Love and life between the censuses: A model of family decision making in Puerto Rico, 1950–1960*. Santa Monica, Calif.: Rand Corporation.

O'Hara, D. J. 1972. *Changes in mortality levels and family decisions regarding children*. Santa Monica, Calif.: Rand Corporation.

Panikar, P. G. K. 1961. Rural savings in India. *Economic Development and Cultural Change* 10 (October): 64–85.

Peek, Peter. 1974. Household savings and demographic change in the Philippines. World Employment Program (mimeographed). Geneva: International Labor Organization.

———. 1975. Family composition and married female employment: The case of Chile. World Employment Program (mimeographed). Geneva: International Labor Organization.

———. 1976. The education and employment of children: A comparative study of San Salvador and Khartoum. World Employment Program (mimeographed). Geneva: International Labor Organization.

Perlman, Mark. 1975. Review of *Economics of the family: Marriage, children and human capital*, ed. T. W. Schultz. *Demography* 13 (August): 549–56.

Perrella, Vera C. 1970. Moonlighters: Their motivations and characteristics. *Monthly Labor Review* 93 (August): 57–63.

Pilarski, Adam. 1976. The impact of fertility in hours of work: A cross-national comparison (mimeographed). University of Illinois.

Pollak, Robert A., and Wachter, Michael L. 1975. The relevance of the household production function and its implications for the allocation of time. *Journal of Political Economy* 83 (April): 255–78.

Preston, Samuel H. 1975. Health programs and population growth. *Population and Development Review* 1 (December): 189–99.

Raju, Beulah M. 1973. *Education in Kenya*. London: Heinemann.

Ramanathan, R. 1968. Estimating the permanent income of a household: An application to Indian data. *Review of Economics and Statistics* 50 (August): 383–87.

Rodgers, G. B. 1974. Population, consumption and employment. World Employment Program (mimeographed). Geneva: International Labor Organization.

Rosenzweig, Mark R. 1975. Female work experience, employment status, and birth expectations: Sequential decision-making in the Philippines (mimeographed). New Haven: Yale University.

Rosenzweig, Mark R., and Evenson, Robert. 1975. Fertility, schooling and the economic contribution of children in rural India: An econometric analysis (mimeographed). New Haven: Yale University.

Ryder, Norman B. 1973. Comment on "A new approach to the economic theory of fertility behavior," by Robert J. Willis. *Journal of Political Economy* 81, part 2 (March/April): S65–69.

Schultz, T. Paul. 1969. An economic model of family planning and fertility. *Journal of Political Economy* 77 (March/April): 153–80.

———. 1971*a*. An economic perspective on population growth. In *Rapid population growth*. Baltimore: Johns Hopkins University Press (for the National Academy of Sciences).

———. 1971*b*. The effectiveness of population policies: Alternative methods of statistical inferences (mimeographed). Santa Monica, Calif.: Rand Corporation.

———. 1973. Explanation of birth rate changes over space and time: A study of Taiwan. *Journal of Political Economy* 81, part 2 (March/April): S238–74.

———. 1974. *Fertility determinants: A theory, evidence, and an application to policy evaluation*. Santa Monica, Calif.: Rand Corporation.

Schultz, T. Paul, and DaVanzo, J. 1970. *Analysis of demographic change in East Pakistan: Retrospective survey data*. Santa Monica, Calif.: Rand Corporation.

Schultz, Theodore W. 1961. Investment in human capital. *American Economic Review* 51 (March): 1–17.

———. 1973. *The value of children: An economic perspective. Journal of Political Economy* 81, part 2 (March/April): S2–13.

———. ed. 1974. *Economics of the family: Marriage, children, and human capital*. Chicago: University of Chicago Press.

Scully, John J. 1962. The influence of family size on efficiency within the farm: An Irish study. *Journal of Agricultural Economics* 14 (May): 116–21.

Shapiro, S.; Schlesinger, E. R.; and Nesbitt, R. E., Jr. 1968. *Infant, perinatal, maternal and childhood mortality in the United States*. Cambridge: Harvard University Press.

Simon, Julian L. 1969. The effect of income upon fertility. *Population Studies* 23 (November): 327–41.

———. 1971. The influence of population growth on per-worker income in developed economies (mimeographed). Urbana: University of Illinois.

———. 1974. *The effects of income on fertility*. Chapel Hill: Carolina Population Center.

———. 1976. Population growth may be good for LDCs in the long run: A richer simulation model. *Economic Development and Cultural Change* 24 (January): 309–37.

———. 1977. *The economics of population growth*. Princeton: Princeton University Press.

Simon, Julian L., and Aigner, Dennis J. 1970. Cross sectional budget studies, aggregate time-series studies, and the permanent income hypothesis. *American Economic Review* 60 (June): 341–51.

Simon, Julian L., and Pilarski, Adam. 1976. The effect of fertility on the amount of education. *Review of Economics and Statistics.* Forthcoming.

Snyder, Donald. 1971. An econometric analysis of consumption and saving in Sierra Leone. Ph.D. diss., Pennsylvania State University.

———. 1974*a*. Econometric studies of household saving behavior in developing countries: A survey. *Journal of Development Studies* 10 (January): 138–51.

———. 1974*b*. Economic determinants of family size in West Africa. *Demography* 11 (November): 613–28.

Stycos, J. Mayone. 1967. Education and fertility in Puerto Rico. In *World Population Conference*, vol. 4. New York: United Nations.

Sweet, James A. 1970. Family composition and the labor force activity of American wives. *Demography* 7: 195–209.

Thias, Hans H., and Carnoy, Martin. 1972. *Cost benefit analysis in education.* Baltimore: Johns Hopkins University Press.

Turchi, Boone. 1975. *The demand for children: The economics of fertility in the U.S.* Cambridge, Mass.: Ballinger.

Watts, H. 1960. An objective permanent income concept for the household. Cowles Foundation Discussion Paper no. 99 (mimeographed). New Haven: Yale University.

Williamson, Jeffrey G. 1961. Public expenditure and revenue: An international comparison. *Manchester School of Economics and Social Studies*, January, pp. 43–56.

———. 1968. Personal saving in developing nations: An intertemporal cross-section from Asia. *Economic Record* 44 (June): 194–210.

Willis, Robert J. 1973. A new approach to the economic theory of fertility behavior. *Journal of Political Economy* 81, part 2 (March/April): S14–64.

Yaukey, David. 1971. *Fertility differences in a modernizing country.* Princeton: Princeton University Press.

8 Recent Population Trends in Less Developed Countries and Implications for Internal Income Inequality

Simon Kuznets

In a recent paper (Kuznets 1976) I explored the effects on the conventional measures of distribution of income among households of demographic elements such as the size and changing composition of households through their life cycle. The exploration emphasized the need to take explicit account of these demographic elements in any attempt to observe trends in the long-term levels of income differentials—particularly those associated with economic growth, since the latter is usually accompanied by marked shifts in the size and age-of-head distributions of households. Of particular interest was the negative association between per capita income and size of the household or family, found also within the age-of-head classes and thus persisting through the household's life-span. If this cross-sectional association is translated into comparisons of per capita income for households of differing average size over the life-span, the result is a negative association between the per capita income and size variables. Since, in turn, size of households or families is largely a function of the number of children, the negative association just noted is also one between lifetime per capita income and fertility—*provided* that the differentials in fertility dominate differentials in mortality, as they did in the small sample of countries for recent years used in the cross section in my recent paper.

The present paper deals with a different, though related, question. Given the major population trends observable in recent decades in the

Simon Kuznets is professor of economics, emeritus, Harvard University, and consultant to the Economic Growth Center, Yale University

This research was supported in part by AID contract otr-1432 and aided by the Rockefeller Foundation grant RF 70051 to Yale's Economic Demography program.

The author is indebted to Yoram Ben-Porath of the Hebrew University of Jerusalem for helpful comments on an earlier draft of this paper.

economically less developed countries (LDCs), what can one infer about the possible effects on long-term levels or changes in them in the internal distribution of income? For obvious reasons of scarcity of relevant data, and even more of the complex interactions between the population trends and the concurrent structural changes in the economy and society of the countries involved, any answer to the question just raised is bound to be speculative. But there may be value in at least trying to formulate the question unambiguously and in attempting some explicit, relevant speculation.

8.1 The Major Population Trends

One must begin by stressing that the acceleration in the population growth rate in the LDCs, and their markedly higher rate of natural increase than in the economically more developed countries (MDCs), are recent historical trends—as is clearly indicated in table 8.1. Such recency, and the brevity of the period over which these trends have prevailed, compared with the preceding centuries of quite different demographic patterns, are basic to the understanding and evaluation of both the trends and their implications.

Table 8.1 shows that from the mid-eighteenth century through 1920, the rate of increase (overwhelmingly, of *natural* increase) in the LDCs was at relatively low level, varying from less than a 0.1% to about 0.5% per year (see col. 5, lines 12–24).[1] Throughout this long period of some seventeen to eighteen decades, the population growth rate in the MDCs was substantially higher—ranging from over 0.4% to well over 1% per year; and showed a marked acceleration already in the first half of the nineteenth century. It is only since the 1920s that the rates of natural increase in the LDCs rose to approach those in the MDCs; they began to exceed the latter in the 1930s and 1940s, when severe economic recession and then World War II reduced population growth in the developed countries; and only since the 1950s have the annual growth rates of the LDCs climbed to well over 2%, while those in the MDCs declined by the early 1970s to less than 1%. Thus, the acceleration and growth excess of population movements in the LDCs were within a relatively short span of about five decades, following centuries of growth at low rates that would look like stagnation by modern standards.

The second important aspect of these recent trends is that the acceleration, and the resulting excess in the rates of natural increase in the LDCs over those in the MDCs, was due wholly, or almost wholly, to the decline in the death rates—rather than to any movements in the birthrates. A summary of the trends of these vital rates taken separately, but unfortunately limited to the years since 1937, is presented in table

Table 8.1 **Growth of Population, Economically Less Developed (LDC) and More Developed (MDC) Countries, 1750–1975**

	Dates	World (1)	MDCs (2)	LDCs (3)	China (4)	Other LDCs (5)
			A. *Absolute Totals (in millions)*			
1.	1750	791	201	590	200	390
2.	1800	978	248	730	323	407
3.	1850	1,262	347	915	430	485
4.	1900	1,650	573	1,077	436	641
5.	1920	1,860	673	1,187	476	711
6.	1930	2,069	758	1,311	502	809
7.	1940	2,295	821	1,474	533	941
8*a*.	1950*a*	2,515	858	1,658	563	1,095
9*a*.	1960*a*	2,998	976	2,022	654	1,368
8*b*.	1950*b*	2,501	857	1,644	558	1,086
9*b*.	1960*b*	2,986	976	2,010	654	1,356
10.	1970	3,610	1,084	2,526	772	1,754
11.	1975 (proj. med. var.)	3,967	1,132	2,835	838	1,997
			B. *Rates of Increase (per year, per 1,000)*			
12.	1750–1800	4.3	4.2	4.3	9.6	0.9
13.	1800–1850	5.1	6.7	4.5	5.2	3.5
14.	1850–1900	5.4	10.6	3.3	0.3	5.6
15.	1900–1950	8.4	8.1	8.3	4.9	10.7
16.	1950–75	18.6	11.2	22.0	16.4	24.7
17.	1900–1920	6.0	8.1	4.9	4.4	5.2
18.	1920–30	10.8	12.0	10.0	5.3	13.0
19.	1930–40	10.4	8.0	11.8	6.0	15.2
20.	1940–50	9.2	4.4	11.8	5.5	15.3
21.	1950–60	17.7	13.0	20.0	15.1	22.5
22.	1950–60	17.9	13.1	20.3	16.0	22.5
23.	1960–70	19.2	10.6	23.1	16.7	26.1
24.	1970–75	19.0	8.7	23.3	16.5	26.3

Notes

MDCs include Europe, the USSR, North America, temperate South America (Argentina, Uruguay, Chile), Australia, and New Zealand. LDCs include all others.

Lines 1–4: from United Nations, *The Population Debate: Dimensions and Perspectives,* vol. 1 (New York 1975), table 1, pp. 3–4, and the original paper by John Durand cited there. The estimates for China used here are from the Durand paper.

Lines 5–9a: United Nations, *World Population Prospects* (New York, 1966), table A.3.1, p. 133.

Lines 8b–11: United Nations, *Selected World Demographic Indicators, 1950–2000,* mimeographed working paper ESA/P/WP.55, May 1975.

Lines 12–16: Calculated from lines 1–4, 8*b*, and 11.

Lines 17–21: Calculated from lines 5–9*a*.

Lines 22–24: Calculated from lines 8*b*–11.

8.2. Part of this table refers to observed changes, to 1970–75;[2] the other part refers to projections to the year 2000. We deal with the observed changes first.

Between 1937 and 1970–75, a span of about 35 to 36 years, the rise in the rate of natural increase for LDCs (excluding China) from 11.7 to 26.1, some 14.4 points, resulted from a combination of a decline in the crude death rate from 30.8 to 16.0, 14.8 points, and a drop in the birthrate of only 0.4 points. A similar dominance of the drop in the death rate as the overwhelming factor in the rise in the rate of natural increase over the period from 1937 to 1970–75 is also true of LDCs including China (for both comparisons see lines 15–20, cols. 2 and 5). By contrast, whatever movements occurred in the rate of natural increase in the MDCs have been due at least as much to declines in birthrates as to declines in death rates (see lines 12–14, cols. 2 and 5).

It is interesting to estimate the trend were we to extend the view to 1920, the date that is the dividing line before the acceleration in the growth rate of LDC populations. In line 17 of table 8.1 we observe that the growth rate for LDCs for 1900–1920 was about 0.5% per year, meaning a rate of natural increase of 5.0 per 1,000. Assuming that the crude birthrate in 1900–1920 averaged about the same as in 1937 (42.5 per 1,000), we would obtain an implicit crude death rate (CDR) for 1900–1920 of 37.5 per thousand—compared with a CDR in 1937 between 31 and 32 per 1,000. If we assume that the recent downward trend in the crude death rate for the LDCs did not begin until the 1920s, the conclusion is that over a decade to a decade and a half before 1937, the drop in the CDR for LDCs was about 6 to 7 points per 1,000—of the same order of magnitude found in the somewhat longer periods from 1937 to 1950–55, and from 1950–55 to 1970–75 (see line 19, cols. 2 and 4). And while the calculation is obviously approximate, it is reasonable to conclude that the estimated decline in the crude death rates was most likely much greater over that period than any reasonably assumed change in birthrates.[3]

Using the evidence in table 8.2, and the approximate calculations in the text, one may summarize by saying that over the fifty years terminating in 1970–75, that is, between 1920–25 and 1970–75, crude death rates in the LDCs must have declined from more than 37.5 to between 14 and 16 per 1,000 (see table 8.2, lines 16 and 19, col. 5); whereas the crude birthrates may have moved from 42.5 per 1,000 to either 42.1 (LDCs excluding China) or 37.5 (LDCs including China). The drop over the five decades was thus about 22.5 points in the crude death rate, and between 0.4 and 5 points in the crude birthrate—the rise in the rate of natural increase almost completely dominated by the downtrend in the death rate.

Several aspects of this recent decline in death rates in the LDCs should be noted. These and other aspects of what appeared to be the

Table 8.2 **Growth Trends and Vital Rates (per 1,000), Observed 1937–75 and Projected 1975–2000**

A. *Absolute Totals and Growth Rates*

	1937 (1)	1955 (2)	1975 (3)	1985 (4)	2000 (5)
Total (in millions)					
1. World	2,225	2,722	3,967	4,816	6,253
2. MDCs	802	915	1,132	1,231	1,361
3. LDCs	1,423	1,808	2,835	3,585	4,893
4. LDCs, except China	899	1,203	1,997	2,612	3,745
Rates of Increase (per year, per 1,000, successive intervals)					
5. World		11.3	19.0	18.6	17.6
6. MDCs		7.4	10.7	8.4	6.7
7. LDCs		13.4	22.7	23.8	21.4
8. LDCs except China		16.3	25.7	27.2	24.3

B. *Vital Rates, Levels, and Changes*

	1937 (1)	Change to 1950–55 (2)	1950–55 (3)	Change to 1970–75 (4)	1970–75 (5)	Change to 1995–2000 (6)	1995–2000 (7)	Total Change (8)
World								
9. CBR	35.8	−0.2	35.6	−4.1	31.5	−6.4	25.1	−10.7
10. CDR	25.7	−6.9	18.8	−6.0	12.8	−3.9	8.9	−16.8
11. CRNI	10.1	+6.7	16.8	+1.9	18.7	−2.5	16.2	+6.1
MDCs								
12. CBR	24.1	−1.2	22.9	−5.7	17.2	−1.6	15.6	−8.5
13. CDR	15.5	−5.4	10.1	−0.9	9.2	+0.7	9.9	−5.6
14. CRNI	8.6	+4.2	12.8	−4.8	8.0	−2.3	5.7	−2.9
LDCs								
15. CBR	42.5	−0.4	42.1	−4.6	37.5	−9.7	27.8	−14.7
16. CDR	31.6	−8.3	23.3	−9.0	14.3	−5.7	8.6	−23.0
17. CRNI	10.9	+7.9	18.8	+4.4	23.2	−4.0	19.2	+8.3
LDCs except China								
18. CBR	42.5	+2.0	44.5	−2.4	42.1	−11.3	30.8	−11.7
19. CDR	30.8	−6.4	24.4	−8.4	16.0	−7.1	8.9	−21.9
20. CRNI	11.7	+8.4	20.1	+6.0	26.1	−4.2	21.9	+10.2

Notes

Panel A: The estimates for 1937, lines 1–4, col. 1, are logarithmic interpolations between the totals for 1930 and 1940 shown in lines 6–7 of table 8.1. The other entries in lines 1–4 are from the source used for table 8.1, lines 8*b*–11, with the use of the medium variant projection throughout.

The rates of increase in lines 5–8 are from lines 1–4, with due allowance for the varying durations of the intervals (which are 18, 20, 10, and 15 years respectively).

Panel B:

Col. 1: Data from United Nations, *World Population Trends, 1920–1947* (New York, 1949); table 2, p. 10, shows the vital rates, and we took the mid-value of major demographic revolution in world population have been widely discussed in the literature;[4] but they deserve at least brief explicit mention here.

The first aspect of the recent declines in death rates in the LDCs is that they proceeded at a rate far exceeding that of the past declines in death rates in the currently developed countries. Table 8.3 illustrates the contrast with the older European countries. A drop of 22.5 points in the rates in the LDCs over five decades meant a decline per decade of 4.5 points. For the five northern European countries, the rates of decline per decade were, for the successive intervals in columns 5–7, 0.76, 0.84, and 1.80. For the other four European countries, the declines per decade in the death rates were 1.11 points for the interval 1850–95, and 2.10 for the interval 1895–1925. If the initial position of the LDCs in 1920–25 is compared with that of the European countries either in 1800 or in 1850, the rate of decline in the LDCs over the first five decades of their demographic transition was from four to five times as high as that for the older, settled, currently developed European countries.

One should also note that, in the *earlier* phases of the shift in demographic patterns, the movements of the birthrates in the currently developed countries were also at rates much lower than those in the death rates—so that the initial rises in the crude rates of natural increase were, as in the case of the recent trends for the LDCs, due predominantly to the declines in mortality.

The second distinctive feature of the recent major drop in death rates in the LDCs is that it occurred in regions where the basic economic and institutional structures were little affected by industrialization and modernization—whereas the trends in death rates that we observed for the currently developed countries in table 8.3 occurred largely in association with marked upward movements in per capita product and, more important, advances of the countries in the economic and institutional transformation associated with modern economic growth. This was certainly true beginning with the mid-nineteenth century. And, one should add, both the rapidity of the recent decline in death rates in the LDCs and its occurrence without association, in many of the regions involved, with any significant economic and institutional changes, can be credited to

the ranges shown. MDCs here include North America, Japan, Europe, and Oceania (but exclude temperate South America, a minor omission here and a minor inclusion under the LDCs). China is identified with "Remaining Far East" (after exclusion of Japan). The population weights used to combine the rates are in the source, table 1, p. 3.

Cols. 2–8: Based on data from the United Nations working paper used for lines 8*b*–11 of table 8.1 (on *Selected World Demographic Indicators by Countries, 1950–2000*).

Table 8.3 **Long-term Trends in Crude Vital Rates (per 1,000), Currently Developed Countries (for Comparison with Recent Trends in the LDCs)**

	Levels of Vital Rates				*Changes in Rates*		
	1800 (1)	1850 (2)	1895 (3)	1925 (4)	1800–1850 (5)	1850–95 (6)	1895–1925 (7)
Five Northern European Countries							
1. CBR	34.0	32.8	29.8	20.6	−1.2	−3.0	−9.2
2. CDR	25.2	21.4	17.6	12.2	−3.8	−3.8	−5.4
3. CRNI	8.8	11.4	12.2	8.4	+2.6	+0.8	−3.8
Four Other European Countries							
4. CBR	n.a.	31.5	30.0	21.2	n.a.	−1.5	−8.8
5. CDR	n.a.	25.0	20.0	13.7	n.a.	−5.0	−6.3
6. CRNI	n.a.	6.5	10.0	7.5	n.a.	+3.5	−2.5

Notes

The averages in lines 1–6 are calculated from the vital rates summarized in Simon Kuznets, *Modern Economic Growth* (New Haven: Yale University Press, 1966), table 2.3, pp. 42–44. Lines 1–3 include England and Wales, Denmark, Finland, Norway and Sweden; lines 4–6 include Belgium, France, Germany, and the Netherlands. For all countries the year indicated represents the midpoint of a long interval over which the crude rates were averaged, the interval varying between sixty, forty, and ten years. The entries represent unweighted arithmetic means of the values for the individual countries included.

The changes in columns 5–7 are derived directly from the averages in columns 1–4.

the nature of the technological revolution in dealing with infectious diseases and with the major health problems of the LDCs, which apparently began after World War I and attained its most striking successes shortly after World War II.

Third, granted the importance of major innovations in the technology related to control of diseases and of mortality, and the pervasive spread of declines in mortality to LDC regions and countries differing widely in institutional and economic structure, complementary effects of other technologies were required and differences in exposure to modernizing influences continued to affect death rates. After all, the new medical and public health tools had to be made accessible to all population groups in the LDCs to produce the wide effects observed (see comment below); here the technological revolution in transport and communication played an important role. And differences in extent and duration of exposure to modernizing influences are reflected even now in death rate differentials among major groups of LDCs (and would be even more prominent in single-country comparisons). Thus, table 8.4 below shows that, even by 1970–75, crude death rates in sub-Saharan Africa (excluding the southern region) were, at 22 per 1,000, more than twice as high as those for Latin America (excluding the Temperate Zone) at somewhat over 9 per 1,000.

Finally, one should note that declines in death rates (as in other vital rates) of the magnitude suggested for the LDCs over the last fifty years—and perhaps even for each of the quarter-century subperiods separately—mean that the demographic trends involved must have necessarily affected large proportions of the total population involved. For each of these vital rates is a weighted average of group-specific rates, weighted by the groups' proportions in the total. Thus, a decline in the crude death rate of a few points, say from 32 to 30 per 1,000, could well be accounted for by a decline of 6 points for a group whose mortality declined from 32 to 26 per 1,000 while that of the remaining group stayed constant—the two groups accounting for one-third and two-thirds of the total population respectively. But a much larger decline, and conditions in which the death rate of a small group in the total population cannot be sharply reduced while mortality remains high in the rest of the population, mean that the impact of the decline must necessarily have been widespread. This point is of analytical importance, considering the contrast between the sharp downtrends in the death rates and the minor declines in birthrates—with implications for the possible differential effects of the two sets of trends on the various groups in the population, particularly the smaller economic and social groups at the top and the much larger proportions of the population at middle and below-average economic and social levels.

In turning now to the sections of table 8.2 that relate to population and vital rate *projections* to the year 2000, we may view the latter as informed judgments of the likely demographic trends—on the assumption that no great catastrophes or miraculous boons introduce major discontinuities, and the more interesting assumption that economic and social progress will take place at a feasible pace to warrant expectation that the growing populations will be sustained at acceptable levels.[5] From our standpoint, the major interest in these projections is their indication that while the growth rates and the vital rates in the developed countries will move slowly downward over the last quarter of this century—and show no declines in the death rates—for LDCs (excluding China) death rates will still decline substantially (see line 19, col. 6). And while the birthrates for the LDCs are assumed to drop even more (see line 18, col. 6), the projections for the last quinquennium still show a rate of natural increase over 2% per year and well above the initial rates either in 1937 or even in 1950–55.

But given the large magnitudes of, and some significant disparities within, the total of LDCs, it is useful to consider the magnitudes and projections separately for the major LDC regions—and with some time break from 1950–75 to 1995–2000 (table 8.4). The total LDC population for 1975 accounted for in this table can be compared with that in table 8.2, for LDCs excluding China—and it is 1,918 million compared with 1,997 in line 4, column 3 of table 8.2.

One should begin by noting the dominance of the South Asian region in the 1975 total, and the Asian contribution would become all the larger were we to include China. In 1975, the population for China implicit in table 8.2 is 838 million. Of the total for South Asia, the contribution of what might be called the clearly Hindic group (Bangladesh, Pakistan, and India) was 758 million. Thus, of the total in 1975 of the four regions shown in table 8.3 plus China—2,746 million—as much as 1,596 million was accounted for by the two areas that could be designated centers of the centuries-old Sinic and Hindic civilizations. Of the total additions over the twenty-five year period from 1975 onward—some 1,984 million—310 million are projected for China (see table 8.2) and another 593 million for the three Indian countries listed above. Thus, by the year 2000, the areas that are the centers of these two old civilizations would still account for 1,148 plus 1,351 billion, or a total of some 2.5 billion out of an aggregate of 4.74 billion for all LDCs in the four regions plus China. The emphasis on this large contribution of these two old civilizations to the population bulk, and to current and projected excess growth of the LDCs, points to a consideration of the past economic and social innovations that permitted the sustained growth of this population mass on an area far smaller than that occupied by the other LDCs—innovations in agriculture and institutional devices. These would presumably affect the responses of the relevant populations to the declines in the death rates and to the changing role of the next generation in the adjustment to widening economic opportunities associated with industrialization and modernization.[6]

There were marked differences among the regions in the levels of death rates in 1950–55, the earliest quinquennium for which the comparison is easily made. In Latin America, these death rates were as low as 15.2, as result of preceding declines that proceeded at a slow pace to the 1930s and accelerated thereafter (Arriaga and Davis 1969). In the same quinquennium, the crude death rates ranged from 22.5 to 28.5 per 1,000 in the three other LDC regions. With the crude birthrates at roughly similar levels, the result was a substantial range in rates of natural increase, from 19 to 28.5 per 1,000.

Over the twenty-five-year period to 1975, there were substantial declines in the crude death rates in all four LDC regions, leaving the differentials in death rates in 1975 even wider, at least proportionally, than they were in 1950–55 (see col. 3, which shows a range of 9.3 for Latin America to 21.8 for sub-Saharan Africa), and the declines in death rates were substantially larger than the declines in birthrates, leading to a rise

Table 8.4 **Vital Rates (per 1,000), Observed (to 1970–75) and Projected (to 1995–2000, medium variant), LDC Regions**

	1950–55 (1)	Change to 1970–75 (2)	1970–75 (3)	Change to 1980–85 (4)	1980–85 (5)	Change to 1995–2000 (6)	1995–2000 (7)	Total Change (8)
East and middle South Asia (1,162; 2,093)								
1. CBR	44.1	−2.2	41.9	−3.5	38.4	−10.2	28.2	−15.9
2. CDR	25.2	−8.7	16.5	−3.8	12.7	−3.9	8.8	−16.4
3. CRNI	18.9	+6.5	25.4	+0.3	25.7	−6.3	19.4	+0.5
Middle East (186; 366)								
4. CBR	47.1	−4.0	43.1	−2.4	40.7	−9.1	31.6	−15.5
5. CDR	22.4	−7.6	14.8	−3.1	11.7	−3.8	7.9	−14.5
6. CRNI	24.7	+3.6	28.3	+0.7	29.0	−5.3	23.7	−1.0
Sub-Saharan Africa (275; 566)								
7. CBR	48.7	−1.1	47.6	−1.0	46.6	−4.7	41.9	−6.8
8. CDR	28.6	−6.8	21.8	−3.6	18.2	−5.4	12.8	−15.8
9. CRNI	20.1	+5.7	25.8	+2.6	28.4	+0.7	29.1	+9.0
Latin America, except temperate zone (285; 567)								
10. CBR	43.7	−4.8	38.9	−2.3	36.6	−6.0	30.6	−13.1
11. CDR	15.2	−6.0	9.2	−2.0	7.2	−1.9	5.3	−9.9
12. CRNI	28.5	+1.2	29.7	−0.3	29.4	−4.1	25.3	−3.2
LDCs, four regions above (1,908; 3,592)								
13. CBR	45.0	−2.6	42.4	−2.8	39.6	−8.7	30.9	−14.1
14. CDR	23.9	−7.9	16.0	−3.4	12.6	−3.8	8.8	−15.1
15. CRNI	21.1	+5.3	26.4	+0.6	27.0	−4.9	22.1	+1.0

Notes:

The underlying data are all from the United Nations working paper cited in the notes to tables 8.1 and 8.2.

The totals entered in parentheses following the designation of regions are the 1975 and year 2000 populations of the region, in millions.

East and middle South Asia is a combination of east South Asia and middle South Asia. The internal weights, based on the 1975 population, are 3 and 7 for the two subregions respectively.

Middle East comprises western South Asia and North Africa, with approximately equal weights.

Sub-Saharan Africa includes three subregions—eastern Africa, middle Africa, and western Africa (with approximate weights of 4, 2, and 4). Southern Africa was omitted because of the weight in it of the Union of South Africa and the mixed composition of its population with different levels of economic development.

Latin America comprises the Caribbean, Middle America, and Tropical South America, with approximate weights of 1, 3, and 6. The Temperate Zone (Argentina, Uruguay, and Chile) was omitted.

The total of LDCs is a weighted average of the four regions (with weights of 60, 10, 15, and 15, for the regions in the order listed).

For more detail concerning inclusion of individual countries, see the source. China and East Asia, in general, are omitted, and so are some LDCs in Oceania.

in the rate of natural increase in all four regions. Yet for Latin America, the region furthest along in the demographic transition, the decline in birthrates was more substantial and the rise in rates of natural increase rather minor. The result was that by 1975 the regional differentials in rates of natural increase were narrow (from 25.5 to 29.5)—the rates being at relatively high levels in all four regions.

But the most interesting part of table 8.4 is the indication that for three of the four regions, excluding Latin America, the next decade, to the mid-1980s, will again show greater declines in death rates than in birthrates—with consequent further rises, even though minor, in the rates of natural increase. It is only in the period after the mid-1980s that the birthrates are expected to decline substantially enough to exceed the still-expected further declines in the death rates. Even so, one region—sub-Saharan Africa—is, according to the present projections, to show rising rates of natural increase practically to the end of the century.

Further subdivisions within the regions would reveal even further differences among various groups of the LDCs in the levels of their vital rates, and distinction of narrower time periods would more clearly reveal differences in past and projected changes in these basic demographic trends. Thus, the differences among the currently distinguished four regions with respect to the timing in the demographic transition—from Latin America as the most advanced to sub-Saharan Africa as the least—would be refined further; and so would the difference in timing in reaching the peak rate of natural increase, and the peaks and troughs in the underlying birthrates and death rates. But the distinctions in table 8.4 are sufficient to indicate both the similarities and the major differences in the movements of the death rates, in their relation to the levels and changes in the birthrates; and to remind us of the diversity of the demographic, and implicitly economic and institutional patterns, among the major groups within the LDC universe. The recognition of this diversity is particularly important, as we shift now to an exploration of the possible implications these movements in death rates, in their relation to those in birthrates, have for the internal economic distributions in the countries affected.

8.2 Some Implications

What were the likely effects of the recent population trends in the LDCs, summarized in the preceding section? In attempting to formulate some speculative but plausible answers to this question, it seemed best to start with (*a*) the effects of the rapid and striking declines in the death rates; and then turn to (*b*) the possible reasons for the lag in the declines of the birthrates. The separation between the two trends may seem artificial; and yet I will argue below that the choices with respect to the downward movement of death rates were more limited than those with respect to the adaptive movement of birthrates. If only for this reason, one is warranted in considering the two sets of trends separately before attempting to combine their possible effects.

8.2.1 Declines in Death Rates

In dealing with the effects of the recent major declines in mortality in the LDCs, we may ask first what kind of demographic patterns prevailed in these countries before, when high death rates and birthrates yielded low rates of natural increase. Were there substantial *within-country* differences among the various economic and social groups, in demographic structure and in the rates of natural increase?

No adequate direct evidence on this question is available to me, although a long search in the literature and greater familiarity with the sources might have provided it. But some plausible conjectures can be suggested. First, in these pre-1920 decades, as table 8.1 indicated, the MDCs were characterized by markedly lower death rates than the LDCs, so that the rate of natural increase in the former was substantially higher —*despite* the fact that their birthrates were substantially lower. This suggests that, with death rates in the LDCs at these high levels, even a moderate proportional lowering of the death rate could allow for a moderate decrease in the birthrate and still result in a substantial rise in the rate of natural increase. With CDR at, say, 40 and a CBR at 45, a drop in the former to 36 and in the latter to 42 would mean a rise in the rate of natural increase to 6 per 1,000—by a full fifth. One may reasonably assume that also *within* the LDC country or region there could have been differences among economic and social groups, where greater wealth and easier access to means of subsistence could have resulted in appreciably lower death rates—and, even if these led to somewhat lower fertility, the more favored economic of social groups might have attained a higher rate of natural increase—just as the MDCs did in the comparison with the LDCs. This would be particularly likely so long as higher economic and social status was not connected with greater health risks in urban conditions (if urban living was a prerequisite of higher income). But in the countries and times of which we are speaking, urban populations constituted a minor fraction of total population.[7]

The implication is that in the earlier decades of high levels of both mortality and fertility, before 1920, differences within the LDCs in economic and social status may have been associated with reductions in mortality that were substantial and larger than the likely restraints on fertility (if any)—thus yielding a higher rate of natural increase among the upper social and economic groups than among the lower ones. If this implication is valid, the resulting contrast with the conditions in times and countries in which the overall level of death rates has been reduced sufficiently so that large *relative* mortality differentials could not convert even minor birthrate excesses into equality or shortage of the rates of natural increase, is of major analytical importance.

Unfortunately, I can find only illustrative evidence, relating primarily to differentials in death rates in one or two less developed countries by economic or social status (directly given, or associated with some ethnic group distinctions), or separate evidence on birthrates by social status or ethnic grouping—but not the two bodies of evidence together. Thus, to cite an example for India, in 1931 the expectation of life at birth for Parsis was (combined with equal weight for men and women) as high as 53 years—compared with 32 years for total population—and the difference is "attributed in large measure to the relatively advantageous position of the Parsis" (United Nations 1953, p. 63). If we apply crude conversion ratios to expectation of life at birth to derive crude death rates as used by Kingsley Davis (that is, setting the latter to 1,000 divided by expectation of life),[8] the corresponding CDRs are 19 per 1,000 for the Parsis (a small group in the large total) compared with more than 31 per 1,000 for total population—a difference that may or may not have been fully compensated by the difference in crude birthrates. Similar evidence of substantial differences in death rates appear in the summary of a sample survey of rural families in Punjab in 1931. One may note that in the 1973 edition of United Nations, *The Determinants* . . . , the relevant section on mortality differentials in less developed countries (par. 132, p. 139) begins with a statement that information on these "differentials by occupation, income, and education is . . . sparse" and quotes only a few cases, mostly for the late 1950s or early 1960s.

A related illustration of interest can be derived from the vital rates for the United States when the distinction is made between the white population and the nonwhite (the latter predominantly Negro). For 1905–10 (the earliest period for which the comparison is given) the *gross* reproduction rate was shown at 1,740 for the white population and 2,240 for the nonwhite—an excess of the latter of some 30%; but the *net* reproduction rate, that is, the one that takes account of mortality, was 1,339 for the white population and 1,329, somewhat lower, for the nonwhite population. This is an illustration of greater mortality in the economically and socially disadvantaged group more than offsetting a much higher fertility; and it is shown for a period when crude death rates averaged (for 1900–1904) 16 per 1,000 for the white population and about 26 per 1,000 for the nonwhite.[9] It is plausible to assume that further back in time, when the level of death rates was appreciably higher, their excess may have produced an even greater differential in rate of natural increase in favor of the white population. By contrast, in the later period, when death rates declined for both white and nonwhite populations, the *net* reproduction rate of the nonwhite population began to exceed that of the white by a large margin. Thus, by 1957 (the peak year in the United States reproduction rates in recent times) the gross rate of the nonwhite population, at 2,371, exceeded that of the white, at 1,764, by almost 40%; the net rates were 2,206 and 1,701 respectively, an excess of almost 30%.

Finally, one should note briefly the data on demography of peasant communities.[10] They deal largely with fertility, strongly suggesting, though with some exceptions, that fertility is higher among the richer (in terms of land) peasants than among the poorer; with mortality, at least in children, also being distinctly lower among the rich. The result, then, is a positive association within the peasantry between higher economic position and rate of natural increase. But the findings are qualified by sparsity of coverage, particularly for LDCs in the premodern periods of high mortality; the limitation of the data largely to fertility; the absence of data on per capita income of the peasant families classified by size over the life cycle; and the difficulty of assigning weights to the peasant population (distinctly smaller than the rural) within the total. A further exploration of the field, not feasible here, may yield significant findings.

If we assume that the rate of natural increase *within* the LDCs, before the recent sharp decline in death rates, was greater among the upper economic and social groups, the situation would have been in sharp contrast to that in the MDCs for a number of decades and that in the LDCs once overall death rate levels have been substantially reduced. The more familiar finding is that the birthrates *and* the rates of natural increase have been greater among the lower income groups—associated with the greater lag in the declines of birthrates among the former, in conditions under which a generally lower level of death rates reduced the weight of the death variable in offsetting births. This also meant that in the earlier times in the LDCs, the number of *surviving* children per family—once it reached a decade or more beyond the marriage date—was greater among the upper economic and social groups than among the lower, with the necessary qualification concerning the urban death rate excess over the rural. Since the number of surviving children is in turn a major factor in determining the size of the family (the other being the degree of "jointness"), it is possible that the average size of the family was larger among the upper than among the lower economic and social groups; and that the average income of this larger family, even on a *per capita* basis, was significantly greater than that of the smaller family among the lower economic and social groups. Such *positive* association between the size of family and *per capita* income is not found in recent cross-sectional studies, which are naturally limited either to MDCs or to LDCs with death rates already substantially reduced recent advances in health technology. On the contrary, the negat association between size of family or household and its per capita come is a common finding; and while qualified by changes in income levels over the life cycle, still remained a major result in the analysis in the recent paper cited in note 1 (see section III, pp. 23–48, on the size of family or household effects).

But more important here is the implication that this situation of higher death rates and lower rates of natural increase among the lower economic and social groups meant a serious aggravation of already existing inequalities, in that shorter life-spans, greater morbidity, and fewer children surviving to productive ages were both cause and effect of lower economic returns over the family's productive life-span. This association of lower economic position with higher rates of death and morbidity persisted, of course, beyond the transition in the population patterns from premodern to modern times; and it is still found in the MDCs in recent decades. But the effects of this association must have been far greater when death and morbidity rates were so high, and when substantial reductions in them could be attained by more food, better clothing and shelter, and greater mobility for protection against epidemics or famines. Of course, we cannot now gauge these differentials in death rate and rate of natural increase or test their persistence in conditions of frequent short-term rises in death rates that might have swept over rich and poor alike. But one may assume that if there were these death and natural increase differentials in the pre-modern LDCs, they served only to aggravate long-term economic inequalities rather than to temper them.

In this connection, the exploratory illustration of economic losses represented by the deaths of children and young adults in the Appendix to this paper is of interest. These explorations compare the losses of past inputs into children and young adults (the latter dying before their net contribution might have fully covered the past inputs into their consumption), in a less developed and a developed country in the 1930s—relating these annual losses to the total annual product of each of the two countries. The results of the comparison, indicating that relative losses involved in such deaths are more than five times as great in the less developed as in the developed country, only suggest what might be found by comparing similar losses from deaths for the richer (lower mortality) and poorer (higher mortality) groups *within* a premodern LDC. Clearly, the burden of such losses was proportionally much greater among the lower-income groups, representing a greater relative drain on their long-term economic capacity and resources.

The comments above are meant to provide a tentative base for evaluating the effects of the striking declines in death rates that we find in the tables in section 8.1. Given their magnitude and the character of the major causal factors involved, it is reasonable to infer that these reductions in death rates were widespread; that their absolute magnitude was greater among those groups in the population for whom the initial levels were higher; and that consequently their effects on the rates of natural increase were far greater for those groups in the population for whom these rates were initially lower—the larger groups at the lower economic and social levels. If the death rates for the upper and lower groups could differ by as much as 10 points (e.g., 30 to 40), it could be expected that a major step forward in health care and medical technology applicable without a major input of scarce resources and without requiring major changes in patterns of life would affect the higher death rates absolutely more than it would affect the lower death rates already reduced by more favorable economic conditions in the past. And one could also argue that the benefit would be greater to those who have sustained the losses caused by higher death rates in the past. The immediate implication, subject to a major qualification noted below, is that the differential reduction in death rates plausibly assumed above, the resulting convergence of internal death rates among various economic and social groups, meant the reduction of an important aspect of persisting inequality that loomed large in the premodern LDC societies.

Before we consider the possible qualification on the equalizing effects of the internal differentials in reduction of death rates in the LDCs once the major declines began, we should stress two aspects of the trends under discussion. The first, already noted, is that little choice was possible, or wanted, in incurring these declines. If they came, largely as effects of developments in the MDCs brought into the LDCs from the outside, as it were, relieving sickness and death without incurring perceptible economic and social costs, there was no incentive for resisting the much-desired opportunity for longer and healthier life. In that sense the situation was quite different from the choices relating to birthrates: reducing these involved a variety of alternatives within limits that could spell substantial differences in population growth rates, for countries or for groups within them. Second, and more important, once contacts with the developed parts of the world were increasingly numerous, it became obvious that the reduction in death rates (and associated reduction in rates of morbidity) was a *necessary* if not sufficient requirement for a healthier, long-lived, population—with the possibility of longer investment in the training and education of the younger generation preserved from demographic calamities, with the chances of developing a forward spirit in a population justifiably believing in man's control over his destiny, and with a family structure in which smaller size and fewer children would make possible a better adjustment to widening economic and social opportunities. Rejecting the contacts that reduced the death rates would thus mean also rejecting the possibility of shifting to a modern demographic pattern and modernization of society that could also mean better use of the potentials of economic growth.[11]

The conclusion is that the reduction of the death rates in the LDCs from their initial high levels in the 1920s was an indispensable condition for eventual modernization and participation in modern economic growth—while the rapidity and magnitudes of the declines were unavoidable (were anybody willing to avoid it) effects of the new technology in situations of a backlog of high mortality and high morbidity problems. Whatever the immediate, or shorter-term, consequences of these trends, particularly those when the failure of birthrates to decline resulted in a rapid acceleration of the rates of natural increase, in the longer run the major declines in death rates were a precondition of the declines in birthrates and of other adjustments to the modern demographic patterns of population growth.

The major qualification alluded to above is, of course, the consequence of lag of the decline in birthrates—in conditions where the basic innovation introduced by the reduction in death rates was not accompanied by sufficient changes in other aspects of social and material technology. In such conditions, and provided there was—as there was likely to be with stagnant social structure and production technology—scarcity of the traditional resources (whether land or reproducible capital), a rapid acceleration of rates of natural increase among the groups hitherto below the upper economic and social levels may have meant suddenly increased pressures of augmented labor supplies on scarce complementary resources. Whether under these conditions a longer and healthier working life of the members of a family compensated, over the life cycle, for the greater pressure of labor on resources is a question that does not admit of an easy answer; and the answer would vary among various groups of LDCs, depending upon the initial resource endowments and the degree to which further advances in traditional technology were possible with augmented labor. Here the added knowledge concerning the demographic and economic structures of LDCs before the recent declines in death rates would be required to provide even tentative answers. But one cannot exclude the possibility that in some cases the longer productive life-span and greater increase of the lower economic and social groups may still have resulted in some widening of internal income inequality because upper groups took advantage of the greater pressure of labor on land or on other capital, while in other cases the inequality-reducing internal convergence of rates of mortality and morbidity among the several economic groups might have reduced internal income inequality—even if the crude birthrates continued at high levels and failed for some time to respond to the declines in death rates.

On this uncertain conclusion, I end the discussion of the effects of declines in mortality in the LDCs. One should emphasize to the end the indispensable—and in the longer run beneficial—effects of the declines in the death rates, regardless of whether their immediate and direct effect was to widen or to narrow internal income inequalities. This emphasis might have been superfluous except that much recent discussion of the problems created by rapid population growth tends to neglect the source of the latter in the declines in mortality and morbidity—and thus to understate, by omission, their vitally important and beneficial long-term effects.[12]

8.2.2 Lags in the Decline of Birthrates

The long lag in fertility decline behind the downtrend in mortality is illustrated in Professor Lindert's paper for this conference, on "Child Costs and Economic Development" (chap. 1) and is strongly suggested for the LDCs in the initial section of this paper, with its emphasis on the dominance of declines in mortality in contribution to a rising rate of natural increase in the face of constant or only slightly dropping birthrates. This section deals with a few aspects of the response of birthrates to the major declines in death rates in the LDCs.

Even though the would-be parental pair is the immediate decision unit in this response, one must allow for the wider, blood-related groups (an extended family, a tribe, an ethnic group, a caste) that may set the norms for the would-be parents. In addition, there are the large non-blood collectives, particularly the government, that may react to declining death rates and accelerating population growth in a variety of ways, all of which involve modifications of conditions under which the family unit would make decisions concerning more or fewer children—whether the steps are limited to exhortation and to providing cheaper methods of birth control or extend to drastic policy measures affecting the costs of more children. On the other hand, the effects of declining deaths include more than just increase in numbers of surviving children. The underlying innovation in health and medical technology may reduce involuntary sterility formerly associated with widely prevalent debilitating diseases; it may raise intramarital fertility by prolonging the duration of marriage (within the childbearing span of the wife) through the reduction of mortality (particularly male) in the procreative ages—just as it may eventually, by reducing uncontrollable and unpredictable diseases, introduce changes in would-be parents' outlook on the future and the role of the next generation. Given the diversity of possible sources of decisions in response to declining death rates, the variety of direct and indirect effects of the latter on the birthrate response, and finally our inadequate knowledge of the parameters of demographic processes and of economic and institutional patterns in various LDC regions, we can attempt only a limited probing.

This is true even if we eliminate from consideration the communist societies, in which the power of the single-party, ideologically motivated government is such that *its* responses to declining death rates and accelerating population growth may dominate whatever free responses could have originated within the population masses of the country. Such domination is suggested by the power of intensive propaganda, control over location and migration of the population, disposition of the basic consumer goods, particularly housing, needed for a growing population, and the like. I would find it difficult, for lack of adequate knowledge of societies so organized, to formulate a rational basis for evaluating the planned response that the governmental decision centers of these countries would make to declining death rates and rising rates of natural increase. The same criterion might also lead to exclusion of noncommunist, dictatorially organized LDCs, in which a similar domination of the state over the free responses of the population might be expected; but there are no clear relevant measures for drawing the line. The purpose of the comment is to call attention to the possible policy interventions of groups not related by blood, particularly those endowed with internal sovereignty. They may be important in both dictatorially and democratically organized societies; but their weight seems more dominant in the former—sufficiently so to warrant limiting further discussion by concentrating on the societies with relative freedom of decision by families and related blood groups.

The importance of the wider, blood-related groups that encompass the individual families is clearly great in LDCs, whether they be the tribal groupings in much of Africa, the racial-ethnic divisions within many Latin American countries, or the groupings in Asian countries where limited intermarriage among groups (say, among castes in India) is still the norm. In conditions of relative weakness and instability of the country's collective institutions, particularly the state, such wider blood-related groups serve an important function in providing long-term security to individual families in conditions of group competition. The response of a family to declining death rates and more surviving children would, with reference to the wider group norms, differ from that of an individual family within a stable political framework, relying securely on the protection and stability of a strong government representing the interests of the community and of all its parts. An adequate analysis would require taking specific account of these various blood-related subgroups within the populations of the several LDC regions in the process of their reaction to declines in death rates. But for obvious reasons our discussion can take only general cognizance of these sources of influence on the decisions of would-be parents.

We may now face a limited question. Assume that the individual families, the pairs of would-be parents, either experience or observe a perceptible reduction in death rates, both through the reduction of infant and child mortality and through declines in deaths of adults. Under what conditions would we expect a relatively prompt and full response of birthrates such as would prevent the rate of natural increase from rising substantially over a relatively long period? These conditions would presumably bear on (1) firmness of judgment with respect to continuity (irreversibility) of the observed declines in mortality; (2) the relation of the resulting numbers of surviving children to the desired numbers; and (3) the identity of the population group in a position to realize an effective birthrate response and the limits of their possible perception of mortality declines.[13]

1. Given the emergence of a marked downturn in death rates as a novel phenomenon for populations and countries that for centuries have experienced a much higher average mortality, and, most important, with instability characterized by sharp short-term declines and equally short-term larger rises, a fairly long period of observation and experience at lower and stable death rates would be required before a response could be expected. This is particularly true at the later stages of the woman's childbearing span, when a decision to forego another child, in reliance on the persistence of low death rates for children, may be beyond repair if the expectation proves false. How long a period of waiting to test the persistence of the mortality trend one should reasonably assume would have to be estimated from an analytical case in which all other factors affecting the decision (except the decline in mortality itself) have been removed (i.e., held constant)—not an easy task. A span of well over a decade seems a minimum, and one could perhaps argue that, ruling out downward revisions in numbers of desired surviving children, a whole generation might have to pass before the next parental generation could react significantly. Yet, given the declines in crude death rates averaging between 4 and 5 points per 1,000 per decade over the last half-century (in the LDCs from the mid-1920s to the mid-1970s), a lag of only one decade would mean a substantial addition to the rate of natural increase—which would continue so long as the death rates continued to decline, even though persistence of the latter would, as time goes on, raise confidence and reduce the lag.

The judgment of confidence in the continuity and irreversibility of a new social trend is hardly susceptible of tests for either ex ante or post facto validity, and one hesitates to assign a large weight to it. Yet complete neglect of it implies a neglect of a possibly major problem of the channels by which effective perception of, and response to, new social processes is attained within the traditional, and later transitional, framework of LDCs. It may well be that a long delay in response to new trends is a rational reaction, due partly to limitation of information, partly to lack of resources for taking chances on uncertain trends and for overcoming the fear of the unknown.

2. The conjecture under (1) becomes less relevant if we can assume that over a long initial period of the decline in mortality in the LDCs, the desired number of surviving children remains higher than, or in the neighborhood of, the actual number (as perceived by the family). Given targets or norms, whether individually elaborated or more realistically set as norms in the form of socially approved patterns; whether hard or, more realistically, with soft margins, it is not difficult to see that *beginning* at the premodern levels of death rates and birthrates, there might be a long period of sustained mortality declines—and yet the resulting number of surviving children would remain short of or close to the desired target, thus providing no incentive for a response decline in birthrates.

To begin with, the declines in mortality and morbidity permit those groups in the population that formerly could not reach their fertility targets—either because of involuntary sterility or because of institutional constraints on remarriage of widows or because of other similar consequences of past mortality and morbidity—to start approximating them. Far more important, quantitatively, is the condition of the large economic and social groups below the narrowly defined top. Given the rather low rate of natural increase of LDCs just before the initiation of the recent downtrends in mortality (of about 0.5% in the 1920s), it is reasonable to suggest that for the majority of the population the number of surviving children was below the desired number. This suggestion is strengthened if we assume the earlier conjecture (discussed in section 8.2.1 above) that at the top economic and social levels in the premodern LDCs death rates and rates of natural increase were substantially lower and greater respectively than at the lower levels. For this would mean a long-persisting pattern of association of a much larger number of surviving children with the higher economic and social status, which would most likely be carried over into the initial decades of the declines of death rates in the LDCs—unless there are prompt and major changes in the desired numbers, a possibility that largely depends on underlying major changes in the economy and institutions of the country, a shift at high gear into modernization that is likely to be the exception rather than the rule.

If so, a substantial phase of the long-term decline in death rates in the LDCs would also be a phase of catching up with formerly unavailable potentials of desired number of surviving children. The length of this catching-up phase, representing lack of incentive for a response of birthrates, is a matter for conjecture. It might differ from one group of LDCs to another; and it would certainly differ in its historical chronology, with disparities in the dates when the major mortality declines began among the different groups of LDCs. But if the natural-increase differences in premodern LDCs were as large as they seem from the scattered data on mortality (and some on fertility, particularly for the peasant communities), being at a minimum 10 points per 1,000, it might take at least two decades for the catching-up phase to be completed; nor should the possibility of a longer period be ruled out. If so, this phase would largely overlap with any lag due to lack of confidence in the persistence and irreversibility of the mortality trends, discussed under (1) above.

3. The perception of a trend like that in the death rates in the LDCs in recent decades may be limited to that of major *absolute* declines—which were concentrated in the early childhood ages, at one end, and in the age brackets beyond the early 50s at the other. Following the comment made above, we may ask how the population groups who are in a position to affect birthrates, either because they are of childbearing age or because they exercise influence on those who are, perceive the demographic trends. In the LDCs, in the transition period, and outside the limited upper circles of government, this is hardly done by scrutinizing aggregative statistics or observing graphs. But the answer to how families and the blood-related groups to which they may belong attain their perception of major demographic trends would have to come from greater familiarity with the LDC societies and their mechanisms for ascertaining and diffusing major social data than is possessed here.

One part of the answer is that reduction in the mortality of children, sizable only in the very early ages (below 5), is surely observed by those families in procreative phases of their life cycle that enjoy the benefits of such decreased mortality. And it may be legitimately argued that the knowledge of, and reaction to, this part of the downtrend in mortality could be expected to be more direct and potentially effective (other conditions being favorable) than the knowledge of, and reaction to, the decline in mortality at the advanced adult ages. It also follows that if the knowledge of trends is extrapolated into the future, in the process of formulating birth decisions, the reduction in early childhood mortality would be far more likely to form the basis for such an extrapolation than the changes at the advanced adult ages—which would relate to the role of children four or five decades after their birth. To be sure, neglecting these latter, as we do in the statistical illustration that follows, means neglecting the insurance motive of assuring survival of children to ages when they could support their aged parents. But, granted this limitation, it is of interest to explore what an instantaneous and complete response to declines in early child mortality would mean for the movements of the rates of natural increase.

The estimates of what we may designate the offset response of birthrates to declines in death rates, presented in table 8.5, are based on two assumptions: that the response is to reduction in death rates at ages under 5; that the response is prompt and full, allowing for no lag in the process. Both assumptions are unrealistic, the second far more so than the first. But the result is an extreme version of a full major response of birthrates; and it is of interest, in deriving it, to compare it with the actual movement of the birthrates and the trend in the rates of natural increase.

Given these assumptions, we need measures not only of the decline in crude death rates for total population, but also of the decline in the death rates of the population 0–4. Panel A of table 8.5 summarizes the results of utilizing the rich data in the United Nations Working Paper repeatedly used here, which shows for individual countries and for regions not only crude birthrates and death rates and total population at quinquennial intervals beginning with 1950, but also the proportions, in total population, of the 0–4 group (as well as of other age groups—5–14, etc.). On the reasonable premise that all these demographic parameters are consistent with each other, it is possible to derive, by comparing the cumulated crude birthrates over the quinquennium (related to total population at midpoint of the period) with the surviving 0–4 population at the end of the quinquennium (related to the population at the end of the quinquennium) the proportional attrition (per 1,000). If the population is closed, with no emigration or immigration, this attrition rate is identical with the crude death rate for the 0–4 group. Given the size of the regions we deal with, and the demonstrated closeness between the growth rates in total population and the rates of natural increase, it seemed justifiable to identify the attrition rates thus calculated with death rates relating to the 0–4 population. The estimates are clearly approximate, but the resulting orders of magnitude are plausible.[14]

With the results in panel A, which show the declines in death rates of 0–4 population between 1950–55 and 1970–75 and the proportions of that population in the total at the start of each quinquennium, we can estimate the offset response of birthrates—on the assumption that birthrates would decline, without any lag, to offset fully the experienced reduction in childhood deaths (panel B). It will be noted that the derived response was only somewhat larger than the actual decline in birthrates in three of the four LDC regions—a rough agreement that, however, cannot be interpreted to mean that the observed drop in the birthrates *did* represent the assumed offset response. It could well have

Table 8.5 **Estimated Offset Response of Birthrates to Declines in Death Rates of Children 0–4, 1950–55 to 1970–75, for the Four LDC Regions of Table 8.4**

	East and Middle South Asia (1)	Middle East (2)	Sub-Saharan Africa (3)	Latin America (4)	All Four (5)
A. *The Relevant Demographic Parameters* (per 1,000 of underlying population)					
Data for 1950–55					
1. Proportion of 0–4 to total population, 1950	153	164	170	169	160
2. Proportion of 0–4 to total population, 1955	162	169	180	178	168
3. CRNI, 1950–55	18.9	24.7	20.1	28.5	21.1
4. 0–4 population in 1955 as proportion of total in 1950 (per 1,000)	178.3	190.9	198.8	204.9	186.5
5. CBR, 1950–55	44.1	47.1	48.7	43.7	45.0
6. CBR in line 5, shifted to the base of 1950	46.26	50.06	51.18	46.88	47.41
7. Cumulative births, 1950–55, as proportion of 1950 population	247.8	276.6	283.5	257.5	260.5
8. Attrition (death rate) per 1,000 of 0–4 population in 1950–55, per year (from lines 4 and 7)	63.0	71.4	68.0	42.5	64.1
9. CDR, total population, 1950–55	25.2	22.4	28.6	15.2	23.9
Data for 1970–75					
10. Proportion of 0–4 to total population, 1970	169	173	178	171	171
11. Proportion of 0–4 to total population, 1975	167	171	181	167	170
12. CRNI, 1970–75	25.4	28.3	25.8	29.7	26.4
13. 0–4 population in 1975 as proportion of total in 1970	190.3	196.8	205.6	193.3	193.7
14. CBR, 1970–75	41.9	43.1	47.6	38.9	42.4
15. CBR, to the base of 1970 population	44.51	46.19	50.73	41.85	45.25
16. Cumulative births, 1970–75, as proportion of 1970 population	240.8	252.9	280.7	230.0	247.7
17. Attrition (death rate) of population 0–4, in 1970–75	45.4	48.1	59.8	33.3	47.4
18. CDR, 1970–75	16.5	14.8	21.8	9.2	16.0

Table 8.5 (continued)

	East and Middle South Asia (1)	Middle East (2)	Sub-Saharan Africa (3)	Latin America (4)	All Four (5)
B. *Derivation of Offset Response in Birthrates to Decline in Death Rates of 0–4 Population* (all entries per 1,000 of relevant population)					
19. Decline in death rates of 0–4 population from 1950–55 to 1970–75	17.6	23.3	8.2	9.2	16.7
20. Proportion of 0–4 population to total at initial date	0.17	0.17	0.18	0.18	0.17
21. Decline in death rates of 0–4 population related to total population (line 19 × line 20) = full offset response	3.0	4.0	1.5	1.7	2.8
22. Observed decline in CBR	2.2	4.0	1.1	4.8	2.6
23. Observed change in CRNI	+6.5	+3.6	+5.7	+1.2	+5.3
24. Derived change in CRNI with full offset response	+5.7	+3.6	+5.3	+4.3	+5.1

Notes

All the underlying data are from the United Nations working paper cited and used in connection with table 8.4.

Panel A, lines 4 and 13—The estimates are the proportions in lines 2 and 11, raised by the cumulative growth of population (cumulative natural increase) over the quinquennium, using the entries in lines 3 and 12 respectively.

Panel A, lines 6 and 15—The estimates use the rise of the base (total) population, but over half rather than the full quinquennium (as it was used for lines 4 and 13).

Panel A, lines 8 and 17—The entries in lines 4 and 7, and 13 and 16 respectively, were used first to derive attrition (deaths) as the difference between lines 7 and 4, and 13 and 6, related to the initial base (1950 and 1970 respectively) and representing the proportion over the quinquennium. Then the proportion was adjusted for a shift from the 1950 or 1970 base to the 1950–55 and 1970–75, using the entries for 0–4 population in lines 1 and 4, and 10 and 13 respectively. The adjusted proportions, now to the base of 1950–55 and 1970–75 respectively, were then converted into death rates per year.

Panel B—for the rationale, see discussion in the text. Line 19 is the difference between lines 8 and 17 of panel A. Line 20 is based on the shares as shown in lines 1 and 4, and 10 and 13, of panel A. Line 22 was derived from the observed CBRs in lines 3 and 14 of panel A. Line 23 was derived from the observed CRNIs in lines 3 and 12 of panel A. Line 24 equals line 23 reduced by the excess of line 21 over line 22 (or raised by the shortage of line 21 relative to line 22).

been due to a substantial decline in birthrates of the top economic and social groups, only partly offset by the constancy or slight rise in birthrates among the lower economic groups. In Latin America, the observed decline in birthrates, almost 5 points, greatly exceeded the derived offset of 1.7 points; and this finding is plausible, considering the much longer period over which declines in mortality occurred in Latin America and the greater movement toward the demographic transition that began to affect the birthrates.

But the major aspect of the finding in panel B is that even if we assume full and instantaneous response to declines in child mortality, such a response will not be sufficient to prevent a major rise in the rate of natural increase. As line 24 shows, the *derived* rate of natural increase shows a substantial rise over the two-decade span in *all* of the four LDC regions.

The results are as one would expect. If the birthrates respond to declines in child mortality alone, the rates of natural increase will be raised by the declines in mortality in ages *above* those of childhood—and largely by reduced mortality in the advanced adult ages. If we were to allow for effects of deaths also of children 5 years of age and over, there would be a somewhat larger, but not much larger, offset response. If, as partial data indicate, total deaths of children under 15 were only about 60% of total deaths, while the share of the 0–14 group ranged about 42% of total population, the implicitly more moderate level and decline of death rates for ages 5–14 than for the 0–4 populations might, if taken into account, raise the estimated offset decline in line 21 by about a tenth, but not more than that.

The major conclusion is that if it is largely childhood deaths that affect the birthrate response, then even a full and prompt response (neither likely) would be insufficient to prevent a substantial rise in the rates of natural increase. Under the assumed conditions, the latter will cease rising only when the death rates above the childhood ages cease declining. Or, to put the conclusion in its converse form, while death rates are declining—sharply and with the usual concentration in early and advanced ages—the possibility of avoiding large rises in the rates of natural increase would lie not so much in a response of birthrates to child mortality (a most likely response, yet even so not promptly or fully) as in changing conditions that would affect the total number of surviving children desired. Such changes in conditions are not automatically provided by declines in death rates and by those factors behind them that appeared to operate in the LDCs in recent decades. On the contrary, the conjectures under (2) suggest a long initial period in the decline of death rates when the desired number of surviving children may continue to remain above that yielded by declining child mortality levels.

But what are the implications of our discussion of the responses of birthrates to the declines in death rates? At the end of the preceding subsection, which dealt with the declines in death rates, we came to a rather uncertain conclusion on the effects of the greater declines in death rates among the lower economic and social groups than among the upper groups, for whom death rates were already appreciably lower because of better nutrition, housing, and so on. We argued that prolongation of life, and closer convergence of death rates among various economic and social groups, removed one major aspect of long-term inequality. This reduction could be offset by greater pressure of higher rates of population growth on scarce traditional resources, unless such pressure was relieved by economic and social innovations associated with modern economic growth. We now add the conclusion that even with full and prompt offset response of birthrates to declines in death rates of 0–4 population, there will be acceleration of rates of natural increase; and such acceleration will be greater among those groups for whom the declines in death rates were greater, that is, among the lower economic and social strata. And this should mean that instead of a positive association between economic and social levels and group rates of natural increase, the trends discussed will produce an inverse association between economic and social levels and rates of natural increase. But this does not imply a necessary widening of per capita income inequalities if we deal with long-term levels of life-cycle income—which will be sustained by the longer span over which life and productivity can now be maintained among the lower income groups, as they could not be so maintained in the pretransition past. The conclusion is still uncertain; but one may argue that both the trends in the birthrates and the trends in income inequality depend heavily on economic and social transformations that relieve the pressure of growing population on the scarcity of traditional resources and that induce downtrends in the birthrates beyond those derivable as offset responses to declines in child mortality.

This latter argument could be developed further by indicating that the technological innovations associated with modern economic growth, which are the main source of the economic advance, depend heavily upon new knowledge; and that they and the associated social innovations require a much greater emphasis on higher levels of education and training of the younger generation that would be carrying the innovational process further. Once this connection between investment in the younger generation and further economic and social advance is established, there will be a shift toward greater investment by the older generation in the young (away from the earlier pattern of the younger generation contributing to their elders within the wider family),[15] with a resulting change in the number of desired surviving children, having major effects on birthrates. The important link in this argument is between the *sources* of economic advance and the contribution needed from the younger generation if these sources are to be maintained—a contribution that demands greater investment in education and training.

And it is in this connection that a decline in death rates of the type that has occurred in LDCs in recent decades looms as an indispensable condition. How the eventual declines in birthrates develop, whether they begin at the top, and how rapidly they spread through the wider groups in the population are questions and possibilities with obvious bearing upon income distribution while the transition process is taking place. But these arguments take us well beyond the immediate effects of the death rate trends in the LDCs, the major movement so far observed. And it would require more analysis of the differential death rate movements and of the related movements in birthrates to permit adequate discussion of the wider interconnections just suggested.

Appendix. Economic Losses Represented by Deaths: Exploratory Illustrations

In this appendix we discuss economic losses represented by deaths, with special attention to the differences between the high death rates of the LDCs and the much lower mortality of the MDCs. The discussion is directly relevant to the effects of the major declines of the death rates in the LDCs emphasized in the text. But, in view of the complexity and the difficulty of arriving at defensible approximations even of the order of magnitudes, it seemed best to shift the exploration to a separate appendix.

The discussion is limited to direct *economic* costs or losses. No attempt is, or can be, made to attach magnitudes to the psychological and emotional effects of death upon members of the family. Nor can we deal with indirect negative effects—for example, the greater unpredictability and variability over time of mortality in conditions of limited control over disease.

An even more important exclusion is the neglect of the association between high death rates and high levels of morbidity—that is, incidence of disease apart from higher mortality. Given this association, the level of death rates clearly suggests the level of morbidity; and higher incidence of disease either in childhood or in adulthood would presumably have negative effects on productivity, either because of the lasting debilitating effects of an earlier disease (even if incurred in childhood) or because of direct consequences of such diseases affecting adults of working age. Any attempt to measure the losses so involved in LDCs, in comparison with those in the MDCs, would run into the difficulty of separating the effects of health conditions from those of nutrition and other components of the standard of living. But it is reasonable to assume that these losses from higher morbidity associated with higher death rates in the LDCs are significantly greater than similar relative losses in the MDCs. If so, the comparison of economic losses suggested by deaths in the discussion that follows underestimates the excess relative loss in the less developed countries.

In dealing here with direct economic losses debited to deaths, we use for illustration the relevant demographic data for 1937 for two countries, Egypt and the Netherlands (see table 8.A.1, panel A). With

Table 8.A.1 Economic Losses Implicit in Death Rates: An Illustrative Calculation, Egypt and the Netherlands, 1937

A. *Distributions of Population and Deaths by Age Classes, and the Age-Specific Death Rates*

	Egypt			*The Netherlands*		
Age Class	% Share Population by Age (1)	% Share Deaths by Age (2)	ASDR per 1,000 (3)	% Share Population by Age (4)	% Share Deaths by Age (5)	ASDR per 1,000 (6)
1. Below 1	3.1	26.5	234.4	2.2	8.6	34.3
2. 1–4	10.2	29.5	78.9	8.1	2.6	2.8
3. 5–9	14.0	3.9	7.6	9.8	1.2	1.1
4. 10–14	12.1	2.0	4.5	9.2	0.9	0.9
5. 0–14	39.4	61.9		29.3	13.3	
6. 15–24	15.4	3.2	5.6	17.8	3.1	1.5
7. 25–34	15.7	4.4	7.7	15.4	3.6	2.1
8. 35–44	13.1	4.9	10.1	13.0	4.8	3.2
9. 45–54	8.3	4.5	14.7	10.3	7.7	6.6
10. 55–64	4.5	4.1	24.8	7.5	14.4	16.9
11. 15–64	57.0	21.1		64.0	33.6	
12. 65 and over	3.6	17.0	127.2	6.7	53.1	69.6
13. Total	100.0	100.0	27.27	100.0	100.0	8.78

B-1. *Economic Losses from Child Mortality*

	Egypt			*The Netherlands*		
Age Class	Deaths, % of Total Population (1)	Loss Multiple (2)	Loss, % of 100 CU (3)	Deaths, % of Total Population (4)	Loss Multiple (5)	Loss, % of 100 CU (6)
14. Below 1	0.7266	0.25	0.1817	0.0755	0.25	0.0189
15. 1–4	0.8048	1.50	1.2072	0.0227	1.50	0.0340
16. 5–9	0.1064	3.75	0.3990	0.0108	3.75	0.0405
17. 10–14	0.0545	6.25	0.3406	0.0083	6.25	0.0519
18. 0–14	1.6923		2.1205 (2.681)	0.1173		0.1453 (0.174)

Table 8.A.1 (continued)

B-2. *Residual Economic Losses, Adult Mortality*

	Egypt				*The Netherlands*			
Class Age	Deaths, % of Total Population (1)	Assumed Output per Person (CU) (2)	Residual Cost Beginning of Age Class CU's (3)	Residual Loss, % of 100 CU (4)	Deaths (5)	Output (6)	Residual Cost (7)	Residual Loss (8)
19. 15–24	0.0862	1.000	7.50	0.6465	0.0267	1.000	7.50	0.2002
20. 25–34	0.1209	1.322	7.50	0.7121	0.0327	1.224	7.50	0.2061
21. 35–44	0.1323	1.644	4.28	0.1402	0.0416	1.449	5.26	0.1256
22. 45–54		1.644	−2.16			1.449	0.77	
23. Total				1.4988				0.5319
				(1.888)				(0.636)
24. Total, for panels B-1 and B-2, % of total product				4.57				0.81

Notes

Panel A—The data used here are taken, or calculated, from United Nations, *Demographic Yearbooks, 1949–1950, and 1951* (New York, 1950, 1951). The distribution of the population by age for Egypt is for late March 1937, and is from the *1949–50 Yearbook*, table 4, pp. 104 ff.; that for the Netherlands is the average of the percentage shares for 1930 and 1945, from the same table. The small fraction of age-unknown is allocated proportionately. The distribution of deaths by age is from United Nations, *Demographic Yearbook, 1951* (New York 1951), table 16, pp. 216 ff., and relates to the deaths in 1937 for both countries.

The age-specific death rates in column 3 are derived by relating the absolute numbers of deaths to the relevant population; but the multiplication of the ratio of column 2 to column 1 by the crude death rate (line 13, col. 3) yields identical results, except for errors of rounding. The age-specific death rates in col. 6 were derived by multiplying the ratio of col. 5 to col. 4, by the crude death rate in line 13, col. 6 (8.78).

Panel B-1, cols. 1 and 4—The entries were derived by multiplying the age-specific death rates (see panel A, cols. 3 and 6), expressed as proper fractions, by the percentage share of the age-class in total population (see panel A, cols. 1 and 4).

Panel B-1, cols. 2 and 5—Entries were calculated on three assumptions: (*a*) Consumption per child is 0.5 of that for the adult in working ages (15–64). (*b*) Total income of the country is the sum of all consumption units, the latter being 0.5 per child; 1.00 per adult in working ages; 0.75 per adult aged 65 and over. (*c*) The number of years within the life-span of the children dying is 0.5, 3.0, 7.5, and 12.5 respectively for each successive age class under 15—representing linear interpolation and cumulation of the age-class limits. The entries in cols. 2 and 5 are then the products of 0.5 by the number of years.

Panel B-1, cols. 3 and 6—The entries are the products of those in cols. 1–2, and 4–5—for lines 14–17; and direct sums in line 18. The entries in parentheses in line 8, cols. 3 and 6, are the total loss related to the total number of consuming units. Based on the assumptions stated above, the latter total for Egypt is: (39.4%) (0.5) + (57.0%)(1.0) + (3.6%)(0.75) = 79.4; and for the Netherlands, using a similar equation—83.675. Division by these totals used as proper fractions (to 100) yields the percentages in the parentheses.

Panel B-2, cols. 1 and 5—These again are the products of the age-specific death further search, we probably could have found the data for a wider contrast with respect to death rates, both crude and age-specific. But the contrast observed in panel A in the crude death rates, between 27.3 per 1,000 for Egypt and fewer than 9 per 1,000 for the Netherlands, is wide enough for our purposes. The intention is to suggest the wider ramifications of the comparison with respect to the economic losses involved—rather than attempt a full estimate of the orders of magnitude.

A glance at the age-specific death rates in columns 3 and 6 of panel A reveals that these rates are higher in Egypt than in the Netherlands for *each* age class distinguished; that the ratios of the age-specific death rates in Egypt to those in the Netherlands tend to be higher in the early ages than at later ages, the decline in these ratios being interrupted only by the extremely high ratio for the 1–4 age class; and that the greater share of the younger age groups—particularly those below 15—in the total population, in Egypt than in the Netherlands, tends to accentuate the disparity in the crude death rates. Whatever losses are represented by deaths are bound to be much greater in a high death rate country like Egypt, at least in relation to its total economic magnitude, than in a low death rate country like the Netherlands. It also follows that if the

---

rates by the proportion of the age class in total population, both being taken from panel A (see notes to panel A).

Panel B-2, cols. 2 and 6—The life-cycle pattern of product per capita in the working ages (and also for age 65 and over) is based on the following assumptions: (*a*) The product per capita in age 65 and over is 0.75 CU, just sufficient to cover consumption. It follows that the product per capita for ages 15–64 must cover more than the per capita CU, to compensate for the consumption of children under 15. The average excess in per capita product in ages 15–64 is given by the ratio of all consumption units for people under 65 to the number of people of working age (i.e., for Egypt [(39.4 × 0.5) + (57.0 × 1.0)] divided by 57.0; for the Netherlands [(29.3 × 0.5) + (64.0 × 1.0)] divided by 64.0. (*b*) It is assumed that in the age class 15–24 product per capita just equals consumption, i.e., 1.0; that there is a peaking plateau in ages 35–44 and 45–54, per capita product being equally high in the two age classes; and that in the intermediate age classes (25–34 and 55–64), the per capita product is a simple average of the preceding and following class means. Given assumptions (*a*) and (*b*), it is possible to solve a one-variable equation to find the value of the peak level (which proves to be 1.644 in Egypt and 1.449 in the Netherlands), and thus of all the lower-class product per capita.

Panel B-2, cols. 3 and 7—The initial value here is the product of 0.5 CU (consumption per person per year) by 15, the number of years elapsing to the beginning of the 15–24 age class. From then on the cumulated past costs are affected by the surplus of product over assumed consumption in the successive age classes of adults of working age—the surplus being the difference between the entries in cols. 2 and 6, and 1.00.

Panel B-2, cols. 4 and 8—The entries are product of the entries in cols. 1 and 4, by the *average* of those in cols. 3 and 7 (e.g., for line 20, it would be the average of 7.50 and 4.28, in col. 4; and of 7.50 and 5.26 in col. 8)—all of this for lines 19 through 22.

For entries in lines 23 and 24, whether the sums are in top lines or in the parentheses, see notes to the relevant part of panel B-1.

recent major declines in the LDCs proceeded on the path suggested in the text, with larger declines among the lower economic and social groups with initially much higher mortality than among the more favored, upper economic groups, the resulting convergence within the country among group death rates would also mean convergence in the relative burden of losses represented by deaths. But how do we estimate, as a first approximation, the direct economic losses that deaths represent?

Two approaches may be followed. In the first, the losses represented by deaths would be defined as inputs into past consumption of children and young adults offset by productive contributions that the deceased might have made. The question being answered, then, is What unoffset consumption inputs might have been avoided if the children and young adults whose deaths we are considering had never been born? In the other approach, the losses represented by deaths are viewed as the *projected* net productive contribution of the deceased that could have been expected but for the irreversible loss. This is the lost opportunities, rather than the lost costs, approach; but both deal only with economic costs, opportunities, and returns, not with the psychic. We follow here the first approach, carried through more easily and dealing with historical facts and incurred burdens, rather than with extrapolated possibilities and lost future opportunities.[16]

Panel B-1, columns 1 and 3, reveals that total childhood deaths in a year account for 1.7% of total population in Egypt, but only 0.117% in the Netherlands (line 18)—a ratio of more than 14 to 1. To estimate the input into these children to whose death we are trying to assign an economic weight, we are assuming that the annual consumption per child amounted to 0.5 of the consumption of an adult of working age; that the productive contribution of children was negligible and that no offset to the input of past costs is thus to be entered; that with stable prices, there was no rise over time in per capita consumption of the adults of working age; and that with savings minimal (and disregarded for simplicity), total income (or net product of the nation) was the sum of all consumption (calculated by assigning 1.0 per adult of working age, 0.50 to those below 15, and 0.75 to those 65 and over). Given these assumptions, and cumulation of inputs into children who died after year 0, we can calculate the cost as a percentage of total current product. It works out to 2.68% for Egypt and 0.17% for the Netherlands (see line 18, cols. 3 and 6, in parentheses).

It is of interest to compare the results in table 8.A.1 with those in Hansen's note (Hansen 1957), which reports measures for India similar to those for the United Kingdom and the United States, for 1931 and 1951 (see table 8.A.2).

Table 8.A.2 Major Results of Hansen's Calculations of Costs of Childhood Deaths

	India (1)	United Kingdom (2)	United States (3)
Deaths before age 15 as % of total population			
1. 1931	1.58	0.17	0.18
2. 1951	1.31	0.07	0.08
Costs of childhood deaths, child-adult consumption ratio set at 0.5			
3. 1931	2.81	0.26	0.32
4. 1951	2.83	0.07	0.09
Costs of childhood deaths, child-adult consumption ratio variable			
5. 1931	2.78	0.35	0.40
6. 1951	2.82	0.09	0.12

Notes

Taken or calculated from tables 2 and 3, pp. 259–60, of the paper cited in note 19.

The costs of childhood deaths are expressed in percentages of the country's total product, equated to aggregate consumption.

The variable child-adult consumption ratios in lines 5 and 6 were as follows. For India, the ratio was set at 0.5 through age class 5–9, and at 0.8 for age class 10–14. For the United Kingdom and the United States, the ratios for the four successive age classes (the same as used here) were 0.6, 0.7, 0.8, and 0.9.

The comparison with the results here confirms the general orders of magnitude and indicates how differences in the assumed child-adult consumption ratios affect the cost of childhood mortality expressed as a percentage of total product. While we have assumed here the child-adult consumption ratio of 0.5, adults defined as people of working age (and with the consumption level per person of 65 and over set at 0.75), the resulting cost estimate for Egypt, at 2.7%, is close to that for India, either in 1931 or 1951—see lines 3–4, col. 1). And the introduction of a somewhat greater consumption allowance for the age group 10–14 in India does not change the cost estimate significantly (see lines 5–6, col. 1). In contrast, introducing higher child-adult consumption ratios for the United Kingdom and the United States raises the cost estimates by a substantial proportion (from 0.26 to 0.35 in United Kingdom in 1931, and from 0.32 to 0.40 for the United States in the same year; the proportional changes in 1951 are almost as great, see columns 2 and 3, lines 3–6). Yet, even with the allowance for much higher consumption levels (relative to adults) of children in the United Kingdom and the United States, the relative costs of childhood deaths for India are still much greater in 1931 and 1951.

But if deaths of children represent an economic loss because of past input of resources that cannot be recovered, the same is true of the deaths of adults of working age—so long as the surplus of their contribution to product beyond their own consumption fails to cover past historical costs incurred in raising them to productive ages. This is the rationale for panel B-2 of table 8.A.1, in which the cumulative input in past consumption (at 0.5 units until age 15, and at 1.0 through the successive ages until age 65) is compared with the cumulative total output credited to the adults. The latter output is estimated on two assumptions: (*a*) that it is the adult population of working age, 15–64, who produce the goods sufficient for their consumption *and* that of children under 15; (*b*) that within the working life-span, output per person age 15–24 just equals per capita consumption (i.e., 1.0); that the peak per capita output is a plateau at ages 35–44 and 45–54; and that per capita product in the intermediate age classes (25–34 and 55–64) is at an arithmetic mean of the per capita products in the preceding and folling age classes. This is clearly only a rough approximation to the life cycle of product per adult; but some such pattern is needed for a proper view of the time span within which the accumulated excess of output over consumption begins to match the accumulated past input into consumption—for the proportion of population that dies and for whom full recovery of past costs cannot be attained.

The results of the estimates in panel B-2 (for details of the procedure see the notes to the table) suggest that for Egypt the costs of mortality in the adult ages when past costs are recovered adds an item equivalent to 2% of product, raising the total past costs of child and early adult mortality to 4.6% (see lines 23–24, col. 4). For the Netherlands, the addition, while smaller absolutely (0.64%), is far greater relative to cost of child mortality. This is due to the much greater weight of costs in col. 7, lines 19–22, than in col. 5, lines 14–17; whereas total mortality (as percentage of total population) in ages 15–44, of 0.1010 (see col. 5, lines 19–21) is not much lower than the corresponding total of 0.1173 for ages 0–14 (see line 18, col. 4).

Only further exploration, involving many more countries, would reveal whether the approximation to unrequited past costs represented by child and early adult mortality (introduced by the estimates in panel B-2) is typical of less developed and developed countries respectively. But there is one aspect of the estimates underlying panel B-2 that is likely to be typical and deserves explicit note. If the adult population of working age is assumed to produce sufficiently to cover both its own consumption *and* that of the population ages 0–14, the average per capita output for the adult working-age population of Egypt would have to be 76.7/57.0 = 1.346; whereas that for the Netherlands would have to be 78.65/64.0 = 1.229. In other words, the excess output demanded from adults of working age in Egypt is proportionately greater than that demanded from the adults of working age in the Netherlands. This reflects a dependency ratio that, whether or not we exclude dependency in ages of 65 and over (it was excluded by our assumption), is significantly greater in LDCs than in MDCs. The source lies in the higher ratio of children to adults of working age—which, for Egypt, amounted to 39.4/57.0 = 0.69; whereas in the Netherlands it was 29.3/64.0 = 0.46. It is the difference in these two ratios, combined with assumptions concerning the life-cycle pattern of product per capita within the working ages, that results in a contrast, at the peak plateau, between an output index of 1.664 for Egypt and one of 1.449 for the Netherlands. The implicit question is whether, given average levels of productivity, it is possible to muster such a high excess ratio, or whether, in order to achieve the latter, the whole average level of output in the productive ages would have to be lowered. If both the child-adult consumption ratios and the proportions of children to working-age adults are fixed, the adjustment may be either in the average level of the product or in the pattern; and if the pattern is fixed, the adjustment is limited to the average level—implicitly involving the lowering of consumption for both children and adults.

Assuming for purposes of argument that the results in both panel B-1 and panel B-2 can be viewed as typical, what importance can be assigned to the indicated differences in the economic costs of child and early adult mortality between a less developed and a more developed country? The answer can be suggested only after we take a brief account of the major omissions in the calculations, even allowing (as Hansen did) for a higher child-adult consumption ratio in a developed than in a less developed country.

The first major omission is neglect of the contribution of the mother's engagement in pregnancy, birth, and the immediate burdens of care in infancy—the cost estimates here relating only to the consumption of goods and services by children. The weight of such omission would vary even among less developed countries, depending on institutional practices and the role of women in productive activity; and it is not clear that differences in the weight of this particular cost component can be surmised in comparisons between less developed and developed countries (such costs always viewed as proportions of some overall economic product magnitude). It clearly adds to the absolute costs of child mortality in both groups of countries and thus adds to the accumulated costs that would have to be debited against the output in the early working ages (in estimating the costs of deaths at those age levels); but we have no basis here for any plausible comparisons.

The second omission is of a possible allowance for effects of growth in per capita product on the estimate of past costs embodied in economic loss from childhood (or young adult) mortality. If such growth does occur, the current burden is lessened, since past consumption of children and younger adults is lower in proportion to *current* per capita consumption, and hence in relation to current product. Here the difference in this respect between LDCs, with their much lower growth rates in per capita product (or even absence of growth in many cases in premodern periods), and the MDCs, with their higher and steadier rates of growth in per capita product, is clearly in favor of the latter—reducing more appreciably the ratio of past costs to current output. The magnitudes, and their differences as between LDCs and MDCs, could be calculated using assumptions now used in table 8.A.1 and introducing illustrative rates of past growth in per capita product.

The third omission, of potentially large magnitude, is that of foregone yields on past costs. These yields are possible even if we retain the oversimplified assumption that equates total product with total consumption and thus completely neglects savings and capital. Even under such conditions, were it have been possible to dispense with past consumption of children or young adults whose deaths we are evaluating, the consumption of surviving adults would have been greater—with effects on productivity, which would be likely to have been greater in LDCs than in MDCs. This greater consumption foregone would also have meant greater productivity in the past—a loss that presumably would be, in terms of current product, proportionately greater in LDCs than in MDCs. An alternative way to evaluate this omission is to allow for interest yield on past costs, and for the presence of capital returns in the economy. If, for the sake of an illustration, we allow for an addition of returns on capital equal to a quarter of total consumption, and use a 5% return rate on past consumption in children viewed as an investment, the application of these rates to panel B-1, columns 2–3 and 5–6, lines 14–17 would yield an estimate of accumulated losses (to age 15) of 3.5014 in column 3 for Egypt and of 0.2165 in column 6 for the Netherlands, which—with rough allowance for the rise in the total product denominators by 25%—would work out to percentages of 3.528 and 0.207 respectively, a wider contrast than between the entries in parentheses in line 8, columns 3 and 6. This would also affect estimates of losses in the younger adult age classes in panel B-2.

Finally, there is a question similar to that discussed in the text in connection with the focus of decision in the response of birthrates to the declines in death rates. Here the question is who bears the costs of childhood mortality or the residual losses involved in the death of adults in the younger working ages. The question may not be relevant for the economy as a whole. But if we are concerned with differential effects of these losses on different economic and social groups within the population, the question of who bears them becomes relevant. Thus in many developed countries the state, in various ways, assumes part of the costs of children and young adults—that is, part of their consumption —even though it may finance the activity from taxes on the income of adults and families, with the burden perhaps falling more heavily on the higher-income families. In many less developed countries, there may also be sharing of such costs within the larger blood group, rather than the full cost falling on the individual family unit. These comments suggest that the question of how the economic losses of mortality have been shared involves complicated effects of benefits and incidence of taxes in those developed societies where the state assumes increasing responsibility; of separation or jointness between the parental family and that of the next generation (bearing particularly on the locus of mortality costs for the younger age classes within the working life-span); and of the relation between the single family, no matter how widely defined, and the wider blood-related group of which it may be a member.

It is not feasible here to explore the variety of omissions just indicated and to probe the interrelated and intricate questions they suggest. The discussion of differential costs of mortality, like that of the offset response of birthrates to declines in death rates, emphasizes that the analysis must take account of the wide variety of institutional, economic, and social groupings that condition the impact of losses involved in deaths at different ages or that shape the response of birthrates to declines in mortality. With inadequate data to indicate the differences in the framework among various groups of LDCs and MDCs, and with limited command over the monographic literature, the probing had to be limited and constrained by oversimplifying assumptions.

Despite these limitations, the discussion above is, I believe, sufficient to suggest the minimum relative magnitudes of the losses represented by deaths of children and younger adults—and the large differences in these losses between MDCs and LDCs on the eve of the recent major downtrends of the death rates in LDCs. The proportionate losses represented by the death rates in the LDCs relating to children and younger adults approximate at least 5% of the current product, compared with probably less than a fifth of that proportion in the developed countries; and reasonable adjustments of these shares, to take account of the omissions, could easily raise these minimal ratios to twice their indicated levels.

Comparisons of LDCs and MDCs are only suggestive of comparisons *within* a less developed country between the mortality experience of the lower economic and social groups and that of the higher, more favorably situated. Yet given the possibility of substantial differences in mortality within the LDCs, associated before the 1920s largely with disparities in economic and social status, one can reasonably assume that in those earlier decades the burden of economic losses of mortality were much heavier relative to the consumption and income levels of the lower income groups than they were for the upper economic and social groups; and that the convergence in death rates, and reduction in overall levels associated with the recent technological breakthroughs in control of death and of public health, also meant reduction in the inequality of the burden of relative losses of mortality at these different economic and social levels. And one must repeat, in conclusion, the comment made at the outset—that death rates are significant as indexes of morbidity and that declining and converging morbidity rates may have direct effects on related disparities in productivity among the various economic and social groups within a less developed country as it benefits from declining mortality.

Notes

1. We prefer to emphasize the total for LDCs, excluding China. The estimates for the latter before the 1950s were always subject to debate; and there has been ever greater scarcity of data for China since the 1950s. Yet the estimated population for the country accounted for 0.2 of world population for 1975, and about 0.3 of the population total for the LDCs.

2. The quinquennium 1970–75 and the estimate for 1975 are described as a projection even in the more recent United Nations sources; and we used the medium variant. But since estimates for this recent period could not deviate substantially from the actual, at least with respect to change from the preceding two decades, we felt justified in including them to form an observed 25-year span, 1950–75.

3. Kingsley Davis (1951) estimated the death rate for India by decades from 1881–91 to 1931–41, showing a level of about 43 per 1,000 in the first three decades, a bulge in 1911–21 (associated with the influenza pandemic of 1918) to 48.6, and a decline to 36.3 in 1921–31 and to 31.3 in 1931–41 (p. 37). The estimated crude birthrates were set at between 46 and 49 in the first four of the six decades, and then at 46 in 1921–31 and 45 in 1931–41 (p. 69). This combination of relative constancy of the birthrate between 1920 and 1940, with a substantial decline in the death rate, is what we are assuming in the tentative calculation in the text.

4. See particularly the paper in this volume by Samuel H. Preston (chap. 5), "Causes and Consequences of Mortality Declines in Less Developed Countries during the Twentieth Century," for a wide-ranging summary and bibliography. I also found a wealth of data and interpretation in the articles by George H. Stolnitz, beginning with the two-part paper "A Century of International Mortality Trends" (Stolnitz 1955, 1956), reviewing the evidence to 1950, and concluding

with the latest, "International Mortality Trends: Some Main Facts and Implications" (Stolnitz 1975).

5. A useful *brief* description of the assumptions underlying the projections, and the criteria of plausibility used in selecting them, is in United Nations (1966, chap. 2, pp. 6–7). A wider review of the field is in United Nations (1973, 1:558–88).

6. It is possible to secure from United Nations, *Demographic Yearbook 1957*, the distribution of population among continents and subcontinents in 1920, as well as of the land area (including internal waters); and we find in Clark (1957) a distribution of land among major parts of the world, the land evaluated with respect to rainfall, temperature, and other climatic factors that affect suitability for intensive cultivation (table 33, inset before p. 309). Comparing the large areas within the group that comprises the LDCs we find the following percentage distributions (LDCs, comprising the regions distinguished = 100):

	Population (1920)	*Total Land*	*Land in Standard Units*
East and Southeast Asia	77.0	24.8	29.4
Southwest Asia	3.7	8.2	1.3
Africa	11.7	39.4	31.8
Latin America	7.6	27.6	37.5

East and Southeast Asia in the first line is dominated by the Sinic and Hindic group; and the capacity shown to sustain enormous populations with a land endowment that is less than a third of that in the rest of the less developed world is striking.

7. In 1920, of some 1,187 million population estimated in the less developed regions (defined as countries outside of Europe, North America, Japan, the Soviet Union, Australia and New Zealand, and temperate South America), only 69 million were living in places with populations of 20,000 or more. While this low percentage—less than 6%—was largely due to the dominance of Asia, a level of slightly over 10% was the highest shown for any subregion. See United Nations (1969, tables 47–49, pp. 115–17).

8. See Davis (1951); the conversion ratio used in the text is described on p. 36. The data on children born and surviving to rural families in Punjab in 1939 for various occupational class groups are in table 26, p. 78, with discussion in the text (p. 76) stressing some limitations of the data.

9. The data are from U.S. Bureau of the Census (1975). The series on gross and net reproduction rates are series B36–41, p. 53; those on crude birthrates are series B5–10, p. 49; and those on crude death rates are series B167–80, p. 59.

10. See, e.g., a recent paper by Ajami (1976, pp. 453–63), and the literature cited therein, particularly the early paper by Stys (1957, pp. 136–48).

11. For a brief discussion of the relation between the health revolution and economic development, see the paper by the World Health Organization, "Health Trends and Prospects in Relation to Population and Development," in United Nations (1975). The same paper contains some discussion of the relation between the decline in infant mortality and the birthrate.

12. In this connection one may refer to two papers on population growth and income distribution in the United Nations volume, *Population Debate* (1975, vol. 1). The first, by Dharam P. Ghai, "Population Growth, Labour Absorption, and Income Distribution" (pp. 502–9), summarizes the conclusions by listing in table 2 (p. 509) the effects of population growth on income distribution—under two major headings of "high fertility" and "reduced fertility"—with the levels and trends

of mortality not mentioned. In the other paper, by H. W. Singer, "Income Distribution and Population Growth" (pp. 510–17), there is explicit mention of lower mortality as "a necessary first step towards achieving the more desirable low birth rate/low death rate type of equilibrium" (p. 516). But the author follows this statement by considering effects of a more equal distribution on death rates, with no discussion of the reverse, the possible effects of declines in mortality on the income distribution in the LDCs. Yet, with all the interest in the latter, the possible effects of the trends in mortality rather than in fertility that dominated the demographic changes in the LDCs in the last few decades seem to be neglected.

13. Much of the literature on the response of fertility to mortality declines concentrates on the response of families to the actually incurred death of a child (or children) and the observed reaction. See in this connection Preston's chapter in this volume and the paper for this conference by Yoram Ben-Porath on "Fertility and Child Mortality—Issues in the Demographic Transition of a Migrant Population." Of particular interest also are Preston (1975, pp. 189–200); and his summary introduction to the volume of proceedings of the CICRED seminar on Infant Mortality in Relation to the Level of Fertility (the proceedings were not available to me at the time of writing). For lack of familiarity with the details of most of the sample studies involved, one cannot judge whether the failure to completely "replace" children who die can be translated into an effective absence of a desired number of children as a target firm enough to explain the failure to reduce the birthrate in response to a perceived decline in mortality. There is an apparent lack of symmetry between a situation in which birth frequency has to be raised in an active response to the loss of a child and a situation in which births have to be reduced in response to an increased number of surviving children.

At any rate, it seemed of interest to stress in the brief discussion here aspects of lag, of perception of mortality declines, and of persistence of an excess in the possible number of desired surviving children over that actually resulting through much of the early phase of the downtrend in mortality in the LDCs.

14. The death rates derived for 0–4 population in lines 8 and 17 exceed the crude death rates for total population by factors of 2.4 to 3.2 in 1950–55 and 2.7 to 3.6 in 1970–75. Multiplying these ratios by the proportion of 0–4 to total population, averaged over each of the two quinquennia, we can derive the proportions of deaths of children 0–4 to all deaths, which would range from well over 40% to 50% or more. The direct data on distribution of deaths by age for various countries in the United Nations *Demographic Yearbook* (various years) suggest proportions for recent years, back to the 1950s, of between 40% and somewhat over 50%. The agreement cannot be checked fully because of scarcity of data on distribution of deaths by age and the indication that in many countries the deaths of infants are particularly underreported (a bias that would affect death rates for 0–4 population much more than total crude death rates). For the present illustrative purposes, further effort at assembling data on deaths by age, or at using direct information on age-specific death rates for LDCs, did not seem worthwhile. A more intensive study of the effects of declines in death rates would warrant such further effort.

15. See a recent paper by Caldwell (1976), which stresses the "flow from the younger generation to the older" in pretransition society and the reverse flow in the posttransition, nucleated families.

16. This choice follows the approach in an earlier brief paper by W. Lee Hansen (1957). This paper was stimulated by a desire to correct an exaggerated and erroneous estimate of the proportional cost of child mortality made rather casually for India by D. Ghosh, who set this cost as high as 22.5% of national income

(compared with Hansen's medium estimate of less than 3%). Hansen's note employed somewhat more elaborate assumptions than are followed here and used data for other countries and dates. But, as will be seen below, the general order of conclusions, when limited to child mortality, is about the same.

The topic here is clearly a part of the wider theme of the economics of family formation in the demographic transition, subject of a brief and illuminating paper by Frank Lorimer (1967).

Comment Albert Fishlow

Simon Kuznets has made a significant contribution in this essay to the discussion of the economic consequences of recent demographic trends in developing countries. He starts from the dominant role played by mortality decline in bringing about the rapid increase in population in the postwar decades. That enables him to advance three novel propositions relating population growth to the level and internal distribution of income of LDCs.

First, he shows that even instantaneous fertility adjustment to declines in early childhood mortality would not have prevented much of the population expansion actually experienced. Second, he calculates a large economic loss caused by high rates of child and young adult mortality. Third, he conjectures that the reduction in such losses may have accrued disproportionately to poorer families, thereby potentially reducing the inequality of income, especially if measured over the life cycle.

Taken together, these conclusions add up to a rather less negative view of the acceleration of rates of natural increase experienced by developing countries. "One should emphasize to the end the indispensable —and in the longer run beneficial—effects of the declines in the death rates." That perspective, at a time when there is much hand-wringing concerning the population problem, alone is sufficient to make the paper important.

Without denying the positive aspects of mortality decline, I believe casual readers may come away perhaps too persuaded by Kuznets's subtle revisionism. Careful examination of each of the three central propositions is therefore indicated.

The limited potential offset to natural increase afforded by fertility adjustment to declining mortality in the age group 0–4 is the least controversial conclusion. It follows directly from the historical shift downward of the mortality schedule as a whole, not merely at the youngest ages. What Kuznets perhaps does not emphasize enough is that his

Albert Fishlow is professor of economics and director of the Concilium on International and Area Studies at Yale University.

calculations in table 8.5 imply that the age-specific death rates in the group age 0–4 declined even proportionally *less* than for older ages: 26% (for all regions together) compared with 40%. For Latin America alone, starting from a more favorable initial level, the disparity is much greater: 22% versus 55%. The recent mortality experience in developing countries has therefore not been dominated by declines in infant and early childhood mortality. That, of course, is why the calculated fertility offset, defined as a response to fewer deaths only in those years, is so limited.

This pattern of mortality decline has not been sufficiently commented upon. One reason is limited information. The Kuznets technique itself is based on age distribution and fertility estimates, not mortality data. Yet the direct calculations reported by the United Nations for those few countries with the requisite information seem to support the Kuznets results. Mortality decline does seem to have been more rapid between ages 15 and 34 than for younger groups.

The disparity with the historical experience of the developed countries is noteworthy. Its implication in this context is that the lag in fertility adjustment to mortality decline will be greater than if improvement had been more concentrated at the youngest ages. It is reasonable to suppose that private calculations aimed at achieving a desired family size will not take into account the improved survival rates of young adults. Completed families may thus come to be larger than anticipated. But since the young adults can go off and be productive, there may well be benefits rather than costs associated with the excess. The survival of these young adults means that a larger number of families, not merely an increase in average size, will characterize the population acceleration. It is only through an indirect route—diffusion of educational and economic opportunities, and increased labor force participation of women, among others—that the countervailing reduction in desired family size can come about.

The characteristics of mortality decline thus influence the extent of resulting population growth. Kuznets contends, however, that reduced mortality produces economic savings. His Appendix details a method for quantifying the reduced wastage. Those calculations seem to me deficient because they do not really measure the economic consequences of mortality decline. The question posed, rather, is What net "consumption inputs might have been avoided if the children and young adults whose deaths we are considering *had never been born*?" (italics mine). That is, the benefits are contingent upon a simultaneous decline in mortality *and* fertility, leaving natural increase unchanged. A reduction in mortality alone does not free up resources; the investment in consumption inputs has already been made. Rather, lower death rates influence the potential future return on such streams of inputs. Instead of a zero or small return for those dying in childhood or young adulthood, survival extends the period over which surplus may be produced.

There are not two alternative approaches to the measure of the benefits of mortality decline as Kuznets suggests. One cannot use the averted losses, because there is no reason to presume that the realized returns on the surviving investment exactly equal their original cost. The difficult task of identifying the consequences of a higher rate of natural increase emanating from mortality decline is precisely the one of "historical facts and incurred burdens." Kuznets's procedure of fewer births is the one not experienced. Because population increased, supplementary resources had to be found to complement the investments already made. When that occurred, the returns may well have increased; if they did not, then the effects could well have been adverse.

The concentration of mortality decline in the young adult ages is clearly a most favorable one for reaping positive benefits. Much of the investment has already been made, and a productive return upon it has been made possible. The aggregate counterpart is an initial increase in the relative size of the potentially productive population. Even if diminishing returns were encountered, there would be a net gain so long as the survivors produced more than their own consumption requirements. But if they could not, then the decline in mortality will have worsened the situation by reducing the surplus produced.

The issue cannot be settled without resort to the facts. The variety of theoretical arguments about savings, investment, and production relationships are not in themselves decisive. Assuming a life-cycle pattern of returns determines the outcome. The relevant question is what form it historically took as population increased. While there is no question that an identical rate of population growth generated by mortality decline rather than fertility increase is economically more favorable, there can still be legitimate doubt about the direction of influence of the greater population size.

One is therefore back to the familiar and fundamental problem. We can approach it more intelligently by appreciating that the pattern of mortality decline actually experienced by developing countries may have permitted them to cope with the population explosion more effectively. What is called for is systematic analysis of the economic circumstances of countries whose patterns of mortality decline differed.

Kuznets's final conjecture about possible improvement in the internal income distribution follows from his emphasis upon the economic wastage inherent in high levels of mortality: "The benefit to those who have sustained the losses in the past caused by higher death rates among various economic and social groups meant the reduction of an important aspect of persisting inequality that loomed large in the premodern LDC societies." Our stress upon the resource *using* character of mortality decline makes such a logical sequence more dubious. This is quite apart from the Kuznets qualification of changing factor prices deriving from the relative scarcity of other factors as labor supply increased.

Three points may be noted. First, it is the richer families that can more easily cope with the greater strains imposed by larger family size resulting from lower death rates. Additional mouths must be fed from the same family output if the potential returns are to be realized. This puts a premium upon access to finance for marginal investment in consumption. Poor families may simply not be able to afford it. Lower levels of average consumption for all survivors likely means inability to take advantage of what opportunities there are. Education will be sacrificed, health will remain poor, skills will continue undeveloped relative to those surviving in families initially better able to respond. Then inequality among incomes over the life cycle will increase. Second, the assumption of uniformity in the pattern of mortality decline is not necessarily correct. Richer families probably already start with much lower infant mortality because of better nutrition; the improvement they experience from improved public health measures may be relatively concentrated in the most productive ages. This could lead to higher returns to them, and again to an increase in inequality. Finally, it may well be that higher-income (and better educated) families are first to adjust their fertility to mortality decline. Then there *are* tangible savings to be achieved that would accrue to those with higher initial incomes.

This analysis, like that of Kuznets, is couched in terms of income per family member over the life cycle. It therefore abstracts from any instantaneous deterioration in the income distribution of those gainfully employed. The trends here are real in welfare terms and are further aggravated by the increase in land rentals and returns to capital that greater population may be expected to induce, especially where traditional social and economic structures remain intact.

I therefore conclude more pessimistically than he. The inevitable decline in mortality and increase in population, however necessary to modern economic growth, need not have had beneficial consequences for the distribution and level of per capita incomes. But my counterarguments, like his, are very much conjectural. His paper opens up fresh and promising areas for further research. More careful specification of the underlying life-cycle economic-demographic models and their empirical test both rank high on the agenda. It is not the first time, or surely the last, that he has reframed the questions those interested in the process of economic development might fruitfully explore.

References

Ajami, I. 1976. Differential fertility in peasant communities: A study of six Iranian villages. *Population Studies* 30, no. 3 (November): 453–63.

Arriaga, Eduardo E., and Davis, Kingsley. 1969. The pattern of mortality change in Latin America. *Demography* 6, no. 3 (August): 223–42.

Caldwell, John C. 1976. Toward a restatement of demographic transition theory. *Population and Development Review* 2, nos. 3–4 (September, December): 321–66.

Clark, Colin. 1957. *Conditions of economic progress.* 3d ed. London.

Davis, Kingsley. 1951. *Population of India and Pakistan.* Princeton: Princeton University Press.

Hansen, W. Lee. 1957. A note on the cost of children's mortality. *Journal of Political Economy* 65, no. 3 (June): 257–62.

Kuznets, Simon. 1976. Demographic aspects of the size distribution of income. *Economic Development and Cultural Change* 25, no. 1 (October): 1–94.

Lorimer, Frank. 1967. The economics of family formation under different conditions. In *World population conference, 1965*, 2:92–95. New York: United Nations.

Preston, Samuel H. 1975. Health programs and population growth. *Population and Development Review* 1, no. 2 (December): 189–200.

Stolnitz, George H. 1955. A century of international mortality trends. Part 1. *Population Studies*, vol. 9 (July).

———. 1956. A century of international mortality trends. Part 2. *Population Studies*, vol. 10 (July).

———. 1975. International mortality trends: Some main facts and implications. In *The population debate*, 1:220–36. New York: United Nations.

Stys, W. 1957. The influence of economic conditions on the fertility of peasant women. *Population Studies* 11, no. 2 (November): 136–48.

United Nations. 1953. *The determinants and consequences of population trends.* 1st ed. New York: United Nations.

United Nations. 1966. *World population prospects as assessed in 1963.* New York: United Nations.

United Nations. 1969. *Growth of the world's urban and rural population, 1920–2000.* New York: United Nations.

———. 1973. *The determinants and consequences of population trends.* New York: United Nations.

U.S. Bureau of the Census. 1975. *Historical statistics of the United States, colonial times to 1970, bicentennial edition, part 1.* Washington, D.C.

9 A Historical Perspective on Economic Aspects of the Population Explosion: The Case of Preindustrial England

Ronald Demos Lee

9.1 Introduction

The preindustrial context offers particular advantages for the study of population change and its consequences. Over the course of centuries the effects of population pressure on resources have a chance to emerge and to dominate the more transitory influences. And other sources of long-run economic change, such as technology, capital accumulation, education, and institutional reorganization, were formerly weaker or absent. Thus history may provide us with an actual ceteris paribus situation where statistical attempts to control for extraneous influences on contemporary development have failed. Of course there is always the risk that changing circumstances may have rendered the lessons of history obsolete, but one has to start someplace; the drunk looks for his dime under the lamppost, though he lost it down the street.

There have been many studies of the effects of population growth on economic development, but only a few of these studies are empirical.

Ronald Demos Lee is associated with the Department of Economics and the Population Studies Center, the University of Michigan.

This research was funded by NICHD grant HD 08586–03. I am very grateful to Professor E. A. Wrigley and Professor R. Schofield of the Cambridge Group for the History of Population and Social Structure for making the aggregate parish data set available to me. Philip Mirowski provided valuable research assistance at all stages of this project, and I also profited from his knowledge of English history and his creative insights. Professors Gavin Wright, Gary Saxonhouse, C. K. Harley, and Albert Fishlow made helpful comments on earlier drafts. I am particularly indebted to Professor Marc Nerlove for his detailed comments and his solutions to some of the analytic problems.

Theoretical studies, and the many simulation studies in the tradition of the classic work by Coale and Hoover (1958), can be queried on their premises (see Simon 1976). Cost-benefit studies of marginal lives, pioneered by Enke (1960), are empirical only in appearance; their results can actually be derived a priori for virtually any country, regardless of its economic situation, as Ohlin (1969) has shown in an ingenious article.[1] Cross-national studies, seeking correlations of population growth rates and growth rates of per capita income (see, e.g., Kuznets 1967; Chesnai and Sauvy 1973; Easterlin 1972) have invariably found no significant association.[2] Leff's (1969) well-known article on savings rates and dependency rates has been so heavily criticized as to leave the results in serious doubt. So although most economists and almost all demographers believe high population growth rates are a problem, there is a surprising shortage of empirical evidence. A study of the consequences of population change in a historical context may help demonstrate the importance of the variable in at least the simplest case.

Historical studies may also aid our understanding of the causes of population change. It is sometimes suggested that until a couple of centuries ago the size of human populations in relation to resources was effectively regulated by socioeconomic institutions, but that in recent times these mechanisms have broken down under the influences of mortality decline, urbanization, technical change, and modernization in general. However, there is little understanding of how such mechanisms functioned in the past, how effective they were, and how they reacted to various kinds of external shocks. An examination of these historical mechanisms should help us understand to what extent modern and historical experience differ qualitatively, and should provide some perspective on current high rates of population growth.

This paper has three major parts. The first discusses the consequences of population change in preindustrial England, concentrating on wages, rents, and the ratio of industrial to agricultural prices. A simple two-sector model is developed to organize the analysis. The second part discusses the cause of population change, focusing on the nature of the social mechanisms that controlled it and their reaction to variations in mortality and productivity. In the third part, a simple model of economic-demographic equilibrium is developed, in which steady shifts in labor demand are the main determinant of sustained population growth, while the equilibrium living standards maintained during expansion result from the interplay of largely exogenous mortality and institutionally regulated fertility. These three parts are followed by a brief summary and conclusion. Appendixes describe the data sources and the formal development of the dual-sector model.

9.2 Effects of Population Change

9.2.1 Overview

> For those who care for the overmastering pattern, the elements are evidently there for a heroically simplified version of English history before the nineteenth century in which the long-term movements in prices, in income distribution, in investment, in real wages, and in migration are dominated by changes in the growth of population. [Habakkuk 1965, p. 148]

This "heroically simplified version" of English history, which gives the central role to population change, appears to be accepted by a majority of economic historians. And since there was a rough synchronism of changes in population, wages, rents, and industrial and agricultural prices across Western Europe, many economic historians extend the same argument to the Continent as well.[3] The assertion is that when population grew, the additional labor that was applied to a relatively fixed amount of land brought diminishing returns, leading to falling real wages and rising real rents. Since industry's main input was labor, industrial prices closely followed the real wage. Thus a large population caused low prices for industrial goods relative to agricultural ones. Since, however, total agricultural incomes rose with population, so did the demand for industrial goods; thus industrial output—and with it urbanization—increased when population grew. This extension of the market encouraged specialization and trade.

Figure 9.1 shows the basic data series for England over the period 1250 to 1800. This analysis will focus on the latter part, from 1540 to 1800, for which better data are available; however, the earlier data help put this later period into perspective and strengthen the findings by suggesting their wider applicability. The data plotted in figure 9.1 are described in Appendix 9.1; however, the population series merits special mention. It is based on data from 404 parishes, collected and aggregated by the Cambridge Group for the History of Population and Social Structure. Although the population estimates used here are still preliminary, they are far superior to the demographic data previously available.

The series in figure 9.1 shows that the population-induced changes in the preindustrial economy were not trivial; rather, they were of fundamental importance to the people of the time. For example, the segment of society dependent primarily on wage income was comfortably off at the end of the fifteenth century; after a century of population growth their wages had fallen by 60% and their situation was desperate. Landlords were enriched over this period; industry grew rapidly; and industrial prices plummeted in relation to agricultural prices.

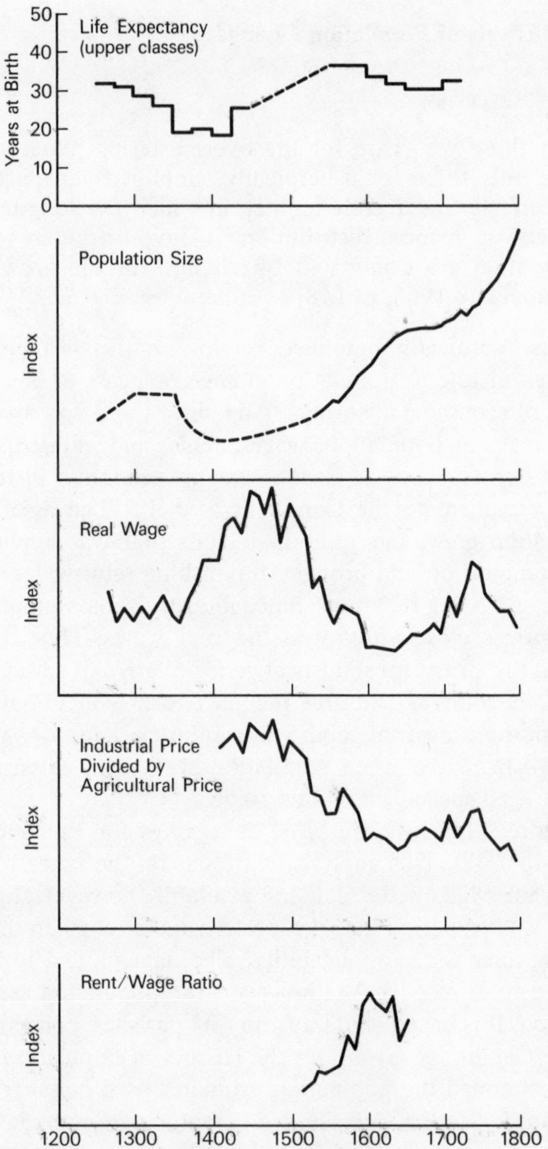

Fig. 9.1 Basic data for England, 1250–1800. For a description of the data and sources, see Appendix 9.1.

9.2.2 Population and Wages

Before developing and estimating the dual-sector model, I will examine the relation between population and wages in a simpler context. This will allow me to use annual data and to develop results comparable to my earlier work.

The wage is of interest because it reflects the marginal product of labor throughout the economy. It is also of interest because it represents the chief source of income for a large and growing segment of the population, rising from about 30% in rural areas in the sixteenth century to about 50% in 1700, and perhaps 75% in 1800 (Everitt 1967, pp. 397–99). While the wages of labor varied by skill and location, the various wage rates seem to have maintained rather fixed ratios one to the other (see Finberg 1967, p. 599, and Phelps-Brown and Hopkins 1955), so that a single wage can be used to represent changes over time in the experience of most workers.

Under competitive conditions, the real wage is determined by the intersection of the schedules relating labor supply and demand to the real wage. The labor demand schedule corresponds to the relation between the amount of labor utilized in the economy and its marginal productivity. This will depend on available land, capital, and technology, among other things, and in England during this period it is reasonable to expect changes in these to have increased the demand for labor in a cumulative manner. If the demand schedule shifts outward at a constant rate ρ, while maintaining its shape, then its position over time will be indexed by $e^{\rho t}$.

Now consider labor supply. In the short run, the labor services provided by the population might depend positively or negatively on the real wage, but there is no possibility of identifying such an effect empirically with these data. Over the longer run, the supply of labor varies roughly in proportion to population size, although the age-sex distribution of the population should also be taken into account.

The combined effects of the shifting supply and demand schedules on the short-run equilibrium wage may be expressed as:

$$(1) \qquad w_t = e^{\mu + \rho t + \epsilon_t} N_t^{-\eta},$$

or, in log form, as:

$$(2) \qquad ln\, w_t = \mu + \rho t - \eta ln N_t + \epsilon_t.$$

If the the short-run labor supply schedule is inelastic to the wage, then η measures the elasticity of the labor-demand schedule. The rate of shift of labor demand is ρ; μ is a scale parameter; and ϵ_t reflects the influence of climate and other omitted variables. The rate at which population can grow without altering the wage, or the rate of population "absorption," is ρ/η.

Note that from equation 2 the rate of change of wages $(\dot{w}/w)$ should be related to the rate of population change $(\dot{N}/N)$ by: $\dot{w}/w = \rho + \eta\dot{N}/N$. The data on w and N that were plotted in figure 9.1 can be used to get a rough idea of η and ρ/η. Inspection of the population series suggests the following periodization:

Date	*Population Growth Rate (% per year)*	*Rate of Change of Wages (% per year)*
1535–1605	.65	—.72
1605–45	.49	.15
1645–95	.08	.54
1695–1745	.23	.60
1745–95	.58	—.86

Figure 9.2 plots $\dot{w}/w$ against $\dot{N}/N$, treating each subperiod as an observation. There is indeed a clear negative relationship between the growth rates of population and wages, and the slope suggests that η is about —2 or —2.5. The rate of absorption is apparently about 0.4% per year, since at that rate of population growth, $\dot{w}/w = 0$. More rapid population growth sharply depresses wages; slower growth allows wages to rise.

The relation of wages to population over this period can be explored more exactly with regression analysis. For this purpose I have used not the real wage series shown in figure 9.1, which is deflated by agricultural prices alone, but the Phelps-Brown and Hopkins (1956) series, which is deflated by the cost of a mixed basket of goods including both agricultural and industrial commodities. This deflator is more appropriate for measuring welfare changes. The estimated equation is similar to equation 2, but somewhat more flexible. In addition to N, population size, I included variables $N1$ and $N2$, which give population size in subperiods, allowing the wage-population elasticities to be different in 1539–1638, 1639–1745, and 1746–1839. In addition to t, I also included t^3. This allows for the *rate* of shift to be quadratic in time, accelerating in the eighteenth century. Omitting the t^2 term constrains the rate of shift to change monotonically over the period. A special time variable, Dt, allows the period after 1809 to have a different rate of shift; this was included after inspection of residuals from earlier specifications. Finally, the error term was corrected for first-order autocorrelation, using the noniterative Cochrane-Orcutt procedure. The equation was fitted to annual data for 1539–1839, with the following result:

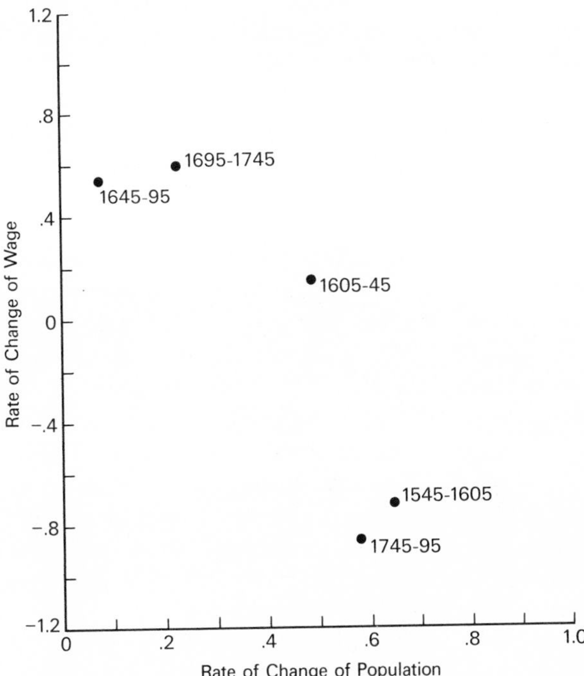

Fig. 9.2 Rates of change for population and wages in England, 1540–1800. Rates are given in percentage per year. Rates of change of wages are calculated from centered thirty-year averages of wages, except for 1795.

(3)

$$\underset{}{1nw_t} = \underset{(7.27)}{6.81} + \underset{(3.16)}{.0057t} - \underset{(.13)}{.18 \times 10^{-8}\, t^3} + \underset{(3.77)}{.008Dt}$$

$$- \underset{(5.61)}{1.51\, lnN_t} + \underset{(.87)}{.0071\, lnN1_t} + \underset{(.58)}{.0075\, lnN2_t}$$

$R^2 = .161$ (for changes in *lnw*);

t-statistics are given in parentheses below each estimate.

The results may be interpreted as follows:

i. Real wage levels were very sensitive to population size, with an elasticity of —1.5; thus a 10% increase in population caused a 15% decrease in real wages. This estimate is significant at the .001 level. The elasticity is lower than that suggested by figure 9.2 because of the difference in deflators.

ii. Surprisingly, there is virtually no change in this elasticity from subperiod to subperiod, as is shown by the small and insignificant coefficients for $1nN1$ and $1nN2$.

iii. The coefficients of t and t^3 show that the rate of shift in the relation between population and wages, reflecting technical change and capital accumulation, did not accelerate in the eighteenth century with early stages of the industrial revolution. This also is a surprising result.

iv. From 1539 to 1810, a population growth rate of 0.38% per year would have been consistent with a constant real wage. After the Napoleonic wars, the rate of shift more than doubled, and a growth rate of 0.88% per year would have left wages unchanged. This shows a dramatic alteration in the growth rate of the demand for labor.

v. The low R^2 is due to the Cochrane-Orcutt transformation, which causes quasi-differences in the data, emphasizing their short-run variability.

Perhaps the most striking aspect of all these estimates is the size of the wage-population elasticity. If production obeyed a Cobb-Douglas production function, these elasticities would equal minus the share of nonlabor inputs, or 0.4 to 0.6. The estimate above is about three times this great, suggesting that the Cobb-Douglas interpretation is incorrect. I will discuss this point in detail in the next section.

Since t^3, $N1$, and $N2$ all had insignificant effects, and the period after 1809 seemed quite different, I reestimated a simpler version of equation 3 for 1539–1809, correcting for second-order autocorrelation using an iterative Cochrane-Orcutt procedure.

$$(4) \qquad lnw_t = \underset{(11.73)}{25.59} + \underset{(10.03)}{.00645t} - \underset{(9.23)}{1.62\, lnN_t}$$

$$R^2 = .75 \qquad DW = 1.97$$

$$R^2 \text{ for changes} = .19;$$

t-statistics are given in parentheses. These estimates are consistent with equation 3. The implied rate of absorption is 0.4% per year, and the wage-population elasticity is —1.62.

It is interesting to compare the results of this part with previous work I have done using less satisfactory demographic data[4] (see table on next page).

The elasticities estimated in equations 3 and 4 are larger in absolute value than the earlier estimates, but given the differences in data, time periods, and time units, I do not find the differences troubling. The principal inconsistency arises from the estimates of rate of population absorption. The previous studies, taken together, suggest a fivefold in-

Source	Period Covered	Time Units	Wage-Population Elasticity (η)	Annual Rate of Absorption
Lee 1973	1250–1700	50 years	−1.10 (7.05)	.00089
Lee 1977	1705–89	5 years	−1.29 (3.69)	.0046
Equation 4	1539–1809	1 year	−1.62 (9.23)	.0040

crease in this rate between 1250–1700 and 1705–89. This increase seems a plausible reflection of the agricultural and industrial revolutions. However the estimate in equation 3 shows no sign of an accelerating rate of shift. I have no explanation for this inconsistency, although the estimated dual-sector model will show that this constant rate of absorption masks important differences in rates of shift between sectors.

9.2.3 A Dual-Sector Model

The effects of population growth on the economy can be understood in richer detail if we distinguish between the agricultural and nonagricultural sectors. In this section I will develop a simple model of a dual-sector economy; in a subsequent section I will test it empirically. In the model, agricultural production exhibits sharply diminishing returns to labor, owing to the relatively fixed supply of land. Industrial production, which uses labor and agricultural output in fixed proportions, encounters no such bottleneck. The demand for industrial and agricultural output is such as to leave their shares in national income constant, when valued at current prices.

Throughout I will assume that the English economy was closed. In fact, exports made up about 5% or 6% of national income in 1688, rising to 14% by 1800 (see Deane and Cole 1969, p. 309). Some justification for the closure assumption is given by Kelley and Williamson in the context of Meiji Japan (1974, chap. 12).[5]

Capital and capitalists are ignored completely by the model, except that land-augmenting investment and technical progress at a constant rate are allowed in agriculture.[6] This is a model of a preindustrial economy; the industrial sector is largely passive and is not intended to provide insights into the beginnings of the industrial revolution. Details of the development of the model are given in Appendix 9.2; here I will discuss only the assumptions and the main results.

Industrial Production

The nonagricultural sector, which I will for convenience call "industrial," provides such diverse items as domestic service, buildings, textiles, lace, household goods, iron products, and so on.[7] Production in this sector directly requires only trivial amounts of land. The main inputs are labor and agricultural output, such as skins, wool, and grain. I assume that these inputs are combined in fixed proportions.

By appropriate choice of units of measure for agricultural output, A, and labor, N, the fixed input coefficients can be made to equal unity. Thus,

$$I = min(N_I, A_I), \tag{5}$$

where I is "industrial" output, N_I is labor employed in the industrial sector, and A_I is agricultural output used in the industrial sector. If no inputs are wasted, then:

$$I = N_I = A_I. \tag{6}$$

I will further assume that there are no profits in this sector, so that the price of industrial output, P_I, just equals the cost of inputs, $W_I + P_A$, where W_I is the industrial-sector wage and P_A is the price of agricultural output. A comparison of the wages of builders' helpers (Phelps-Brown and Hopkins 1955) and agricultural laborers employed in nonseasonal work without remuneration in kind (Finberg 1967) shows that these were equal in southern England from 1450 to 1650. I will therefore assume that $W_I = W_A$ and drop the subscript. Thus:

$$P_I = W + P_A, \tag{7}$$

or, taking A as the numeraire, as I will throughout,

$$p = w + 1, \tag{8}$$

where $p = PA/PI$ and $w = W/P_A$.

From equation 8 it is easy to determine the effect of population change on the terms of trade between industry and agriculture. Let $\gamma_I = w/p$ be labor costs as a proportion of total costs in industry. Then, if $N = N_A + N_I$ is the total labor force (by assumption, fully employed), and E denotes "elasticity,"

$$E_{p,N} = \gamma_I E_{w,N}. \tag{9}$$

Changes in technology and formation of industrial capital can best be described as labor-saving rather than material-saving. This was particularly true for textile manufacture but probably was false for the iron industry, which became important only at the very end of the period. Labor-augmenting change at the constant rate ρ has the effect of reducing labor requirements by a factor of $e^{-\rho t}$. Thus, for example, equation 8 can be rewritten:

$$p = e^{-\rho t} w + 1. \tag{10}$$

The Demand for Industrial Output

The amount of industrial output demanded by a household typically depends on its income, with an elasticity greater than 1, and on the relative price of industrial goods, with an elasticity less than 0. These effects can be incorporated at the household level by a linear expenditure system, which has the advantage of being aggregable. Although it would be desirable to incorporate such a demand specification, in the present model I assume that the shares of agriculture and industry in national income, valued at current prices, are fixed. This is equivalent to assuming income elasticities of unity for both kinds of goods, and price elasticities of minus one. The assumption is not so implausible as it may first appear, since the incomes of landlords and laborers typically moved in opposite directions. Historical data suggest a major decline in agriculture's share at the end of the eighteenth century but have been interpreted in conflicting ways concerning earlier changes.[8]

Final product in agriculture is total product less the portion used in the industrial sector: $A - I$. The value of total output is: $A - I + pI = A + I\,(p - 1)$. The assumption of constant shares can conveniently be written:

$$pI = \lambda(A - I), \tag{11}$$

since this yields a share of final product in agriculture of $1/(1 + \lambda)$, a constant.

This does not mean, of course, that in real terms the ratio of nonagricultural to agricultural consumption was constant; quite the contrary. Growing population would confront diminishing returns in agriculture, depressing wages and industrial prices, as indicated by equation 9. The assumption of a constant share of industry in national income would therefore require an increasing share of industry in *real* output, when population grew. And indeed this is historically accurate (see Deane and Cole 1969, p. 162).

The ratio of industrial to agricultural output, both intermediate and final, I/A, turns out to be:

$$I/A = \lambda/(w + 1 + \lambda). \tag{12}$$

This clearly increases as w falls; therefore, when population grows, industrial output increases more, proportionately, than does agricultural output. For a detailed discussion, see Appendix 2F.

Agricultural Production

Unlike industry, agricultural production is constrained by a relatively invariant supply of potentially arable land. However, conditions of agricultural production certainly did not remain static over the period under consideration. On the one hand, new rotations were adopted and new crops sown, land tenure arrangements were altered, and greater use was made of farm animals and fertilizer. Some of these changes may be regarded as reactions to changing factor prices, themselves due to population change; others represent genuine technological progress. On the other hand, the supply of land was increased through investment in such projects as draining the fens; and investments also facilitated the more efficient use of existing arable land, particularly in association with enclosure. These changes can be described as "land-augmenting." Lacking detailed information on the timing and extent of these changes, I will attempt to capture them by an exponential trend.

As noted above, the large (in absolute value) estimated wage-population elasticity is inconsistent with a Cobb-Douglas production function; so a CES (constant elasticity of substitution) production function will be assumed in agriculture. Denoting by F the initial quantity of land, and by ρ the rate at which land is augmented by reclamation, investment, and technological progress, the CES production function can be written:

$$(13) \qquad A = \mu_0[\mu_1 (Fe^{\rho t})^{-\beta} + (1 - \mu_1) N_A{}^{-\beta}]^{-1/\beta}.$$

If agricultural labor is paid its marginal product, then $w = [(1 - \mu_1)/\mu_0{}^\beta](A/N_A)^{1+\beta}$ or, alternatively, for appropriate a and b:

$$(14) \qquad w = a[N_A{}^\beta e^{-\beta\rho t} + b]^{-(1+\beta)/\beta}.$$

This relation can be estimated from data on real wages and employment in agriculture.

Total rents—whether explicitly treated as such or merely imputed to land—are the remainder after labor has been paid: $R = A - wN_A$, where R is total money rents divided by P_A. In a CES production function, the ratio of returns to inputs is simply related to the ratio of input quantities; here:

$$(15) \qquad R/w = [(1 - \mu_1)/\mu_1]N_A{}^{1+\beta}e^{-\beta\rho t} F^{-(1+\beta)}.$$

Alternatively, the rent per efficiency-unit of land, $r = R/(Fe^{\rho t})$, is related to wages by:

$$(16) \qquad r/w = [(1 - \mu_1)/\mu_1]N_A{}^{1+\beta}e^{-(\beta+1)\rho t} F^{-(1+\beta)}.$$

These equations are easily estimable after a log transformation. However, it is impossible to know for any particular rent series whether it indexes R or r, since it may or may not include the return to new investments in the land.

An important shortcoming of this analysis is that investment in agriculture is left exogenous and is indeed assumed to take place at a constant rate. But it is clear that agricultural investment and also perhaps technical change was more rapid when rents and agricultural prices were relatively high, and these themselves depended on population. It might be possible to get at these issues empirically through analysis of bills of enclosure. By ignoring these effects, I have surely overstated the long-run negative effects of population growth in England. However, regressions that do not include a shift term do not suffer from this bias, and they confirm the negative effects of population, although with a lower elasticity (see Lee 1973, p. 588).

Labor Force Allocation

In this model, wages vary because of variation in the labor employed in agriculture, N_A. However, data on N_A are not available; there are only data on N, the total labor force. Estimated relations between w and N reflect in part the effect of N on the allocation of labor between the two sectors. For this reason it is important to analyze the determinants of sectoral labor force allocation.

In Appendix 9.2.B it is shown that:

$$N_A/N = \gamma_A/[\gamma_A + \lambda w/(p+\lambda)], \tag{17}$$

where γ_A is labor's proportional share of agricultural output, which makes it possible to calculate the implied labor force share of agriculture.

In Appendix 9.2.C, following Marc Nerlove's analysis of this model, it is shown that:

$$E_{N_A,N} = \left\{1 + E_{w,N}\frac{N_I}{N}\frac{w}{(p+\lambda)}\right\} / \left\{1 - (1-\gamma_A)\frac{N_I}{N}\right\}. \tag{18}$$

This result is particularly useful, because it makes possible the calculation of E_{w,N_A} and $\sigma = 1/(1+\beta)$. In Appendix 9.2.D it is shown that:

$$\sigma = -(1-\gamma_A)E_{N_A,N}/E_{w,N}. \tag{19}$$

9.2.4 Empirical Results for the Two-Sector Model

Population and Wages

Under the CES specification, the elasticity of wages with respect to labor is a variable, not a constant. It is therefore inappropriate to estimate log-linear equations such as equations 1 through 4 above. The appropriate procedure is to estimate the highly nonlinear equation 14, using maximum likelihood methods. My attempts to do so failed; the program encountered nearly singular matrixes it could not invert. An alternative approach is to estimate a log-quadratic approximation (see

Kmenta 1971, pp. 462–65); my attempts to estimate β and σ in this way were also unsuccessful. Therefore I reverted to estimates of the log-linear equation, a decidedly inferior procedure.

In the dual-sector context, the log-linear wage-population regressions discussed above in section 9.2.2 are *not* appropriate, since the real wage employed there was based on a fixed basket of goods that included both industrial and agricultural products. This is an appropriate standard to use for welfare comparisons, but for the purpose at hand the money wage should be deflated by agricultural prices alone. The regression reported below uses decadal averages of money wages from Phelps-Brown and Hopkins (1955) for 1540 through 1700, and for the eighteenth century uses a series reported in Deane and Cole (1969, p. 19), which takes into account regional differences in wages and population growth. The wage is deflated using the agricultural price index described in Appendix 1.

Rather than using total population as a proxy for labor supply, it was possible to take account of age structure, as estimated by the inverse projection method (see Lee 1974). Ages 0–14 were weighted by zero, 15–64 by 1, and 65+ by 0.5.

Several versions of the log-linear regression were run. The one reported below allows for different $E_{w,N}$ in three time periods: 1540–1629, 1630–1719, and 1720–1800. It also includes linear and cubic shift terms.

(20)
$$\begin{aligned} ln(w) = {} & \underset{(9.16)}{14.6} + \underset{(5.21)}{.0103t} - \underset{(3.43)}{.533 \times 10^{-7}t^3} \\ & - \underset{(7.08)}{2.22\, lnN} + \underset{(1.20)}{.0197\, lnN1} + \underset{(2.31)}{.0596\, lnN2} \\ & R^2 = .832 \qquad D.W. = 2.14. \end{aligned}$$

There are several points worth noting. First, the estimates of $E_{w,N}$, which range from -2.22 to -2.16 depending on the period, are even greater in absolute value than those in section 9.2.2. In other specifications of this equation, not reported here, they reach -2.7. There is a simple explanation for the discrepancy between these and the earlier results: when the cost of a mixed bundle of commodities is used to deflate the money wage, population change induces partially offsetting variations in the costs of the industrial and agricultural components. Therefore the estimated elasticity is closer to zero.

Second, although there is a statistically significant change in $E_{w,N}$ for the last subperiod, the effect is numerically inconsequential.

Third, and quite striking, the initial annual rate of land-augmenting change, measured as ρ/η, is 0.45%, but by 1800 it has declined to zero (that is, for fixed N, $\partial lnw/\partial t$ evaluated at $t = 260$ is roughly zero).

In other specifications the rate of shift also declines, but only by about two-thirds. This eighteenth-century retardation in agricultural progress is consistent with the view of Deane and Cole (1969, p. 75), which was based on quite different evidence.

Population and Terms of Trade

Data for constructing the terms-of-trade index were available for ten-year periods from 1541–50 to 1791–1800, giving 26 observations. Some splicing was necessary, and the last 100 years of the series are not completely comparable with the first 160. This is a serious difficulty with the results presented below, since different industrial commodities have different labor intensities. Nonetheless, I have taken the data at face value for present purposes.

In developing the model, I made simplifying assumptions about units of measure. In practice the simplifying transformations can be made only after estimation has taken place. The equation estimated, therefore, was not equation 10; two scaling parameters were added, as well as a more flexible rate of labor-saving progress. The following are maximum likelihood estimates:

$$p_t = \underset{(4.24)}{12.8} + \underset{(14.1)}{1.63}e^{-\underset{(2.49)}{.0017t}-\underset{(2.79)}{.243\times 10^{-7}t^3}}w_t \qquad (21)$$

$$R^2 = .91 \qquad D.W. = 1.58.$$

This estimated equation can be transformed to the form of (10) by defining: $\tilde{p} = p/12.8$ and $\tilde{w} = (1.63/12.8)w = .127w$. Then:

$$\tilde{p}_t = 1 + e^{-.00117t-.243\times 10^{-7}t^3}\tilde{w}_t. \qquad (22)$$

The estimated coefficients of t and t^3 imply an annual rate of labor-saving change of only 0.117% in 1540, rising to 0.304% in 1700 and 0.061% in 1800. Thus, while the rate of progress in agriculture was declining, that in industry was accelerating. The cumulative effect of this change was to reduce the labor inputs per unit of output by 25% between 1540 and 1700, and between 1700 and 1800 by a further 36%. Over the entire 260-year period, labor requirements were reduced to 48% of their initial level.

The rates of shift in the two sectors, and their changes over time, are plotted in figure 9.3. The time paths appear to be mirror images, and the sum of the two rates is nearly constant. This reveals clearly the sectoral differences that were concealed by the constant rate of absorption.

The parameter estimates in equation 21 can also be used to estimate γ_I, labor's share of costs in industry. The average wage was 29.5, which transforms to $.127 \times 29.5 = 3.75$. Initially, therefore, $\gamma_I = 3.75/4.75 = .79$; labor costs were about 80% of total costs of industrial produc-

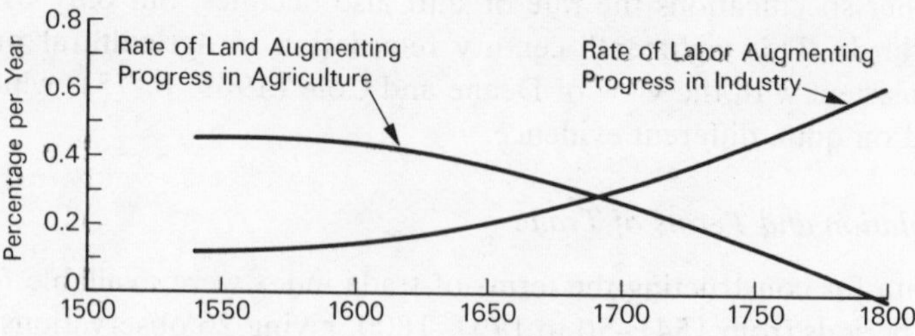

Fig. 9.3 Estimated rates of progress in agriculture and industry. Calculated from equations 20 and 21.

tion. By 1800, however, γ_I had fallen to $.48 \times 3.75/(.48 \times 3.75 + 1) = .64$. These estimates suggest that the effect of population change on terms of trade also declined (see eq. 9). In 1540, $E_{p,N} = .79(-2.22) = -1.75$; in 1800, $E_{p,N} = .64(-2.16) = -1.38$. These estimates seem on the high side (in absolute value) when compared directly with historical evidence (see Lee 1973, p. 591).

I should caution that domestic service, which made up a large proportion of the nonagricultural sector, is not included in the industrial price index. The effect of its inclusion would doubtless be to raise γ, labor's share of the cost inputs.

Population and Rent

Of all the data series, that for rent is undoubtedly the worst (see Appendix 1E). It is the shortest, covering only the period 1540 to 1660, in time units of ten years; thus there are only twelve observations. It is also unclear just what theoretical concept is represented: Does the series include rents on marginal lands brought into cultivation only under pressure of rising agricultural prices? If so, the increase in rents as population grows will be understated. Does it include rent changes reflecting investment in the land?

I used the rent series to form the ratio R/w, which under the CES specification is log-linearly related to N_A, as in equations 14 and 15. The actual regression uses N, not N_A; results can be interpreted with the help of $E_{N_A,N}$ (see Appendix 2E).

$$(23) \qquad ln(R_t/w_t) = -36.6 - .0420t + 7.50\, lnN_t$$
$$(2.99) \quad (2.63) \quad (3.08)$$
$$R^2 = .77 \qquad D.W. = 2.60.$$

Because the time period is relatively short, and population was growing fairly rapidly over most of it, time is quite colinear with lnN. When a quadratic or cubic time-shift term is included, population's coefficient becomes small and insignificant.

The implied annual rate of land augmenting change is roughly .042/ 7.50 = 0.56%, compared with an estimate of 0.44% for this period from equation 20.

From equation 20 or equation 23, we can derive an estimate of the elasticity of substitution in agriculture. First, however, $E_{N_A,N}$ must be evaluated using equation A20 in Appendix 2. This requires estimates of N_I/N, γ_A, $E_{w,N}$, and $w/(p+\lambda)$. Reasonable mean values of these variables are $N_I/N = .35$, $\gamma_A = .45$, $E_{w,N} = -2.22$, and $w/(p+\lambda) = .6$.[9] These imply $E_{N_A,N} = .66$, so that as population rises, the proportion of the labor force agriculture declines quite markedly. Using equations A22 and A27, the implied estimates of σ can be derived. These are 0.16 from equation 20 or 0.09 from equation 23. The first figure is surely more accurate, since it is based on the full 260 years, while the second is based on only 120 years.

Is an estimated elasticity of substitution as low as 0.16 at all plausible? I am not sufficiently familiar with the agricultural techniques used to be able to form a judgment. Most modern studies of agricultural production report values in the neighborhood of unity, although low values, near 0.2, have been estimated for Meiji Japan (Sawada 1970) and India (Srivastava and Heady 1973).

The reader may have noted that all the estimates of population's effects were made using single-equation methods. However, if population growth rates are themselves dependent on economic welfare, then the system is simultaneously determined, and single equation methods will yield biased parameter estimates. In previous work (1973, 1978*a*, *b*) I have dealt with this problem at length. It turns out that simultaneity bias is not very important when estimating *effects* of population change; it is, however, a serious problem when examining the causes of population change. So the results reported in this part should not have been seriously biased by the use of single-equation methods.

Miscellaneous Effects of Population Growth

I have already discussed the effects of population growth, relative to augmented land, on wages, rents, and the terms of trade. Population also affected the composition of output. In Appendix 2, expressions for the effect of population on I and on I/A are derived (see eq. A29, A30). Evaluating these expressions gives $E_{I/A,N} = 1.33$ and $E_{I,N} = 1.65$. Thus a 10% increase in population would increase I/A by 13% and increase I by 16.5%.

Labor-saving progress in industry has a similar effect on the composition of output. Evaluating expression A42 yields $E_{I,\alpha} = -.85$; thus almost all the labor released by progress in industry is used to boost output in industry.

The effects of technical change and population growth taken together go a long way toward explaining the rapid industrial growth of the late eighteenth century. Using expression A28 for I/A and evaluating it in 1731–40 and in 1791–1800, I find that over this sixty-year period, industrial output in *real* terms should have increased by 60% more than did agricultural output. This compares with a figure of 90% derived from Deane and Cole (1969, p. 78). Thus the combination of rapid population growth, rapid improvement in industrial technology, and slowing change in agricultural technology accounts for much of the increased importance of industry.

Population growth also had an important effect on the factor distribution of income. For farmers working their own land, these effects would have been relatively unimportant; but for landlords and laborers the effects were very large. Evaluating expression A37, I find $E_{S,N} = -1.4$, where S is labor's share of total output. Thus a 10% increase in population would reduce S from perhaps 55% to 47%.

Finally, I should stress that the estimated value of $E_{w,N} = -2.22$ greatly *overstates* the effect of population change on material welfare, because the wage is expressed in terms of the agricultural commodity. Consider instead a wage deflator based on a 50-50 mix (in terms of mean value) of agricultural and industrial commodities. This is essentially the real wage concept measured by Phelps-Brown and Hopkins (1956), and used in section 9.2.2 above. Call this real wage w^*. Then, given actual mean values for w and p, it can be shown that $E_{w^*,N} \doteq (5/8)E_{w,N} \doteq -1.4$.[10] This agrees very well with the estimates of section 9.2.2 above (−1.5 and −1.6).

9.3 Causes of Population Change

9.3.1 A Test of Two Simple Theories

The broad issues were already sketched in the Introduction: Is population an endogenous element in the socioeconomic system, regulated by norms and institutions so as to establish and protect a culturally defined standard of living? Or is population an independent force that determines levels of living, and to which the society and economy must adjust as best they can? The former view has been held by many classical and neoclassical economists from Malthus to Harberger (1958, pp. 109–10), and by many biologists and ecologists as well (e.g., Dubos 1965, pp. 286–87). The latter view is generally held by historians, demographers, and some economists.

In its simplest form the classical theory—which makes population endogenous—posits a functional relation between the population growth rate and the level of wages. There will be some wage corresponding to zero population growth; this equilibrium wage is the conventional living standard or natural price of labor. In figure 9.4 I have plotted population growth rates against the wage level for twenty-five-year periods, 1550 to 1799, using the data introduced above. It is clear that there is no strong relation between the two; the scatter provides no support for the classical theory as applied to this period. In fact, similar results hold for the entire period 1250 to 1789 (see Lee 1973, 1978*a*).

The alternate theory holds that population varied independently. The simplest version argues that fertility is maintained at relatively fixed levels by institutions and customs that have evolved over the long run to ensure population replacement. Over the shorter run, population growth rates are determined by variations in mortality, since fertility does not change. In figure 9.5 I have plotted English population growth rates against the life expectancy of the British aristocracy (see Appendix 1A) for twenty-five-year periods, 1550 to 1724. After 1724, this life-expectancy series is no longer representative of the general population; before then, it compares well with other series in so far as changes are concerned, if not levels.[11] Figure 9.5 shows a very close relation between mortality and population change over this 175-year period. And since the data come from totally different sources, there is no possibility that the relation is an artifact due to errors in measurement.

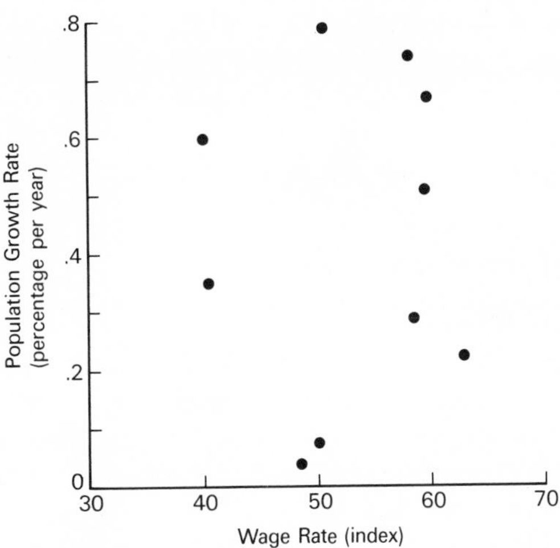

Fig. 9.4 Population growth rates and the real wage for twenty-five year periods, 1550–74 to 1775–1799.

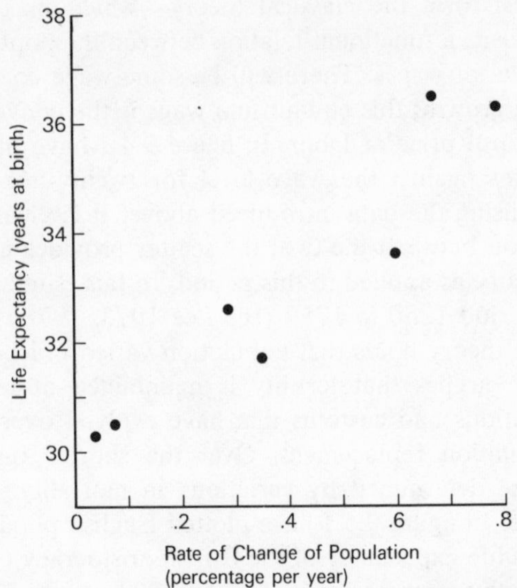

Fig. 9.5 Population growth rates and life expectancy of the British aristocracy, by twenty-five-year periods 1550–74 to 1700–1724.

This is strong support for the view that population growth rates varied independently, not primarily in response to changes in wages or the demand for labor (for formal tests of these hypotheses see Lee 1973, 1978*a*, *b*). But how then are we to explain the broad historical agreement of economic and demographic trends? In subsequent sections I will discuss in more detail the mechanisms thought to have regulated population in relation to resources in preindustrial Western Europe and attempt to reconcile the dependent and independent aspects of population change.

9.3.2 Fertility and Mortality

The Preventive Check

To the extent that European societies controlled population, it was almost entirely through regulation of fertility, not mortality. The conventional view of the mechanism linking fertility to resources in preindustrial Western Europe has not changed in broad outline since Malthus: Marriage required a sufficient livelihood, in the form of property or an adequate wage income. "Sufficiency" was defined by longstanding norms and institutions, which varied from country to country. Thus Malthus thought that the English were more prosperous than other Europeans *because* they regarded wheat and meat as necessities and would not marry without income enough to provide them for their families. Europeans in general were regarded as more prosperous than other peoples *because* they required more comfortable circumstances before they were willing to marry. Once married, couples were believed to bear children at a "natural" rate, while making no efforts to control family size. Such a system would relate aggregate fertility rates to per capita income or wealth, and to wage rates.

Whereas historical demographers have confirmed the general outline of the natural fertility theory, a number of studies have shown that in the eighteenth and nineteenth centuries, at least, marital fertility as well as nuptiality responded positively to the harvest cycle. There is also some mixed evidence that on balance suggests that wealthier couples may not only have married earlier, but also have had higher fertility within marriage (see Smith 1977).

The Cambridge Group's aggregate parish register data set makes it possible to analyze the effect on vital rates of short-run variations in the real wage. It provides series of the annual numbers of baptisms, burials, and marriages in 404 parishes from 1539 to 1839. In theoretical work described elsewhere (Lee 1975, 1978*a*) I have shown that short-run fluctuations in such series can be interpreted as fluctuations in marital fertility, mortality, and nuptiality. This enables us to draw demographic inferences from changes in the numbers of events without bothering about the size and structure of the population at risk. I have also shown (Lee 1978*a*) that short-run fluctuations can be used to study the causes of population change without contamination by the simultaneity in the system.

I have used cross-spectral analysis to estimate these relations, in part because for compelling reasons the theoretical analysis mentioned above had to be carried out in spectral terms.[12] However, given the theoretical results, the empirical work could have been carried out by regression analysis after suitable "filtering" of the series.

Spectral analysis examines the variances and covariances of sets of series by frequency or periodicity. Any detrended series may be examined in this way; there is no presumption that there are cycles in the data. It is convenient, although not entirely accurate, to think of frequency here as distinguishing, say, between long-run (low-frequency) and short-run (high-frequency) components of variation in the series. My previous work has established that for wavelengths of less than fifteen years or so, the population size and age structure, and the duration structure of marriages, have only negligible effects on births, deaths, and marriages. For my purposes, therefore, I will refer to these as "short run."

I will use three basic cross-spectral concepts in this paper. The first is "coherence squared," denoted $C^2(\lambda)$, which is analogous to R^2 in regression analysis but is specific to wavelength λ. The second is phase shift, $\phi(\lambda)$, which measures the lag of one series behind the other in radians at each wavelength. The third is "gain squared," $G^2(\lambda)$, which is analogous to the square of a regression coefficient, again specific to wavelength.

Estimated cross spectra for births and marriages in relation to wages are presented in figure 9.6. First consider births. For periods of thirteen years or less, $C^2(\lambda)$ is typically significantly greater than zero, indicating that wage fluctuations did indeed affect marital fertility, explaining perhaps 25% of the variance. The phase shift diagram indicates that marital fertility lagged slightly behind the wage rate, by something less than a year. I have not drawn in confidence bands for the phase estimates, but

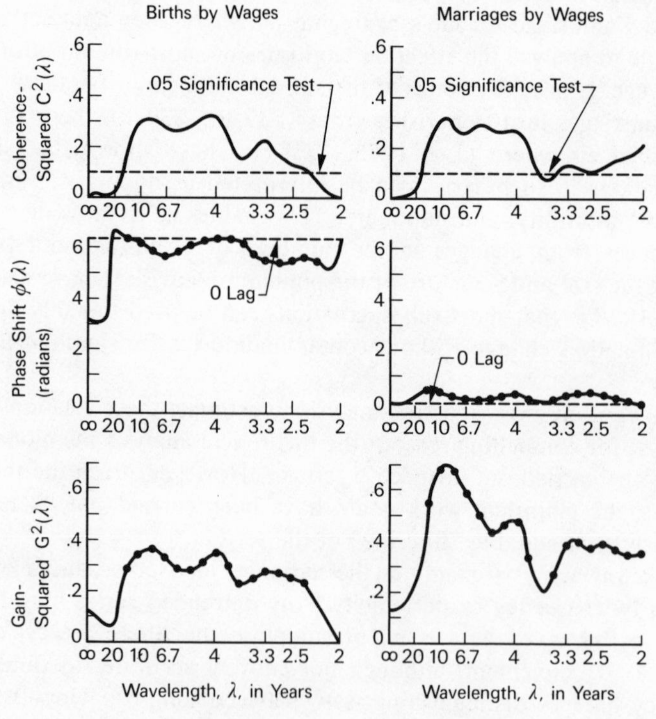

Fig. 9.6 Cross-spectral estimates of births and marriages by wages for England, 1539–1839. Phase estimates indicated by solid circles correspond to significant estimates of coherence squared and are more accurate than others. Estimates were made using a Parzen window with T = 301, M = 20. Births, marriages, and wages were measured as the residuals from a regression of the lag of the basic series on time.

they are very narrow, typically about ± 0.3 radians. The estimates of $G^2(\lambda)$ can here be interpreted as elasticities,[13] suggesting a value of 0.3. I also estimated separate cross spectra for each of the periods 1539–1638, 1639–1745, and 1746–1839 and found virtually identical results within each subperiod. This establishes the existence of a procyclical response of marital fertility to wages as far back as the sixteenth century, with no noticeable change in the timing or sensitivity of the relationship.

The estimated cross spectrum for marriages and wages shows a coherence-squared very similar to that for fertility. The phase diagram shows that nuptiality responded to wages with no lag at all, in contrast to fertility. The gain-squared estimates show that the elasticity for nuptiality was on the order of 0.5, or nearly twice as high as that of fertility. Generally, the association was closer and more sensitive for fluctuations of about ten years' periodicity than it was for very short-run fluctuations. To summarize, these results show that as far back as the sixteenth century, both marital fertility and nuptiality were strongly influenced by short-run variations in the real wage, which explained 20% to 30% of their short-run variance. Without making any judgment on whether the association of marital fertility with wage variations was due to voluntary limitation of fertility, these results provide some support for the existence of an aggregate relation between general fertility and wages.[14]

The Positive Check

While the role of exogenous mortality decline in the current LDCs' rapid population growth is widely acknowledged, it is less well known that large exogenous changes in mortality occurred in the past, leading to major population swings in Europe from the thirteenth through the eighteenth centuries. And I refer not to catastrophic mortality associated with periodic harvest failure or epidemic, but rather to long-run changes persisting for decades or centuries. The causes of these shifts are obscure; they may have been climatic, or the by-product of independent epidemiological and ecological changes, or the result of voyages of exploration. But that these changes occurred is clear; their magnitude is suggested by the life expectancy series for upper-class Englishmen shown in figure 9.1. Other confirming evidence is found both for England and for the Continent in reconstitution studies based on parish registers, in data from religious orders and the professions, and in the analysis of wills and death taxes. The exogeneity of the changes is clear from their temporal relation to changes in wages and population size, and from their disregard for class distinctions (see Chambers 1972; Lee 1973, 1978*a* and 1978*b*).

I do not mean to suggest that mortality was completely independent of income; but the importance of this endogenous component has been greatly exaggerated. The extent to which mortality was associated with wages in the short-run can be studied with the Cambridge Group's parish data; figure 9.7 shows the relevant cross-spectral estimates. The coherence-squared indicates that only about 10% of the variance is explained, less than half the amount explained for nuptiality and marital fertility. The phase diagram is somewhat erratic but suggests that mortality and wages were negatively related, with mortality lagging by from zero to one year. The squared gain, not shown here, suggests an elasticity of about —0.5. (For an analysis of wages and mortality by cause of death in sixteenth- and seventeenth-century London, see Mirowski 1976.)

I have also analyzed the relation of wages to the rate of natural increase; these results are also shown in figure 9.7. The coherence-squared averages about 0.15, with a very small lag of growth behind wages. The elasticity is not a useful measure of sensitivity in this case. It is more helpful to note that a doubling of the real wage would increase the population growth rate by about 1.25% per year, ceteris paribus.

Direct Links of Fertility to Mortality

I have so far discussed the relations of fertility and mortality to wages. Now I will briefly consider the possibility that there were direct links of fertility to mortality, such that fertility would adjust to changes in mortality. Several such links have been suggested in the literature. One is that, through inheritance, high mortality resulted in the transfer of assets to the nubile, thus increasing nuptiality, then fertility (Ohlin 1961). The cross spectrum of marriages and deaths lends some support to this hypothesis. However, it is only the redistributive effect that should be counted here; changes in the population/wealth ratio are an indirect influence of mortality on fertility, already reflected in the wage rate. Another suggested link is that couples may have attempted to replace unexpected infant and child deaths and that, when mortality changed, they would eventually revise their mortality expectations and adjust their fertility accordingly. This argument requires the assumption that couples controlled their fertility and strove for some number of surviving children, in contrast to the natural-fertility hypothesis. Knodel (1975) has shown that this "replacement hypothesis" is false for a sample of preindustrial European parish populations. My own studies of the short-run relation of fertility to mortality show a very strong *negative* relation. Perhaps the most convincing evidence that fertility did not strongly compensate for mortality changes even over the long run is given by figure 9.5, which shows a very close correlation of mortality and population growth rates over a period of 175 years.

To sum up section 9.3, I have shown that, at least in the short-run, there was an endogenous component to population change, operating through nuptiality, marital fertility, and mortality. Presumably these

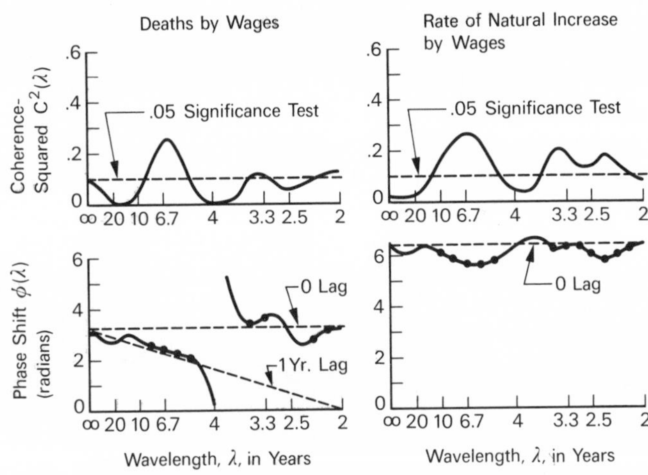

Fig. 9.7 Cross-spectral estimates of deaths and rate of natural increase in relation to real wages for England, 1539–1839. Phase estimates indicated by solid circles correspond to significant estimates of coherence-squared and are more accurate than the others. Estimates were made using a Parzen window with T = 301, M = 20. Deaths and wages were measured as residuals from the regression of the log of the basic series on time. Natural increase was used untransformed.

short-run relations also held over the long run, although these data provide no evidence on this point. Even in the short run, however, wages account for only about 15% of the variance in growth rates, so that most of the variation is exogenous. Furthermore, inspection of long-run life-expectancy series, as in figures 9.1 and 9.4, suggests that long-run variation in population growth rates was also dominated by exogenous variation.

Under these circumstances, over the very long run, the average wage level will be an important determinant of average population growth rates. But even over the course of centuries, fluctuations of growth rates about that average level may be largely exogenous.

9.4 A Model of Economic-Demographic Equilibrium

At this point it will be helpful to introduce a simple equilibrating model relating fertility, mortality, wages, and population. Rent and terms of trade could also be added, but they play an essentially passive role and would only clutter the diagram.

The relation of fertility and mortality to wages, measured by their crude rates b and d, may be plotted as in the top half of figure 9.8. The

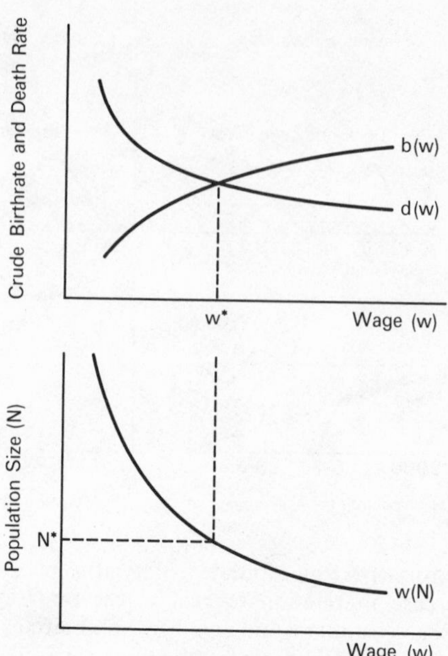

Fig. 9.8 Economic-demographic equilibrium.

level and curvature of the birthrate curve are determined primarily by norms and institutions, although at very low wages biological considerations may become important. Some societies might have horizontal fertility curves, if neither nuptiality nor marital fertility depended on material well-being. Societies with institutional arrangements conducive to high fertility, such as the extended family system, would have higher birthrate curves than those with less pronatalist institutions, such as the nuclear family. The death-rate curve is primarily biologically determined, although such additional factors as income distribution, centralized famine precautions, and in some cases infanticide and geronticide are also important.

The population growth rate, equal to $b - d$, is given by the difference between the two schedules; where they intersect, the growth rate is zero and the population is stationary. The corresponding wage, w^*, is variously known as the "long-run equilibrium wage," the "natural wage," the "conventional standard of living," or "subsistence."

The lower half of the diagram shows the relation between the wage rate and the size of the population; it corresponds to the demand for labor, which I assume is fixed. Corresponding to the equilibrium wage is an equilibrium size of population, N^*. There will also be equilibrium levels of rent and terms of trade, which are not shown. Evidently the equilibrium is stable; when population size is below N^* its growth rate will be positive, and conversely.

Now consider the effect of a once-for-all shift in the demand for labor; this situation is shown in figure 9.9. When $w(N)$ shifts out to $w_1(N)$, the wage will initially rise, inducing population growth until population attains its new equilibrium at the old wage level. Thus, over the long run, population responds passively to economic advance, while a roughly constant level of material well-being is maintained; this is the "iron law of wages."

Now consider the effect of a permanent exogenous decline in mortality, shifting the schedule from $d(w)$ to $d_1(w)$. This is shown in figure 9.10.[15] The decline in mortality lowers the equilibrium wage and population size; growth rates are initially positive until a new equilibrium is established with lower fertility and wages and larger population size. The point to note is that the equilibrium wage is not a culturally determined parameter, as the classical economists thought; it depends also on a level of mortality that was subject to autonomous long-run change. It is this that gives population an independent role in history: within broad limits, the equilibrium population and living standard changed when mortality changed, even if institutions and the economic base of society remained completely unaltered.

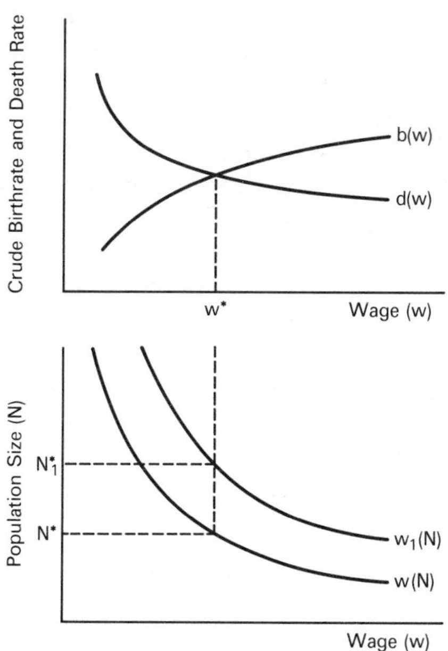

Fig. 9.9 Increased demand for labor.

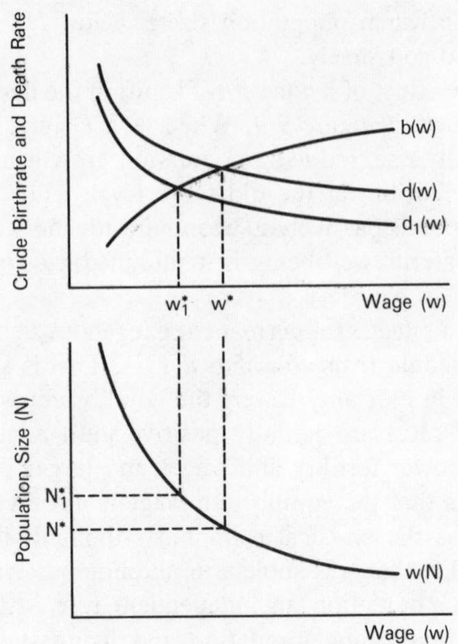

Fig. 9.10 Exogenous mortality decline.

I have simplified here by ignoring the direct links of fertility to mortality; these would cause the fertility curve to shift in response to shifts in the mortality curve. However, such direct links were very weak (see Lee 1973, p. 598; 1978*a*, p. 167). Therefore it was only through long-run change in the norms and institutions themselves that society could maintain constant population and wages in the face of exogenous change in mortality. The automatic homeostatic mechanisms were not adequate in these circumstances.

In earlier papers (Lee, 1973, 1978*a*, *b*) I used estimated forms of this model to simulate the course of wages, population, and fertility, assuming that only mortality varied exogenously. These simulations fit the historical data remarkably well for 1250 to 1700 and 1705 to 1784.

The diagram can also be used to illustrate the effect of a steady rate of shift of the demand for labor, of the sort included in the equations estimated earlier. Suppose that this rate of shift is such that population growth at rate r leaves wages unchanged; the estimates suggested $r = 0.4\%$ per year. Then in steady state growth, population will grow at rate r, and the wage will be constant at a level such that $b(w) - d(w) = r$. This situation is shown in figure 9.11. Evidently the wage will have to be a bit above its "natural" level in order to induce growth. Exogenous change in mortality will alter the steady-state wage but will only temporarily affect the population's growth rate.

Finally, consider a simultaneous decline in mortality and initiation of growth at rate *r* in the demand for labor. This situation is shown in figure 9.12. In this case we might observe constant fertility, low mortality, and population growth with no diminution in wages. This is the situation T. H. Marshall had in mind when he wrote of eighteenth-century England (1965, p. 248):

> The obvious temptation is to assert that the death rate was not only the variable, but also the determining, factor in the increase of population, and that, to understand the causes of this increase, we should study the deaths rather than the births. But, clearly, a horizontal line on a graph may be as dynamic as a diagonal; the forces that prevent a birth rate from falling may be as significant as those that make it rise.

Ordinarily, one would expect a fall in the death rate to be followed by a fall in fertility, as equilibrium is attained at a lower rate and larger population; if this does not happen, it suggests that the underlying cause of continuing population growth is economic progress, not the mortality decline.

Might this be similar to the situation in today's LDCs? We often observe exogenously declining mortality, relatively constant fertility and per capita income, and rapid population growth. Without the concurrent

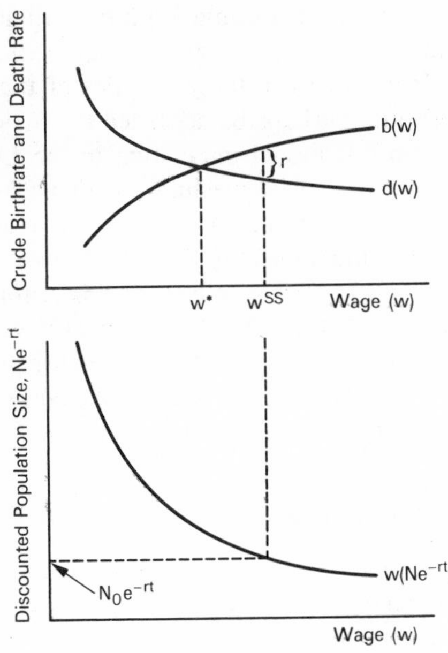

Fig. 9.11 Labor demand increasing at a constant rate.

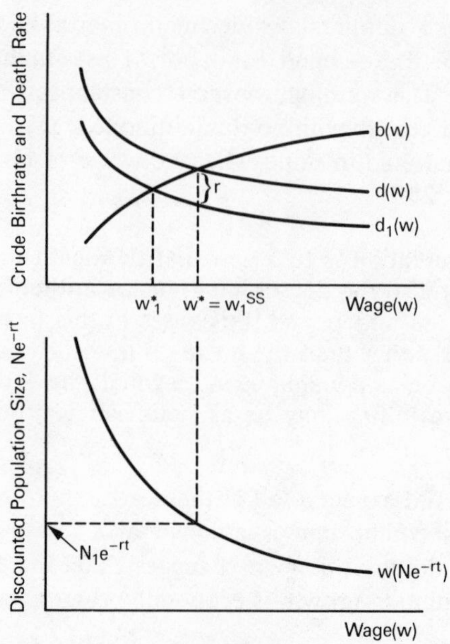

Fig. 9.12 Offsetting changes in growth of labor demand and mortality.

economic development, surely by now incomes and fertility would have fallen and mortality risen. It is not quite right to attribute the population growth to the mortality decline, although this may be the most conspicuous exogenous change; growth in the capacities of these economies to sustain population should perhaps be accorded the major responsibility.

A final comment on this model in relation to the LDCs is in order. Whatever the nature of the social mechanisms that may have regulated population in Asia, it is clear that a balance was reached at a much higher level of fertility and mortality than in Europe. Apparently life expectancy in China and India at the turn of this century was about 23 years (see Barclay et al. 1976; Das Gupta 1971), versus perhaps 30 years in Europe; the total fertility rate must consequently have been about 6.5 versus 4.5 in Europe. The necessary change in fertility-regulating institutions, in response to declining mortality, is staggering.

9.5 Summary and Conclusions

For today's LDCs there is little empirical evidence on the economic effects of population change. For the economy of preindustrial England and perhaps Europe, on the other hand, population emerges clearly as the dominant cause of long-run change in wages, rents, industrial prices, and income distribution. The economy could absorb population growth at about 0.4% per year with little effect; deviations of population size above or below this trend line, however, had dramatic consequences. And perhaps more striking than the existence of these effects is the extreme sensitivity of the economy's reaction: reckoning in terms of agricultural goods, a 10% increase in population depressed wages by 22%; raised rents by 19%; lowered industrial prices relative to agricultural prices by 17%; raised the ratio of industrial to agricultural production by 13%; and lowered labor's share of national income by 14%. This sensitivity of response poses the principal puzzle to emerge from this research. My attempt to account for these large (in absolute value) elasticities by means of a very low elasticity of substitution of labor for land is not altogether convincing without corroborating evidence.

In this study I looked for negative consequences of population growth, and I found them. However, I made no effort to analyze such positive effects as the stimulation of agricultural investment or of technical change, the role of rising domestic demand for basic industrial commodities, or industrial wage rates held down by population growth and sharply diminishing returns in agriculture.[16] Nor can these possible positive effects be brushed aside as merely partially offsetting reactions to dominant adverse effects; if they in any way brought on the industrial revolution, then their net effect was overwhelmingly positive. But surely the links of today's LDCs with the world economy greatly reduce the advantages of scale, home demand, and home-produced technology. Perhaps after all it is the centuries before the industrial revolution that are most relevant for the LDCs, when population growth did have strong and predictable effects, beneficial for some social classes and damaging for others. In any event, a more balanced treatment of these issues would require a second paper.

Now let me turn to the causes of population change. There is a notion that social mechanisms cause population to grow and decline in response to changes in productive capacity, in such a way as to keep incomes close to a culturally defined standard of well-being. And some who reject this model as descriptive of the present still believe it is appropriate for the past. In fact it is a poor description of both. In preindustrial Europe, as far back as records will take us, population swings were largely autonomous, not a response to economic variation. Their active determinant was mortality, which then as now experienced large exogenous variation. Our current experience is not unique in this respect, and, indeed, though the present decline in mortality has been much greater and more sudden than those of the past, its effects on welfare have so far been much less.

On the other hand, it would be a mistake to ignore the institutional mechanisms of population control that existed in preindustrial times. The point is not that they were absent, but that the equilibriums to which they steered society were largely accidental, resulting as they did from the interaction of cultural control with independent mortality. And while mortality largely determined the equilibrium and actual standard of living, it was the social mechanisms that produced sustained population growth in response to economic progress.

In short, the social protection of living standards through population regulation has always been vulnerable to mortality change, and it would be folly to expect longstanding demographic adjustment mechanisms to prevent population growth from forcing material welfare below some conventional standard in today's LDCs.

It is only in the *very* long run, over which the institutional mechanisms are themselves variable, that such automaticity can be expected, and the European experience suggests that even centuries may not suffice.

Appendix 1. Data Used in Figure 9.1 and Section 9.2

A. Life Expectancy

For 1250–1450, estimates are based on J. C. Russell's (1958) life tables that refer to the mortality experience of a predominantly upper-class, geographically dispersed group of English males holding property granted by the king. Some errors in the original tables were corrected; the infant mortality rates in the tables were revised; and estimates were converted from a cohort to a period basis. These estimates appear consistent with scattered evidence for other social classes. For details on all this, see Lee (1978*b*, appendix 4).

For 1550 to 1725, the estimates are based on Hollingsworth's study of the British peerage (1964). These estimates refer to the mortality of male peers. I have converted them from a cohort to a period basis. Extensive comparisons suggest that these estimates accurately reflect relative changes in the mortality of other social groups through 1725. For details, see Lee (1978*b*, appendix 2). Between 1450 and 1550, life expectancy estimates are not available.

B. Population Size

From 1250 to 1540, the dotted line indicates rough estimates of population size, based principally on Russell's work (1948); for details see Lee (1978*b*, appendix 1).

The remaining population estimates for 1540 to 1800 are based on a preliminary version of the Cambridge Group's aggregate parish register series. These series, generously made available to me by E. A. Wrigley and Roger Schofield, give the annual number of baptisms and burials for a nonrandom sample of 404 English parishes, covering about 6 or 7% of the total population. Various adjustments were made to correct for gaps, underregistration, and the entry and departure of parishes to and from the sample. Using a variety of methods, population size for the sample was estimated to be roughly 230,000 at the beginning of the period. Annual population estimates were formed by cumulating the difference between adjusted baptisms and burials, resulting in a population size of 1,055,000 for 1840. This implies a 4.6-fold increase over the three centuries, agreeing well with estimates from other sources. Estimates for the sample were inflated to the national scale using a ratio calculated for the end of the period when national population data are available. These estimates are preliminary. Figure 9.1 shows population size at five-year intervals, for 1540, 1545, . . . , 1800.

C. Real Wage (w)

The numerator (W) of the real wage series is taken from Phelps-Brown and Hopkins (1955), with some interpolation, for 1261 through 1700. It is the wage for building craftsmen. Thereafter, it is taken from Deane and Cole (1969, p. 19) and represents a population-weighted average of regions. A splicing ratio was derived from the overlap. The figure for 1790–99 was again taken from Phelps-Brown and Hopkins (1955).

For 1261–1400, the deflator of the real wage series is the Phelps-Brown and Hopkins (1956) cost of a composite basket of consumables including both agricultural and industrial commodities.

For 1401 to 1800, the deflator is an agricultural price index (P_A). It is taken from Phelps-Brown and Hopkins (1957), through 1700. From 1701 to 1760 it is based on the Phelps-Brown and Hopkins grain index as reported in A. H. John (1967, p. 191), using the overlap 1671–1700 to derive a splicing ratio. For 1761–1800, a wheat price index from Deane and Cole (1969, p. 91), is used, with splicing ratio based on 1641–70.

D. Terms of Trade (P_I/P_A)

The denominator, P_A, is exactly as described above in section C. The numerator, P_I, is taken from Phelps-Brown and Hopkins (1957) through 1700; thereafter the series is based on the average of the Schumpeter-Gilboy producers' goods index and consumers' goods other-than-cereals index, as reported in Deane and Cole (1969, p. 91). Because this average gives animal products a weight of 1/11, I assumed animal products were similar to wheat and subtracted 1/11 of the wheat price series from it. The splicing ratio was calculated from the Gilboy-Schumpeter index for 1680–1710, as reported in Mitchell and Deane (1962, p. 468). The price ratio, p, was calculated as $p = 100(P_I/P_A)$.

E. Rent/Wage Ratio (R/w)

The nominal rent index (RP_A) is taken from Kerridge (1953) and is an average of the two series for the Herbert estates (with weight 1/4 each) and the Seymour estate (with weight 1/2). The ratio R/w is calculated as RP_A/W times 100.

Appendix 2. Formal Development of the Two-Sector Model

This appendix sets out the assumptions of the model explicitly and develops a number of results that are used in the main body of the paper. The development presented here owes much to Marc Nerlove, particularly the material in section C. In what follows, agricultural output is the numeraire.

A. Assumptions

(A1) $$A = \mu_0(\mu_1 F^{-\beta} + (1 - \mu_1)N_A{}^{-\beta})^{-1/\beta}.$$

Agricultural production follows a constant return to scale, constant elasticity of substitution production function, with inputs of labor and land-plus-other factors.

(A2) $$I = min\{N_I, A_I\}.$$

Nonagricultural production follows a fixed-coefficients production function with inputs of labor and agricultural output; units of measure for labor and agricultural output are chosen so that the production coefficients are unity.

(A3) $$w_I = w_A = w.$$

Wages are equal in the two sectors.

(A4) $$w = \partial A/\partial N_A.$$

The wage in agriculture is competitively determined.

(A5) $$p = w + 1.$$

The price of industrial output equals its cost of production.

(A6) $$N = N_A + N_I.$$

There is full employment (or employment of a constant proportion of the working-age population).

(A7) $pI = \lambda(A - I)$ or, equivalently, $(A - I)/(A - I + pI) = 1/(1 + \lambda)$.

The demand for nonagricultural output is such that net agricultural output is a constant proportion of total net output, valued at current prices.

B. Derivation of the Sectoral Allocation of Labor

Let γ_A be labor's proportional share of agricultural product; by (A4) this equals $E_{A,N_A} \times N_A$ can be expressed as:

(A8) $$N_A = A\gamma_A/w.$$

From equation A2 it follows that $I = N_I$, and combining this with equation A7 and solving for N_I yields:

(A9) $$N_I = \lambda A/(p + \lambda).$$

From equations A8, A9, and A6 it follows that:

(A10) $$N_A/N = \gamma_A/[\gamma_A + \lambda w/(p + \lambda)],$$

which gives agricultural employment as a proportion of the total labor force.

C. The Effect of Population Growth on the Sectoral Allocation of Labor

The goal here is to derive an explicit expression for the elasticity of N_A with respect to N. From equations A6 and A9 it follows that:

(A11) $$N_A = N - \lambda A/(p + \lambda).$$

Differentiating with respect to N gives:

(A12) $$\frac{\partial N_A}{\partial N} = 1 - \lambda \frac{\partial N_A}{\partial N}\left\{\frac{\partial A/\partial N_A}{p + \lambda} - \frac{A\partial w/\partial N_A}{(p + \lambda)^2}\right\}.$$

Solving equation A12 for $\partial N_A/\partial N$ yields:

(A13) $$\frac{\partial N_A}{\partial N} = 1/\left\{1 + \frac{\lambda\partial A/\partial N_A}{p + \lambda} - \frac{\lambda A\partial w/\partial N_A}{(p + \lambda)^2}\right\}.$$

From equation A9:

(A14) $$\lambda/(p + \lambda) = N_I/A.$$

Substituting in equation A13 yields:

(A15)
$$\frac{\partial N_A}{\partial N} = 1/\left\{1 + \frac{N_I \partial A/\partial N_A}{A} - \frac{N_I \partial w/\partial N_A}{p+\lambda}\right\}.$$

Multiplying by N/N_A on both sides yields:

(A16)
$$E_{N_A,N} = 1/\left\{\frac{N_A}{N} + \frac{N_A N_I \partial A/\partial N_A}{AN} - \frac{N_A N_I \partial w/\partial N_A}{N(p+\lambda)}\right\}$$

This can be rewritten:

(A17)
$$E_{N_A,N} = 1/\left\{1 - (1-\gamma_A)\frac{N_I}{N} - \frac{N_I}{N} E_{w,N_A} \frac{w}{(p+\lambda)}\right\}$$

Equation A17 relates two unknown and unobservable elasticities, $E_{N_A,N}$ and E_{w,N_A}. Fortunately these same two elasticities are also related by the identity:

(A18)
$$E_{w,N_A} = E_{w,N}/E_{N_A,N},$$

where $E_{w,N}$ is directly estimable. Substituting from equation A18 into equation A17 yields:

(A19)
$$E_{N_A,N} = 1/\left\{1 - (1-\gamma_A)\frac{N_I}{N} - \frac{E_{w,N} N_I}{E_{N_A,N} N} \frac{w}{p+\lambda}\right\}.$$

Solving for $E_{N_A,N}$ yields:

(A20)
$$E_{N_A,N} = \left\{1 + E_{w,N}\frac{N_I}{N}\frac{w}{(p+\lambda)}\right\} / \left\{1 - (1-\gamma_A)\frac{N_I}{N}\right\}.$$

This last equation permits estimation of $E_{N_A,N}$ from estimable quantities. And it is also true, of course, that:

(A21)
$$E_{N_A/N,N} = E_{N_A,N} - 1.$$

D. Estimation of E_{w,N_A} and the Elasticity of Substitution in Agriculture

Once we have derived the effect of population change on the sectoral allocation of labor, $E_{N_A,N}$, it is simple to find E_{w,N_A} and $\sigma = 1/(1+\beta)$. In fact, E_{w,N_A} can be calculated directly from equations A20 and A18. Since the elasticity of substitution equals $-(1-\gamma_A)/E_{w,N_A}$, it is also true that:

(A22)
$$\sigma = -(1-\gamma_A)E_{N_A,N}/E_{w,N}.$$

Substituting from equation A20, this gives:

(A23)
$$\sigma = -(1-\gamma_A)\left\{1 + E_{w,N}\frac{N_I}{N}\frac{w}{(p+\lambda)}\right\} / \left\{E_{w,N}[1-(1-\gamma_A)\frac{N_I}{N}]\right\},$$

or

(A24)
$$\sigma = -(1-\gamma_A)\left\{1/E_{w,N} + \frac{N_I}{N}\frac{w}{(p+\lambda)}\right\} / \left\{1-(1-\gamma_A)\frac{N_I}{N}\right\}.$$

E. Rent and Population

From equations A1 and A4 it follows that:

(A25)
$$R/w = [(1-\mu_1)/\mu_1](N_A/F)^{1+\beta}.$$

This could be estimated in log-linear form, except that N_A is not directly observed. However if $E_{R/w,N}$ is estimated, then $E_{R/w,N_A} = 1+\beta = 1/\sigma$ can be calculated as:

(A26)
$$1+\beta = E_{R/w,N}/E_{N_A,N},$$

or

(A27)
$$\sigma = E_{N_A,N}/E_{R/w,N}.$$

F. The Effect of Population on the Ratio of Industrial to Agricultural Output in Real Terms

Solving equation A7 for I, and dividing by A, gives:

(A28)
$$I/A = \lambda/(\lambda+p).$$

Calculation of the elasticity of I/A with respect to N yields:

(A29)
$$E_{I/A,N} = -wE_{w,N}/(p+\lambda).$$

Inspection shows that this is a positive number; population growth increases industrial output more, proportionately, than agricultural output. In fact, since $I = N_I$, and $N_I = N - N_A$, the elasticity of I with respect to N is easily shown to be:

(A30)
$$E_{I,N} = 1 + (N_A/N_I)(1-E_{N_A,N}).$$

Thus, to a first approximation, industrial output increases in proportion to population; more accurately, it increases *more* than proportionately when $E_{N_A,N}$ is less than one.

G. Population and Terms of Trade

Since $p = 1 + w$, it is easily shown that:

$$E_{p,N} = \gamma_I E_{w,N}, \tag{A31}$$

where γ_I is $w/(1 + w)$, the share of labor in the cost of industrial production.

H. Population and Income Distribution

In the model, all income accrues either to labor or to "land" (which includes all agricultural nonlabor inputs). Labor's share of output in proportionate terms, denoted S, is therefore:

$$S = wN/(wN + R) = 1/[1 + R/(wN)]. \tag{A32}$$

Dividing numerator and denominator of $R/(wN)$ by A gives $(1 - \gamma_A)/(\gamma_A N/N_A)$, so equation A32 can be rewritten:

$$S = \gamma_A/[\gamma_A + (1 - \gamma_A)\,(N_A/N)], \tag{A33}$$

so that labor's share in all output is greater than it share in agricultural output.

Equation A33 can also be used to calculate γ_A, which is unobserved, from S and N_A/N, for which estimates exist. Solving for γ_A yields:

$$\gamma_A = (SN_A/N)/(1 - SN_I/N). \tag{A34}$$

The elasticity of labor's proportionate share with respect to population size can be calculated from equation A32 as follows:

$$\frac{\partial S}{\partial N}\frac{N}{S} = \frac{-\{[\partial(R/w)/\partial N](1/N) + [\partial(1/N)/\partial N](R/w)\}N}{[1 + R/(wN)]^2\{1/[1 + R/(wN)']\}}. \tag{A35}$$

This simplifies to:

$$E_{S,N} = -\{\partial(R/w)/\partial N - R/(wN)\} /[1 + R/(wN)], \tag{A36}$$

which further simplifies to:

$$E_{S,N} = (1 - E_{R/w,N})(1 - S), \tag{A37}$$

which is easily evaluated.

I. Nonagricultural Technical Change, Wages, and Labor Force Allocation

Suppose equation A2 is altered to: $I = \min\,(N_I/\alpha, A_I)$, so that $\alpha I = N_I$ and $p = \alpha w + 1$. Then equation A11 becomes:

(A38) $$N_A = N - \alpha\lambda A/(\alpha w + 1 + \lambda).$$

This can be differentiated to find the effect of a change in α on labor force allocation, for constant N.

(A39) $$\frac{\partial N_A}{\partial \alpha} = \frac{-\lambda}{(p+\lambda)^2}\{(A + \frac{\partial A}{\partial N_A}\frac{\partial N_A}{\partial w}\alpha)(p+\lambda) - (w + \alpha\frac{\partial w}{\partial N_A}\frac{\partial N_A}{\partial \alpha})\alpha A\}.$$

After solving for $\partial N_A/\partial\alpha$ and simplifying:

(A40) $$\frac{\partial N_A}{\partial \alpha} = \frac{-\lambda A(1+\lambda)/(p+\lambda)^2}{1 + \frac{\lambda\alpha w}{p+\lambda} - \frac{\lambda\alpha^2 A \partial w/\partial N_A}{(p+\lambda)^2}}.$$

Further simplifying, and expressing as an elasticity, this gives:

(A41) $$E_{N_A,\alpha} = -1/\{pN_A/N_I - [\alpha w/(1+\lambda)]E_{w,N_A}\}.$$

It is also easily shown that $E_{N_I,\alpha} = -(N_A/N_I)E_{N_A,\alpha}$ so that:

(A42) $$E_{I,\alpha} = -[(N_A/N_I)E_{N_A,\alpha} + 1].$$

And, finally, the effect of changes in α on w are easily assessed, since:

(A43) $$E_{w,\alpha} = E_{w,N_A} \times E_{N_A,\alpha}.$$

Notes

1. He has shown that in a stable population with growth rate r, whose economy has a rate of disembodied technological progress s, and in which savings are less than or equal to profits, the internal rate of return to a marginal birth, viewed as an investment, is less than or equal to $r + s$. If r is 0.02 and s is 0.01, then discounting over a life cycle at a rate above 3% yields a negative present value of a birth.

2. This may in part reflect their methodology. In a single-sector neoclassical growth model, rates of population growth have no effect on steady-state growth rates. Weak negative effects arise in transitional disequilibriums, and strong effects occur in nonneoclassical economies with surplus labor. It might be worth redoing the analysis while distinguishing among these three categories.

3. See, for example, Van Bath (1963); North and Thomas (1973); and Phelps-Brown and Hopkins (1959). Properly put, the argument is that population change accounted for changes in relative prices over the period; some historians, however, go too far and suggest that population growth caused the general price inflation of the sixteenth century. For a perceptive review see McCloskey (1972). In a recent paper, Cohen and Weitzman (1975) have suggested that the process of enclosure might also explain these changes; however, they have drastically underestimated the strength of the demographic data.

4. For the regression covering the years 1250 to 1700, the Phelps-Brown and Hopkins (1956) real wage series was used, which is money wages deflated by the price of a basket of goods including both agricultural and industrial items. The wage series used for 1705–89 was deflated in a similar manner; it is based on data given in Deane and Cole (1969, p. 19) and takes account of regional differences in wages and population growth rates.

5. In any case, if the economy is viewed as open, then relative prices are determined in large measure exogenously. But until midway through the eighteenth century, Europe accounted for most of England's trade (see Deane and Cole 1969, p. 34), and changes in European factor supplies and factor prices paralleled those in England (see e.g. Phelps-Brown and Hopkins 1959).

6. This view of the English economy, which emphasizes land and labor to the total exclusion of capital, receives some support from estimates of the capital stock in the late seventeenth century. From Gregory King's tabulations, Deane and Cole (1969, p. 270) estimate that 64% of capital was in land, 8% in livestock, 17.5% in buildings, and only 10.5% in transportation, inventories, machines, and the military. The saving rate was 3 to 6%, and savings went to a considerable extent into agriculture.

By 1698, the "industrial" category had risen to about 21%, while land had fallen to 55%; but the economy's capital was still largely agricultural (Deane and Cole 1969, p. 271).

7. In 1798, roughly 12% to 16% of the population were "living-in" employees; of these, domestic servants were the largest group. See Mathias (1969, p. 25). In 1801, according to Colquhoun, about 7.5% of the population were personal and household servants.

8. According to Deane and Cole (1969, p. 154–64) the proportional share of agriculture in national income was 40–45% in 1688 and in 1770; by 1801 it had declined to about 32–36%. Pollard and Crossley (1968), put the 1688 figure at 56%, which if correct would change the picture considerably.

9. Mean values are needed for the variables N_I/N, γ_A, $E_{w,N}$ and $w/(p+\lambda)$, all of which are actually endogenous. Based on Gregory King, Deane and Cole (1969, p. 137) estimate that 60 to 80% of the labor force was primarily engaged in agriculture in 1688. Since many of those primarily engaged in agriculture nonetheless did nonagricultural work as by-employment or for their own consumption, I will take 65% as the proportion of labor services engaged in agriculture: so $N_I/N = .35$.

An estimate of γ_A can be derived from an estimate of S, labor's share of total national income, using equation A34. For 1688 Deane and Cole, based on Gregory King, estimate that between 25% and 39% of national income was wages and salaries. However, not included is the labor contribution of farmers and freeholders, whose income accounts for about 40% of national income. I will somewhat arbitrarily take $S = .55$, which implies that $\gamma_A = .45$. $E_{w,N}$ has been estimated to be -2.22 in equation 20; $w/(p+\lambda)$ should be estimated for the mean amount of labor augmentation. Taking $\lambda = 1$ (i.e., 50% of final product is in agriculture), and $w = 3$, gives $w/(p+\lambda) = .6$.

10. In transformed terms, $w = 3$ and $p = w+1 = 4$. Since agricultural prices are by definition 1, the quantity of I consumed must be 1/4 as large as that of A. Thus $w^* = w/[c + (c/4)p] = (4/c)[w/(w+5)]$. From this, $E_{w,N} = [5/(5+w)]$ $E_{w,N} = (5/8)E_{w,N}$ evaluated at $w = 3$.

11. See Lee (1971) for a comparison of this series with others for Colyton, a small rural parish, and for "professional men" in England.

12. The theoretical cross spectrum is ideally suited to analyze the interactions of two series that are related to one another approximately linearly with known sets of lagged coefficients, as is the case with demographic series.

13. The variables are measured as residuals from the regression of the log of the basic series on time.

14. Many dozens of previous studies of populations, in many social contexts and time periods, have demonstrated this sort of procyclical response, including situations in which the cross-sectional and secular relationship of fertility to income appears to be negative. Therefore this cross-spectral evidence is weak support at best for the existence of a long-run positive aggregate relation of fertility and income.

15. For diagrammatic simplicity, I have assumed that fertility is completely independent of mortality, so that $b(w)$ remains unchanged. The results are not qualitatively different so long as compensation is less than perfect.

16. These positive effects of population growth have been stressed by Boserup (1965) and others and have been modeled and simulated in a recent article by Simon (1976).

Comment Nathan Keyfitz

Is population growth the cause or the result of economic change? Ronald Lee tackles nothing smaller than this central problem of demography. The answer he provides is limited in space and time, but his analysis is nonetheless a tour de force combining economic time series, parish records, and simple models.

Everyone wants to endogenize population in his economic model, but there are doubts whether the real world is made in a way that permits this. Adam Smith seemed to do it: for him the production of people responded to the demand, just like the supply of shoes. For Malthus the number of people the landscape could support was limited just like the number of animals that could be sustained on a given food supply. Though they did not use the expression, Smith and Malthus in their different ways both saw a negative feedback by which the family received signals either from the larger society or from the environment, and so family behavior could never be destabilizing.

Neither view is wholly inapplicable—places and times can be found to illustrate both. So can places and times be found in which they do not apply. The Kung Bushmen, with densities of about one person per two square miles, do not seem to produce people up to either the economic or the biological limit. They avoid any sense of population pressure, keeping their numbers below the physiological maximum—by what means and under what motivation no one seems to know.

Nathan Keyfitz is professor of sociology at Harvard University.

Thus population in some places goes up either with capital (Smith) or with land (Malthus); among the Kung and elsewhere it stays well below the limits set by either. To make matters more difficult, the dominant tendency in most industrial societies has been for the birthrate to go *down* with the increase of income, a social mobility effect that overcomes the Smith and Malthus effects. The would-be endogenizer does not even know whether to insert in his model a positive, zero, or negative relation of population to income, let alone how strong to make that relation.

Lee's empirical finding that in preindustrial Europe income does not affect population accords with the theoretical ambiguity. However, in the other direction there does appear to be clear causation both theoretically and empirically. The result that when population rose by 10%, as it could easily do in a period of low mortality, wages went down by 15%, is surprising and important. The two-sector model is simple and convincing. My only wish is that he could reassure us more about the quality of the wage and other data to which it was fitted.

What is implicit in Lee's paper, as in other work, is two systems: the small system of the family and the large system of the population, whether it be parish, county, nation, or world. Each of the two systems has its own laws and variables, and the two sets of variables mesh differently in different circumstances. This paper tells us something important about both the small and the large systems as well as about the relation between them in preindustrial England.

It considers Smith's device for linking the two through the birthrate: with more capital and hence more jobs, young people will be able to marry earlier and so will have children sooner. Lee shows that the number of children within marriage did vary with jobs, a feature Smith did not recognize. But this and marriage seem to have been less important than the exogenously caused fluctuations in the death rates whose action is the main feature of the paper.

Lee mentions at the beginning of his paper the belief that in modern times the old regulatory mechanisms have broken down under the influences of mortality decline, urbanization, technical change, and modernization in general. He speaks of the finite world of preindustrial England with limits not yet rendered flexible by technology, and of how ancient regulatory mechanisms fail to operate in the twentieth century. But then at the end of the paper he transfers his major result from preindustrial England to the present LDCs. I am more convinced by his initial reservation than by his later transfer. For various reasons it seems unlikely that the currently developing countries will duplicate Europe's early experience.

The most conspicuous difference is in the rapid urbanization of the LDCs. In past centuries when remnants of feudal class respect were still controlling, communication was slow, and most of the population worked on the land, fluctuations of income were accepted even when they brought part of the population below the starvation line. In the 1970s, with huge migration to the cities—Cairo, Calcutta, Mexico City each have as many people as the whole of England and ten times as many as London—surplus population has a social and political visibility that daily reminds the elite of the importance of birth control. Each day's newspapers tell us about a turnaround or accentuation of birth-control policy in one or another country, conspicuously in certain countries where urbanization is most rapid.

But this does not say anything about the smaller system—it refers only to the policy of the larger society. Does the turnaround that is occurring in elite views tell us what will happen within the smaller system of the family? How can the elite control the family-building practices of their masses? Certainly they cannot do so directly or immediately. By the 1990s we should have a clear idea of the manner and degree in which currently visible economic and political forces of the larger society will penetrate the family. Sooner or later they will; it is the timing that is important. How much will the current fall in mortality and rapid population growth affect wages in the LDCs? One has trouble seeing how such a question can be answered by analysis of the forces operating in preindustrial England.

But this doubt about generalizing to the late twentieth century in no way lessens my admiration of Lee's historical work. His choice of models is judicious, and the method will be exemplary for others who use time series and parish registers to answer real questions.

Comment Marc Nerlove

In 1973 Lee published a paper entitled "Population in Preindustrial England: An Econometric Analysis," based on his 1971 dissertation.[1] In that paper Lee presented a model relating crude birthrates and death rates, population size, and the real wage rate that is the same in all essentials as that underlying figures 9.7, 9.8, 9.9 and 9.10 in the present paper. In the model of economic demographic equilibrium, real wages and population sizes are inversely related, whereas fertility, as measured by the crude birthrate, is positively related and mortality, as measured by the crude death rate, is negatively related to real wages. Population size is simply connected with the crude birthrate and death rate by the identity

Marc Nerlove is associated with Northwestern University.

$$(1) \qquad \frac{dP}{dt}/P = b - d,$$

where P is population size and b and d are the crude birthrate and death rate, respectively.

Lee estimated the basic relationships of his model using fifty-year averages of population size (aggregate data from Wrigley and Russell), a wage index (from Phelps-Brown and Hopkins) deflated by an index of prices for both agricultural and nonagricultural commodities, and life expectancies at birth for the peerage (from Russell and Hollingsworth). Assuming a stable population, Lee was able to derive estimates of the crude birthrate and death rate from the growth of population over time. The basic equations of the model—real wages as a function of population size, and crude birthrate and death rate as functions of the real wage rate—were estimated for the period 1250–1700 using both ordinary least squares and two-stage least squares, assuming mortality to be exogenous.[2] Indeed, the simple correlation between mortality and the real wage turns out to be positive in this period, a result that can be attributed almost entirely to the simultaneity of the system Lee considers. It is also possible to estimate many of the basic parameters of the system without using the wage data at all, or without using the population or fertility data but only the crude death rates related to the life-expectancy data, by exploiting the overidentification of Lee's system. These estimates provide tests of the overidentification of the system and its consistency with the data, unreliable as these may be.

On the basis of his 1973 analysis, Lee concluded that "long-run changes in the real wage are adequately accounted for by changes in population size" and that "there were no dramatic shifts in the demand for labor over this period. . . . The relationship between population and the real wage was stable until the beginning of the eighteenth century, at which time it began to change markedly. . . . The great swings in population during this period were due to swings in mortality." These latter were largely exogenous according to Lee (1973, pp. 604–5). Lee found a "highly variable equilibrium wage in conjunction with a relatively constant demand for labor" (1973, p. 606).

It is worth stressing two aspects of Lee's earlier paper in conjunction with the one presented at this conference. First, "The end point, 1700 [of the period analyzed], was chosen because the relation between wages and population size began to shift unmistakably after this, and because the mortality of the aristocracy, from which we have derived our estimates, was no longer representative of that of the general population" (Lee 1973, p. 583). Second, the interpretation of the wage-population relationship, in terms of a one-sector model with a Cobb-Douglas production function, is a key element in assessing the adequacy of this central relationship of the economic-demographic model. Lee's difficulties in this connection have led to an extensive investigation, in the present paper, of a two-sector model with a CES production function for agriculture and fixed-coefficients technology for the nonagricultural sector. This two-sector model was discussed in detail at the conference in an appendix to these comments. That material, however, has been largely incorporated in Lee's Appendix 2 and is therefore omitted here.

The paper under discussion contains four important innovations:

1. Lee utilizes greatly superior population data derived from the sample of 404 parish registers collected by the Cambridge Group for the History of Population and Social Structure, spanning the period 1538–1840. For some analyses Lee has used decadal averages, for others the annual data themselves, and the latter are clearly essential to the cross-spectral statistical analyses he carries out in section 9.3.2.

2. This paper focuses on a later period, 1530–1800 (sometimes 1839) for which the clearly superior data are available. Use of better data is certainly desirable, but, especially in view of Lee's earlier cautionary statement concerning the noncomparability of the period after 1700 with the period before, combining data for the period after industrialization had clearly gotten under way with prior data may raise some serious questions about the stability of the relationships estimated. To some degree Lee tries to handle this problem in his regression (eq. 3), but he succeeds only in capturing an acceleration of the trend in real wages after 1809 and does not detect a significant shift in the two subperiods 1639–1745 and 1746–1839. However, this analysis should be reworked using real wage data more appropriate to the two-sector model (deflating money wages by agricultural prices alone rather than an index of both agricultural and industrial prices). The regression result reported in equation 20 uses data from 1540 only to 1800 and omits a variable designed to detect acceleration of the trend in the demand for labor after the Napoleonic wars and is thus not so directly comparable.

Using the older set of data, Lee reports a significant shift of the wage-population relation between 1250–1700 and 1705–89 in the form of a fivefold increase in the rate of exponential trend.

3. A central, and most attractive, feature of the present paper is its attempt to interpret the real wage-population relation within the framework of a two-sector model that assumes CES technology in the agricultural sector and fixed coefficients in the nonagricultural sector. Despite several limitations, this new model allows a much richer set of tests for consistency of the relationship between real wages and population important in Lee's later analysis of economic-demographic interactions. The two-sector model and its implications are described in detail in Appendix 2 to Lee's paper.

Major limitations in the model and its estimation, of which Lee is aware, include: (*a*) The fact that under CES technology, in either a two-sector or a one-sector model, the elasticity of the real wage with respect to the labor force is not constant and should not be treated as such in estimating the relationship between real wages and population. (*b*) The assumption that net agricultural production is a constant proportion of total output valued at market prices is surely a poor one during a period that encompasses the beginning of rapid industrialization. Moreover, two-sector model results tend to be quite sensitive to assumptions on the demand side. (*c*) The inverse projection method used to estimate labor force from population size by taking age structure into account may not be entirely adequate when using data for relatively short periods during which fertility and mortality may be changing rapidly. (*d*) Finally, the use of OLS instead of simultaneous-equations estimation procedures in a model in which population or labor force or both is, potentially at least, endogenous is inappropriate. This treatment contrasts with Lee's 1973 paper, in which both OLS and two-state least-squares procedures were used in some of the estimations. Lee, however, does go to some lengths in section 9.3 to show that population may be treated exogenously and that it varied largely in response to variations in mortality, which was not itself affected by the real wage.

4. The discussion in section 9.3 of the interrelations among fluctuations in mortality, marital fertility, nuptiality, and real wages represents an important modification and amplification of Lee's earlier work, although much of this material has been developed in subsequent papers presented at MSSB conferences or published elsewhere. All of this work relies heavily on cross-spectral analysis, which Lee argues has to be used because "for compelling reasons, the theoretical analysis had to be carried out in spectral terms." I would be the last person to argue against use of frequency domain techniques in appropriate circumstances, but I have yet to see a distributed lag relationship that could not be more easily interpreted in the time than in the frequency domain. Moreover, cross-spectral estimates, especially of phase, are notoriously difficult to interpret when the coherence between the two series analyzed is highly variable and frequently low. In addition, it is not at all clear to me that Lee's general finding that marital fertility and nuptiality were related to real wages and the population size and age structure only at high frequencies (1/15 cycle/year and higher) is evidence that such relations are not important for the wage population and other relations that Lee fits in section 9.2 and interprets further in section 9.3.3. In the first place, Lee has not used ten-year averages throughout, although he might argue that use of such averages constitutes a low frequency band-pass filter that allows him to look only at movements unaffected by the feedback between real wages and population size and structure. In the sec-

ond place, even if he had used such averages, they do not constitute an appropriate filter, and substantial "contamination" of his estimates is likely to occur. And finally, as Lee recognizes, low and high frequencies do not represent appropriately the economist's intuitive distinction between long- and short-run movements and relations, nor is filtering by band-pass filters a good way to get at the dynamic lag structure that must surely lie at the heart of a useful formulation of the nexus of economic-demographic interactions.

Lee concludes his paper with the comment that, "For the economy of preindustrial England . . . population emerges clearly as the dominant source of long-run changes in wages, rents, industrial prices, and income distribution," whereas, "For today's LDCs there is little convincing empirical evidence of the economic effects of population change." From what I have heard at this conference and read elsewhere, I would say, quite to the contrary, there is plenty of empirical evidence that population change and economic growth and development are intimately related—only lots of it is conflicting! Perhaps what Lee means to say, and I would heartily agree, is that we have a long way to go before we really understand these connections for today's LDCs. I add that, despite Lee's pioneering work, we also have some distance to go in understanding the nexus for preindustrial and industrializing England.

Notes

1. Lee (1973). The dissertation, *Econometric Studies of Topics in Demographic History* (Harvard University) has been published as Lee (1978*b*).

2. There is a great deal of discussion in Lee's paper about the possibility that mortality is not exogenous and that that of the peerage may not reflect mortality in the population at large. Obviously it is not possible to do justice to Lee's lengthy and complex discussion in this brief summary.

References

Barclay, George; Coale, Ansley; Stoto, Michael; and Trussell, James. 1976. A reassessment of the demography of traditional rural China. *Population Index* 42, no. 4 (October): 606–35.

Boserup, Ester. 1965. *The conditions of agricultural growth.* Chicago: Aldine-Atherton.

Chambers, J. D. 1972. *Population, economy and society in preindustrial England.* Oxford: Oxford University Press.

Chesnai, Jean-Claude, and Sauvy, Alfred. 1973. Progrès économique et accroisement de la population: Une expérience commentée. *Population* 28 (July/October): 843–57.

Coale, Ansley, and Hoover, Edgar. 1958. *Population growth and eco-*

nomic development in low-income countries. Princeton: Princeton University Press.

Cohen, Jon, and Weitzman, Martin. 1975. A Marxian model of enclosures. *Journal of Development Economics* 1:287–336.

Das Gupta, Prithwis. 1971. Estimation of demographic measures for India, 1881–1961, based on census age distributions. *Population Studies* 25, no. 3 (March): 395–415.

Deane, Phyllis, and Cole, W. A. 1969. *British economic growth 1688–1959.* 2d ed. Cambridge: Cambridge University Press.

Dubos, Rene. 1965. *Man adapting.* New Haven: Yale University Press.

Easterlin, Richard. 1972. Population. In *Contemporary economic issues,* ed. Neil Chamberlin. Homewood, Ill.: Richard Irwin.

Enke, S. 1960. The gains to India from population control. *Review of Economics and Statistics* (May): 175–81.

Everitt, Alan. 1967. Farm labourers. In *The agrarian history of England and Wales.* Vol. 4. *1500–1640,* ed. H. P. R. Finberg. Cambridge: Cambridge University Press.

Finberg, H. P. R., ed. 1967. *The agrarian history of England and Wales.* Vol. 4. *1500–1640.* Cambridge: Cambridge University Press.

Habakkuk, H. J. 1965. The economic history of modern Britain. In *Population in history,* ed. D. V. Glass and D. E. C. Eversley. Chicago: Aldine.

Harberger, A. 1958. Variations on a theme by Malthus. In *The population ahead,* ed. Roy Francis. Minneapolis: Minnesota University Press.

Hollingsworth, T. H. 1964. *The demography of the British peerage.* Supplement to *Population Studies* 18, no. 2 (November): 1964.

John, A. H. 1967. Agricultural productivity and economic growth in England 1700–1760 (with a Postscript). In *Agriculture and economic growth in England 1650–1815,* ed. E. L. Jones. London: Methuen.

Kelley, Allen, and Williamson, Jeffrey. 1974. *Lessons from Japanese development.* Chicago: University of Chicago Press.

Kerridge, E. 1953. The movement of rent, 1540–1640. *Economic History Review,* 2d ser., 6, no. 1 (August): 16–34.

Kmenta, Jan. 1971. *Elements of econometrics.* New York: Macmillan.

Knodel, John. 1975. Influence of child mortality on fertility in European populations in the past: Results from individual data." In *Seminar on infant mortality in relation to the level of fertility,* ed. Committee for International Coordination of National Research in Demography, pp. 103–18. Paris: CICRED.

Kuznets, S. 1967. Population and economic growth. *Proceedings of the American Philosophical Society* 3, no. 3 (June): 170–93.

Lee, Ronald. 1973. Population in preindustrial England: An econometric analysis. *Quarterly Journal of Economics* 87, no. 4 (November): 581–607.

———. 1974. Estimating series of vital rates and age structures from baptisms and burials: A new technique, with applications to pre-industrial England. *Population Studies* 28, no. 3 (November): 495–512.

———. 1975. Natural fertility, population cycles, and the spectral analysis of births and marriages. *Journal of the American Statistical Association* 70, no. 350 (June): 295–304.

———. 1977. Methods and models for analyzing historical series of births, deaths and marriages. In *Population patterns in the past*, ed. Ronald Lee. New York: Academic Press.

———. 1978*a*. Models of preindustrial population dynamics, with applications to England. In *Historical studies of changing fertility*, ed. Charles Tilly. Princeton: Princeton University Press.

———. 1978*b*. *Econometric studies of topics in demographic history*. New York: Arno Press.

Leff, Nathaniel. 1969. Dependency rates and savings rates. *American Economic Review* 54, no. 5 (December): 886–96.

McCloskey, Donald. 1972. Review of Peter Ramsey, ed., *The price revolution in sixteenth-century England. Journal of Political Economy* 80, no. 6 (November/December): 1332–35.

Marshall, T. H. 1965. The population problem during the industrial revolution: A note on the present state of the controversy. In *Population in history*, ed. D. V. Glass and D. E. C. Eversley, pp. 247–68. Chicago: Aldine.

Mathias, Peter. 1969. *The first industrial revolution*. London: Methuen.

Mirowski, Philip. 1976. The plague and the penny-loaf: The disease-dearth nexus in Stuart and Hanoverian London. Unpublished manuscript, Department of Economics, University of Michigan, presented at the 1976 meetings of the Cleometric Society, Madison.

Mitchell, B. R., and Deane, Phyllis. 1962. *Abstract of British historical statistics*. Cambridge: Harvard University Press.

North, Douglass, and Thomas, Robert. 1973. *The rise of the Western world*. Cambridge: Cambridge University Press.

Ohlin, Goran. 1961. Mortality, marriage, and growth in pre-industrial population. *Population Studies* 14, no. 3 (March): 190–97.

———. 1969. Population pressure and alternative investments. In *International Population Conference*, 3:1703–28. London, 1969.

Phelps-Brown, E. H., and Hopkins, S. V. 1955. Seven centuries of building wages. *Economica*, n.s., 22: 195–206.

———. 1956. Seven centuries of the prices of consumables, compared with builders' wage rates. *Economica* 23 (November): 296–314.

———. 1957. Wage-rates and prices: Evidence for population pressure in the sixteenth century. *Economica* 24 (November): 289–306.

———. 1959. Builders' wage-rates, prices and population: Some further evidence. *Economica* 26, no. 101 (February): 18–38.

Pollard, Sidney, and Crossley, David W. 1968. *The wealth of Britain 1085–1966.* New York: Schocken Books.

Russell, J. C. 1948. *British medieval population.* Albuquerque: University of New Mexico Press.

———. 1958. *Late ancient and medieval population, comprising transactions of the American Philosophical Society*, n.s., vol. 48, no. 3.

Sauvy, Alfred. 1969. *General theory of population.* New York: Basic Books.

Sawada, Shujiro. 1970. Technological change in Japanese agriculture. In *Agriculture and economic growth: Japan's experience*, ed. K. Ohkawa, B. Johnston and H. Kaneda. Princeton: Princeton University Press.

Simon, Julian. 1976. Population growth may be good for LDCs in the long run: A richer simulation model. *Economic Development and Cultural Change* 24, no. 2 (January): 309–38.

Smith, Daniel Scott. 1977. A homeostatic demographic regime: Patterns in West European family reconstitution studies. In *Population Patterns in the Past*, ed. Ronald Lee. New York: Academic Press.

Srivastava, Uma, and Heady, Earl. 1973. Technological change and relative factor shares in Indian agriculture: An empirical analysis. *American Journal of Agricultural Economics* 55, no. 3 (August): 509–14.

Van Bath, B. H. Slicher. 1963. *The agrarian history of Western Europe 500–1850.* London: Edward Arnold.

Contributors

Yoram Ben-Porath
Department of Economics
Hebrew University
Jerusalem, Israel

Paul Demeny
Center for Policy Studies
The Population Council
One Dag Hammarskjöld Plaza
New York, New York 10017

John Durand
Population Studies Center
University of Pennsylvania
3718 Locust Walk/CR
Philadelphia, Pennsylvania 19104

Richard A. Easterlin
Department of Economics
University of Pennsylvania
3718 Locust Walk/CR
Philadelphia, Pennsylvania 19104

Gary S. Fields
New York State School of Industrial
and Labor Relations
Cornell University
Ithaca, New York 14853

Albert Fishlow
Department of Economics
Yale University
New Haven, Connecticut 06520

Ronald Freedman
Population Studies Center
University of Michigan
1225 South University Avenue
Ann Arbor, Michigan 48109

Victor R. Fuchs
Center for Advanced Study in
Behavioral Sciences
202 Junipero Serra Boulevard
Stanford, California 94305

Allen C. Kelley
Department of Economics
Duke University
Durham, North Carolina 27706

Nathan Keyfitz
Center for Population Studies
Harvard University
9 Bow Street
Cambridge, Massachusetts 02138

Simon Kuznets
67 Francis Avenue
Cambridge, Massachusetts 02138

Ronald D. Lee
Population Studies Center
University of Michigan
1225 South University Avenue
Ann Arbor, Michigan 48109

Harvey Leibenstein
Department of Economics
Harvard University
Cambridge, Massachusetts 02138

Peter H. Lindert
Department of Economics
University of California
Davis, California 95616

Eva Mueller
Department of Economics
University of Michigan
Ann Arbor, Michigan 48109

Marc Nerlove
Department of Economics
Northwestern University
629 Noyes Street
Evanston, Illinois 60201

Richard W. Parks
Department of Economics/DK-30
University of Washington
Seattle, Washington 98195

Robert A. Pollak
Department of Economics
University of Pennsylvania
3718 Locust Walk/CR
Philadelphia, Pennsylvania 19104

Samuel H. Preston
Population Division
United Nations
New York, New York 10017

Warren C. Robinson
Population Group
Burrowes Building
Pennsylvania State University
University Park, Pennsylvania 16802

Warren Sanderson
Department of Economics
Stanford University
Stanford, California 94305

T. Paul Schultz
Department of Economics
Economic Growth Center
Box 1987, Yale Station
Yale University
New Haven, Connecticut 06520

Julian L. Simon
Department of Economics
University of Illinois
Urbana, Illinois 61801

Riad Tabbarah
Chief, Population Division
Economic Commission for Western Asia
United Nations Building
P.O. Box 4656
Beirut, Lebanon

Michael P. Todaro
Center for Policy Studies
The Population Council
One Dag Hammarskjöld Plaza
New York, New York 10017

Etienne van de Walle
Population Studies Center
University of Pennsylvania
3718 Locust Walk/CR
Philadelphia, Pennsylvania 19104

Michael L. Wachter
Department of Economics
University of Pennsylvania
3718 Locust Walk/CR
Philadelphia, Pennsylvania 19104

Anne D. Williams
Department of Economics
University of Pennsylvania
3718 Locust Walk/CR
Philadelphia, Pennsylvania 19104

Robert J. Willis
Department of Economics
State University of New York
Stony Brook, New York 11794

Author Index

Subject Index

UNIVERSITY LIBRARY
NOTTINGHAM